Proofs, Arguments, and Zero-Knowledge

Other titles in Foundations and Trends® in Privacy and Security

Assured Autonomy Survey
Christopher Rouff and Lanier Watkins
ISBN: 978-1-63828-038-5

Hardware Platform Security for Mobile Devices
Lachlan J. Gunn, N. Asokan, Jan-Erik Ekberg, Hans Liljestrand,
Vijayanand Nayani and Thomas Nyman
ISBN: 978-1-68083-976-0

Cloud Computing Security: Foundations and Research Directions
Anrin Chakraborti, Reza Curtmola, Jonathan Katz, Jason Nieh,
Ahmad-Reza Sadeghi, Radu Sion and Yinqian Zhang
ISBN: 978-1-68083-958-6

Expressing Information Flow Properties
Elisavet Kozyri, Stephen Chong and Andrew C. Myers
ISBN: 978-1-68083-936-4

Accountability in Computing: Concepts and Mechanisms
Joan Feigenbaum, Aaron D. Jaggard and Rebecca N. Wright
ISBN: 978-1-68083-784-1

Proofs, Arguments, and Zero-Knowledge

Justin Thaler
Georgetown University
jt1157@georgetown.edu

the essence of knowledge

Boston — Delft

Foundations and Trends® in Privacy and Security

Published, sold and distributed by:
now Publishers Inc.
PO Box 1024
Hanover, MA 02339
United States
Tel. +1-781-985-4510
www.nowpublishers.com
sales@nowpublishers.com

Outside North America:
now Publishers Inc.
PO Box 179
2600 AD Delft
The Netherlands
Tel. +31-6-51115274

The preferred citation for this publication is

J. Thaler. *Proofs, Arguments, and Zero-Knowledge.* Foundations and Trends® in
Privacy and Security, vol. 4, no. 2–4, pp. 117–660, 2022.

ISBN: 978-1-63828-124-5
© 2022 J. Thaler

Foundations and Trends® in Privacy and Security
Volume 4, Issue 2–4, 2022
Editorial Board

Editorial Scope

Topics

Foundations and Trends® in Privacy and Security publishes survey and tutorial articles in the following topics:

- Access control
- Accountability
- Anonymity
- Application security
- Artifical intelligence methods in security and privacy
- Authentication
- Big data analytics and privacy
- Cloud security
- Cyber-physical systems security and privacy
- Distributed systems security and privacy
- Embedded systems security and privacy
- Forensics
- Hardware security

- Human factors in security and privacy
- Information flow
- Intrusion detection
- Malware
- Metrics
- Mobile security and privacy
- Language-based security and privacy
- Network security
- Privacy-preserving systems
- Protocol security
- Security and privacy policies
- Security architectures
- System security
- Web security and privacy

Information for Librarians

Foundations and Trends® in Privacy and Security, 2022, Volume 4, 4 issues. ISSN paper version 2474-1558. ISSN online version 2474-1566. Also available as a combined paper and online subscription.

Contents

Proofs, Arguments, and Zero-Knowledge

Justin Thaler

Georgetown University, USA; jt1157@georgetown.edu

ABSTRACT

Interactive proofs (IPs) and arguments are cryptographic protocols that enable an untrusted prover to provide a guarantee that it performed a requested computation correctly. Introduced in the 1980s, IPs and arguments represented a major conceptual expansion of what constitutes a "proof" that a statement is true.

Traditionally, a proof is a static object that can be easily checked step-by-step for correctness. In contrast, IPs allow for interaction between prover and verifier, as well as a tiny but nonzero probability that an invalid proof passes verification. Arguments (but not IPs) even permit there to be "proofs" of false statements, so long as those "proofs" require exorbitant computational power to find. To an extent, these notions mimic in-person interactions that mathematicians use to convince each other that a claim is true, without going through the painstaking process of writing out and checking a traditional static proof.

This work is supported by NSF CAREER award CCF-1845125 and by DARPA under Agreement No. HR00112020022. Any opinions, findings and conclusions or recommendations expressed in this material are those of the author and do not necessarily reflect the views of the United States Government or DARPA.

Justin Thaler (2022), "Proofs, Arguments, and Zero-Knowledge", Foundations and Trends® in Privacy and Security: Vol. 4, No. 2–4, pp 117–660. DOI: 10.1561/3300000030.

Celebrated theoretical results from the 1980s and 1990s such as **IP** = **PSPACE** and **MIP** = **NEXP** showed that, in principle, surprisingly complicated statements can be verified efficiently. What is more, any argument can in principle be transformed into one that is *zero-knowledge*, which means that proofs reveal no information other than their own validity. Zero-knowledge arguments have a myriad of applications in cryptography.

Within the last decade, general-purpose zero-knowledge arguments have made the jump from theory to practice. This has opened new doors in the design of cryptographic systems, and generated additional insights into the power of IPs and arguments (zero-knowledge or otherwise). There are now no fewer than five promising approaches to designing efficient, general-purpose zero-knowledge arguments. This survey covers these approaches in a unified manner, emphasizing commonalities between them.

1

Introduction

This monograph is about verifiable computing (VC). VC refers to cryptographic protocols called interactive proofs (IPs) and arguments that enable a prover to provide a guarantee to a verifier that the prover performed a requested computation correctly. Introduced in the 1980s, IPs and arguments represented a major conceptual expansion of what constitutes a "proof" that a statement is true. Traditionally, a proof is a static object that can be easily checked step-by-step for correctness, because each individual step of the proof should be trivial to verify. In contrast, IPs allow for interaction between prover and verifier, as well as a tiny but nonzero probability that an invalid proof passes verification. The difference between IPs and arguments is that arguments (but not IPs) permit the existence of "proofs" of incorrect statements, so long as those "proofs" require exorbitant computational power to find.[1]

Celebrated theoretical results from the mid-1980s and early 1990s indicated that VC protocols can, at least in principle, accomplish amazing feats. These include enabling a cell phone to monitor the execution of a powerful but untrusted (even malicious) supercomputer, enabling

---

[1]For example, an argument, but not an IP, might make use of a cryptosystem, such that it is possible for a cheating prover to find a convincing "proof" of a false statement if (and only if) the prover can break the cryptosystem.

computationally weak peripheral devices (e.g., security card readers) to offload security-critical work to powerful remote servers, or letting a mathematician obtain a high degree of confidence that a theorem is true by looking at only a few symbols of a purported proof.[2]

VC protocols can be especially useful in cryptographic contexts when they possess a property called *zero-knowledge*. This means that the proof or argument reveals nothing but its own validity.

To give a concrete sense of why zero-knowledge protocols are useful, consider the following quintessential example from authentication. Suppose that Alice chooses a random password x and publishes a hash $z = h(x)$, where h is a one-way function. This means that given $z = h(x)$ for a randomly chosen x, enormous computational power should be required to find a preimage of z under h, i.e., an x' such that $h(x') = z$. Later, suppose that Alice wants to convince Bob that she is the same person who published z. She can do this by proving to Bob that she knows an x' such that $h(x') = z$. This will convince Bob that Alice is the same person who published z, since it means that either Alice knew x to begin with, or she inverted h (which is assumed to be beyond the computational capabilities of Alice).

How can Alice convince Bob that she knows a preimage of z under h? A trivial proof is for Alice to send x to Bob, and Bob can easily check that $h(x) = z$. But this reveals much more information than that Alice knows a preimage of z. In particular it reveals the preimage itself. Bob can use this knowledge to impersonate Alice forevermore, since now he too knows the preimage of z.

In order to prevent Bob from learning information that can compromise the password x, it is important that the proof reveals nothing beyond its own validity. This is exactly what the zero-knowledge property guarantees.

A particular goal of this survey is to describe a variety of approaches to constructing so-called zero-knowledge Succinct Non-interactive Arguments of Knowledge, or zk-SNARKs for short. "Succinct" means that the proofs are short. "Non-interactive" means that the proof is

---

[2]So long as the proof is written in a specific, mildly redundant format. See our treatment of *probabilistically checkable proofs* (PCPs) in Section 9.

static, consisting of a single message from the prover. "Of Knowledge" roughly means that the protocol establishes not only that a statement is true, but also that the prover *knows* a "witness" to the veracity of the statement.[3] Argument systems satisfying all of these properties have a myriad of applications throughout cryptography.

Practical zero-knowledge protocols for highly specialized statements of cryptographic relevance (such as proving knowledge of a discrete logarithm [223]) have been known for decades. However, general-purpose zero-knowledge protocols have only recently become plausibly efficient enough for cryptographic deployment. By general-purpose, we mean protocol design techniques that apply to arbitrary computations. This exciting progress has involved the introduction of beautiful new protocols, and brought a surge of interest in zero-knowledge proofs and arguments. This survey seeks to make accessible, in a unified manner, the main ideas and approaches to the design of these protocols.

Background and Context. In the mid-1980s and 1990s, theoretical computer scientists showed that IPs and arguments can be vastly more efficient (at least, in an asymptotic sense) than traditional **NP** proofs,[4] which are static and information-theoretically secure.[5] The foundational results characterizing the power of these protocols (such as **IP** = **PSPACE** [186], [231], **MIP** = **NEXP** [17], and the PCP theorem [10], [11]) are some of the most influential and celebrated in computational complexity theory.[6]

Despite their remarkable asymptotic efficiency, general-purpose VC protocols were long considered wildly impractical, and with good reason: naive implementations of the theory would have had comically high

---

[3] For example, the authentication scenario above really requires a zero-knowledge proof *of knowledge* for the statement "there exists a password x such that $h(x) = z$". This is because the application requires that Bob be convinced not just of the fact that there *exists* a preimage x of z under h (which will always be true if h is a surjective function), but also that Alice knows x.

[4] We formally define notions such as **NP** and **IP** in Section 3.3.

[5] The term information-theoretically secure here refers to the fact that **NP** proofs (like IPs, but unlike arguments) are secure against computationally unbounded provers.

[6] The results **IP** = **PSPACE** and **MIP** = **NEXP** are both covered in this survey (see Sections 4.5.5 and 8.5 respectively).

concrete costs (trillions of years for the prover, even for very short computations). But the last decade has seen major improvements in the costs of VC protocols, with a corresponding jump from theory to practice. Even though implementations of general-purpose VC protocols remain somewhat costly (especially for the prover), paying this cost can often be justified if the VC protocol is zero-knowledge, since zero-knowledge protocols enable applications that may be totally impossible without them. Moreover, emerging applications to public blockchains have elevated the importance of proving relatively simple statements, on which it is feasible to run modern VC protocols despite their costs.

Approaches to Zero-Knowledge Protocol Design, and Philosophy of This Survey. Argument systems are typically developed in a two-step process. First, an information-theoretically secure protocol, such as an IP, *multi-prover interactive proof* (MIP), or *probabilistically checkable proof* (PCP), is developed for a model involving one or more provers that are assumed to behave in some restricted manner (e.g., in an MIP, the provers are assumed not to send information to each other about the challenges they receive from the verifier). Second, the information-theoretically secure protocol is combined with cryptography to "force" a (single) prover to behave in the restricted manner, thereby yielding an argument system. This second step also often endows the resulting argument system with important properties, such as zero-knowledge, succinctness, and non-interactivity. If the resulting argument satisfies all of these properties, then it is in fact a zk-SNARK.

By now, there are a variety promising approaches to developing efficient zk-SNARKs, which can be categorized by the type of information-theoretically secure protocol upon which they are based. These include (1) IPs, (2) MIPs, (3) PCPs, or more precisely a related notion called *interactive oracle proofs* (IOPs), which is a hybrid between an IP and a PCP, and (4) *linear PCPs*. Sections 1.2.1–1.2.3 below give a more detailed overview of these models. This survey explains in a unified manner how to design efficient protocols in all four information-theoretically secure models, emphasizing commonalities between them.

IPs, MIPs, and PCPs/IOPs can all be transformed into succinct interactive arguments by combining them with a cryptographic primitive called a *polynomial commitment scheme*; the interactive arguments can then be rendered non-interactive and publicly verifiable by applying a cryptographic technique called the *Fiat-Shamir transformation* (Section 5.2), yielding a SNARK. Transformations from linear PCPs to arguments are somewhat different, though closely related to certain polynomial commitment schemes. As with the information-theoretically secure protocols themselves, this survey covers these cryptographic transformations in a unified manner.

Because of the two-step nature of zk-SNARK constructions, it is often helpful to first understand proofs and arguments *without* worrying about zero-knowledge, and then at the very end understand how to achieve zero-knowledge as an "add on" property. Accordingly, we do not discuss zero-knowledge until relatively late in this survey (Section 11). Earlier sections are devoted to describing efficient protocols in each of the information-theoretically secure models, and explaining how to transform them into succinct arguments.

By now, zk-SNARKs have been deployed in a number of real-world systems, and there is a large and diverse community of researchers, industry professionals, and open source software developers working to improve and deploy the technology. This survey assumes very little formal mathematical background—mainly comfort with modular arithmetic, some notions from the theory of finite fields and groups, and basic probability theory—and is intended as a resource for anyone interested in verifiable computing and zero-knowledge. However, it does require significant mathematical maturity and considerable comfort with theorems and proofs. Also helpful (but not strictly necessary) is knowledge of standard complexity classes like $\mathbf{P}$ and $\mathbf{NP}$, and complexity-theoretic notions such as $\mathbf{NP}$-completeness.

Ordering of Information-Theoretically Secure Models in This Survey.
We first cover IPs, then MIPs, then PCPs and IOPs, then linear PCPs. This ordering roughly follows the chronology of the models' introduction to the research literature. Perhaps ironically, the models have been applied to practical SNARK design in something resembling *reverse*

chronological order. For example, the first practical SNARKs were based on linear PCPs. In fact, this is not a coincidence: a primary motivation for introducing linear PCPs in the first place was the goal of obtaining simpler and more practical succinct arguments, and specifically the *impracticality* of arguments derived from PCPs.

Section-by-section Outline. Section 2 familiarizes the reader with randomness and the power of probabilistic proof systems, through two easy but important case studies. Section 3 introduces technical notions that will be useful throughout the survey. Sections 4 describes state-of-the-art interactive proofs. Section 5 describes the Fiat-Shamir transformation, a key technique that is used to remove interaction from cryptographic protocols. Section 7 introduces the notion of a polynomial commitment scheme, and combines it with the IPs of Section 4 and the Fiat-Shamir transformation of Section 5 to obtain the first SNARK covered in the survey. Section 8 describes state-of-the-art MIPs and SNARKs derived thereof. Sections 9–10 describe PCPs and IOPs, and SNARKs derived thereof.

Section 6 is a standalone section describing techniques for representing computer programs in formats amenable to application of such SNARKs.

Section 11 introduces the notion of zero-knowledge. Section 12 describes a particularly simple type of zero-knowledge argument called Σ-protocols, and uses them to derive commitment schemes. These commitment schemes serve as important building blocks for more complicated protocols covered in subsequent sections. Section 13 describes efficient techniques for transforming non-zero-knowledge protocols into zero-knowledge ones. Sections 14–16 cover practical polynomial commitment schemes, which can be used to turn any IP, MIP, or IOP into a succinct zero-knowledge argument of knowledge (zkSNARK). Section 17 covers our final approach to designing zkSNARKs, namely through linear PCPs. Section 18 describes how to recursively compose SNARKs to improve their costs and achieve important primitives such as so-called *incrementally verifiable computation*. Finally, Section 19 provides a taxonomy of design paradigms for practical zkSNARKs, and delineates the pros and cons of each approach.

Suggestions for Reading the Monograph. The monograph may happily be read from start to finish, but non-linear paths may offer a faster route to a big-picture understanding of SNARK design techniques. Suggestions to this effect are as follows.

Sections 2 and 3 introduce basic technical notions used throughout all subsequent sections (finite fields, IPs, arguments, low-degree extensions, the Schwartz-Zippel lemma, etc.), and should not be skipped by readers unfamiliar with these concepts.

Readers may next wish to read the *final* section, Section 19, which provides a birds-eye view of all SNARK design approaches and how they relate to each other. Section 19 uses some terminology that may be unfamiliar to the reader at this point, but it should nonetheless be understandable and it provides context that is helpful to have in mind when working through more technical sections.

After that, there are many possible paths through the monograph. Readers specifically interested in the SNARKs that were the first to be deployed in commercial settings can turn to Section 17 on linear PCPs. This section is essentially self-contained but for its use of pairing-based cryptography that is introduced in Section 15.1 (and, at the very end, its treatment of zero-knowledge, a concept introduced formally in Section 11).

Otherwise, readers should turn to understanding the alternative approach to SNARK design, namely to combine a *polynomial IOP* (of which IPs, MIPs, and PCPs are special cases) with a *polynomial commitment scheme.*

To quickly understand polynomial IOPs, we suggest a careful reading of Section 4.1 on the sum-check protocol, followed by Section 4.6 on the GKR interactive proof protocol for circuit evaluation, or Section 8.2 giving a 2-prover MIP for circuit satisfiability. Next, the reader can turn to Section 7, which explains how to combine such protocols with polynomial commitments to obtain succinct arguments.

To understand polynomial commitment schemes, the reader can either tackle Sections 10.4 and 10.5 to understand IOP-based polynomial commitments, or instead turn to Sections 12 and 14–16 (in that order) to understand polynomial commitments based on the discrete logarithm problem and pairings.

A compressed overview of polynomial IOPs and polynomial commitments is provided in a sequence of three talk videos posted on this monograph's webpage.[7] Readers may find it useful to watch these videos prior to a detailed reading of Sections 4–10.

Material That can be Skipped on a First Reading. Sections 4.2–4.5 are devoted to detailed example applications of the sum-check protocol and explaining how to efficiently implement the prover within it. While these sections contain interesting results and are useful for familiarizing oneself with the sum-check protocol, subsequent sections do not depend on them. Similarly, Section 5 on the Fiat-Shamir transformation and Section 6 on front-ends are optional on a first reading. Sections 9.3 and 9.4 provide PCPs that are mainly of historical interest and can be skipped.

Sections 11 and 13 offer treatments of zero-knowledge that largely stand on their own. Similarly, Section 18 discusses SNARK composition and stands on its own.

1.1 Mathematical Proofs

This survey covers different notions of *mathematical proofs* and their applications in computer science and cryptography. Informally, what we mean by a proof is anything that convinces someone that a statement is true, and a "proof system" is any procedure that decides what is and is not a convincing proof. That is, a proof system is specified by a verification procedure that takes as input any statement and a claimed "proof" that the statement is true, and decides whether or not the proof is valid.

What properties do we want in a proof system? Here are four obvious ones.

- Any true statement should have a convincing proof of its validity. This property is typically referred to as *completeness*.

- No false statement should have a convincing proof. This property is referred to as *soundness*.

---

[7]https://people.cs.georgetown.edu/jthaler/ProofsArgsAndZK.html.

- Ideally, the verification procedure will be "efficient". Roughly, this means that simple statements should have short (convincing) proofs that can be *checked* quickly.

- Ideally, proving should be efficient too. Roughly, this means that simple statements should have short (convincing) proofs that can be *found* quickly.

Traditionally, a mathematical proof is something that can be written and checked line-by-line for correctness. This traditional notion of proof is precisely the one captured by the complexity class **NP**.[8] However, over the last 30+ years, computer scientists have studied much more general and exotic notions of proofs. This has transformed computer scientists' notions of what it means to prove something, and has led to major advances in complexity theory and cryptography.

1.2 What Kinds of Non-Traditional Proofs Will We Study?

All of the notions of proofs that we study in this survey will be probabilistic in nature. This means that the verification procedure will make random choices, and the soundness guarantee will hold with (very) high probability over those random choices. That is, there will be a (very) small probability that the verification procedure will declare a false statement to be true.

1.2.1 Interactive Proofs (IPs)

To understand what an interactive proof is, it is helpful to think of the following application. Imagine a business (verifier) that is using a commercial cloud computing provider to store and process its data. The business sends all of its data up to the cloud (prover), which stores it, while the business stores only a very small "secret" summary of the data (meaning that the cloud does not know the user's secret summary). Later, the business asks the cloud a question about its data, typically

---

[8]Roughly speaking, the complexity class **NP** contains all problems for which the correct answer on any input is either YES or NO, and for all YES instances, there is an efficiently-checkable (traditional) proof that the correct answer is YES. See Section 3.3 for details.

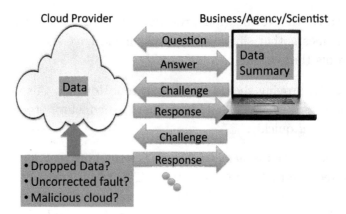

Figure 1.1: Depiction of an interactive proof or argument used to check that a cloud computing provider is storing and processing a user's data correctly.

in the form of a computer program f that the business wants the cloud to run on its data using the cloud's vast computing infrastructure. The cloud does so, and sends the user the claimed output of the program, $f(\mathsf{data})$. Rather than blindly trust that the cloud executed the program on the data correctly, the business can use an interactive proof system (IP) to obtain a formal *guarantee* that the claimed output is correct.

In the IP, the business interrogates the cloud, sending a sequence of challenges and receiving a sequence of responses. At the end of the interrogation, the business must decide whether to accept the answer as valid or reject it as invalid. See Figure 1.1 for a diagram of this interaction.

Completeness of the IP means that if the cloud correctly runs the program on the data and follows the prescribed protocol, then the user will be convinced to accept the answer as valid. Soundness of the IP means that if the cloud returns the wrong output, then the user will reject the answer as invalid with high probability *no matter how hard the cloud works to trick the user* into accepting the answer as valid. Intuitively, the interactive nature of the IP lets the business exploit the element of surprise (i.e., the fact that the cloud cannot predict the business's next challenge) to catch a lying cloud in a lie.

It is worth remarking on an interesting difference between IPs and traditional static proofs. Static proofs are *transferrable*, meaning that if

Peggy (prover) hands Victor (verifier) a proof that a statement is true, Victor can turn around and convince Tammy (a third party) that the same statement is true, simply by copying the proof. In contrast, an interactive proof may not be transferrable. Victor can try to convince Tammy that the statement is true by sending Tammy a transcript of his interaction with Peggy, but Tammy will not be convinced unless Tammy trusts that Victor correctly represented the interaction. This is because soundness of the IP only holds if, every time Peggy sends a response to Victor, Peggy does not know what challenge Victor will respond with next. The transcript alone does not give Tammy a guarantee that this holds.

1.2.2 Argument Systems

Argument systems are IPs, but where the soundness guarantee need only hold against cheating provers that run in polynomial time.[9] Argument systems make use of cryptography. Roughly speaking, in an argument system a cheating prover cannot trick the verifier into accepting a false statement unless it breaks some cryptosystem, and breaking the cryptosystem is assumed to require superpolynomial time.

1.2.3 Multi-Prover Interactive Proofs, Probabilistically Checkable Proofs, etc.

An MIP is like an IP, except that there are multiple provers, and these provers are assumed not to share information with each other regarding what challenges they receive from the verifier. A common analogy for MIPs is placing two or more criminal suspects in separate rooms before interrogating them, to see if they can keep their story straight. Law enforcement officers may be unsurprised to learn that the study of MIPs has lent theoretical justification to this practice. Specifically, the study of MIPs has revealed that if one locks the provers in separate rooms and then interrogates them separately, they can convince their

---

[9]Roughly speaking, this means that if the input has size n, then the prover's runtime (for sufficiently large values of n) should be bounded above by some constant power of n, e.g., n^{10}.

interrogators of much more complicated statements than if they are questioned together.

In a PCP, the proof is static as in a traditional mathematical proof, but the verifier is only allowed to read a small number of (possibly randomly chosen) characters from the proof.[10] This is in analogy to a lazy referee for a mathematical journal, who does not feel like painstakingly checking the proofs in a submitted paper for correctness. The PCP theorem [10], [11] essentially states that *any* traditional mathematical proof can be written in a format that enables this lazy reviewer to obtain a high degree of confidence in the validity of the proof by inspecting just a few words of it.

Philosophically, MIPs and PCPs are extremely interesting objects to study, but they are not directly applicable in most cryptographic settings, because they make unrealistic or onerous assumptions about the prover(s). For example, soundness of any MIP only holds if the provers do not share information with each other regarding what challenges they receive from the verifier. This is not directly useful in most cryptographic settings, because typically in these settings there is only a single prover, and even if there is more than one, there is no way to force the provers not to communicate. Similarly, although the verifier only reads a few characters of a PCP, a direct implementation of a PCP would require the prover to transmit the whole proof to the verifier, and this would be the dominant cost in most real-world scenarios (the example of a lazy journal referee notwithstanding). That is, once the prover transmits the whole proof to the verifier, there is little real-world benefit to having the verifier avoid reading the whole proof.

However, by combining MIPs and PCPs with cryptography, we will see how to turn them into argument systems, and these *are* directly applicable in cryptographic settings. For example, we will see in Section 9.2 how to turn a PCP into an argument system in which the prover does *not* have to send the whole PCP to the verifier.

---

[10]More precisely, a PCP verifier is allowed to read as much of the proof as it wants. However, for the PCP to be considered efficient, it must be the case that the verifier only needs to read a tiny fraction of the proof to ascertain with high confidence whether or not the proof is valid.

Section 10.2 of this survey in fact provides a unifying abstraction, called *polynomial IOPs*, of which all of the IPs, MIPs, and PCPs that we cover are a special case. It turns out that any polynomial IOP can be transformed into an argument system with short proofs, via a cryptographic primitive called a polynomial commitment scheme.

2

The Power of Randomness: Fingerprinting and Freivalds' Algorithm

2.1 Reed-Solomon Fingerprinting

The proof systems covered in this survey derive much of their power and efficiency from their use of randomness. Before we discuss the details of such proof systems, let us first develop an appreciation for how randomness can be exploited to dramatically improve the efficiency of certain algorithms. Accordingly, in this section, there are no untrusted provers or computationally weak verifiers. Rather, we consider two parties, Alice and Bob, who trust each other and want to cooperate to jointly compute a certain function of their inputs.

2.1.1 The Setting

Alice and Bob live across the country from each other. They each hold a very large file, each consisting of n characters (for concreteness, suppose that these are ASCII characters, so there are $m = 128$ possible characters). Let us denote Alice's file as the sequence of characters $(a_1, \ldots, a_n)$, and Bob's as $(b_1, \ldots, b_n)$. Their goal is to determine whether their files are *equal*, i.e., whether $a_i = b_i$ for all $i = 1, \ldots, n$. Since the files are large, they would like to minimize *communication*, i.e., Alice would like to send as little information about her file to Bob as possible.

A trivial solution to this problem is for Alice to send her entire file to Bob, and Bob can check whether $a_i = b_i$ for all $i = 1, \ldots, n$. But this requires Alice to send all n characters to Bob, which is prohibitive if n is very large. It turns out that no *deterministic* procedure can send less information than this trivial solution.[1]

However, we will see that if Alice and Bob are allowed to execute a *randomized* procedure that might output the wrong answer with some tiny probability, say at most 0.0001, then they can get away with a much smaller amount of communication.

2.1.2   The Communication Protocol

The High-Level Idea. The rough idea is that Alice is going to pick a hash function h at random from a (small) family of hash functions $\mathcal{H}$. We will think of $h(x)$ as a very short "fingerprint" of x. By fingerprint, we mean that $h(x)$ is a "nearly unique identifier" for x, in the sense that for any $y \neq x$, the fingerprints of x and y differ with high probability over the random choice of h, i.e.,

$$\text{for all } x \neq y, \Pr_{h \in \mathcal{H}} [h(x) = h(y)] \leq 0.0001.$$

Rather than sending a to Bob in full, Alice sends h and $h(a)$ to Bob. Bob checks whether $h(a) = h(b)$. If $h(a) \neq h(b)$, then Bob *knows* that $a \neq b$, while if $h(a) = h(b)$, then Bob can be very confident (but not 100% sure) that $a = b$.

The Details. To make the above outline concrete, fix a prime number $p \geq \max\{m, n^2\}$, and let $\mathbb{F}_p$ denote the set of integers modulo p. For the remainder of this section, we assume that all arithmetic is done *modulo p* without further mention.[2] This means that all numbers are

---

[1] The interested reader is directed to [177, Example 1.21] for a proof of this fact, based on the so-called *fooling set method* in communication complexity.

[2] The reason to perform all arithmetic modulo p rather than over the integers is to ensure that all numbers arising in the protocol can always be represented using just $\log_2(p) = O(\log(n) + \log(m))$ bits. If arithmetic were performed over the integers rather than modulo p, then the protocol covered in this section would require Alice

replaced with their remainder when divided by p. So, for example, if $p = 17$, then $(2 \cdot 3^2 + 4) \pmod{17} = 22 \pmod{17} = 5$.

The reason p must be chosen larger than n^2 is that the error probability of the protocol we are about to describe is less than n/p, and we wish this quantity to be bounded above by $1/n$ (larger choices of p will result in yet smaller error probabilities). The reason p must be chosen larger than the number of possible characters m is that the protocol will interpret Alice and Bob's inputs as vectors in $\mathbb{F}_p^n$ and check whether these vectors are equal. This means that we need a way to associate each possible character in Alice and Bob's inputs with a different element of $\mathbb{F}_p$, which is possible if and only if p is greater than or equal to m.

For each $r \in \mathbb{F}_p$, define $h_r(a_1, \ldots, a_n) = \sum_{i=1}^{n} a_i \cdot r^{i-1}$. The family $\mathcal{H}$ of hash functions we will consider is

$$\mathcal{H} = \{h_r : r \in \mathbb{F}_p\}. \tag{2.1}$$

Intuitively, each hash function h_r interprets its input $(a_1, \ldots, a_n)$ as the coefficients of a degree $n-1$ polynomial, and outputs the polynomial evaluated at r. That is, in our communication protocol, Alice picks a random element r from $\mathbb{F}_p$, computes $v = h_r(a)$, and sends v and r to Bob. Bob outputs EQUAL if $v = h_r(b)$, and outputs NOT-EQUAL otherwise.

2.1.3 The Analysis

We now prove that this protocol outputs the correct answer with very high probability. In particular:

- If $a_i = b_i$ for all $i = 1, \ldots, n$, then Bob outputs EQUAL for every possible choice of r.

- If there is even one i such that $a_i \neq b_i$, then Bob outputs NOT-EQUAL with probability at least $1 - (n-1)/p$, which is at least $1 - 1/n$ by choice of $p \geq n^2$.

---

to send to Bob an integer that may have magnitude more than 2^n, which would require more than n bits to represent. This is nearly as expensive as having Alice send her entire input to Bob.

The first property is easy to see: if $a = b$, then obviously $h_r(a) = h_r(b)$ for every possible choice of r. The second property relies on the following crucial fact, whose validity we justify later in Section 2.1.6.

Fact 2.1. For any two distinct (i.e., unequal) polynomials p_a, p_b of degree at most n with coefficients in $\mathbb{F}_p$, $p_a(x) = p_b(x)$ for at most n values of x in $\mathbb{F}_p$.

Let $p_a(x) = \sum_{i=1}^{n} a_i \cdot x^{i-1}$ and similarly $p_b(x) = \sum_{i=1}^{n} b_i \cdot x^{i-1}$. Observe that both p_a and p_b are polynomials in x of degree at most $n - 1$. The value v that Alice sends to Bob in the communication protocol is precisely $p_a(r)$, and Bob compares this value to $p_b(r)$.

By Fact 2.1, if there is even one i such that $a_i \neq b_i$, then there are at most $n - 1$ values of r such that $p_a(r) = p_b(r)$. Since r is chosen at random from $\mathbb{F}_p$, the probability that Alice picks such an r is thus at most $(n - 1)/p$. Hence, Bob outputs NOT-EQUAL with probability at least $1 - (n - 1)/p$ (where the probability is over the random choice of r).

2.1.4   Cost of the Protocol

Alice sends only two elements of $\mathbb{F}_p$ to Bob in the above protocol, namely v and r. In terms of bits, this is $O(\log n)$ bits assuming $p \leq n^c$ for some constant c. This is an *exponential improvement* over the $n \cdot \log m$ bits sent in the deterministic protocol (all logarithms in this monograph are to base 2 unless the base is explicitly specified otherwise). This is an impressive demonstration of the power of randomness.[3]

---

[3] Readers familiar with cryptographic hash functions such as SHA-3 may be in the habit of thinking of such a hash function as a fixed, deterministic function, and hence perplexed by the characterization of our protocol as randomized (as Alice just sends the hash function h and the evaluation $h(a)$ to Bob, where a is Alice's input vector). To this, we offer two clarifications. First, the communication protocol in this section actually does not require a cryptographic hash function. Rather, it uses a function chosen at random from the hash family given in Equation (2.1), which is in fact far simpler than any cryptographic hash family, e.g., it is not collision-resistant or one-way. Second, cryptographic hash functions such as SHA-3 really should be modeled as having been sampled at random from some large family. Otherwise, properties such as collision-resistance would be broken against non-uniform adversaries (i.e., adversaries permitted unlimited pre-processing). For example, collision-resistance

2.1.5 Discussion

We refer to the above protocol as Reed-Solomon fingerprinting because $p_a(r)$ is actually a random entry in an *error-corrected encoding* of the vector $(a_1, \ldots, a_n)$. The encoding is called the Reed-Solomon encoding. Several other fingerprinting methods are known. Indeed, all that we really require of the hash family $\mathcal{H}$ used in the protocol above is that for any $x \neq y$, $\Pr_{h \in \mathcal{H}}[h(x) = h(y)]$ is small. Many hash families are known to satisfy this property,[4] but Reed-Solomon fingerprinting will prove particularly relevant in our study of probabilistic proof systems, owing to its algebraic structure.

A few sentences on finite fields. A *field* is any set equipped with addition, subtraction, multiplication, and division operations, and such that these operations behave roughly the same as they do over the rational numbers.[5] So, for example, the set of real numbers is a field, because for any two real numbers c and d, it holds that $c+d$, $c-d$, $c \cdot d$, and (assuming $d \neq 0$) c/d are themselves all real numbers. The same holds for the set of complex numbers, and the set of rational numbers. In contrast, the set of integers is *not* a field, since dividing two integers does not necessarily yield another integer.

For any prime number p, $\mathbb{F}_p$ is also a field (a *finite* one). Here, the field operations are simply addition, subtraction, multiplication, and

---

of any fixed deterministic function h is broken by simply "hard-coding" into the adversary two distinct inputs x, x' such that $h(x) = h(x')$. This pre-processing attack does not work if h is chosen at random from a large family of functions, and the pre-processing has to occur prior to the random selection of h.

[4]Such hash families are called *universal*. The excellent Wikipedia article on universal hashing contains many constructions https://en.wikipedia.org/wiki/Universal_hashing.

[5]In more detail, the addition and multiplication operations in any field must be associative and commutative. They must also satisfy the distributive law, i.e., $a \cdot (b + c) = a \cdot b + a \cdot c$. Moreover, there must be two special elements in the field, denoted 0 and 1, that are additive and multiplicative identity elements, i.e., for all field elements a, it must hold that $a + 0 = a$ and $a \cdot 1 = a$. Every field element a must have an additive inverse, i.e., a field element $-a$ such that $a + (-a) = 0$. This ensures that subtraction can be defined in terms of addition of an additive inverse, i.e., $b - a$ is defined as $b + (-a)$. And every *nonzero* field element a must have a multiplicative inverse a^{-1} such that $a \cdot a^{-1} = 1$. This ensures that division by a nonzero field element a can be defined as multiplication by a^{-1}.

division modulo p. What we mean by division modulo p requires some explanation: for every $a \in \mathbb{F}_p \setminus \{0\}$, there is a unique element $a^{-1} \in \mathbb{F}_p$ such that $a \cdot a^{-1} = 1$. For example, if $p = 5$ and $a = 3$, then $a^{-1} = 2$, since $3 \cdot 2 \ (\mathrm{mod} \ 5) = 6 \ (\mathrm{mod} \ 5) = 1$. Division by a in $\mathbb{F}_p$ refers to multiplication by a^{-1}. So if $p = 5$, then in $\mathbb{F}_p$, $4/3 = 4 \cdot 3^{-1} = 4 \cdot 2 = 3$.

Much later in this monograph (e.g., Section 15.1), we will exploit the fact that for any prime *power* (i.e., p^k for some prime p and positive integer k), there is a unique finite field of size p^k, denoted $\mathbb{F}_{p^k}$.[6]

2.1.6　Establishing Fact 2.1

Fact 2.1 is implied by (in fact, equivalent to) the following fact.

Fact 2.2. Any nonzero polynomial of degree at most n over any field has at most n roots.

A simple proof of Fact 2.2 can be found online at [208]. To see that Fact 2.2 implies Fact 2.1, observe that if p_a and p_b are *distinct* polynomials of degree at most n, and $p_a(x) = p_b(x)$ for more than n values of $x \in \mathbb{F}_p$, then $p_a - p_b$ is a *nonzero* polynomial of degree at most n with more than n roots.

2.2　Freivalds' Algorithm

In this section, we see our first example of an efficient probabilistic proof system.

2.2.1　The Setting

Suppose we are given as input two $n \times n$ matrices A and B over $\mathbb{F}_p$, where $p > n^2$ is a prime number. Our goal is to compute the product matrix $A \cdot B$. Asymptotically, the fastest known algorithm for accomplishing this task is very complicated, and runs in time roughly $O(n^{2.37286})$ [5], [178]. Moreover, the algorithm is not practical. But for the purposes of this monograph, the relevant question is not how fast can one multiply

---

[6]More precisely, all finite fields of size p^k are isomorphic, roughly meaning they have the exact same structure, though they may not assign names to elements in the same manner.

two matrices—it's how efficiently can one *verify* that two matrices were multiplied correctly. In particular, can verifying the output of a matrix multiplication problem be done faster than the fastest known algorithm for actually multiplying the matrices? The answer, given by Freivalds in 1977 [115], is yes.

Formally, suppose someone hands us a matrix C, and we want to check whether or not $C = A \cdot B$. Here is a very simple randomized algorithm that will let us perform this check in $O(n^2)$ time.[7] This is only a constant factor more time than what is required to simply read the matrices A, B, and C.

2.2.2 The Algorithm

First, choose a random $r \in \mathbb{F}_p$, and let $x = (1, r, r^2, \ldots, r^{n-1})$. Then compute $y = Cx$ and $z = A \cdot Bx$, outputting YES if $y = z$ and NO otherwise.

2.2.3 Runtime

We claim that the entire algorithm runs in time $O(n^2)$. It is easy to see that generating the vector $x = (1, r, r^2, \ldots, r^{n-1})$ can be done with $O(n)$ total multiplication operations (r^2 can be computed as $r \cdot r$, then r^3 can be computed as $r \cdot r^2$, then r^4 as $r \cdot r^3$, and so on). Since multiplying an $n \times n$ matrix by an n-dimensional vector can be done in $O(n^2)$ time, the remainder of the algorithm runs in $O(n^2)$ time: computing y involves multiplying C by the vector x, and computing $A \cdot Bx$ involves multiplying B by x to get a vector $w = Bx$, and then multiplying A by w to compute $A \cdot Bx$.

2.2.4 Completeness and Soundness Analysis

Let $D = A \cdot B$, so that our goal is to determine whether the *claimed* product matrix C actually equals the *true* product matrix D. Letting $[n]$ denote the set $\{1, 2, \ldots, n\}$, we claim that the above algorithm satisfies the following two conditions:

---

[7]Throughout this monograph, we assume that addition and multiplication operations in finite fields take constant time.

- If $C = D$, then the algorithm outputs YES for every possible choice of r.

- If there is even one $(i, j) \in [n] \times [n]$ such that $C_{i,j} \neq D_{i,j}$, then Bob outputs NO with probability at least $1 - (n-1)/p$.

The first property is easy to see: if $C = D$, then clearly $Cx = Dx$ for all vectors x, so the algorithm will output YES for every choice of r. To see that the second property holds, suppose that $C \neq D$, and let C_i and D_i denote the ith row of C and D respectively. Obviously, since $C \neq D$, there is some row i such that $C_i \neq D_i$. Recalling that $x = (1, r, r^2, \ldots, r^{n-1})$, observe that $(Cx)_i$ is precisely $p_{C_i}(r)$, the Reed-Solomon fingerprint of C_i as in the previous section. Similarly, $(A \cdot B \cdot x)_i = p_{D_i}(r)$. Hence, by the analysis of Section 2.1.3, the probability that $(Cx)_i \neq (A \cdot B \cdot x)_i$ is at least $1 - (n-1)/p$, and in this event the algorithm outputs NO.

2.2.5 Discussion

Whereas fingerprinting saved communication compared to a deterministic protocol, Freivalds' algorithm saves *runtime* compared to the best known deterministic algorithm. We can think of Freivalds' algorithm as our first probabilistic proof system: here, the proof is simply the answer C itself, and the $O(n^2)$-time verification procedure simply checks whether $Cx = A \cdot Bx$.

Freivalds actually described his algorithm with a perfectly random vector $x \in \mathbb{F}_p^n$, rather than $x = (1, r, r^2, \ldots, r^{n-1})$ for a random $r \in \mathbb{F}_p$ (see Exercise 3.1). We chose $x = (1, r, r^2, \ldots, r^{n-1})$ to ensure that $(Cx)_i$ is a Reed-Solomon fingerprint of row i of C, thereby allowing us to invoke the analysis from Section 2.1.

2.3 An Alternative View of Fingerprinting and Freivalds' Algorithm

Recall from Section 2.1.5 that the fingerprinting protocol for equality testing can be viewed as follows. Alice and Bob replace their length-n vectors $a, b \in \mathbb{F}_p^n$ with so-called Reed-Solomon encodings of these vectors. These encodings are vectors of length $p \gg n$. They interpret a and b as

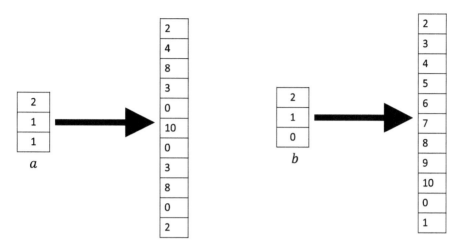

Figure 2.1: On the left is the vector $a = (2, 1, 1)$ of length 3 with entries interpreted as elements of the field $\mathbb{F}_{11}$, as well as its Reed-Solomon encoding. The Reed-Solomon encoding interprets a as the polynomial $p_a(x) = 2 + x + x^2$ and lists all evaluations of p_a over the field $\mathbb{F}_{11}$. On the right is the vector $b = (2, 1, 0)$ and its Reed-Solomon encoding.

specifying polynomials p_a and p_b over $\mathbb{F}_p$, and for each $r \in \mathbb{F}_p$, the r'th entry of the encodings of a and b are respectively $p_a(r)$ and $p_b(r)$. See Figure 2.1 for an example.

The Reed-Solomon encoding of a vector a is a *much* larger vector than a itself—whereas a has length n, the encoding of a has length p. The encoding is *distance-amplifying*: if a and b differ on even a single coordinate, then their encodings will differ on a $1 - (n-1)/p$ fraction of coordinates.[8] Due to the distance-amplifying nature of the code, it is enough for Alice to pick a single random entry of the encoding of her vector a and send it to Bob, who compares it to the corresponding entry of b's encoding.

---

[8] Reed-Solomon codes, and other encoding procedures used in this monograph, are typically called *error-correcting* codes rather than *distance-amplifying* codes. Distance-amplification of the encodings in fact implies error-correcting properties, meaning that if some entries of an encoding are corrupted, the "true" encoding can be recovered. However, no parties in any of the protocols in this monograph ever need to correct errors—only the distance-amplifying properties of the encoding procedure are exploited by the protocols.

Hence, checking equality of two vectors a and b was reduced to checking equality of a *single* (randomly chosen) entry of the encodings. Note that while the encodings of a and b are huge vectors, neither Alice nor Bob ever needed to materialize the full encodings—they both only needed to "access" a single random entry of each encoding.

Similarly, Freivalds' algorithm can be thought of as evaluating a single randomly chosen entry of the Reed-Solomon encoding of each row of the claimed answer C and the true answer D, and comparing the results. Evaluating just a single entry of the encoding of each row of D can be done in just $O(n^2)$ time, which is much faster than any known algorithm to compute D from scratch.

In summary, both protocols reduced the task of checking equality of two large objects (the vectors a and b in the fingerprinting protocol, and the claimed answer matrix and true answer matrix in Freivalds' algorithm) to checking equality of just a single random entry of distance-amplified encodings of those objects. While deterministically checking equality of the two large objects would be very expensive in terms of either communication or computation time, evaluating a single entry of the each object's encoding can be done with only logarithmic communication or in just linear time.

2.4   Univariate Lagrange Interpolation

The Reed-Solomon encoding of a vector $a = (a_1, \ldots, a_n) \in \mathbb{F}^n$ described in Section 2.3 interprets a as the *coefficients* of a univariate polynomial p_a of degree $n - 1$, i.e., $p_a(X) = \sum_{i=1}^n a_i X^{i-1}$. There are other ways to interpret a as the description of a univariate polynomial q_a of degree $n - 1$. The most natural such alternative is to view $a_1, \ldots, a_n$ as the *evaluations* of q_a over some canonical set of inputs, say, $\{0, 1, \ldots, n-1\}$. Indeed, as we now explain, for any list of n (input, output) pairs, there is a unique univariate polynomial of degree $n - 1$ consistent with those pairs. The process of defining this polynomial q_a is called *Lagrange interpolation* for univariate polynomials.

Lemma 2.3 (Univariate Lagrange Interpolation). Let p be a prime larger than n and $\mathbb{F}_p$ be the field of integers modulo p. For any vector $a =$

$(a_1, \ldots, a_n) \in \mathbb{F}^n$, there is a unique univariate polynomial q_a of degree at most $n - 1$ such that

$$q_a(i) = a_{i+1} \text{ for } i = 0, \ldots, n - 1. \tag{2.2}$$

Proof. We give an explicit expression for the polynomial q_a with the behavior claimed in Equation (2.2). To do so, we introduce the notion of Lagrange basis polynomials.

Lagrange basis polynomials. For each $i \in \{0, \ldots, n - 1\}$, define the following univariate polynomial δ_i over $\mathbb{F}_p$:

$$\delta_i(X) = \prod_{k=0,1,\ldots,n-1: \, k \neq i} (X - k)/(i - k). \tag{2.3}$$

It is straightforward to check that $\delta_i(X)$ has degree at most $n - 1$, since the product on the right hand side of Equation (2.3) has $n - 1$ terms, each of which is a polynomial in X of degree 1. Moreover, it can be checked that δ_i maps i to 1 and maps all other points in $\{0, 1, \ldots, n-1\}$ to 0.[9] In this way, δ_i acts as an "indicator function" for input i, in that it maps i to 1 and "kills" all other inputs in $\{0, 1, \ldots, n - 1\}$. δ_i is referred to as the i'th *Lagrange basis polynomial*.

For example, if $n = 4$, then

$$\delta_0(X) = \frac{(X - 1) \cdot (X - 2) \cdot (X - 3)}{(0 - 1) \cdot (0 - 2) \cdot (0 - 3)} = -6^{-1} \cdot (X - 1)(X - 2)(X - 3), \tag{2.4}$$

$$\delta_1(X) = \frac{(X - 0) \cdot (X - 2) \cdot (X - 3)}{(1 - 0) \cdot (1 - 2) \cdot (1 - 3)} = 2^{-1} \cdot X(X - 2)(X - 3), \tag{2.5}$$

$$\delta_2(X) = \frac{(X - 0) \cdot (X - 1) \cdot (X - 3)}{(2 - 0) \cdot (2 - 1) \cdot (2 - 3)} = -2^{-1} \cdot X(X - 1)(X - 3), \tag{2.6}$$

and

$$\delta_3(X) = \frac{(X - 0) \cdot (X - 1) \cdot (X - 2)}{(3 - 0) \cdot (3 - 1) \cdot (3 - 2)} = 6^{-1} \cdot X(X - 1)(X - 2). \tag{2.7}$$

Expressing q_a in terms of the Lagrange basis polynomials. Recall that we wish to identify a polynomial q_a of degree $n - 1$ such that

---

[9]Note, however, that $\delta_i(r)$ does *not* equal 0 for any points $r \in \mathbb{F}_p \setminus \{0, 1, \ldots, n-1\}$.

$q_a(i) = a_{i+1}$ for $i \in \{0, 1, \ldots, n-1\}$. We can define such a polynomial q_a in terms of the Lagrange basis polynomials as follows:

$$q_a(X) = \sum_{j=0}^{n-1} a_{j+1} \cdot \delta_j(X). \tag{2.8}$$

Indeed, for any $i \in \{0, 1, \ldots, n-1\}$, every term in the sum on the right hand side of Equation (2.8) other than the i'th evaluates to 0, because $\delta_j(i) = 0$ for $j \neq i$. Meanwhile, the i'th term evaluates to $a_{i+1} \cdot \delta_i(i) = a_{i+1}$ as desired. See Figure 2.2 for examples.

Establishing uniqueness. The fact that q_a defined in Equation (2.8) is the unique polynomial of degree at most $n-1$ satisfying Equation (2.2) holds because any two distinct polynomials of degree at most $n-1$ can agree on at most $n-1$ inputs. Since Equation (2.2) specifies the behavior of q_a on n inputs, this means that there cannot be two distinct polynomials of degree at most $n-1$ that satisfy the equation. □

Specifying a Polynomial Via Evaluations vs. Coefficients. Readers are likely already comfortable with univariate polynomials p of degree

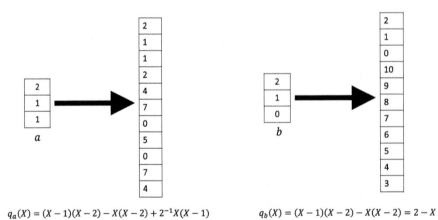

$$q_a(X) = (X-1)(X-2) - X(X-2) + 2^{-1}X(X-1) \qquad q_b(X) = (X-1)(X-2) - X(X-2) = 2 - X$$

Figure 2.2: On the left is the vector $a = (2, 1, 1)$ of length 3 with entries interpreted as elements of the field $\mathbb{F}_{11}$, as well as its univariate low-degree extension encoding. This encoding interprets a as the evaluations of a univariate polynomial q_a over the input set $\{0, 1, 2\} \subseteq \mathbb{F}_{11}$, and the encoding lists all evaluations of q_a over the field $\mathbb{F}_{11}$. On the right is the vector $b = (2, 1, 0)$ and its low-degree extension encoding.

$(n-1)$ that are specified via coefficients in the standard monomial basis, meaning $c_0, \ldots, c_{n-1}$ such that

$$p(X) = c_0 + c_1 X + \cdots + c_{n-1} X^{n-1}.$$

As indicated before the statement of Lemma 2.3, the n evaluations $\{p(0), p(1), \ldots, p(n-1)\}$ can be thought of as an alternative specification of p. Just as the standard coefficients $c_0, c_1, \ldots, c_{n-1}$ uniquely specify p, so do prescribed evaluations at the n inputs $0, 1, \ldots, n-1$.

In fact, Equation (2.8) shows that these n evaluations of p can themselves be interpreted as coefficients for p, not over the standard monomial basis $\{1, X, X^2, \ldots, X^{n-1}\}$, but rather over the Lagrange polynomial basis $\{\delta_0, \delta_1, \ldots, \delta_{n-1}\}$. In other words, for $i \in \{0, 1, \ldots, n-1\}$, $p(i)$ is the coefficient of δ_i in the unique representation of p as a linear combination of Lagrange basis polynomials.

A Coding-Theoretic View. Given a vector $a = (a_1, \ldots, a_n) \in \mathbb{F}_p^n$, the polynomial q_a given in Lemma 2.3 is often called the *univariate low-degree extension* of a.[10] The viewpoint underlying this terminology is as follows. Consider the vector $\mathrm{LDE}(a)$ of length $p = |\mathbb{F}_p|$ whose ith entry is $q_a(i)$. If $p \gg n$, then $\mathrm{LDE}(a)$ is vastly longer than a itself. But $\mathrm{LDE}(a)$ contains a as a sub-vector, since, by design, $q_a(i) = a_{i+1}$ for $i \in \{0, \ldots, n-1\}$. One thinks of $\mathrm{LDE}(a)$ as an "extension" of a: $\mathrm{LDE}(a)$ "begins" with a itself, but includes a large number of additional entries. See Figure 2.2.

Such encoding functions, in which the vector a is a subset of its encoding $\mathrm{LDE}(a)$ are called *systematic*. The systematic nature of the low-degree extension encoding turns out to render it more useful in the context of interactive proofs and arguments than the Reed-Solomon encoding of Section 2.3 (see, for example, Section 10.3.2).

---

[10] Actually, many authors refer to *any* "reasonably low-degree" polynomial q satisfying $q(i) = a_{i+1}$ for $i \in \{0, 1, \ldots, n-1\}$ as a low-degree extension of a (however, there is always a *unique* extension polynomial q_a of a of degree at most $n-1$). What "reasonably low-degree" means varies by context, but typically the asymptotic costs of probabilistic proof systems that use univariate extension polynomials are unchanged so long as the extension polynomial has degree $O(n)$. At the bare minimum, the degree of the extension polynomial should be smaller than the size of the field over which the polynomial is defined. Otherwise, encoding a via the evaluation table of the extension polynomial will not be a distance-amplifying procedure.

Exactly as for the Reed-Solomon code in Section 2.3, $\text{LDE}(a)$ is a distance-amplified encoding of a, in the sense that, for any two vectors $a, b \in \mathbb{F}_p^n$ that differ in even a single coordinate, $\text{LDE}(a)$ and $\text{LDE}(b)$ differ in at least a $1 - (n-1)/p$ fraction of entries. This fraction is very close to 1 if $p \gg n$.

A Note on Terminology.   In the coding theory literature, a is referred to as a *message* and the encoding $\text{LDE}(a)$ is called as the *codeword* corresponding to message a. Many authors use the term Reed-Solomon encoding and low-degree extension encoding interchangeably. Often, the distinction does not matter, as the set of codewords is the same regardless, namely the set of all evaluation tables of polynomials of degree at most $n - 1$ over $\mathbb{F}_p$. All that differs between the two is the correspondence between messages and codewords, i.e., whether the message is interpreted as the coefficients of a polynomial of degree $n - 1$, vs. as the evaluations of the polynomial over a canonical set of inputs such as $\{0, 1, \ldots, n - 1\}$.

Algorithms for Evaluating $q_a(r)$.   Suppose that, given a vector $a \in \mathbb{F}_p^n$, one wishes to evaluate the univariate low-degree extension q_a at some input $r \in \mathbb{F}$. How quickly can this be done? It turns out that $O(n)$ field additions, multiplications, and inversions are sufficient.[11]

If $r \in \{0, 1, \ldots, n - 1\}$, then by definition, $q_a(r) = a_{r+1}$. So let us assume henceforth that $r \in \mathbb{F} \setminus \{0, 1, \ldots, n - 1\}$.

Equation (2.8) offers an expression for $q_a(r)$ in terms of the Lagrange basis polynomials, namely

$$q_a(r) = \sum_{j=0}^{n-1} a_{j+1} \cdot \delta_j(r). \tag{2.9}$$

There are only n terms of this sum. However, evaluating the j'th term requires evaluating $\delta_j(r)$, and if this is done directly via its definition

---

[11] A single field inversion is a slower operation than a field addition or multiplication operation, often performed via the so-called Extended Euclidean algorithm. However, there are batch inversion algorithms that can perform n field inversions with roughly $3n$ field multiplications and one field inversion.

(Equation (2.3)), this requires $O(n)$ field operations per term, for a total time bound of $O(n \cdot n) = O(n^2)$.

Fortunately, it turns out that the n values $\delta_0(r), \delta_1(r), \ldots, \delta_{n-1}(r)$ can all be evaluated using just $O(n)$ additions, multiplications, and inversions *in total*. Once these values are all computed, the right hand side of Equation (2.9) can be computed with $O(n)$ additional field operations.

Here is how to evaluate $\delta_0(r), \delta_1(r), \ldots, \delta_{n-1}(r)$ with $O(n)$ additions, multiplications, and inversions. First, $\delta_0(r)$ can be evaluated with $O(n)$ such operations directly via its definition (Equation (2.3)).

Then, for each $i > 0$, given $\delta_{i-1}(r)$, $\delta_i(r)$ can be computed with a constant number of additional field subtractions, multiplications, and inversions. This is because the products defining $\delta_i(r)$ and $\delta_{i-1}(r)$ involve almost all of the same terms. For example, relative to

$$\delta_0(r) = \left(\prod_{k=1,\ldots,n-1} (r-k) \right) \left(\prod_{k=1,\ldots,n-1} (0-k)^{-1} \right),$$

the definition of

$$\delta_1(r) = \left(\prod_{k=0,2,3,\ldots,n-1} (r-k) \right) \cdot \left(\prod_{k=0,2,3,\ldots,n-1} (1-k)^{-1} \right)$$

is "missing" a factor of

$$(r-1) \cdot \left(-(n-1) \right)^{-1},$$

and has an "extra" factor of

$$(r-0)(1-0)^{-1} = r.$$

In other words, $\delta_1(r) = \delta_0(r) \cdot r \cdot (r-1)^{-1} \cdot (-(n-1))$. In general, for $i \geq 1$, the following key equation ensures that $\delta_i(r)$ can be computed from $\delta_{i-1}(r)$ with just $O(1)$ field additions, multiplications, and inversions:

$$\delta_i(r) = \delta_{i-1}(r) \cdot (r - (i-1)) \cdot (r-i)^{-1} \cdot i^{-1} \cdot (-(n-i)). \quad (2.10)$$

Theorem 2.4. Let $p \geq n$ be a prime number. Given as input $a_1, \ldots, a_n \in \mathbb{F}_p$, and $r \in \mathbb{F}_p$, there is an algorithm that performs $O(n)$ additions, multiplications, and inversions over $\mathbb{F}_p$, and outputs $q(r)$ for the unique univariate polynomial q of degree at most $n-1$ such that $q(i) = a_{i+1}$ for $i \in \{0, 1, \ldots, n-1\}$.

A Worked Example of Equation (2.10).   When $n = 4$, explicit expressions for δ_0, δ_1, δ_2, and δ_3 were given in Equations (2.4)–(2.7). One can check that Equation (2.10) holds for each of these Lagrange basis polynomials. Indeed,

$$\delta_0(r) = -6^{-1} \cdot (r-1)(r-2)(r-3),$$
$$\delta_1(r) = 2^{-1} \cdot r(r-2)(r-3) = \delta_0(r) \cdot r \cdot (r-1)^{-1} \cdot 1^{-1} \cdot (-(n-1)),$$
$$\delta_2(r) = -2^{-1} \cdot r(r-1)(r-3) = \delta_1(r) \cdot (r-1) \cdot (r-2)^{-1} \cdot 2^{-1} \cdot (-(n-2)),$$

and

$$\delta_3(r) = 6^{-1} \cdot r(r-1)(r-2) = \delta_2(r) \cdot (r-2) \cdot (r-3)^{-1} \cdot 3^{-1} \cdot (-(n-3)).$$

3

Definitions and Technical Preliminaries

3.1 Interactive Proofs

Given a function f mapping $\{0,1\}^n$ to a finite range $\mathcal{R}$, a k-message *interactive proof system* (IP) for f consists of a probabilistic verifier algorithm $\mathcal{V}$ running in time $\mathrm{poly}(n)$ and a prescribed ("honest") deterministic prover algorithm $\mathcal{P}$.[1,2] Both $\mathcal{V}$ and $\mathcal{P}$ are given a common input $x \in \{0,1\}^n$, and at the start of the protocol $\mathcal{P}$ provides a value y claimed to equal $f(x)$. Then $\mathcal{P}$ and $\mathcal{V}$ exchange a sequence of messages $m_1, m_2, \ldots, m_k$ that are determined as follows. The IP designates one of the parties, either $\mathcal{P}$ or $\mathcal{V}$, to send the first message m_1. The party

---

[1]In general, one may consider defining IPs to permit probabilistic prover strategies. However, as explained in Section 3.3, it is without loss of generality to restrict attention to deterministic prover strategies.

[2]The choice of domain $\{0,1\}^n$ in this section is not essential, but rather made by convention and for convenience. One reason $\{0,1\}^n$ is a convenient domain is that, in order to express a proof system's costs (e.g., prover time and verifier time) in terms of the size of the input, we need a well-defined notion of input size, and if the input domain is all n-bit strings, then n is the natural such measure.

sending each message alternates, meaning for example that if $\mathcal{V}$ sends m_1, then $\mathcal{P}$ sends m_2, $\mathcal{V}$ sends m_3, $\mathcal{P}$ sends m_4, and so on.[3]

Both $\mathcal{P}$ and $\mathcal{V}$ are thought of as "next-message-computing algorithms", meaning that when it is $\mathcal{V}$'s (respectively, $\mathcal{P}$'s) turn to send a message m_i, $\mathcal{V}$ (respectively, $\mathcal{P}$) is run on input $(x, m_1, m_2, \ldots, m_{i-1})$ to produce message m_i. Note that since $\mathcal{V}$ is probabilistic, any message m_i sent by $\mathcal{V}$ may depend on both $(x, m_1, m_2, \ldots, m_{i-1})$ and on the verifier's internal randomness.

The entire sequence of k messages $t := (m_1, m_2, \ldots, m_k)$ exchanged by $\mathcal{P}$ and $\mathcal{V}$, along with the claimed answer y, is called a *transcript*. At the end of the protocol, $\mathcal{V}$ must output either 0 or 1, with 1 indicating that the verifier accepts the prover's claim that $y = f(x)$ and 0 indicating that the verifier rejects the claim. The value output by the verifier at the end of the protocol may depend on both the transcript t and the verifier's internal randomness.

Denote by $\mathrm{out}(\mathcal{V}, \mathrm{x}, \mathrm{r}, \mathcal{P}) \in \{0, 1\}$ the output of verifier $\mathcal{V}$ on input x when interacting with deterministic prover strategy $\mathcal{P}$, with $\mathcal{V}$'s internal randomness equal to r. For any fixed value r of $\mathcal{V}$'s internal randomness, $\mathrm{out}(\mathcal{V}, \mathrm{x}, \mathrm{r}, \mathcal{P})$ is a deterministic function of x (as we have restricted our attention to deterministic prover strategies $\mathcal{P}$).

Definition 3.1. An interactive proof system $(\mathcal{V}, \mathcal{P})$ is said to have completeness error δ_c and soundness error δ_s if the following two properties hold.

(1) *(Completeness)* For every $x \in \{0, 1\}^n$,

$$\Pr_r[\mathrm{out}(\mathcal{V}, \mathrm{x}, \mathrm{r}, \mathcal{P}) = 1] \geq 1 - \delta_c.$$

(2) *(Soundness)* For every $x \in \{0, 1\}^n$ and *every* deterministic prover strategy $\mathcal{P}'$, if $\mathcal{P}'$ sends a value $y \neq f(x)$ at the start of the

---

[3]Without loss of generality, the final message m_k is sent by the prover. There is no point in having the verifier send a message to the prover if the prover is not going to respond to it.

protocol, then

$$\Pr_r[\text{out}(\mathcal{V}, x, r, \mathcal{P}') = 1] \le \delta_s.$$

An interactive proof system is valid if $\delta_c, \delta_s \le 1/3$.

Intuitively, for any input x, the completeness condition requires that there be a convincing proof for what is the value of f on input x. The soundness condition requires that false statements of the form "$f(x) = y$" for any $y \ne f(x)$ lack a convincing proof. That is, there is no cheating prover strategy $\mathcal{P}'$ that can convince $\mathcal{V}$ to accept a false claim with probability more than $1/3$.

The two costs of paramount importance in any interactive proof are $\mathcal{P}$'s runtime and $\mathcal{V}$'s runtime, but there are other important costs as well: $\mathcal{P}$'s and $\mathcal{V}$'s space usage, the total number of bits communicated, and the total number of messages exchanged. If $\mathcal{V}$ and $\mathcal{P}$ exchange k messages, then $\lceil k/2 \rceil$ is referred to as the *round complexity* of the interactive proof system.[4] The round complexity is the number of "back-and-forths" in the interaction between $\mathcal{P}$ and $\mathcal{V}$. If k is odd, then the final "back-and-forth" in the interaction is really just a "back" with no "forth", i.e., it consists of only one message from prover to verifier.

Interactive proofs were introduced in 1985 by Goldwasser *et al.* [133] and Babai [15].[5]

3.2 Argument Systems

Definition 3.2. An *argument system* for a function f is an interactive proof for f in which the soundness condition is only required to hold against prover strategies that run in polynomial time.

---

[4]Be warned that the literature is not consistent with regard to the meaning of the term "rounds". Vexingly, many papers use the terms rounds and messages interchangeably.

[5]More precisely, [133] introduced IPs, while Babai (with different motivations) introduced the so-called *Arthur-Merlin class hierarchy*, which captures constant-round interactive proof systems, with the additional requirement that the verifier's randomness is public—that is, any coin tossed by $\mathcal{V}$ is made visible to the prover as soon as it is tossed. See Section 3.3 for discussion of public vs. private verifier randomness.

The notion of soundness in Definition 3.2 is called *computational soundness*. Computational soundness should be contrasted with the notion of soundness in Definition 3.1, which is required to hold even against computationally unbounded provers $\mathcal{P}'$ that might be devoting enormous computational resources to trying to trick $\mathcal{V}$ into accepting an incorrect answer. The soundness notion from Definition 3.1 is referred to as *statistical soundness* or *information-theoretic soundness*.

Argument systems were introduced by Brassard *et al.* in 1986 [77]. They are sometimes referred to as *computationally sound proofs*, but in this monograph we will mainly use the term "proof" to refer to statistically sound protocols.[6] Unlike interactive proofs, argument systems are able to utilize cryptographic primitives. While a super-polynomial time prover may be able to break the primitive and thereby trick the verifier into accepting an incorrect answer, a polynomial time prover will be unable to break the primitive. The use of cryptography often allows argument systems to achieve additional desirable properties that are unattainable for interactive proofs, such as reusability (i.e., the ability for the verifier to reuse the same "secret state" to outsource many computations on the same input), public verifiability, etc. These properties will be discussed in more detail later in this survey.

3.3 Robustness of Definitions and the Power of Interaction

At first glance, it may seem that a number of aspects of Definitions 3.1 and 3.2 are somewhat arbitrary or unmotivated. For example, why does Definition 3.1 insist that the soundness and completeness errors be at most $1/3$, and not some smaller number? Why does the completeness condition in Definition 3.1 demand that the honest prover is deterministic? And so forth. As we explain in this section, many of these choices are made for convenience or aesthetic reasons—the power of IPs and arguments are largely unchanged if different choices are made in the

---

[6]The main exception is in Section 18, where we use the term "SNARK proof π" to refer to a string π that convinces the verifier of a non-interactive argument system to accept. This terminology is unambiguous because the acronym SNARK, which is short for Succinct Non-interactive ARgument of Knowledge, clarifies that the protocol at hand is an argument system.

definitions.[7] The remarks in this section are somewhat technical and may be skipped with no loss of continuity.

- (Perfect vs. Imperfect Completeness) While Definition 3.1 required that the completeness error $\delta_c < 1/3$, all of the interactive proofs that we will see in this monograph actually satisfy *perfect* completeness, meaning that $\delta_c = 0$. That is, the honest prover in our IPs and arguments will *always* convince the verifier that it is honest.

  It is actually known [119] that any IP for a function f with $\delta_c \leq 1/3$ can be transformed into an IP for f with perfect completeness, with a polynomial blowup in the verifier's costs (e.g., verifier time, round complexity, communication complexity).[8] We will not need such transformations in this monograph, because the IPs we give will naturally satisfy perfect completeness.

- (Soundness Error) While Definition 3.1 required the soundness error δ_s to be at most $1/3$, the constant $1/3$ is merely chosen by convention. In all of the interactive proofs that we see in this survey, the soundness error will always be proportional to $1/|\mathbb{F}|$, where $\mathbb{F}$ is the field over which the interactive proof is defined. In practice, the field will typically be chosen large enough so that the soundness error is astronomically small (e.g., smaller than, say, 2^{-128}). Such tiny soundness error is essential in cryptographic applications, where a cheating prover successfully tricking a verifier to accept a false claim can have catastrophic effects. Soundness error of any IP or argument can also be generically reduced from δ_s to δ_s^k by

---

[7]Generally speaking, robustness to tweaks in the definition is a hallmark of a "good" notion or model in complexity theory. If the power of a model is highly sensitive to idiosyncratic or arbitrary choices in its definition, then the model may have limited utility and be unlikely to capture fundamental real-world phenomena. After all, the real world is messy and evolving—the hardware people use to compute is complicated and changes over time, protocols get used in a variety of different settings, etc. Robustness of a model to various tweaks helps ensure that any protocols in the model are useful in a variety of different settings and will not be rendered obsolete by future changes in technology.

[8]The transformation does *not* necessarily preserve the prover's runtime.

repeating the protocol $\Theta(k)$ times in sequence and rejecting unless the verifier accepts in a majority of the repetitions.[9]

- (Public vs. Private Randomness) In an interactive proof system, $\mathcal{V}$'s randomness is internal, and in particular is not visible to the prover. This is referred to in the literature as *private randomness*. One can also consider IPs in which the verifier's randomness is public—that is, any coin tossed by $\mathcal{V}$ is made visible to the prover as soon as it is tossed. We will see that such *public-coin* IPs are particularly useful, because they can be combined with cryptography to obtain argument systems with important properties (see Section 5 on the Fiat-Shamir transformation).

  Goldwasser and Sipser [136] showed that the distinction between public and private coins is not crucial: any private coin interactive proof system can be simulated by a public coin system (with a polynomial blowup in costs for the verifier, and a small increase in the number of rounds). As with perfect vs. imperfect completeness, we will not need to utilize such transformations in this monograph because all of the IPs that we give are naturally public coin protocols.

- (Deterministic vs. Probabilistic Provers) Definition 3.1 demands that the honest prover strategy $\mathcal{P}$ be deterministic, and only requires soundness to hold against deterministic cheating prover strategies $\mathcal{P}'$. Restricting attention to deterministic prover strategies in this manner is done only for convenience, and does not alter the power of interactive proofs.

  Specifically, if there is a probabilistic prover strategy $\mathcal{P}'$ that convinces the verifier $\mathcal{V}$ to accept with probability at least p (with the probability taken over both the prover's internal randomness and the verifier's internal randomness), then there is a deterministic prover strategy achieving the same. This follows from an averaging argument over the prover's randomness: if a probabilistic prover $\mathcal{P}'$ convinces $\mathcal{V}$ to accept a claim "$f(x) = y$" with probability p,

---

[9]For perfectly complete protocols, the verifier may reject unless *every* repetition of the base protocol leads to acceptance.

there must be at least one setting of the internal randomness r' of $\mathcal{P}'$ such that the deterministic prover strategy obtained by fixing the randomness of $\mathcal{P}'$ to r' also convinces the verifier to accept the claim "$f(x) = y$" with probability p. (Note that the value r' may depend on x). In this monograph, the honest prover in all of our IPs and arguments will naturally be deterministic, so we will have no need to exploit this generic transformation from randomized to deterministic prover strategies.[10]

Interactive Proofs for Languages Versus Functions. Complexity theorists often find it convenient to study *decision problems*, which are functions f with range $\{0, 1\}$. We think of decision problems as "yes-no questions", in the following manner: any input x to f is interpreted as a question, namely: "Does $f(x)$ equal 1?". Equivalently, we can associate any decision problem f with the subset $\mathcal{L} \subseteq \{0, 1\}^n$ consisting of "yes-instances" for f. Any subset $\mathcal{L} \subseteq \{0, 1\}^n$ is called a *language*.

The formalization of IPs for languages differs slightly from that for functions (Definition 3.1). We briefly describe this difference because celebrated results in complexity theory regarding the power of IPs and their variants (e.g., **IP = PSPACE** and **MIP = NEXP**) refer to IPs for languages.

In an interactive proof for the language $\mathcal{L}$, given a public input $x \in \{0, 1\}^n$, the verifier $\mathcal{V}$ interacts with a prover $\mathcal{P}$ in exactly the same manner as in Definition 3.1 and at the end of the protocol $\mathcal{V}$ must output either 0 or 1, with 1 corresponding to "accept" and 0 corresponding to "reject". The standard requirements of an IP for the language $\mathcal{L}$ are:

- **Completeness.** For any $x \in \mathcal{L}$, there is some prover strategy that will cause the verifier to accept with high probability.

- **Soundness.** For any $x \notin \mathcal{L}$, then for *every* prover strategy, the verifier rejects with high probability.

---

[10] An important caveat is that for most of the *zero-knowledge* proofs and arguments considered in Sections 11–17 in this monograph, the prover will be randomized. This randomization of the proof has no bearing on the completeness or soundness of the protocol, but rather is incorporated as a means of ensuring that the proof leaks no information to the verifier (other than its own validity).

Given a language $\mathcal{L}$, let $f_{\mathcal{L}}\colon \{0,1\}^n \to \{0,1\}$ be the corresponding decision problem, i.e., $f_{\mathcal{L}}(x) = 1$ if x is in $\mathcal{L}$, and $f_{\mathcal{L}}(x) = 0$ if x is not in $\mathcal{L}$. Note that for $x \notin \mathcal{L}$, the above definition of an IP for $\mathcal{L}$ does *not* require that there be a "convincing proof" of the fact that $f_{\mathcal{L}}(x) = 0$. This is in contrast to the definition of IPs for the *function* $f_{\mathcal{L}}$ (Definition 3.1), for which the completeness requirement insists that for *every* input x (even those for which $f_{\mathcal{L}}(x) = 0$), there be a prover strategy that convinces the verifier of the value of $f(x)$.

The motivation behind the above formalization of IPs for languages is as follows. One may think of inputs in the language $\mathcal{L}$ as *true statements*, and inputs not in the language as *false statements*. The above completeness and soundness properties require that all true statements have convincing proofs, and all false statements do not have convincing proofs. It is natural *not* to require that false statements have convincing refutations (i.e., convincing proofs of their falsity).

While the notions of interactive proofs for languages and functions are different, they are related in the following sense: given a *function* f, an interactive proof for f is equivalent to an interactive proof for the *language* $\mathcal{L}_f := \{(x,y)\colon y = f(x)\}$.

As indicated above, in this monograph we will primarily be concerned with interactive proofs for functions instead of languages. We only talk about interactive proofs for languages when referring to complexity classes such as **NP** and **IP**, defined next.

NP and IP. Let **IP** be the class of all languages solvable by an interactive proof system with a polynomial time verifier. The class **IP** can be viewed as an interactive, randomized variant of the classical complexity class **NP** (**NP** is the class obtained from **IP** by restricting the proof system to be non-interactive and deterministic, meaning that the completeness and soundness errors are 0).

We will see soon that the class **IP** is in fact equal to **PSPACE**, the class of all languages solvable by algorithms using polynomial space (and possibly exponential time). **PSPACE** is believed to be a vastly bigger class of languages than **NP**, so this is one formalization of the statement that "interactive proofs are far more powerful than classical static (i.e, **NP**) proofs".

By Your Powers Combined, I am IP. The key to the power of interactive proofs is the *combination* of randomness and interaction. If randomness is disallowed (equivalently, if perfect soundness $\delta_s = 0$ is required), then interaction is pointless, because the prover can predict the verifier's messages with certainty, and hence there is no reason for the verifier to send the messages to the prover. In more detail, the proof system can be rendered non-interactive by demanding that the (non-interactive) prover send a transcript of the interactive protocol that would cause the (interactive) verifier to accept, and the (non-interactive) verifier can check that indeed the (interactive) verifier would have accepted this transcript. By perfect soundness of the interactive protocol, this non-interactive proof system is perfectly sound.

On the other hand if no interaction is allowed, but the verifier is allowed to toss random coins and accept an incorrect proof with small probability, the resulting complexity class is known as **MA** (short for *Merlin-Arthur*). This class is widely believed to be equal to **NP** (see for example [155]), which as stated above is believed by many researchers to be a much smaller class of problems than **IP = PSPACE**.[11]

3.4 Schwartz-Zippel Lemma

Terminology. For an m-variate polynomial g, the degree of a term of g is the sum of the exponents of the variables in the term. For example if $g(x_1, x_2) = 7x_1^2 x_2 + 6x_2^4$, then the degree of the term $7x_1^2 x_2$ is 3, and the degree of the term $6x_2^4$ is 4. The total degree of g is the maximum of the degree of any term of g, which in the preceding example is 4.

---

[11]More precisely, it is widely believed that for every non-interactive randomized proof system $(\mathcal{V}, \mathcal{P})$ for a language $\mathcal{L}$, there is a non-interactive deterministic proof system $(\mathcal{V}', \mathcal{P}')$ for $\mathcal{L}$ in which the runtime of the deterministic verifier $\mathcal{V}'$ is at most polynomially larger than that of the randomized verifier $\mathcal{V}$. This would not necessarily mean that the deterministic verifier $\mathcal{V}'$ is *just as fast* as the randomized verifier $\mathcal{V}$. See for example Freivald's non-interactive randomized proof system for matrix multiplication in Section 2.2—the verifier there runs in $O(n^2)$ time, which is faster than any known deterministic verifier for the same problem, but "only" by a factor of about $O(n^{0.3728639})$, which is a (small) polynomial in the input size. This is in contrast to the transformation of the preceding paragraph from deterministic interactive proofs to non-interactive proofs, which introduces no overhead for either the verifier or the prover.

The lemma itself. Interactive proofs frequently exploit the following basic property of polynomials, which is commonly known as the Schwartz-Zippel lemma [224], [260].

Lemma 3.3 (Schwartz-Zippel Lemma). Let $\mathbb{F}$ be any field, and let $g \colon \mathbb{F}^m \to \mathbb{F}$ be a nonzero m-variate polynomial of total degree at most d. Then on any finite set $S \subseteq \mathbb{F}$,

$$\Pr_{x \leftarrow S^m}[g(x) = 0] \leq d/|S|.$$

Here, $x \leftarrow S^m$ denotes an x drawn uniformly at random from the product set S^m, and $|S|$ denotes the size of S. In words, if x is chosen uniformly at random from S^m, then the probability that $g(x) = 0$ is at most $d/|S|$. In particular, any two distinct polynomials of total degree at most d can agree on at most a $d/|S|$ fraction of points in S^m.

We will not prove the lemma above, but it is easy to find a proof online (see, e.g., the wikipedia article on the lemma, or an alternative proof due to Moshkovitz [194]). An easy implication of the Schwartz-Zippel lemma is that for any two distinct m-variate polynomials p and q of total degree at most d over $\mathbb{F}$, $p(x) = q(x)$ for at most a $d/|\mathbb{F}|$ fraction of inputs. Section 2.1.1 on Reed-Solomon fingerprinting exploited precisely this implication in the special case of univariate polynomials (i.e., $m = 1$).

3.5   Low Degree and Multilinear Extensions

Motivation and Comparison to Univariate Lagrange Interpolation. In Section 2.4, we considered any *univariate* function f mapping $\{0, 1, \ldots, n - 1\}$ to $\mathbb{F}_p$, and studied the univariate low-degree extension of f. This was the unique univariate polynomial g over $\mathbb{F}_p$ of degree at most $n - 1$ such that $g(x) = f(x)$ for all $x \in \{0, 1, \ldots, n - 1\}$. In this section, we consider *multivariate* functions f, more specifically defined over the v-variate domain $\{0, 1\}^v$. Note that when $v = \log n$, the domain $\{0, 1\}^v$ has the same size as the univariate domain $\{0, 1, \ldots, n - 1\}$.

As we will see, functions defined over the domain $\{0, 1\}^v$ have extension polynomials that have much lower degree than in the univariate case. Specifically, any function f mapping $\{0, 1\}^v \to \mathbb{F}$ has an extension polynomial that is *multilinear*, meaning it has degree at most 1 in each variable. This implies that the *total degree* of the polynomial is at most v, which is logarithmic in the domain size 2^v. In contrast, univariate low-degree extensions over a domain of size n require degree $n - 1$. Multivariate polynomials with ultra-low degree in each variable turn out to be especially useful when designing interactive proofs with small communication and fast verification.

Details of Polynomial Extensions for Multivariate Functions. Let $\mathbb{F}$ be any finite field, and let $f: \{0,1\}^v \to \mathbb{F}$ be any function mapping the v-dimensional Boolean hypercube to $\mathbb{F}$. A v-variate polynomial g over $\mathbb{F}$ is said to be an *extension* of f if g agrees with f at all Boolean-valued inputs, i.e., $g(x) = f(x)$ for all $x \in \{0,1\}^v$. Here, the domain of the v-variate polynomial g over $\mathbb{F}$ is $\mathbb{F}^v$, and 0 and 1 are respectively associated with the additive and multiplicative identity elements of $\mathbb{F}$.

As with univariate low-degree extensions, one can think of a (low-degree) extension g of a function $f: \{0,1\}^v \to \mathbb{F}$ as a distance-amplifying encoding of f: if two functions $f, f': \{0,1\}^v \to \mathbb{F}$ disagree at even a single input, then any extensions g, g' of total degree at most d must differ *almost everywhere*, assuming $d \ll |\mathbb{F}|$.[12] This is made precise by the Schwartz-Zippel lemma above, which guarantees that g and g' agree on at most $d/|\mathbb{F}|$ fraction of points in $\mathbb{F}^v$. As we will see throughout this survey, these distance-amplifying properties give the verifier surprising power over the prover.[13]

---

[12] As with Footnote 10 in Section 2.4, the univariate setting, precisely how small d must be for a degree-d extension polynomial g to be called "low-degree" is deliberately left vague and may be context-dependent. At a minimum, d should be less than $|\mathbb{F}|$ to ensure that the probability $d/|\mathbb{F}|$ appearing in the Schwartz-Zippel lemma is less than 1; otherwise, the Schwartz-Zippel lemma is vacuous. When a low-degree extension g is used in interactive proofs or arguments, various costs of the protocol, such as proof size, verifier time, or prover time, often grow linearly with the degree d of g, and hence the smaller d is, the lower these costs are.

[13] In fact, the use of low-degree extensions in many of the interactive proofs and arguments we describe in this survey could in principle be replaced with different distance-amplifying encodings that do not correspond to polynomials at all (see for example [190], [215] for papers in this direction). However, we will see that low-degree extensions have nice structure that enables the prover and verifier to run especially efficiently when we use low-degree extensions rather than general distance-amplifying

Definition 3.4. A multivariate polynomial g is *multilinear* if the degree of the polynomial in each variable is at most one.

For example, the polynomial $g(x_1, x_2) = x_1 x_2 + 4x_1 + 3x_2$ is multilinear, but the polynomial $h(x_1, x_2) = x_2^2 + 4x_1 + 3x_2$ is not. Throughout this survey, we will frequently use the following fact.

Fact 3.5. Any function $f \colon \{0, 1\}^v \to \mathbb{F}$ has a unique *multilinear extension* (MLE) over $\mathbb{F}$, and we reserve the notation $\widetilde{f}$ for this special extension of f.

That is, $\widetilde{f}$ is the unique multilinear polynomial over $\mathbb{F}$ satisfying $\widetilde{f}(x) = f(x)$ for all $x \in \{0, 1\}^v$. See Figures 3.1 and 3.2 for an example of a function and its multilinear extension.

The first step in the proof of Fact 3.5 is to establish the existence of a multilinear polynomial extending f. In fact, we give an explicit expression for this polynomial, via Lagrange interpolation. This is analogous to Lemma 2.3 in Section 2.3, which considered the case of univariate rather than multilinear polynomials.

Lemma 3.6 (Lagrange Interpolation of Multilinear Polynomials). Let $f \colon \{0, 1\}^v \to \mathbb{F}$ be any function. Then the following multilinear polynomial $\widetilde{f}$ extends f:

$$\widetilde{f}(x_1, \ldots, x_v) = \sum_{w \in \{0,1\}^v} f(w) \cdot \chi_w(x_1, \ldots, x_v), \tag{3.1}$$

where, for any $w = (w_1, \ldots, w_v)$,

$$\chi_w(x_1, \ldots, x_v) := \prod_{i=1}^{v} (x_i w_i + (1 - x_i)(1 - w_i)). \tag{3.2}$$

The set $\{\chi_w \colon w \in \{0, 1\}^v\}$ is referred to as the set of *multilinear Lagrange basis polynomials* with interpolating set $\{0, 1\}^v$.

Proof. For any vector $w \in \{0, 1\}^v$, χ_w satisfies $\chi_w(w) = 1$, and $\chi_w(y) = 0$ for all other vectors $y \in \{0, 1\}^v$. To see that the latter property holds,

---

encodings. It remains an important research direction to obtain IPs and arguments with similar (or better!) efficiency by using non-polynomial encodings—Section 10.5 of this survey covers one result in this vein.

	0	1
0	1	2
1	1	4

Figure 3.1: All evaluations of a function f mapping $\{0,1\}^2$ to the field $\mathbb{F}_5$.

observe that if $w_i \neq y_i$, then either $w_i = 1$ and $y_i = 0$ or $w_i = 0$ and $y_i = 1$. Either way, the ith term on the right hand side of Equation (3.2), namely $(x_i w_i + (1 - x_i)(1 - w_i))$, equals 0. This ensures that the entire product on the right hand side of Equation (3.2) equals 0.

It follows that $\sum_{w \in \{0,1\}^v} f(w) \cdot \chi_w(y) = f(y)$ for all Boolean vectors $y \in \{0,1\}^v$. In addition, the right hand side of Equation (3.1) is a multilinear polynomial in $(x_1, \ldots, x_v)$, as each term of the sum is clearly a multilinear polynomial, and a sum of multilinear polynomials is itself multilinear. Putting these two statements together, the right hand side of Equation (3.1) is a multilinear polynomial extending f. $\square$

Lemma 3.6 demonstrated that for any function $f \colon \{0,1\}^v \to \mathbb{F}$, there is some multilinear polynomial that extends f. To complete the proof of Fact 3.5, we must establish that there is only one such polynomial.

	0	1	2	3	4
0	1	2	3	4	0
1	1	4	2	0	3
2	1	1	1	1	1
3	1	3	0	2	4
4	1	0	4	3	2

Figure 3.2: All evaluations of the multilinear extension, $\widetilde{f}$ of f over $\mathbb{F}_5$. Via Lagrange interpolation (Lemma 3.6), $\widetilde{f}(x_1, x_2) = (1 - x_1)(1 - x_2) + 2(1 - x_1)x_2 + x_1(1 - x_2) + 4x_1 x_2$.

Completing the Proof of Fact 3.5. To show that there is a unique multilinear polynomial extending f, we show that if p and q are two multilinear polynomials such that $p(x) = q(x)$ for all $x \in \{0,1\}^v$, then p and q are in fact the same polynomial, i.e., $p(x) = q(x)$ for all $x \in \mathbb{F}^v$. Equivalently, we want to show that the polynomial $h := p - q$ is the identically 0 polynomial.

Observe that h is also multilinear, because it is the difference of two multilinear polynomials. Furthermore, the assumption that $p(x) = q(x)$ for all $x \in \{0,1\}^v$ implies that $h(x) = 0$ for all $x \in \{0,1\}^v$. We now show that any such polynomial is identically 0.

Assume that h is a multilinear polynomial that vanishes on $\{0,1\}^v$, meaning that $h(x) = 0$ for all $x \in \{0,1\}^v$. If h is not the identically zero polynomial, then consider any term t in h of minimal degree. h must have at least one such term since h is not identically 0. For example, if $h(x_1, x_2, x_3) = x_1 x_2 x_3 + 2x_1 x_2$, then the term $2x_1 x_2$ is of minimal degree, since it has degree 2, and h has no terms of degree 1 or 0.

Now consider the input z obtained by setting all of the variables in t to 1, and all other variables to 0 (in the example above, $z = (1, 1, 0)$). At input z, term t is nonzero because all of the variables appearing in term t are set to 1. For instance, in the example above, the term $2x_1 x_2$ evaluates to 2 at input $(1, 1, 0)$).

Meanwhile, by multilinearity of h, all other terms of h contain at least one variable that is not in term t (otherwise, t would not be of minimal degree in h). Since z sets all variables not in t to 0, this means that all terms in h other than t evaluate to 0 at z. It follows that $h(z) \neq 0$ (e.g., in the example above, $h(z) = 2$).

This contradicts the assumption that $h(x) = 0$ for all $x \in \{0,1\}^v$. We conclude that any multilinear polynomial h that vanishes on $\{0,1\}^v$ must be identically zero, as desired. $\qquad\square$

While any function $f\colon \{0,1\}^v \to \mathbb{F}$ has many polynomials that extend it, Fact 3.5 states that exactly one of those extension polynomials is multilinear. For example, if $f(x) = 0$ for all $x \in \{0,1\}^v$, then the multilinear extension of f is just the 0 polynomial. But $p(x_1, \ldots, x_v) = x_1 \cdot (1 - x_1)$ is one example of a non-multilinear polynomial that also extends f.

Algorithms for Evaluating the Multilinear Extension of f. Suppose that the verifier is given as input the values $f(w)$ for all $n = 2^v$ Boolean vectors $w \in \{0,1\}^v$. Equation (3.1) yields two efficient methods for evaluating $\widetilde{f}$ at any point $r \in \mathbb{F}^v$, The first method was described in [103]: it requires $O(n \log n)$ time, and allows $\mathcal{V}$ to make a single streaming pass over the $f(w)$ values while storing just $v + 1 = O(\log n)$ field elements. The second method is due to Vu *et al.* [241]: it shaves a logarithmic factor off of $\mathcal{V}$'s runtime, bringing it down to linear time, i.e., $O(n)$, but increases $\mathcal{V}$'s space usage to $O(n)$.

Lemma 3.7 ([103]). Fix a positive integer v and let $n = 2^v$. Given as input $f(w)$ for all $w \in \{0,1\}^v$ and a vector $r \in \mathbb{F}^{\log n}$, $\mathcal{V}$ can compute $\widetilde{f}(r)$ in $O(n \log n)$ time and $O(\log n)$ words of space[14] with a single streaming pass over the input (regardless of the order in which the $f(w)$ values are presented).

Proof. $\mathcal{V}$ can compute the right hand side of Equation (3.1) incrementally from the stream by initializing $\widetilde{f}(r) \leftarrow 0$, and processing each update $(w, f(w))$ via:

$$\widetilde{f}(r) \leftarrow \widetilde{f}(r) + f(w) \cdot \chi_w(r).$$

$\mathcal{V}$ only needs to store $\widetilde{f}(r)$ and r, which requires $O(\log n)$ words of memory (one for each entry of r). Moreover, for any w, $\chi_w(r)$ can be computed in $O(\log n)$ field operations (see Equation (3.2)), and thus $\mathcal{V}$ can compute $\widetilde{f}(r)$ with one pass over the stream, using $O(\log n)$ words of space and $O(\log n)$ field operations per update. $\square$

The algorithm of Lemma 3.7 computes $\widetilde{f}(r)$ by evaluating each term on the right hand side of Equation (3.1) independently in $O(v)$ time and summing the results. This results in a total runtime of $O(v \cdot 2^v)$. The following lemma gives an even faster algorithm, running in time $O(2^v)$. Its speedup relative to Lemma 3.7 is obtained by *not* treating each term of the sum independently. Rather, using dynamic programming, Lemma 3.8 computes $\chi_w(r)$ *for all* 2^v vectors $w \in \{0,1\}^v$ in time $O(2^v)$.

---

[14] A "word of space" refers to the amount of data processed by a machine in one step. It is often 64 bits on modern processors. For simplicity, we assume throughout that a field element can be stored using a constant number of machine words.

Lemma 3.8 ([241]). Fix a positive integer v, and let $n = 2^v$. Given as input $f(w)$ for all $w \in \{0,1\}^v$ and a vector $r = (r_1, \ldots, r_v) \in \mathbb{F}^{\log n}$, $\mathcal{V}$ can compute $\widetilde{f}(r)$ in $O(n)$ time and $O(n)$ space.

Proof. Notice the right hand side of Equation (3.1) expresses $\widetilde{f}(r)$ as the inner product of two n-dimensional vectors, where (associating $\{0,1\}^v$ and $\{0, \ldots, 2^v - 1\}$ in the natural way) the w'th entry of the first vector is $f(w)$ and the w'th entry of the second vector is $\chi_w(r)$. This inner product can be computed in $O(n)$ time given a table of size n whose wth entry contains the quantity $\chi_w(r)$. Vu *et al.*, show how to build such a table in time $O(n)$ using memoization.

The memoization procedure consists of $v = \log n$ stages, where Stage j constructs a table $A^{(j)}$ of size 2^j, such that for any $(w_1, \ldots, w_j) \in \{0,1\}^j$, $A^{(j)}[(w_1, \ldots, w_j)] = \prod_{i=1}^j \chi_{w_i}(r_i)$. Notice $A^{(j)}[(w_1, \ldots, w_j)] = A^{(j-1)}[(w_1, \ldots, w_{j-1})] \cdot (w_j r_j + (1 - w_j)(1 - r_j))$, and so the jth stage of the memoization procedure requires time $O(2^j)$. The total time across all $\log n$ stages is therefore $O(\sum_{j=1}^{\log n} 2^j) = O(2^{\log n}) = O(n)$. An example of this memoization procedure for $v = 3$ is given in Figure 3.3.

Conceptually, the above algorithm in Stage 1 evaluates all one-variate multilinear Lagrange basis polynomials at the input r_1. There are two such basis polynomials, namely $\chi_0(x_1) = x_1$ and $\chi_1(x_1) = (1 - x_1)$, and hence the algorithm in Stage 1 computes and stores two values: r_1 and $(1 - r_1)$. In Stage 2, the algorithm evaluates all two-variate multilinear Lagrange basis polynomials at the input (r_1, r_2). There are four such values, namely $r_1 r_2$, $r_1(1 - r_2)$, $(1 - r_1)r_2$ and $(1 - r_1)(1 - r_2)$. In general,

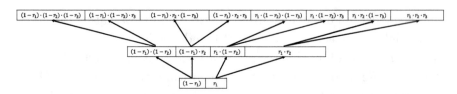

Figure 3.3: Evaluating all eight three-variate Lagrange basis polynomials at input $r = (r_1, r_2, r_3) \in \mathbb{F}^3$ via the memoization procedure in the proof of Lemma 3.8. The algorithm uses 12 field multiplications in total. In contrast, the algorithm given in Lemma 3.7 independently evaluates each Lagrange basis polynomial at r independently. This requires 2 field multiplications per basis polynomial, or $8 \cdot 2 = 16$ multiplications in total.

Stage i of the algorithm evaluates all i-variate multilinear Lagrange basis polynomials at the input $(r_1, r_2, \ldots, r_i)$. Figure 3.3 illustrates the entire procedure when the number of variables is $v = 3$. $\square$

3.6   Exercises

Exercise 3.1. Let A, B, C be $n \times n$ matrices over a field $\mathbb{F}$. In Section 2.2, we presented a randomized algorithm for checking that $C = A \cdot B$. The algorithm picked a random field element r, let $x = (r, r^2, \ldots, r^n)$, and output EQUAL if $Cx = A \cdot (Bx)$, and output NOT-EQUAL otherwise. Suppose instead that each entry of the vector x is chosen independently and uniformly at random from $\mathbb{F}$. Show that:

- If $C_{ij} = (AB)_{ij}$ for all $i = 1, \ldots, n, j = 1, \ldots, n$, then the algorithm outputs EQUAL for every possible choice of x.

- If there is even one $(i, j) \in [n] \times [n]$ such that $C_{ij} \neq (AB)_{ij}$, then the algorithm outputs NOT-EQUAL with probability at least $1 - 1/|\mathbb{F}|$.

Exercise 3.2. In Section 2.1, we described a communication protocol of logarithmic cost for determining whether Alice's and Bob's input vectors are equal. Specifically, Alice and Bob interpreted their inputs as degree-n univariate polynomials p_a and p_b, chose a random $r \in \mathbb{F}$ with $|\mathbb{F}| \gg n$, and compared $p_a(r)$ to $p_b(r)$. Give a different communication protocol in which Alice and Bob interpret their inputs as multilinear rather than univariate polynomials over $\mathbb{F}$. How large should $\mathbb{F}$ be to ensure that the probability Bob outputs the wrong answer is at most $1/n$? What is the communication cost in bits of this protocol?

Exercise 3.3. Let $p = 11$. Consider the function $f: \{0,1\}^2 \to \mathbb{F}_p$ given by $f(0,0) = 3$, $f(0,1) = 4$, $f(1,0) = 1$ and $f(1,1) = 2$. Write out an explicit expression for the multilinear extension $\tilde{f}$ of f. What is $\tilde{f}(2,4)$?

Now consider the function $f: \{0,1\}^3 \to \mathbb{F}_p$ given by $f(0,0,0) = 1$, $f(0,1,0) = 2$, $f(1,0,0) = 3$, $f(1,1,0) = 4$, $f(0,0,1) = 5$, $f(0,1,1) = 6$, $f(1,0,1) = 7$, $f(1,1,1) = 8$. What is $\tilde{f}(2,4,6)$? How many field multiplications did you perform during the calculation? Can you work through a calculation of $\tilde{f}(2,4,6)$ that uses "just" 20 multiplication operations? Hint: see Lemma 3.8.

Exercise 3.4. Fix some prime p of your choosing. Write a Python program that takes as input an array of length 2^ℓ specifying all evaluations of a function $f\colon \{0,1\}^\ell \to \mathbb{F}_p$ and a vector $\mathbf{r} \in \mathbb{F}_p^\ell$, and outputs $\tilde{f}(\mathbf{r})$.

4

Interactive Proofs

The first interactive proof that we cover is the sum-check protocol, due to Lund *et al.* [186]. The sum-check protocol has served as the single most important "hammer" in the design of efficient interactive proofs. Indeed, after introducing the sum-check protocol in Section 4.1, the remaining sections of this section apply the protocol in clean (but non-trivial) ways to solve a variety of important problems.

4.1 The Sum-Check Protocol

Suppose we are given a v-variate polynomial g defined over a finite field $\mathbb{F}$. The purpose of the sum-check protocol is for prover to provide the verifier with the following sum:

$$H := \sum_{b_1 \in \{0,1\}} \sum_{b_2 \in \{0,1\}} \cdots \sum_{b_v \in \{0,1\}} g(b_1, \ldots, b_v). \qquad (4.1)$$

Summing up the evaluations of a polynomial over all Boolean inputs may seem like a contrived task with limited practical utility. But to the contrary, later sections of this section will show that many natural problems can be directly cast as an instance of Equation (4.1).

Remark 4.1. In full generality, the sum-check protocol can compute the sum $\sum_{b \in B^v} g(b)$ for any $B \subseteq \mathbb{F}$, but most of the applications covered in this survey will only require $B = \{0, 1\}$.

What does the verifier gain by using the sum-check protocol? The verifier could clearly compute H via Equation (4.1) on her own by evaluating g at 2^v inputs (namely, all inputs in $\{0, 1\}^v$), but we are thinking of 2^v as an unacceptably large runtime for the verifier. Using the sum-check protocol, the verifier's runtime will be

$$O(v + [\text{the cost to evaluate } g \text{ at a single input in } \mathbb{F}^v]).$$

This is much better than the 2^v evaluations of g required to compute H unassisted.

It also turns out that the prover in the sum-check protocol can compute all of its prescribed messages by evaluating g at $O(2^v)$ inputs in $\mathbb{F}^v$. This is only a constant factor more than what is required simply to compute H without proving correctness.

For presentation purposes, we assume for the rest of this section that the verifier has oracle access to g, i.e., $\mathcal{V}$ can evaluate $g(r_1, \ldots, r_v)$ for a randomly chosen vector $(r_1, \ldots, r_v) \in \mathbb{F}^v$ with a single query to an oracle.[1] A self-contained description of the sum-check protocol is provided in the codebox below. This is followed by a more intuitive, recursive description of the protocol.

Description of the Start of the Protocol. At the start of the sum-check protocol, the prover sends a value C_1 claimed to equal the true answer (i.e., the quantity H defined in Equation (4.1)). The sum-check

---

[1]This will not be the case in the applications described in later sections of this section. In our applications, $\mathcal{V}$ will either be able to efficiently evaluate $g(r_1, \ldots, r_v)$ unaided, or if this is not the case, $\mathcal{V}$ will ask the prover to *tell her* $g(r_1, \ldots, r_v)$, and $\mathcal{P}$ will subsequently prove this claim is correct via further applications of the sum-check protocol.

Description of Sum-Check Protocol.

- At the start of the protocol, the prover sends a value C_1 claimed to equal the value H defined in Equation (4.1).

- In the first round, $\mathcal{P}$ sends the univariate polynomial $g_1(X_1)$ claimed to equal

$$\sum_{(x_2,\ldots,x_v)\in\{0,1\}^{v-1}} g(X_1, x_2, \ldots, x_v).$$

  $\mathcal{V}$ checks that
  $$C_1 = g_1(0) + g_1(1),$$
  and that g_1 is a univariate polynomial of degree at most $\deg_1(g)$, rejecting if not. Here, $\deg_j(g)$ denotes the degree of $g(X_1, \ldots, X_v)$ in variable X_j.

- $\mathcal{V}$ chooses a random element $r_1 \in \mathbb{F}$, and sends r_1 to $\mathcal{P}$.

- In the jth round, for $1 < j < v$, $\mathcal{P}$ sends to $\mathcal{V}$ a univariate polynomial $g_j(X_j)$ claimed to equal

$$\sum_{(x_{j+1},\ldots,x_v)\in\{0,1\}^{v-j}} g(r_1, \ldots, r_{j-1}, X_j, x_{j+1}, \ldots, x_v).$$

  $\mathcal{V}$ checks that g_j is a univariate polynomial of degree at most $\deg_j(g)$, and that $g_{j-1}(r_{j-1}) = g_j(0) + g_j(1)$, rejecting if not.

- $\mathcal{V}$ chooses a random element $r_j \in \mathbb{F}$, and sends r_j to $\mathcal{P}$.

- In Round v, $\mathcal{P}$ sends to $\mathcal{V}$ a univariate polynomial $g_v(X_v)$ claimed to equal

$$g(r_1, \ldots, r_{v-1}, X_v).$$

  $\mathcal{V}$ checks that g_v is a univariate polynomial of degree at most $\deg_v(g)$, rejecting if not, and also checks that $g_{v-1}(r_{v-1}) = g_v(0) + g_v(1)$.

- $\mathcal{V}$ chooses a random element $r_v \in \mathbb{F}$ and evaluates $g(r_1, \ldots, r_v)$ with a single oracle query to g. $\mathcal{V}$ checks that $g_v(r_v) = g(r_1, \ldots, r_v)$, rejecting if not.

- If $\mathcal{V}$ has not yet rejected, $\mathcal{V}$ halts and accepts.

protocol proceeds in v rounds, one for each variable of g. At the start of the first round, the prover sends a polynomial $g_1(X_1)$ *claimed* to equal the polynomial $s_1(X_1)$ defined as follows:

$$s_1(X_1) := \sum_{(x_2,\ldots,x_v)\in\{0,1\}^{v-1}} g(X_1, x_2, \ldots, x_v). \qquad (4.2)$$

$s_1(X_1)$ is defined to ensure that

$$H = s_1(0) + s_1(1). \qquad (4.3)$$

Accordingly, the verifier checks that $C_1 = g_1(0) + g_1(1)$, i.e., the verifier checks that g_1 and the claimed answer C_1 are consistent with Equation (4.3).

Throughout, let $\deg_i(g)$ denote the degree of variable i in g. If the prover is honest, the polynomial $g_1(X_1)$ has degree $\deg_1(g)$. Hence g_1 can be specified with $\deg_1(g) + 1$ field elements, for example by sending the evaluation of g_1 at each point in the set $\{0, 1, \ldots, \deg_1(g)\}$, or by specifying the $d + 1$ coefficients of g_1.

The Rest of Round 1. Recall that the polynomial $g_1(X_1)$ sent by the prover in round 1 is claimed to equal the polynomial $s_1(X_1)$ defined in Equation (4.2). The idea of the sum-check protocol is that $\mathcal{V}$ will probabilistically check this equality of polynomials holds by picking a random field element $r_1 \in \mathbb{F}$, and confirming that

$$g_1(r_1) = s_1(r_1). \qquad (4.4)$$

Clearly, if g_1 is as claimed, then this equality holds for all $r_1 \in \mathbb{F}$ (i.e., this probabilistic protocol for checking that $g_1 = s_1$ as formal polynomials is complete). Meanwhile, if $g_1 \neq s_1$, then with probability at least $1 - \deg_1(g)/|\mathbb{F}|$ over the verifier's choice of r_1, Equation (4.4) fails to hold. This is because two distinct degree d univariate polynomials agree on at most d inputs. This means that this protocol for checking that $g_1 = s_1$ by confirming that equality holds at a random input r_1 is sound, so long as $|\mathbb{F}| \gg \deg_1(g)$.

The remaining issue is the following: can $\mathcal{V}$ efficiently compute both $g_1(r_1)$ and $s_1(r_1)$, in order to check that Equation (4.4) holds? Since $\mathcal{P}$ sends $\mathcal{V}$ an explicit description of the polynomial g_1, it is possible for $\mathcal{V}$

to evaluate $g_1(r_1)$ in $O(\deg_1(g))$ time.[2] In contrast, evaluating $s_1(r_1)$ is not an easy task for $\mathcal{V}$, as s_1 is defined as a sum over 2^{v-1} evaluations of g. This is only a factor of two smaller than the number of terms in the sum defining H (Equation (4.1)). Fortunately, Equation (4.2) expresses s_1 as the sum of the evaluations of a $(v-1)$-variate polynomial over the Boolean hypercube (the polynomial being $g(r_1, X_2, \ldots, X_v)$ that is defined over the variables $X_2, \ldots, X_v$). This is exactly the type of expression that the sum-check protocol is designed to check. Hence, rather than evaluating $s_1(r_1)$ on her own, $\mathcal{V}$ instead *recursively* applies the sum-check protocol to evaluate $s_1(r_1)$.

Recursive Description of Rounds $2, \ldots, v$. The protocol thus proceeds in this recursive manner, with one round per recursive call. This means that in round j, variable X_j gets *bound* to a random field element r_j chosen by the verifier. This process proceeds until round v, in which the prover is forced to send a polynomial $g_v(X_v)$ claimed to equal $s_v := g(r_1, \ldots, r_{v-1}, X_v)$. When the verifier goes to check that $g_v(r_v) = s_v(r_v)$, there is no need for further recursion: since the verifier is given oracle access to g, $\mathcal{V}$ can evaluate $s_v(r_v) = g(r_1, \ldots, r_v)$ with a single oracle query to g.

Iterative Description of the Protocol. Unpacking the recursion described above, here is an equivalent description of what happens in round j of the sum-check protocol. At the start of round j, variables $X_1, \ldots, X_{j-1}$ have already been bound to random field elements $r_1, \ldots, r_{j-1}$. The prover sends a polynomial $g_j(X_j)$, and claims that

$$g_j(X_j) = \sum_{(x_{j+1}, \ldots, x_v) \in \{0,1\}^{v-j}} g(r_1, \ldots, r_{j-1}, X_j, x_{j+1}, \ldots, x_v). \quad (4.5)$$

The verifier compares the two most recent polynomials by checking

$$g_{j-1}(r_{j-1}) = g_j(0) + g_j(1), \quad (4.6)$$

---

[2]One may wonder, if the prover specifies g_1 via its evaluations at each input $i \in \{0, \ldots, \deg_1(g)\}$ rather than via its coefficients, how efficiently can the verifier evaluate $g_1(r_1)$? This is just Lagrange interpolation of a univariate polynomial (Section 2.4), which costs $O(\deg(g_1))$ field additions, multiplications, and inversions. In practical applications of the sum-check protocol, g will often have degree at most 2 or 3 in each of its variables, and hence this is very fast.

and rejecting otherwise (for round $j = 1$, the left hand side of Equation (4.6) is replaced with the claimed answer C_1). The verifier also rejects if the degree of g_j is too high: each g_j should have degree at most $\deg_j(g)$, the degree of variable x_j in g. If these checks pass,, $\mathcal{V}$ chooses a value r_j uniformly at random from $\mathbb{F}$ and sends r_j to $\mathcal{P}$.

In the final round, the prover has sent $g_v(X_v)$ which is claimed to be $g(r_1, \ldots, r_{v-1}, X_v)$. $\mathcal{V}$ now checks that $g_v(r_v) = g(r_1, \ldots, r_v)$ (recall that we assumed $\mathcal{V}$ has oracle access to g). If this check succeeds, and so do all previous checks, then the verifier is convinced that $H = g_1(0) + g_1(1)$.

Example Execution of the Sum-Check Protocol.   Let $g(X_1, X_2, X_3) = 2X_1^3 + X_1X_3 + X_2X_3$. The sum of g's evaluations over the Boolean hypercube is $H = 12$. When the sum-check protocol is applied to g, the honest prover's first message in the protocol is the univariate polynomial $s_1(X_1)$ equal to:

$$g(X_1, 0, 0) + g(X_1, 0, 1) + g(X_1, 1, 0) + g(X_1, 1, 1)$$
$$= (2X_1^3) + (2X_1^3 + X_1) + (2X_1^3) + (2X_1^3 + X_1 + 1)$$
$$= 8X_1^3 + 2X_1 + 1.$$

The verifier checks that $s_1(0) + s_1(1) = 12$, and then sends the prover r_1. Suppose that $r_1 = 2$. The honest prover would then respond with the univariate polynomial

$$s_2(X_2) = g(2, X_2, 0) + g(2, X_2, 1) = 16 + (16 + 2 + X_2) = 34 + X_2.$$

The verifier checks that $s_2(0) + s_2(1) = s_1(r_1)$, which amounts in this example to confirming that $34 + (34 + 1) = 8 \cdot (2^3) + 4 + 1$; indeed, both the left hand side and right hand side equal 69. The verifier then sends the prover r_2. Suppose that $r_2 = 3$. The honest prover would respond with the univariate polynomial $s_3(X_3) = g(2, 3, X_3) = 16 + 2X_3 + 3X_3 = 16 + 5X_3$, and the verifier confirms that $s_3(0) + s_3(1) = s_2(r_2)$, which amounts in this example to confirming that $16 + 21 = 37$. The verifier picks a random field element r_3. Suppose that $r_3 = 6$. The verifier confirms that $s_3(6) = g(2, 3, 6)$ by making one oracle query to g.

Completeness and Soundness.   The following proposition formalizes the completeness and soundness properties of the sum-check protocol.

Proposition 4.1. Let g be a v-variate polynomial of degree at most d in each variable, defined over a finite field $\mathbb{F}$. For any specified $H \in \mathbb{F}$, let $\mathcal{L}$ be the language of polynomials g (given as an oracle) such that

$$H = \sum_{b_1 \in \{0,1\}} \sum_{b_2 \in \{0,1\}} \cdots \sum_{b_v \in \{0,1\}} g(b_1, \ldots, b_v).$$

The sum-check protocol is an interactive proof system for $\mathcal{L}$ with completeness error $\delta_c = 0$ and soundness error $\delta_s \leq vd/|\mathbb{F}|$.

Proof. Completeness is evident: if the prover sends the prescribed polynomial $g_j(X_j)$ at all rounds j, then $\mathcal{V}$ will accept with probability 1. We offer two proofs of soundness, the first of which reasons in a manner analogous to the iterative description of the protocol, and the second of which reasons in a manner analogous to the recursive description.

Non-Inductive Proof of Soundness. One way to prove soundness conceptually follows the iterative description of the sum-check protocol. Specifically, if $H \neq \sum_{(x_1,\ldots,x_v) \in \{0,1\}^v} g(x_1, x_2, \ldots, x_v)$, then the only way the prover can convince the verifier to accept is if there is at least one round i such that the prover sends a univariate polynomial $g_i(X_i)$ that does not equal the prescribed polynomial

$$s_i(X_i) = \sum_{(x_{i+1},\ldots,x_v) \in \{0,1\}^{v-i}} g(r_1, r_2, \ldots, r_{i-1}, X_i, x_{i+1}, \ldots, x_v),$$

and yet $g_i(r_i) = s_i(r_i)$. For every round i, g_i and s_i both have degree at most d, and hence if $g_i \neq s_i$, the probability that $g_i(r_i) = s_i(r_i)$ is at most $d/|\mathbb{F}|$. By a union bound over all v rounds, the probability that there is any round i such that the prover sends a polynomial $g_i \neq s_i$ yet $g_i(r_i) = s_i(r_i)$ is at most $dv/|\mathbb{F}|$.

Inductive Proof of Soundness. A second way to prove soundness is by induction on v (this analysis conceptually follows the recursive description of the sum-check protocol). In the case $v = 1$, $\mathcal{P}$'s only message specifies a degree d univariate polynomial $g_1(X_1)$. If $g_1(X_1) \neq g(X_1)$, then because any two distinct degree d univariate polynomials can agree on at most d inputs, $g_1(r_1) \neq g(r_1)$ with probability at least

$1 - d/|\mathbb{F}|$ over the choice of r_1, and hence $\mathcal{V}$'s final check will cause $\mathcal{V}$ to reject with probably at least $1 - d/|\mathbb{F}|$.

For $v \geq 2$, assume by way of induction that for all $v - 1$-variate polynomials of degree at most d in each variable, the sum-check protocol has soundness error at most $(v-1)d/|\mathbb{F}|$. Let

$$s_1(X_1) = \sum_{x_2,\ldots,x_v \in \{0,1\}^{v-1}} g(X_1, x_2, \ldots, x_v).$$

Suppose $\mathcal{P}$ sends a polynomial $g_1(X_1) \neq s_1(X_1)$ in Round 1. Then because any two distinct degree d univariate polynomials can agree on at most d inputs, $g_1(r_1) = s_1(r_1)$ with probability at most $d/|\mathbb{F}|$. Conditioned on this event, $\mathcal{P}$ is left to prove the false claim in Round 2 that $g_1(r_1) = \sum_{(x_2,\ldots,x_v) \in \{0,1\}^{v-1}} g(r_1, x_2, \ldots, x_v)$. Since $g(r_1, x_2, \ldots, x_v)$ is a $(v-1)$-variate polynomial of degree at most d in each variable, the inductive hypothesis implies that $\mathcal{V}$ will reject at some subsequent round of the protocol with probability at least $1 - d(v-1)/|\mathbb{F}|$. Therefore, $\mathcal{V}$ will reject with probability at least

$$\Pr[s_1(r_1) \neq g_1(r_1)] - (1 - \Pr[\mathcal{V} \text{ rejects in some Round}$$
$$j > 1 | s_1(r_1) \neq g_1(r_1)])$$
$$\geq \left(1 - \frac{d}{|\mathbb{F}|}\right) - \frac{d(v-1)}{|\mathbb{F}|} = 1 - \frac{dv}{|\mathbb{F}|}.$$

$\square$

Discussion of Costs. There is one round in the sum-check protocol for each of the v variables of g. The total prover-to-verifier communication is $\sum_{i=1}^{v} (\deg_i(g) + 1) = v + \sum_{i=1}^{v} \deg_i(g)$ field elements, and the total verifier-to-prover communication is v field elements (one per round).[3] In particular, if $\deg_i(g) = O(1)$ for all j, then the communication cost is $O(v)$ field elements.[4]

---

[3]More precisely, the verifier does not need to send to the prover the random field element r_v chosen in the final round. However, when the sum-check protocol is used as a "subroutine" in a more involved protocol (e.g., the GKR protocol of Section 4.6), the verifier will often have to send that last field element to the prover to "continue" the more involved protocol.

[4]In practical applications of the sum-check protocol, $\mathbb{F}$ will often be a field of size between 2^{128} and 2^{256}, meaning that any field element can be specified with between

The running time of the verifier over the entire execution of the protocol is proportional to the total communication, plus the cost of a single oracle query to g to compute $g(r_1, \ldots, r_v)$.

Determining the running time of the prover is less straightforward. Recall that $\mathcal{P}$ can specify g_j by sending for each $i \in \{0, \ldots, \deg_j(g)\}$ the value:

$$g_j(i) = \sum_{(x_{j+1}, \ldots, x_v) \in \{0,1\}^{v-j}} g(r_1, \ldots, r_{j-1}, i, x_{j+1}, \ldots, x_v). \qquad (4.7)$$

An important insight is that the number of terms defining the value $g_j(i)$ in Equation (4.7) falls geometrically with j: in the jth sum, there are only $(1+\deg_j(g)) \cdot 2^{v-j}$ terms, with the 2^{v-j} factor due to the number of vectors in $\{0,1\}^{v-j}$. Thus, the total number of terms that must be evaluated over the course of the protocol is $\sum_{j=1}^{v} (1 + \deg_j(g)) 2^{v-j}$. If $\deg_j(g) = O(1)$ for all j, this is $O(1) \cdot \sum_{j=1}^{v} 2^{v-j} = O(1) \cdot (2^v - 1) = O(2^v)$. Consequently, if $\mathcal{P}$ is given oracle access to g, then $\mathcal{P}$ will require just $O(2^v)$ time.

In all of the applications covered in this survey, $\mathcal{P}$ will not have oracle access to the evaluation table of g, and the key to many of the results in this survey is to show that $\mathcal{P}$ can nonetheless evaluate g at all of the necessary points in close to $O(2^v)$ total time.

The costs of the sum-check protocol are summarized in Table 4.1. Since $\mathcal{P}$ and $\mathcal{V}$ will not be given oracle access to g in applications, the table makes the number of oracle queries to g explicit.

Remark 4.2. An important feature of the sum-check protocol is that the verifier's messages to the prover are simply random field elements, and hence entirely independent of the input polynomial g. In fact, the only information $\mathcal{V}$ needs about the polynomial g to execute its part of the protocol is an upper bound on the degree of g in each of its v variables, and the ability to evaluate g at a random point $r \in \mathbb{F}^v$.[5]

---

16 and 32 bytes. These field sizes are large enough to ensure very low soundness error of the sum-check protocol, while being small enough that field operations remain fast.

[5] And $g(r)$ is needed by $\mathcal{V}$ only in order for the verifier to perform its final check of the prover's final message in the protocol. All other checks that $\mathcal{V}$ performs on the messages sent by $\mathcal{P}$ can be performed with no knowledge of g.

Table 4.1: Costs of the sum-check protocol when applied to a v-variate polynomial g over $\mathbb{F}$. Here, $\deg_i(g)$ denotes the degree of variable i in g, and T denotes the cost of an oracle query to g.

Communication	Rounds	$\mathcal{V}$ time	$\mathcal{P}$ time
$O\left(\sum_{i=1}^{v} \deg_i(g)\right)$	v	$O\left(v + \sum_{i=1}^{v} \deg_i(g)\right) + T$	$O\left(\sum_{i=1}^{v} \deg_i(g) \cdot 2^{v-i} \cdot T\right)$
field elements			$= O\left(2^v \cdot T\right)$ if $\deg_i(g)$ $= O(1)$ for all i

This means that $\mathcal{V}$ can apply the sum-check protocol *even without knowing the polynomial g to which the protocol is being applied*, so long as $\mathcal{V}$ knows an upper bound on the degree of the polynomial in each variable, and later obtains the ability to evaluate g at a random point $r \in \mathbb{F}^v$. In contrast, the prover does need to know the precise polynomial g in order to compute each of its messages over the course of the sum-check protocol.

Preview: Why multilinear extensions are useful: ensuring a fast prover. We will see several scenarios where it is useful to compute $H = \sum_{x \in \{0,1\}^v} f(x)$ for some function $f: \{0,1\}^v \to \mathbb{F}$ derived from the verifier's input. We can compute H by applying the sum-check protocol to any low-degree extension g of f. When g is itself a product of a small number of multilinear polynomials, then the prover in the sum-check protocol applied to g can be implemented extremely efficiently. Specifically, as we show later in Lemma 4.5, Lemma 3.6 (which gave an explicit expression for $\tilde{f}$ in terms of Lagrange basis polynomials) can be exploited to ensure that enormous cancellations occur in the computation of the prover's messages, allowing fast computation.

Preview: Why using multilinear extensions is not always possible: ensuring a fast verifier. Although the use of the MLE $\tilde{f}$ typically ensures fast computation for the prover, $\tilde{f}$ cannot be used in all applications. The reason is that the verifier has to be able to evaluate $\tilde{f}$ at a random point $r \in \mathbb{F}^v$ to perform the final check in the sum-check protocol, and in some settings, this computation would be too costly.

Lemma 3.8 gives a way for $\mathcal{V}$ to evaluate $\tilde{f}(r)$ in time $O(2^v)$, given all evaluations of f at Boolean inputs. This might or might not be an acceptable runtime, depending on the relationship between v and the verifier's input size n. If $v \leq \log_2 n + O(\log \log n)$, then $O(2^v) = \tilde{O}(n),^6$ and the verifier runs in quasilinear time.[7] But we will see some applications where $v = c \log n$ for some constant $c > 1$, and others where $v = n$ (see, e.g., the #SAT protocol in Section 4.2). In these settings, $O(2^v)$ runtime for the verifier is unacceptable, and we will be forced to use an extension g of f that has a succinct representation, enabling $\mathcal{V}$ to compute $g(r)$ in much less than 2^v time. Sometimes $\tilde{f}$ itself has such a succinct representation, but other times we will be forced to use a higher-degree extension of f. See Exercise 4.2 and Exercise 4.3 (Parts (d) and (e)) for further details.

4.2 First Application of Sum-Check: #SAT ∈ IP

Boolean Formulas and Circuits. A Boolean formula over variables $x_1, \ldots, x_n$ is a binary tree with each leaf labeled by a variable x_i or its negation, and each non-leaf node computing the AND or OR of its two children. Each node of the tree is also called a *gate*. The root of the tree is the output gate of the formula. The size S of the formula is the number of leaves of the tree. Note that many leaves of the formula may be labeled by the same variable x_i or its negation, so S may be much larger than n (see Figure 4.1 for an example).

A Boolean formula is identical to a Boolean *circuit*, except that in a formula, non-output gates are required to have fan-out 1, while in a circuit the fan-out of each gate can be unbounded. Here, the fan-out of a gate g in a circuit or formula refers to the number of other gates that g feeds into, i.e., the number of gates for which g is itself an input. See Figure 4.2 for an example of a Boolean circuit.[8]

---

[6] The notation $\tilde{O}(\cdot)$ hides polylogarithmic factors. So, for example, $n \log^4 n = \tilde{O}(n)$.

[7] Quasilinear time means time $\tilde{O}(n)$; i.e., at most a polylogarithmic factor more than linear.

[8] By convention, variable negation in Boolean circuits is typically depicted via explicit NOT gates, whereas in formulas, variable negation is depicted directly at the leaves.

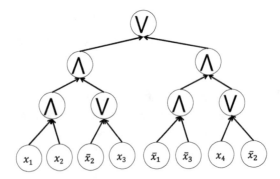

Figure 4.1: A Boolean formula ϕ over 4 variables of size 8. Here, $\lor$ denotes OR, $\land$ denotes AND, and $\bar{x}_i$ denotes the negation of variable x_i.

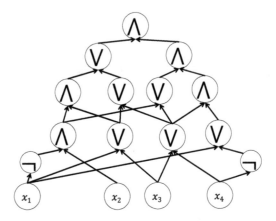

Figure 4.2: A Boolean circuit over 4 input variables. Here, $\lor$ denotes OR, $\land$ denotes AND, and $\neg$ denotes negation.

This means that circuits can "reuse intermediate values", in the sense that the value computed by one gate can be fed to multiple downstream gates. Whereas if a formula wants to reuse a value, it must recompute it from scratch, owing to the requirement that every AND and OR gate have fan-out 1. Visualized graph-theoretically, formulas have a binary-tree wiring pattern, while circuits can be arbitrary directed acyclic graphs. See Figure 4.2 for an example of a Boolean circuit.

The #SAT Problem. Let ϕ be any Boolean formula on n variables of size $S = \text{poly}(n)$.[9] Abusing notation, we will use ϕ to refer to both the formula itself and the function on $\{0,1\}^n$ that it computes. In the #SAT problem, the goal is to compute the number of satisfying assignments of ϕ. Equivalently, the goal is to compute

$$\sum_{x \in \{0,1\}^n} \phi(x). \tag{4.8}$$

#SAT is believed to be a very difficult problem, with the fastest known algorithms requiring time exponential in the number of variables n. This means that known algorithms do not do much better than the "brute force" approach of spending time $O(S)$ to evaluate the formula gate-by-gate at each of the 2^n possible assignments to the inputs. Even determining whether there exists one or more satisfying assignments to the formula is widely believed to require exponential time.[10] Nonetheless, there is an interactive proof protocol for #SAT in which the *verifier* runs in polynomial time.

The Interactive Proof for #SAT. Equation (4.8) sums up the evaluations of ϕ over all vectors in $\{0,1\}^n$. This is highly reminiscent of the kind of function that Lund et al. [186] designed the sum-check protocol to compute, namely the sum of g's evaluations over $\{0,1\}^n$ for some *low-degree polynomial* g. In order to apply the sum-check protocol to compute Equation (4.8), we need to identify a polynomial extension g of ϕ of total degree $\text{poly}(S)$ over a suitable finite field $\mathbb{F}$. The fact that g extends ϕ will ensure that $\sum_{x \in \{0,1\}^n} g(x) = \sum_{x \in \{0,1\}^n} \phi(x)$.[11] Moreover, we need the verifier to be able to evaluate g at a random point r in

---

[9] $S = \text{poly}(n)$ means that S is bounded above by $O(n^k)$ for some constant $k \geq 0$. We will assume $S \geq n$ to simplify statements of protocol costs—this will always be the case if ϕ depends on all n input variables.

[10] Readers familiar with the notion of **NP**-completeness will recognize formula satisfiability as an **NP**-complete problem, meaning that it has a polynomial time algorithm if and only if **P** = **NP**.

[11] More precisely, if the field $\mathbb{F}$ is of some prime size p, then $\sum_{x \in \{0,1\}^n} g(x)$ will equal the number of satisfying assignments of ϕ modulo p. There are a number of ways to address this issue if the exact number of satisfying assignments is desired. The simplest is to choose p larger than the maximum number of possible satisfying assignments, namely 2^n. This will still ensure a polynomial time verifier, as elements

polynomial time. Together with the fact that g has total degree poly(S), this will ensure that the verifier in the sum-check protocol applied to g runs in time poly(S). We define g as follows.

Let $\mathbb{F}$ be a finite field of size at least, say, S^4. In the application of the sum-check protocol below, the soundness error will be at most $S/|\mathbb{F}|$, so the field should be big enough to ensure that this quantity is acceptably small. If $|\mathbb{F}| \approx S^4$, then the soundness error is at most $1/S^3$. Bigger fields will ensure even smaller soundness error.

We can turn ϕ into an *arithmetic* circuit ψ over $\mathbb{F}$ that computes the desired extension g of ϕ. Here, an arithmetic circuit $\mathcal{C}$ has input gates, output gates, intermediate gates, and directed wires between them. Each gate computes addition or multiplication over a finite field $\mathbb{F}$. The process of replacing the Boolean formula ϕ with an arithmetic circuit ψ computing an extension polynomial of ϕ is called *arithmetization*.

For any gate in ϕ computing the AND of two inputs y, z, ψ replaces AND(y, z) with multiplication of y and z over $\mathbb{F}$. It is easy to check that the bivariate polynomial $y \cdot z$ extends the Boolean function AND(y, z), i.e., AND$(y, z) = y \cdot z$ for all $y, z \in \{0, 1\}$. Likewise, ψ replaces any gate computing OR(y, z) by $y + z - y \cdot z$. Any formula leaf of the form $\bar{y}$ (i.e., the negation of variable y) is replaced by $1 - y$, This transformation is depicted in Figures 4.3 and 4.4. It is easy to check that $\psi(x) = \phi(x)$ for all $x \in \{0, 1\}^n$, and that the number of gates in the arithmetic circuit ψ is at most $3S$.

For the polynomial g computed by ψ, $\sum_{i=1}^{n} \deg_i(g) \le S$.[12] Thus, the total communication cost of the sum-check protocol applied to g

---

of a field of this size can be written down and operated upon in time polynomial in n. Similar overflow issues arise frequently when designing proof systems that work over finite fields yet are meant to capture integer arithmetic. For other examples, see Footnote 19 and Sections 6.5.4.1 and 6.6.3.

[12]Here is an inductive proof of this fact. It is clearly true if ϕ consists of just one leaf. Suppose by way of induction that it is true when ϕ consists of at most $S/2$ leaves, and suppose that the output gate of ϕ is an AND gate (a similar argument applies if the output gate is an OR gate). The two in-neighbors of the output gate partition ϕ into two disjoint subformulas ϕ_1, ϕ_2 of sizes S_1, S_2 such that $S_1 + S_2 = S$ and $\phi(x) = \text{AND}(\phi_1(x), \phi_2(x))$. By the induction hypothesis, arithmetizing the two subformulas yields extension polynomials g_1, g_2 such that for $j = 1, 2$, $\sum_{i=1}^{n} \deg_i(g_j) \le S_j$. The arithmetization of ϕ is $g = g_1 \cdot g_2$, which satisfies $\sum_{i=1}^{n} \deg_i(g) \le S_1 + S_2 = S$.

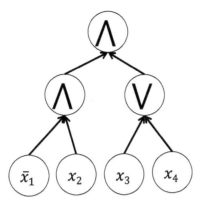

Figure 4.3: A Boolean formula ϕ over 4 variables of size 4. Here, $\vee$ denotes OR, $\wedge$ denotes AND, and $\bar{x}_1$ denotes the negation of variable x_1.

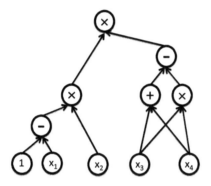

Figure 4.4: An arithmetic circuit ψ computing a polynomial extension g of ϕ over a finite field $\mathbb{F}$.

is $O(S)$ field elements, and $\mathcal{V}$ requires $O(S)$ time in total to check the first $n - 1$ messages from $\mathcal{P}$. To check $\mathcal{P}$'s final message, $\mathcal{V}$ must also evaluate $g(r)$ for the random point $r \in \mathbb{F}^n$ chosen during the sum-check protocol. $\mathcal{V}$ can clearly evaluate $g(r)$ gate-by-gate in time $O(S)$. Since the polynomial g has n variables and $\sum_{i=1}^{n} \deg_i(g) \leq S$, the soundness error of the sum-check protocol applied to g is at most $S/|\mathbb{F}|$.

As explained in Section 4.1, the prover runs in time (at most) $2^n \cdot T \cdot (\sum_{i=1}^{n} \deg_i(g))$, where T is the cost of evaluating g at a point. Since g can be evaluated at any point in time $O(S)$ by evaluating ψ

Table 4.2: Costs of the #SAT protocol of Section 4.2 when applied to a Boolean formula $\phi : \{0,1\}^n \to \{0,1\}$ of size S.

Communication	Rounds	$\mathcal{V}$ time	$\mathcal{P}$ time
$O(S)$ field elements	n	$O(S)$	$O\left(S^2 \cdot 2^n\right)$

gate-by-gate, the prover in the #SAT protocol runs in time $O(S^2 \cdot 2^n)$. The costs of this protocol are summarized in Table 4.2.

IP = PSPACE. The above #SAT protocol comes quite close to establishing a famous result, namely that **IP = PSPACE** [186], [231].[13] That is, the class of problems solvable by interactive proofs with a polynomial-time verifier is exactly equal to the class of problems solvable in polynomial space. Here, we briefly discuss how to prove both directions of this result, i.e., that **IP $\subseteq$ PSPACE** and that **PSPACE $\subseteq$ IP**.

To show that **IP $\subseteq$ PSPACE**, one needs to show that for any constant $c > 0$ and any language $\mathcal{L}$ solvable by an interactive proof in which the verifier's runtime is at most $O(n^c)$ there is an algorithm $\mathcal{A}$ that solves the problem in space at most, say, $O(n^{3c})$. Since c is a constant independent of n, so is $3c$ (albeit a larger one), and hence the space bound $O(n^{3c})$ is a polynomial in n.

Note that the resulting space-$O(n^{3c})$ algorithm might be *extremely* slow, potentially taking time *exponential* in n. That is, the inclusion **IP $\subseteq$ PSPACE** does *not* state that any problem solvable by an interactive proof with an efficient verifier necessarily has a *fast* algorithm, but does state that the problem has a reasonably small-space algorithm.

Very roughly speaking, the algorithm $\mathcal{A}$ on input x will determine whether $x \in \mathcal{L}$ by ascertaining whether or not there is a prover strategy that causes the verifier to accept with probability at least $2/3$. It does this by actually identifying an optimal prover strategy, i.e., finding the prover that maximizes the probability the verifier accepts on input x, and determining exactly what that probability is.

---

[13]Here, **PSPACE** is the class of decision problems that can be solved by some algorithm whose memory usage is bounded by some constant power of n.

In slightly more detail, it suffices to show that for any interactive proof protocol with the verifier running in time $O(n^c)$, that (a) an optimal prover strategy can be computed in space $O(n^{3c})$ and (b) the verifier's acceptance probability when the prover executes that optimal strategy can also be computed in space $O(n^{3c})$. Together, (a) and (b) imply that **IP** ⊆ **PSPACE** because $x \in \mathcal{L}$ if and only if the optimal prover strategy induces the verifier to accept input x with probability at least $2/3$.

Property (b) holds simply because for any fixed prover strategy $\mathcal{P}$ and input x, the probability the verifier accepts when interacting with $\mathcal{P}$ can be computed in space $O(n^c)$ by enumerating over every possible setting of the verifier's random coins and computing the fraction of settings that lead the verifier to accept. Again, note that this enumeration procedure is *extremely* slow—requiring time exponential in n—but can be done in space just $O(n^c)$, because if the verifier runs in time $O(n^c)$ then it also uses space at most $O(n^c)$. For a proof of Property (a), the interested reader is directed to [176, Lecture 17].[14]

The more challenging direction is to show that **PSPACE** ⊆ **IP**. The #SAT protocol of Lund *et al.* [186] described above already contains the main ideas necessary to prove this. Shamir [231] extended the #SAT protocol to the **PSPACE**-complete language TQBF, and Shen [232] gave a simpler proof. We do not cover Shamir or Shen's extensions of the #SAT protocol here, since later (Section 4.5.5), we will provide a different and quantitatively stronger proof that **PSPACE** ⊆ **IP**.

---

[14] As stated in [176, Lecture 17], the result that **IP** ⊆ **PSPACE** is attributed to a manuscript by Paul Feldman in a paper by Goldwasser and Siper [136], and also follows from the analysis in [136].

4.3 Second Application: A Simple IP for Counting Triangles in Graphs

Section 4.2 used the sum-check protocol to give an IP for the #SAT problem, in which the verifier runs in time polynomial in the input size, and the prover runs in time exponential in the input size. This may not seem particularly useful, because in the real-world an exponential-time prover simply will not scale to even moderately-sized inputs. Ideally, we want provers that run in polynomial rather than exponential time, and we want verifiers that run in *linear* rather than polynomial time. IPs achieving such time costs are often called *doubly-efficient*, with the terminology chosen to highlight that both the verifier and prover are highly efficient. The remainder of this section is focused on developing doubly-efficient IPs.

As a warmup, in this section, we apply the sum-check protocol in a straightforward manner to give a simple, doubly-efficient IP for an important graph problem: counting triangles. We give an even more efficient (but less simple) IP for this problem in Section 4.5.1.

To define the problem, let $G = (V, E)$ be a simple graph on n vertices.[15] Here, V denotes the set of vertices of G, and E denotes the edges in G. Let $A \in \{0, 1\}^{n \times n}$ be the adjacency matrix of G, i.e., $A_{i,j} = 1$ if and only if $(i, j) \in E$. In the counting triangles problem, the input is the adjacency matrix A, and the goal is to determine the number of unordered node triples $(i, j, k) \in V \times V \times V$ such that i, j, and k are all connected to each other, i.e., (i, j), (j, k) and (i, k) are all edges in E.

At first blush, it is totally unclear how to express the number of triangles in G as the sum of the evaluations of a low-degree polynomial g over all inputs in $\{0, 1\}^v$, as per Equation (4.1). After all, the counting triangles problem itself makes no reference to any low-degree polynomial g, so where will g come from? This is where multilinear extensions come to the rescue.

For it to make sense to talk about multilinear extensions, we need to view the adjacency matrix A not as a matrix, but rather as a function

---

[15] A simple graph is one that is undirected and unweighted, with no self-loops or repeat edges.

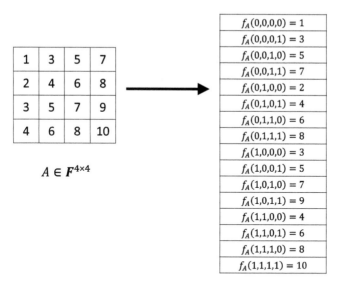

Figure 4.5: Example of how to view an $n \times n$ matrix A with entries from $\mathbb{F}$ as a function f_A mapping the domain $\{0,1\}^{\log_2(n)} \times \{0,1\}^{\log_2(n)}$ to $\mathbb{F}$, when $n = 4$. Note that there are n^2 entries of A, and n^2 vectors in $\{0,1\}^{\log_2(n)} \times \{0,1\}^{\log_2(n)}$. The entries of A are interpreted as the list of all n^2 evaluations of f_A.

f_A mapping $\{0,1\}^{\log n} \times \{0,1\}^{\log n}$ to $\{0,1\}$. The natural way to do this is to define $f_A(x,y)$ so that it interprets x and y as the binary representations of some integers i and j between 1 and n, and outputs $A_{i,j}$. See Figure 4.5 for an example.[16]

Then the number of triangles, Δ, in G can be written:

$$\Delta = \frac{1}{6} \sum_{x,y,z \in \{0,1\}^{\log n}} f_A(x,y) \cdot f_A(y,z) \cdot f_A(x,z). \qquad (4.9)$$

To see that this equality is true, observe that the term for x, y, z in the above sum is 1 if edges (x,y), (y,z), and (x,z) all appear in G, and is 0 otherwise. The factor $1/6$ comes in because the sum over *ordered* node triples (i,j,k) counts each triangle 6 times, once for each permutation of i, j, and k.

---

[16]Figure 4.5 depicts a matrix A with arbitrary entries from some field $\mathbb{F}$. In the counting triangles problem as defined above, each entry of A is either 0 or 1, not an arbitrary field element.

Let $\mathbb{F}$ be a finite field of size $p \geq 6n^3$, where p is a prime, and let us view all entries of A as elements of $\mathbb{F}$. Here, we are choosing p large enough so that 6Δ is guaranteed to be in $\{0, 1, \ldots, p-1\}$, as the maximum number of triangles in any graph on n vertices is $\binom{n}{3} \leq n^3$. This ensures that, if we associate elements of $\mathbb{F}$ with integers in $\{0, 1, \ldots, p-1\}$ in the natural way, then Equation (4.9) holds even when all additions and multiplications are done in $\mathbb{F}$ rather than over the integers. (Choosing a large field to work over has the added benefit of ensuring good soundness error, as the soundness error of the sum-check protocol decreases linearly with field size.)

At last we are ready to describe the polynomial g to which we will apply the sum-check protocol to compute 6Δ. Recalling that $\tilde{f}_A$ is the multilinear extension of f_A over $\mathbb{F}$, define the $(3 \log n)$-variate polynomial g to be:

$$g(X, Y, Z) = \tilde{f}_A(X, Y) \cdot \tilde{f}_A(Y, Z) \cdot \tilde{f}_A(X, Z).$$

Equation (4.9) implies that:

$$6\Delta = \sum_{x,y,z \in \{0,1\}^{\log n}} g(x, y, z),$$

so applying the sum-check protocol to g yields an IP computing 6Δ.

Example. Consider the smallest non-empty graph, namely the two-vertex graph with a single undirected edge connecting the two vertices. There are no triangles in this graph. This is because there are fewer than three vertices in the entire graph, and there are no self-loops. That is, by the pigeonhole principle, for every triple of vertices (i, j, k), at least two of the vertices are the *same* vertex (i.e., at least one of $i = j$, $j = k$, or $i = k$ holds), and since there are no self-loops in the graph, these two vertices are not connected to each other by an edge. In this example, the adjacency matrix is

$$A = \begin{bmatrix} 0 & 1 \\ 1 & 0 \end{bmatrix}.$$

In this case,

$$\tilde{f}_A(a, b) = a \cdot (1 - b) + b \cdot (1 - a),$$

and g is the following 3-variate polynomial:

$$g(X, Y, Z) = (X \cdot (1 - Y) + Y \cdot (1 - X)) (Y \cdot (1 - Z)$$
$$+ Z \cdot (1 - Y)) (X \cdot (1 - Z) + Z \cdot (1 - X)).$$

It is not hard to see that $g(x, y, z) = 0$ for all $(x, y, z) \in \{0, 1\}^3$, and hence applying the sum-check protocol to g reveals that the number of triangles in the graph is $\frac{1}{6} \cdot \sum_{(x,y,z) \in \{0,1\}^3} g(x, y, z) = 0$.

Costs of the Protocol. Since the polynomial g is defined over $3 \log n$ variables, there are $3 \log n$ rounds. Since g has degree at most 2 in each of its $3 \log n$ variables, the total number of field elements sent by the prover in each round is at most 3. This means that the communication cost is $O(\log n)$ field elements ($9 \log n$ elements sent from prover to verifier, and at most $3 \log n$ sent from verifier to prover).

The verifier's runtime is dominated by the time to perform the final check in the sum-check protocol. This requires evaluating g at a random input $(r_1, r_2, r_3) \in \mathbb{F}^{\log n} \times \mathbb{F}^{\log n} \times \mathbb{F}^{\log n}$, which in turn requires evaluating $\tilde{f}_A(r_1, r_2)$, $\tilde{f}_A(r_2, r_3)$ and $\tilde{f}_A(r_1, r_3)$. Each of these 3 evaluations can be computed in $O(n^2)$ field operations using Lemma 3.8, which is linear in the size of the input matrix A.

The prover's runtime is clearly at most $O(n^5)$. This is because, since there are $3 \log_2 n$ rounds of the protocol, it is sufficient for the prover to evaluate g at $O(n^3)$ inputs (see Table 4.1), and as explained in the previous paragraph, g can be evaluated at any input in $\mathbb{F}^{3 \log n}$ in $O(n^2)$ time. In fact, more sophisticated algorithmic insights introduced in the next section can bring the prover runtime down to $O(n^3)$, which is competitive with the naive unverifiable algorithm for counting triangles that iterates over every triple of vertices and checks if they form a triangle. We omit further discussion of how to achieve prover time $O(n^3)$ in the protocol of this section, as Section 4.5.1 gives a different IP for counting triangles, in which the prover's runtime is much less than $O(n^3)$.

A Bird's Eye View. Hopefully the above protocol for counting triangles gives a sense of how problems that people care about in practice can be expressed as instances of Equation (4.1) in non-obvious ways. The general paradigm works as follows. An input x of length n is viewed as a function f_x mapping $\{0,1\}^{\log n}$ to some field $\mathbb{F}$. And then the multilinear extension $\tilde{f}_x$ of f_x is used in some way to construct a low-degree polynomial g such that, as per Equation (4.1), the desired answer equals the sum of the evaluations of g over the Boolean hypercube. The remaining sections of this section cover additional examples of this paradigm.

4.4 Third Application: Super-Efficient IP for MatMult

This section describes a highly optimized IP protocol for matrix multiplication (MATMULT) from [237]. While this MATMULT protocol is of interest in its own right, it is included here for didactic reasons: it displays, in a clean and unencumbered setting, all of the algorithmic insights that are exploited later in this survey to give more general IP and MIP protocols.

Given two $n \times n$ input matrices A, B over field $\mathbb{F}$, the goal of MATMULT is to compute the product matrix $C = A \cdot B$.

4.4.1 Comparison to Freivalds' Protocol

Recall from Section 2.2 that, in 1977, Freivalds [115] gave the following verification protocol for MATMULT: to check that $A \cdot B = C$, $\mathcal{V}$ picks a random vector $x \in \mathbb{F}^n$, and accepts if $A \cdot (Bx) = Cx$. $\mathcal{V}$ can compute $A \cdot (Bx)$ with two matrix-vector multiplications, which requires just $O(n^2)$ time. Thus, in Freivelds' protocol, $\mathcal{P}$ simply finds and sends the correct answer C, while $\mathcal{V}$ runs in optimal $O(n^2)$ total time. Today, Freivalds' protocol is regularly covered in introductory textbooks on randomized algorithms.

At first glance, Freivalds' protocol seems to close the book on verification protocols for MATMULT, since the runtimes of both $\mathcal{V}$ and $\mathcal{P}$ are optimal: $\mathcal{P}$ does *no* extra work to prove correctness of the answer matrix C, $\mathcal{V}$ runs in time linear in the input size, and the protocol is even non-interactive ($\mathcal{P}$ just sends the answer matrix C to $\mathcal{V}$).

However, there is a sense in which it is possible to improve on Freivalds' protocol by introducing interaction between $\mathcal{P}$ and $\mathcal{V}$. In many settings, algorithms invoke MATMULT, but they are not really interested in the full answer matrix. Rather, they apply a simple post-processing step to the answer matrix to arrive at the quantity of true interest. For example, the best-known graph diameter algorithms repeatedly square the adjacency matrix of the graph, but ultimately they are not interested in the matrix powers—they are only interested in a single number. As another example, discussed in detail in Section 4.5.1, the fastest known algorithm for counting triangles in dense graphs invokes matrix multiplication, but is ultimately only interested in a single number, namely the number of triangles in the graph.

If Freivalds' protocol is used to verify the matrix multiplication steps of these algorithms, the actual product matrices must be sent for each step, necessitating $\Omega(n^2)$ communication. In practice, this can easily be many terabytes of data, even on graphs G with a few million nodes. Also, even if G is sparse, powers of G's adjacency matrix may be dense.

This section describes an interactive matrix multiplication protocol from [237] that preserves the runtimes of $\mathcal{V}$ and $\mathcal{P}$ from Freivalds' protocol, but avoids the need for $\mathcal{P}$ to send the full answer matrix in the settings described above—in these settings, the communication cost of the interactive protocol is just $O(\log n)$ field elements per matrix multiplication.

Preview: The Power of Interaction. This comparison of the interactive MATMULT protocol to Freivalds' non-interactive one exemplifies the power of interaction in verification. Interaction buys the verifier the ability to ensure that the prover correctly materialized intermediate values in a computation (in this case, the entries of the product matrix C), without requiring the prover to explicitly materialize those values to the verifier. This point will become clearer later, when we cover the counting triangles protocol in Section 4.5.1. Roughly speaking, in that protocol, the prover convinces the verifier it correctly determined the squared adjacency matrix of the input graph, without ever materializing the squared adjacency matrix to the verifier.

Preview: Other Protocols for MatMult. An alternate interactive MATMULT protocol can be obtained by applying the GKR protocol (covered later in Section 4.6) to a circuit $\mathcal{C}$ that computes the product C of two input matrices A, B. The verifier in this protocol runs in $O(n^2)$

time, and the prover runs in time $O(S)$, where S is the number of gates in $\mathcal{C}$.

The advantage of the MATMULT protocol described in this section is two-fold. First, it does not care how the prover finds the right answer. In contrast, the GKR protocol demands that the prover compute the answer matrix C in a prescribed manner, namely by evaluating the circuit $\mathcal{C}$ gate-by-gate. Second, the prover in the protocol of this section simply finds the right answer and then does $O(n^2)$ extra work to prove correctness. This $O(n^2)$ term is a low-order additive overhead, assuming that there is no linear-time algorithm for matrix multiplication. In contrast, the GKR protocol introduces at least a constant factor overhead for the prover. In practice, this is the difference between a prover that runs many times slower than an (unverifiable) MATMULT algorithm, and a prover that runs a fraction of a percent slower [237].

4.4.2   The Protocol

Given $n \times n$ input matrix A, B, recall that we denote the product matrix $A \cdot B$ by C. And as in Section 4.3, we interpret A, B, and C as functions f_A, f_B, f_C mapping $\{0,1\}^{\log n} \times \{0,1\}^{\log n}$ to $\mathbb{F}$ via:

$$f_A(i_1, \ldots, i_{\log n}, j_1, \ldots, j_{\log n}) = A_{ij}.$$

As usual, $\tilde{f}_A$, $\tilde{f}_B$, and $\tilde{f}_C$ denote the MLEs of f_A, f_B, and f_C.

It is cleanest to describe the protocol for MATMULT as a protocol for evaluating $\tilde{f}_C$ at any given point $(r_1, r_2) \in \mathbb{F}^{\log n \times \log n}$. As we explain later (see Section 4.5), this turns out to be sufficient for application problems such as graph diameter and triangle counting.

The protocol for computing $\tilde{f}_C(r_1, r_2)$ exploits the following explicit representation of the polynomial $\tilde{f}_C(x, y)$.

Lemma 4.2. $\tilde{f}_C(x, y) = \sum_{b \in \{0,1\}^{\log n}} \tilde{f}_A(x, b) \cdot \tilde{f}_B(b, y)$. Here, the equality holds as formal polynomials in the coordinates of x and y.

Proof. The left and right hand sides of the equation appearing in the lemma statement are both multilinear polynomials in the coordinates of x and y. Since the MLE of C is unique, we need only check that the left and right hand sides of the equation agree for all *Boolean* vectors $i, j \in \{0, 1\}^{\log n}$. That is, we must check that for Boolean vectors $i, j \in \{0, 1\}^{\log n}$,

$$f_C(i, j) = \sum_{k \in \{0,1\}^{\log n}} f_A(i, k) \cdot f_B(k, j). \tag{4.10}$$

But this is immediate from the definition of matrix multiplication. $\square$

With Lemma 4.2 in hand, the interactive protocol is immediate: we compute $\tilde{f}_C(r_1, r_2)$ by applying the sum-check protocol to the $(\log n)$-variate polynomial $g(z) := \tilde{f}_A(r_1, z) \cdot \tilde{f}_B(z, r_2)$.

Example. Consider the 2×2 matrices $A = \begin{bmatrix} 0 & 1 \\ 2 & 0 \end{bmatrix}$ and $B = \begin{bmatrix} 1 & 0 \\ 0 & 4 \end{bmatrix}$ over $\mathbb{F}_5$. One can check that

$$A \cdot B = \begin{bmatrix} 0 & 4 \\ 2 & 0 \end{bmatrix}.$$

Viewing A and B as a functions mapping $\{0, 1\}^2 \to \mathbb{F}_5$,

$$\tilde{f}_A(x_1, x_2) = (1 - x_1)x_2 + 2x_1(1 - x_2) = -3x_1x_2 + 2x_1 + x_2,$$

and

$$\tilde{f}_B(x_1, x_2) = (1 - x_1)(1 - x_2) + 4x_1x_2 = 5x_1x_2 - x_1 - x_2 + 1 = 1 - x_1 - x_2,$$

where the final equality used the fact that we are working over $\mathbb{F}_5$, so the coefficient 5 is the same as the coefficient 0.

Observe that

$$\sum_{b \in \{0,1\}} \tilde{f}_A(x_1, b) \cdot \tilde{f}_B(b, x_2) = \tilde{f}_A(x_1, 0) \cdot \tilde{f}_B(0, x_2) + \tilde{f}_A(x_1, 1) \cdot \tilde{f}_B(1, x_2)$$

$$= 2x_1 \cdot (1 - x_2) + (-x_1 + 1) \cdot (-x_2) = -x_1x_2 + 2x_1 - x_2. \tag{4.11}$$

Meanwhile, viewing C as a function f_C mapping $\{0, 1\}^2 \to \mathbb{F}_5$, we can calculate via Lagrange Interpolation:

$$\tilde{f}_C(x_1, x_2) = 4(1 - x_1)x_2 + 2x_1(1 - x_2) = -6x_1x_2 + 2x_1 + 4x_2$$

$$= -x_1x_2 + 2x_1 - x_2,$$

where the final equality uses that $6 \equiv 1$ and $4 \equiv -1$ when working modulo 5. Hence, we have verified that Lemma 4.2 indeed holds for this particular example.

4.4.3 Discussion of Costs

Rounds and Communication Cost.   Since g is a $(\log n)$-variate polynomial of degree 2 in each variable, the total communication is $O(\log n)$ field elements, spread over $\log n$ rounds.

$\mathcal{V}$**'s Runtime.**   At the end of the sum-check protocol, $\mathcal{V}$ must evaluate $g(r_3) = \tilde{f}_A(r_1, r_3) \cdot \tilde{f}_B(r_3, r_2)$. To perform this evaluation, it suffices for $\mathcal{V}$ to evaluate $\tilde{f}_A(r_1, r_3)$ and $\tilde{f}_B(r_3, r_2)$. Since $\mathcal{V}$ is given the matrices A and B as input, Lemma 3.8 implies that both evaluations can be performed in $O(n^2)$ time.

$\mathcal{P}$**'s Runtime.**   Recall that in each round k of the sum-check protocol $\mathcal{P}$ sends a quadratic polynomial $g_k(X_k)$ claimed to equal:

$$\sum_{b_{k+1} \in \{0,1\}} \cdots \sum_{b_{\log n} \in \{0,1\}} g(r_{3,1}, \ldots, r_{3,k-1}, X_i, b_{k+1}, \ldots b_{\log n}),$$

and to specify $g_k(X_k)$, $\mathcal{P}$ can just send the values $g_i(0), g_i(1)$, and $g_i(2)$. Thus, it is enough for $\mathcal{P}$ to evaluate g at all points of the form

$$(r_{3,1}, \ldots, r_{3,k-1}, \{0, 1, 2\}, b_{k+1}, \ldots, b_{\log n}) : (b_{k+1}, \ldots, b_{\log n})$$
$$\in \{0, 1\}^{\log n - k}. \tag{4.12}$$

There are $3 \cdot n/2^k$ such points in round k.

We describe three separate methods to perform these evaluations. The first method is the least sophisticated and requires $\Theta(n^3)$ total time. The second method reduces the runtime to $\Theta(n^2)$ per round, for a total runtime bound of $\Theta(n^2 \log n)$ over all $\log n$ rounds. The third method is more sophisticated still—it enables the prover to *reuse work* across rounds, ensuring that $\mathcal{P}$'s runtime in round k is bounded by $O(n^2/2^k)$. Hence, the prover's total runtime is $O(\sum_k n^2/2^k) = O(n^2)$.

Method 1. As described when bounding $\mathcal{V}$'s runtime, g can be evaluated at any point in $O(n^2)$ time. Since there are $3 \cdot n/2^k$ points at which $\mathcal{P}$ must evaluate g in round k, this leads to a total runtime for $\mathcal{P}$ of $O(\sum_k n^3/2^k) = O(n^3)$.

Method 2. To improve on the $O(n^3)$ runtime of Method 1, the key is to exploit the fact that $3 \cdot n/2^k$ points at which $\mathcal{P}$ needs to evaluate

g in round k are not arbitrary points in $\mathbb{F}^{\log n}$, but are instead highly structured. Specifically, each such point z is in the form of Equation (4.12), and hence the trailing coordinates of z are all Boolean (i.e., $\{0, 1\}$-valued). As explained below, this property ensures that **each entry A_{ij} of A contributes to** $g\left(r_{3,1}, \ldots, r_{3,k-1}, \{0, 1, 2\}, b_{k+1}, \ldots, b_{\log n}\right)$ **for only one tuple** $(b_{k+1}, \ldots, b_{\log n}) \in \{0, 1\}^{\log n - k}$, **and similarly for each entry of B_{ij}.** Hence, $\mathcal{P}$ can make a single pass over the matrices A and B, and for each entry A_{ij} or B_{ij}, $\mathcal{P}$ only needs to update $g(z)$ for the three relevant tuples z of the form $(r_{3,1}, \ldots, r_{3,k-1}, \{0, 1, 2\}, b_{k+1}, \ldots, b_{\log n})$.

In more detail, in order to evaluate g at any input z, it suffices for $\mathcal{P}$ to evaluate $\widetilde{f}_A(r_1, z)$ and $\widetilde{f}_B(z, r_2)$. We explain the case of evaluating $\widetilde{f}_A(r_1, z)$ at all relevant points z, since the case of $\widetilde{f}_B(z, r_2)$ is identical. From Lemma 3.6 (Lagrange Interpolation), $\widetilde{f}_A(r_1, z) = \sum_{i,j \in \{0,1\}^{\log n}} A_{ij} \chi_{(i,j)}(r_1, z)$. For any input z of the form $(r_{3,1}, \ldots, r_{3,k-1}, \{0, 1, 2\}, b_{k+1}, \ldots, b_{\log n})$, notice that $\chi_{i,j}(r_1, z) = 0$ unless $(j_{k+1}, \ldots, j_{\log n}) = (b_{k+1}, \ldots, b_{\log n})$. This is because, for any coordinate ℓ such that $j_\ell \neq b_\ell$, the factor $(j_\ell b_\ell + (1 - j_\ell)(1 - b_\ell))$ appearing in the product defining $\chi_{(i,j)}$ equals 0 (see Equation (3.1)).

This enables $\mathcal{P}$ to evaluate $\widetilde{f}_A(r_1, z)$ in round k at all points z of the form of Equation (4.12) with a single pass over A: when $\mathcal{P}$ encounters entry A_{ij} of A, $\mathcal{P}$ updates $\widetilde{f}_A(z) \leftarrow \widetilde{f}_A(z) + A_{ij} \chi_{i,j}(z)$ for the three relevant values of z.

Method 3. To shave the last factor of $\log n$ off $\mathcal{P}$'s runtime, the idea is to have $\mathcal{P}$ reuse work across rounds. Very roughly speaking, the key fact that enables this is the following:

Informal Fact. If two entries $(i, j), (i', j') \in \{0, 1\}^{\log n} \times \{0, 1\}^{\log n}$ agree in their last ℓ bits, then $A_{i,j}$ and $A_{i',j'}$ contribute to the same three points in each of the final ℓ rounds of the protocol.

The specific points that they contribute to in each round $k \geq \log(n) - \ell$ are the ones of the form

$$z = (r_{3,1}, \ldots, r_{3,k-1}, \{0, 1, 2\}, b_{k+1}, \ldots, b_{\log n}),$$

where $b_{k+1} \ldots b_{\log n}$ equal the trailing bits of (i, j) and (i', j'). This turns out to ensure that $\mathcal{P}$ can treat (i, j) and (i', j') as a single entity thereafter. There are only $O(n^2/2^k)$ entities of interest after k variables have been bound (out of the $2 \log n$ variables over which $\widetilde{f_A}$ is defined). So the total work that $\mathcal{P}$ invests over the course of the protocol is

$$O\left(\sum_{k=1}^{2 \log n} n^2/2^k\right) = O(n^2).$$

In more detail, the **Informal Fact** stated above is captured by the proof of the following lemma.

Lemma 4.3. Suppose that p is an ℓ-variate multilinear polynomial over field $\mathbb{F}$ and that A is an array of length 2^ℓ such that for each $x \in \{0,1\}^\ell$, $A[x] = p(x)$.[17] Then for any $r_1 \in \mathbb{F}$, there is an algorithm running in time $O(2^\ell)$ that, given r_1 and A as input, computes an array B of length $2^{\ell-1}$ such that for each $x' \in \{0,1\}^{\ell-1}$, $B[x'] = p(r_1, x')$.

Proof. The proof is reminiscent of that of Lemma 3.8. Specifically, we can express the multilinear polynomial $p(x_1, x_2, \ldots, x_\ell)$ via:

$$p(x_1, x_2, \ldots, x_\ell) = x_1 \cdot p(1, x_2, \ldots, x_\ell) + (1 - x_1) \cdot p(0, x_2, \ldots, x_\ell). \quad (4.13)$$

Indeed, the right hand side is clearly a multilinear polynomial that agrees with p at all inputs in $\{0,1\}^\ell$, and hence must equal p by Fact 3.5. The algorithm to compute B iterates over every value $x' \in \{0,1\}^{\ell-1}$ and sets $B[x'] \leftarrow r_1 \cdot A[1, x'] + (1 - r_1) \cdot A[0, x']$.[18] □

Lemma 4.3 captures Informal Fact because, while inputs $(0, x')$ and $(1, x')$ to p both contribute to $B[x']$, they contribute to no other entries of the array B. As we will see when we apply Lemma 4.3 repeatedly to compute the prover's messages in the sum-check protocol, once $B[x']$ is computed, the prover only needs to know $B[x']$, not $p(0, x')$ or $p(1, x')$ individually.

---

[17] Here, we associate bit-vectors x of length ℓ with indices into the array A of length 2^ℓ in the natural way.

[18] As in the statement of the lemma, here we associate bit-vectors x of length ℓ with indices into the array A of length 2^ℓ in the natural way, and similarly bit-vectors x' of length $\ell - 1$ with indices into the array B of length $2^{\ell-1}$.

Lemma 4.4. Let h be any ℓ-variate multilinear polynomial over field $\mathbb{F}$ for which all evaluations of $h(x)$ for $x \in \{0,1\}^\ell$ can be computed in time $O(2^\ell)$. Let $r_1, \ldots, r_\ell \in \mathbb{F}$ be any sequence of ℓ field elements. Then there is an algorithm that runs in time $O(2^\ell)$ and computes the following quantities:

$$\{h(r_1, \ldots, r_{i-1}, \{0,1,2\}, b_{i+1}, \ldots, b_\ell)\}_{i=1,\ldots,\ell;\ b_{i+1},\ldots,b_\ell \in \{0,1\}} \qquad (4.14)$$

Proof. Let

$$S_i = \{h(r_1, \ldots, r_{i-1}, b_i, b_{i+1}, \ldots, b_\ell)\}_{b_i,\ldots,b_\ell \in \{0,1\}}.$$

Given all values in S_i, applying Lemma 4.3 to the $(\ell - i + 1)$-variate multilinear polynomial $p(X_i, \ldots, X_\ell) = h(r_1, \ldots, r_{i-1}, X_i, \ldots, X_\ell)$ implies that all values in S_{i+1} can be computed in time $O(2^{\ell-i})$.

Equation (4.13) further implies

$$h(r_1, \ldots, r_{i-1}, 2, b_{i+1}, \ldots, b_\ell) = 2 \cdot h(r_1, \ldots, r_{i-1}, 1, b_{i+1}, \ldots, b_\ell)$$
$$- h(r_1, \ldots, r_{i-1}, 0, b_{i+1}, \ldots, b_\ell),$$

and hence the values

$$\{h(r_1, \ldots, r_{i-1}, 2, b_{i+1}, \ldots, b_\ell)\}_{b_i,\ldots,b_\ell \in \{0,1\}}$$

can also be computed in $O(2^{\ell-i})$ time given the values in S_i.

It follows the total time required to compute all values in Equation (4.14) is $O(\sum_{i=1}^{\ell} 2^{\ell-i}) = O(2^\ell)$. $\qquad \square$

Lemma 4.5. (Implicit in [103, Appendix B], see also [237], [251]) Let $p_1, p_2, \ldots, p_k$ be ℓ-variate multilinear polynomials. Suppose that for each p_i there is an algorithm that evaluates p_i at all inputs in $\{0,1\}^\ell$ in time $O(2^\ell)$. Let $g = p_1 \cdot p_2 \cdots \cdots p_k$ be the product of these multilinear polynomials. Then when the sum-check protocol is applied to the polynomial g, the honest prover can be implemented in $O(k \cdot 2^\ell)$ time.

Proof. As explained in Equation (4.12), the dominant cost in the honest prover's computation in the sum-check protocol lies in evaluating g at points of the form referred to in Lemma 4.4 (see Equation (4.14)). To obtain these evaluations, it clearly suffices to evaluate $p_1, \ldots, p_k$ at each one of these points, and multiply the results in time $O(k)$ per point.

Lemma 4.4 guarantees that each p_i can be evaluated at the relevant points in $O(2^\ell)$ time, yielding a total runtime of $O(k \cdot 2^\ell)$. See Figure 4.6 for a depiction of the honest prover's computation in the case $\ell = 3$. $\square$

In the matrix multiplication protocol of this section, the sum-check protocol is applied to the $(\log_2 n)$-variate polynomial $g(X_3) = \widetilde{f_A}(r_1, X_3) \cdot \widetilde{f_B}(X_3, r_2)$. The multilinear polynomial $\widetilde{f_A}(r_1, X_3)$ can be evaluated at all inputs in $\{0,1\}^{\log n}$ in $O(n^2)$ time, by applying Lemma 4.4 with $h = \widetilde{f_A}$, and observing that the necessary evaluations of $\widetilde{f_A}(r_1, X_3)$ are a subset of the points in Equation (4.14) (with i in Equation (4.14) equal to $\log n$, and $(r_1, \ldots, r_{\log n})$ in Equation (4.14) equal to the entries of r_1). Similarly, $\widetilde{f_B}(X_3, r_2)$ can be evaluated at all inputs in $\{0,1\}^{\log n}$ in $O(n^2)$ time. Given all of these evaluations, Lemma 4.5 implies that the prover can execute its part of the sum-check protocol in just $O(n)$ additional time.

This completes the explanation of how the prover in the matrix multiplication protocol of this section executes its part of the sum-check protocol in $O(n^2)$ total time. All costs of the protocol are summarized in Table 4.3.

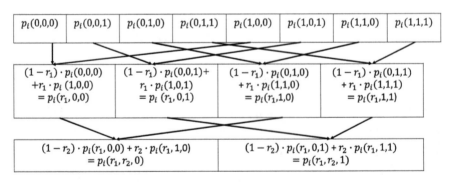

Figure 4.6: Depiction of the round-by-round evolution of the honest prover's internal data structure devoted to the polynomial p_i in Lemma 4.5 in the case $\ell = 3$ (recall this lemma considers the sum-check protocol applied to compute $\sum_{x \in \{0,1\}^\ell} p_1(x) \cdot \cdots \cdot p_k(x)$ when each p_i is multilinear). The top row is used by the prover to compute its prescribed message in the first round, the middle row for the second round, and the bottom row for the third round.

Table 4.3: Costs of the MATMULT protocol of Section 4.4 when applied to $n \times n$ matrices A and B. Here, T is the time required by $\mathcal{P}$ to compute the product matrix $C = A \cdot B$.

Communication	Rounds	$\mathcal{V}$ time	$\mathcal{P}$ time
$O(\log n)$ field elements	$\log n$	$O\left(n^2\right)$	$T + O(n^2)$

4.5 Applications of the Super-Efficient MatMult IP

Why does an IP for computing $\tilde{f}_C(r_1, r_2)$ rather than the full product matrix $C = A \cdot B$ suffice in applications? This section answers this question via several examples. With the exception of Section 4.5.5, all of the protocols in this section enable the honest prover to run the best-known algorithm to solve the problem at hand, and then do a low-order amount of extra work to prove the answer is correct. We refer to such IPs as *super-efficient* for the prover. There are no other known IPs or argument systems that achieve this super-efficiency while keeping the proof length sublinear in the input size.

4.5.1 A Super-Efficient IP For Counting Triangles

Algorithms often invoke MATMULT to generate crucial *intermediate values* compute some product matrix C, but are not interested in the product matrix itself. For example, the fastest known algorithm for counting triangles in dense graphs works as follows. If A is the adjacency matrix of a simple graph, the algorithm first computes A^2 (it is known how to accomplish this in time $O(n^{2.3728639})$ [178]), and then outputs (1/6 times)

$$\sum_{i,j \in \{1,\dots,n\}} (A^2)_{ij} \cdot A_{ij}. \tag{4.15}$$

It is not hard to see that Equation (4.15) quantity is six times the number of triangles in the graph, since $(A^2)_{i,j}$ counts the number of common neighbors of vertices i and j, and hence $A_{ij}^2 \cdot A_{ij}$ equals the number of vertices k such that (i, j), (j, k) and (k, j) are all edges in the graph.

Clearly, the matrix A^2 is not of intrinsic interest here, but rather is a useful intermediate object from which the final answer can be quickly derived. As we explain in this section, it is possible to give an IP for counting triangles in which $\mathcal{P}$ essentially establishes that he correctly materialized A^2 and used it to generate the output via Equation (4.15). Crucially, $\mathcal{P}$ will accomplish this with only logarithmic communication (i.e., without sending A^2 to the verifier), and while doing very little extra work beyond determining A^2.

The Protocol. As in Section 4.3, let $\mathbb{F}$ be a finite field of size $p \geq 6n^3$, where p is a prime, and let us view all entries of A as elements of $\mathbb{F}$. Define the functions $f_A(x, y), f_{A^2}(x, y) \colon \{0, 1\}^{\log n} \times \{0, 1\}^{\log n} \to \mathbb{F}$ that interprets x and y as the binary representations of some integers i and j between 1 and n, and outputs $A_{i,j}$ and $(A^2)_{i,j}$ respectively. Let $\widetilde{f}_A$ and $\widetilde{f}_{A^2}$ denote the multilinear extensions of f_A and f_{A^2} over $\mathbb{F}$.

Then the expression in Equation (4.15) equals $\sum_{x,y \in \{0,1\}^{\log n}} \widetilde{f}_{A^2}(x, y) \cdot \widetilde{f}_A(x, y)$. This quantity can be computed by applying the sum-check protocol to the multi-quadratic polynomial $\widetilde{f}_{A^2} \cdot \widetilde{f}_A$. At the end of this protocol, the verifier needs to evaluate $\widetilde{f}_{A^2}(r_1, r_2) \cdot \widetilde{f}_A(r_1, r_2)$ for a randomly chosen input $(r_1, r_2) \in \mathbb{F}^{\log n} \times \mathbb{F}^{\log n}$. The verifier can evaluate $\widetilde{f}_A(r_1, r_2)$ unaided in $O(n^2)$ time using Lemma 3.8. While the verifier cannot evaluate $\widetilde{f}_{A^2}(r_1, r_2)$ without computing the matrix A^2 (which is as hard as solving the counting triangles problem on her own), evaluating $\widetilde{f}_{A^2}(r_1, r_2)$ is exactly the problem that the MatMult IP of Section 4.4.2 was designed to solve (as $A^2 = A \cdot A$), so we simply invoke that protocol to compute $\widetilde{f}_{A^2}(r_1, r_2)$.

Example. Consider the example from Section 4.3, in which the input matrix is

$$A = \begin{bmatrix} 0 & 1 \\ 1 & 0 \end{bmatrix}.$$

In this case,

$$A^2 = \begin{bmatrix} 1 & 0 \\ 0 & 1 \end{bmatrix}.$$

One can check that

$$\widetilde{f}_A(X, Y) = X \cdot (1 - Y) + Y \cdot (1 - X),$$

and

$$\tilde{f}_{A^2}(X, Y) = X \cdot Y + (1 - Y) \cdot (1 - X).$$

The counting triangles protocol in this section first applies the sum-check protocol to the following bivariate polynomial that has degree 2 in both of its variables:

$$\tilde{f}_{A^2}(X, Y) \cdot \tilde{f}_A(X, Y) = (X \cdot (1 - Y) + Y \cdot (1 - X))$$
$$\cdot (X \cdot Y + (1 - X) \cdot (1 - Y)).$$

It is easy to check that this polynomial evaluates to 0 for all four inputs in $\{0, 1\}^2$, so applying the sum-check protocol to this polynomial reveals to the verifier that $\sum_{(x,y) \in \{0,1\}^2} \tilde{f}_{A^2}(x, y) \cdot \tilde{f}_A(x, y) = 0$.

At the end of the sum-check protocol applied to this polynomial, the verifier needs to evaluate $\tilde{f}_{A^2}$ and $\tilde{f}_A$ at a randomly chosen input $(r_1, r_2) \in \mathbb{F}^{\log n} \times \mathbb{F}^{\log n}$. The verifier evaluates $\tilde{f}_A(r_1, r_2)$ on its own. To compute $\tilde{f}_{A^2}(r_1, r_2)$, the matrix multiplication IP is invoked. This protocol applies the sum-check protocol a second time, to the univariate quadratic polynomial

$$s(X) := \tilde{f}_A(r_1, X) \cdot \tilde{f}_A(X, r_2) = (r_1(1 - X) + (1 - r_1)X) \cdot (X(1 - r_2)$$
$$+ r_2(1 - X)).$$

This reveals to the verifier that

$$\tilde{f}_{A^2}(r_1, r_2) = s(0) + s(1) = r_1 r_2 + (1 - r_1)(1 - r_2).$$

At the end of this second invocation of the sum-check protocol, the verifier needs to evaluate $s(r_3)$ for a randomly chosen $r_3 \in \mathbb{F}$. To do this, it suffices to evaluate $\tilde{f}_A(r_1, r_3)$ and $\tilde{f}_A(r_3, r_2)$, both of which the verifier computes on its own.

Costs of the Counting Triangles Protocol. The number of rounds, communication size, and verifier runtime of the IP of this section are all identical to the counting triangles protocol we saw earlier in Section 4.3 (namely, $O(\log n)$ rounds and communication, and $O(n^2)$ time verifier). The big advantage of the protocol of this section is in prover time: the prover in this section merely has to compute the matrix A^2 (it does not matter how $\mathcal{P}$ chooses to compute A^2), and then does $O(n^2)$ extra work to compute the prescribed messages in the two invocations of the sum-check protocol. Up to the additive $O(n^2)$ term, this matches the amount of work performed by the fastest known (unverifiable) algorithm for counting triangles. The additive $O(n^2)$ is a low-order cost for $\mathcal{P}$, since computing A^2 with the fastest known algorithms requires super-linear time.

Communication and Rounds. In more detail, the application of sum-check to the polynomial $\widetilde{f}_{A^2} \cdot \widetilde{f}_A$ requires $2 \log n$ rounds, with 3 field elements sent from prover to verifier in each round. The matrix multiplication IP used to compute $\widetilde{f}_{A^2}(r_1, r_2)$ requires an additional $\log n$ rounds, with 3 field elements sent from the prover to verifier in each round. This means there are $3 \log n$ rounds in total, with $9 \log n$ field elements sent from the prover to the verifier (and $3 \log n$ sent from the verifier to the prover). This round complexity and communication cost is identical to the counting triangles protocol from Section 4.3.

Verifier runtime. The verifier is easily seen to run in $O(n^2)$ time in total–it's runtime is dominated by the cost of evaluating $\widetilde{f}_A$ at three inputs in $\mathbb{F}^{\log n} \times \mathbb{F}^{\log n}$, namely (r_1, r_2), (r_2, r_3), and (r_1, r_3). This too is identical to the verifier cost in the counting triangles protocol from Section 4.3.

Prover runtime. Once the prover knows A^2, the prover's messages in both the sum-check protocol applied to the polynomial $\widetilde{f}_{A^2} \cdot \widetilde{f}_A$, and in the matrix multiplication IP of Section 4.4.2, can be derived in $O(n^2)$ time. Specifically, Method 3 of Section 4.4.3 achieves an $O(n^2)$ time prover in the matrix multiplication IP, and the same techniques show that, if $\mathcal{P}$ knows all of the entries of the matrix A^2, then in $O(n^2)$ time $\mathcal{P}$ can compute the prescribed messages when applying the sum-check protocol to the polynomial $\widetilde{f}_{A^2} \cdot \widetilde{f}_A$.

4.5.2 A Useful Subroutine: Reducing Multiple Polynomial Evaluations to One

In the counting triangles protocol just covered, at the end of the protocol the verifier needs to evaluate $\widetilde{f}_A$ at *three* points, (r_1, r_2), (r_2, r_3), and (r_1, r_3). This turns out to be a common occurrence: the sum-check protocol is often applied to some polynomial g such that, in order to evaluate g at a single point, it is necessary to evaluate some other multilinear polynomial $\tilde{W}$ at multiple points.

For concreteness, let us begin by supposing that $\tilde{W}$ is a multilinear polynomial over $\mathbb{F}$ with $\log n$ variables, and the verifier wishes to evaluate $\tilde{W}$ at just two points, say $b, c \in \mathbb{F}^{\log n}$—we consider the case of three or more points at the end of this section. We cover a simple one-round interactive proof with communication cost $O(\log n)$ that reduces the evaluation of $\tilde{W}(b)$ and $\tilde{W}(c)$ to the evaluation of $\tilde{W}(r)$ for a *single* point $r \in \mathbb{F}^{\log n}$. What this means is that the protocol will force the prover $\mathcal{P}$ to send claimed values v_0 and v_1 for $\tilde{W}(b)$ and $\tilde{W}(c)$, as well as claimed values for many other points chosen by the verifier $\mathcal{V}$ in a specific manner. $\mathcal{V}$ will then pick r at random from those points, and it will be safe for $\mathcal{V}$ to believe that $v_0 = \tilde{W}(b)$ and $v_1 = \tilde{W}(c)$ so long as $\mathcal{P}$'s claim about $\tilde{W}(r)$ is valid. In other words, the protocol will ensure that if either $v_0 \neq \tilde{W}(b)$ or $v_1 \neq \tilde{W}(c)$, then with high probability over the $\mathcal{V}$'s choice of r, it will also be the case that the prover makes a false claim as to the value of $\tilde{W}(r)$.

The protocol. Let $\ell : \mathbb{F} \to \mathbb{F}^{\log n}$ be some canonical line passing through b and c. For example, we can let $\ell \colon \mathbb{F} \to \mathbb{F}^{\log n}$ be the unique line such that $\ell(0) = b$ and $\ell(1) = c$. $\mathcal{P}$ sends a univariate polynomial q of degree at most $\log n$ that is claimed to be $\widetilde{W} \circ \ell$, the restriction of $\widetilde{W}$ to the line ℓ. $\mathcal{V}$ interprets $q(0)$ and $q(1)$ as the prover's claims v_0 and v_1 as to the values of $\widetilde{W}(b)$ and $\widetilde{W}(c)$. $\mathcal{V}$ picks a random point $r^* \in \mathbb{F}$, sets $r = \ell(r^*)$, and interprets $q(r^*)$ as the prover's claim as to the value of $\tilde{W}(r)$.

A picture and an example. This technique is depicted pictorially in Figure 4.7. For a concrete example of how this technique works, suppose that $\log n = 2$, $b = (2, 4)$, $c = (3, 2)$, and $\widetilde{W}(x_1, x_2) = 3x_1 x_2 + 2x_2$. Then the unique line $\ell(t)$ with $\ell(0) = b$ and $\ell(1) = c$ is $t \mapsto (t + 2, 4 - 2t)$. The restriction of $\widetilde{W}$ to ℓ is $3(t+2)(4-2t) + 2(4-2t) = -6t^2 - 4t + 32$. If $\mathcal{P}$ sends a degree-2 univariate polynomial q claimed to equal $\widetilde{W} \circ \ell$, the verifier will interpret $q(0)$ and $q(1)$ as claims about the values $\widetilde{W}(b)$ and $\widetilde{W}(c)$ respectively. The verifier will then pick a random $r^* \in \mathbb{F}$, set

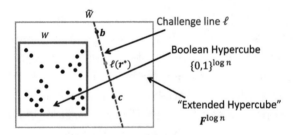

Figure 4.7: Schematic of how to reduce verifying claims about the values of $\tilde{W}(b)$ and $\tilde{W}(c)$ to a single claim about the value of $\tilde{W}(r)$. Here, $\tilde{W}$ is the multilinear extension of W, ℓ is the unique line passing through b and c, and $r = \ell(r^*)$ is a random point on ℓ.

$r = \ell(r^*)$, and interpret $q(r^*)$ as the claimed value of $\widetilde{W}(r)$. Observe that $\ell(r^*) = (r^* + 2, 4 - 2r^*)$ is a random point on the line ℓ.

The following claim establishes completeness and soundness of the above protocol.

Claim 4.6. Let $\tilde{W}$ be a multilinear polynomial over $\mathbb{F}$ in $\log n$ variables. If $q = \widetilde{W} \circ \ell$, then $q(0) = \tilde{W}(b)$, $q(1) = \tilde{W}(c)$, and $q(r^*) = \tilde{W}(\ell(r^*))$ for all $r^* \in \mathbb{F}$. Meanwhile, if $q \neq \widetilde{W} \circ \ell$, then with probability at least $1 - \log n/|\mathbb{F}|$ over a randomly chosen $r^* \in \mathbb{F}$, $q(r^*) \neq \tilde{W}(\ell(r^*))$.

Proof. The first claim is immediate from the fact that $\ell(0) = b$ and $\ell(1) = c$. For the second claim, observe that both q and $\widetilde{W} \circ \ell$ are univariate polynomials of degree at most $\log n$. If they are not the same polynomial, then the Schwartz-Zippel Lemma (even its simple special case for univariate polynomials) implies that when r^* is chosen at random from $\mathbb{F}$, $q(r^*) \neq \tilde{W}(\ell(r^*))$ with probability at least $1 - \log(n)/|\mathbb{F}|$. $\qquad\square$

Reducing Three or More Evaluations to One. If the verifier needs to evaluate $\tilde{W}$ at more than two points, a similar protocol still applies. For example, suppose the verifier needs to know $\widetilde{W}(a)$, $\widetilde{W}(b)$, $\widetilde{W}(c)$. This time, let ℓ be a canonical *degree-two curve* passing through a, b, and c. For concreteness, we can let ℓ be the unique degree-2 curve with $\ell(0) = a$ and $\ell(1) = b$ and $\ell(2) = c$. For example, if $a = (0, 1)$, $b = (2, 2)$ and $c = (8, 5)$, then $\ell(t) = (2t^2, t^2 + 1)$.

Then $\mathcal{P}$ sends a univariate polynomial q of degree at most $2\log n$ that is claimed to be $\widetilde{W} \circ \ell$. $\mathcal{V}$ interprets $q(0)$, $q(1)$ $q(2)$ as the prover's claims as to the values of $\widetilde{W}(a)$, $\widetilde{W}(b)$, and $\widetilde{W}(c)$. $\mathcal{V}$ picks a random point $r^* \in \mathbb{F}$, sets $r = \ell(r^*)$, and interprets $q(r^*)$ as the prover's claim as to the value of $\tilde{W}(r)$. Compared to the protocol for reducing two evaluations of $\widetilde{W}$ to one, the degree of q doubled from $\log n$ to $2\log n$, and hence the prover-to-verifier communication increased by a factor of roughly 2, but remains $O(\log n)$. The protocol remains perfectly complete, and the soundness error increases from $1 - \log(n)/|\mathbb{F}$ to $1 - 2\log(n)/\mathbb{F}$.

This protocol could be applied at the end of both of the counting triangles protocols that we have covered, with $\tilde{W}$ equal to $\tilde{f}_A$, to reduce the number of points at which $\mathcal{V}$ needs to evaluate $\tilde{f}_A$ from three to one. As these evaluations are the dominant cost in $\mathcal{V}$'s runtime, this reduces $\mathcal{V}$ time by a factor of essentially 3. In the matrix powering protocol of the next section, the technique will be used to obtain more dramatic improvements in verification costs, and it will recur in the GKR protocol for circuit evaluation of Section 4.6.

4.5.3 A Super-Efficient IP for Matrix Powers

Let A be an $n \times n$ matrix with entries from field $\mathbb{F}$, and suppose a verifier wants to evaluate a single entry of the powered matrix A^k for a large integer k. For concreteness, let's say $\mathcal{V}$ is interested in learning entry $(A^k)_{n,n}$, and k and n are powers of 2. As we now explain, the MatMult IP of Section 4.4 gives a way to do this, with $O(\log(k) \cdot \log(n))$ rounds and communication, and a verifier that runs in $O(n^2 + \log(k)\log(n))$ time.

Clearly we can express the matrix A^k as a product of smaller powers of A:

$$A^k = A^{k/2} \cdot A^{k/2}. \tag{4.16}$$

Hence, letting g_ℓ denote the multilinear extension of the matrix A^ℓ, we can try to exploit Equation (4.16) by applying the MatMult IP to compute $(A^k)_{n,n} = g_k(1,1)$.

At the end of the MatMult IP applied to two $n \times n$ matrices A', B', the verifier needs to evaluate $\tilde{f}_{A'}$ and $\tilde{f}_{B'}$ at the respective points (r_1, r_2) and (r_2, r_3), both in $\mathbb{F}^{\log n} \times \mathbb{F}^{\log n}$. In the invocation of the MatMult IP above, both A' and B' equal $A^{k/2}$. Hence, at the end of the MatMult IP, the verifier has to evaluate the polynomial $f_{A^{k/2}} = g_{k/2}$ at the two points (r_1, r_2) and (r_2, r_3). Unfortunately, the verifier cannot do this since she doesn't know $A^{k/2}$.

Reducing Two Points to One.   Via the one-round interactive proof of Section 4.5.2 (see Claim 4.6 with $\tilde{W}$ equal to $g_{k/2}$), the verifier reduces evaluating a polynomial $g_{k/2}$ at the two points to evaluating $g_{k/2}$ at a single point.

Recursion to the Rescue.   After reducing two points to one, the verifier is left with the task of evaluating $g_{k/2}$ at a single input, say $(r_3, r_4) \in \mathbb{F}^{\log n} \times \mathbb{F}^{\log n}$. Since $g_{k/2}$ is the multilinear extension of the matrix $A^{k/2}$ (viewed in the natural way as a function $f_{A^{k/2}}$ mapping $\{0,1\}^{\log n} \times \{0,1\}^{\log n} \to \mathbb{F}$), and $A^{k/2}$ can be decomposed as $A^{k/4} \cdot A^{k/4}$, the verifier can recursively apply the MatMult protocol to compute $g_{k/2}(r_3, r_4)$. This runs into the same issues as before, namely that to run the MatMult protocol, the verifier needs to evaluate $g_{k/4}$ at two points, which can in turn be reduced to the task of evaluating $g_{k/4}$ at a single point. This can again be handled recursively as above. After $\log k$ layers of recursion, there is no need to recurse further since the verifier can evaluate $g_1 = \tilde{f}_A$ at any desired input in $O(n^2)$ time using Lemma 3.8.

4.5.4   A General Paradigm for IPs with Super-Efficient Provers

Beyond algorithms for counting triangles, there are other algorithms that invoke MATMULT to compute some product matrix C, and then apply some post-processing to C to compute an answer that is much smaller than C itself (often the answer is just a single number, rather than an $n \times n$ matrix). In these settings, $\mathcal{V}$ can apply a general-purpose protocol, such as the GKR protocol that will be presented in Section 4.6, to verify that the post-processing step was correctly applied to the product matrix C. As we will see in Section 4.6, at the end of the application of the GKR protocol, $\mathcal{V}$ needs to evaluate $\tilde{f}_C(r_1, r_2)$ at a randomly chosen point $(r_1, r_2) \in \mathbb{F}^{\log n \times \log n}$. $\mathcal{V}$ can do this using the MATMULT protocol described above.

Crucially, this post-processing step typically requires time linear in the size of C. So $\mathcal{P}$'s runtime in this application of the GKR protocol will be proportional to the size of (a circuit computing) the post-processing step, which is typically just $\tilde{O}(n^2)$.

As a concrete example, consider the problem of computing the diameter of a directed graph G. Let A denote the adjacency matrix of G, and let I denote the $n \times n$ identity matrix. Then the diameter of G is the least positive number d such that $(A + I)_{ij}^d \neq 0$ for all (i, j). This yields the following natural protocol for diameter. $\mathcal{P}$ sends the claimed output d to V, as well as an (i, j) such that $(A + I)_{ij}^{d-1} = 0$. To confirm that d is the diameter of G, it suffices for V to check two things: first, that all entries of $(A + I)^d$ are nonzero, and second that $(A + I)_{ij}^{d-1}$ is indeed zero.[19]

The first task is accomplished by combining the MATMULT protocol with the GKR protocol as follows. Let d_j denote the jth bit in the binary representation of d. Then $(A + I)^d = \prod_j^{\lceil \log d \rceil} (A + I)^{d_j 2^j}$, so computing the number of nonzero entries of $D_1 = (A + I)^d$ can be computed via a sequence of $O(\log d)$ matrix multiplications, followed by a post-processing step that computes the number of nonzero entries of D_1. We can apply the GKR protocol to verify this post-processing step, but at the end of the protocol, V needs to evaluate the multilinear extension of D_1 at a random point (as usual, when we refer to the multilinear extension of D_1, we are viewing D_1 as a function mapping $\{0, 1\}^{\log n} \times \{0, 1\}^{\log n} \to \mathbb{F}$ in the natural way). V cannot do this without help, so V outsources even this computation to $\mathcal{P}$, by using $O(\log d)$ invocations of the MATMULT protocol described above.

The second task, of verifying that $(A + I)_{ij}^{d-1} = 0$, is similarly accomplished using $O(\log d)$ invocations of the MATMULT protocol— since V is only interested in one entry of $(A + I)^{d-1}$, $\mathcal{P}$ need not send the matrix $(A + I)^{d-1}$ in full, and the total communication here is just polylog(n).

---

[19] If the interactive proof works over field $\mathbb{F}_p$, one does need to be careful that $(A + I)_{ij}^{d-1}$ is not positive and divisible by p. One technique for dealing with this is to have the verifier, after the prover sends (i, j), choose p to be a random prime in an appropriate interval. We omit further details for brevity.

Ultimately, $\mathcal{V}$'s runtime in this diameter protocol is $O(m \log n)$, where m is the number of edges in G. $\mathcal{P}$'s runtime in the above diameter protocol matches the best known unverifiable diameter algorithm up to a low-order additive term [225], [254], and the communication is just polylog(n).

4.5.5   An IP for Small-Space Computations (and IP = PSPACE)

In this section, we use the matrix-powering protocol to re-prove the following important result of Goldwasser *et al.* [135]: all problems solvable in logarithmic space have an IP with a quasilinear-time verifier, polynomial time prover, and polylogarithmic proof length.

The basic idea of the proof is that executing any Turing Machine M that uses s bits of space can be reduced to the problem of computing a single entry of A^{2^s} for a certain matrix A (A is in fact the configuration graph of M). So one can just apply the matrix-powering IP to A to determine the output of M. While A is a huge matrix (it has at least 2^s rows and columns), configuration graphs are highly structured, and this enables the verifier to evaluate $\tilde{f}_A$ at a single input in $O(s \cdot n)$ time. If s is logarithmic in the input size, then this means that the verifier in the IP runs in $O(n \log n)$ time.

The original paper of GKR proved the same result by constructing an arithmetic circuit for computing A^{2^s} and then applying a sophisticated IP for arithmetic circuit evaluation to that circuit (we cover this IP in Section 4.6 and the arithmetic circuit for computing A^{2^s} in Section 6.4). The approach described in this section is simpler, in that it directly applies a simple IP for matrix-powering, rather than the more complicated IP for the general circuit-evaluation problem.

Details. Let M be a Turing Machine that, when run on an m-bit input, uses at most s bits of space. Let $A(x)$ be the adjacency matrix of its *configuration graph* when M is run on input $x \in \{0, 1\}^m$. Here, the configuration graph has as its vertex set all of the possible states and memory configurations of the machine M, with a directed edge from vertex i to vertex j if running M for one step from configuration i on input x causes M to move to configuration j. Since M uses s bits of space, there are $O(2^s)$ many vertices of the configuration graph. This means that $A(x)$ is an $N \times N$ matrix for some $N = O(2^s)$. Note that if M never enters an infinite loop (i.e., never enters the same configuration twice), then M must trivially run in time at most N.

We can assume without loss of generality that M has a unique starting configuration and a unique accepting configuration; say for concreteness that these configurations correspond to vertices of the configuration graph with labels 1 and N. Then to determine whether M accepts input x, it is enough to determine whether there is a length-N path from vertex 0 to vertex N in the configuration graph of M. This is equivalent to determining the $(1, N)$'th entry of the matrix $(A(x))^N$.[20]

This quantity can be computed with the matrix power protocol of the previous section, which uses $O(s \cdot \log N)$ rounds and communication. At the end of the protocol, the verifier does need to evaluate the MLE of the matrix $A(x)$ at a randomly chosen input. This may seem like it should take up to $O(N^2)$ time, since A is a $N \times N$ matrix. However, the configuration matrix of any Turing Machine is highly structured, owing to the fact that at any time step, the machine only reads or writes to $O(1)$ memory cells, and only moves its read and write heads at most one cell to the left or right. This turns out to imply that the verifier can evaluate the MLE of A in $O(s \cdot m)$ time (we omit these details for brevity).

In total, the costs of the IP are as follows. The rounds and number of field elements communicated is $O(s \log N)$, the verifier's runtime is $O(s \log N + m \cdot s)$ and the prover's runtime is $\text{poly}(N)$. If $s = O(\log m)$, then these three costs are respectively $O(\log^2 m)$, $O(m \log m)$, and $\text{poly}(m)$. That is, the communication cost is polylogarithmic in the input size, the verifier's runtime is quasilinear, and the prover's runtime is polynomial.

Note that if $s = \text{poly}(m)$, then the verifier's runtime in this IP is $\text{poly}(m)$, recovering the famous result of LFKN [186] and Shamir [231] that **IP = PSPACE**.

---

[20]Since the configuration graph of M is acyclic (except for all halting states having self-loops), the entries of any power of $A(x)$ are all 0 or 1. This means that, unlike in Footnote 19 that discussed computing the diameter of general graphs, one does not need to worry about the possibility that $(1, N)$'th entry of $(A(x))^N$ is nonzero but divisible by the size p of the field over which the IP is defined.

Additional Discussion. One disappointing feature of this IP is that, if the runtime of M is significantly less than $N \geq 2^s$, the prover will still take time at least N, because the prover has to explicitly generate powers of the configuration graph's adjacency matrix. This is particularly problematic if the space bound s is superlogarithmic in the input size m, since then 2^s is not even a polynomial in m. Effectively, the IP we just presented forces the prover to explore all possible configurations of M, even though when running M on input x, the machine will only enter a tiny fraction of such configurations. A breakthrough complexity-theory result of [214] gave a very different IP that avoids this inefficiency for P. Remarkably, their IP also requires only a constant number of rounds of interaction.

4.6   The GKR Protocol and Its Efficient Implementation

4.6.1   Motivation

The goal of Section 4.2 was to develop an interactive proof for an intractable problem (such as #SAT [186] or TQBF [231]), in which the verifier ran in polynomial time. The perspective taken in this section is different: it acknowledges that there are no "real world" entities that can act as the prover in the #SAT and TQBF protocols of earlier sections, since real world entities cannot solve large instances of **PSPACE**-complete or #**P**-complete problems in the worst case. We would really like a "scaled down" result, one that is useful for problems that can be solved in the real world, such as problems in the complexity classes **P**, or **NC** (capturing problems solvable by efficient parallel algorithms), or even **L** (capturing problems solvable in logarithmic space).

One may wonder what is the point of developing verification protocols for such easy problems. Can't the verifier just ignore the prover and solve the problem without help? One answer is that this section will describe protocols in which the verifier runs much faster than would be possible without a prover. Specifically, $\mathcal{V}$ will run linear time, doing little more than just reading the input.[21, 22]

Meanwhile, we will require that the prover not do much more than solve the problem of interest. Ideally, if the problem is solvable by a Random Access Machine or Turing Machine in time T and space s, we want the prover to run in time $O(T)$ and space $O(s)$, or as close to it as possible. At a minimum, $\mathcal{P}$ should run in polynomial time.

Can the TQBF and #SAT protocols of prior sections be scaled down to yield protocols where the verifier runs in (quasi-)linear time for a "weak" complexity class like $\mathbf{L}$? It turns out that it can, but the prover is not efficient.

Recall that in the #SAT protocol (as well as in the TQBF protocol of [231]), $\mathcal{V}$ ran in time $O(S)$, and $\mathcal{P}$ ran in time $O(S^2 \cdot 2^N)$, when applied to a Boolean formula ϕ of size S over N variables. In principle, this yields an interactive proof for any problem solvable in space s: given an input $x \in \{0,1\}^n$, $\mathcal{V}$ first transforms x to an instance ϕ of TQBF (see, e.g., [9, Section 4] for a lucid exposition of this transformation, which is reminiscent of Savitch's Theorem [222]), and then applies the interactive proof for TQBF to ϕ.

However, the transformation yields a TQBF instance ϕ over $N = O(s \cdot \log T)$ variables when applied to a problem solvable in time T and space s. This results in a prover that runs in time in time $2^{O(s \cdot \log T)}$. This is superpolynomial (i.e., $n^{\Theta(\log n)}$), even if $s = O(\log n)$ and $T = \text{poly}(n)$. Until 2007, this was the state of the art in interactive proofs.

---

[21] The protocols for counting triangles, matrix multiplication and powering, and graph diameter of Sections 4.3–4.5 also achieved a linear-time verifier. But unlike the GKR protocol, those protocols were not general-purpose. As we will see, the GKR protocol is general-purpose in the sense that it solves the problem of arithmetic *circuit evaluation*, and any problem in $\mathbf{P}$ can be "efficiently" reduced to circuit evaluation (these reductions and the precise meaning of "efficiently" will be covered in Section 6).

[22] Another answer is that interactive proofs for "easy" problems can be combined with cryptography to turn them into succinct non-interactive arguments of knowledge (SNARKs), which allow the prover to establish that it knows a witness satisfying a specified property. In such SNARKs, the interactive proof only needs to solve the "easy" problem of checking that a purported witness satisfies the specified property.

4.6.2   The GKR Protocol and Its Costs

Goldwasser *et al.* [135] described a remarkable interactive proof protocol that does achieve many of the goals set forth above. The protocol is best presented in terms of the (arithmetic) *circuit evaluation* problem. In this problem, $\mathcal{V}$ and $\mathcal{P}$ first agree on a *log-space uniform* arithmetic circuit $\mathcal{C}$ of fan-in 2 over a finite field $\mathbb{F}$, and the goal is to compute the value of the output gate(s) of $\mathcal{C}$. A log-space uniform circuit $\mathcal{C}$ is one that possesses a succinct implicit description, in the sense that there is a logarithmic-space algorithm that takes as input the label of a gate a of $\mathcal{C}$, and is capable of determining all relevant information about that gate. That is, the algorithm can output the labels of all of a's neighbors, and is capable of determining if a is an addition gate or a multiplication gate.

Letting S denote the size (i.e., number of gates) of $\mathcal{C}$ and n the number of variables, the key feature of the GKR protocol is that the prover runs in time poly(S). We will see that $\mathcal{P}$'s time can even be made *linear* in S [102], [237], [251]. If $S = 2^{o(n)}$, then this is much better than the #SAT protocol that we saw in an earlier section, where the prover required time exponential in the number of variables over which the #SAT instance was defined.

Moreover, the costs to the verifier in the GKR protocol is $O(d \log S)$, which grows linearly with the *depth* d of $\mathcal{C}$, and only logarithmically with S. Crucially, this means that $\mathcal{V}$ can run in time *sublinear* in the size S of the circuit. At first glance, this might seem impossible—how can the verifier make sure the prover correctly evaluated $\mathcal{C}$ if the verifier never even "looks" at all of $\mathcal{C}$? The answer is that $\mathcal{C}$ was assumed to have a succinct implicit description in the sense of being log-space uniform. This enables $\mathcal{V}$ to "understand" the structure of $\mathcal{C}$ without ever having to look at every gate individually. The costs of the protocol are summarized in Table 4.4.

Application: An IP for Parallel Algorithms.   The complexity class **NC** consists of languages solvable by parallel algorithms in time polylog(n) and total work poly(n). Any problem in **NC** can be computed by a

Table 4.4: Costs of the original GKR protocol [135] when applied to any log-space uniform layered arithmetic circuit C of size S and depth d over n variables defined over field $\mathbb{F}$. Section 4.6.5 describes methods from [102] for reducing $\mathcal{P}$'s runtime to $O(S \log S)$, and reducing the polylog(S) terms in the remaining costs to $O(\log S)$. It is now known how to achieve prover runtime of $O(S)$ for arbitrary layered arithmetic circuits C (see Remark 4.5).

Communication	Rounds	$\mathcal{V}$ Time	$\mathcal{P}$ Time	Soundness error
$d \cdot$ polylog(S) field elements	$d \cdot$ polylog(S)	$O(n + d \cdot$ polylog(S))	poly(S)	$O(d \log(S) / \|\mathbb{F}\|)$

log-space uniform arithmetic circuit C of polynomial size and polylog-arithmetic depth. Applying the GKR protocol to C yields a polynomial time prover and a linear time verifier.

4.6.3 Protocol Overview

As described above, $\mathcal{P}$ and $\mathcal{V}$ first agree on an arithmetic circuit C of fan-in 2 over a finite field $\mathbb{F}$ computing the function of interest. C is assumed to be in layered form, meaning that the circuit can be decomposed into layers, and wires only connect gates in adjacent layers (if C is not layered it can easily be transformed into a layered circuit C' with at most a factor-d blowup in size).[23] Suppose that C has depth d, and number the layers from 0 to d with layer d referring to the input layer, and layer 0 referring to the output layer.

In the first message, $\mathcal{P}$ tells $\mathcal{V}$ the (claimed) output(s) of the circuit. The protocol then works its way in iterations towards the input layer, with one iteration devoted to each layer. We describe the gates in C as having values: the value of an addition (respectively, multiplication) gate is set to be the sum (respectively, product) of its in-neighbors. The purpose of iteration i is to reduce a claim about the values of the gates at layer i to a claim about the values of the gates at layer $i + 1$, in the sense that it is safe for $\mathcal{V}$ to assume that the first claim is true as long as the second claim is true. This reduction is accomplished by applying the sum-check protocol.

---

[23] Recent work gives a variant of the GKR protocol that applies directly to non-layered circuits [255], avoiding a factor-d blowup in prover time.

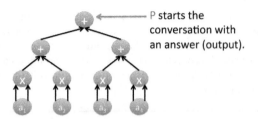

Figure 4.8: Start of GKR Protocol.

More concretely, the GKR protocol starts with a claim about the values of the output gates of the circuit, but $\mathcal{V}$ cannot check this claim without evaluating the circuit herself, which is precisely what she wants to avoid. So the first iteration uses a sum-check protocol to reduce this claim about the outputs of the circuit to a claim about the gate values at layer 2 (more specifically, to a claim about an evaluation of the multilinear extension of the gate values at layer 2). Once again, $\mathcal{V}$ cannot check this claim herself, so the second iteration uses another sum-check protocol to reduce the latter claim to a claim about the gate values at layer 3, and so on. Eventually, $\mathcal{V}$ is left with a claim about the inputs to the circuit, and $\mathcal{V}$ can check this claim without any help. This outline is depicted in Figures 4.8–4.11.

4.6.4 Protocol Details

Notation. Suppose we are given a layered arithmetic circuit $\mathcal{C}$ of size S, depth d, and fan-in two ($\mathcal{C}$ may have more than one output gate). Number the layers from 0 to d, with 0 being the output layer and d being the input layer. Let S_i denote the number of gates at layer i of

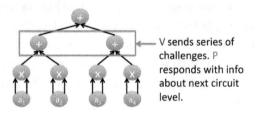

Figure 4.9: Iteration 1 reduces a claim about the output of $\mathcal{C}$ to one about the MLE of the gate values in the previous layer.

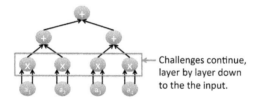

Figure 4.10: In general, iteration i reduces a claim about the MLE of gate values at layer i, to a claim about the MLE of gate values at layer $i+1$.

the circuit C. Assume S_i is a power of 2 and let $S_i = 2^{k_i}$. The GKR protocol makes use of several functions, each of which encodes certain information about the circuit.

Number the gates at layer i from 0 to $S_i - 1$, and let $W_i : \{0,1\}^{k_i} \to \mathbb{F}$ denote the function that takes as input a binary gate label, and outputs the corresponding gate's value at layer i. As usual, let $\widetilde{W}_i$ denote the multilinear extension of W_i. See Figure 4.12, which depicts an example circuit C and input to C and describes the resulting function W_i for each layer i of C.

The GKR protocol also makes use of the notion of a "wiring predicate" that encodes which pairs of wires from layer $i+1$ are connected to a given gate at layer i in C. Let $\text{in}_{1,i}, \text{in}_{2,i} : \{0,1\}^{k_i} \to \{0,1\}^{k_{i+1}}$ denote the functions that take as input the label a of a gate at layer i of C,

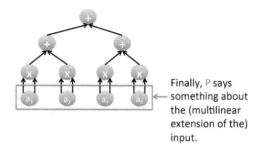

Figure 4.11: In the final iteration, $\mathcal{P}$ makes a claim about the MLE of the input (here, the input of length n with entries in $\mathbb{F}$ is interpreted as a function mapping $\{0,1\}^{\log_2 n} \to \mathbb{F}$. Any such function has a unique MLE by Fact 3.5). $\mathcal{V}$ can check this claim without help, since $\mathcal{V}$ sees the input explicitly.

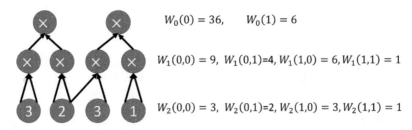

Figure 4.12: Example circuit $\mathcal{C}$ and input x, and resulting functions W_i for each layer i of $\mathcal{C}$. Note that $\mathcal{C}$ has two output gates.

and respectively output the label of the first and second in-neighbor of gate a. So, for example, if gate a at layer i computes the sum of gates b and c at layer $i+1$, then $\text{in}_{1,i}(a) = b$ and $\text{in}_{2,i}(a) = c$.

Define two functions, add_i and mult_i, mapping $\{0,1\}^{k_i+2k_{i+1}}$ to $\{0,1\}$, which together constitute the wiring predicate of layer i of $\mathcal{C}$. Specifically, these functions take as input three gate labels (a, b, c), and return 1 if and only if $(b, c) = (\text{in}_{1,i}(a), \text{in}_{2,i}(a))$ and gate a is an addition (respectively, multiplication) gate. As usual, let $\widetilde{\text{add}}_i$ and $\widetilde{\text{mult}}_i$ denote the multilinear extensions of add_i and mult_i.

For an example, consider the circuit depicted in Figure 4.12. Since the circuit contains no addition gates, add_0 and add_1 are the constant 0 function. Meanwhile, mult_0 is the function defined over domain $\{0,1\} \times \{0,1\}^2 \times \{0,1\}^2$ as follows. mult_0 evaluates to 1 on the following two inputs: $(0, (0,0), (0,1))$ and $(1, (1,0), (1,1))$. On all other inputs, mult_0 evaluates to zero. This is because the first and second in-neighbors of gate 0 at layer 0 are respectively gates $(0,0)$ and $(0,1)$ at layer 1, and similarly the first and second in-neighbors of gate 1 at layer 0 are respectively gates $(1,0)$ and $(1,1)$ at layer 1.

Similarly, mult_1 is a function on domain $\{0,1\}^2 \times \{0,1\}^2 \times \{0,1\}^2$. It evaluates to 0 on all inputs except for the following four, on which it evaluates to 1:

- $((0,0), (0,0), (0,0))$.

- $((0,1), (0,1), (0,1))$.

- $((1,0),(0,1),(1,0))$.

- $((1,1),(1,1),(1,1))$.

Note that for each layer i, add_i and mult_i depend only on the circuit $\mathcal{C}$ and not on the input x to $\mathcal{C}$. In contrast, the function W_i does depend on x. This is because W_i maps each gate label at layer i to the value of the gate when $\mathcal{C}$ is evaluated on input x.

Detailed Description. The GKR protocol consists of d iterations, one for each layer of the circuit. Each iteration i starts with $\mathcal{P}$ claiming a value for $\widetilde{W}_i(r_i)$ for some point in $r_i \in \mathbb{F}^{k_i}$.

At the start of the first iteration, this claim is derived from the claimed outputs of the circuit. Specifically, if there are $S_0 = 2^{k_0}$ outputs of $\mathcal{C}$, let $D: \{0,1\}^{k_0} \to \mathbb{F}$ denote the function that maps the label of an output gate to the claimed value of that output. Then the verifier can pick a random point $r_0 \in \mathbb{F}^{k_0}$, and evaluate $\tilde{D}(r_0)$ in time $O(S_0)$ using Lemma 3.8. By the Schwartz-Zippel lemma, if $\tilde{D}(r_0) = \widetilde{W}_0(r_0)$ (i.e., if the multilinear extension of the claimed outputs equals the multilinear extension of the correct outputs when evaluated at a randomly chosen point), then it is safe for the verifier to believe that $\tilde{D}$ and $\widetilde{W}_0$ are the same polynomial, and hence that all of the claimed outputs are correct. Unfortunately, the verifier cannot evaluate $\widetilde{W}_0(r_0)$ without help from the prover.[24]

The purpose of iteration i is to reduce the claim about the value of $\widetilde{W}_i(r_i)$ to a claim about $\widetilde{W}_{i+1}(r_{i+1})$ for some $r_{i+1} \in \mathbb{F}^{k_{i+1}}$, in the sense that it is safe for $\mathcal{V}$ to assume that the first claim is true as long as the second claim is true. To accomplish this, the iteration applies the sum-check protocol to a specific polynomial derived from $\widetilde{W}_{i+1}$,

---

[24]Throughout this survey, a statement of the form "if $p(r) = q(r)$ for a random r, then it is safe for the verifier to believe that $p = q$ as formal polynomials" is shorthand for the following: if $p \neq q$, then the former equality fails to hold with overwhelming probability over the random choice of r, i.e., the prover would have to "get unreasonably lucky" to pass the check.

$\widetilde{\text{add}}_i$, and $\widetilde{\text{mult}}_i$. Our description of the protocol actually makes use of a simplification due to Thaler [238].

Applying the Sum-Check Protocol. The GKR protocol exploits an ingenious explicit expression for $\tilde{W}_i(r_i)$, captured in the following lemma.

Lemma 4.7.

$$\tilde{W}_i(z) = \sum_{b,c \in \{0,1\}^{k_{i+1}}} \widetilde{\text{add}}_i(z, b, c) \left(\tilde{W}_{i+1}(b) + \tilde{W}_{i+1}(c) \right)$$
$$+ \widetilde{\text{mult}}_i(z, b, c) \left(\tilde{W}_{i+1}(b) \cdot \tilde{W}_{i+1}(c) \right) \tag{4.17}$$

Proof. It is easy to check that the right hand side is a multilinear polynomial in the entries of z, since $\widetilde{\text{add}}_i$ and $\widetilde{\text{mult}}_i$ are multilinear polynomials. (Note that, just as in the matrix multiplication protocol of the Section 4.4, the function being summed over is *quadratic* in the entries of b and c, but this quadratic-ness is "summed away", leaving a multilinear polynomial only in the variables of z).

Since the multilinear extension of a function with domain $\{0,1\}^{k_i}$ is unique, it suffices to check that the left hand side and right hand side of the expression in the lemma agree for all $a \in \{0,1\}^{k_i}$. To this end, fix any $a \in \{0,1\}^{s_i}$, and suppose that gate a in layer i of $\mathcal{C}$ is an addition gate (the case where gate a is a multiplication gate is similar). Since each gate a at layer i has two unique in-neighbors, namely $\text{in}_1(a)$ and $\text{in}_2(a)$;

$$\text{add}_i(a, b, c) = \begin{cases} 1 & \text{if } (b, c) = (\text{in}_1(a), \text{in}_2(a)) \\ 0 & \text{otherwise} \end{cases}$$

and $\text{mult}_i(a, b, c) = 0$ for all $b, c \in \{0,1\}^{k_{i+1}}$.

Hence, since $\widetilde{\text{add}}_i$, $\widetilde{\text{mult}}_i$, $\tilde{W}_{i+1}$, and $\tilde{W}_i$ extend add_i and mult_i, W_{i+1}, and W_i respectively,

$$\sum_{b,c \in \{0,1\}^{k_{i+1}}} \widetilde{add}_i(a,b,c)$$

$$\left(\tilde{W}_{i+1}(b) + \tilde{W}_{i+1}(c)\right) + \widetilde{mult}_i(a,b,c)\left(\tilde{W}_{i+1}(b) \cdot \tilde{W}_{i+1}(c)\right)$$
$$= \tilde{W}_{i+1}(in_1(a)) + \tilde{W}_{i+1}(in_2(a)) = W_{i+1}(in_1(a))$$
$$+ W_{i+1}(in_2(a)) = W_i(a) = \tilde{W}_i(a).$$

$\square$

Remark 4.3. Lemma 4.7 is actually valid using any extensions of add_i and $mult_i$ that are multilinear in the first k_i variables.

Remark 4.4. Goldwasser *et al.* [135] use a slightly more complicated expression for $\tilde{W}_i(a)$ than the one in Lemma 4.7. Their expression allowed them to use even more general extensions of add_i and $mult_i$. In particular, their extensions do not have to be multilinear in the first k_i variables.

However, the use of the multilinear extensions $\widetilde{add}_i$ and $\widetilde{mult}_i$ turns out to be critical to achieving a prover runtime that is nearly *linear* in the circuit size S, rather than a much larger polynomial in S as achieved by [135] (cf. Section 4.6.5 for details).

Therefore, in order to check the prover's claim about $\tilde{W}_i(r_i)$, the verifier applies the sum-check protocol to the polynomial

$$f_{r_i}^{(i)}(b,c) = \widetilde{add}_i(r_i,b,c)\left(\tilde{W}_{i+1}(b) + \tilde{W}_{i+1}(c)\right)$$
$$+ \widetilde{mult}_i(r_i,b,c)\left(\tilde{W}_{i+1}(b) \cdot \tilde{W}_{i+1}(c)\right). \tag{4.18}$$

Note that *the verifier does not know the polynomial $\tilde{W}_{i+1}$* (as this polynomial is defined in terms of gate values at layer $i+1$ of the circuit, and unless $i+1$ is the input layer, the verifier does not have direct access to the values of these gates), and hence the verifier does not actually know the polynomial $f_{r_i}^{(i)}$ that it is applying the sum-check protocol to. Nonetheless, it is possible for the verifier to apply the sum-check protocol to $f_{r_i}^{(i)}$ because, until the final round, the sum-check protocol does not require the verifier to know anything about the polynomial other than its degree in each variable (see Remark 4.2). However, there remains the issue that $\mathcal{V}$ can only execute the final check in the sum-check protocol if she can evaluate the polynomial $f_{r_i}^{(i)}$ at a random point. This is handled as follows.

Let us denote the random point at which $\mathcal{V}$ must evaluate $f_{r_i}^{(i)}$ by (b^*, c^*), where $b^* \in \mathbb{F}^{k_{i+1}}$ is the first k_{i+1} entries and $c^* \in \mathbb{F}^{k_{i+1}}$ the last k_{i+1} entries. Note that b^*, and c^* may have non-Boolean entries. Evaluating $f_{r_i}^{(i)}(b^*, c^*)$ requires evaluating $\widetilde{\text{add}}_i(r_i, b^*, c^*)$, $\widetilde{\text{mult}}_i(r_i, b^*, c^*)$, $\widetilde{W}_{i+1}(b^*)$, and $\widetilde{W}_{i+1}(c^*)$.

For many circuits, particularly those whose wiring pattern displays repeated structure, $\mathcal{V}$ can evaluate $\widetilde{\text{add}}_i(r_i, b^*, c^*)$ and $\widetilde{\text{mult}}_i(r_i, b^*, c^*)$ on her own in $O(k_i + k_{i+1})$ time as well. For now, assume that $\mathcal{V}$ can indeed perform this evaluation in $\text{poly}(k_i, k_{i+1})$ time, but this issue will be discussed further in Section 4.6.6.

$\mathcal{V}$ cannot however evaluate $\widetilde{W}_{i+1}(b^*)$, and $\widetilde{W}_{i+1}(c^*)$ on her own without evaluating the circuit. Instead, $\mathcal{V}$ asks $\mathcal{P}$ to simply provide these two values, say, z_1 and z_2, and uses iteration $i+1$ to *verify* that these values are as claimed. However, one complication remains: the precondition for iteration $i+1$ is that $\mathcal{P}$ claims a value for $\widetilde{W}_{i+1}(r_{i+1})$ for a single point $r_{i+1} \in \mathbb{F}^{k_{i+1}}$. So $\mathcal{V}$ needs to reduce verifying both $\widetilde{W}_{i+1}(b^*) = z_1$ and $\widetilde{W}_{i+1}(c^*) = z_2$ to verifying $\widetilde{W}_{i+1}(r_{i+1})$ at a single point $r_{i+1} \in \mathbb{F}^{k_{i+1}}$, in the sense that it is safe for $\mathcal{V}$ to accept the claimed values of $\widetilde{W}_{i+1}(b^*)$ and $\widetilde{W}_{i+1}(c^*)$ as long as the value of $\widetilde{W}_{i+1}(r_{i+1})$ is as claimed. As per Section 4.5.2 this is done as follows.

Reducing to Verification of a Single Point. Let $\ell \colon \mathbb{F} \to \mathbb{F}^{k_{i+1}}$ be the unique line such that $\ell(0) = b^*$ and $\ell(1) = c^*$. $\mathcal{P}$ sends a univariate polynomial q of degree at most k_{i+1} that is claimed to be $\widetilde{W}_{i+1} \circ \ell$, the restriction of $\widetilde{W}_{i+1}$ to the line ℓ. $\mathcal{V}$ checks that $q(0) = z_1$ and $q(1) = z_2$ (rejecting if this is not the case), picks a random point $r^* \in \mathbb{F}$, and asks $\mathcal{P}$ to prove that $\widetilde{W}_{i+1}(\ell(r^*)) = q(r^*)$. By Claim 4.6, as long as $\mathcal{V}$ is convinced that $\widetilde{W}_{i+1}(\ell(r^*)) = q(r^*)$, it is safe for $\mathcal{V}$ to believe that q does in fact equal $\widetilde{W}_{i+1} \circ \ell$, and hence that $\widetilde{W}_{i+1}(b^*) = z_1$ and $\widetilde{W}_{i+1}(c^*) = z_2$ as claimed by $\mathcal{P}$. See Section 4.5.2 for a picture and example of this sub-protocol.

This completes iteration i; $\mathcal{P}$ and $\mathcal{V}$ then move on to the iteration for layer $i+1$ of the circuit, whose purpose is to verify that $\widetilde{W}_{i+1}(r_{i+1})$ has the claimed value, where $r_{i+1} := \ell(r^*)$.

The Final Iteration. At the final iteration d, $\mathcal{V}$ must evaluate $\widetilde{W}_d(r_d)$ on her own. But the vector of gate values at layer d of $\mathcal{C}$ is simply the input x to $\mathcal{C}$. By Lemma 3.8, $\mathcal{V}$ can compute $\widetilde{W}_d(r_d)$ on her own in $O(n)$ time, where recall that n is the size of the input x to $\mathcal{C}$.

A self-contained description of the GKR protocol is provided in Figure 4.13.

4.6.5 Discussion of Costs and Soundness

$\mathcal{V}$'s **Runtime.** Observe that the polynomial $f_{r_i}^{(i)}$ defined in Equation (4.18) is a $(2k_{i+1})$-variate polynomial of degree at most 2 in each variable, and so the invocation of the sum-check protocol at iteration i requires $2k_{i+1}$ rounds, with three field elements transmitted per round. Thus, the total communication cost is $O(S_0 + d \log S)$ field elements where S_0 is the number of outputs of the circuit. The time cost to $\mathcal{V}$ is $O(n + d \log S + t + S_0)$, where t is the amount of time required for $\mathcal{V}$ to evaluate $\widetilde{\text{add}}_i$ and $\widetilde{\text{mult}}_i$ at a random input, for each layer i of $\mathcal{C}$. Here the n term is due to the time required to evaluate $\widetilde{W}_d(r_d)$, the S_0 term is the time required to read the vector of claimed outputs and evaluate the corresponding multilinear extension, the $d \log S$ term is the time required for $\mathcal{V}$ to send messages to $\mathcal{P}$ and process and check the messages from $\mathcal{P}$. For now, let us assume that t is a low-order cost and that $S_0 = 1$, so that $\mathcal{V}$ runs in total time $O(n + d \log S)$; we discuss this issue further in Section 4.6.6.

$\mathcal{P}$'s **Runtime.** Analogously to the MATMULT protocol of Section 4.4, we give two increasingly sophisticated implementations of the prover when the sum-check protocol is applied to the polynomial $f_{r_i}^{(i)}$.

Method 1: $f_{r_i}^{(i)}$ is a v-variate polynomial for $v = 2k_{i+1}$. As in the analysis of Method 1 for implementing the prover in the matrix multiplication protocol from Section 4.4, $\mathcal{P}$ can compute the prescribed method in round j by evaluating $f_{r_i}^{(i)}$ at $3 \cdot 2^{v-j}$ points. It is not hard to see that

Description of the GKR protocol, when applied to a layered arithmetic circuit $\mathcal{C}$ of depth d and fan-in two on input $x \in \mathbb{F}^n$. Throughout, k_i denotes $\log_2(S_i)$ where S_i is the number of gates at layer i of $\mathcal{C}$.

- At the start of the protocol, $\mathcal{P}$ sends a function $D \colon \{0,1\}^{k_0} \to \mathbb{F}$ claimed to equal W_0 (the function mapping output gate labels to output values).

- $\mathcal{V}$ picks a random $r_0 \in \mathbb{F}^{k_0}$ and lets $m_0 \leftarrow \tilde{D}(r_0)$. The remainder of the protocol is devoted to confirming that $m_0 = \tilde{W}_0(r_0)$.

- **For** $i = 0, 1, \ldots, d-1$:

  - Define the $(2k_{i+1})$-variate polynomial

  $$f_{r_i}^{(i)}(b,c) := \widetilde{\text{add}}_i(r_i, b, c) \left(\tilde{W}_{i+1}(b) + \tilde{W}_{i+1}(c) \right)$$
  $$+ \widetilde{\text{mult}}_i(r_i, b, c) \left(\tilde{W}_{i+1}(b) \cdot \tilde{W}_{i+1}(c) \right).$$

  - $\mathcal{P}$ claims that $\sum_{b,c \in \{0,1\}^{k_{i+1}}} f_{r_i}^{(i)}(b,c) = m_i$.

  - So that $\mathcal{V}$ may check this claim, $\mathcal{P}$ and $\mathcal{V}$ apply the sum-check protocol to $f_{r_i}^{(i)}$, up until $\mathcal{V}$'s final check in that protocol, when $\mathcal{V}$ must evaluate $f_{r_i}^{(i)}$ at a randomly chosen point $(b^*, c^*) \in \mathbb{F}^{k_{i+1}} \times \mathbb{F}^{k_{i+1}}$. See Remark (a) at the end of this codebox.

  - Let ℓ be the unique line satisfying $\ell(0) = b^*$ and $\ell(1) = c^*$. $\mathcal{P}$ sends a univariate polynomial q of degree at most k_{i+1} to $\mathcal{V}$, claimed to equal $\tilde{W}_{i+1}$ restricted to ℓ.

  - $\mathcal{V}$ now performs the final check in the sum-check protocol, using $q(0)$ and $q(1)$ in place of $\tilde{W}_{i+1}(b^*)$ and $\tilde{W}_{i+1}(c^*)$. See Remark (b) at the end of this codebox.

  - $\mathcal{V}$ chooses $r^* \in \mathbb{F}$ at random and sets $r_{i+1} = \ell(r^*)$ and $m_{i+1} \leftarrow q(r_{i+1})$.

- $\mathcal{V}$ checks directly that $m_d = \tilde{W}_d(r_d)$ using Lemma 3.8.

  Note that $\tilde{W}_d$ is simply $\tilde{x}$, the multilinear extension of the input x when x is interpreted as the evaluation table of a function mapping $\{0,1\}^{\log n} \to \mathbb{F}$.

Remark a. Note that $\mathcal{V}$ does not actually know the polynomial $f_{r_i}^{(i)}$, because $\mathcal{V}$ does not know the polynomial $\tilde{W}_{i+1}$ that appears in the definition of $f_{r_i}^{(i)}$. However, the sum-check protocol does not require $\mathcal{V}$ to know anything about the polynomial to which it is being applied, until the very final check in the protocol (see Remark 4.2).

Remark b. We assume here that for each layer i of $\mathcal{C}$, $\mathcal{V}$ can evaluate the multilinear extensions $\widetilde{\text{add}}_i$ and $\widetilde{\text{mult}}_i$ at the point (r_i, b^*, c^*) in polylogarithmic time. Hence, given $\tilde{W}_{i+1}(b^*)$ and $\tilde{W}_{i+1}(c^*)$, $\mathcal{V}$ can quickly evaluate $f_{r_i}^{(i)}(b^*, c^*)$ and thereby perform its final check in the sum-check protocol applied to $f_{r_i}^{(i)}$.

Figure 4.13: Self-contained description of the GKR protocol for arithmetic circuit evaluation.

$\mathcal{P}$ can evaluate $f_{r_i}^{(i)}$ at any point in $O(S_i + S_{i+1})$ time using techniques similar to Lemma 3.8. This yields a runtime for $\mathcal{P}$ of $O\left(2^v \cdot (S_i + S_{i+1})\right)$. Over all d layers of the circuit, $\mathcal{P}$'s runtime is bounded by $O(S^3)$.

Method 2: Cormode *et al.* [102] improved on the $O(S^3)$ runtime of Method 1 by observing, just as in the matrix multiplication protocol from Section 4.4, that the $3 \cdot 2^{v-j}$ points at which $\mathcal{P}$ must evaluate $f_{r_i}^{(i)}$ in round j of the sum-check protocol are highly structured, in the sense that their trailing entries are Boolean. That is, it suffices for $\mathcal{P}$ to evaluate $f_{r_i}^{(i)}(z)$ for all points z of the form: $z = (r_1, \ldots, r_{j-1}, \{0, 1, 2\}, b_{j+1}, \ldots, b_v)$, where $v = 2k_{i+1}$ and each $b_k \in \{0, 1\}$.

For each such point z, the bottleneck in evaluating $f_{r_i}^{(i)}(z)$ is in evaluating $\widetilde{\text{add}}_i(z)$ and $\widetilde{\text{mult}}_i(z)$. A direct application of Lemma 3.8 implies that each such evaluation can be performed in $2^v = O(S_{i+1}^2)$ time. However, we can do much better by observing that the functions add_i and mult_i are *sparse*, in the sense that $\text{add}_i(a, b, c) = \text{mult}_i(a, b, c) = 0$ for all Boolean vectors $(a, b, c) \in \mathbb{F}^v$ except for the S_i vectors of the form $(a, \text{in}_{1,i}(a), \text{in}_{2,i}(a)): a \in \{0, 1\}^{k_i}$.

Thus, by Lagrange Interpolation (Lemma 3.6), we can write $\widetilde{\text{add}}_i(z) = \sum_{a \in \{0,1\}^{k_i}} \chi_{(a, \text{in}_{1,i}(a), \text{in}_{2,i}(a))}(z)$, where the sum is only over addition gates a at layer i of $\mathcal{C}$, and similarly for $\widetilde{\text{mult}}_i(z)$ (recall that the multilinear Lagrange basis polynomial $\chi_{(a, \text{in}_{1,i}(a), \text{in}_{2,i}(a))}$ was defined in Equation (3.2) of Lemma 3.6). Just as in the analysis of Method 2 for implementing the prover in the matrix multiplication protocol of Section 4.4, for any input z of the form $z = (r_1, \ldots, r_{j-1}, \{0, 1, 2\}, b_{j+1}, \ldots, b_v)$, it holds that $\chi_{(a, \text{in}_{1,i}(a), \text{in}_{2,i}(a))}(z) = 0$ unless the last $v - j$ entries of z and $(a, \text{in}_{1,i}(a), \text{in}_{2,i}(a))$ are equal (here, we are exploiting the fact that the trailing entries of z are Boolean). Hence, $\mathcal{P}$ can evaluate $\widetilde{\text{add}}_i(z)$ at all the necessary points z in each round of the sum-check protocol with a single pass over the gates at layer i of $\mathcal{C}$: for each gate a in layer i, $\mathcal{P}$ only needs to update $\widetilde{\text{add}}_i(z) \leftarrow \widetilde{\text{add}}_i(z) + \chi_{(a, \text{in}_{1,i}(a), \text{in}_{2,i}(a))}(z)$ for the three values of z whose trailing $v - j$ entries equal the trailing entries of $(a, \text{in}_{1,i}(a), \text{in}_{2,i}(a))$.

Round Complexity and Communication Cost. By direct inspection of the protocol description, there are $O(d \log S)$ rounds in the GKR protocol, and the total communication cost is $O(d \log S)$ field elements.

Soundness Error. The soundness error of the GKR protocol is $O(d \log(S)/|\mathbb{F}|)$. The idea of the soundness analysis is that, if the prover begins the protocol with a false claim as to the output value(s) $C(x)$, then for the verifier to be convinced to accept, there must be at least one round j of the interactive proof in which the following occurs. The prover sends a univariate polynomial g_j that differs from the prescribed polynomial s_j that the honest prover would have sent in that round, yet $g_j(r_j) = s_j(r_j)$, where r_j is a random field element chosen by the verifier in round j. For rounds j of the GKR protocol corresponding to a round within an invocation of the sum-check protocol, g_j and s_j are polynomials of degree $O(1)$, and hence if $g_j \neq s_j$ then the probability (over the random choice of r_j) that $g_j(r_j) = s_j(r_j)$ is at most $O(1/|\mathbb{F}|)$.

In rounds j of the GKR protocol corresponding to the "reducing to verification of a single point" technique, g_j and s_j have degree at most $O(\log S)$, and hence if $g_j \neq s_j$, the probability that $g_j(r_j) = s_j(r_j)$ is at most $O(\log(S)/|\mathbb{F}|)$. Note that there are at most d such rounds over the course of the entire protocol, since this technique is applied at most once per layer of C.

By applying a union bound over all rounds in the protocol, we conclude that the probability there is *any* round j such that $g_j \neq s_j$ yet $g_j(r_j) = s_j(r_j)$ is at most $O(d \log(S)/|\mathbb{F}|)$.

Additional Intuition and Discussion of Soundness. In summary, the GKR protocol prover begins by sending the claimed values of the output gates, thereby specifying the vector of output values W_0, and the verifier evaluates $\tilde{W}_0$ at a random point. Similarly, at the end of the ith iteration of the protocol, the prover is forced to make a claim about a single randomly chosen evaluation of $\tilde{W}_i$. In this way, the prover gradually transitions from making a claim about (one evaluation of the multilinear extension of) the output layer to an analogous claim about the input layer, which the verifier can check directly in linear time.

A common source of confusion is to suspect that "checking the prover's claim" about a random evaluation of $\tilde{W}_i$ is the same as *selecting a random gate* at layer i at confirming that the prover evaluated that one gate correctly (e.g., if the gate is a multiplication gate, checking that the prover indeed assigned a value to the selected gate that is equal to the product of the values assigned to the gate's inputs). If this interpretation were accurate, the protocol would not be sound, because a cheating prover that "alters" the value of a single gate in the circuit would only be caught by the verifier if that gate happens to be the one selected at random from its layer.

The above interpretation is inaccurate: these two processes would only be equivalent if each entry of r_i were chosen at random from $\{0, 1\}$, rather than at random from the entire field $\mathbb{F}$.

Indeed, if even a *single* gate value of layer i is corrupted, then by the Schwartz-Zippel lemma, *almost all* evaluations of $\tilde{W}_i$ must change.[25] By "spot-checking" the *multilinear extension encoding* of the gate values of each layer of the circuit, the GKR verifier is able to detect even tiny deviations of the prover from correct gate-by-gate evaluation of the circuit. See Figure 4.14 for a depiction.

4.6.6 Evaluating $\widetilde{\text{add}}_i$ and $\widetilde{\text{mult}}_i$ Efficiently

The issue of the verifier efficiently evaluating $\widetilde{\text{add}}_i$ and $\widetilde{\text{mult}}_i$ at a random point $\omega \in \mathbb{F}^{k_i + 2k_{i+1}}$ is a tricky one. While there does not seem to be a clean characterization of precisely which circuits have $\widetilde{\text{add}}_i$'s and $\widetilde{\text{mult}}_i$'s that can be evaluated in $O(\log S)$ time, most circuits that exhibit any kind of repeated structure satisfy this property. In particular, the papers [102], [237] show that the evaluation can be computed in $O(k_i + k_{i+1}) = O(\log S)$ time for a variety of common wiring patterns and specific circuits. This includes specific circuits computing functions such as MATMULT, pattern matching, Fast Fourier Transforms, and various problems of interest in the streaming literature, like frequency moments and distinct elements (see Exercise 4.4). In a similar vein, Holmgren and Rothblum [152, Section 5.1] show that as long as add_i

---

[25] So long as the field size is significantly larger than the logarithm of the number of gates at layer i of the circuit.

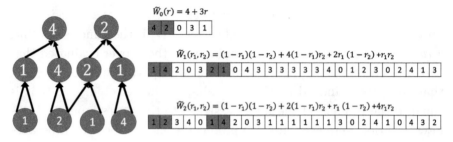

Figure 4.14: Depiction of a circuit over $\mathbb{F}_5$ consisting entirely of multiplication gates, and the multilinear extension encodings $\tilde{W}_i$ of each layer i when the circuit is evaluated on the length-4 input $(1, 2, 1, 4)$ (see Figure 3.2). Due to there being two outputs, $\tilde{W}_0$ is a univariate polynomial, and hence its evaluation table consists of $|\mathbb{F}_5| = 5$ values. The other two layers have four gates each, and hence $\tilde{W}_1$ and $\tilde{W}_2$ are bivariate polynomials, the evaluations tables of which each contain $5^2 = 25$ values, indexed from $(0, 0)$ to $(4, 4)$. Entries of the multilinear extension encodings indexed by Boolean vectors are highlighted in blue. In the GKR protocol applied to this circuit on this input, the prover begins by sending the claimed values of the two output gates, thereby specifying W_0, and the verifier evaluates $\tilde{W}_0$ at a random point. Then at the end of each iteration i of the for loop in Figure 4.13, the prover is forced to make a claim about a single (randomly chosen) evaluation of $\tilde{W}_i$.

and mult_i are computable within a computational model called read-once branching programs, then $\widetilde{\text{add}}_i$ and $\widetilde{\text{mult}}_i$ can be evaluated at any desired point in logarithmic time, and observe that this condition indeed captures common wiring patterns. Moreover, we will see in Section 4.6.7 that $\widetilde{\text{add}}_i$ and $\widetilde{\text{mult}}_i$ can be evaluated efficiently for any circuit that operates in a *data parallel* manner.

In addition, various suggestions have been put forth for what to do when $\widetilde{\text{add}}_i$ and $\widetilde{\text{mult}}_i$ cannot be evaluated in time $O(\log S)$. For example, as observed by Cormode *et al.* [102], these computations can always be done by $\mathcal{V}$ in $O(\log S)$ *space* as long as the circuit is log-space uniform. This is sufficient in streaming applications where the space usage of the verifier is paramount [102]. Moreover, these computations can be done offline before the input is even observed, because they only depend on the wiring of the circuit, and not on the input [102], [135].

An additional proposal appeared in [135], where Goldwasser *et al.* considered the option of outsourcing the computation of $\widetilde{\text{add}}_i(r_i, b^*, c^*)$ and $\widetilde{\text{mult}}_i(r_i, b^*, c^*)$ themselves. In fact, this option plays a central role in obtaining their result for general log-space uniform circuits. Specifically, GKR's results for general log-space uniform circuits are obtained via a two-stage protocol. First, they give a protocol for any problem computable in (non-deterministic) logarithmic space by applying their protocol to the canonical circuit for simulating a space-bounded Turing machine. This circuit has a highly regular wiring pattern for which $\widetilde{\text{add}}_i$ and $\widetilde{\text{mult}}_i$ can be evaluated in $O(\log S)$ time.[26] For a general log-space uniform circuit $\mathcal{C}$, it is not known how to identify low-degree extensions of add_i and mult_i that can be evaluated at w in polylogarithmic time. Rather, Goldwasser *et al.* outsource computation of $\widetilde{\text{add}}_i(r_i, b^*, c^*)$ and $\widetilde{\text{mult}}_i(r_i, b^*, c^*)$ themselves. Since $\mathcal{C}$ is log-space uniform, $\widetilde{\text{add}}_i(r_i, b^*, c^*)$ and $\widetilde{\text{mult}}_i(r_i, b^*, c^*)$ can be computed in logarithmic space, and the protocol for logspace computations applies directly.

A closely related proposal to deal with the circuits for which $\widetilde{\text{add}}_i$ and $\widetilde{\text{mult}}_i$ cannot be evaluated in time sublinear in the circuit size S leverages cryptography. Specifically, later in this monograph we introduce a cryptographic primitive called a *polynomial commitment scheme* and explain how this primitive can be used to achieve the following. A trusted party (e.g., the verifier itself) can spend $O(S)$ time in pre-processing and produce a short *cryptographic commitment* to the polynomials $\widetilde{\text{add}}_i$ and $\widetilde{\text{mult}}_i$ for all layers i of $\mathcal{C}$. After this pre-processing stage, the verifier $\mathcal{V}$ can apply the IP of this section to evaluate $\mathcal{C}$ on many different inputs, and $\mathcal{V}$ can use the cryptographic commitment to force the prover to accurately evaluate $\widetilde{\text{add}}_i$ and $\widetilde{\text{mult}}_i$ on its behalf. Due to its use of cryptography, this proposal results in an argument system as opposed to an interactive proof. Argument systems that handle pre-processing in this manner are sometimes called *holographic*, or referred to as using *computation commitments*. See Sections 10.3.2 and 16.2 for details.

---

[26] In [135], Goldwasser *et al.* actually use higher degree extensions of add_i and mult_i obtained by arithemetizing a Boolean formula of size $\text{polylog}(S)$ computing these functions (see Remark 4.4). The use of these extensions results in a prover whose runtime is a large polynomial in S (i.e., $O(S^4)$). Cormode *et al.* [102] observe that in fact the multilinear extensions of add_i and mult_i can be used for this circuit, and that with these extensions the prover's runtime can be brought down to $O(S \log S)$.

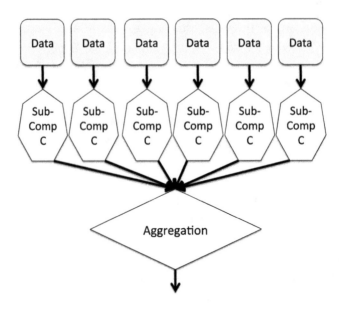

Figure 4.15: Schematic of a data parallel computation.

4.6.7   Leveraging Data Parallelism for Further Speedups

Data parallel computation refers to any setting in which the same sub-computation is applied independently to many pieces of data, before possibly aggregating the results. The protocol of this section makes no assumptions on the sub-computation that is being applied. In particular, it handles sub-computations computed by circuits with highly irregular wiring patterns, but does assume that the sub-computation is applied independently to many pieces of data. Figure 4.15 gives a schematic of a data parallel computation.

Data parallel computation is pervasive in real-world computing. For example, consider any *counting query* on a database. In a counting query, one applies some function independently to each row of the database and sums the results. For example, one may ask "How many people in the database satisfy Property P?" The protocol below allows one to verifiably outsource such a counting query with overhead that depends minimally on the size of the database, but that necessarily depends on the complexity of the property P. In Section 6.5, we will see that data parallel computations are in some sense "universal", in that efficient transformations from high-level computer programs to circuits often yield data parallel circuits.

The Protocol and its Costs. Let C be a circuit of size S with an arbitrary wiring pattern, and let C' be a "super-circuit" that applies C independently to $B = 2^b$ different inputs before aggregating the results in some fashion. For example, in the case of a counting query, the aggregation phase simply sums the results of the data parallel phase. Assume that the aggregation step is sufficiently simple that the aggregation itself can be verified using the techniques of Section 4.6.5.

If one naively applies the GKR protocol to the super-circuit C', $\mathcal{V}$ might have to perform an expensive pre-processing phase to evaluate the wiring predicates $\widetilde{\text{add}}_i$ and $\widetilde{\text{mult}}_i$ of C' at the necessary locations—this would require time $\Omega(B \cdot S)$. Moreover, when applying the basic GKR protocol to C' using the techniques of [102], $\mathcal{P}$ would require time $\Theta\left(B \cdot S \cdot \log(B \cdot S)\right)$. A different approach was taken by Vu *et al.* [241], who applied the GKR protocol B independent times, once for each copy of C. This causes both the communication cost and $\mathcal{V}$'s online check time to grow linearly with B, the number of sub-computations, which is undesirable.

In contrast, the protocol of this section (due to [242], building on [237]) achieves the best of both worlds, in that the overheads for the prover and verifier have no dependence on the number of inputs B to which C is applied. More specifically, the preprocessing time of the verifier is at most $O(S)$, independent of B. The prover runs in time $O(BS + S \log S)$. Observe that as long as $B > \log S$ (i.e., there is a sufficient amount of data parallelism in the computation), $O(BS + S \log S) = O(B \cdot S)$, and hence the prover is only a constant factor slower than the time required to evaluate the circuit gate-by-gate with no guarantee of correctness.

The idea of the protocol is that although each sub-computation C can have a complicated wiring pattern, the circuit is maximally regular between sub-computations, as the sub-computations do not interact at all. It is possible to leverage this regularity to minimize the pre-processing time of the verifier, and to significantly speed up the prover.

4.6.7.1 Protocol Details

Let $\mathcal{C}$ be an arithmetic circuit over $\mathbb{F}$ of depth d and size S with an arbitrary wiring pattern, and let $\mathcal{C}'$ be the circuit of depth d and size $B \cdot S$ obtained by laying B copies of $\mathcal{C}$ side-by-side, where $B = 2^b$ is a power of 2. We will use the same notation as in Section 4.6.4, using apostrophes to denote quantities referring to $\mathcal{C}'$. For example, layer i of $\mathcal{C}$ has size $S_i = 2^{k_i}$ and gate values specified by the function W_i, while layer i of $\mathcal{C}'$ has size $S_i' = 2^{k_i'} = 2^{b+k_i}$ and gate values specified by W_i'.

Consider layer i of $\mathcal{C}'$. Let $a = (a_1, a_2) \in \{0,1\}^{k_i} \times \{0,1\}^b$ be the label of a gate at layer i of $\mathcal{C}'$, where a_2 specifies which "copy" of $\mathcal{C}$ the gate is in, while a_1 designates the label of the gate within the copy. Similarly, let $b = (b_1, b_2) \in \{0,1\}^{k_{i+1}} \times \{0,1\}^b$ and $c = (c_1, c_2) \in \{0,1\}^{k_{i+1}} \times \{0,1\}^b$ be the labels of two gates at layer $i+1$. The key to achieving the speedups for data parallel circuits relative to the interactive proof described in Section 4.6.4 is to tweak the expression in Lemma 4.7 for $\tilde{W}_i$. Specifically, Lemma 4.7 represents $\tilde{W}_i'(z)$ as a sum over $(S_{i+1}')^2$ terms. In this section, we leverage the data parallel structure of $\mathcal{C}'$ to represent $\tilde{W}_i'(z)$ as a sum over $S_{i+1}' \cdot S_{i+1}$ terms, which is smaller than $(S_{i+1}')^2$ by a factor of B.

Lemma 4.8. Let h denote the polynomial $\mathbb{F}^{k_i \times b} \to \mathbb{F}$ defined via

$$h(a_1, a_2) := \sum_{b_1, c_1 \in \{0,1\}^{k_{i+1}}} g(a_1, a_2, b_1, c_1),$$

where

$$g(a_1, a_2, b_1, c_1) := \widetilde{\mathrm{add}}_i(a_1, b_1, c_1)\left(\widetilde{W}_{i+1}'(b_1, a_2) + \widetilde{W}_{i+1}'(c_1, a_2)\right)$$
$$+ \widetilde{\mathrm{mult}}_i(a_1, b_1, c_1) \cdot \widetilde{W}_{i+1}'(b_1, a_2) \cdot \widetilde{W}_{i+1}'(c_1, a_2).$$

Then h extends W_i'.

Proof Sketch. Essentially, Lemma 4.8 says that an addition (respectively, multiplication) gate $a = (a_1, a_2) \in \{0,1\}^{k_i+b}$ of $\mathcal{C}'$ is connected to gates

$b = (b_1, b_2) \in \{0, 1\}^{k_{i+1}+b}$ and $c = (c_1, c_2) \in \{0, 1\}^{k_{i+1}+b}$ of $\mathcal{C}'$ if and only if a, b, and c are all in the same copy of $\mathcal{C}$, and a is connected to b and c within the copy. $\qquad\square$

The following lemma requires some additional notation. Let $\beta_{k_i'}(a, b)$: $\{0, 1\}^{k_i'} \times \{0, 1\}^{k_i'} \rightarrow \{0, 1\}$ be the function that evaluates to 1 if $a = b$, and evaluates to 0 otherwise, and define the formal polynomial

$$\tilde{\beta}_{k_i'}(a, b) = \prod_{j=1}^{k_i'} \left((1 - a_j)(1 - b_j) + a_j b_j \right). \tag{4.19}$$

It is straightforward to check that $\tilde{\beta}_{k_i'}$ is the multilinear extension $\beta_{k_i'}$. Indeed, $\tilde{\beta}_{k_i'}$ is a multilinear polynomial. And for $a, b \in \{0, 1\}^{k_i'}$, it is easy to check that $\tilde{\beta}_{k_i'}(a, b) = 1$ if and only if a and b are equal coordinate-wise.

Lemma 4.9. (Restatement of [216, Lemma 3.2.1].) For *any* polynomial $h \colon \mathbb{F}^{k_i'} \rightarrow \mathbb{F}$ extending W_i', the following polynomial identity holds:

$$\tilde{W}_i'(z) = \sum_{a \in \{0,1\}^{k_i'}} \tilde{\beta}_{k_i'}(z, a) h(a). \tag{4.20}$$

Proof. It is easy to check that the right hand side of Equation (4.20) is a multilinear polynomial in z, and that it agrees with W_i' on all Boolean inputs. Thus, the right hand side of Equation (4.20), viewed as a polynomial in z, must be the (unique) multilinear extension $\tilde{W}_i'$ of W_i'. $\qquad\square$

Intuitively, Lemma 4.9 achieves "multi-linearization" of the higher-degree extension h. That is, it expresses the *multilinear* extension of any function W_i' in terms of *any* extension h of W_i', regardless of the degree of h.

Combining Lemmas 4.8 and 4.9 implies that for any $z \in \mathbb{F}^{k_i'}$,

$$\tilde{W}_i'(z) = \sum_{(a_1, a_2, b_1, c_1) \in \{0,1\}^{k_i+b+2k_{i+1}}} g_z^{(i)}(a_1, a_2, b_1, c_1), \tag{4.21}$$

where

$$g_z^{(i)}(a_1, a_2, b_1, c_1) := \widetilde{\beta}_{k_i'}(z, (a_1, a_2)) \cdot \left[\widetilde{\mathrm{add}}_i(a_1, b_1, c_1) \right.$$
$$\times \left(\widetilde{W}_{i+1}'(b_1, a_2) + \widetilde{W}_{i+1}'(c_1, a_2) \right) + \widetilde{\mathrm{mult}}_i(a_1, b_1, c_1)$$
$$\left. \cdot \widetilde{W}_{i+1}'(b_1, a_2) \cdot \widetilde{W}_{i+1}'(c_1, a_2) \right].$$

Thus, to reduce a claim about $\widetilde{W}_i'(r_i)$ to a claim about $\widetilde{W}_{i+1}'(r_{i+1})$ for some point $r_{i+1} \in \mathbb{F}^{k_{i+1}'}$, it suffices to apply the sum-check protocol to the polynomial $g_{r_i}^{(i)}$, and then use the "Reducing to Verification of a Single Point" protocol from Section 4.5.2. That is, the protocol is the same as in Section 4.6.4, except that, at layer i, rather than applying the sum-check protocol to the polynomial $f_{r_i}^{(i)}$ defined in Equation (4.18) to compute $\widetilde{W}_i'(r_i)$, the protocol instead applies the sum-check protocol to the polynomial $g_{r_i}^{(i)}$ (Equation (4.21)).

Costs for $\mathcal{V}$. To bound $\mathcal{V}$'s runtime, observe that $\widetilde{\mathrm{add}}_i$ and $\widetilde{\mathrm{mult}}_i$ can be evaluated at a random point in $\mathbb{F}^{k_i+2k_{i+1}}$ in pre-processing in time $O(S_i)$ by enumerating the in-neighbors of each of the S_i gates at layer i in order to apply Lemma 3.8. Adding up the pre-processing time across all iterations i of our protocol, $\mathcal{V}$'s pre-processing time is $O(\sum_i S_i) = O(S)$ as claimed. Notice this pre-processing time is independent of B, the number of copies of the subcircuit.

Outside of pre-processing, the costs to the verifier are similar to Section 4.6.5, with the main difference being that now the verifier needs to also evaluate $\widetilde{\beta}_{k_i}$ at a random point at each layer i. But the verifier can evaluate $\widetilde{\beta}_{k_i}$ at any input with $O(\log S_i)$ additions and multiplications over $\mathbb{F}$, using Equation (4.19). This does not affect the verifier's asymptotic runtime.

Costs for $\mathcal{P}$. The insights that go into implementing the honest prover in time $O(B \cdot S + S \log S)$ build on ideas related the Method 3 for implementing the prover in the Matrix Multiplication protocol of Section 4.4, and heavily exploit the fact that Equation (4.21) represents $\widetilde{W}_i'(z)$ as a sum over just $S_{i+1}' \cdot S_{i+1}$ terms, rather than the $(S_{i+1}')^2$ terms in the sum that would be obtained by applying Equation (4.17) to $\mathcal{C}'$. The costs of the protocol are summarized in Table 4.5.

Table 4.5: Costs of the IP of Section 4.6.7 when applied to any log-space uniform arithmetic circuit $\mathcal{C}$ of size S and depth d over n variables, that is applied B times in a data parallel manner (cf. Figure 4.15).

Communication	Rounds	$\mathcal{V}$ Time	$\mathcal{P}$ Time
$O(d \cdot \log$ $(B \cdot S))$ field elements	$O\,(d \cdot$ $(\log\,(B \cdot S)))$	online time: $O\,(B \cdot n + d \cdot (\log(B \cdot S)))$ pre-processing time: $O(S)$	$O(B \cdot S + S$ $\cdot \log(S))$

Remark 4.5. Recent work [251] has shown how to use Lemma 4.5 to implement the prover in the IP of Section 4.6.4 in time $O(S)$ for *arbitrary* arithmetic circuits of size S (not just circuits with a sufficient amount of data parallelism as in Section 4.6.7).[27] For brevity, we do not elaborate here upon how to achieve this result. The same result in fact follows (with some adaptation) from Section 8.4 in Section 8, where we explain how to achieve an $O(S)$-time prover in a (two-prover) interactive proof for a *generalization* of arithmetic circuits, called *rank-one constraint systems* (R1CS).

4.6.8   Tension Between Efficiency and Generality

The GKR protocol and its variants covered in this section is an example of a *general-purpose* technique for designing VC protocols. Specifically, the GKR protocol can be used to verifiably outsource the evaluation of an arbitrary arithmetic circuit, and as we will see in the next section, arbitrary computer programs can be turned into arithmetic circuits. Such general-purpose techniques are the primary focus of this survey.

However, there is often a tension between the generality and efficiency of VC protocols. That is, the general-purpose techniques should sometimes be viewed as heavy hammers that are capable of pounding arbitrary nails, but are not necessarily the most efficient way of hammering any particular nail.

---

[27]To clarify, this does not address the issue discussed in Section 4.6.6 that for arbitrary arithmetic circuits, the verifier may need time linear in the circuit size S to evaluate $\widetilde{\text{add}}_i$ and $\widetilde{\text{mult}}_i$ as required by the protocol.

This point was already raised in Section 4.4.1 in the context of matrix multiplication (see the paragraph "Preview: Other Protocols for Matrix Multiplication"). That section described an interactive proof for matrix multiplication that is far more concretely efficient, especially in terms of prover time and communication cost, than applying the GKR protocol to any known arithmetic circuit computing matrix multiplication. As another example, the circuit depicted in Figures 4.8–4.11 computes the sum of the squared entries of the input in $\mathbb{F}^n$. This is an important function in the literature on streaming algorithms, called the second frequency moment. Applying the GKR protocol to this circuit (which has logarithmic depth and size $O(n)$) would result in communication cost of $\Theta(\log^2 n)$. But the function can be computed much more directly, and with total communication $O(\log n)$, by a single application of the sum-check protocol. Specifically, if we interpret the input as specifying a function $f\colon \mathbb{F}^{\log n} \to \mathbb{F}$ in the natural way, then we can simply apply the sum-check protocol to the polynomial $\left(\tilde{f}\right)^2$, the square of the multilinear extension of f. This requires the verifier to evaluate $\left(\tilde{f}\right)^2$ at a single point r. The verifier can compute $\left(\tilde{f}\right)^2(r)$ by evaluating $\tilde{f}(r)$ in linear or quasilinear time using Lemma 3.7 or Lemma 3.8, and then squaring the result.

To summarize, while this survey is primarily focused on general-purpose VC protocols, these do not represent the most efficient solutions in all situations. Those interested in specific functionalities may be well-advised to consider whether less general but more efficient protocols apply to the functionality of interest. Even when using a general-purpose VC protocol, there are typically many optimizations a protocol designer can identify (e.g., expanding the gate set within the GKR protocol from addition and multiplication gates to other types of low-degree operations tailored to the functionality of interest, see for example [102, Section 3.2], [251, Section 5], and [30]).

4.7   Exercises

Exercise 4.1. Recall that Section 4.3 gave a doubly-efficient interactive proof for counting triangles. Given as input the adjacency matrix A

of a graph on n vertices, the IP views A as a function over domain $\{0,1\}^{\log_2 n} \times \{0,1\}^{\log_2 n}$, lets $\tilde{A}$ denote its multlinear extension, and applies the sum-check protocol to the $(3 \log n)$-variate polynomial

$$g(X, Y, Z) = \tilde{A}(X, Y) \cdot \tilde{A}(Y, Z) \cdot \tilde{A}(X, Z).$$

A 4-cycle in a graph is a quadruple of vertices (a, b, c, d) such that (a, b), (b, c), (c, d), and (a, d) are all edges in the graph. Give a doubly-efficient interactive proof that, given as input the adjacency matrix A of a simple graph, counts the number of 4-cycles in the graph.

Exercise 4.2. Here is yet another interactive proof for counting triangles given as input the adjacency matrix A of a graph on n vertices: For a sufficiently large prime p, define $f: \{0,1\}^{\log_2 n} \times \{0,1\}^{\log_2 n} \times \{0,1\}^{\log_2 n} \to \mathbb{F}_p$ via $f(i, j, k) = A_{i,j} \cdot A_{j,k} \cdot A_{k,i}$, where here we associate vectors in $\{0,1\}^{\log_2 n}$ with numbers in $\{1, \ldots, n\}$ in the natural way, and interpret entries of A as elements of $\mathbb{F}_p$ in the natural way. Apply the sum-check protocol to the multilinear extension $\tilde{f}$. Explain that the protocol is complete, and has soundness error at most $(3 \log_2 n)/p$.

What are the fastest runtimes you can give for the prover and verifier in this protocol? Do you think the verifier would be interested in using this protocol?

Exercise 4.3. This question has 5 parts.

- (Part a) Section 4.2 gave a technique to take any Boolean formula $\phi: \{0,1\}^n \to \{0,1\}$ of size S and turn ϕ into a polynomial g over field $\mathbb{F}$ that extends ϕ (the technique represents g via an arithmetic circuit over $\mathbb{F}$ of size $O(S)$).

  Apply this technique to the Boolean formula in Figure 4.16. You may specify the resulting extension polynomial g by drawing the arithmetic circuit computing g or by writing out some other representation of g.

- (Part b) Section 4.2 gives an interactive proof for counting the number of satisfying assignments to ϕ by applying the sum-check protocol to g. For the polynomial g you derived in Part a that extends the formula in Figure 4.16, provide the messages sent by the honest prover if the random field element chosen by the verifier in round 1 is $r_1 = 3$ and the random field element chosen by the verifier in round 2 is $r_2 = 4$. You may work over the field $\mathbb{F}_{11}$ of integers modulo 11.

- (Part c) Imagine you are a cheating prover in the protocol of Part b above and somehow you know at the start of the protocol that in round 1 the random field element r_1 chosen by the verifier will be 3. Give a sequence of messages that you can send that will convince the verifier that the number of satisfying assignments of ϕ is 6 (the verifier should be convinced regardless of the random field elements r_2 and r_3 that will be chosen by the verifier in rounds 2 and 3).

- (Part d) You may notice that the extension polynomial g derived in Part a is *not* multilinear. This problem explains that there is a good reason for this.

Show that the ability to evaluate the *multilinear* extension $\tilde{\phi}$ of a formula ϕ at a randomly chosen point in $\mathbb{F}^n$ allows one to determine whether or not ϕ is satisfiable. That is, give an efficient randomized algorithm that, given $\tilde{\phi}(\mathbf{r})$ for a randomly chosen $\mathbf{r} \in \mathbb{F}^n$, outputs SATISFIABLE with probability at least $1 - n/|\mathbb{F}|$ over the random choice of $\mathbf{r}$ if ϕ has one or more satisfying assignments, and outputs UNSATISFIABLE with probability 1 if ϕ has no satisfying assignments. Explain why your algorithm achieves this property.

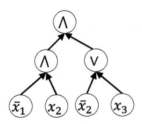

Figure 4.16: A Boolean formula ϕ over $n = 3$ variables.

- (Part e) Let $p > 2^n$ be a prime, and as usual let $\mathbb{F}_p$ denote the field of order p. This question establishes that the ability to evaluate $\tilde{\phi}$ at a certain specific input implies the ability not only to determine whether or not ϕ is satisfiable, but in fact to *count* the number of satisfying assignments to ϕ. Specifically, prove that

$$\sum_{x \in \{0,1\}^n} \phi(x) = 2^n \cdot \tilde{\phi}(2^{-1}, 2^{-1}, \ldots, 2^{-1}).$$

Hint: Lagrange Interpolation.

Exercise 4.4. One of the more challenging notions to wrap one's head around regarding the GKR protocol is that, when applying it to a circuit C with a "nice" wiring pattern, the verifier never needs to materialize the full circuit. This is because the only information about the circuit's wiring pattern of C that the verifier needs to know in order to run the protocol is to evaluate $\widetilde{add}_i$ and $\widetilde{mult}_i$ at a random point, for each layer i of C. And $\widetilde{add}_i$ and $\widetilde{mult}_i$ often have nice, simple expressions that enable them to be evaluated at any point in time logarithmic in the size of C. (See Section 4.6.6).

This problem asks you to work through the details for a specific, especially simple, wiring pattern. Figures 4.8–4.11 depict (for input size $n = 4$) a circuit that squares all of its inputs, and sums the results via a binary tree of addition gates.

Recall that for a layered circuit of depth d, the layers are numbered from 0 to d where 0 corresponds to the output layer and d to the input layer.

- Assume that n is a power of 2. Give expressions $\widetilde{add}_i$ and $\widetilde{mult}_i$ for layers $i = 1, \ldots, d - 2$ such that the expressions can both be evaluated at any point in time $O(\log n)$ (layer i consists of 2^i addition gates, where for $j \in \{0, 1, \ldots, 2^i - 1\}$, the jth addition gate has as its in-neighbors gates $2j$ and $2j + 1$ at layer $i + 1$).

- Assume that n is a power of two. Give expressions for $\widetilde{add}_{d-1}$ and $\widetilde{mult}_{d-1}$ that can both be evaluated at any point in time $O(\log n)$. (This layer consists of $n = 2^{d-1}$ multiplication gates, where the jth multiplication gate at layer $d - 1$ has both in-neighbors equal to the jth input gate at layer d).

Exercise 4.5. Write a Python program implementing the prover and verifier in the interactive proof for counting triangles from Section 4.3 (say, over the prime field $\mathbb{F}_p$ with $p = 2^{61} - 1$). Recall that in this interactive proof, the message from the prover in each round i is a univariate polynomial s_i of degree at most 2. To implement the prover $\mathcal{P}$, you may find it simplest for $\mathcal{P}$ to specify each such polynomial via its evaluations at 3 designated inputs (say, $\{0, 1, 2\}$), rather than via its (at most) 3 coefficients. For example, if $s_i(X) = 3X^2 + 2X + 1$, it may be simplest if, rather than sending the coefficients 3, 2, and 1, the prover sends $s_i(0) = 1$, $s_i(1) = 6$ and $s_i(2) = 17$. The verifier can then evaluate $s_i(r_i)$ via Lagrange interpolation:

$$s_i(r_i) = 2^{-1} \cdot s_i(0) \cdot (r_i - 1)(r_i - 2) - s_i(1) \cdot r_i(r_i - 2) + 2^{-1} \cdot s_i(2) \cdot r_i(r_i - 1).$$

5

Publicly Verifiable, Non-Interactive Arguments via Fiat-Shamir

---

Recall from Section 3.3 that in a public-coin interactive proof or argument, any coin tossed by the verifier $\mathcal{V}$ is made visible to the prover $\mathcal{P}$ as soon as it is tossed. These coin tosses are interpreted as "random challenges" sent by $\mathcal{V}$ to $\mathcal{P}$, and in a public-coin protocol they are, without loss of generality, the only messages sent from $\mathcal{V}$ to $\mathcal{P}$.[1]

The Fiat-Shamir transformation [111] takes any public-coin protocol $\mathcal{I}$ and transforms it into a non-interactive, publicly verifiable protocol $\mathcal{Q}$. To describe the transformation and analyze its security, it is helpful to introduce an idealized setting called the random oracle model.

5.1 The Random Oracle Model

The random oracle model (ROM) [29], [111] is an idealized setting meant to capture the fact that cryptographers have developed hash functions (e.g., SHA-3 or BLAKE3) that efficient algorithms seem totally unable to distinguish from random functions. By a random function R mapping some domain $\mathcal{D}$ to the κ-bit range $\{0,1\}^{\kappa}$, we mean the following: on

---

[1] In a public-coin protocol, any $\mathcal{V} \to \mathcal{P}$ messages other than $\mathcal{V}$'s random coin tosses can be omitted: they must be deterministic functions of $\mathcal{V}$'s coin tosses, and hence $\mathcal{P}$ can derive such messages on its own.

any input $x \in \mathcal{D}$, R chooses its output $R(x)$ uniformly at random from $\{0,1\}^\kappa$.

Accordingly, the ROM simply assumes that the prover and verifier have query access to a random function R. This means that there is an oracle (called a random oracle) such that the prover and verifier can submit any query x to the oracle, and the oracle will return $R(x)$. That is, for each query $x \in \mathcal{D}$ posed to the oracle, the oracle makes an independent random choice to determine $R(x)$ and responds with that value. It keeps a record of its responses to make sure that it repeats the same response if x is queried again.

The random oracle assumption is not valid in the real world, as specifying a random function R requires $|\mathcal{D}| \cdot \kappa$ bits—essentially one must list the value $R(x)$ for every input $x \in \mathcal{D}$—which is totally impractical given that $|\mathcal{D}|$ must be huge to ensure cryptographic security levels (e.g., $|\mathcal{D}| \geq 2^{256}$ or larger). In the real world, the random oracle is replaced with a concrete hash function like SHA-3, which is succinctly specified via, e.g., a small circuit or computer program that evaluates the hash function on any input. In principle, it may be possible for a cheating prover in the real world to exploit access to this succinct representation to break the security of the protocol, even if the protocol is secure in the random oracle model. However, protocols that are proven secure in the random oracle model are often considered secure in practice, and indeed no deployed protocols have been broken in this manner.[2]

---

[2]The relationship between security in the random oracle model and security in the real world has been the subject of considerable debate and criticism. Indeed, a series of works has established very strong negative results regarding the (lack of) implications of random oracle model security. In particular, various protocols have been constructed that are secure in the random oracle model but not secure when the random oracle is replaced with *any* concrete hash function [26], [91], [134], [139], [199]. However, these protocols and functionalities are typically contrived [170]. For two entertaining and diametrically opposed perspectives, the interested reader is directed to [129], [170].

5.2 The Fiat-Shamir Transformation

Recall that the purpose of the Fiat-Shamir transformation [111] is to take any public-coin IP or argument $\mathcal{I}$ and transform it into a non-interactive, publicly verifiable protocol $\mathcal{Q}$ in the random oracle model.

Some Approaches That Do Not Quite Work. The Fiat-Shamir transformation mimics the transformation described in Section 3.3 that transforms any interactive proof system with a deterministic verifier into a non-interactive proof system. In that transformation, the non-interactive prover leverages the total predictability of the interactive verifier's messages to compute those messages itself on behalf of the verifier. This eliminates the need for the verifier to actually send any messages to the prover. In particular, it means that the non-interactive proof can simply specify an accepting transcript from the interactive protocol (i.e., specify the first message sent by the prover in the interactive protocol, followed by the verifier's response to that message, followed by the prover's second message, and so on until the protocol terminates).

In the setting of this section, the verifier's messages in $\mathcal{I}$ are not predictable. But since $\mathcal{I}$ is public coin, the verifier's messages in $\mathcal{I}$ come from a known distribution; specifically, the uniform distribution. So a naive attempt to render the protocol non-interactive would be to ask the prover to determine the verifier's messages itself, by drawing each message at random from the uniform distribution, independent of all previous messages sent in the protocol. But this does not work because the prover is untrusted, and hence there is no way to force the prover to actually draw the verifier's challenges from the appropriate distribution.

A second approach that attempts to address the above issue is to have $\mathcal{Q}$ use the random oracle to determine the verifier's message r_i in round i of $\mathcal{I}$. This will ensure that each challenge is indeed uniformly distributed. A naive attempt at implementing this second approach would be to select r_i in $\mathcal{Q}$ by evaluating the random oracle at input i. But this attempt is also unsound. The problem is that, although this ensures each of the verifier's messages r_i are uniformly distributed, it does not ensure that they are independent of the prover's messages $g_1, \ldots, g_i$ from rounds $1, 2, \ldots, i$ of $\mathcal{I}$. Specifically, the prover in $\mathcal{Q}$ can learn all of the verifier's messages $r_1, r_2, \ldots$ in advance (by simply querying the random oracle at the predetermined points $1, 2, \ldots$) and then choose the prover messages in $\mathcal{I}$ in a manner that depends on these values. Since the IP $\mathcal{I}$ is not sound if the prover knows r_i in advance of sending its ith message g_i, the resulting non-interactive argument is not sound.

The above issue can be made more concrete by imagining that $\mathcal{I}$ is the sum-check protocol applied to an ℓ-variate polynomial g over $\mathbb{F}$. Consider a cheating prover $\mathcal{P}$ who begins the protocol with a false claim C for the value $\sum_{x \in \{0,1\}^\ell} g(x)$. Suppose in round one of the sum-check protocol, before sending its round-one message polynomial g_1, $\mathcal{P}$ knows what will be the verifier's round-one message $r_1 \in \mathbb{F}$. Then the prover can trick the verifier as follows. If s_1 is the message that the *honest* prover would send in round one, $\mathcal{P}$ can send a polynomial g_1 such that

$$g_1(0) + g_1(1) = C \quad \text{and} \quad g_1(r_1) = s_1(r_1), \tag{5.1}$$

where recall (Equation (4.2)) that

$$s_1(X_1) := \sum_{(x_2,\ldots,x_v) \in \{0,1\}^{v-1}} g(X_1, x_2, \ldots, x_v).$$

Note that such a polynomial is guaranteed to exist so long as g_1 is permitted to have degree at least one. From that point on in $\mathcal{I}$, the cheating prover $\mathcal{P}$ can send the same messages as the honest prover, and thereby pass all of the verifier's checks. In the naive attempt at implementing the second approach to obtaining a non-interactive protocol above, the prover in $\mathcal{Q}$ will be able to simulate this attack on $\mathcal{I}$. This is because the prover in $\mathcal{Q}$ can learn r_1 by simply querying the random oracle at the input 1, and then choosing g_1 to satisfy Equation (5.1) above.

To prevent this attack on soundness, the Fiat-Shamir transformation ensures that the verifier's challenge r_i in round i of $\mathcal{I}$ is determined by querying the random oracle at an input that depends on the prover's i'th message g_i. This means that the prover in $\mathcal{Q}$ can only simulate the aforementioned attack on $\mathcal{I}$ if the prover can find a g_1 satisfying Equation (5.1) with r_1 equal to evaluation of the random oracle at the appropriate query point (which, as previously mentioned, includes g_1). Intuitively, for the prover in $\mathcal{Q}$ to find such a g_1, a vast number of queries to the random oracle are required, because the output of the random oracle is totally random, and for each g_1 there are a tiny number of values of r_1 satisfying Equation (5.1).

Complete Description of the Fiat-Shamir Transformation. The Fiat-Shamir transformation replaces each of the verifier's messages from the interactive protocol $\mathcal{I}$ with a value derived from the random oracle in the following manner: in $\mathcal{Q}$, the verifier's message in round i of $\mathcal{I}$ is determined by querying the random oracle, where the query point is the the list of messages sent by the prover in rounds $1, \ldots, i$. As in the naive attempt above, this eliminates the need for the verifier to send any information to the prover—the prover can simply send a single message containing the transcript of the entire protocol (i.e., a list of all messages exchanged by the prover in the interactive protocol, with the verifier's random coin tosses in the transcript replaced with the random oracle evaluations just described). See Figure 5.1.

A Concrete Optimization. When applying the Fiat-Shamir transformation to many-round interactive protocols, it is often implemented using a technique called *hash chaining*. This means that, rather than choosing the round-i verifier challenge r_i in the interactive protocol to be the hash (or random oracle evaluation) of all preceding prover messages

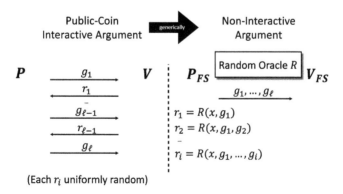

Figure 5.1: Depiction of the Fiat-Shamir transformation. Image courtesy of Ron Rothblum [218].

$g_1, \ldots, g_i$, one instead chooses r_i to be a hash only of (i, r_{i-1}, g_i). This reduces the cost of hashing in practice, because it keeps the inputs at which the hash function is evaluated short. This variant of Fiat-Shamir also shown secure in the random oracle model.

Avoiding a Common Vulnerability. For the Fiat-Shamir transformation to be secure in settings where an adversary can choose the input x to the IP or argument, it is essential that x be appended to the list that is hashed in each round. This property of soundness against adversaries that can choose x is called adaptive soundness. Some real-world implementations of the Fiat-Shamir transformation have missed this detail, leading to attacks [51], [146]. In fact, this precise error was recently identified in several popular SNARK deployments, leading to critical vulnerabilities.[3] Sometimes, the version of Fiat-Shamir that includes x in the hashing is called *strong* Fiat-Shamir, while the version that omits it is called *weak* Fiat-Shamir.

Here is a sketch of the attack if the adversary can choose x and x is not hashed within the Fiat-Shamir transformation. For concreteness, consider a prover applying the GKR protocol to establish that $\mathcal{C}(x) = y$. In the GKR protocol, the verifier $\mathcal{V}$ completely ignores the input $x \in \mathbb{F}^n$ until the final check in the protocol, when $\mathcal{V}$ checks that the multilinear extension $\tilde{x}$ of x evaluated at some randomly chosen point r equals some value c derived from previous rounds. The adversary can easily generate a transcript for the Fiat-Shamir-ed protocol that passes all of the verifier's checks except the final one. To pass the final check, the adversary can choose any input $x \in \mathbb{F}^n$ such that $\tilde{x}(r) = c$ (such an input $\tilde{x}$ can be identified in linear time). The transcript convinces the verifier of the Fiat-Shamir-ed protocol to accept the claim that $\mathcal{C}(x) = y$. Yet there is no guarantee that $\mathcal{C}(x) = y$, as x may be an arbitrary input satisfying $\tilde{x}(r) = c$. See Exercise 5.2, which asks the reader to work through the details of this attack.

Note that in this attack, the prover does not necessarily have "perfect control" over the inputs x for which it is able to produce convincing

---

[3]https://blog.trailofbits.com/2022/04/13/part-1-coordinated-disclosure-of-vulnerabilities-affecting-girault-bulletproofs-and-PlonK/.

"proofs" that $\mathcal{C}(x) = y$. This is because x is constrained to satisfy $\tilde{x}(r) = c$ for some values r and c that depend on the random oracle. This may render the attack somewhat benign in some applications.[4] Nonetheless, practitioners should take care to avoid this vulnerability, especially since including x in the hashing is rarely a significant cost in practice.

5.3 Security of the Transformation

It has long been known that when the Fiat-Shamir transformation is applied to a *constant-round* public-coin IP or argument $\mathcal{I}$ with negligible soundness error,[5] the resulting non-interactive proof $\mathcal{Q}$ in the random oracle model is sound against cheating provers that run in polynomial time [211]. More quantitatively, if $\mathcal{I}$ consists of t rounds, any prover $\mathcal{P}$ for $\mathcal{Q}$ that can convince the verifier to accept input x with probability ε and runs in time T can be transformed into a prover $\mathcal{P}'$ for $\mathcal{I}$ that convinces the verifier to accept input x with probability at least $(\varepsilon/T)^{O(t)}$. If t is constant, this is $\text{poly}(1/\varepsilon, 1/T)$, which is non-negligible.[6] In fact, we prove this result at the end of this section for 3-message protocols $\mathcal{I}$ (Theorem 5.1). However, the runtime of $\mathcal{P}'$ grows exponentially with the number of rounds t in $\mathcal{I}$, and the IPs covered in this section all require at least logarithmically many rounds. Recently, a better understanding of the soundness of $\mathcal{Q}$ has been developed for such many-round protocols $\mathcal{I}$.

Specifically, it is now known that if a public-coin interactive proof $\mathcal{I}$ for a language $\mathcal{L}$ satisfies a property called *round-by-round soundness*

---

[4] An illustrative example: in some applications the only "sensible" inputs x are bit-vectors $x \in \{0,1\}^n$. The attack described above will efficiently identify an $x \in \mathbb{F}^n$ along with a convincing "proof" that $\mathcal{C}(x) = y$, but it may not be the case that all entries of x are in $\{0,1\}$. This may mean that the attacker is only able to generate "convincing proofs" for false statements about "nonsense vectors" $x \in \mathbb{F}^n \setminus \{0,1\}^n$.

[5] Throughout this monograph, negligible means any quantity smaller than the reciprocal of any fixed polynomial in the input length n or a security parameter λ. Non-negligible means any quantity that is *at least* the reciprocal of some fixed polynomial in n or λ. Computationally-bounded adversaries are assumed to run in time polynomial in λ and n.

[6] If $\mathcal{I}$ is an argument rather than a proof, then soundness of $\mathcal{Q}$ in the random oracle model will also inherit any computational hardness assumptions on which soundness of $\mathcal{I}$ is based.

then $\mathcal{Q}$ is sound in the random oracle model [44], [88]. Here, $\mathcal{I}$ satisfies round-by-round soundness if the following properties hold: (1) At any stage of any execution of $\mathcal{I}$, there is a well-defined state (depending on the partial transcript at that stage of the execution) and some states are "doomed", in the sense that once the protocol $\mathcal{I}$ is in a doomed state, it will (except with negligible probability) forever remain doomed, no matter the strategy executed by the prover in $\mathcal{I}$. (2) If $x \notin \mathcal{L}$, then the initial state of $\mathcal{I}$ is doomed. (3) If at the end of the interaction the state is doomed, then the verifier will reject.[7]

Canetti *et al.* [88] showed that the GKR protocol (and any other interactive proof based on the sum-check protocol) satisfy round-by-round soundness, and hence applying the Fiat-Shamir transformation to it yields a non-interactive proof that is secure in the random oracle model.[8]

Here is some rough intuition for why round-by-round soundness of the IP $\mathcal{I}$ implies soundness of the non-interactive proof $\mathcal{Q}$ in the random oracle model. The only way a cheating prover in $\mathcal{I}$ can convince the verifier of a false statement is to "get lucky", in the sense that the verifier's random coin tosses in $\mathcal{I}$ happen to fall into some small set of "bad" coin tosses B that eventually force the protocol into a *non-doomed* state. Round-by-round soundness implies that B is small. Because a random oracle is by definition totally unpredictable and unstructured, in $\mathcal{Q}$ roughly speaking all that a cheating prover can do to find an accepting transcript is to iterate over possible prover messages/transcripts for the IP $\mathcal{I}$ in an arbitrary order, and stop when he identifies one where the random oracle happens to return a sequence of values falling in B. Of course, this isn't quite true: a malicious prover in $\mathcal{Q}$ is also capable of executing a so-called *state-restoration* attack [44]

---

[7]For illustration, the canonical example of an IP with negligible soundness error that does *not* satisfy round-by-round soundness is to take any IP with soundness error $1/3$, and sequentially repeat it n times. This yields a protocol with at least n rounds and soundness error $1/3^{-\Omega(n)}$, yet it is not round-by-round sound. And indeed, applying the Fiat-Shamir transformation to this protocol does *not* yield a sound argument system in the random oracle model [218]. See Exercise 5.1.

[8]In fact, Canetti *et al.* [88] also show that, using parallel repetition, *any* public-coin IP can be transformed into a different public-coin IP that satisfies round-by-round soundness.

(also sometimes called a *grinding attack*), which means that the prover in $\mathcal{Q}$ can "rewind" any interaction with the verifier of $\mathcal{I}$ to an earlier point of the interaction and "try out" sending a different response to the last message sent by the verifier in this partial transcript for $\mathcal{I}$ (see Section 5.3.1 for additional discussion of this attack). The prover may hope that by trying out a different response, this will cause the random oracle to output a non-doomed value. However, round-by-round soundness of $\mathcal{I}$ precisely guarantees that such an attack is unlikely to succeed: once in a doomed state of $\mathcal{I}$, no prover strategy can "escape" doom except with negligible probability.

In summary, applying the Fiat-Shamir Transformation to a public coin interactive protocol with negligible round-by-round soundness error yields a non-interactive argument in the random oracle model with negligible soundness error against efficient provers. The protocol can then be heuristically instantiated in the "real world" by replacing the random oracle with a cryptographic hash function.

As discussed next, there are nuances regarding what is an appropriate level of security for interactive protocols vs. the non-interactive arguments that result after applying the Fiat-Shamir transformation.

5.3.1 "Bits of Security": Statistical vs. Computational

Statistical, Computational, and Interactive Security. As we have seen (Section 4), interactive protocols can satisfy *statistical* (i.e., information-theoretic) security. The logarithm of the soundness error of an information-theoretically secure protocol is referred to as the number of *bits of statistical security.*

In contrast, the security level of a non-interactive argument is measured by the amount of work that must be done to find a convincing "proof" of a false statement. Similar to other cryptographic primitives like digital signatures and collision-resistant hash functions, the logarithm of this amount of work is referred to as the number of *bits of computational security.* For example, 30 bits of security implies that $2^{30} \approx 1$ billion "steps of work" are required to attack the argument system. This is inherently an approximate measure of real-world security because the notion of one step of work can vary, and practical considerations like memory requirements or opportunities for parallelism are not considered.

Later in this text, we will see many examples of succinct *interactive* arguments. Although only computationally rather than statistically sound, many of these arguments have the property that adversaries that cannot break a cryptographic primitive (e.g., cannot find a collision in a collision-resistant hash function) also cannot convince the argument-system verifier to accept a false statement with probability more than 2^{-s} for some value s. In this situation, some practitioners refer informally to s as the number of *bits of interactive security* of the argument.

Appropriate Security Levels for Interactive vs. Non-Interactive Arguments.   For reasons discussed shortly, non-interactive arguments are generally recommended to be deployed with at least 100 or 128 bits of computational security [261]. In contrast, it may be appropriate in some contexts to set statistical or interactive security levels lower.

The key difference is that, with statistical or interactive security, the cheating prover has to actually interact with the verifier in order to "attempt" an attack that will succeed with only tiny probability. This is because the cheating prover in an interactive protocol is hoping to get a "lucky" verifier challenge (i.e., one that leads the verifier to accept the prover's false claim), and the prover does not know whether or not the verifier's challenge will be lucky until after sending one or more messages to the verifier and receiving challenges in response.

For example, suppose that an interactive protocol is run at 60 bits of statistical or interactive security. This means that each attempted attack succeeds with probability at most 2^{-60}. So after, say, 2^{30} attempted attacks, the probability that *any* of the attempts succeed is at most $2^{-60} \cdot 2^{30} = 2^{-30}$. It is unlikely that a verifier will continue interacting with a prover that has tried and failed to convince her to accept false statements 2^{30} times. Moreover, due to round-trip delays involved in interactive protocols, executing a large number of attacks may take an infeasibly large amount of time. For example, if every attempted attack executes in one second, then 2^{30} attempts would take more than 30 years to execute. For these reasons, 60 bits of statistical or interactive security may be sufficient in some contexts—specifically, those where a successful attack would not be totally catastrophic, and where, for the reasons above, attacks cannot be attempted too many times.

In contrast, with non-interactive arguments, a cheating prover can "silently" attack a protocol, without any interaction with the verifier. For example, if applying the Fiat-Shamir transformation to a 3-message interactive protocol as considered in Figure 5.2 below, the canonical "grinding attack" on the resulting non-interactive argument involves the prover attempting to "guess" a first message α that yields a "lucky" verifier message $R(x, \alpha)$, in the sense that the prover can efficiently find a response γ such that $(\alpha, R(x, \alpha), \gamma)$ is an accepting transcript.

Suppose the original protocol had only 60 bits of statistical or interactive security. Then a cheating prover executing a grinding attack on the non-interactive argument only needs to try about 2^{60} first messages α before it finds one such that $R(x, \alpha)$ is "lucky". When instantiating the Fiat-Shamir transformation with a concrete hash function, the computational bottleneck in this attack may be simply performing 2^{60} hash evaluations. This number of hash evaluations is entirely feasible for modern computers.[9] Indeed, in 2020, the cost of computing just shy of 2^{64} SHA-1 evaluations using GPUs was \$45,000 [181]. As another data point, as of 2022, bitcoin's network hash rate was about 2^{67} hash evaluations per second, meaning bitcoin miners as a whole were performing 2^{80} SHA-256 evaluations every 2 hours. Of course, this very large number of hashes is due to vast investment in ASICs for bitcoin mining.

In summary, if one is applying the Fiat-Shamir transformation to render an interactive protocol non-interactive, the interactive protocol should be configured to over 80 bits of statistical or interactive security if one wishes to ensure that the canonical grinding attack on the resulting non-interactive protocol is out of the reach of modern hardware.

---

[9]More precisely, a grinding attack that tries $T < 2^{60}$ different values of α succeeds with probability roughly $T \cdot 2^{-60}$. This matches the lower bound shown in the proof of Theorem 5.1. Specifically, Theorem 5.1 shows that if the Fiat-Shamir transformation is applied to a 3-message interactive protocol with statistical soundness error 2^{-60}, then any attack on the Fiat-Shamir-ed protocol that treats the hash function as a random oracle, runs in time at most T, and succeeds with probability ϵ must satisfy $\epsilon/T < 2^{-60}$.

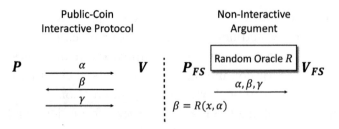

Figure 5.2: Depiction of the Fiat-Shamir transformation applied to a 3-message interactive proof or argument as in the proof of Theorem 5.1. Image courtesy of Ron Rothblum [218].

5.3.2 Soundness in the Random Oracle Model for Constant-Round Protocols

Theorem 5.1. Let $\mathcal{I}$ be a *constant-round* public-coin IP or argument with negligible soundness error, and let $\mathcal{Q}$ be the non-interactive protocol in the random oracle model obtained by applying the Fiat-Shamir transformation to $\mathcal{I}$. Then $\mathcal{Q}$ has negligible computational soundness error. That is, no prover running in polynomial time can convince the verifier in $\mathcal{Q}$ of a false statement with non-negligible probability.

Proof. For simplicity, we will only prove the result in the case where $\mathcal{I}$ is a 3-message protocol where the prover speaks first. See Figure 5.2 for a depiction of the Fiat-Shamir transformation in this setting and the notation we will use during the proof.

We will show that, for any input x, if $\mathcal{P}_{FS}$ is a prover that runs in time T and convinces the verifier in $\mathcal{Q}$ to accept on input x with probability at least ϵ (where the probability is over the choice of random oracle), then there is a prover $\mathcal{P}^*$ for $\mathcal{I}$ that convinces the verifier in $\mathcal{I}$ to accept with probability at least $\varepsilon^* \geq \Omega(\varepsilon/T)$ (where the probability is over the choice of the verifier's random challenges in $\mathcal{I}$). Moreover, $\mathcal{P}^*$ has essentially the same runtime as $\mathcal{P}_{FS}$. The theorem follows, because if ϵ is non-negligible and T is polynomial in the size of the input, then ε^* is non-negligible as well.

Handling Restricted $\mathcal{P}_{FS}$ Behavior. The rough idea is that there isn't much $\mathcal{P}_{FS}$ can do to find an accepting transcript (α, β, γ) with

$\beta = R(x, \alpha)$ other than to mimic a successful prover strategy $\mathcal{P}$ for $\mathcal{Q}$, setting α to be the first message sent by $\mathcal{P}$, setting β to be $R(x, \alpha)$, and setting γ to be $\mathcal{P}$'s response to the challenge β.[10] If this is indeed how $\mathcal{P}_{\mathcal{FS}}$ behaved, it would be easy for $\mathcal{P}^*$ to "pull" the prover strategy $\mathcal{P}$ for $\mathcal{Q}$ out of $\mathcal{P}_{\mathcal{FS}}$ as follows: $\mathcal{P}^*$ runs $\mathcal{P}_{\mathcal{FS}}$, up until the point where $\mathcal{P}_{\mathcal{FS}}$ makes its (only) query, of the form (x, α), to the random oracle. $\mathcal{P}^*$ sends α to the verifier $\mathcal{V}$ in $\mathcal{I}$, who responds with a challenge β. $\mathcal{P}^*$ uses β as the response of the random oracle to $\mathcal{P}_{\mathcal{FS}}$'s query. $\mathcal{P}^*$ then continues running $\mathcal{P}_{\mathcal{FS}}$ until $\mathcal{P}_{\mathcal{FS}}$ terminates.

Since $\mathcal{I}$ is public coin, $\mathcal{V}$ chooses β uniformly random, which means that β is distributed appropriately to be treated as a response of the random oracle. Hence, with probability at least ε, $\mathcal{P}_{\mathcal{FS}}$ will produce an accepting transcript of the form (α, β, γ). In this case, $\mathcal{P}^*$ sends γ as its final message in $\mathcal{I}$, and the verifier accepts because (α, β, γ) is an accepting transcript. This ensures that $\mathcal{P}^*$ convinces the verifier in $\mathcal{I}$ to accept with the same probability that $\mathcal{P}_{\mathcal{FS}}$ outputs an accepting transcript, which is at least ε by assumption.

The General Case: Overview. In the general case, $\mathcal{P}_{\mathcal{FS}}$ may not behave in the manner above. In particular, $\mathcal{P}_{\mathcal{FS}}$ may ask the random oracle *many* queries, though no more than T of them, since $\mathcal{P}_{\mathcal{FS}}$ runs in time at most T. This means that it is not obvious which of the queries (x, α) $\mathcal{P}^*$ should forward to $\mathcal{V}$ as its first message α. Fortunately, we will show that it suffices for $\mathcal{P}^*$ to simply pick one of $\mathcal{P}_{\mathcal{FS}}$'s queries at random. Essentially, $\mathcal{P}^*$ will pick the "right" query with probability at least $1/T$, leading $\mathcal{P}^*$ to convince $\mathcal{V}$ to accept input x with probability at least ε/T.

What We Can Assume About $\mathcal{P}_{\mathcal{FS}}$ Without Loss of Generality. Let us assume that $\mathcal{P}_{\mathcal{FS}}$ always makes exactly T queries to the random oracle (this can be ensured modifying $\mathcal{P}_{\mathcal{FS}}$ to ask "dummy queries" as necessary to ensure that it always makes exactly T queries to the random oracle R). Let us further assume that all queries $\mathcal{P}_{\mathcal{FS}}$ makes

---

[10] As explained in Section 5.3.1, this isn't actually true, as $\mathcal{P}_{\mathcal{FS}}$ can also run state-restoration attacks a.k.a. grinding attacks, an issue with which the formal proof below must grapple.

are distinct (there is never a reason for $\mathcal{P}_{\mathcal{FS}}$ to query the oracle at the same location twice, since the oracle will respond with the same value both times). Finally, we assume that whenever $\mathcal{P}_{\mathcal{FS}}$ successfully outputs an accepting transcript (α, β, γ) with $\beta = R(x, \alpha)$, then at least one of $\mathcal{P}_{\mathcal{FS}}$'s T queries to R was at point (x, α). This can be ensured by modifying $\mathcal{P}_{\mathcal{FS}}$ to always query (x, α) before outputting the transcript (α, β, γ), if (x, α) has not already been queried, and making a "dummy query" otherwise.

Complete Description of $\mathcal{P}^*$. $\mathcal{P}^*$ begins by picking a random integer $i \in \{1, \ldots, T\}$. $\mathcal{P}^*$ runs $\mathcal{P}_{\mathcal{FS}}$ up until its i'th query to the random oracle, choosing the random oracle's responses to queries $1, \ldots, i-1$ uniformly at random. If the ith query is of the form (x, α) for some α, $\mathcal{P}^*$ sends α to $\mathcal{V}$ as its first message, and receives a response β from $\mathcal{V}$.[11] $\mathcal{P}^*$ uses β as the response of the random oracle to query (x, α). $\mathcal{P}^*$ then continues running $\mathcal{P}_{\mathcal{FS}}$, choosing the random oracle's responses to queries $i + 1, \ldots, T$ uniformly at random. If $\mathcal{P}_{\mathcal{FS}}$ outputs an accepting transcript of the form (α, β, γ), then $\mathcal{P}^*$ sends γ to $\mathcal{V}$, which convinces $\mathcal{V}$ to accept.

Analysis of Success Probability for $\mathcal{P}^*$. As in the restricted case, since $\mathcal{I}$ is public coin, $\mathcal{V}$ chooses β uniformly random, which means that β is distributed appropriately to be treated as a response of the random oracle. This means that $\mathcal{P}_{\mathcal{FS}}$ outputs an accepting transcript of the form $(\alpha, R(x, \alpha), \gamma)$ with probability at least ε. In this event, $\mathcal{P}^*$ convinces $\mathcal{V}$ to accept whenever $\mathcal{P}_{\mathcal{FS}}$'s ith query to R was (x, α). Since we have assumed that $\mathcal{P}_{\mathcal{FS}}$ makes exactly T queries, all of which are distinct, and one of those queries is of the form (x, α), this occurs with probability exactly $1/T$. Hence, $\mathcal{P}^*$ convinces $\mathcal{V}$ to accept with probability at least ε/T. □

---

[11] If the ith query is not of the form (i, α), $\mathcal{P}^*$ aborts, i.e., $\mathcal{P}^*$ gives up trying to convince $\mathcal{V}$ to accept.

5.3.3 Fiat-Shamir Preserves Knowledge-Soundness in the Random Oracle Model

Theorem 5.1 roughly shows that the Fiat-Shamir transformation renders any constant-round IP or argument non-interactive in the random oracle model while preserving soundness. Later in this monograph, we will be concerned with a strengthening of soundness called *knowledge-soundness* that is relevant when the prover is claiming to *know* a witness satisfying a specified property (see Section 7.4). In the random oracle model, the Fiat-Shamir transformation does preserve knowledge-soundness, at least when applied to specific important argument systems. We cover two important examples of these results later in this survey: Section 9.2.1 shows that the Fiat-Shamir transformation preserves knowledge-soundness when applied to succinct arguments obtained from *PCPs* and *IOPs*. Section 12.2.3 establishes a similar result when the transformation is applied to a different class of arguments, called Σ-*protocols* (introduced in Section 12.2.1). A brief discussion of extensions to super-constant round variants of Σ-protocols can be found at the end of Section 14.4.2.

5.3.4 Fiat-Shamir in the Plain Model

Chaum and Impagliazzo, and Canetti *et al.* [91] identified a property called correlation-intractability (CI) such that instantiating the Fiat-Shamir transformation in the plain model results in a sound argument when the concrete hash function h is chosen at random from a hash family $\mathcal{H}$ satisfying CI. Below, we explain in more detail what CI means, before describing recent results that construct CI hash families based on standard cryptographic assumptions.

What is Correlation-Intractability? Let R denote some *property* of pairs $(y, h(y))$. A hash family $\mathcal{H}$ satisfies CI for R if it is computationally infeasible to find a pair $(y, h(y))$ satisfying property R.

Suppose $\mathcal{I}$ is an IP or argument for a language $\mathcal{L}$ such that $\mathcal{I}$ satisfies round-by-round soundness. Let R denote the relation capturing "success" of a cheating prover for the Fiat-Shamir transformation $\mathcal{Q}$ of $\mathcal{I}$. That is, R consists of all tuples $(y, h(y))$ such that $y = (x, g_1, \ldots, g_i)$ with

$x \notin \mathcal{L}$ and the following holds. Let $g_1, \ldots, g_i$ be interpreted as prover messages in the first i rounds of $\mathcal{I}$ when run on input x, with round-j verifier message equal to $h(x, g_1, \ldots, g_j)$. Then we define R to include $(y, h(y))$ if $\mathcal{I}$ is in a doomed state at the start of round i, but enters a non-doomed state if the ith verifier challenge is $h(y)$.

A cheating prover in the Fiat-Shamir-ed protocol $\mathcal{Q}$ *must* find some pair $(y, h(y))$ satisfying property R to find a convincing "proof" of membership in $\mathcal{L}$ for some $x \notin \mathcal{L}$. If $\mathcal{H}$ satisfies CI for R, then this task is intractable—no polynomial time cheating prover can find a convincing proof of a false statement with non-negligible probability.

Recent Results Constructing CI Hash Families.   An exciting recent line of work [76], [88]–[90], [150], [151], [158], [161], [185], [207] has constructed CI hash families for various natural classes of IPs and arguments, with the CI property holding under standard cryptographic assumptions. In particular, [151], [207] construct CI families for various natural classes of IPs and arguments assuming the Learning With Errors (LWE) assumption, upon which many lattice-based cryptosystems are based. The constructions of CI hash families in the aforementioned works have the flavor of *fully homomorphic encryption* (FHE) schemes, which are currently highly computationally intensive, much more so than the prover and verifier in interactive proofs such as the GKR protocol. Hence, these hash families are not practical for use in obtaining non-interactive arguments. However, it is plausible that cryptographic hash families used in practice actually satisfy the relevant notions of correlation-intractability.

The aforementioned results apply, for example, to the GKR protocol. They also apply to various zero-knowledge proofs of theoretical and historical (but not practical) importance for **NP**-complete languages [58], [131] (we formally introduce the notion of zero-knowledge in Section 11). Note that these zero-knowledge proofs are not *succinct*. This means that the proof length is not shorter than the trivial (non-zero-knowledge) **NP** proof system in which the prover sends a classical static proof, i.e., an **NP** witness, for the validity of the claim at hand, and the verifier deterministically checks the proof.

Fiat-Shamir and succinct public-coin arguments. There is great interest in obtaining analogous results for the *succinct* public-coin interactive arguments described later in this survey, to obtain succinct non-interactive arguments that are secure in the plain model under standard cryptographic assumptions. Unfortunately, the results that have been obtained on this topic have so far been negative [21], [126]. For example, Bartusek *et al.* [21] show, roughly speaking, that obtaining non-interactive arguments in this manner would require exploiting some special structure in both the underlying interactive argument and in the concrete hash function used to implement the random oracle in the Fiat-Shamir transformation.

5.4 Exercises

Exercise 5.1. Section 5.2 described the Fiat-Shamir transformation and asserted that if the Fiat-Shamir transformation is applied to any IP with negligible soundness error that satisfies an additional property called round-by-round soundness, then the resulting argument system is computationally sound in the random oracle model. One may wonder if in fact the Fiat-Shamir transformation yields a computationally sound argument for any IP with negligible soundness error, not just those that are round-by-round sound. In this problem, we will see that the answer is no.

Take any IP with perfect completeness and soundness error $1/3$, and sequentially repeat it n times, having the verifier accept if and only if all n invocations of the base IP lead to acceptance. This yields an IP with soundness error 3^{-n}. Explain why applying the Fiat-Shamir transformation to this IP does *not* yield a sound argument system in the random oracle model, despite the fact that the soundness error 3^{-n} is negligible.

You may assume that the prover in the IP is permitted to pad messages with nonces if it so desires, i.e., the prover may append extra symbols to any message and the verifier will simply ignore those symbols. For example, if the prover in the IP wishes to send message $m \in \{0,1\}^b$, the prover could choose to send (m, m') for an arbitrary string m', and the IP verifier will simply ignore m'.

Exercise 5.2. Recall that the GKR protocol for circuit evaluation is used to verify the claim that $C(x) = y$, where C is an arithmetic circuit over field $\mathbb{F}$, x is a vector in $\mathbb{F}^n$, and C, x, and y are all known to both the prover and the verifier. Consider applying the Fiat-Shamir transformation in the random oracle model to the GKR protocol, but suppose that when applying the Fiat-Shamir transformation, the input x is *not* included in the partial transcripts fed into the random oracle. Show that the resulting non-interactive argument is *not* adaptively sound. That is, for a circuit C and claimed output y of your choosing, explain how a cheating prover can, in time proportional to the size of C and with overwhelming probability, find an input $x \in \mathbb{F}^n$ such that $C(x) \neq y$, along with a convincing "proof" for the claim that $C(x)$ in fact equals y.

6

Front Ends: Turning Computer Programs Into Circuits

6.1 Introduction

In Section 4.6, we saw a very efficient interactive proof, called the GKR protocol, for verifiably outsourcing the evaluation of large arithmetic circuits, as long as the circuit is not too deep. But in the real world, people are rarely interested in evaluating giant arithmetic circuits. Rather, they typically have a computer program written in a high-level programming language like Java or Python, and want to execute the program on their data. In order for the GKR protocol to be useful in this setting, we need an efficient way to turn high-level computer programs into arithmetic circuits. We can then apply the GKR protocol (or any other interactive proof or argument system for circuit evaluation) to the resulting arithmetic circuit.

Most general purpose argument system implementations work in this two-step manner. First, a computer program is compiled into a model amenable to probabilistic checking, such as an arithmetic circuit or arithmetic circuit satisfiability instance.[1] Second, an interactive proof or

---

[1] Many argument systems prefer to work with models such "Rank-1 Constraint Systems" that are generalizations of arithmetic circuits. These alternative models are discussed later in this survey (see Section 8.4).

argument system is applied to check that the prover correctly evaluated the circuit. In these implementations, the program-to-circuit compiler is referred to as the *front end* and the argument system used to check correct evaluation of the circuit is called the *back end*.

Some computer programs naturally lend themselves to implementation via arithmetic circuits, particularly programs that only involve addition and multiplication of integers or elements of a finite field. For example, the following layered arithmetic circuit of fan-in two implements the standard naive $O(n^3)$ time algorithm for multiplying two $n \times n$ matrices, A and B.

Let $[n] := \{1, \ldots, n\}$. Adjacent to the input layer of the circuit is a layer of n^3 multiplication gates, each assigned a label $(i, j, k) \in [n] \times [n] \times [n]$. Gate (i, j, k) at this layer computes the product of $A_{i,k}$ and $B_{k,j}$. Following this layer of multiplication gates lies a binary tree of addition gates of depth $\log_2(n)$. This ensures that there are n^2 output gates, and if we assign each output gate a label $(i, j) \in [n] \times [n]$, then the (i, j)'th output gate computes $\sum_{k \in [n]} A_{i,k} \cdot B_{k,j}$ as required by the definition of matrix multiplication. See Figure 6.1.

As another example, Figures 4.8–4.11 portray an arithmetic circuit implementing the same functionality as the computer program depicted in Algorithm 1 (with $n = 4$). The circuit devotes one layer of gates to squaring each input entry, and then sums up the results via a complete binary tree of addition gates of fan-in two.

Algorithm 1 Algorithm Computing the Sum of Squared Entries of Input Vector

---

Input: Array $a = (a_1, \ldots, a_n)$
  1: $b \leftarrow 0$
  2: **for** $i = 1, 2, \ldots, n$ **do**
  3:     $b \leftarrow b + a_i^2$
Output: b

While it is fairly straightforward to turn the algorithm for naive matrix multiplication into an arithmetic circuit as above, other kinds of computer programs that perform "non-arithmetic" operations, such as

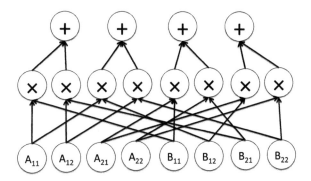

Figure 6.1: An arithmetic circuit implementing the naive matrix multiplication algorithm for 2×2 matrices.

evaluating complicated conditional statements, seem to be much more difficult to turn into small arithmetic circuits.

In Sections 6.3 and 6.4, we will see two techniques for turning arbitrary computer programs into circuits. In Section 6.5, we will see a third technique, which is far more practical, but makes use of what are sometimes called "non-deterministic circuits" and "circuits with auxiliary input". Equivalently, the third technique produces instances of the circuit *satisfiability* problem, rather than of the circuit *evaluation* problem.

We would like to make statements like "Any computer programming that halts within T time steps can be turned into a low-depth, layered, fan-in two arithmetic circuit of size at most $O(T \log T)$." In order to make statements of this form, we first have to be precise about what it means to say that a computer programs has runtime T.

6.2 Machine Code

Modern compilers are very good at efficiently turning high-level computer programs into *machine code*, which is a set of basic instructions that can each be executed in unit time on the machine's hardware. When we say that a program runs in $T(n)$ time steps, we mean that it can be compiled into a sequence of machine instructions of length at most $T(n)$. But for this statement to be precise, we have to decide precisely what is a machine instruction. That is, we have to specify a model of the hardware on which we will think of our programs as running.

Our hardware model will be a simple *Random Access Machine* (RAM). A RAM consists of the following components.

- (Main) Memory. That is, it will contain s cells of storage, where each cell can store, say, 64 bits of data.

- A constant number (say, 8) of registers. Registers are special memory cells with which the RAM can manipulate data. That is, whereas Main Memory cells can only store data, the RAM is allowed to perform operations on data in registers, such as "add the numbers in Registers 1 and 2, and store the result in Register 3".

- A set of $\ell = O(1)$ allowed machine instructions. Typically, these instructions are of the form:

  - Write the value currently stored in a given register to a specific location in Main Memory.

  - Read the value from a specific location in Main Memory into a register.

  - Perform basic manipulations of data in registers. For example, adding, subtracting, multiplying, dividing, or comparing the values stored in two registers, and storing the result in a third register. Or doing bitwise operations on the values stored in two registers (e.g., computing the bit-wise AND of two values).

- A program counter. This is a special register that tells the machine what is the next instruction to execute.

6.3 A First Technique For Turning Programs Into Circuits [Sketch]

Our first technique for turning computer programs into circuits yields the following.[2] If a computer program runs in time $T(n)$ on a RAM with at most $s(n)$ cells of memory, then the program can be turned into a layered, fan-in 2 arithmetic circuit of depth not much more than $T(n)$ and *width* of about $s(n)$ (i.e., the number of gates at each layer of the circuit is not much more than $s(n)$).

Observe that such a transformation from programs to circuits is useless in the context of the GKR protocol, because the verifier's time complexity in the GKR protocol is at least the circuit depth, which is about $T(n)$ in this construction. In time $T(n)$, the verifier could have executed the entire program on her own, without any help from the prover. We describe this circuit-generation technique because it is conceptually important, even though it is useless in the context of the GKR protocol.

This program-to-circuit transformation makes use of the notion of a machine *configuration*. A machine configuration tells you everything about the state of a RAM at a given time. That is, it specifies the input, as well as the value of every single memory cell, register, and program counter. Observe that if a RAM has a memory of size s, then a configuration can be specified with roughly $64s$ bits (where 64 is the number of bits that can fit in one memory cell), plus some extra bits to specify the input and the values stored in the registers and program counter.

The basic idea of the transformation is to have the circuit proceed in iterations, one for each time step of the computer program. The ith iteration takes as input the configuration of the RAM after i steps of the program have been executed, and "executes one more step of the

---

[2]The transformation described in this section can yield either Boolean circuits (with AND, OR, or NOT gates) or arithmetic circuits (whose inputs are elements of some finite field $\mathbb{F}$ and whose gates compute addition and multiplication over the field). In fact, any transformation to Boolean circuits implies one to arithmetic circuits, since we know from Section 4.2 that any Boolean circuit can be transformed into an equivalent arithmetic circuit over any field, with at most a constant-factor blowup in size.

program". That is, it determines what the configuration of the RAM would be after the $(i + 1)$'st machine instruction is executed. This is displayed pictorially in Figure 6.2.

A key point that makes this transformation work is that there is only a constant number of possible machine instructions, each of which is very simple (operating on only a constant number of registers, in a simple manner). Hence, the circuitry that maps the configuration of the machine after i steps of the program to the configuration after the $(i + 1)$'st step is very simple.

Unfortunately, the circuits that are produced by this transformation have size $\tilde{\Theta}(T(n) \cdot s(n))$, meaning that, relative to running the computer program (which takes time $T(n)$), even writing down or reading the circuit is more expensive by a factor of $s(n)$.[3] The source of the inefficiency is that, for each time step of the RAM, the circuit produces an entire new machine configuration. Each configuration has size $\tilde{\Theta}(s)$, as a configuration must specify the state of the RAM's memory at that time step. Conceptually, while each step of the program only alters a constant number of memory cells in each time step, the circuit does not "know in advance" which memory cells will be updated. Hence, the circuit has to explicitly check, for each memory cell at each time step, whether or not the memory cell should be updated. This causes the circuit to be at least $s(n)$ times bigger than the runtime $T(n)$ of the RAM that the circuit simulates. This overhead renders this program-to-circuit transformation impractical.

---

[3]A second issue is that the circuit is very deep, i.e., depth at least $T(n)$. Because the GKR protocol's (Section 4.6) communication cost grows linearly with circuit depth, applying the GKR protocol to this circuit leads to communication cost at least $T(n)$, which is trivial (in the time required to read the prover's message, the verifier could afford to execute M on its own). This issue will be addressed in Section 6.4 below, which reduces the circuit depth to polynomial in the *space* usage rather than *runtime* of the RAM. However, this comes at the cost of increasing the circuit size from $\text{poly}(T, s)$ to $2^{\Theta(s)}$. Note that argument systems covered later in this monograph do not have communication cost growing linearly with circuit depth, and hence applying these arguments to deep circuits such as those described in this section does yield non-trivial protocols.

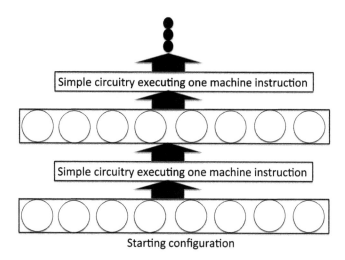

Figure 6.2: A caricature of a technique for turning any program running in time $T(n)$ and space $s(n)$ into a circuit of depth not much more than $T(n)$ and width not much more than $s(n)$.

6.4 Turning Small-Space Programs Into Shallow Circuits

The circuits that come out of the program-to-circuit transformation of Section 6.3 are useless in the context of the GKR protocol because the circuits have depth at least T. When applying the GKR protocol to such a deep circuit, the runtime of the verifier is at least T. It would be just as fast for the verifier to simply run the computer program on its own, without bothering with a prover.

A second technique for turning computer programs generates shallower circuits as long as the computer program doesn't use much space. Specifically, it is capable of taking any program that runs in time T and space s, and turning it into a circuit of depth roughly $s \cdot \log T$ and size $2^{\Theta(s)}$.

Section 4.5.5 explained how we can determine whether a Turing Machine M outputs 1 on input x in less than T time steps by determining whether there is a directed path of length at most T in M's configuration graph from the starting configuration to the accepting configuration. While that section discussed Turing Machines, the same result also applies to Random Access Machines, because both Turing Machine or Random Access Machine using s bits of space have at most $2^{O(s)}$ configurations.

To solve this directed-path problem, it suffices to compute a single entry of the T'th power of A, where A be the adjacency matrix of M's configuration graph; that is, $A_{i,j} = 1$ if configuration i has a directed edge to configuration j in M's configuration graph, and $A_{i,j} = 0$ otherwise. This is because the (i,j)'th entry of the T'th power of A equals the number of directed paths of length T from node i to node j in the configuration graph of M. Hence, in order to determine whether there is a directed path of length T from the starting configuration of M to the accepting configuration, it is enough for the circuit to repeatedly square the adjacency matrix $\log_2 T$ times. We have seen in Section 6.1 that there is a circuit of size $O(N^3)$ and depth $O(\log N)$ for multiplying two $N \times N$ matrices. Since the configuration graph of M on input x is an $2^{\Theta(s)} \times 2^{\Theta(s)}$ matrix, the circuit that squares the adjacency matrix of the configuration graph of M $O(\log T)$ times has depth $O(\log(2^{\Theta(s)}) \cdot \log T) = O(s \log T)$, and size $2^{\Theta(s)}$.[4]

Hence, one can obtain an IP for determining the output of the RAM M by applying the GKR protocol to this circuit. However, the IP of Section 4.5.5 solves the same problem in a more direct and efficient manner.

6.5 Turning Computer Programs Into Circuit Satisfiability Instances

6.5.1 The Circuit Satisfiability Problem

In Sections 6.3 and 6.4, we saw two methods for turning computer programs into arithmetic circuits. The first method was undesirable for two reasons. First, it yielded circuits of very large depth. So large, in fact, that applying the GKR protocol to the resulting circuits led to a verifier runtime that was as bad as just having the verifier run the

---

[4]To be more precise, the circuit takes as input x, and first computes the adjacency matrix A of the configuration graph of M on input x. Each entry of A is a simple function of x. Then the circuit repeatedly squares A to compute the $T(n)$'th power of A and the outputs the (i,j)'th entry, where i indexes the starting configuration and j the ending configuration.

entire program without any help from a prover. Second, if the computer program ran in time T and space s, the circuit had size at least $T \cdot s$, and we'd really prefer to have circuits with close to T gates.

In this section, we are going to address both of these issues. However, to do so, we are going to have to shift from talking about circuit *evaluation* to talking about circuit *satisfiability*.

Recall that in the arithmetic circuit evaluation problem, the input specifies an arithmetic circuit C, input x, and output(s) y, and the goal is to determine whether $C(x) = y$. In the arithmetic circuit *satisfiability* problem (circuit-SAT for short), the circuit C takes *two inputs*, x and w. The first input x is public and fixed, i.e., known to both the prover and verifier. The second input w is often called the *witness*, or sometimes the *non-deterministic input* or *auxiliary input*. Given the first input x and output(s) y, the goal is to determine whether *there exists* a w such that $C(x, w) = y$.

Preview: Succinct Arguments for Circuit Satisfiability, and Outline for the Remainder of the Section.   After this section, the remainder of the monograph is devoted to developing succinct arguments, especially so-called *SNARKs*, for circuit satisfiability and generalizations thereof. These protocols will enable the untrusted prover $\mathcal{P}$ to prove that it *knows* a witness w such that $C(x, w) = y$. Ideally, the proof size and verification time of the SNARK will be far smaller than they are in the naive proof system, in which $\mathcal{P}$ sends the witness w to $\mathcal{V}$ and $\mathcal{V}$ evaluates $C(x, w)$ on its own. And ideally, if $\mathcal{P}$ already knows the witness—and hence does not have to spend any time to find it—$\mathcal{P}$ will run in time close to that required just to evaluate C on input (x, w).

In applications, $\mathcal{P}$ will typically already know w. For example, Section 1 discussed an application in which Alice chooses a random password w, publishes a cryptographic hash $y = h(w)$, and later wants to prove to Bob that she knows a pre-image of y under h. The witness in this application is w. Effectively, Alice herself generated the statement she wishes to prove, and hence she knows the witness without needing to spend massive compute power to compute it "from scratch", which in this example would entail inverting the hash function h at y.

Such applications entail a major shift in thinking, compared to the interactive proofs for circuit *evaluation* already covered. No longer is $\mathcal{P}$ claiming to have applied a specific circuit $\mathcal{C}$ or run a specific RAM M on a public input x that is known to both verifier and prover. Rather, $\mathcal{P}$ is claiming it knows *some* witness w (not known to the verifier) such that applying $\mathcal{C}$ to (x, w), or running M on (x, w), yields output y.

But as we will see, arguments for circuit satisfiability are useful *even when* $\mathcal{P}$ is only claiming to have run a specific RAM M on a public input x. In this case, the witness w is "used" merely to enable more efficient transformations of the machine M into an "equivalent circuit" $\mathcal{C}$. By this, we mean that the output of the RAM M on input x equals y if and only if there exists a w such that $\mathcal{C}(x, w) = y$.

In more detail, the remainder of the section explains that any computer program running in time T can be efficiently transformed into an equivalent instance $(\mathcal{C}, x, y)$ of arithmetic circuit satisfiability, where the circuit $\mathcal{C}$ has size close to T, and depth close to $\log T$. The output of the program on input x equals y if and only if there exists a w such that $\mathcal{C}(x, w) = y$. Moreover, any party (such as a prover) that actually runs the program on input x can easily construct a w satisfying $\mathcal{C}(x, w) = y$.

Why Circuit-SAT Instances Are Expressive.   Intuitively, circuit satisfiability instances should be "more expressive" than circuit evaluation instances, for the same reason that *checking* a proof of a claim tends to be easier then discovering the proof in the first place. In the coming sections, the claim at hand is "running a designated computer program on input x yields output y". Conceptually, the witness w in the circuit satisfiability instances that we construct in the remainder of this section will represent a traditional, static *proof* of the claim, and the circuit $\mathcal{C}$ will simply check that the proof is valid. Unsurprisingly, we will see that *checking validity of a proof* can be done by much smaller circuits than circuit evaluation instances that determine the veracity of the claim "from scratch".

To make the above intuition more concrete, here is a specific, albeit somewhat contrived, example of the power of circuit satisfiability instances. Imagine a straightline program in which all inputs are elements of some finite field $\mathbb{F}$, and all operations are addition, multiplication, and division (by division a/b, we mean multiplying a by the multiplicative inverse of b in $\mathbb{F}$). Suppose one wishes to turn this straightline program into an equivalent arithmetic circuit *evaluation* instance $\mathcal{C}$. Since the gates of $\mathcal{C}$ can only compute addition and multiplication operations (not division), $\mathcal{C}$ would need to replace every division operation a/b with an explicit computation of the multiplicative inverse b^{-1} of b, where the computation of b^{-1} is only able to invoke addition and multiplication operations. This is expensive, leading to huge circuits. In contrast, to turn the straightline program into an equivalent circuit *satisfiability* instance, we can demand that the witness w contain a field element e for every division operation a/b where e should be set to b^{-1}. The circuit can "check" that $e = b^{-1}$ by adding an output gate that computes $e \cdot b - 1$. This output gate will equal 0 if and only if $e = b^{-1}$. In this manner, each division operation in the straightline program translates into only $O(1)$ additional gates and witness elements in the circuit satisfiability instance.

One may initially be worried that this techniques introduces a "checker" output gate for each division operation in the straightline program, and that consequently, if there are many division operations the prover will have to send a very long message to the verifier in order to inform the verifier of the claimed output vector y of $\mathcal{C}$. However, since any "correct" witness w causes these "checker" gates to evaluate to 0, their claimed values are implicitly 0. This means that the size of the prover's message specifying the claimed output vector y is independent of the number of "checker" output gates in $\mathcal{C}$.

6.5.2 Preview: How Do Succinct Arguments for Circuit Satisfiability Operate?

One way we could design an efficient IP for the claim that there exists a w such that $\mathcal{C}(x, w) = y$ is to have the prover send w to the verifier, and run the GKR protocol to efficiently check that $\mathcal{C}(x, w) = y$. This would be enough to convince the verifier that indeed the program outputs y on input (x, w). This approach works well if the witness w is small. But in the computer-program-to-circuit-satisfiability transformation that we're about to see, the witness w will be very large, of size roughly T, the runtime of the computer program. So even asking the verifier to read the claimed witness w is as expensive as asking the verifier to simply run the program herself without the help of a prover.

Fortunately, we will see in Section 7.3 that we can combine the GKR protocol with a cryptographic primitive called a *polynomial commitment scheme* to obtain an argument system that avoids having the prover send the entire witness w to the verifier. The high-level idea is as follows (see Section 7.3 for details).

In the IP for circuit satisfiability described two paragraphs above, it was essential that the prover sent the witness w at the start of the protocol, so that the prover was not able to base the choice of w on the random coin tosses of the verifier within the circuit evaluation IP to confirm that $C(x, w) = y$. Put another way, the point of sending w at the start of the protocol was that it *bound* the prover to a specific choice of w *before* the prover knew anything about the verifier's random coin tosses in the subsequent IP for circuit evaluation.

We can mimic the above, without the prover having to send w in full, using cryptographic commitment schemes. These are cryptographic protocols that have two phases: a commit phase, and a reveal phase. In a sense made precise momentarily, the commit phase binds the prover to a witness w without requiring the prover to send w in full. In the reveal phase, the verifier asks the prover to reveal certain entries of w. The required binding property is that, unless the prover can solve some computational task that is assumed to be intractable, then after executing the commit phase, there must be some fixed string w such that the prover is forced to answer all possible reveal-phase queries in a manner consistent with w. Put another way, the prover is not able to choose w in a manner that depends on the questions asked by the verifier in the reveal phase.

This means that to obtain a succinct argument for circuit satisfiability, one can first have the prover run the commit phase of a cryptographic commitment scheme to bind itself to the witness w, then run an IP or argument for circuit evaluation to establish that $C(x, w) = y$, and over the course of the protocol the verifier can force the prover as necessary to reveal any information about w that the verifier needs to know to perform its checks.

If the GKR protocol is used as the circuit evaluation protocol, what information does the verifier need to know about w to perform its checks? Recall that in order to run the GKR protocol on circuit C with input $u = (x, w)$, the only information about the input that the verifier needs to know is the evaluation of the multilinear extension $\tilde{u}$ of u at a random point. Moreover, this evaluation is only needed by the verifier at the very end of the protocol.

We explain in Section 7 that in order to quickly evaluate $\tilde{u}$ at any point, it is enough for the verifier to know the evaluation of the multilinear extension $\tilde{w}$ of w at a related point.

Hence, the cryptographic commitment scheme should bind the prover to the multilinear polynomial $\tilde{w}$, in the sense that in the reveal phase of the commitment scheme, the verifier can ask the prover to tell her $\tilde{w}(r)$ for any desired input r to w. The prover will respond with $\tilde{w}(r)$ and a small amount of "authentication information" that the verifier insists be included to enforce binding. The required binding property roughly ensures that when the verifier asks the prover to reveal $\tilde{w}(r)$, the prover will not be able to "change" its answer in a manner that depends on r.

To summarize the resulting argument system, after the prover commits to the multilinear polynomial $\tilde{w}$, the parties run the GKR protocol to check that $C(x, w) = y$. The verifier can happily run this protocol even though it does not know w, until the very end when the verifier has to evaluate $\tilde{u}$ at a single point. This requires the verifier to learn $\tilde{w}(r)$ for some point r. The verifier learns $\tilde{w}(r)$ from the prover, by having the prover decommit to $\tilde{w}$ at input r.

All told, this approach (combined with the Fiat-Shamir transformation, Section 5.2) will lead to a non-interactive argument system of knowledge for circuit satisfiability, i.e., for the claim that the prover knows a witness w such that $C(x, w) = y$. If a sufficiently efficient polynomial commitment scheme is used, the argument system is nearly optimal in the sense that the verifier runs in linear time in the size of the input x, and the prover runs in time close to the size of C.

6.5.3   The Transformation From Computer Programs To Arithmetic Circuit Satisfiability

Before describing the transformation, it is helpful to consider why the circuit generated in Method 1 of Section 6 (see Section 6.3) had at least $T \cdot s$ gates, which is significantly larger than T if s is large. The answer is that that circuit consisted of T "stages" where the ith stage computed each bit of the machine's configuration—which includes the entire contents of its main memory—after i machine instructions had been executed.

But each machine instruction affects the value of only $O(1)$ registers and memory cells, so between any two stages, almost all bits of the configuration remain unchanged. This means that almost all of the gates and wires in the circuit are simply devoted to copying bits from the configuration after i steps to the configuration after step $i + 1$. This is highly wasteful, and in order to obtain a circuit of size close to T, rather than $T \cdot s$, we will need to cut out all of this redundancy.

To describe the main idea in the transformation, it is helpful to introduce the notion of the *transcript* (sometimes also called a *trace*) of a Random Access Machine M's execution on input x. Roughly speaking, the transcript describes just the *changes* to M's configuration at each step of its execution. That is, for each step i that M takes, the transcript lists just the value of each register and the program counter at the end of step i. Since M has only $O(1)$ registers, the transcript can be specified using $O(T)$ words, where a *word* refers to a value that can be stored in a single register or memory cell.

The basic idea is that the transformation from RAM execution to circuit satisfiability produces a circuit satisfiability instance $(\mathcal{C}, x, y)$, where x is the input to M, y is the claimed output of M, and the witness w is supposed to be the transcript of M's execution of input x. The circuit $\mathcal{C}$ will simply check that w is indeed the transcript of M's execution on input x, and if this check passes, then $\mathcal{C}$ outputs the same value as M does according to the ending configuration in the transcript. If the check fails, $\mathcal{C}$ outputs a special rejection symbol.

A schematic of $\mathcal{C}$ is depicted in Figure 6.3.

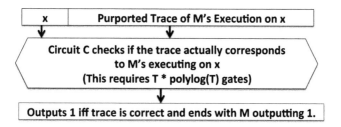

Figure 6.3: Sketch of the transformation From RAM execution on input x to an instance of circuit satisfiability.

6.5.4 Details of the Transformation

The circuit C takes an entire transcript of the entire execution of M on x as a non-deterministic input, where a transcript consists of (timestamp, list) pairs, one for each step taken by M. Here, a list specifies the bits contained in the current program counter and the values of all of M's registers. If a read or write operation occurs at the associated timestep of M's execution, the list also includes the memory location accessed and the value returned if a read operation occurs or written to memory if a write operation occurs. Timesteps at which no read or write operation occurs contain a special memory address indicating as much.

The circuit then checks that the transcript is valid. Details of the validity check follow.

Conceptually, one can think of a RAM running in time T as comprised of two independent pieces:

- The maintenance of its Main Memory, meaning correctly implementing all memory reads and writes. Each memory read should return the most recent value written to that memory cell.

- Assuming memory is maintained correctly, execute each of the T steps of the program. Each step of the program is simple, as it only affects the machine's registers, of which there are only a constant number, and performs at most one read or write operation to Main Memory.

Following the above conceptual partition of a RAM's operation, checking the validity of a purported transcript amounts to checking that it satisfies the following two properties.

- Memory consistency: whenever a value is read from a memory location, check that the value that the transcript claims is returned is equal to the last value written to that location.

- Time consistency: *assuming that memory consistency holds*, check that for each timestep $i \in \{1, \ldots, T-1\}$, the claimed state of the machine at time $i+1$ correctly follows from the machine's claimed state at time i.

The circuit checks time-consistency by representing the transition function of the RAM as a small sub-circuit. We provide some details of this representation in Section 6.5.4.1. It then applies this sub-circuit to each entry i of the transcript and checks that the output is equal to entry $i+1$ of the transcript. That is, for each time step i in $1, \ldots, T-1$, the circuit will have an output gate that will equal 0 if and only if entry $i+1$ of the transcript equals that application of the transition function to entry i of the transcript.

The circuit checks memory consistency by reordering the transcript entries based on the memory location read from or written to, with ties broken by time. That is, for each memory location, the read and write operations for that location appear in increasing order of timestamp. We refer to this reordering of the transcript as *memory ordering*. Transcript entries that do not perform either a memory read or write operation can be grouped together in any order and placed at the end of the reordered transcript–these entries will be ignored by the part of the circuit that checks memory consistency.

Given the memory-ordered transcript, it is straightforward for the circuit to check that every memory read from a given location returns the last value written to that location. For any two adjacent entries in the memory-ordered transcript, the circuit checks whether the associated memory locations are equal, and whether the latter entry contains a read operation. If so, it checks that the value returned by the read operation equals the value read or written in the preceding operation.

The sorting step is the most conceptually involved part of the construction of $\mathcal{C}$, and is discussed in Section 6.5.4.2. Note that all of the at most T time-consistency checks and memory-consistency checks can be done in parallel. As we will see, sorting can also be done in logarithmic depth. All together, this ensures that $\mathcal{C}$ has polylogarithmic depth.

6.5.4.1 *Representing Transition Functions of RAMs as Small Arithmetic Circuits*

Depending on the field over which the circuit $\mathcal{C}$ is defined, certain operations of the RAM are easy to compute inside $\mathcal{C}$ using a single gate. For example, if $\mathcal{C}$ is defined over a prime-order field $\mathbb{F}_p$ of order p, then this field naturally simulates integer addition and multiplication so long as one is guaranteed that the values arising in the computation always lie in the range $[-\lfloor p/2 \rfloor, \lfloor p/2 \rfloor].$[5] If the values grow outside of this range, then the field, by reducing all values modulo p, will no longer simulate integer arithmetic. In contrast, fields of characteristic 2 are not able to simulate integer addition or multiplication on numbers of magnitude 2^W without spending (at least) $\Omega(W)$ gates by operating on the bit-representations of the integers. On the other hand, if $\mathcal{C}$ is defined over a field of characteristic two, then addition of two field elements is equivalent to bitwise-XOR of the binary representations of the field operations. The message here is that integer arithmetic, but not bitwise operations, are simulated very directly over fields of large prime order (up to overflow issues), whereas bitwise operations, but not integer arithmetic, are simulated very directly over fields of characteristic 2.

In general, if a Random Access Machine has word size W then any primitive instruction other than memory accesses (e.g., integer arithmetic, bitwise operations, integer comparisons, etc.) can be implemented in a circuit-satisfiability instance using $\text{poly}(W)$ many gates. This works by representing each bit of each register with a separate field element, and implementing the instruction bitwise. To give some simple examples,

---

[5]If operating over unsigned integers rather than signed integers, the integer values arising in the computation may lie in the range $[0, p-1]$ rather than $[-\lfloor p/2 \rfloor, \lfloor p/2 \rfloor]$.

one can compute the bitwise-AND of two values $x, y \in \{0, 1\}^W$ with W multiplication gates over a large prime-order field, where the ith multiplication gate multiplies x_i by y_i. Bitwise-OR and Bitwise-XOR can be computed in a similar manner, replacing $x_i \cdot y_i$ with $x_i + y_i - x_i y_i$ and $x_i + y_i - 2x_i y_i$ respectively.

As a more complicated example, suppose the circuit is defined over a field $\mathbb{F}_p$ of large prime order. Let a and b be two field elements interpreted as integers in $\{0, 1, \ldots, p-1\}$, and suppose that one wishes to determine whether $a > b$. Let $\ell := \lceil \log_2 p \rceil$. The circuit can ensure that the witness contains 2ℓ bits $a_0, \ldots, a_{\ell-1}, b_1, \ldots, b_{\ell-1}$ representing the binary representations of a and b respectively as follows. First, to check that a_i is in $\{0, 1\}$ for all $i = 0, \ldots, \ell - 1$, the circuit can include an output gate computing $a_i^2 - a_i$. This gate will evaluate to 0 if and only if $a_i \in \{0, 1\}$. Second, to check that $(a_0, \ldots, a_{\ell-1})$ is indeed the binary representation of $a \in \mathbb{F}_p$, the circuit can include an output gate computing $a - \sum_{i=0}^{\ell} a_i 2^i$. Assuming each $a_i \in \{0, 1\}$, this output gate equals 0 if and only if $(a_0, \ldots, a_{\ell-1})$ is the binary representation of a_i. Analogous checks can be included in the circuit to ensure that $(b_0, \ldots, b_{\ell-1})$ is the binary representation of b.

Finally, the circuit can include an output gate computing an arithmetization of the Boolean circuit that checks bit-by-bit whether $a > b$. Specifically, for $j = \ell - 2, \ell - 3, \ldots, 1$, define

$$A_j := \prod_{j'>j} (a_{j'} b_{j'} + (1 - a_{j'})(1 - b_{j'}))$$

so that $A_j = 1$ if the $\ell - j$ high-order bits of a and b are equal. Then the following expression equals 1 if $a > b$ and 0 otherwise:

$$a_{\ell-1}(1 - b_{\ell-1}) + A_{\ell-2} a_{\ell-2}(1 - b_{\ell-2}) + \cdots + A_0 \cdot a_0 (1 - b_0).$$

It can be checked that the above expression (which can be computed by an arithmetic circuit of depth $O(\ell) = O(\log p)$ consisting of $O(\ell)$ gates) equals 1 if $a > b$ and 0 otherwise. Indeed, if $a_{\ell-1} = 1$ and $b_{\ell-1} = 0$, then the first term evaluates to 1 and all other terms evaluate to 0, while if $a_{\ell-1} = 0$ and $b_{\ell-1} = 1$, then all terms evaluate to 0. Otherwise, if $a_{\ell-2} = 1$ and $b_{\ell-2} = 0$, then the second term evaluates to 1 and all other terms evaluate to 0, while if $a_{\ell-2} = 0$ and $b_{\ell-2} = 1$ then all terms evaluate to 0. And so on.

There has been considerable effort devoted to developing techniques to more efficiently simulate non-arithmetic operations over fields of large prime order. Section 6.6.3 sketches an important result in this direction, due to Bootle *et al.* [68].

6.5.4.2 *How to Sort with a Non-Deterministic Circuit*

Recall that to check that a purported transcript for RAM M satisfies memory consistency, the transcript entries must be reordered so that they are grouped by the memory cell read from or written to, with ties broken by time. Below, we describe a method based on so-called *routing networks* that enable such reordering.

The use of routing networks to check memory consistency is conceptually involved, and typically yields larger circuits than simpler alternatives discussed in Section 6.6.1, which uses Merkle trees, and Section 6.6.2, which uses fingerprinting techniques originally introduced in Section 2.1. The reader may skip this section's discussion of routing networks with no loss of continuity.

We cover routing networks both for historical context, and because the alternative transformations do not actually yield a circuit C such that $M(x) = y$ if and only if there exists a w satisfying $C(x, w) = y$. The Merkle-trees approach yields a "computationally-sound" transformation. This means that even if $M(x) \neq y$, there will exist witnesses w such that $C(x, w) = y$, but such witnesses will be computationally infeasible to find—doing so will require finding collisions in a cryptographic hash function. Meanwhile, the fingerprinting techniques use a random field element $r \in \mathbb{F}$ to check memory-consistency. Even if $M(x) \neq y$, for any *fixed* r, it will be easy to find a witness w such that $C(x, w) = y$. Fingerprinting techniques are therefore only useful in settings where the prover can be forced to "choose" the witness w *before* a random r is selected. Fortunately, neither of the above issues with Merkle-hashing and fingerprinting turns out not to be an obstacle to using such techniques in SNARK design.

Routing Networks.   A routing network is a graph with a designated set of T source vertices and a designated set of T sink vertices (both sets of the same cardinality) satisfying the following property: for any perfect matching between sources and sinks (equivalently, for any desired sorting of the sources), there is a set of node-disjoint[6] paths that connects each source to the sink to which it is matched. Such a set of node-disjoint paths is called a *routing*. The specific routing network used in $\mathcal{C}$ is derived from a *De Bruijn* graph G. G consists of $\ell = O(\log T)$ layers, with T nodes at each layer. The first layer consists of the source vertices, and the last layer consists of the sinks. Each node at intermediate layers has exactly two in-neighbors and exactly two out-neighbors.

The precise definition of the De Bruijn graph G is not essential to the discussion here. What is important is that G satisfies the following two properties.

- Property 1: Given any desired sorting of the sources, a corresponding routing can be found in $O(|G|) = O(T \cdot \log T)$ time using known routing algorithms [31], [40], [180], [245].

- Property 2: The multilinear extension of the wiring predicate of G can be evaluated in polylogarithmic time. By wiring predicate of G, we mean the Boolean function (analogous to the functions add_i and mult_i in the GKR protocol) that takes as input the labels (a, b, c) of three nodes in G, and outputs 1 if and only if b and c are the in-neighbors of a in G.

  Roughly speaking, Property 2 holds because in a De Bruijn graph, the neighbors of a node with label v are obtained from v by simple bit shifts, which is a "degree-1 operation" in the following sense. The function that checks whether two binary labels are bit-shifts of each other is an AND of pairwise disjoint bit-equality checks. The direct arithmetization of such a function (replacing the AND gate with multiplication, and the bitwise equality checks with their multilinear extensions) is multilinear.

In a routing of G, each node v other than the source nodes has exactly one in-neighbor in the routing—we think of this in-neighbor as forwarding its packet to v—and each node v other than the sink nodes

---

[6]Two length-ℓ paths $u_1 \to u_2 \to \cdots \to u_\ell$ and $v_1 \to v_2 \to \cdots \to v_\ell$ are node-disjoint if there does not exist a pair $(i, j) \in [\ell] \times [\ell]$ such that $u_i = v_j$.

has exactly one out-neighbor in the routing. Thus, a routing in G can be specified by assigning each non-source node v a single bit b_v that specifies which of v's two in-neighbors in G is forwarding a packet to v.

To perform the sorting step, the circuit will take additional bits as non-deterministic input (i.e., as part of the witness w), called *routing bits*, which give the bit-wise specification of a routing as just described. To check memory consistency of a purported transcript, the circuit $\mathcal{C}$ sorts the (timestamp, list) pairs of the transcript into memory order by implementing the routing. This means that for each node v in G, $\mathcal{C}$ contains a "gadget" of logarithmically many gates. The gadget for v takes as input the two (timestamp, list) pairs and the routing bit b_v. Based on the routing bit, it outputs one of the two input pairs. In $\mathcal{C}$, the gadget for v is connected to the gadgets for its two in-neighbors in G. This ensures that the two inputs to v's gadget in $\mathcal{C}$ are the pairs output by v's two in-neighbors in G. One thinks of each (timestamp, list) pair of the transcript as a packet, and of v's gadget outputting a (timestamp, list) pair as v forwarding the packet it receives in the routing to the appropriate out-neighbor of v in G.

Putting Everything Together. For any RAM M running in time T, we have now sketched all of the components of a circuit $\mathcal{C}$ of size $O(T \cdot \text{polylog}(T))$ such that $M(x) = y \iff$ there exists a w satisfying $\mathcal{C}(x, w) = y$. The witness w specifies a purported transcript for M. $\mathcal{C}$ first checks the transcript for time consistency. It then uses a routing network to sort the transcript entries into memory order, meaning sorted by the memory location read from or written to, with ties broken by time. Any routing computes *some* reordering of the original transcript, and the circuit can check with $O(T \cdot \text{polylog} T)$ gates that the reordered transcript is indeed in the prescribed order—this amounts to interpreting the (memory location, timestamp) pair associated with each transcript entry as an integer, and performing one integer comparison for every adjacent pair, to confirm that they are sorted in increasing order (see Section 6.5.4.1 for details of how to implement integer comparisons in arithmetic circuits). Finally, given that the reordered transcript is in the prescribed order, the circuit can easily check that every memory read returns the last value written to that location.

Intuitively, when applying a succinct argument for circuit-satisfiability to $\mathcal{C}$, the verifier is forcing the prover not only to run the RAM M on input x, but also to produce a transcript of the execution and then *confirm* via the circuit $\mathcal{C}$ that the transcript contains no errors. Fortunately, it does not require much more work for the prover to produce the transcript and confirm its correctness then it does to run M on x in the first place.

The Wiring Predicates of $\mathcal{C}$. The circuit $\mathcal{C}$ has a very regular wiring structure, with lots of repeated structure. Specifically, its time-consistency-checking circuitry applies the same small sub-circuit (capturing the transition function of the RAM) independently to every two adjacent (timestep, list) pairs in the time-ordered transcript specified by the witness, and (after resorting the witness into memory order), the memory-consistency-checking circuitry also applies a small sub-circuit independently to adjacent (timestamp, list) pairs in the memory-ordered transcript to check that every memory read from a given location returns the last value written to that location. That is, the parts of the circuit devoted to both time-consistency and memory-consistency checking are data parallel in the sense of Section 4.6.7.

All told, it is possible to exploit this data parallel structure—and Property 2 of the routing network G above, which ensures that the sorting circuitry also has a nice, regular wiring structure—to show that (a slight modification of) the multilinear extensions $\widetilde{\text{add}}_i$ and $\widetilde{\text{mult}}_i$ of $\mathcal{C}$ can be evaluated in polylogarithmic time.

This ensures that if one applies the GKR protocol (in combination with a commitment scheme as described in Section 6.5.2) that the verifier can run in time $O(n + \text{polylog}(T))$, without ever having to explicitly enumerate over all gates of $\mathcal{C}$. Moreover, the prover can generate the entire circuit $\mathcal{C}$ and the witness w, and perform its part of the GKR protocol applied to $\mathcal{C}(x, w)$ in time $O(T \cdot \text{polylog}(T))$.

6.6 Alternative Transformations and Optimizations

The previous section gave a way to turn any RAM M with runtime T into a circuit $\mathcal{C}$ of size $\tilde{O}(T)$ such that the output of M on input

x equals y if and only if there exists a w such that $\mathcal{C}(x, w) = y$. In this section, we relax this requirement on $\mathcal{C}$ in one of two ways. First, in Section 6.6.1 we permit there to be values $y \neq M(x)$ such that there exists a w satisfying $\mathcal{C}(x, w) = y$, but we insist that if there is a polynomial-time prover capable of *finding* a w satisfying $\mathcal{C}(x, w) = y'$, then $y = M(x)$. Satisfying this requirement is still sufficient to ultimately obtain argument systems for RAM execution, by applying an argument system for circuit satisfiability to $\mathcal{C}$.[7] Second, in Section 6.6.2, we permit prover and verifier to interact while performing the transformation from M into $\mathcal{C}$—the interaction can then be removed via the Fiat-Shamir transformation.

In both of these settings, we avoid the use of routing networks in the construction of $\mathcal{C}$. This is desirable because routing networks lead to noticeable concrete and asymptotic overheads in circuit size—routing T items requires a routing network of size $\Omega(T \log T)$, which is superlinear in T.

6.6.1 Ensuring Memory Consistency via Merkle Trees

The point of using routing networks in $\mathcal{C}$ was to ensure memory consistency of the execution trace specified by the witness. An alternative technique for ensuring memory consistency is to use Merkle trees, which are covered later in this survey in Section 7.3.2.2. Roughly speaking, the idea is that $\mathcal{C}$ will insist that every memory read in the transcript is immediately followed by "authentication information" that a polynomial-time prover is only capable of producing if the value returned by the memory read is in fact the last value written to that memory location.[8],[9] This leads to a circuit $\mathcal{C}$ such that the only *computationally tractable* method

---

[7]More precisely, the argument system must be an argument of knowledge. See Section 7.4 for details.

[8]Each write operation must also be accompanied by authentication information to enable appropriately updating the Merkle tree. We omit details for brevity.

[9]A Merkle tree is an example of a cryptographic object called an *accumulator*, which is simply a commitment to a set that furthermore supports succinct proofs of membership in the set. In this section, the relevant set is the (memory location, value) pairs comprising the RAM's memory at a given step of the RAM's execution during which a memory read occurs. In some applications, there can be concrete efficiency advantages to using accumulators other than Merkle trees [200].

of finding a satisfying assignment w for C is to provide an execution trace that indeed satisfies memory consistency. That is, while there will *exist* satisfying assignments w for C that do not satisfy memory consistency, finding such assignments w would require identifying collisions in a collision-resistant family of hash functions. This technique can lead to very large circuits if there are many memory operations, because each memory operation must be followed by a full authentication path in the Merkle tree, which consists a sequence of cryptographic hash evaluations (the number of hash evaluations is logarithmic in the size of the memory). All of these hash values must be included in the witness w, and the circuit C must check that the hash evaluations are computed correctly, which requires the cryptographic hash function to be repeatedly evaluated inside C. Cryptographic hash evaluations can require many gates to implement in an arithmetic circuit. For this and related reasons, there have been significant efforts to identify collision-resistant hash functions that are "SNARK-friendly" in the sense that they can implemented inside arithmetic circuits using few gates [4], [6], [47], [138], [153], [171], [173]. For machines M that perform relatively few memory operations, Merkle trees built with such SNARK-friendly hash functions can be a cost-effective technique for checking memory consistency.

6.6.2 Ensuring Memory Consistency via Fingerprinting

Another technique for checking memory consistency is to use simple fingerprinting-based memory checking techniques (recall that we discussed Reed-Solomon fingerprinting in Section 2.1). The circuit C resulting from this procedure implements a *randomized* algorithm, in the following sense. In addition to public input x and witness w, C takes a third input $r \in \mathbb{F}$ and the guarantee is the following: for any pair x, y,

- if $M(x) = y$ then there exists a w such that for every $r \in \mathbb{F}$ such that $C(x, w, r) = 1$. Moreover, such a w can be easily derived by any prover running M on input x.

- if $M(x) \neq y$, then for *every* w, the probability over a randomly chosen $r \in \mathbb{F}$ that $C(x, w, r) = 1$ is at most $\tilde{O}(T)/|\mathbb{F}|$.

An important aspect of this transformation to be aware of is that, for any known r, it is easy for a cheating prover to find a w such that $C(x, w, r) = y$. However, if r is chosen at random from $\mathbb{F}$ independently of w (say, because the prover commits to w and only then is public randomness used to select r), then learning that $C(x, w, r) = y$ does give very high confidence that in fact $M(x) = y$. This is sufficient to combine the transformation described below with the approach described in Section 6.5.2 to obtain a succinct argument for proving that $M(x) = y$. Indeed, after the prover commits to w (or more precisely to the multilinear extension $\tilde{w}$ of w, using a polynomial commitment scheme), the verifier can then select r at random, and the prover can then run the GKR protocol to convince the verifier that $C(x, w, r) = 1$. The resulting interactive protocol is public coin, so the interaction can be removed using the Fiat-Shamir transformation.

The idea of the randomized fingerprinting-based memory-consistency-checking procedure implemented within the circuit C is the following. As we explain shortly, by tweaking the behavior of the machine M (without increasing its runtime by more than a constant factor) it is possible to ensure the following key property holds: a time-consistent transcript for M is also memory consistent if and only if the multiset of (memory location, value) pairs written from memory equals the multiset of (memory location, value) pairs read from memory. This property turns the problem of checking memory consistency into the problem of checking whether two multisets are equal—equivalently, checking whether two lists of (memory location, value) pairs are permutations of each other—and the latter can be solved with fingerprinting techniques.

We now explain how to tweak the behavior of M so as to ensure the problem of checking memory-consistency amounts to checking equality of two multisets, and then explain how to use fingerprinting to solve this latter task.

Reducing memory-consistency-checking to multiset equality checking. Here is how to tweak M to ensure that any time-consistent transcript for M is memory-consistent if and only if the multisets of (memory location, value) pairs written vs. read from memory are identical. This technique dates to work of Blum *et al.* [59] who referred to it as an *offline memory checking* procedure. At the start of the computation (time step 0), we have M initialize memory by writing an arbitrary value to each memory location, without preceding these initialization-writes with reads. After this initialization phase, suppose that we insist that every time the machine M writes a value to a memory location, it precedes the write with a read operation from the same location (the result of which is simply ignored by M), and every time M reads a value from a memory location, it follows the read with a write operation (writing the same value that was just read). Moreover, let us insist that every time a value is written to memory, M includes in the value the current timestamp. Finally, just before M terminates, it makes a linear reading scan over every memory location. Unlike all other memory reads by M, the reads during this scan are *not* followed with a matching write operation. M also halts and outputs "reject" if a read ever returns a timestamp greater than current timestamp.

With these modifications, if M does not output "reject" then the set of (memory location, value) pairs returned by all the read operations equals the set of (memory location, value) pairs written during all the write operations if and only if every write operation returns the value that was last written to that location. Clearly these tweaks only increase M's runtime by a constant factor, as the tweak turns each read operation and each write operation of M into both a read and a write operation.

Multiset equality checking (a.k.a. permutation checking) via fingerprinting. Recall that in Section 2.1 we gave a probabilistic procedure called Reed-Solomon fingerprinting for determining whether two vectors a and b are equal entry-by-entry: a is interpreted as specifying the coefficients of a polynomial $p_a(x) = \sum_{i=1}^{n} a_i x^i$ over field $\mathbb{F}$, and similarly for b, and the equality-checking procedure picks a random $r \in \mathbb{F}$ and checks whether $p_a(r) = p_b(r)$. The guarantee of this procedure is that if $a = b$ entry-by-entry, then the equality holds for every possible choice of r, while if a and b disagree in even a single entry i (i.e., $a_i \neq b_i$), then with probability at least $1 - n/|\mathbb{F}|$ over the random choice of r, the equality fails to hold.

To perform memory-checking, we do not want to check equality of vectors, but rather of multisets, and this requires us to tweak to the fingerprinting procedure from Section 2.1. That is, the above reduction from memory-consistency-checking to multiset equality checking produced two lists of (memory location, value) pairs, and we need to determine whether the two lists specify the same *set* of pairs, i.e., whether they are permutations of each other. This is different than determining whether the lists agree entry-by-entry.

To this end, let us interpret each (memory location, value) pair as a field element, via any arbitrary injection of (memory location, value) pairs to $\mathbb{F}$. This does require the field size $|\mathbb{F}|$ to be at least as large as the number of possible (memory location, value) pairs. For example, if the memory has size, say, 2^{64}, and values consist of 64 bits, it is sufficient for $|\mathbb{F}|$ to be at least 2^{128}. Under this interpretation, we can think of our task as follows. We are given two length-m lists of field elements $a = (a_1, \dots, a_m)$ and $b = (b_1, \dots, b_m)$, where m is the number of read and write operations performed by the machine M. We want to determine whether the lists a and b are permutations of each other, i.e., whether for every possible field element $z \in \mathbb{F}$, the number of times z appears in list a equals the number of times that z appears in list b.

Here is a randomized algorithm that accomplishes this task. Interpret a as a polynomial p_a whose roots are $a_1, \dots, a_m$ (with multiplicity), i.e., define

$$p_a(x) := \prod_{i=1}^{m} (a_i - x),$$

and similarly

$$p_b(x) := \prod_{i=1}^{m} (b_i - x).$$

Now evaluate both p_a and p_b at the same randomly chosen input $r \in \mathbb{F}$, and output 1 if and only if the evaluations are equal. Clearly p_a and p_b are the same polynomial if and only if a and b are permutations of each other. Hence, this randomized algorithm satisfies:

- if a and b are permutations of each other then this algorithm outputs 1 with probability 1.

- if a and b are not permutations of each other, then this algorithm outputs 1 with probability at most $m/|\mathbb{F}|$. This is because p_a and p_b are distinct polynomials of degree at most m and hence can agree at at most m inputs (Fact 2.1).

We can think of $p_a(r)$ and $p_b(r)$ as fingerprints of the lists a and b that captures "frequency information" about a and b (i.e., how many times each field element z appears in the two lists), but deliberately ignores the order in which A and B are presented. A key aspect of this fingerprinting procedure is that it lends itself to highly efficient implementation within arithmetic circuits. That is, given as input lists A and B of field elements, along with a field element $r \in \mathbb{F}$, an arithmetic circuit can easily evaluate $p_a(r)$ and $p_b(r)$. For example, computing $p_a(r)$ amounts to subtracting r from each input $a_i \in a$, and then computing the product of the results via a binary tree of multiplication gates. This requires only $O(m)$ gates and logarithmic depth. Hence, this randomized algorithm for permutation checking can be efficiently implemented within the arithmetic circuit $\mathcal{C}$.

Historical Notes and Optimizations. Techniques for memory-consistency-checking closely related to those described above were given in [259] and also exploited in subsequent work [172]. Specifically, [259] checks memory consistency of an execution trace for a RAM within a circuit by exploiting permutation-invariant fingerprinting to check that claimed time-ordered and memory-ordered descriptions of the execution trace are permutations of each other. While the fingerprints can be computed within the circuit with $O(T)$ gates, this does not reduce total circuit size or prover runtime below $O(T \log T)$.[10] This holds for two reasons. First, to compute a satisfying assignment for the circuit constructed in [259], the prover must sort the transcript based on memory location, and this takes $O(T \log T)$ time. Second, there is still a need for the circuit to implement comparison operations on timestamps associated with each memory operation, and [259] uses $\Theta(\log T)$

---

[10][259] asserts a prover running in time $O(T)$, but this assertion hides a factor that is linear in the word length of the RAM. [259] considers this to be a constant such as 32 or 64, but in general this word length must be $\Omega(\log T)$ to write down timestamps and index into memory, if the memory has size $\Omega(T)$.

many gates to implement each comparison operation bit-wise inside the circuit-satisfiability instance (see the final paragraph of Section 6.5.4.1).

Both sources of overhead just described were addressed in two works [68], [226]. Setty [226] observes that (as described above in this section), the need for the prover to sort the transcript based on memory location can be avoided by modifying the RAM as per the offline memory checking technique of Blum *et al.* [59]. This does not in general avoid the need to perform comparison operations on timestamps inside the circuit, because the modified RAM constructed by Blum *et al.* [59] requires checking that the timestamp returned by every read operation is smaller than the timestamp at which the read operation occurs. However, there are contexts in which such comparison operations are not necessary (see, e.g., Section 16.2), and this implies $O(T)$-sized circuits in such contexts.[11] Even outside such contexts, work of Bootle *et al.* [68] (which we sketch in Section 6.6.3 below) give a technique for reducing the *amortized* gate-complexity of performing many integer comparison operations inside a circuit over a field prime order. Specifically, they shows how to perform $O(T)$ comparison operations on integers of magnitude $\text{poly}(T)$ using $O(T)$ gates in arithmetic circuits over any prime-order field $\mathbb{F}_p$ of size at least T.[12] In summary, both sources of "superlinearity" in the size of the memory-consistency-checking circuit and prover runtime can be removed using the techniques of [68], [226], reducing both circuit size and prover runtime to $O(T)$.

Setty [226] and Campanelli *et al.* [87] observe that this fingerprinting procedure can be verified efficiently using optimized variants of succinct arguments derived from the GKR protocol [237], [244], because $p_A(r)$ can be computed via a small, low-depth arithmetic circuit with a regular wiring pattern, that simply subtracts r from each input and multiplies the results via a binary tree of multiplication gates. This ensures that

---

[11]Specifically, if the memory access pattern of the RAM is independent of the input, then the use of timestamps and the need to perform comparisons on them can be eliminated using a pre-processing phase requiring time $O(T)$. See Section 16.2 for details.

[12]The techniques of [68] build on permutation-invariant fingerprinting, and hence are interactive.

the circuit-satisfiability instances resulting from the transformation above can be efficiently verified via such arguments.

Additional Applications of Fingerprinting-based Permutation Checking. The above fingerprinting procedure for checking whether two vectors are permutations of each other has a long history in algorithms and verifiable computing and has been rediscovered many times. It was introduced by Lipton [183] as a hash function that is invariant to permutations of the input, and later applied in the context of interactive and non-interactive proofs with small-space streaming verifiers [92], [184], [220].

Permutation-invariant fingerprinting techniques were also applied to give zero-knowledge arguments that two encrypted vectors are permutations of each other [24], [140], [144], [198]. Such zero-knowledge arguments are also called shuffle arguments, and are directly applicable to construct an anonymous routing primitive called a mix network, a concept introduced by Chaum [94]. The ideas in these works were in turn built upon to yield SNARKs for circuit satisfiability with proofs that consist of a constant number of field or group elements [66], [123], [187]. Roughly speaking, these works use variants of permutation checking to ensure that a purported circuit transcript assigns consistant values to all output wires of each gate, i.e., to confirm that the transcript respects the wiring pattern of the circuit. Other uses of permutation-invariant fingerprinting in the context of zero-knowledge proofs were given in [229].[13]

Additional Discussion. We remark that there are other permutation-invariant fingerprinting algorithms that do *not* lend themselves to efficient implementation within arithmetic circuits, and hence are not useful for transforming an instance of RAM execution to an instance

---

[13] [229], like earlier work [101], uses a collision-resistant permutation-invariant hash function to check multiset equality, rather than the simple (non-collision-resistant) permutation-invariant fingerprinting function described in this section. Such hash functions are secure against polynomial time cheating provers even when the prover knows the hash function being used in the permutation-checking procedure and can choose the inputs to the procedure.

of arithmetic circuit satisfiability. An instructive example is as follows. Let $\mathbb{F}$ be a field of prime order, and suppose that it is known that all entries of the lists a and b are positive integers with magnitude at most B, where $B \ll |\mathbb{F}|$. Then we can define the polynomial $q_a(x)$ over $\mathbb{F}$ via

$$q_a(x) := \sum_{i=1}^{m} x^{a_i},$$

and similarly

$$q_b(x) := \sum_{i=1}^{m} x^{b_i}.$$

Clearly q_a and q_b are polynomials of degree at most B, and they satisfy properties analogous to p_a and p_b, namely:

- if a and b are permutations of each other then $q_a(r) = q_b(r)$ with probability 1 over a random choice $r \in \mathbb{F}$.

- if a and b are not permutations of each other, then $q_a(r) = q_b(r)$ with probability at most $B/|\mathbb{F}| \ll 1$. This is because q_a and q_b are distinct polynomials of degree at most B and hence can agree at at most B inputs (Fact 2.1).

However, given as input the entries of a and b, interpreted as field elements in $\mathbb{F}$, an arithmetic circuit cannot efficiently evaluate $q_a(r)$ or $q_b(r)$, as this would require raising r to the power of input entries, which is not a low-degree operation.

6.6.3 Efficiently Representing Non-Arithmetic Operations Over Large Prime-Order Fields

Recall from Section 6.5.4.1 that when operating over a field of large prime order p, it is convenient to interpret field elements as integers in $[0, p-1]$ or $[-\lfloor p/2 \rfloor, \lfloor p/2 \rfloor]$, as then integer addition and multiplication corresponds directly to field addition and multiplication, up to overflow issues. This means (again, ignoring overflow issues) integer addition and multiplication operations can be implemented with a *single* gate in the corresponding circuit satisfiability instance.

Non-arithmetic operations on integer values are more challenging to implement inside an arithmetic circuit. Section 6.5.4.1 described a straightforward approach, which broke field elements into their binary representation, and computed the non-arithmetic operations by operating over these bits. The reason that this bit-decomposition approach is expensive is that it transforms an integer (which for a Random Access Machine M is a primitive data type, consuming just one machine register) into at least $\log_2 p$ field elements, and hence at least $\log_2 p$ gates. In practice, $\log_2 p$ might be roughly 128 or 256, which is a very large constant. In theory, since we would like to be able to represent timestamps via a single field element, we typically think of $\log_2 p$ as at least $\Omega(\log T)$, and hence superconstant. From either perspective, turning a single machine operation such as integer comparison into (at least) 256 gates is painfully expensive.

Ideally, we would like to replace the $\Omega(\log p)$ cost of the bit-decomposition approach to implementing these operations inside a circuit with a constant independent of p. Bootle *et al.* [68] develop techniques for achieving this in an amortized sense. That is, they showed how to simulate non-arithmetic operations over integers (e.g., integer comparisons, range queries, bit-wise operations, etc.) by arithmetic circuit-satisfiability instances working over a field of large prime order. Before providing details, here is the rough idea. The bit-decomposition approach represents integers in base-b for $b = 2$, and this means that logarithmically many field elements are required to represent a single integer. The convenient feature about using base-2 was that it was easy to check that a list of field elements represented a valid base-2 representation; in particular, that every field element in the list was either 0 or 1. This is because the low-degree expression $x \mapsto x^2 - x$ equals 0 if and only if x is in $\{0, 1\}$. Instead, Bootle *et al.* represent integers $y \in [0, 2^W]$ in a far larger base, namely base $b = 2^{W/c}$ for some specified integer constant $c > 1$. This has the benefit that y is represented via only c field elements, rather than W field elements. However, working over such a large base b means that there is no longer a degree-2 polynomial $q(x)$ that evaluates to 0 if and only if x is in $\{0, 1, \ldots, b-1\}$—the lowest-degree polynomial q with this property has degree b. Bootle *et al.* work around this issue by turning the task of checking whether a field element x is in the set $\{0, 1, \ldots, b-1\}$ into a *table lookup*, and then giving an efficient procedure for performing such lookups inside an arithmetic circuit satisfiability instance. That is, conceptually, they have the circuit initialize a table containing the values $\{0, 1, \ldots, b-1\}$, and then have the witness include a proof that all values appearing in the base-b decomposition of any integer y arising in the computation reside in the table. As we will see, the number of gates required to initialize the table and specify and check the requisite lookup proof is roughly $\tilde{O}(b)$, so a key point is that c will be chosen to be a large enough constant so that b is smaller than the runtime T of the Random Access Machine M whose execution the circuit is simulating. This ensures constant *amortized* cost of all the $O(T)$ decomposition operations that the circuit has to perform. Details follow.

Let 2^W be a bound on the magnitude of integers involved in each non-arithmetic operation (assume 2^W is significantly smaller than the size of the prime order field over which the circuits we generate will be defined), and let T be an upper bound on the number of operations to be simulated. In the context of Section 6.6.2, T is a bound on the runtime of the Random Access Machine, and W is the word-size. This is because, if a register of the RAM contains W bits, then the RAM is incapable of representing integers larger than 2^W without resorting to approximate arithmetic. In this context, one would need to choose W at least as large as $\log_2 T$ to ensure that a timestamp can be stored in one machine word.

As sketched above, Bootle *et al.* effectively reduces each non-arithmetic operation to a lookup into a table of size $2^{W/c}$, where $c \geq 1$ is any integer parameter. For example, if $W = \ell \log_2 T$ for some constant $\ell \geq 1$, then setting $c = \ell/4$ ensures that the lookup table has size at most $T^{1/4}$. The lookup table is initialized to contain a certain set of $2^{W/c}$ pre-determined values (i.e., the values are independent of the input to the computation). In the technique of [68], the length of the witness w of $\mathcal{C}$ grows linearly in c. This is because, in order to keep the table to size $2^{W/c}$, each W-bit word of memory is represented via c field elements. That is, each W-bit word is broken into c blocks of length W/c, ensuring that each block can only take on $2^{W/c}$ possible values. This means that if a transcript for a time-T computation consists of, say, $k \cdot T$ words of memory—because each time step of the transcript requires specifying k register values—the transcript will be represented by $k \cdot c \cdot T$ field elements in the witness for $\mathcal{C}$.

Before describing the reduction of Bootle *et al.* from non-arithmetic operations to lookups in a pre-determined table, we explain how to efficiently verify a long sequence of lookup operations.

Checking many lookup operations efficiently. Bootle *et al.* develop a technique for checking that many values all reside in the lookup table. The technique builds on the permutation-invariant fingerprinting function of Section 6.6.2. Specifically, to show that a sequence of values $\{f_1, \ldots, f_N\}$ only contains elements from a lookup table containing values $\{s_1, \ldots, s_B\}$ where $B \leq 2^{W/c}$ is the size of the lookup table, it is enough to show that there are non-negative integers $e_1, \ldots, e_B$ such that the polynomials $h(X) := \prod_{i=1}^{N}(X - f_i)$ and $q(X) := \prod_{i=1}^{B}(X - s_i)^{e_i}$ are the same polynomial. To establish this, the witness will specify the bit-representation of the exponents $e_1, \ldots, e_B$ (each $e_i \in \{0,1\}^{\log_2 N}$), and the circuit confirms that $h(r) = q(r)$ for an $r \in \mathbb{F}_p$ randomly chosen by the verifier after the prover commits to the witness. As usual, Fact 2.1 implies that if this check passes then up to soundness error N/p, h and q are the same polynomial. A crucial fact that enables the circuit to efficiently implement this check is that $q(r)$ can be computed by an arithmetic circuit using $O(B \log(N))$ gates, as

$$\prod_{i=1}^{B} \prod_{j=1}^{\log_2 N} (r - s_i)^{2^j \cdot e_{i,j}}.$$

In summary, this lookup table technique permits Bootle *et al.* to implement a sequence of $O(N)$ non-arithmetic operations inside an arithmetic circuit-satisfiability instance using just $O(N + B \log N)$ gates. So long as $N = O(T)$ and $B = 2^{W/c} \leq N/\log N$, this is $O(T)$ operations in total.

Gabizon and Williamson [122] describe a variant transformation they call *plookup* that reduces the number of gates to $O(N)$, which is an improvement by a logarithmic factor if $B = \Theta(N)$. To give an idea of how *plookup* works, we sketch a simplified variant due to Cairo that works under two assumptions: first, that each value s_i appearing in the lookup table appears at least once in the sequence $\{f_1, \ldots, f_N\}$, and second that that the elements $\{s_1, \ldots, s_B\}$ cover a contiguous interval such as $\{1, 2, \ldots, B\}$, i.e., $s_i = s_1 + i - 1$ for all $i = 1, \ldots, B$.

Under these assumptions, the witness can simply consist of a sequence $\{w_1, \ldots, w_N\}$ of field elements claimed to equal $\{f_1, \ldots, f_N\}$ in sorted order, i.e., such that:

- $\{w_1, \ldots, w_N\}$ is a permutation of $\{f_1, \ldots, f_N\}$.

- When $w_1, \ldots, w_N$ are interpreted as integers,

$$s_1 = w_1 \leq w_2 \leq \ldots \leq w_N = s_B. \tag{6.1}$$

The circuit can apply permutation-invariant fingerprinting to confirm (with overwhelming probability) that the first bullet point above holds. To confirm that Equation (6.1) holds, the circuit checks that the following equalities hold:

- $w_1 = s_1$.

- $w_N = s_B$.

- For each $i = 2, \ldots, N$, $(w_i - w_{i-1}) \cdot (w_i - (w_{i-1} + 1)) = 0$.

Here, the constraints captured in the final bullet point ensure that as i ranges from 1 up to N, the w_i values start at s_1 and proceed to s_B in a non-decreasing manner. Under the two assumptions made above, this is equivalent to checking that for each $i > 1$, either $w_i = w_{i-1}$ or $w_i = w_{i-1} + 1$, which is exactly what is captured by the quadratic constraint in the final bullet point.

Reducing non-arithmetic operations to lookups. To give a sense of the main ideas of the reduction of [68], we sketch the reduction in the context of two specific non-arithmetic operations: range proofs and integer comparisons.

For simplicity, let us assume that $c = 2$. To confirm that a field element v is in the range $[0, 2^W]$, one can have the witness specify v's unique representation as a pair of field elements (a, b) such that $v = 2^{W/2} \cdot a + b$ and $a, b \in \{0, \ldots, 2^{W/2} - 1\}$. The circuit then just checks that indeed $v = 2^{W/2} \cdot a + b$ and that a and b both reside in a lookup table of size $2^{W/2}$ initialized to store all field elements y between 0 and $2^{W/2} - 1$.

As another example, doing an integer comparison reduces to a range proof. Indeed, to prove that $a > c$ when a and c are guaranteed to be in $[0, 2^W]$, it is enough to show that the difference $a - c$ is positive, which is a range proof described above, albeit under the weaker guarantee that the input $v = a - c$ to the range proof is in $[-2^W, 2^W]$ rather than $[0, 2^W]$.

6.6.4   CPU-Like vs. ASIC-Like Program-to-Circuit Transformations

This section described frontends that produce circuit-satisfiability instances that essentially execute step-by-step some simple CPU. The idea is that frontend designers will specify a set of "primitive operations" (also known as an *instruction set*) analogous to assembly instructions for real computer processors. Developers who want to use the frontend will either write "witness-checking programs" directly in the assembly language or else in some higher-level language, and have their programs automatically compiled into assembly code and then transformed into an equivalent circuit-satisfiability instance by the front-end.

At the time of writing, several prominent projects are taking this CPU-oriented approach to front-end design. For example, StarkWare's Cairo [128] is a very limited assembly language in which assembly instructions roughly permit addition and multiplication over a finite field, function calls, and reads and writes to an immutable (i.e., write-once) memory. The Cairo CPU is a von Neumann architecture, meaning that the circuits produced by the frontend essentially take a Cairo program as public input and "run" the program on the witness. The Cairo language is Turing Complete—despite its limited instruction set, it can simulate more standard architectures, although doing so may be expensive. Another example project is called RISC-Zero.[14] which targets a CPU called the so-called *RISC-V architecture*,[15] an open-source architecture with a rich software ecosystem that is growing in popularity.

---

[14]https://github.com/risc0/risc0.
[15]https://riscv.org/.

For sufficiently simple instruction sets, the front-end techniques described in this section produce circuits over fields of large prime order, with $O(T)$ gates, where T is the runtime of the CPU whose execution we wish to verify. This is clearly optimal up to a constant factor. Moreover, it is possible to ensure that the wiring of the circuit is sufficiently regular that the verifier in argument systems derived from (for example) the GKR protocol can run in time polylogarithmic in T, i.e., the verifier need not materialize the entire circuit itself. However, these transformations can still be expensive in practice.

"CPU emulator" projects such as RISC-Zero and Cairo produce a single circuit that can handle all programs in the associated assembly language. Alternative approaches are "ASIC-like," producing different circuits for different programs [79], [243], [259]. This ASIC-like approach can yield smaller circuits for some programs, especially when the assembly instruction that the program executes at each timestep does not depend on the program's input. For example, it can potentially avoid frontend overhead entirely for straight-line programs such as naive matrix multiplication (Figure 6.1). But the ASIC approach may be limited; for example, at the time of writing, it's not known how to use it to support loops without predetermined iteration bounds. It seems likely that additional progress will be made to improve the generality of ASIC-like approaches, as well as the efficiency of CPU emulator approaches.

6.7 Exercises

Exercise 6.1. Describe a layered arithmetic circuit of fan-in three that takes as input a matrix $A \in \{0, 1\}^{n \times n}$, interprets A as the adjacency matrix of a graph G, and outputs the number of triangles in G. You may assume that n is a power of three.

Exercise 6.2. Describe a layered arithmetic circuit of fan-in two that, given as input an $n \times n$ matrix A with entries from some field $\mathbb{F}$, computes $\sum_{i,j,k,\ell \in \{1,\dots,n\}} A_{i,j} \cdot A_{k,\ell}$. The smaller your circuit is, the better.

Exercise 6.3. Fix an integer $k > 0$. Assume that k is a power 2 and let $p > k$ be a large prime number. Describe an arithmetic circuit of fan-in 2 that takes as input n elements of the field $\mathbb{F}_p$, $a_1, a_2, \ldots, a_n$, and outputs the n field elements $a_1^k, a_2^k, \ldots, a_n^k$.

What is the verifier's asymptotic runtime when the GKR protocol is applied to this circuit (express your answer in terms of k and n)? Would the verifier be interested in using this protocol if n is very small (say, if $n = 1$)? What if n is very large?

Exercise 6.4. Let $p > 2$ be prime. Draw an arithmetic circuit $\mathcal{C}$ over $\mathbb{F}_p$ that takes as input one field element $b \in \mathbb{F}_p$ and evaluates to 0 if and only if $b \in \{0, 1\}$.

Exercise 6.5. Let $p = 11$. Draw an arithmetic circuit $\mathcal{C}$ over $\mathbb{F}_p$ that takes as input one field element a followed by four field elements b_0, b_1, b_2, b_3, and such that all output gates of $\mathcal{C}$ evaluate to 0 if and only if (b_0, b_1, b_2, b_3) is the binary representation of a. That is, $b_i \in \{0, 1\}$ for $i = 1, \ldots, 4$, and $a = \sum_{i=0}^{3} b_i \cdot 2^i$.

Exercise 6.6. Let $p = 11$. Let $x = (a, b)$ consist of two elements of the field $\mathbb{F}_p$. Draw an arithmetic circuit satisfiability instance that is equivalent to the conditional $a \geq b$. That is, interpreting a and b as integers in $\{0, 1, \ldots, p - 1\}$, the following two properties should hold:

- $a \geq b \Longrightarrow$ there exists a witness w such that evaluating $\mathcal{C}$ on input (x, w) produces the all-zeros output.

- $a < b \Longrightarrow$ there does not exist a witness w such that evaluating $\mathcal{C}$ on input (x, w) produces the all-zeros output.

Additional Exercises. The interested reader can find a sequence of additional exercises on front ends at https://www.pepper-project.org/tutorials/t3-biu-mw.pdf. These exercises discuss transforming computer programs into equivalent R1CS-satisfiability instances, a generalization of arithmetic circuit-satisfiability that we discuss further in Section 8.4.

7

A First Succinct Argument for Circuit Satisfiability, from Interactive Proofs

Arguments for Circuit-SAT. Recall from Section 6.5.1 that in the arithmetic circuit *satisfiability* problem, a designated circuit C takes two inputs, x and w. The first input x is public and fixed, i.e., known to both the prover and verifier. The second input w is often called the *witness*, or sometimes the *non-deterministic input* or *auxiliary input*. Given the first input x and output(s) y, the prover in an argument system for circuit-satisfiability wishes to establish that *there exists* a witness w such that $C(x, w) = y$.

In Section 6.5 we saw an efficient way to turn any computer program into an equivalent instance of the arithmetic circuit satisfiability problem. Roughly, we showed that the problem of checking whether a Random Access Machine M taking at most T steps on an input of size x produces output y can be reduced to a circuit satisfiability instance (C, x, y), where C has size close to T and depth close to $O(\log T)$. That is, M outputs y on x if and only if there exists a w such that $C(x, w) = y$.

This transformation is only useful in the context of interactive proofs and arguments if we can design efficient proof systems for solving instances of circuit satisfiability. In this section, we will see our first example of such an argument system, by combining the GKR protocol with a cryptographic primitive called a *polynomial commitment scheme*, in a manner that was already outlined in detail in Section 6.5.2. The polynomial commitment scheme we describe in this section is conceptually appealing but highly impractical; more practical polynomial commitment schemes will be covered later in this monograph.

Specifically, the polynomial commitment scheme in this section combines a technique called Merkle-hashing with a protocol called a *low-degree test*. Low-degree tests themselves tend to be very simple protocols, though the analysis showing that they work is very complicated and omitted from this survey. More practical commitments that we will see in Section 10 replace the low-degree test with more efficient interactive variants—the interaction can then be removed via the Fiat-Shamir transformation. Other polynomial commitments based on very different techniques are covered in Sections 14–16.

Arguments of Knowledge and SNARKs. Arguments for circuit satisfiability are particularly useful when they satisfy an enhanced soundness property called *knowledge-soundness*. Informally, this means that the prover establishes not only that there *exists* a witness w such that $\mathcal{C}(x, w) = y$, but in fact that the prover *knows* such a w.

Knowledge-soundness can be a meaningful notion even when standard soundness is not. For example, suppose the prover and verifier agree on a cryptographic hash function h and hash value y, and the prover claims to know a w such that $h(w) = y$. The prover can establish this by applying a *knowledge-sound* argument for circuit-satisfiability to a circuit $\mathcal{C}$ that takes w as input and computes $h(w)$.

An argument satisfying standard soundness, which merely guarantees the *existence* of a witness w such that $\mathcal{C}(w) = y$, would be useless in this context. This is because cryptographic hash functions are typically surjective, meaning for *any* y there will *exist* many pre-images w. Accordingly, the trivial proof system where the verifier always accepts satisfies standard soundness in this context, but not knowledge-soundness.

Knowledge-sound arguments can be particularly useful when they are non-interactive, meaning the proof is just a static string that is accepted or rejected by the verifier, and *succinct*, meaning that the proofs are very short. Such arguments are called SNARKs. In Section 7.4, we explain that the succinct arguments we give in this section are in fact SNARKs.

7.1 A Naive Approach: An IP for Circuit Satisfiability

A naive way to use the GKR protocol to solve circuit satisfiability is to have the prover explicitly send to the verifier the witness w satisfying $C(x, w) = y$, and then running the GKR protocol to check that indeed $C(x, w) = y$. The problem with this simple approach is that in many settings w can be very large. For example, in the transformation from Section 6.5, the witness w is supposed to be a transcript of M's entire execution on input x, and hence w has size at least T. This means that in the time that the verifier would take to read the whole witness, the verifier could have run M on x without any help from the prover.

7.2 Succinct Arguments for Circuit Satisfiability

If an argument system for circuit satisfiability avoids the above bottleneck of sending the entire witness to the verifier, then it is called *succinct*. Formally, we say that an argument system for circuit satisfiability is succinct if the total communication is sublinear in the size of the witness $|w|$.[1] Succinctness is important for a variety of reasons:

- Shorter proofs are always better. For example, in some applications to blockchains, proofs may be stored on the blockchain permanently. If proofs are long, it drastically increases the global storage requirements of the blockchain. For many (but not all) argument systems, shorter proofs also result in faster verification.

- In some applications, witnesses are naturally large. For example, consider a hospital that publishes cryptographic hash $h(w)$ of a

---

[1] Here, sublinear in $|w|$ means $o(|w|)$, i.e., any expression that asymptotically is much smaller than the witness length. This use of the term "succinct" is slightly nonstandard, as many works reserve the term *succinct* for any proof or argument systems in which the total communication is polylogarithmic (or even logarithmic) in the witness length (or even in the circuit size). Some others use succinctness more informally to refer broadly to argument systems with short proofs.

massive database w of patient records, and later wants to prove that it ran a specific analysis on w. In this case, the witness is the database w, the public input x is the hash value $h(w)$, and the circuit C should both implement the analysis of w and "check" that $h(w) = x$.

- Efficient transformations from computer programs to circuit satisfiability often produce circuits with very large witnesses (see Section 6.5).

The coming sections will describe a variety of approaches to obtaining succinct arguments.[2] This section will cover one specific approach.

7.3 A First Succinct Argument for Circuit Satisfiability

7.3.1 The Approach

The approach of this section is to "simulate" the trivial application of the GKR protocol to circuit satisfiability described in Section 7.1, but *without* requiring the prover to explicitly send w to the verifier. We will accomplish this by using a cryptographic primitive called a *polynomial commitment scheme*. The idea of combining the GKR protocol with polynomial commitment schemes to obtain succinct arguments was first put forth by Zhang *et al.* [258]. We cover polynomial commitment schemes with state-of-the-art concrete efficiency in Sections 10.4.4 and 10.5, and in Section 14. In this section, we informally introduce the notion of polynomial commitment schemes and sketch a conceptually simple (but impractical) polynomial commitment scheme based on low-degree tests and Merkle trees.

---

[2]There is strong evidence that succinct interactive *proofs* (as opposed to arguments) for circuit satisfiability do not exist [72], [132], [205], [246]. For example, it is known [132] that interactive proofs for circuit satisfiability cannot have communication cost that is *logarithmic* in the witness length unless **coNP** $\subseteq$ **AM**, and this is widely believed to be false (i.e., it is not believed that there are efficient constant-round interactive proofs to establish that a circuit is *unsatisfiable*). Similar, though quantitatively weaker, surprising consequences would follow from the existence of interactive proofs for circuit satisfiability with sublinear (rather than logarithmic) communication cost.

Cryptographic Commitment Schemes. Conceptually, cryptographic commitment schemes can be described via the following metaphor. They allow the committer to take some object b (b could be a field element, vector, polynomial, etc.) place b in a box and lock it, and then send the locked box to a "verifier". The committer holds on to the key to the lock. Later, the verifier can ask the committer to open the box, which the committer can do by sending the verifier the key to the lock. Most commitment schemes satisfy two properties: hiding and binding. In the metaphor, hiding means that the verifier can not "see inside" the locked box to learn anything about the object within it. Binding means that once the box is locked and transmitted to the verifier, the committer cannot change the object within the box. We provide a far more detailed and formal treatment of cryptographic commitment schemes much later in this survey, in Section 12.3, and of polynomial commitment schemes in particular at the start of Section 14.

Polynomial Commitment Schemes. Roughly speaking, a polynomial commitment scheme is simply a commitment scheme in which the object being committed to is (all evaluations of) a low-degree polynomial. That is, a polynomial commitment scheme allows a prover to commit to a polynomial $\tilde{w}$ satisfying a specified degree bound, and later reveal $\tilde{w}(r)$ for a point r of the verifier's choosing. Even though in the commitment phase the prover does *not* send all evaluations of $\tilde{w}$ to the verifier, the commitment still effectively binds the prover to a specific $\tilde{w}$. That is, at a later time, the verifier can ask the prover to reveal $\tilde{w}(r)$ for any desired r of the verifier's choosing, and the prover is effectively forced to reveal $\tilde{w}(r)$ for a fixed polynomial $\tilde{w}$ determined at the time of the original commitment. In particular, the prover is unable to choose the polynomial $\tilde{w}$ to depend on the query point r, at least not without breaking the computational assumption on which security of the commitment scheme is based.

Combining Polynomial Commitment Schemes and the GKR Protocol. When applying the GKR protocol to check that $\mathcal{C}(x, w) = y$, the verifier does not need to know any information whatsoever about w until the very end of the protocol, when (as explained in Section 7.3.2.1

below) the verifier only needs to know $\tilde{w}(r)$ for a randomly chosen input r.

So rather than having the prover send w in full to the verifier as in Section 7.1, we can have the prover merely send a *cryptographic commitment* to $\tilde{w}$ at the start of the protocol. The prover and verifier can then happily apply the GKR protocol to the claim that $C(x, w) = y$, ignoring the commitment entirely until the very end of the protocol. At this point, the verifier needs to know $\tilde{w}(r)$. The verifier can force the prover to reveal this quantity using the commitment protocol.

Because the polynomial commitment scheme *bound* the prover to a fixed multilinear polynomial $\tilde{w}$, the soundness analysis of the argument system is essentially the same as if the prover had sent all of w explicitly to the verifier at the start of the protocol as in Section 7.1 (see Section 7.4 for additional details of how one formally analyzes the soundness of this argument system).

7.3.2 Details

7.3.2.1 What The GKR Verifier Needs to Know About The Witness

In this subsection, we justify the assertion from Section 7.3.1 that the only information the verifier needs about w in order to apply the GKR protocol to check that $C(x, w) = y$ is $\tilde{w}(r_1, \ldots, r_{\log n})$.

Let z denote the concatenation of x and w. Let us assume for simplicity throughout this section that x and w are both of length n, so that each entry of z can be assigned a unique label in $\{0, 1\}^{1+\log n}$, with the ith entry of x assigned label $(0, i)$, and the ith entry of w assigned label $(1, i)$.

A key observation is that when applying the GKR protocol to check that $C(z) = y$, the verifier doesn't need to know the exact value of z. Rather, the verifier only needs to know $\tilde{z}(r_0, \ldots, r_{\log n})$ at a single, randomly chosen input $(r_0, \ldots, r_{\log n})$. Moreover, the verifier doesn't even need to know $\tilde{z}(r)$ until *the very end of the protocol*, after the interaction with the prover has finished. We now explain that in order to calculate $\tilde{z}(r)$, it suffices for the verifier to know $\tilde{w}(r_1, \ldots, r_{\log n})$.

It is straightforward to check that

$$\tilde{z}(r_0, r_1, \ldots, r_{\log n}) = (1 - r_0) \cdot \tilde{x}(r_1, \ldots, r_{\log n}) + r_0 \cdot \tilde{w}(r_1, \ldots, r_{\log n}).$$
$$(7.1)$$

Indeed, the right hand side is a multilinear polynomial in $(r_0, r_1, \ldots, r_{\log n})$ that evaluates to $z(r_0, \ldots, r_{\log n})$ whenever $(r_0, \ldots, r_{\log n}) \in \{0, 1\}^{1+\log n}$.[3] By Fact 3.5, the right hand side of Equation (7.1) must equal the unique multilinear extension of z.

Equation (7.1) implies that, given $\tilde{w}(r_1, \ldots, r_{\log n})$, the verifier can evaluate $\tilde{z}(r_0, \ldots, r_{\log n})$ in $O(n)$ time, since the verifier can evaluate $\tilde{x}(r_1, \ldots, r_{\log n})$ in $O(n)$ time (see Lemma 3.8).

In summary, the GKR protocol has the (a priori) amazing property that in order for the verifier to apply it to a known circuit $\mathcal{C}$ on input $z = (x, w) \in \mathbb{F}^n \times \mathbb{F}^n$, the verifier does not need to know anything at all about w other than a *single* field element, namely a single evaluation of $\tilde{w}$. Moreover, the verifier doesn't even need to know this single field element until the very end of the protocol, after the entire interaction with the prover has terminated.

7.3.2.2   A First (Relaxed) Polynomial Commitment Scheme

There are a number of ways to design polynomial commitment schemes. In this section, we describe a simple, folklore commitment scheme (it was also explicitly proposed by Yael Kalai [160]). This scheme is impractical owing to a large prover runtime (see the paragraph on "Costs of this succinct argument system" later in this section), but it provides a clean and simple introduction to cryptographic commitment schemes. We will see (much) more efficient examples of polynomial commitment schemes later in the survey.[4]

---

[3]To see that the latter statement holds, observe that the right hand side of Equation (7.1) evaluates to $\tilde{x}(r_1, \ldots, r_{\log n})$ when $r_0 = 0$ and to $\tilde{w}(r_1, \ldots, r_{\log n})$ and when $r_0 = 1$. Since $\tilde{x}$ and $\tilde{w}$ extend x and w respectively, this means that the right hand side extends the concatenated input (x, w).

[4]In particular, practical argument systems have replaced low-degree tests with interactive variants that have far superior concrete efficiency (see Sections 10.4.4 and 10.5); the interaction can then be removed from the argument via the Fiat-Shamir transformation. For this reason, we do not cover low-degree tests or their analysis in detail in this survey.

To be more precise, the scheme we give here is not a genuine polynomial commitment scheme, because it only binds the prover to a function that is *close* to a polynomial. We call this a *relaxed* polynomial commitment scheme. As we will see, even this relaxed guarantee is enough to transform the GKR protocol into a succinct argument for circuit-satisfiability.

The scheme makes essential use of two important concepts: Merkle Trees and low-degree tests.

Merkle Trees. A Merkle tree [191] (sometimes also called a hash tree) can be used to design a *string-commitment scheme*, which allows a sender to send a short commitment to a *string* $s \in \Sigma^n$ for any finite alphabet Σ.[5] Later, the sender can efficiently reveal the value of any entries of s that are requested by the receiver.

Specifically, a Merkle tree makes use of a collision-resistant hash function h mapping inputs to $\{0, 1\}^\kappa$ where κ is a security parameter that in practice is typically on the order of several hundred.[6, 7]

---

[5] Many treatments of Merkle trees use the phrase *vector* commitment rather than string commitment. We use the phrase string commitment in this section to clarify that the alphabet Σ need not be numerical in nature, but rather can be any finite set.

[6] For example, SHA-3 allows for several output sizes, from as small as 224 bits to as large as 512 bits.

[7] As discussed in Section 5.1, cryptographic hash functions such as SHA-3 or BLAKE3 are designed with the goal of ensuring that they "behave like" truly random functions. In particular, for such cryptographic hash functions it is typically assumed that the fastest way to find a collision is via exhaustive search, i.e., randomly choosing inputs at which to evaluate the hash function until a collision is found. If the hash function were a truly random function mapping to range $\{0, 1\}^\kappa$, then by the *birthday paradox*, with high probability roughly $\sqrt{2^\kappa} = 2^{\kappa/2}$ evaluations must be performed before exhaustive search finds a collision. This means that for security against attackers running in time, say, 2^{128}, the output size of the hash function should consist of at least $\kappa = 256$ bits. Obtaining security against attackers running in time 2^λ is often referred to by saying the primitive "achieves λ bits of security", and λ is called the *security parameter* (see Section 5.3.1). Quantum algorithms are in principle capable of finding collisions in random functions with codomain $\{0, 1\}^\kappa$ in time $2^{\kappa/3}$ via a combination of Grover's algorithm and random sampling [78], meaning that κ should be set larger by a factor of $\frac{3}{2}$ to achieve security against the same number of quantum rather than classical operations.

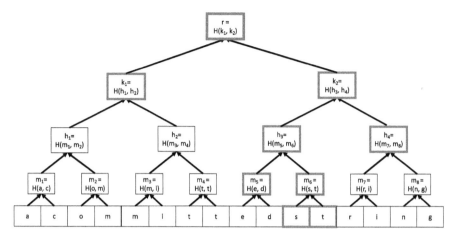

Figure 7.1: A Merkle-tree committing to the string "acommittedstring" using hash function H. Boxes with a red, bold outline represent the authentication path to reveal the twelfth entry of the committed string, namely the letter t. This consists of every node along the path from the root to the twelfth leaf, as well as each such node's sibling.

The leaves of the tree are the symbols of a string s, and every internal node of the tree is assigned the hash of its two children. Figure 7.1 provides a visual depiction of a hash tree.

One obtains a string-commitment protocol from a Merkle tree as follows. In the commitment step, the sender commits to the string s by sending the root of the hash-tree.

If the sender is later asked to reveal the ith symbol in s, the sender sends the value of the ith leaf in the tree (i.e., s_i), as well as the value of every node v along the root-to-leaf path for s_i, and the sibling of each such node v. We call all of this information the *authentication information* for s_i. The receiver checks that the hash of every two siblings sent equals the claimed value of their parent.[8]

Since the tree has depth $O(\log n)$, this translates to the sender sending $O(\log n)$ hash values per symbol of s that is revealed.

---

[8]In fact, it is unnecessary to include in the authentication information the hash values for the nodes along the root-to-leaf path, as for each such node the receiver can infer its claimed values by hashing its two children.

The scheme is binding in the following sense. For each index i, there is at most one value s_i that the sender can successfully reveal without finding a collision under the hash function h. This is because, if the sender is able to send valid authentication information for two different values s_i and s_i', then there must be at least one collision under h along the root-to-leaf path connecting the root to the ith leaf, since the authentication information for both s_i and s_i' result in the same root hash value, but differ in at least one leaf hash value.

A (Relaxed) Polynomial Commitment Scheme From a Merkle Tree?

One could attempt to obtain a polynomial commitment scheme directly from a Merkle tree as follows. To have the prover $\mathcal{P}$ commit to a polynomial p, $\mathcal{P}$ could Merkle-commit to the string consisting of all evaluations of the polynomial, i.e., $p(\ell_1), \ldots, p(\ell_N)$ where $\ell_1, \ldots, \ell_N$ is an enumeration of all possible inputs to the polynomial. This would enable the prover to reveal any requested evaluation of the polynomial: if the verifier asks for $p(\ell_i)$, the prover can reply with $p(\ell_i)$ along authentication information for this value (the authentication information consists of $O(\log N)$ hash values).

Unfortunately, this approach does *not* directly yield a polynomial commitment scheme. The reason is that while the Merkle tree does bind the prover to a fixed string, there is no guarantee that the string is equal to all evaluations of some multilinear polynomial. That is, when the verifier $\mathcal{V}$ asks $\mathcal{P}$ to reveal $p(r)$ for some input r, the binding nature of Merkle trees does force $\mathcal{P}$ to respond with the r'th entry of the committed string and the associated authentication information. But $\mathcal{V}$ has no idea whether the committed string consists of all evaluations of a multilinear polynomial—the committed string could in general consists of all evaluations of some totally arbitrary function.

To address this issue, we combine Merkle trees with a low-degree test. The low-degree test ensures that not only is the prover bound to some (possibly completely unstructured) string, but actually that the string contains all evaluations of a low-degree polynomial. More precisely, it ensures that the string is "close" to the evaluation-table of a low-degree polynomial, so its use here yields a somewhat weaker object than an actual polynomial commitment scheme. The low-degree test guarantees this despite only inspecting a small number of entries of the string—often logarithmic in the length of the string—thereby keeping the amount of authentication information transmitted by the prover low (at least, lower than the communication that would be required to explicitly send a complete description of the polynomial to the verifier). Details follow.

Low-Degree Tests. Suppose a receiver is given oracle access to a giant string s, which is claimed to contain all evaluations of an m-variate function over a finite field $\mathbb{F}$. Note that there are $|\mathbb{F}|^m$ such inputs, so s consists of a list of $|\mathbb{F}|^m$ elements of $\mathbb{F}$. A low-degree test allows one determine to whether or not the string is consistent with a low-degree polynomial, by looking at only a tiny fraction of symbols within the string.

Unfortunately, because the low-degree test only looks at a tiny fraction of s, it cannot determine whether s is *exactly* consistent with a low-degree polynomial. Imagine if s were obtained from a low-degree polynomial p by changing its value on only one input. Then unless the test gets lucky and chooses the input on which s and p disagree, the test has no hope of distinguishing between s and p itself.[9]

What the low-degree test can guarantee, however, is that s is *close* in Hamming distance to (the string of all evaluations of) a low-degree polynomial. That is, if the test passes with probability γ, then there is a low-degree polynomial that agrees with s on close to a γ fraction of points.

Typically, low-degree tests are extremely simple procedures, but they are often very complicated to analyze and existing analyses often involve very large constants that result in weak guarantees unless the field size is very large. An example of such a low-degree test is the point-versus-line test of Rubinfeld and Sudan, with a tighter analysis

---

[9]The word "test" in the phrase low-degree test has precise technical connotations. Specifically, it refers to the fact that if a function passes the test, then the function is only guaranteed to be "close" to a low-degree polynomial, i.e., it may not be exactly equal to a low-degree polynomial. This is the same sense that the word test is used in the field of property testing (see https://en.wikipedia.org/wiki/Property_testing). We reserve the word "test" throughout this monograph to have this technical connotation.

subsequently given by Arora and Sudan [12]. In this test, one evaluates s along a randomly chosen line in $\mathbb{F}^m$, and confirms that s restricted to this line is consistent with a univariate polynomial of degree at most m (see Section 4.5.2). Clearly, if the string s agrees perfectly with a multilinear polynomial then this test will always pass. The works [12], [219] roughly show that if the test passes with probability γ, then there is a low-degree polynomial that agrees with s at close to a γ fraction of points.[10] In this survey, we will not discuss how these results are proved.

A (Relaxed) Polynomial Commitment Scheme by Combining Merkle Trees and Low-Degree Tests. Let $\tilde{w} \colon \mathbb{F}^{\log n} \to \mathbb{F}$ be a $(\log n)$-variate multilinear polynomial over $\mathbb{F}$. Let s be the string consisting of all $|\mathbb{F}|^{\log n}$ evaluations of $\tilde{w}$. One obtains a polynomial commitment scheme by applying the Merkle-tree based string commitment scheme of Section 7.3.2.2, and then applying a low-degree test to s. For example, if the point-versus-line low-degree test is used, then the receiver picks a random line in $\mathbb{F}^{\log n}$, asks the sender to provide authentication information for all points along the line, and checks that the revealed values are consistent with a univariate polynomial of degree at most $\log n$.

The guarantee of this commitment scheme is the same as in the string-commitment scheme of Section 7.3.2.2, except that the use of the low-degree test ensures that if the sender passes all of the receivers checks with probability γ, then not only is the sender bound to a fixed string s, but also that there is some low-degree polynomial that agrees with s at close to a γ fraction of points.

This guarantee is enough to use the commitment scheme in conjunction with the GKR protocol applied to the claim $\mathcal{C}(x, w) = y$, as outlined in Section 7.3.1. Specifically, if the verifier's checks in the polynomial commitment scheme pass with probability at least (say) $1/2$, then the prover is bound to a string s such that there is a multilinear polynomial p that agrees with s on close to a $1/2$ fraction of points. As long as the point $(r_1, \ldots, r_{\log n})$ at which the verifier in the GKR protocol evaluates

---

[10]More precisely, these works show that there is a polynomial of total degree at most d that agrees with s on at least a $\gamma - m^{O(1)}/|\mathbb{F}|^{\Omega(1)}$ fraction of points. This fraction is $\gamma - o(1)$ as long as $|\mathbb{F}|$ is super-polynomially large in m (or even a large enough polynomial in m).

s is not one of the "bad" points on which s and p disagree, then the soundness analysis of the GKR protocol applies exactly as if the prover were bound to the multilinear polynomial p itself.

This is enough to argue that if the prover passes all of the verifier's checks with probability significantly larger than $1/2$, then indeed there exists a w (namely, the restriction of p to the domain $\{0, 1\}^{\log n}$) such that $C(x, w) = y$. The soundness error can be reduced from roughly $1/2$ to arbitrarily close to 0 by repeating the protocol many times and rejecting if any of the executions ever results in a rejection.[11]

Costs of this succinct argument system. In addition to the communication involved in applying the GKR protocol to check that $C(x, w) = y$, the argument system above requires additional communication for the prover to commit to $\tilde{w}$ and execute the point-versus-line low-degree test. The total communication cost due to the (relaxed) polynomial commit scheme is $O(|\mathbb{F}| \cdot \log n)$ hash values (the cost is dominated by the cost of the prover revealing the value of $\tilde{w}$ on all $|\mathbb{F}|$ points along a line chosen by the verifier). This is $O(n)$ hash values as long as $|\mathbb{F}| \leq n/\log n$. Note that, while in practice we prefer to work over large fields, the soundness error of the GKR protocol is $O\left(\frac{d \log |\mathcal{C}|}{|\mathbb{F}|}\right)$ where d is the circuit depth, so working over a field of size $O(n/\log n)$ is enough to ensure non-trivial soundness error in the GKR protocol as long as $d \log |\mathcal{C}| \ll n/\log n$.

The verifier's runtime is the same as in the GKR protocol, plus the time required to play its part of the polynomial commit scheme. Assuming the collision-resistant hash function h can be evaluated in constant time, and the field size is $O(n/\log^2 n)$, the verifier spends $O(n)$ time to execute its part of the polynomial commitment scheme.

The prover's runtime in the above argument system is dominated by the time required to commit to $\tilde{w}$. This requires building a Merkle tree over all possible evaluations of $\tilde{w}$, of which there are $|\mathbb{F}|^{\log n}$. If we work over a field of size (say) $O(n)$, then this runtime is $n^{O(\log n)}$, which is

---

[11] It is possible to use a so-called *list-decoding guarantee* of the low-degree test to argue that the soundness error is much lower than $1/2$ (if the field size is large enough), without the need for repetition of the protocol. See Section 8.2.1.4 for details.

superpolynomial. So, as described, this polynomial commitment scheme is asymptotically efficient for the verifier, but not the prover.

Remark 7.1. It is possible to reduce the prover's runtime to $O(n^c)$ for some constant c in the above argument system. The way to do this is to tweak the parameters within the GKR protocol to enable working over a much smaller field, of size $O(\text{polylog}(n))$. This will be explained in more detail in Section 9.3 when we talk about designing succinct arguments from PCPs and multi-prover interactive proofs. However, the resulting prover runtime will still be impractical (practicality requires a prover runtime close to *linear*, rather than polynomial, in the size of the circuit-satisfiability instance). As indicated above, working over such a small field would also lead to soundness error of $1/\text{polylog}(n)$, and the protocol would have to be repeated many times to drive the soundness error low enough for cryptographic use.

Remark 7.2. An alternative polynomial commitment scheme would be to use Merkle trees to have the prover commit to the string consisting of the n coefficients of the multilinear polynomial $\tilde{w} \colon \mathbb{F}^{\log n}$, rather than to the $|\mathbb{F}|^{\log n}$ evaluations of $\tilde{w}$. This approach would have the benefit of allowing the commitment to be computed with $O(n)$ cryptographic hash evaluations, and the commitment would remain small (consisting simply of the root hash evaluation). However, in order to reveal the evaluation $\tilde{w}(r)$ for a point $r \in \mathbb{F}^n$, the prover would have to reveal all n of the coefficients of $\tilde{w}$, resulting in linear communication complexity and verifier runtime. This is no more efficient than the naive interactive proof from Section 7.1 in which $\mathcal{P}$ simply sends w to $\mathcal{V}$ at the start of the protocol. And the naive approach has the benefit of being statistically rather than computationally sound.

7.4 Knowledge-Soundness

Proofs and Arguments of Knowledge. The notion of a proof or argument of knowledge is meant to capture situations in which a prover establishes not only that a statement is true, but also that the prover *knows* a "witness" w to the validity of the statement. For example, in the authentication application of Section 1, Alice chooses a password

x at random, publishes the hash value $y = h(x)$ of x, and later wants to prove to a verifier that she *knows* a preimage of y under h, i.e., a w such that $h(w) = y$.

A natural attempt to achieve this is for Alice to play the role of the prover in a succinct argument for circuit-satisfiability, applied to a circuit $\mathcal{C}$ that takes an input w and outputs $y = h(w)$. However, if the succinct argument only satisfies standard soundness, then Alice's ability to produce a convincing proof will merely guarantee the *existence* of a witness w such that $y = h(w)$. If h is surjective, such a witness w will *always* exist for *any* y. Hence, it is totally uninteresting for Alice to establish the mere existence of such a pre-image w—the trivial proof system in which the verifier always accepts would satisfy the same property.

If the argument for circuit satisfiability satisfies a strengthened security notion called *knowledge-soundness*, then it will in fact guarantee that Alice *knows* the witness w. What does it mean for Alice to prove that she knows a preimage of y under h? The notion of knowledge-soundness posits the following answer. If Alice convinces a verifier to accept her proof with non-negligible probability, then there should be a polynomial time algorithm $\mathcal{E}$ that, if given the ability to repeatedly interact with Alice, is able to output a preimage w of y under h with non-negligible probability. $\mathcal{E}$ is called an *extractor* algorithm. The idea of this definition is that, since $\mathcal{E}$ is efficient, it can't know anything more than Alice does (i.e., anything $\mathcal{E}$ can compute efficiently by interacting with Alice, Alice could compute efficiently on her own, by simulating $\mathcal{E}$'s interaction with herself). Hence, since $\mathcal{E}$ can efficiently find w by interacting with Alice, then Alice must know w. One may think of $\mathcal{E}$ as "efficiently pulling w out of Alice's head".[12, 13]

---

[12]The interested reader is directed to [130, Section 4.7] for a detailed discussion of how to formalize knowledge-soundness.

[13]The reader may initially suspect that any proof of knowledge cannot be zero-knowledge: if it is possible to "pull a witness w out of the prover's head", doesn't this mean that the proof system reveals the witness to the verifier, grossly violating zero-knowledge? The answer is no. This is because it is not the proof system *verifier* that can extract w from the *proof*, but rather an extractor algorithm $\mathcal{E}$ that can extract w from the *prover*. This means that $\mathcal{E}$ can do things that the verifier cannot. For example, if the proof system is interactive, then $\mathcal{E}$ can run the proof system once

As explained below, the argument system for arithmetic circuit satisfiability in this section (obtained by combining the GKR interactive proof with a commitment c to the multilinear polynomial $\widetilde{w}$) is in fact an argument of knowledge.

Extractable Polynomial Commitments. *Extractability* of a polynomial commitment scheme is a stronger property than mere binding. Roughly, extractability is to binding as knowledge-soundness is to standard soundness. It guarantees that for any efficient prover capable of passing all of the checks performed in the commit and reveal phase of the scheme with non-negligible probability, the prover must actually "know" a polynomial p of the claimed degree that explains its answers to all evaluation queries. That is, if the prover can successfully answer evaluation query z with value v, then $p(z) = v$.

That is, binding of a polynomial commitment scheme guarantees that there is some polynomial p of the appropriate degree that "explains" all of the evaluations that the prover can open the commitment to, but a priori it is possible that the prover itself doesn't actually know what that the polynomial is. Extractability guarantees that in fact the prover does know p. (Section 14.1 later in this monograph contains an example of a polynomial commitment scheme that is binding, but is not extractable).

In more detail, extractability of a polynomial commitment scheme guarantees that for every "efficient committer adversary $\mathcal{A}$" that takes as input the public parameters of the commitment scheme and a degree bound D and outputs a polynomial commitment c, there is an efficient

---

to completion to see what messages the prover $\mathcal{P}$ sends over the course of the protocol, and then "rewind" $\mathcal{P}$ until just before $\mathcal{P}$ receives the verifier's final challenge, and "restart" $\mathcal{P}$ with a fresh random challenge from the verifier to see how $\mathcal{P}$'s response changes. In contrast, the proof system verifier $\mathcal{V}$ only gets to run the protocol once. In particular, $\mathcal{V}$ does not have the ability to rewind $\mathcal{P}$ and restart it with a new verifier challenge. As another example, if the proof system is non-interactive and operates in the random oracle model, then the extractor algorithm can "watch" all of the queries that $\mathcal{P}$ makes to the random oracle while computing the proof, and try to use those queries to identify a witness. In contrast, the proof system verifier just sees the resulting proof, not the random oracle queries $\mathcal{P}$ made en route to computing the proof. See Remark 12.1 in Section 12.2.1 and Section 12.2.3 for additional discussion and examples.

algorithm $\mathcal{E}'$ (which depends on $\mathcal{A}$) that produces a degree-D polynomial p explaining all of $\mathcal{A}$'s answers to evaluation queries in the sense above. Since $\mathcal{E}'$ is efficient, it cannot know anything more than $\mathcal{A}$ does (since $\mathcal{A}$ can afford to run $\mathcal{E}'$), and $\mathcal{E}'$ clearly knows p by virtue of outputting it.[14] This captures the intuition that $\mathcal{A}$ knows a polynomial p that it is using to answer evaluation queries.

The (relaxed) polynomial commitment scheme described in Section 7.3.2.2 is extractable (we justify this assertion in Section 9.2.1).

The extractability guarantee of the polynomial commitment scheme enables one to take any efficient prover $\mathcal{P}^*$ for the argument system that convinces the argument system verifier to accept with non-negligible probability ε, and extract from $\mathcal{P}^*$ a witness w and prover strategy $\mathcal{P}$ that convinces the verifier within the GKR protocol that $\mathcal{C}(x, w) = y$. Details follow.

Notation. In the remainder of the analysis, we use the following notation to identify various parties.

- $\mathcal{V}$ denotes the prescribed GKR verifier.

- $\mathcal{P}$ represents "a successful GKR prover" (either the prescribed one, or another successful proving procedure, i.e., that convinces $\mathcal{V}$ to accept with non-negligible probability).

- $\mathcal{V}'$ and $\mathcal{P}'$ represent the prescribed succinct-argument verifier and prover.

- $\mathcal{P}^*$ represents a generic (potentially malicious) succinct-argument prover.

Recap of the succinct argument system. Recall that the argument-system prover first sends a commitment c to a multilinear polynomial p

---

[14]Calling $\mathcal{E}'$ an extractor might initially be puzzling because we have not stated that $\mathcal{E}'$ operates by repeatedly interacting with $\mathcal{A}$ to "pull the polynomial p out of its head". But the extractors for polynomial commitment schemes that we give in this survey actually do work this way. That is, an efficient procedure is given to pull p out of $\mathcal{A}$'s head, and since $\mathcal{A}$ is efficient, the entire procedure, including any computation done "inside" calls to $\mathcal{A}$, is itself efficient, yielding the desired algorithm $\mathcal{E}'$.

claimed to extend a witness w such that $C(x, w) = y$. After receiving c, the argument system verifier $\mathcal{V}'$ acts identically to the GKR verifier $\mathcal{V}$, i.e., $\mathcal{V}'$ simulates $\mathcal{V}$ and copies its behavior ($\mathcal{V}'$ can do this despite not knowing w, because the GKR verifier $\mathcal{V}$ does not need to know anything about w until the very end of the GKR protocol). Similarly, the honest argument-system prover $\mathcal{P}'$ acts identically to the honest GKR prover for the claim that $C(x, w) = y$.

At the very end of the GKR protocol, the GKR verifier $\mathcal{V}$ being simulated by $\mathcal{V}'$ does need to evaluate the multilinear extension $\tilde{w}$ of w at a random point r in order to make its final accept/reject decision. $\mathcal{V}'$ obtains this evaluation using the evaluation procedure of the polynomial commitment scheme applied to the commitment c, and outputs whatever accept/reject decision $\mathcal{V}$ would output given the evaluation $p(r)$ obtained from the commitment scheme.

Knowledge-soundness of the argument. Now suppose that $\mathcal{P}^*$ is a polynomial time, but possibly malicious argument-system prover strategy that convinces the argument-system verifier $\mathcal{V}'$ to accept with some non-negligible probability ε. To establish knowledge-soundness of the argument system, we need to explain that there is an efficient extraction procedure $\mathcal{E}$ that can pull out of $\mathcal{P}^*$ a witness w^* such that $C(x, w^*) = y$.

The extractability of the polynomial commitment scheme implies that we can efficiently extract a pre-image p of the commitment c sent by $\mathcal{P}^*$ at the start of the argument, i.e., p is a multilinear polynomial that opens to all the same values as c. $\mathcal{E}$ sets w^* to be the witness that p extends, i.e., w^* is the set of all evaluations of p at inputs in the Boolean hypercube, $\{0, 1\}^{\log |w|}$.

We still need to explain that w^* satisfies $C(x, w^*) = y$. To do this, we construct a GKR prover strategy $\mathcal{P}$ that convinces the GKR verifier $\mathcal{V}$ to accept the claim that $C(x, w^*) = y$ with probability ε. The soundness of the GKR protocol then implies that indeed $C(x, w^*) = y$.

$\mathcal{P}$ simply simulates $\mathcal{P}^*$ starting from right after $\mathcal{P}^*$ sent the commitment c. That is, in every round i of the GKR protocol, $\mathcal{P}$ sends to $\mathcal{V}$ the message m_i that $\mathcal{P}^*$ would send in that round of the argument system. The GKR verifier $\mathcal{V}$ will reply to m_i with a response r_i, and

$\mathcal{P}$ then continues simulating $\mathcal{P}^*$ into the next round, using r_i as the response of the argument-system verifier $\mathcal{V}^*$ to m_i.

By construction, $\mathcal{P}$ convinces the GKR verifier $\mathcal{V}$ to accept the claim that $\mathcal{C}(x, w^*) = y$ with exactly the same probability that $\mathcal{P}^*$ convinces the argument-system verifier $\mathcal{V}^*$ to accept, namely ϵ. This concludes the proof.

Because the succinct argument of this section is in fact a public coin argument of knowledge, combining it with the Fiat-Shamir transformation yields our first succinct non-interactive argument of knowledge, or SNARK. This SNARK is publicly verifiable, and unconditionally secure in the random oracle model (see Section 9.2.1 for details).

8

MIPs and Succinct Arguments

Multi-prover interactive proofs (MIPs) grant the verifier access to more than one untrusted prover, and assume the provers cannot tell each other about what challenges they receive from the verifier. While MIPs are of interest in their own right, they are also important building blocks for constructing succinct arguments. In particular, in this section we give 2-prover MIPs for circuit satisfiability (Section 8.2) and its generalization R1CS-satisfiability (Section 8.4), in which the second prover effectively acts as a polynomial commitment scheme, a notion we introduced in Section 7.3. Accordingly, one can obtain a (single-prover) succinct argument with state-of-the-art performance by replacing the second prover with an appropriate polynomial commitment scheme, practical instantiations of which are covered in detail in Sections 10.4.4, 10.5, and Section 14.[1] In particular, the arguments obtained from the

---

[1] When an initial version of this monograph was publicly released in the form of lecture notes in 2018, this approach to obtaining succinct arguments had not been previously published; the only published approach to turning MIPs into succinct arguments at that time [55] made use of a cryptographic primitive known as Fully Homomorphic Encryption, which is currently much too computationally intensive to yield practical SNARKs. Since that time, Setty [226] has implemented and extended the MIP-to-succinct-argument approach described in this monograph, with several follow-on works [137], [230].

MIPs of this section have significantly shorter proofs than those of Section 7.

MIPs are also of significant historical importance, and the state-of-the-art MIPs of this section exhibit several ideas that will recur in our coverage of PCPs and IOPs (Sections 9 and 10).

8.1 MIPs: Definitions and Basic Results

Definition 8.1. A k-prover interactive proof protocol for a language $\mathcal{L} \subseteq \{0,1\}^*$ involves $k+1$ parties: a probabilistic polynomial time verifier, and k provers. The verifier exchanges a sequence of messages with each prover; each prover's message is a function of the input and the messages from $\mathcal{V}$ that it has seen so far. The interaction produces a transcript $t = (\mathcal{V}(r), \mathcal{P}_1, \ldots, \mathcal{P}_k)(x)$, where r denotes $\mathcal{V}$'s internal randomness. After the transcript t is produced, $\mathcal{V}$ decides whether to output accept or reject based on r, t, and x. Denote by $\mathrm{out}(\mathcal{V}, x, r, \mathcal{P}_1, \ldots, \mathcal{P}_k)$ the output of verifier $\mathcal{V}$ on input x given prover strategies $(\mathcal{P}_1, \ldots, \mathcal{P}_k)$ and that $\mathcal{V}$'s internal randomness is equal to r.

The multi-prover interactive proof system has completeness error δ_c and soundness error δ_s if the following two properties hold.

(1) *(Completeness)* There exists a tuple of prover strategies $(\mathcal{P}_1, \ldots, \mathcal{P}_k)$ such that for every $x \in \mathcal{L}$,

$$\Pr[\mathrm{out}(\mathcal{V}, x, r, \mathcal{P}_1, \ldots, \mathcal{P}_k) = \mathrm{accept}] \geq 1 - \delta_c.$$

(2) *(Soundness)* For every $x \notin \mathcal{L}$ and every tuple of prover strategies $(\mathcal{P}'_1, \ldots, \mathcal{P}'_k)$,

$$\Pr[\mathrm{out}(\mathcal{V}, x, r, \mathcal{P}'_1, \ldots, \mathcal{P}'_k) = \mathrm{accept}] \leq \delta_s.$$

Say that a k-prover interactive proof system is valid if $\delta_c, \delta_s \leq 1/3$. The complexity class **MIP** is the class of all languages possessing valid k-prover interactive proof systems, for some $k = \mathrm{poly}(n)$.

The MIP model was introduced by Ben-Or *et al.* [32]. It is crucial in Definition 8.1 that each prover's message is a function only of the input and the messages from $\mathcal{V}$ that it has seen so far. In particular, $\mathcal{P}_i$

cannot tell P_j what messages V has sent it, or vice versa, for any $i \neq j$. If such "cross-talk" between P_i and P_j were allowed, then it would be possible to simulate any MIP by a single-prover interactive proof, and the classes **MIP** and **IP** would become equal.

As discussed in Section 1.2.3, it can be helpful to think of MIP as follows. The provers are like prisoners who are about to be interrogated. The prisoners get placed in separate interrogation rooms. Prior to going into these rooms, the prisoners can talk amongst themselves, plotting a strategy for answering questions. But once they are placed in the rooms, they can no longer talk to each other, and in particular prover i cannot tell the other provers what questions the verifier is asking it. The verifier is like the interrogator, trying to determine if the prover's stories are consistent with each other, and with the claim being asserted.

The next section shows that, up to polynomial blowups in V's runtime, 2-prover MIPs are just as expressive as k-prover MIPs, for any $k = \text{poly}(n)$.

8.1.1 What Does a Second Prover Buy?

Non-Adaptivity. In a single-prover interactive proof, the prover P is allowed to act adaptively, in the sense that P's response to the ith message m_i sent from V is allowed to depend on the preceding $i - 1$ messages. Intuitively, the reason that MIPs are more expressive than IPs is that the presence of a second prover (who does not know V's messages to the first prover) prevents the first prover from behaving in this adaptive manner.[2] This can be formalized via the following easy lemma showing that the complexity class **MIP** is equivalent to the class of languages satisfied by polynomial time randomized *oracle machines*. Here, an oracle machine is essentially a computer that has query access to a giant string $\mathcal{O}$ that is fixed at the start of the computer's execution. The string $\mathcal{O}$ may be enormous, but the computer is allowed to look

---

[2]One may initially have the intuition that, since allowing adaptivity on the part of the prover means allowing "more expressive" prover strategies, prover adaptivity leads to efficient proof systems for more challenging problems. In fact, the opposite is true. Allowing the prover to behave adaptively gives the prover more power to break soundness. Hence, allowing the prover to behave adaptively actually weakens the class of problems that have proof systems with an efficient verifier.

at any desired symbol $\mathcal{O}_i$ (i.e., the ith symbol of $\mathcal{O}$) in unit time. One can think of any query that the computer makes to $\mathcal{O}$ as a question, and $\mathcal{O}_i$ as the answer. Because $\mathcal{O}$ is fixed at the start of the computer's execution, the answers that are returned by $\mathcal{O}$ are non-adaptive in the sense that the answer to the computer's jth question *does not depend on which questions the computer asked previously.*

Lemma 8.2 ([113]). Let $\mathcal{L}$ be a language, and M a probabilistic polynomial time oracle Turing Machine. Let $M^{\mathcal{O}}$ denote M when given query access to oracle $\mathcal{O}$. Suppose that $x \in \mathcal{L} \implies \exists$ an oracle $\mathcal{O}$ such that $M^{\mathcal{O}}$ accepts x with probability 1, and $x \notin \mathcal{L} \implies \forall$ oracles $\mathcal{O}$, $M^{\mathcal{O}}$ rejects x with probability at least $2/3$. Then there is a 2-prover MIP for $\mathcal{L}$.

Remark 8.1. In Lemma 8.2, one can think of $\mathcal{O}$ as a giant purported proof that $x \in \mathcal{L}$, and machine M only looks at a small (i.e., polynomial) number of symbols of the proof. This is the same notion as a *probabilistically checkable proof*, which we introduce formally in Section 9.1. In this terminology, Lemma 8.2 states that any PCP with a polynomial time verifier can be turned into a 2-prover MIP with a polynomial time verifier.

Proof. We first describe a "subroutine" 2-prover MIP that has perfect completeness and high but bounded soundness error. The final 2-prover MIP simply repeats the subroutine MIP independently several times.

The Subroutine MIP. $\mathcal{V}$ simulates M, and every time M poses a query q to the oracle, $\mathcal{V}$ asks the query to $\mathcal{P}_1$, treating $\mathcal{P}_1$'s response as $\mathcal{O}(q)$. At the end of the protocol, $\mathcal{V}$ picks a query q uniformly at random from all queries that were posed to $\mathcal{P}_1$, and poses it to $\mathcal{P}_2$, rejecting if $\mathcal{P}_2$'s response to q does not equal $\mathcal{P}_1$'s.

Completeness of the subroutine is clear: if $x \in \mathcal{L}$, there is some oracle $\mathcal{O}^*$ causing M to accept x with probability 1. If $\mathcal{P}_1$ and $\mathcal{P}_2$ respond to any query q with $\mathcal{O}^*(q)$, then $\mathcal{V}$ will accept x on each of the runs of the protocol with probability 1.

For soundness of the subroutine, observe that since $\mathcal{P}_2$ is only asked a single query, we can treat $\mathcal{P}_2$ as an oracle $\mathcal{O}$. That is, $\mathcal{P}_2$'s answer on query q is a function only of q. On any run of the protocol on input $x \notin \mathcal{L}$, let $q_1, \ldots, q_\ell$ denote the queries that $\mathcal{V}$ poses to $\mathcal{P}_1$ on input x. On the one hand, if $\mathcal{P}_1$ ever answers a query q_i differently than $\mathcal{O}(q_i)$, the verifier will pick that query to pose to $\mathcal{P}_2$ with probability at least $1/\ell$, and in this case the verifier will reject. On the other hand, if $\mathcal{P}_1$ answers every query q_i with $\mathcal{O}(q_i)$, then $\mathcal{V}$ will reject with probability at least $2/3$ because $M^\mathcal{O}$ rejects with that probability. Therefore, $\mathcal{V}$ rejects on each run of the protocol with probability at least $1/\ell$.

The Final MIP. The final MIP repeats the subroutine protocol independently and sequentially 3ℓ times, where ℓ is (an upper bound on) the number of queries that M poses to the oracle on any input $x \in \{0, 1\}^n$ (note that ℓ is at most polynomial in the input size n, since M runs in polynomial time). $\mathcal{V}$ accepts only if all instances accept. Since the subroutine MIP has perfect completeness, so does the final MIP. Since the subroutine has soundness error at most $1 - 1/\ell$, sequentially repeating it k times with independently chosen verifier queries on each repetition ensures that, when given an input $x \notin \mathcal{L}$, $\mathcal{V}$ rejects on at least one run of the subroutine with probability at least $1 - (1 - 1/\ell)^{3\ell} > 2/3$. $\quad\square$

The same argument implies that any k-prover MIP (with completeness error at most $\delta_c \leq 1/(9\ell)$, where ℓ is the total number of queries asked) can be simulated by a 2-prover MIP [32]. In the simulation, $\mathcal{V}$ poses all of the questions from the k-prover MIP to $\mathcal{P}_1$, then picks a question at random and poses it to $\mathcal{P}_2$, rejecting if the answers do not agree. $\mathcal{P}_2$ can be treated as an oracle since $\mathcal{P}_2$ is only posed a single question, and hence has no opportunity to behave adaptively. And if $\mathcal{P}_1$ answers even a single query q_i "adaptively" (i.e., different than how $\mathcal{P}_2$ would answer), the probability this is detected is at least $1/\ell$. The whole 2-prover protocol must be repeated $\Omega(\ell)$ times to drive the soundness error from $1 - 1/\ell$ down to $1/3$.

In summary, one can both force non-adaptivity and reduce the number of provers to 2 by posing all queries to $\mathcal{P}_1$ and choosing one of the queries at random to pose to $\mathcal{P}_2$. While this conveys much of the intuition for why MIPs are more expressive than IPs, the technique is very expensive in practice, due to the need for $\Omega(\ell)$ repetitions—typically, ℓ is on the order of $\log n$, and can easily be in the hundreds in implementations. Fortunately, the MIP that we describe in Section 8.2 requires only two provers without the need for repetition to force non-adaptivity or reduce the number of provers to 2.

But What Does Non-Adaptivity Buy?   We will see in Section 8.2 that non-adaptivity buys *succinctness for NP statements*. That is, we will give an MIP for arithmetic circuit *satisfiability* (as opposed to circuit evaluation) in which the total communication and verifier runtime is sublinear in the size of the witness w.

This should not be surprising, as we saw the same phenomenon in Section 7. There, we used a polynomial commitment scheme to cryptographically *bind* the prover to a multilinear polynomial $\tilde{w}$ that was fixed at the start of the interaction with the verifier. In particular, the polynomial commitment scheme enforced non-adaptivity, i.e., the prover must tell the verifier $\tilde{w}(r)$, and is not able to "change its answer" based on the interaction with the verifier. The addition of a second prover in a 2-prover MIP has exactly the same effect. Indeed, we will see that the second prover in the MIP of Section 8.2 essentially functions as a polynomial commitment scheme. Indeed, we will ultimately obtain a (single-prover) succinct argument from the MIP with state-of-the-art practical performance by replacing the second prover with a polynomial commitment scheme; see Section 8.3.

8.2   An Efficient MIP For Circuit Satisfiability

Warmup: A 2-Prover MIP for Low-Depth Arithmetic Circuit Satisfiability. The succinct argument from Section 7 can be directly adapted to yield a 2-prover MIP. The idea is to use the second prover to function as the polynomial commitment scheme.

In more detail, the verifier uses the first prover to apply the GKR protocol to the claim $\mathcal{C}(x, w) = y$. As explained in Section 7.3.2.1, at the end of this protocol, the prover makes a claim about $\tilde{w}(r)$.

In Section 7, this claim was checked by forcing the prover to reveal $\tilde{w}(r)$ via the polynomial commitment protocol (which itself involved a vector-commitment combined with a low-degree test).

In the MIP, the verifier simply uses the second prover to play the role of the polynomial commitment scheme. This means that the second prover provides claimed value for $\tilde{w}(r)$ that does not depend on the questions the verifier asked to the first prover, and executes a low-degree test. Roughly speaking, this combination ensures that the claimed value $\tilde{w}(r)$ is indeed consistent with the multilinear extension $\tilde{w}$ of some witness w that was fixed at the start of the protocol—in particular, w does not depend on the point r chosen by the verifier.

For example, if the low-degree test used is the point-versus-line test, then the verifier picks a random line λ in $\mathbb{F}^{\log n}$ containing r, and sends λ to the second prover, who is asked to respond with a univariate polynomial of degree $\log n$ claimed to equal $\tilde{w}$ restricted to λ. Since r is on the line λ, this univariate polynomial implicitly specifies $\tilde{w}(r)$, and the verifier checks that this value matches the first prover's claim about $\tilde{w}(r)$.

A downside of the warm-up 2-prover MIP for arithmetic circuit satisfiability is that the communication cost and the verifier's runtime grow linearly with the circuit depth d, i.e., is $O(d \log S)$. Hence, the protocol does not save the verifier time for deep, narrow circuits. Arguably, this is not a major downside, because Section 6.5 explained that *any* computer program running in time T can be turned into an equivalent instance of arithmetic circuit satisfiability where the circuit is short and wide rather than long and narrow (specifically, the circuit has depth roughly $O(\log T)$ and size $\tilde{O}(T)$).

Still, even for reasonably small-depth circuits, the proofs from the warm-up GKR-derived MIP can be rather large. In this section, we give an MIP whose proof length is smaller than the warm-up GKR-based MIP by a factor of close to the circuit depth, i.e., $O(\log S)$ rather than $O(d \log S)$, which can be a substantial concrete improvement even for circuits of quite small depth. In so doing, we will see some ideas that recur in later sections when we study argument systems based on PCPs, IOPs, and linear PCPs.

The 2-Prover MIP described in the remainder of this section is a refinement of one given by Blumberg *et al.* [61], which they called Clover. It combines several new ideas with techniques from the original **MIP = NEXP** proof of [17], as well as the GKR protocol [135] and its refinements by Cormode *et al.* [102].

8.2.1   Protocol Summary

8.2.1.1   Terminology

Let $\mathcal{C}$ be an arithmetic circuit over a field $\mathbb{F}$ taking an explicit input x and a non-deterministic input w. Let $S = 2^k$ denote the number of gates in $\mathcal{C}$, and assign each gate in $\mathcal{C}$ a binary label in $\{0,1\}^k$. Refer to an assignment of values to each gate of $\mathcal{C}$ as a *transcript* of $\mathcal{C}$, and view the transcript as a function $W \colon \{0,1\}^k \to \mathbb{F}$ mapping gate labels to their values.

Given a claim that $\mathcal{C}(x,w) = y$, a *correct transcript* is a transcript in which the values assigned to the input gates are those of x, the intermediate values correspond to the correct operation of each gate in $\mathcal{C}$, and the values assigned to the output gates are y. The arithmetic circuit satisfiability problem on instance $\{\mathcal{C}, x, y\}$ is equivalent to determining whether there is a correct transcript for $\{\mathcal{C}, x, y\}$. See Figure 8.1 for an example.

8.2.1.2   Overview of the MIP

The MIP works by having $\mathcal{P}_1$ claim to "hold" an extension Z of a correct transcript W for $\{\mathcal{C}, x, y\}$. If the prover is honest, then Z will equal $\widetilde{W}$, the multilinear extension of W. The protocol then identifies a polynomial $g_{x,y,Z} \colon \mathbb{F}^{3k} \to \mathbb{F}$ (which depends on x, y, and Z) satisfying the following property: $g_{x,y,Z}(a, b, c) = 0$ for all Boolean inputs $(a, b, c) \in \{0,1\}^{3k}$ $\iff$ Z is indeed an extension of a correct transcript W.

To check that $g_{x,y,Z}$ vanishes at all Boolean inputs, the protocol identifies a related polynomial $h_{x,y,Z}$ such that $g_{x,y,Z}$ vanishes at all Boolean inputs $\iff$ the following equation holds:

$$\sum_{(a,b,c)\in\{0,1\}^{3k}} h_{x,y,Z}(a, b, c) = 0. \tag{8.1}$$

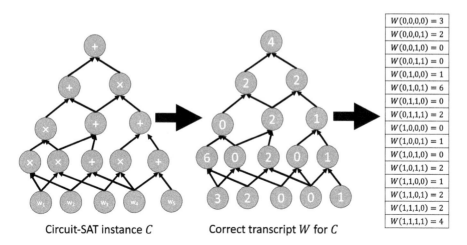

$W(0,0,0,0) = 3$	
$W(0,0,0,1) = 2$	
$W(0,0,1,0) = 0$	
$W(0,0,1,1) = 0$	
$W(0,1,0,0) = 1$	
$W(0,1,0,1) = 6$	
$W(0,1,1,0) = 0$	
$W(0,1,1,1) = 2$	
$W(1,0,0,0) = 0$	
$W(1,0,0,1) = 1$	
$W(1,0,1,0) = 0$	
$W(1,0,1,1) = 2$	
$W(1,1,0,0) = 1$	
$W(1,1,0,1) = 2$	
$W(1,1,1,0) = 2$	
$W(1,1,1,1) = 4$	

Circuit-SAT instance C Correct transcript W for C

Figure 8.1: The leftmost image depicts an arithmetic circuit C over field $\mathbb{F}$ of size 16, with no public input x, and non-deterministic input $w = (w_1, w_2, w_3, w_4, w_5) \in \mathbb{F}^5$. The middle image depicts a correct transcript W for C producing output $y = 4$. The rightmost image is the evaluation table of W when viewed as a function mapping $\{0, 1\}^4$ to $\mathbb{F}$.

Strictly speaking, the polynomial $h_{x,y,Z}$ is randomly generated, and there is a small chance over the random choice of $h_{x,y,Z}$ that Equation (8.1) holds even though $g_{x,y,Z}$ does not vanish at all Boolean inputs. The MIP applies the sum-check protocol to the polynomial $h_{x,y,Z}$ to compute this sum. Note that if Z is a low-degree polynomial, then so is $h_{x,y,Z}$, as is required both to control costs and guarantee soundness in the sum-check protocol.

At the end of the sum-check protocol, $\mathcal{V}$ needs to evaluate $h_{x,y,Z}$ at a random point, which in turn requires evaluating Z at a random point $r \in \mathbb{F}^k$. Unfortunately, $\mathcal{V}$ cannot compute $Z(r)$, since $\mathcal{V}$ does not have access to the polynomial Z (as Z only "exists" in $\mathcal{P}_1$'s head). Instead, $\mathcal{V}$ asks $\mathcal{P}_2$ to send her $Z(r)$, using the point-vs-line low-degree test (see Section 7.3.2.2). Specifically, $\mathcal{P}_2$ is asked to send Z restricted to a line Q, where Q is chosen to be a random line in $\mathbb{F}^k$ containing r. This forces $\mathcal{P}_2$ to implicitly make a claim about $Z(r)$ (note that $\mathcal{P}_2$ does not know *which* point in Q is r); $\mathcal{V}$ rejects if $\mathcal{P}_1$ and $\mathcal{P}_2$'s claims about $Z(r)$ are inconsistent, and accepts otherwise.[3]

The low-degree test cannot guarantee that Z itself is a low-degree polynomial, since $\mathcal{V}$ only ever inspects Z at a small number of points. Hence it is impossible to argue that $h_{x,y,Z}$ itself satisfies Equation (8.1): the soundness analysis for the sum-check protocol breaks down if the polynomial to which it is applied has large degree. However, the low-degree test *does* guarantee that if $\mathcal{P}_1$ and $\mathcal{P}_2$'s claims about $Z(r)$ are consistent with non-negligible probability over the random choice of r, then Z is close to a low-degree polynomial Y, in the sense that $Y(r') = Z(r')$ for a large fraction of points $r' \in \mathbb{F}^k$. Since $h_{x,y,Y}$ is low-degree, it is straightforward to tweak the soundness analysis of the sum-check protocol to argue that $h_{x,y,Y}$ satisfies Equation (8.1), and hence that Y extends a correct transcript for $\{\mathcal{C}, x, y\}$ (cf. Theorem 8.4).

Remark 8.2. The fact that the low-degree test only guarantees that the function Z is *close to* rather than *exactly equal to* a low-degree polynomial substantially complicates the soundness analysis of the MIP (Section 8.2.1.4). In (single-prover) succinct arguments derived from the MIP, the second prover can be replaced with a polynomial commitment scheme that ensures Z is *exactly equal to* a multilinear polynomial, and these complications go away. We cover such polynomial commitment schemes in Sections 10.4.2, 10.5, and Section 14. Accordingly, readers primarily interested in the resulting succinct arguments rather than the MIPs themselves can skip the detailed soundness analysis of Section 8.2.1.4.

Identical complications arose in Section 7, because the polynomial commitment scheme given there used a low-degree test and hence only bound the prover to a function close to a low-degree polynomial.

---

[3]Blumberg *et al.* [61] actually use a different low-degree test called the point-vs-plane test, despite the fact that it leads to asymptotically larger proofs and larger runtime for $\mathcal{P}_2$. They made this choice because the known soundness analyses of the point-vs-line test involve huge constant factors, and hence yield good soundness only over impractically large fields. The constant factors in known analyses of the point-vs-plane test are more reasonable [195], enabling the use of reasonably sized fields in the MIP of [61].

Preview: The importance of checking that a polynomial vanishes on a designated subspace. The problem of checking that a certain polynomial $g_{x,y,Z}$ vanishes on a designated subspace plays a central role in many MIPs and PCPs. The problem is sometimes referred to as checking a *Vanishing Reed-Solomon or Reed-Muller code* [50]. This problem will arise several more times in this survey, including in state of the art PCPs, IOPs, and linear PCPs described in Sections 9, 10, and 17. One difference is that in the PCPs, IOPs, and linear PCPs of later sections, the polynomial $g_{x,y,Z}$ is *univariate*, instead of $(3\log S)$-variate as in the MIP considered here.

Comparison to the GKR Protocol. While the GKR protocol verifies the claim $C(x, w) = y$ layer by layer, with a different instance of the sum-check protocol required for each layer of C, the MIP of this section verifies the whole circuit in one shot, using a single invocation of the sum-check protocol. The reason the GKR protocol must work layer-by-layer is that the verifier must force the prover to make a claim about (the multilinear extension of) *the input alone*, since the verifier never materializes the intermediate gates of the circuit. This is not necessary in the multi-prover setting: in the MIP, $\mathcal{P}_1$ makes a claim about an extension Z of *the entire transcript*. $\mathcal{V}$ cannot check this claim independently, but that is okay because there is a second prover to ask for help.

8.2.1.3 Protocol Details

Notation. Let add, mult: $\{0,1\}^{3k} \to \{0,1\}$ denote the functions that take as input three gate labels (a, b, c) from C and outputs 1 if and only if gate a adds (respectively, multiplies) the outputs of gates b and c. While the GKR protocol had separate functions add_i and mult_i for each layer of C, the MIP of this section arithmetizes all of C at once. We also add a third wiring predicate, which has no analog within the GKR protocol: let io: $\{0,1\}^{3k} \to \{0,1\}$ denote the function that returns 1 when gate a is either a gate from the explicit input x or one of the output gates, and gates b and c are the in-neighbors of a (input gates have in-neighbors $b = c = \mathbf{0}$).

Notice that add, mult, and io are independent of the inputs x and purported outputs y. The final function that plays a role in the MIP does depend on x and y. Define $I_{x,y} \colon \{0,1\}^k \to \mathbb{F}$ such that $I_{x,y}(a) = x_a$ if a is the label of an input gate, $I_{x,y}(a) = y_a$ if a is the label of an output gate, and $I_{x,y}(a) = 0$ otherwise.

Lemma 8.3. For $G_{x,y,W}(a,b,c) \colon \{0,1\}^{3k} \to \mathbb{F}$ defined as below, $G_{x,y,W}$ $(a,b,c) = 0$ for all $(a,b,c) \in \{0,1\}^{3k}$ if and only if W is a correct transcript for $\{C, x, y\}$:

$$
\begin{aligned}
G_{x,y,W}(a,b,c) = {} & \mathrm{io}(a,b,c) \cdot (I_{x,y}(a) - W(a)) + \mathrm{add}(a,b,c) \\
& \cdot (W(a) - (W(b) + W(c))) + \mathrm{mult}(a,b,c) \\
& \cdot (W(a) - W(b) \cdot W(c)).
\end{aligned}
$$

Proof. If W is not a correct transcript, there are five cases:

(1) Suppose $a \in \{0,1\}^k$ is the label of an input gate. If $W(a) \neq x_a$, then $G_{x,y,W}(a,0,0) = I_{x,y}(a) - W(a) = x_a - W(a) \neq 0$.

(2) Suppose $a \in \{0,1\}^k$ is the label of a non-output addition gate with in-neighbors b and c. If $W(a) \neq W(b) + W(c)$, then $G_{x,y,W}(a,b,c) = W(a) - (W(b) + W(c)) \neq 0$.

(3) Suppose $a \in \{0,1\}^k$ is the label of a non-output multiplication gate with in-neighbors b and c. If $W(a) \neq W(b) \cdot W(c)$, then $G_{x,y,W}(a,b,c) = W(a) - (W(b) \cdot W(c)) \neq 0$.

(4) Suppose $a \in \{0,1\}^k$ is the label of an output addition gate with in-neighbors b and c. If $y_a \neq W(b) + W(c)$, then $G_{x,y,W}(a,b,c) = I_{x,y}(a) - W(a) + (W(a) - (W(b) + W(c))) = y_a - (W(b) + W(c)) \neq 0$.

(5) Suppose $a \in \{0,1\}^k$ is the label of an output multiplication gate with in-neighbors b and c. If $y_a \neq W(b) \cdot W(c)$, then $G_{x,y,W}(a,b,c) = I_{x,y}(a) - W(a) + (W(a) - (W(b) \cdot W(c))) = y_a - (W(b) \cdot W(c)) \neq 0$.

On the other hand, if W is a correct transcript then it is immediate from the definition of $G_{x,y,W}$ that $G_{x,y,W}(a,b,c) = 0$ for all $(a,b,c) \in \{0,1\}^{3k}$. $\qquad\square$

For any polynomial $Z \colon \mathbb{F}^k \to \mathbb{F}$, define the associated polynomial:

$$g_{x,y,Z}(a,b,c) = \widetilde{\mathrm{io}}(a,b,c) \cdot (\widetilde{I}_{x,y}(a) - Z(a)) + \widetilde{\mathrm{add}}(a,b,c)$$
$$\cdot (Z(a) - (Z(b) + Z(c))) + \widetilde{\mathrm{mult}}(a,b,c) \cdot (Z(a) - Z(b)$$
$$\cdot Z(c)).$$

It follows from Lemma 8.3 that Z extends a correct transcript W if and only if $g_{x,y,Z}$ vanishes on the Boolean hypercube. We now define a polynomial $h_{x,y,Z}$ such that $g_{x,y,Z}$ vanishes on the Boolean hypercube if and only if $\sum_{u \in \{0,1\}^{3k}} h_{x,y,Z}(u) = 0$.

Defining $h_{x,y,Z}$. As in Lemma 4.9 of Section 4.6.7.1, let $\beta_{3k}(a,b) \colon \{0,1\}^{3k} \times \{0,1\}^{3k} \to \{0,1\}$ be the function that evaluates to 1 if $a = b$, and evaluates to 0 otherwise, and define the formal polynomial

$$\widetilde{\beta}_{3k}(a,b) = \prod_{j=1}^{3k} ((1 - a_j)(1 - b_j) + a_j b_j).$$

It is straightforward to check that $\widetilde{\beta}_{3k}$ is the multilinear extension β_{3k}. Indeed, $\widetilde{\beta}_{3k}$ is a multilinear polynomial. And for $a, b \in \{0,1\}^{3k}$, it is easy to check that $\widetilde{\beta}_{3k}(a,b) = 1$ if and only if a and b are equal coordinate-wise.

Consider the polynomial

$$p(X) := \sum_{u \in \{0,1\}^{3k}} \widetilde{\beta}_{3k}(X,u) \cdot g_{x,y,Z}(u).$$

Clearly p is multilinear since $\widetilde{\beta}$ is, and p vanishes on all inputs in $\{0,1\}^{3k}$ if and only if $g_{x,y,Z}$ does. Since the multilinear extension on domain $\{0,1\}^{3k}$ is unique, this means that p is the *identically zero* polynomial if and only if $g_{x,y,Z}$ vanishes on all inputs in $\{0,1\}^{3k}$. For the verifier to check that p is indeed the zero-polynomial, it is enough for the verifier to pick a random input $r \in \{0,1\}^{3k}$ and confirm that $p(r) = 0$, because if p is any *nonzero* polynomial of total degree at most d, the Schwartz-Zippel lemma implies that $p(r)$ will equal 0 with probability at most $d/|\mathbb{F}|$.

Hence, we define

$$h_{x,y,Z}(Y) := \tilde{\beta}_{3k}(r, Y) \cdot g_{x,y,Z}(Y). \tag{8.2}$$

This definition ensures that $p(r) = \sum_{u \in \{0,1\}^{3k}} h_{x,y,Z}(u)$.

In summary, in the MIP, $\mathcal{V}$ chooses r uniformly at random from the set $\mathbb{F}^{3k}$, defines $h_{x,y,Z}$ based on r as per Equation (8.2), and is convinced that Z extends a correct transcript for $\{\mathcal{C}, x, y\}$ as long as

$$0 = \sum_{u \in \{0,1\}^{3k}} h_{x,y,Z}(u).$$

More formally, if $g_{x,y,Z}$ has total degree at most d, then with probability at least $1 - (d+1)/|\mathbb{F}|$ over the random choice of r, if $g_{x,y,Z}$ does not vanish on the Boolean hypercube then $\sum_{u \in \{0,1\}^{3k}} h_{x,y,Z}(u) \neq 0$. For simplicity, the remainder of the presentation ignores the $(d+1)/|\mathbb{F}|$ probability of error in this step (the $(d+1)/|\mathbb{F}|$ can be absorbed into the soundness error of the entire MIP).

Applying the Sum-Check Protocol to $h_{x,y,Z}$. $\mathcal{V}$ applies the sum-check protocol to $h_{x,y,Z}$, with $\mathcal{P}_1$ playing the role of the prover in this protocol. To perform the final check in this protocol, $\mathcal{V}$ needs to evaluate $h_{x,y,Z}$ at a random point $r \in \mathbb{F}^{3k}$. Let r_1, r_2, r_3 denote the first, second, and third k entries of r. Then evaluating $h_{x,y,Z}(r)$ requires evaluating $K_q(r)$, $\widetilde{\text{io}}(r)$, $\widetilde{\text{add}}(r)$, $\widetilde{\text{mult}}(r)$, $\tilde{I}_{x,y}(r_1)$, $Z(r_1)$, $Z(r_2)$, and $Z(r_3)$. $\mathcal{V}$ can compute the first five evaluations without help in $O(\log(T))$ time, assuming that $\widetilde{\text{add}}$ and $\widetilde{\text{mult}}$ can be computed within this time bound (see Section 4.6.6 for further discussion of this assumption). However, $\mathcal{V}$ cannot evaluate $Z(r_1)$, $Z(r_2)$, or $Z(r_3)$ without help, because $\mathcal{V}$ does not know Z. To deal with this, the verifier first uses the technique from Section 4.5.2 to reduce the evaluation of Z at the three points r_1, r_2, and r_3, to the evaluation of Z at a single point $r_4 \in \mathbb{F}^k$. This reduction forces $\mathcal{P}_1$ to make a claim regarding the value of $Z(r_4)$. Unfortunately, $\mathcal{V}$ does not know Z and hence cannot evaluate $Z(r_4)$ unaided. To obtain the evaluation $Z(r_4)$, $\mathcal{V}$ turns to $\mathcal{P}_2$.

The Low-Degree Test. $\mathcal{V}$ sends $\mathcal{P}_2$ a random line Q in $\mathbb{F}^k$ passing through r_4, and demands that $\mathcal{P}_2$ reply with a univariate polynomial of degree at most k, claimed to equal Z restricted to Q. Note that $\mathcal{P}_2$

does not know *which* of the $|\mathbb{F}|$ many points on the line Q equals r_4. Since r_4 lies on Q, $\mathcal{P}_2$'s response implicitly specifies a value for $Z(r_4)$. $\mathcal{V}$ accepts if this value equals that claimed by $\mathcal{P}_1$ and rejects otherwise.

8.2.1.4 MIP Soundness Analysis

Theorem 8.4. Suppose that $\mathcal{P}_1$ and $\mathcal{P}_2$ convince the MIP verifier to accept with probability $\gamma > .5 + \varepsilon$ for $\varepsilon = \Omega(1)$. Then there is some polynomial Y such that $h_{x,y,Y}$ satisfies Equation (8.1).

Detailed Sketch. Let Z^* denote the function that on input r_4 outputs $\mathcal{P}_1$'s claimed value for $Z(r_4)$.[4] If $\mathcal{P}_1$ and $\mathcal{P}_2$ pass the low-degree test with probability at least γ, known analyses of the low-degree test guarantee that, if working over a sufficiently large field $\mathbb{F}$, there is some polynomial Y of total degree at most k such that Z^* and Y agree on a $p \geq \gamma - o(1)$ fraction of points. Since Y has total degree at most k, $h_{x,y,Y}$ has total degree at most $6k$.

Suppose that $h_{x,y,Y}$ does not satisfy Equation (8.1). Let us say that $\mathcal{P}_1$ *cheats* at round i of the sum-check protocol if he does not send the message that is prescribed by the sum-check protocol in that round, when applied to the polynomial $h_{x,y,Y}$. The soundness analysis of the sum-check protocol (Section 4.1) implies that if $\mathcal{P}_1$ falsely claims that $h_{x,y,Y}$ does satisfy Equation (8.1), then with probability at least $1-(3k)\cdot(6k)/|\mathbb{F}| = 1-o(1)$, $\mathcal{P}_1$ will be forced to cheat at all rounds of the sum-check protocol including the last one. This means that in the last round, $\mathcal{P}_1$ sends a message that is inconsistent with the polynomial Y.

If $\mathcal{P}_1$ does cheat in the last round, the verifier will reject unless, in the final check of the protocol, the verifier winds up choosing a point in $\mathbb{F}^{3k}$ at which $h_{x,y,Y}$ and h_{x,y,Z^*} disagree. This only happens if $\mathcal{V}$ picks a point $r_4 \in \mathbb{F}^k$ for use in the low-degree test such that $Y(r_4) \neq Z(r_4)$. But this occurs with probability only $1 - p = 1 - \gamma + o(1)$. In total, the probability that $\mathcal{P}_1$ passes all tests is therefore at most $1 - \gamma + o(1)$.

---

[4] In principle, $\mathcal{P}_1$'s claim about $Z(r_4)$ could depend on other messages sent to $\mathcal{P}_1$ by $\mathcal{V}$, namely r_1, r_2, and r_3. This turns out not to help $\mathcal{P}_1$ pass the verifier's checks. In our proof sketch, we simply assume for clarity and brevity that $\mathcal{P}_1$'s claim about $Z(r_4)$ depends on r_4 alone.

If $\gamma > \frac{1}{2}$, this contradicts the fact that $\mathcal{P}_1$ and $\mathcal{P}_2$ convince the MIP verifier to accept with probability at least γ.   □

Recall that if $h_{x,y,Y}$ satisfies Equation (8.1), then $g_{x,y,Y}$ vanishes on the Boolean hypercube, and hence Y is an extension of a correct transcript for $\{\mathcal{C}, x, y\}$. So Theorem 8.4 implies that if the MIP verifier accepts with probability $\gamma > \frac{1}{2}$, then there is a correct transcript for $\{\mathcal{C}, x, y\}$.

Although the soundness error can reduced from $\frac{1}{2} + o(1)$ to an arbitrarily small constant with $O(1)$ independent repetitions of the MIP, this would be highly expensive in practice. Fortunately, it is possible to perform a more careful soundness analysis that establishes that the MIP itself, *without repetition*, has soundness error $o(1)$.

The bottleneck in the soundness analysis of Theorem 8.4 that prevents the establishment of soundness error less than $\frac{1}{2}$ is that, if the prover's pass the low-degree test with probability $\gamma < \frac{1}{2}$, then one can only guarantee that there is a polynomial Y that agrees with Z on a γ fraction of points. The verifier will choose a random point r in the sum-check protocol at which Y and Z disagree with probability $1 - \gamma > \frac{1}{2}$, and in this case all bets are off.

The key to the stronger analysis is to use a stronger guarantee from the low-degree test, known as a *list-decoding guarantee*. Roughly speaking, the list-decoding guarantee ensures that if the oracles pass the low-degree test with probability γ, then there is a "small" number of low-degree polynomials $Q_1, Q_2, \dots$ that "explain" essentially all of the tester's acceptance, in the sense that for almost all points r at which the low-degree test passes, $Z^*(r)$ agrees with $Q_i(r)$ for at least one i. This allows one to argue that even if the provers pass the low-degree test with probability only $\gamma < \frac{1}{2}$, the sum-check protocol will still catch $\mathcal{P}_1$ in a lie with probability very close to 1. Here is a very rough sketch of the analysis. For each polynomial Q_i individually, if $\mathcal{P}_1$ were to claim at the end of its interaction with $\mathcal{V}$ that $Z(r_4) = Q_i(r_4)$, then the probability of $\mathcal{P}_1$ passing all of the verifier's checks is negligible. As there are only a small number of Q_i's, a union bound over all Q_i implies that the probability $\mathcal{P}_1$ passes all of the verifier's checks and is able to claim that $Z(r_4) = Q_i(r_4)$ for *some* Q_i is still negligible. Meanwhile, if $\mathcal{P}_1$ does *not* claim that $Z(r_4) = Q_i(r_4)$ for some Q_i, the list-decoding guarantee of the low-degree test states that that the provers will fail the low-degree test except with tiny probability.

8.2.1.5 Protocol Costs

Verifier's Costs. $\mathcal{V}$ and $\mathcal{P}_1$ exchanges two messages for each variable of $h_{x,y,z}$, and where $\mathcal{P}_2$ exchanges two messages in total with $\mathcal{V}$. This is $O(\log S)$ messages in total. Each message from $\mathcal{P}_1$ is a polynomial of degree $O(1)$, while the message from $\mathcal{P}_2$ is a univariate polynomial of total degree $O(\log S)$. In total, all messages can be specified using $O(\log S)$ field elements. As for $\mathcal{V}$'s runtime, the verifier has to process the provers' messages, and then to perform the last check in the sum-check protocol, she must evaluate $\widetilde{\text{add}}$, $\widetilde{\text{mult}}$, $\widetilde{\text{io}}$, and $\widetilde{I}$ at random points. The verifier requires $O(\log S)$ time to process the provers' messages, and Lemma 3.8 implies that $\mathcal{V}$ can evaluate $\widetilde{I}$ at a random point in $O(n)$ time. We assume here that $\widetilde{\text{add}}$, $\widetilde{\text{mult}}$, and $\widetilde{\text{io}}$ can be evaluated at a point in time $\text{polylog}(S)$ as well— see Section 4.6.6 and the end of Section 6.5 for discussion of this assumption, and what to do if it does not hold.

Prover's Costs. Blumberg *et al.* [61] showed that, using the techniques developed to implement the prover in the GKR protocol (Section 4.6), specifically Method 2 described there, $\mathcal{P}_1$ can be implemented in $O(S \log S)$ time. In fact, using more advanced techniques (e.g., Lemma 4.5), it is possible to implement the first prover in $O(S)$ time. $\mathcal{P}_2$ needs to specify $\widetilde{W} \circ Q$, where Q is a random line in $\mathbb{F}^k$. Since $\widetilde{W} \circ Q$ is a univariate polynomial of degree $\log S$, it suffices for $\mathcal{P}_2$ to evaluate $\widetilde{W}$ at $1 + \log S$ many points on the line Q—using Lemma 3.8, this can be done in $O(S)$ time per point, resulting in a total runtime of $O(S \log S)$.

8.3 A Succinct Argument for Deep Circuits

Using any polynomial commitment scheme, one can turn the MIP of the previous section into a succinct argument for deep and narrow arithmetic circuits.[5] Specifically, one gets rid of the second prover, and instead just had the first prover commit to $\tilde{W}$ at the start of the protocol. At the end of the verifier's interaction with the first prover in the MIP above, the first prover makes a claim about $\tilde{W}(r_4)$, which the verifier checks directly by having the prover reveal it via the polynomial commitment protocol.

This succinct argument has an advantage over the approach to succinct argument from Section 7 that was based directly on the GKR protocol: namely, the argument system based on the MIP of the previous section is succinct with a nearly-linear time verifier *even for deep and narrow circuits*. In fact, the MIP-based argument system will have shorter proofs by a factor roughly equal to the depth of the circuit, which can be a significant savings even when the depth is quite small.

The *disadvantage* of the argument system from the previous section is that it applies the polynomial commitment scheme to the entire *transcript extension* $\tilde{W} \colon \mathbb{F}^{\log |\mathcal{C}|} \to \mathbb{F}$, whereas the argument system of Section 7 applied the polynomial commitment scheme only to the multilinear extension of the *witness* $\tilde{w}$. The expense of applying a commitment scheme to $\tilde{w}$ will be much smaller than the expense of applying it to $\tilde{W}$ if the the witness size $|w|$ is much smaller than the circuit size $|\mathcal{C}|$.

Existing polynomial commitment schemes are still the concrete bottlenecks for the prover and verifier in argument systems that use them [226]. Since the witness w can be much smaller than circuit $\mathcal{C}$, applying the polynomial commitment scheme to $\tilde{w}$ can be significantly less expensive than applying it to $\tilde{W}$ (so long as the witness makes up only a small fraction of the total number of gates in the circuit). Besides, we've seen that short, wide circuits are "universal" in the context of succinct arguments, since any RAM running in time T can be turned into an instance of arithmetic circuit satisfiability of size close to T and depth close to $O(\log T)$. In summary, which approach yields a superior argument system for circuit satisfiability in practice depends on many

---

[5]The polynomial commitment scheme should be extractable in addition to binding. See Section 7.4 for details.

factors, including witness size, circuit depth, the relative importance of proof length vs. other protocol costs, etc.

Remark 8.3. Bitansky and Chiesa [55] gave a different way to transform MIPs into succinct arguments, but their transformation used multiple layers of fully homomorphic encryption, rendering it highly impractical. Unlike the MIP-to-argument transformation in this section, Bitansky and Chiesa's transformation works for *arbitrary* MIPs. The transformation in this section exploits additional structure of the specific MIP of this section, specifically the fact that the sole purpose of the second prover in the MIP is to run a low-degree test. In the setting of succinct arguments, this role played by the second prover can be replaced with a polynomial commitment scheme. In summary, while Bitansky and Chiesa's transformation from MIPs to arguments is more general— applying to arbitrary MIPs, not just those in which the second prover is solely used to run a low-degree test—it is also much less efficient than the transformation of this section.

8.4 Extension from Circuit-SAT to R1CS-SAT

Section 6 gave techniques for turning computer programs into equivalent instances of arithmetic circuit satisfiability, and Section 7 and this section gave succinct non-interactive arguments for arithmetic circuit satisfiability. Arithmetic circuit satisfiability is an example of an *intermediate representation*, a term that refers to any model of computation that is directly amenable to application of interactive proof or argument systems.

A related intermediate representation that has proven popular and convenient in practice is *rank-1 constraint system* (R1CS) instances (also sometimes referred to as *Quadratic Arithmetic Programs* (QAPs)). An R1CS instance is specified by three $m \times n$ matrices A, B, C with entries from a field $\mathbb{F}$ and is satisfiable if and only if there is a vector $z \in \mathbb{F}^n$ with $z_1 = 1$ such that

$$(A \cdot z) \circ (B \cdot z) = C \cdot z. \tag{8.3}$$

Here, $\cdot$ denotes matrix-vector product, and $\circ$ denotes entrywise (a.k.a. Hadamard) product. Any vector z satisfying Equation (8.3) is analogous to the notion of a "correct transcript" in the context of arithmetic circuit satisfiability (Section 8.2.1.1). We require that the first entry z_1 of z be fixed to 1 because otherwise the all-zeros vector would trivially satisfy *any* R1CS instance, and to ensure that there are efficient transformations from circuit-SAT to R1CS-SAT (see Section 8.4.1).

8.4.1   Relationship Between R1CS-SAT and Arithmetic Circuit-SAT

The R1CS-SAT problem can be thought of as a generalization of the Arithmetic Circuit-SAT problem in the following sense: any instance of Arithmetic Circuit-SAT can be efficiently transformed into instances of R1CS-SAT. The number of rows and columns of the matrices appearing in the resulting R1CS instance is proportional to the number of gates in $\mathcal{C}$, and the number of nonzero entries in any row of the matrices is bounded above by the fan-in of the circuit $\mathcal{C}$. For fan-in two circuits, this means that the equivalent R1CS-SAT instances are sparse, and hence we will ultimately seek protocols where the prover(s) run in time proportional to the number of nonzero entries of these matrices.

To see this, consider an instance $\{\mathcal{C}, x, y\}$ of arithmetic circuit-SAT, i.e., where the prover wants to convince the verifier that there is a w such that $\mathcal{C}(x, w) = y$. We need to construct matrices A, B, C such that there exists a vector z such that Equation (8.3) holds if and only if the preceding sentence is true.

Let N be the sum of the lengths of x, y, and w, plus the number of gates in $\mathcal{C}$, and let $M = N - |w|$. The R1CS-SAT instance will consist of three $M \times (N + 1)$ matrices A, B, and C. We will fix the first entry z of z to 1, and associate each remaining entry of z with either an entry of x, y, or w, or a gate of $\mathcal{C}$.

For an entry j of z corresponding to an entry x_i of x, we define the jth row of A, B, C to capture the constraint the z_j must equal x_i. That is, we set the jth row of A to be the standard basis vector $e_1 \in \mathbb{F}^{N+1}$, the jth row of B to be the standard basis vector $e_j \in \mathbb{F}^{N+1}$, and the jth row of C to be $x_i \cdot e_1$. This means that the jth constraint in the R1CS system asserts that $z_j - x_i = 0$ which is equivalent to demanding that $z_j = x_i$. We include an analogous constraint for each entry j of z corresponding to an entry of y.

For each entry j of z corresponding to an addition gate of $\mathcal{C}$ (with in-neighbors indexed by $j', j'' \in \{2, \ldots, N+1\}$), we define the jth row of A, B, C to capture the constraint that z_j must equal the sum of the two inputs to that addition gate. That is, we set the jth row of A to be the standard basis vector $e_1 \in \mathbb{F}^{N+1}$, the jth row of B to be $e_{j'} + e_{j''} \in \mathbb{F}^{N+1}$, and the jth row of C to be e_j. This means that the jth constraint in the R1CS system asserts that $(z_{j'} + z_{j''}) - z_j = 0$ which is equivalent to demanding that $z_j = z_{j'} + z_{j''}$.

Finally, for each entry j of z corresponding to a multiplication gate of $\mathcal{C}$ (with in-neighbors indexed by $j', j'' \in \{2, \ldots, N+1\}$), we define the jth row of A, B, C to capture the constraint the z_j must equal the product of the two inputs to that gate. That is, we set the jth row of A to be the standard basis vector $e_{j'} \in \mathbb{F}^{N+1}$, the jth row of B to be the standard basis vector $e_{j''} \in \mathbb{F}^{N+1}$, and the jth row of C to be e_j. This means that the jth constraint in the R1CS system asserts that $(z_{j'} \cdot z_{j''}) - z_j = 0$ which is equivalent to demanding that $z_j = z_{j'} \cdot z_{j''}$.

Figure 8.2 has an example circuit and the R1CS instance resulting from the above transformation.

8.4.2 An MIP for R1CS-SAT

As observed in [226], we can apply the ideas of this section to give an MIP and associated succinct argument for R1CS instances. View the matrices A, B, C as functions $f_A, f_B, f_C \colon \{0, 1\}^{\log_2 m} \times \{0, 1\}^{\log_2 n} \to \mathbb{F}$ in the natural way as per Sections 4.3 and 4.4. Just as in the MIP of this section (Section 8.2.1.2), the prover claims to hold an extension polynomial Z of a correct transcript z for the R1CS instance. Observe that a polynomial $Z \colon \mathbb{F}^{\log_2 m} \times \mathbb{F}^{\log_2 n} \to \mathbb{F}$ extends a correct transcript z for the R1CS instance if and only if the following equation holds for all $a \in \{0, 1\}^{\log_2 m}$:

$$
\left(\sum_{b \in \{0,1\}^{\log_2 n}} \tilde{f}_A(a, b) \cdot Z(b) \right) \cdot \left(\sum_{b \in \{0,1\}^{\log_2 n}} \tilde{f}_B(a, b) \cdot Z(b) \right)
$$

$$
- \left(\sum_{b \in \{0,1\}^{\log_2 n}} \tilde{f}_C(a, b) \cdot Z(b) \right) = 0. \tag{8.4}
$$

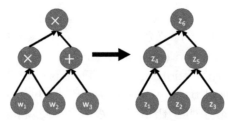

$$\left(\begin{bmatrix} 0 & 1 & 0 & 0 & 0 & 0 & 0 \\ 1 & 0 & 0 & 0 & 0 & 0 & 0 \\ 0 & 0 & 0 & 0 & 1 & 0 & 0 \\ 1 & 0 & 0 & 0 & 0 & 0 & 0 \end{bmatrix} \begin{bmatrix} 1 \\ z_1 \\ z_2 \\ z_3 \\ z_4 \\ z_5 \\ z_6 \end{bmatrix} \right) \circ \left(\begin{bmatrix} 0 & 0 & 1 & 0 & 0 & 0 & 0 \\ 0 & 0 & 1 & 1 & 0 & 0 & 0 \\ 0 & 0 & 0 & 0 & 0 & 1 & 0 \\ 0 & 0 & 0 & 0 & 0 & 0 & 1 \end{bmatrix} \begin{bmatrix} 1 \\ z_1 \\ z_2 \\ z_3 \\ z_4 \\ z_5 \\ z_6 \end{bmatrix} \right) = \begin{bmatrix} 0 & 0 & 0 & 0 & 1 & 0 & 0 \\ 0 & 0 & 0 & 0 & 0 & 1 & 0 \\ 0 & 0 & 0 & 0 & 0 & 0 & 1 \\ y & 0 & 0 & 0 & 0 & 0 & 0 \end{bmatrix} \begin{bmatrix} 1 \\ z_1 \\ z_2 \\ z_3 \\ z_4 \\ z_5 \\ z_6 \end{bmatrix}$$

Equivalently,

$$z_1 \cdot z_2 = z_4$$
$$1 \cdot (z_2 + z_3) = z_5$$
$$z_4 \cdot z_5 = z_6$$
$$1 \cdot z_6 = y$$

Figure 8.2: An arithmetic circuit and an equivalent R1CS instance. Knowing a witness w such that $\mathcal{C}(w) = y$ is equivalent to knowing a vector z that satisfies the constraints of the R1CS. The R1CS instance is expressed in both matrix form and, for readability, as a list of constraints.

Let g_Z denote the $(\log_2(m))$-variate polynomial

$$g_Z(X) = \left(\sum_{b \in \{0,1\}^{\log_2 n}} \tilde{f}_A(X, b) \cdot Z(b) \right) \cdot \left(\sum_{b \in \{0,1\}^{\log_2 n}} \tilde{f}_B(X, b) \cdot Z(b) \right)$$
$$- \left(\sum_{b \in \{0,1\}^{\log_2 n}} \tilde{f}_C(X, b) \cdot Z(b) \right) \tag{8.5}$$

This polynomial has degree at most 2 in each variable (i.e., it is multi-quadratic), and Equation (8.4) holds if and only if g_Z vanishes at all inputs in $\{0, 1\}^{\log_2 m}$.

We obtain an MIP for checking that g_Z vanishes over the Boolean hypercube in a manner analogous to Section 8.2.1.3. Specifically, we can define a related polynomial h_Z by picking a random point $r \in \{0, 1\}^{\log_2 m}$

and, in analogy with Equation (8.2), defining

$$h_Z(Y) = \tilde{\beta}_{\log_2 m}(r, Y) \cdot g_Z(Y).$$

Following the reasoning preceding Equation (8.2), by the Schwartz-Zippel Lemma, it holds that, up to a negligible soundness error (at most $\log_2(m)/|\mathbb{F}|$), g_Z vanishes on the Boolean hypercube if and only if

$$\sum_{a \in \{0,1\}^{\log_2 m}} h_Z(a) = 0.$$

The verifier can compute this last expression by applying the sum-check protocol to the polynomial

$$h_Z(Y) = \tilde{\beta}_{\log_2 m}(r, Y) \cdot g_Z(Y).$$

After applying the sum-check protocol to $h_Z(Y)$, the verifier needs to evaluate $h_Z(Y)$ at a random input $r' \in \mathbb{F}^{\log_2 m}$. To evaluate $h_Z(r')$, it is enough for the verifier to evaluate $\tilde{\beta}_{\log_2 m}(r, r')$ and $g_Z(r')$. The former quantity can be evaluated by the verifier in $O(\log_2 m)$ operations in $\mathbb{F}$ using Equation (4.19). The verifier cannot efficiently evaluate $g_Z(r')$ on its own, but by definition (Equation (8.5)), this quantity equals:

$$\left(\sum_{b \in \{0,1\}^{\log_2 n}} \tilde{f}_A(r', b) \cdot Z(b) \right) \cdot \left(\sum_{b \in \{0,1\}^{\log_2 n}} \tilde{f}_B(r', b) \cdot Z(b) \right)$$
$$- \left(\sum_{b \in \{0,1\}^{\log_2 n}} \tilde{f}_C(r', b) \cdot Z(b) \right). \tag{8.6}$$

This means that to compute $g_Z(r')$, it suffices to apply the sum-check protocol three more times, to the following three $(\log_2(n))$-variate polynomials:

$$p_1(X) = \tilde{f}_A(r', X) \cdot Z(X).$$
$$p_2(X) = \tilde{f}_B(r', X) \cdot Z(X).$$
$$p_3(X) = \tilde{f}_C(r', X) \cdot Z(X).$$

This is because applying the sum-check protocol to $p_1(X)$ computes

$$\left(\sum_{b \in \{0,1\}^{\log_2 n}} \tilde{f}_A(r', b) \cdot Z(b) \right)$$

and similarly applying the sum-check protocol to p_2 and p_3 computes the remaining two quantities appearing in Equation (8.6). As a concrete optimization, all three invocations of sum-check can be executed in parallel, using the same randomness in each of the three invocations.

At the end of these three final invocations of the sum-check protocol, the verifier needs to evaluate each of p_1, p_2, p_3 at a random input r''. To accomplish this, it suffices for the verifier to evaluate $\tilde{f}_A(r', r'')$, $\tilde{f}_B(r', r'')$, $\tilde{f}_C(r', r'')$, and $Z(r'')$.

At this point, the situation is exactly analogous to the MIP for arithmetic circuit-SAT of Section 8.2.1.3, with $\tilde{f}_A$, $\tilde{f}_B$, and $\tilde{f}_C$ playing the roles of the "wiring predicates" $\widetilde{\text{add}}$ and $\widetilde{\text{mult}}$. That is, for many natural R1CS systems, the verifier can evaluate $\tilde{f}_A$, $\tilde{f}_B$, and $\tilde{f}_C$ in logarithmic time unaided, and $Z(r'')$ can be obtained from the second prover using a low-degree test

Regarding the prover's runtime, we claim that the first prover in the MIP, if given a satisfying assignment $z \in \mathbb{F}^n$ for the R1CS instance, can be implemented in time proportional to the number K of nonzero entries of the matrices A, B, and C. Here, we assume without loss of generality that this number is at least $n + m$, i.e., no row or column of any matrix is all zeros.

We begin by showing that in the first invocation of the sum-check protocol within the MIP, to the polynomial $h_Z(Y)$, the prover can be implemented in time proportional to the number of nonzero entries of A, B, and C. This holds by the following reasoning. First, observe that

$$h_Z(Y) = \tilde{\beta}_{\log_2 m}(r, Y) \cdot g_Z(Y) = \tilde{\beta}_{\log_2 m}(r, Y) \cdot q_1(Y) \cdot q_2(Y)$$
$$- \tilde{\beta}_{\log_2 m}(r, Y) \cdot q_3(Y), \tag{8.7}$$

where

$$q_1(Y) = \left(\sum_{b \in \{0,1\}^{\log_2 n}} \tilde{f}_A(Y, b) \cdot Z(b) \right),$$

$$q_2(Y) = \left(\sum_{b \in \{0,1\}^{\log_2 n}} \tilde{f}_B(Y, b) \cdot Z(b) \right),$$

$$q_3(Y) = \left(\sum_{b \in \{0,1\}^{\log_2 n}} \tilde{f}_C(Y, b) \cdot Z(b) \right).$$

We wish to apply Lemma 4.5 to conclude that the prover in the sum-check protocol applied the h_Z can be implemented quickly. Since $\widetilde{\beta}_{\log_2 m}(r, Y)$, $q_1(Y)$, $q_2(Y)$, and $q_3(Y)$ are all multilinear polynomials in the variables Y, to apply Lemma 4.5, it is enough to show that all four of these multilinear polynomials can be evaluated at all inputs $a \in \{0, 1\}^{\log_2 m}$ in time proportional to the number of nonzero entries of A, B, and C.[6]

First, we observe that $\widetilde{\beta}_{\log_2 m}(r, a)$ can be evaluated by the prover at all inputs $a \in \{0, 1\}^{\log_2 m}$ in $O(m)$ total time, as this task is equivalent to evaluating all $(\log m)$-variate Lagrange basis polynomials at input $r \in \mathbb{F}^{\log m}$, which the proof of Lemma 3.8 revealed is possible to achieve in $O(m)$ time.

Second, we turn to the claim that q_1, q_2, and q_3 can be evaluated at all inputs $a \in \{0, 1\}^{\log_2 m}$ in the requisite time bound. This holds because, if we interpret $a \in \{0, 1\}^{\log_2 m}$ as a number in $\{1, ..., m\}$ and let A_a, B_a, and C_a respectively denote the ath row of A, B, and C, then $q_1(a)$ is simply $A_a \cdot z$, and similarly $q_2(a) = B_a \cdot z$ and $q_3(a) = C_a \cdot z$. Hence all three polynomials can be evaluated at *all* $a \in \{0, 1\}^{\log_2(m)}$ in time proportional to the number of nonzero entries of the three matrices A, B, and C.

Similar observations reveal that the prover in the three invocations of the sum-check protocol applied to p_1, p_2, and p_3 can also be implemented in time proportional to the number of nonzero entries of A, B, and C. For example, $p_1(X)$ is a product of two multilinear polynomials $\widetilde{f}_A(r', X)$ and $Z(X)$. To apply Lemma 4.5, the evaluations of $Z(X)$ at all inputs $b \in \{0, 1\}^{\log_2 n}$ are directly given by the satisfying assignment vector z for the R1CS instance. Turning to $\widetilde{f}_A(r', X)$, let $v \in \mathbb{F}^n$ denote the vector of all $(\log_2 n)$-variate Lagrange basis polynomials evaluated at r'. Note that the proof of Lemma 3.8 shows that the vector v can be computed in $O(n)$ time. It can be seen that for $b \in \{0, 1\}^{\log_2 n}$, $\widetilde{f}_A(r', b)$

---

[6]Equation (8.7) represents h_Z as a *sum* of products of $O(1)$ multilinear polynomials, while Lemma 4.5 as stated applies only to products of $O(1)$ multilinear polynomials directly. But the lemma extends easily to sums of polynomials, because the honest prover's messages in the sum-check protocol applied to a sum of two polynomials p and q is just the sum of the messages when the sum-check protocol is applied to p and q individually.

is just the inner product of v with the b'th column of A, which (given v) can be computed in time proportional to the number of nonzero entries in this column of A. This completes the explanation of why $p_1(X)$ can be evaluated at all inputs $b \in \{0,1\}^{\log_2 n}$ in time proportional to the number of nonzero entries of A, and similarly for $p_2(X)$ and $p_3(X)$ (with A replaced with B and C respectively).

8.5 MIP = NEXP

In the MIP for arithmetic circuit-SAT of Section 8.2, if the circuit has size S then the verifier's runtime is $\mathrm{poly}(\log S)$, plus the time required to evaluate $\widetilde{\mathrm{add}}$, $\widetilde{\mathrm{mult}}$, and $\widetilde{\mathrm{io}}$ at random inputs. The transformation from computer programs to circuit-SAT instances sketched in Section 6.5 transforms any non-deterministic Random Access Machine running in time T into an arithmetic circuit of size $\tilde{O}(T)$ in which $\widetilde{\mathrm{add}}$, $\widetilde{\mathrm{mult}}$, and $\widetilde{\mathrm{io}}$ can be evaluated at any desired point in time $O(\log T)$. This means that the verifier in the MIP applied to the resulting circuit runs in polynomial time as long as $T \leq 2^{n^c}$ for some constant $c > 0$. In other words, the class of problems solvable in non-deterministic exponential time (**NEXP**) is contained in **MIP**, the class of languages solvable by a multi-prover interactive proof with a polynomial time verifier [17].

The other inclusion, that **MIP** $\subseteq$ **NEXP**, follows from the following simple reasoning. Given any multi-prover interactive proof system for a language $\mathcal{L}$ and input x, one can in non-deterministic exponential time calculate the acceptance probability of the optimal strategy available to provers attempting to convince the verifier to accept, as follows. First, non-deterministically guess the optimal strategies of the provers. Second, compute the acceptance probability that the strategy induces by enumerating over all possible coin tosses of the verifier and seeing how many lead to acceptance when interacting with the optimal prover strategy [113]. Since the multi-prover interactive proof system is a valid MIP for $\mathcal{L}$ this acceptance probability is at least $2/3$ if and only if $x \in \mathcal{L}$.

9

PCPs and Succinct Arguments

9.1 PCPs: Definitions and Relationship to MIPs

In an MIP, if a prover is asked multiple questions by the verifier, then the prover can behave adaptively, which means that the prover's responses to any question can depend on the earlier questions asked by the verifier. This adaptivity was potentially bad for soundness, because the prover's ability to behave adaptively makes it harder to "pin down" the prover(s) in a lie. But, as will become clear below, it was potentially good for efficiency, since an adaptive prover can be asked a sequence of questions, and only needs to "think up" answers to questions that are actually asked.

In contrast, Probabilistically Checkable Proofs (PCPs) have non-adaptivity baked directly into the definition, by considering a verifier $\mathcal{V}$ who is given oracle access to a static proof string π. Since π is static, $\mathcal{V}$ can ask several queries to π, and π's response to any query q_i can depend only on q_i, and not on q_j for $j \neq i$.

Definition 9.1. A probabilistically checkable proof system (PCP) for a language $\mathcal{L} \subseteq \{0,1\}^*$ consists of a probabilistic polynomial time verifier $\mathcal{V}$ who is given access to an input x, and oracle access to a proof string

223

$\pi \in \Sigma^\ell$. The PCP has completeness error δ_c and soundness error δ_s if the following two properties hold.

(1) *(Completeness)* For every $x \in \mathcal{L}$, there exists a proof string $\pi \in \Sigma^\ell$ such that $\Pr[\mathcal{V}^\pi(x) = \text{accept}] \geq 1 - \delta_c$.

(2) *(Soundness)* For every $x \notin \mathcal{L}$ and every proof string $\pi \in \Sigma^\ell$, $\Pr[\mathcal{V}^\pi(x) = \text{accept}] \leq \delta_s$.

ℓ is referred to as the *length* of the proof, and Σ as the alphabet used for the proof. We think of all of these parameters as functions of the input size n. We refer to the time required to *generate* the honest proof string π as the prover time of the PCP.

Remark 9.1. The PCP model was introduced by Fortnow *et al.* [113], who referred to it as the "oracle" model (we used this terminology in Lemma 8.2). The term Probabilistically Checkable Proofs was coined by Arora and Safra [11].

Remark 9.2. Traditionally, the notation $\mathbf{PCP}_{\delta_c,\delta_s}[r,q]_\Sigma$ is used to denote the class of languages that have a PCP verifier with completeness error δ_c, soundness error δ_s, and in which the verifier uses at most r random bits, and makes at most q queries to a proof string π over alphabet Σ. This notation is motivated in part by the importance of the parameters r, q, and Σ in applications to hardness of approximation. In the setting of verifiable computing, the most important costs are typically the verifier's and prover's runtime, and the total number q of queries (since, when PCPs are transformed into succinct arguments, the proof length of the argument is largely determined by q). Note however that the proof length ℓ is a *lower bound* on the prover's runtime in any PCP system since it takes time at least ℓ to write down a proof of length ℓ. Hence, obtaining a PCP with a small proof length is necessary, but not sufficient, for developing a PCP system with an efficient prover.

PCPs and MIPs are closely related: any MIP can turned into a PCP, and vice versa. However, both transformations can result in a substantial increase in costs. The easier direction is turning an MIP into a PCP. This simple transformation dates back to Fortnow, Rompel, and Sipser, who introduced the PCP model, albeit under a different name.

Lemma 9.2. Suppose $\mathcal{L} \subseteq \{0,1\}^*$ has a k-prover MIP in which $\mathcal{V}$ sends exactly one message to each prover, with each message consisting of at most r_Q bits, and each prover sends at most r_A bits in response to the verifier. Then $\mathcal{L}$ has a k-query PCP system over an alphabet Σ of size 2^{r_A}, where the proof length is $k \cdot 2^{r_Q}$, with the same verifier runtime and soundness and completeness errors as the MIP.

Sketch. For every prover $\mathcal{P}_i$ in the MIP, the PCP proof has an entry for every possible message that $\mathcal{V}$ might send to $\mathcal{P}_i$. The entry is equal to the prover's response to that message from $\mathcal{V}$. The PCP verifier simulates the MIP verifier, treating the proof entries as prover answers in the MIP. $\square$

Remark 9.3. It is also straightforward to obtain a PCP from a k-prover MIP in which $\mathcal{V}$ sends multiple messages to each prover. If each prover $\mathcal{P}_i$ is sent z messages $m_{i,1}, \ldots, m_{i,z}$ in the MIP, obtain a new MIP by replacing $\mathcal{P}_i$ with z provers $\mathcal{P}_{i,1}, \ldots, \mathcal{P}_{i,z}$ who are each sent one message (the message to $\mathcal{P}_{i,j}$ being the concatenation of $m_{i,1}, \ldots, m_{i,j}$).[1] The verifier in the $(z{\cdot}k)$-prover MIP simulates the verifier in the k-prover MIP, treating $\mathcal{P}_{i,j}$'s answer as if it were $\mathcal{P}_i$'s answer to $m_{i,j}$. Completeness of the resulting $(z \cdot k)$-prover MIP follows from completeness of the original k-prover MIP, by having prover $\mathcal{P}_{i,j}$ answer the same as $\mathcal{P}_i$ would upon receiving message $m_{i,j}$. Soundness of the resulting $(z \cdot k)$-prover MIP is implied by soundness of the original k-prover MIP.

Finally, apply Lemma 9.2 to the resulting $(z \cdot k)$-prover MIP.

Lemma 9.2 highlights a fundamental difference between MIPs and PCPs: in a PCP, the prover must pre-compute a response for every possible query of the verifier, which will result in a very large prover runtime unless the number of possible queries from the verifier is small.

---

[1] The reason $\mathcal{P}_{i,j}$ must be sent the concatenation of the first j messages to $\mathcal{P}_i$ rather than just $m_{i,j}$ is to ensure completeness of the resulting $(z \cdot k)$-prover MIP. $\mathcal{P}_i$'s answer to $m_{i,j}$ is allowed to depend on all preceding messages $m_{i,1}, \ldots, m_{i,j-1}$. So in order for $\mathcal{P}_{i,j}$ to be able to determine $\mathcal{P}_i$'s answer to $m_{i,j}$, it may be necessary for $\mathcal{P}_{i,j}$ to know $m_{i,1}, \ldots, m_{i,j-1}$.

Whereas in an MIP, the provers only need to compute responses "on demand", ignoring any queries that the verifier *might* have asked, but did not. Hence, the MIP $\implies$ PCP transformation of Lemma 9.2 may cause a huge blowup in prover runtime.

Lemma 8.2 gave a transformation from a PCP to a 2-prover MIP, but this transformation was also expensive. In summary, the tasks of constructing efficient MIPs and PCPs are incomparable. On the one hand, PCP provers are inherently non-adaptive, but they must pre-compute the answers to all possible queries of the verifier. MIP provers only need to compute answers "on demand", but they can behave adaptively, and while there are generic techniques to force them to behave non-adaptively, these techniques are expensive.

9.2   Compiling a PCP Into a Succinct Argument

We saw in Section 7 that one can turn the GKR interactive proof for arithmetic circuit *evaluation* into a succinct argument for arithmetic circuit *satisfiability* (recall that the goal of a circuit satisfiability instance $\{C, x, y\}$ is to determine whether there exists a witness w such that $C(x, w) = y$). At the start of the argument, the prover sends a cryptographic commitment to the multilinear extension $\tilde{w}$ of a witness w. The prover and verifier then run the GKR protocol to check that $C(x, w) = y$. At the end of the GKR protocol, the prover is forced to make a claim about the value of $\tilde{w}(r)$ for a random point r. The argument system verifier confirms that this claim is consistent with the corresponding claim derived from the cryptographic commitment to $\tilde{w}$.

The polynomial commitment scheme described in Section 7.3.2.2 consisted of two pieces; a *string-commitment* scheme using a Merkle tree, which allowed the prover to commit to *some* fixed function claim to equal $\tilde{w}$, and a low-degree test, which allowed the verifier to check that the function committed to was indeed (close to) a low-degree polynomial.

If our goal is to transform a PCP rather than an interactive proof into a succinct argument, we can use a similar approach, but omit the low-degree test. Specifically, as explained below, Kilian [168] famously showed that any PCP can be combined with Merkle-hashing to yield four-message argument systems for all of **NP**, assuming that collision-resistant hash functions exist. The prover and verifier runtimes are the same as in the underlying PCP, up to low-order factors, and the total communication cost is $O(\log n)$ cryptographic hash values per PCP query. Micali [192] showed that applying the Fiat-Shamir transformation to the resulting four-message argument system yields a *non-interactive* succinct argument in the random oracle model.[2]

The idea is the following. The argument system consists of two phases: commit and reveal. In the commit phase, the prover writes down the PCP π, but doesn't send it to the verifier. Instead, the prover builds a Merkle tree, with the symbols of the PCP as the leaves, and sends the root hash of the tree to the verifier. This binds the prover to the string π. In the reveal phase, the argument system verifier simulates the PCP verifier to determine which symbols of π need to be examined (call the locations that the PCP verifier queries $q_1, \ldots, q_k$). The verifier sends $q_1, \ldots, q_k$ to the prover to $\mathcal{P}$, and the prover sends back the answers $\pi(q_1), \ldots, \pi(q_k)$, along with their authentication paths.

Completeness can be argued as follows. If the PCP satisfies perfect completeness, then whenever there exists a w such that $\mathcal{C}(x, w) = y$, there is always some proof π that would convince the PCP verifier to accept. Hence, if the prover commits to π in the argument system, and executes the reveal phase as prescribed, the argument system verifier will also be convinced to accept.

Soundness can be argued roughly as follows. The analysis of Section 7.3.2.2 showed that the use of the Merkle tree binds the prover to a fixed string π', in the sense that after the commit phase, for each possible query q_i, there is at most one value $\pi'(q_i)$ that the prover can successfully reveal without finding a collision under the hash function used to build the Merkle tree (and collision-finding is assumed to be intractable). Hence, if the argument system prover convinces the argument system verifier to accept, π' would convince the PCP verifier

---

[2]In the non-interactive argument obtained by applying the Fiat-Shamir transformation to Kilian's 4-message argument, the honest prover uses the random oracle in place of a collision-resistant hash function to build the Merkle tree over the PCP proof, and the PCP verifier's random coins are chosen by querying the random oracle at the root hash of the Merkle tree.

to accept. Soundness of the argument system is then immediate from soundness of the PCP system.

Remark 9.4. In order to turn a PCP into a succinct argument, we used a Merkle tree, and did not need to use a low-degree test. This is in contrast to Section 7.3, where we turned an interactive proof into a succinct argument by using a polynomial commitment scheme; the polynomial commitment scheme given in Section 7.3 combined a Merkle tree and a low-degree test.

However, the PCP approach to building succinct arguments has not "really" gotten rid of the low-degree test. It has just pushed it out of the commitment scheme and "into" the PCP. That is, short PCPs are themselves typically based on low-degree polynomials, and the PCP itself typically makes use of a low-degree test.

A difference between the low-degree tests that normally go into short PCPs and the low-degree tests we've already seen is that short PCPs are usually based on low-degree *univariate* polynomials (see Section 9.4 for details). So the low-degree tests that go into short PCPs are targeted at univariate rather than multi-variate polynomials. Low-degree univariate polynomials are codewords in the Reed-Solomon error-correcting code, which is why many papers on PCPs refer to "Reed-Solomon PCPs" and "Reed-Solomon testing". In contrast, efficient interactive proofs and MIPs are typically based on low-degree multivariate polynomials (also known as Reed-Muller codes), and hence use low-degree tests that are tailored to the multivariate setting.

9.2.1 Knowledge-Soundness of Kilian and Micali's Arguments

Recall (see Section 7.4) that an argument system satisfies knowledge-soundness if, for any efficient prover $\mathcal{P}$ that convinces the argument system verifier to accept with non-negligible probability, $\mathcal{P}$ must *know* a witness w to the claim being proven. This is formalized by demanding that there is an efficient algorithm $\mathcal{E}$ that is capable of outputting a valid witness if given the ability to repeatedly "run" $\mathcal{P}$.

Barak and Goldreich [19] showed that Kilian's argument system is not only sound, but in fact knowledge-sound. This assertion assumes that the underlying PCP that the argument system is based on also satisfies an analogous knowledge-soundness property, meaning that given a convincing PCP proof π, one can efficiently compute a witness. All of the PCPs that we cover in this survey have this knowledge-soundness property.

Valiant [239] furthermore showed that applying the Fiat-Shamir transformation to render Kilian's argument system non-interactive (as per Micali [192]) yields a *knowledge-sound* argument in the random oracle model. Recall that the Fiat-Shamir transformation "removes" from Kilian's argument system the verifier's message specifying the symbols of the committed PCP proof that it wishes to query. This message is chosen to equal the evaluation of the random oracle at the argument-system prover's first message, which specifies the Merkle-hash of the committed PCP proof.

The rough idea of Valiant's analysis is to show that, if a prover $\mathcal{P}$ in the Fiat-Shamir-ed protocol produces an accepting transcript for Kilian's interactive protocol, then one of following three events must have occurred: either (1) $\mathcal{P}$ found a "hash collision" enabling it to break binding of the Merkle tree, or (2) $\mathcal{P}$ built Merkle trees over one or more "unconvincing" PCP proofs π, yet applying the Fiat-Shamir transformation to determine which symbols of π are queried caused the PCP verifier to accept π anyway, or (3) $\mathcal{P}$ built a Merkle tree over a "convincing" PCP proof π, and the first message of the transcript produced by $\mathcal{P}$ is the root hash of this Merkle tree.

The first event is unlikely to occur unless the prover makes a huge number of queries to the random oracle. This is because the probability of finding a collision after T queries to the random oracle is at most $T^2/2^\lambda$ where 2^λ is the output length of the random oracle. The second event is also unlikely to occur, assuming the soundness error ε of the PCP is negligible. Specifically, if the prover makes T queries to the random oracle, the probability event (2) occurs is at most $T \cdot \varepsilon$.

This means that (3) must hold (unless $\mathcal{P}$ makes super-polynomially many queries to the random oracle). That is, any prover $\mathcal{P}$ for the non-interactive argument that produces accepting transcripts with non-negligible probability must build a Merkle tree over a convincing PCP proof π and produce a transcript whose first message is the root hash of the Merkle tree. In this case, one can identify the entire Merkle tree by observing $\mathcal{P}$'s queries to the random oracle. For example, if v_0 denotes the root hash provided in the transcript, then one can learn the values v_1, v_2 of the children of the root in the Merkle tree by looking for the (unique) query (v_1, v_2) made by $\mathcal{P}$ to the random oracle R satisfying $R(v_1, v_2) = v_0$. Then one can learn the values of the grandchildren of the root by looking for the (unique) random oracle queries (v_3, v_4) and (v_5, v_6) made by $\mathcal{P}$ such that $R(v_3, v_4) = v_1$ and $R(v_5, v_6) = v_2$. And so on.

The values of the leaves of the Merkle tree are just the symbols of the convincing PCP proof π. By assumption that the PCP system satisfies knowledge-soundness, one can efficiently extract a witness from π.

The next section (Section 10) covers IOPs, an interactive generalization of PCPs. Ben-Sasson *et al.* [44] generalized Micali's PCP-to-SNARK transformation to an IOP-to-SNARK transformation, and via an analysis similar to Valiant's, established that the transformation preserves knowledge-soundness of the IOP.[3] See Section 10.1 for details of the IOP-to-SNARK transformation.

9.3 A First Polynomial Length PCP, From an MIP

In light of Lemma 9.2, it is reasonable to ask whether the MIP of Section 8.2 can be transformed into a PCP for arithmetic circuit satisfiability, of length polynomial in the circuit size S. The answer is yes, though the polynomial is quite large—at least S^3.

Suppose we are given an instance $(\mathcal{C}, x, y)$ of arithmetic circuit satisfiability, where $\mathcal{C}$ is defined over field $\mathbb{F}$. Recall that in the MIP of Section 8.2, the verifier used the first prover to apply the sum-check protocol to a certain $(3 \log S)$-variate polynomial $h_{x,y,z}$ over $\mathbb{F}$, where S is the size of $\mathcal{C}$. This polynomial was itself derived from a polynomial Z, claimed to equal the multilinear extension of a correct transcript for $(\mathcal{C}, x, y)$. The MIP verifier used the second prover to apply the point-vs-line low-degree test to the $O(\log S)$-variate polynomial Z, which required the verifier to send $\mathcal{P}_2$ a random line in $\mathbb{F}^{\log S}$ (such a line can be specified

---

[3]More precisely, knowledge-soundness of the resulting SNARK is characterized by knowledge-soundness of the IOP against a class of attacks called state-restoration attacks, discussed in Section 5.2.

with $2 \log S$ field elements). In order to achieve a soundness error of, say, $1/\log(n)$, it was sufficient to work over a field $\mathbb{F}$ of size at least $\log(S)^{c_0}$ for a sufficiently large constant $c_0 > 0$.[4]

The total number of bits that the verifier sent to each prover in this MIP was $r_Q = \Theta(\log(S) \log |\mathbb{F}|)$, since the verifier had to send a field element for each variable over which $h_{x,y,Z}$ was defined. If $|\mathbb{F}| = \Theta(\log(S)^c)$, then $r_Q = \Theta(\log(S) \log \log(S))$. Applying Lemma 9.2 and Remark 9.3 to transform this MIP into a PCP, we obtain a PCP of length $\tilde{O}(2^{r_Q}) = S^{O(\log \log S)}$. This is slightly superpolynomial in S. On the plus side, the verifier runs in time $O(n + \log S)$, which is linear in the size n of the input assuming $S < 2^n$.

However, by tweaking the parameters used within the MIP itself, we can reduce r_Q from $O(\log(S) \log \log(S))$ to $O(\log S)$. Recall that within the MIP, each gate in $\mathcal{C}$ was assigned a *binary* label, and the MIP made use of functions add_i, mult_i, io, I, and W that take as input $O(\log S)$ binary variables representing the labels of one or more gates. The polynomial $h_{x,y,Z}$ was then defined in terms of the *multilinear* extensions of these functions. This led to an efficient MIP, in which the provers' runtime was $O(S \log S)$. But by defining the polynomials to be over $\Omega(\log S)$ many variables, r_Q becomes slightly super logarithmic, resulting in a PCP of length superpolynomial in S. To rectify this, we must find a way to redefine the polynomials, such that they involve fewer than $\log S$ variables.

To this end, suppose we assign each gate in $\mathcal{C}$ a label in base b instead of base 2. That is, each gate label will consist of $\log_b(S)$ digits, each in $\{0, 1, \ldots, b-1\}$. Then we can redefine the functions add_i, mult_i, io, I, and W to take as input $O(\log_b(S))$ variables representing the b-ary labels of one or more gates. Observe that, the larger b is, the smaller the number of variables these functions are defined over.

---

[4]In cryptographic applications, one would want soundness error $n^{-\omega(1)}$ rather than $1/\log n$. The soundness error of the PCP in this section could be improved to $n^{-\omega(1)}$ by repeating the PCP $O(\log n)$ times independently, and rejecting if the PCP verifier rejects in any one of the runs. Such repetition is expensive in practice, but the PCP of this section is presented for didactic reasons and not meant to be practical.

We can then define $h_{x,y,Z}$ exactly as in Section 8.2, except if $b > 2$ then higher-degree extensions of add_i, mult_i, io, I, and W must be used in the definition, rather than multilinear extensions. Specifically, these functions, when defined over domain $\{0, 1, \ldots, b-1\}^v$ for the relevant value of v, each have a suitable extension of degree at most b in each variable.

Compared to the MIP of Section 8.2, the use of the higher-degree extensions increases the degrees of all of the polynomials exchanged in the sum-check protocol and in the low-degree test by an $O(b)$ factor. Nonetheless, the soundness error remains at most $O\left(b \cdot \log_b(S)/|\mathbb{F}|^c\right)$ for some constant $c > 0$. Recall that we would like to take b as large as possible, but this is in tension with the requirement to keep the soundness error $o(1)$ when working over a field of size polylogarithmic in S. Fortunately, it can be checked that if $b \leq O\left(\log(S)/\log\log(S)\right)$, then $b \cdot \log_b(S) \leq \text{polylog}(S)$, and hence the soundness error is still at most $\text{polylog}(S)/|\mathbb{F}|^c$. In conclusion, if we set b to be on the order of $\log(S)/\log\log(S)$, then as long as the MIP works over a field $\mathbb{F}$ of size that is a sufficiently large polynomial in $\log(S)$, the soundness error of the MIP is still at most, say, $1/\log n$.

For simplicity, let us choose b such that $b^b = S$. This choice of b is in the interval $[b_1, 2b_1]$ where $b_1 = \log(S)/\log\log(S)$.[5] In this modified MIP, the total number of bits sent from the verifier to the provers is $r_Q = O\left(b \cdot \log|\mathbb{F}|\right) = O\left((\log(S)/\log\log(S)) \cdot \log\log S\right) = O(\log S)$. If we apply Lemma 9.2 and Remark 9.3 to this MIP, the resulting PCP length is $\tilde{O}\left(2^{r_Q}\right) \leq \text{poly}(S)$.

Unfortunately, when we write $r_Q = O(\log S)$, the constant hidden by the Big-Oh notation is at least 3. This is because $h_{x,y,Z}$ is defined over $3\log_b(S)$ variables, which is at least $3b$ when $b^b = S$, and applying the sum-check protocol to $h_{x,y,Z}$ requires $\mathcal{V}$ to send at least one field element per variable. Meanwhile, the field size must be at least $3\log_b(S) \geq 3b$ to ensure non-trivial soundness. Hence, $2^{r_Q} \geq (3b)^{3b} \geq S^{3-o(1)}$. So while the proof length of the PCP is polynomial in S, it is a large polynomial in S.

---

[5]Indeed, $b_1^{b_1} \leq S$, while $(2b_1)^{2b_1} \geq S^{2-o(1)}$.

Table 9.1: Costs of PCP of Section 9.3 for arithmetic circuit satisfiability (obtained from the MIP of Section 8.2), when run on a circuit C of size S. The stated bound on P's time assumes P knows a witness w for C.

Communication	Queries	V Time	P Time
polylog(S) bits	$O(\log S / \log \log S)$	$O(n + \text{polylog}(S))$	poly(S)

Nonetheless, this yields a non-trivial result: a PCP for arithmetic circuit satisfiability in which the prover's runtime is poly(S), the verifier's is $O(n)$, and the number of queries the verifier makes to the proof oracle is $O(\log(S)/\log\log(S))$. As the total communication cost of the MIP is at most polylog(S), all of the answers to the verifier's queries can be communicated in polylog(S) bits in total (i.e., the alphabet size of the PCP is $|\Sigma| \leq 2^{\text{polylog}(S)}$). The costs of the PCP are summarized in Table 9.1. Applying the PCP-to-argument compiler of Section 9.2 yields a succinct argument for arithmetic circuit satisfiability with a verifier that runs in time $O(n)$ and a prover that runs in time poly(S).

Remark 9.5. To clarify, the use of labels in base $b = 2$ rather than base $b = \Theta\left(\log(S)/\log\log(S)\right)$ is the superior choice in interactive settings such as IPs and MIPs, if the goal is to minimize total communication. The reason is that binary labels allow the IP or MIP prover(s) to send polynomials of degree $O(1)$ in each round, and this keeps the communication costs low.

To recap, we have obtained a PCP for arithmetic circuit satisfiability with a linear time verifier, and a prover who can generate the proof in time *polynomial* in the size of the circuit. But to get a PCP that has any hope of being practical, we really need the prover time to be very close to *linear* in the size of the circuit. Obtaining such PCPs is quite complicated and challenging. Indeed, researchers have not had success in building plausibly practical VC protocols based on "short" PCPs, by which we mean PCPs for circuit satisfiability whose length is close to linear in the size of the circuit. To mitigate the bottlenecks in known short PCP constructions, researchers have turned to the more general *interactive oracle proof* (IOP) model. The following section and section cover highlights from this line of work. Specifically, Section 9.4

sketches the construction of PCPs for arithmetic circuit satisfiability where the PCP can be generated in time *quasilinear* in the size of the circuit. This construction remains impractical and is included in this survey primarily for historical context. Section 10 describes IOPs that come closer to practicality.

9.4   A PCP of Quasilinear Length for Arithmetic Circuit Satisfiability

We have just seen (Sections 9.1 and 9.3) that known MIPs can fairly directly yield a PCP of polynomial size for simulating a (non-deterministic) Random Access Machine (RAM) M, in which the verifier runs in time linear in the size of the input x to M. But the proof length is a (possibly quite large) polynomial in the runtime T of M, and the length of a proof is of course a lower bound on the time required to generate it. This section describes how to use techniques tailored specifically to the PCP model to reduce the PCP length to $T \cdot \text{polylog}(T)$, while maintaining a verifier runtime of $n \cdot \text{polylog}(T)$.

The PCP described here originates in work of Ben-Sasson and Sudan [50]. Their work gave a PCP of size $\tilde{O}(T)$ in which the verifier runs in time $\text{poly}(n)$ and makes only a polylogarithmic number of queries to the proof oracle. Subsequent work by Ben-Sasson *et al.* [48] reduced the verifier's time to $n \cdot \text{polylog}(T)$. Finally, Ben-Sasson *et al.* [41] showed how the prover can actually generate the PCP in $T \cdot \text{polylog}(T)$ time using FFT techniques, and provided various concrete optimizations and improved soundness analysis. This PCP system is fairly involved, so we elide some details in this survey, seeking only to convey the main ideas. The PCP's costs are summarized in Table 9.2.

9.4.1   Step 1: Reduce to Checking That a Polynomial Vanishes on a Designated Subspace

In Ben-Sasson and Sudan's PCP, the claim that $M(x) = y$ is first turned into an equivalent circuit satisfiability instance $\{C, x, y\}$, and the prover (or more precisely, the proof string π) claims to be holding a low-degree extension Z of a correct transcript W for $\{C, x, y\}$, just like in the MIP of Section 8.2. And just as in the MIP, the first step of Ben-Sasson and

Table 9.2: Costs of PCP from Section 9.4 when run on a non-deterministic circuit $\mathcal{C}$ of size S. The PCP is due to Ben-Sasson and Sudan [50], as refined by Ben-Sasson *et al.* [48] and [41]. The stated bound on $\mathcal{P}$'s time assumes $\mathcal{P}$ knows a witness w for $\mathcal{C}$

Communication	Queries	$\mathcal{V}$ Time	$\mathcal{P}$ Time
polylog(S) bits	polylog(S)	$O(n \cdot \text{polylog}(S))$	$O(S \cdot \text{polylog}(S))$

Sudan's PCP is to construct a polynomial $g_{x,y,Z}$ such that Z extends a correct transcript for $\{\mathcal{C}, x, y\}$ if and only if $g_{x,y,Z}(a) = 0$ for all a in a certain set H.

The details, however, are different and somewhat more involved than the construction in the MIP. We elide several of these details here, and focus on highlighting the primary similarities and differences between the constructions in the PCP and the MIP of Section 8.2.

Most importantly, in the PCP, $g_{x,y,Z}$ **is a univariate polynomial.** The PCP views a correct transcript as a univariate function $W \colon [S] \to \mathbb{F}$ rather than as a v-variate function (for $v = \log S$) mapping $\{0, 1\}^v$ to $\mathbb{F}$ as in the MIP. Hence, any extension Z of W is a univariate polynomial, and $g_{x,y,Z}$ is defined to be a univariate polynomial too. (The reason for using univariate polynomials is that it allows the PCP to utilize low-degree testing techniques in Steps 2 and 3 below that are tailored to univariate rather than multivariate polynomials. It is not currently known how to obtain PCPs of quasilinear length based on multivariate techniques, where by quasilinear length, we mean quasilinear in T, the runtime of the RAM that the prover is supposed to execute). Note that even the lowest-degree extension Z of W may have degree $|S| - 1$, which is much larger than the degrees of the multivariate polynomials that we've used in previous sections, and $g_{x,y,Z}$ will inherit this degree.

The univariate nature of $g_{x,y,Z}$ forces several additional differences in its construction, compared to the $O(\log S)$-variate polynomial used in the MIP. In particular, in the univariate setting, $g_{x,y,Z}$ is specifically defined over a field of characteristic $2.$[6] The structure of fields of characteristic 2 are exploited multiple times in the construction of $g_{x,y,Z}$ and in the PCP as a whole. For example:

- Let us briefly recall a key aspect of the transformation from Section 6.5 that turned a RAM M into an equivalent circuit satisfiability instance $\{\mathcal{C}, x, y\}$. De Bruijn graphs played a role in the construction of $\mathcal{C}$, where they were used to "re-sort" a purported trace of the execution of M from time order into memory order.

  To ensure that the MIP or PCP verifier does not have to fully materialize $\mathcal{C}$ (which is of size at least T, far larger than the verifier's allowed runtime of $n \cdot \mathrm{polylog}(T)$), it is essential that $\mathcal{C}$ have an "algebraically regular" wiring pattern. In particular, in both the PCP of this section and the MIP of Section 8.2, it is important that $\mathcal{C}$'s wiring pattern be "capturable" by a low-degree polynomial that the verifier can quickly evaluate. This is essential for ensuring that the polynomial $g_{x,y,Z}$ used within the MIP or PCP satisfies the following two essential qualities: (1) the degree of $g_{x,y,Z}$ is not much larger than that of Z (2) the verifier can efficiently evaluate $g_{x,y,Z}(r)$ at any point r, if given Z's values at a handful of points derived from r.

  In Ben-Sasson and Sudan's PCP, the construction of $g_{x,y,Z}$ exploits the fact that there is a way to assign labels from $\mathbb{F} = \mathbb{F}_{2^\ell}$ to nodes in a De Bruijn graph such that, for each node v, the labels of the neighbors of v are *affine* (i.e., degree 1) functions of the label of v. (Similar to Section 6.5, the reason this holds boils down to the fact that the neighbors of a node with label v are simple bit-shifts of v. When v is an element of $\mathbb{F}_{2^\ell}$, a bit-shift of v is an affine function of v.).

---

[6] The characteristic of a field $\mathbb{F}$ is the smallest number n such that $\underbrace{1 + 1 + \cdots + 1}_{n \text{ times}} = 0$. If a $\mathbb{F}$ has size p^k for prime p and integer $k > 0$, then its characteristic is p. In particular, any field of size equal to a power of 2 has characteristic 2. We denote the field of size 2^k as $\mathbb{F}_{2^k}$.

This is crucial for ensuring that the degree of $g_{x,y,Z}$ is not much larger than the degree of Z itself. In particular, the univariate polynomial $g_{x,y,Z}$ over $\mathbb{F}$ used in the PCP has the form

$$g_{x,y,Z}(z) = A(z, Z(N_1(z)), \ldots, Z(N_k(z))), \qquad (9.1)$$

where $(N_1(z), \ldots, N_k(z))$ denotes the neighbors of node z in the De Bruijn graph, and A is a certain "constraint polynomial" of polylogarithmic degree. Since $N_1, \ldots, N_k$ are affine over $\mathbb{F}_{2^\ell}$, $\deg(g_{x,y,Z})$ is at most a polylogarithmic factor larger than the degree of Z itself. Moreover, the verifier can efficiently evaluate each affine function $N_1, \ldots, N_k$ at a specified input r [48].

- The set H on which $g_{x,y,Z}$ should vanish if Z extends a correct transcript is chosen to ensure that the polynomial $\mathbb{Z}_H(z) = \prod_{\alpha \in H}(z - \alpha)$ is *sparse* (having $O(\text{polylog}(S))$ nonzero coefficients). The polynomial $\mathbb{Z}_H$ is referred to as the *vanishing polynomial* for H, and via Lemma 9.3 in the next section, it plays a central role in the PCPs, IOPs (Section 10), and linear PCPs (Section 17.4) described hereafter in this survey. The sparsity of $\mathbb{Z}_H$ ensures that it can be evaluated an any point in polylogarithmic time, even though H is a very large set (of size $\Omega(S)$). This will be crucial to allowing the verifier to run in polylogarithmic time in Step 2 of the PCP, discussed below. It turns out that if $\mathbb{F}$ has characteristic $O(1)$ and H is a linear subspace of $\mathbb{F}$, then $\mathbb{Z}_H(z)$ has sparsity $O(\log S)$ as desired. Later in this monograph (e.g., in the IOP of Section 10.3.2), H will instead consist of all n'th roots of unity in $\mathbb{F}$, in which case $\mathbb{Z}_H(z) = z^n - 1$ is clearly sparse.

The final difference worth highlighting is that the field $\mathbb{F}_{2^\ell}$ over which $g_{x,y,Z}$ is defined must be small in the PCP (or, at least, the set of inputs at which the verifier might query $g_{x,y,Z}$ must be a small). In particular, the set must be of size $O(S \cdot \text{polylog}(S))$, since the proof length is lower bounded by the size of the set of inputs at which the verifier might ask for any evaluation of $g_{x,y,Z}$. This is in contrast to the MIP setting, where we were happy to work a very large field size (of size, say, 2^{128} or larger) to ensure negligible soundness error. This is a manifestation of the fact (mentioned in Section 9.1) that in an MIP the prover only has to "think up" answers to queries that the verifier actually asks, while in a PCP, the prover has to write down the answer to every possible query that the verifier *might* ask.

9.4.2   Step 2: Reduce to Checking That a Related Polynomial is Low-Degree

Note that checking whether a low-degree polynomial $g_{x,y,W}$ vanishes on H is very similar to the core statement checked in our MIP from Section 8.2. There, we checked that a *multilinear* polynomial derived from x, y, and W vanished on all Boolean inputs. Here, we are checking whether a *univariate* polynomial $g_{x,y,W}$ vanishes on all inputs in a pre-specified set H. We will rely on the following simple but essential lemma, which will arise several other times in this survey (including when we cover linear PCPs in Section 17).

Lemma 9.3. (Ben-Sasson and Sudan [50]) Let $\mathbb{F}$ be a field and $H \subseteq \mathbb{F}$. For $d \geq |H|$, a degree-d univariate polynomial g over $\mathbb{F}$ vanishes on H if and only if the polynomial $\mathbb{Z}_H(t) := \prod_{\alpha \in H}(t - \alpha)$ divides g, i.e., if and only if there exists a polynomial h^* with $\deg(h^*) \leq d - |H|$ such that $g = \mathbb{Z}_H \cdot h^*$.

Proof. If $g = \mathbb{Z}_H \cdot h^*$, then for any $\alpha \in H$, it holds that $g(\alpha) = \mathbb{Z}_H(\alpha) \cdot h^*(\alpha) = 0 \cdot \alpha = 0$, so g indeed vanishes on H.

For the other direction, observe that if $g(\alpha) = 0$, then the polynomial $(t - \alpha)$ divides $g(t)$. It follows immediately that if g vanishes on H, then g is divisible by $\mathbb{Z}_H$.   □

So to convince $\mathcal{V}$ that $g_{x,y,Z}$ vanishes on H, the proof merely needs to convince $\mathcal{V}$ that $g_{x,y,Z}(z) = \mathbb{Z}_H(z) \cdot h^*(z)$ for some polynomial h^* of degree $d - |H|$. To be convinced of this, $\mathcal{V}$ can pick a random point $r \in \mathbb{F}$ and check that

$$g_{x,y,Z}(r) = \mathbb{Z}_H(r) \cdot h^*(r). \tag{9.2}$$

Indeed, if $g_{x,y,Z} \neq \mathbb{Z}_H \cdot h^*$, then this equality will fail with probability $\frac{999}{1000}$ as long as $|\mathbb{F}|$ is at least 1000 times larger than the degrees of $g_{x,y,Z}$ and $\mathbb{Z}_H \cdot h^*$.

A PCP convincing $\mathcal{V}$ that Equation (9.2) holds consists of four parts. The first part contains the evaluations of $Z(z)$ for all $z \in \mathbb{F}$. The second part contains a proof π_Z that Z has degree at most $|H| - 1$, and hence that $g_{x,y,Z}$ has degree at most $d = |H| \cdot \text{polylog}(S)$. The third part contains the evaluation of $h^*(z)$ for all $z \in \mathbb{F}$. The fourth part purportedly contains a proof π_{h^*} that $h^*(z)$ has degree at most $d - |H|$, and hence that $\mathbb{Z}_H \cdot h^*$ has degree at most d.

Let us assume that the verifier can efficiently check π_Z and π_{h^*} to confirm that Z and $h^*(z)$ have the claimed degrees (this will be the purpose of Step 3 below). $\mathcal{V}$ can evaluate $g_{x,y,Z}(r)$ in quasilinear time after making a constant number of queries to the first part of the proof specifying Z. $\mathcal{V}$ can compute $h^*(r)$ with a single query to the third part of the proof. Finally, $\mathcal{V}$ can evaluate $\mathbb{Z}_H(r)$ without help in polylogarithmic time as described in Step 1 (Section 9.4.1). The verifier can then check that $g_{x,y,W}(r) = h^*(r) \cdot \mathbb{Z}_H(r)$.

In actuality, Step 3 will not be able to guarantee that π_Z and π_{h^*} are *exactly* equal to low-degree polynomials, but will be able to guarantee that, if the verifier's checks all pass, then they are each close to some low-degree polynomial Y and h' respectively. One can then argue that $g_{x,y,Y}$ vanishes on H, analogously to the proof of Theorem 8.4 in the context of the MIP from Section 8.2.

9.4.3 Step 3: A PCP for Reed-Solomon Testing

Overview. The meat of the PCP construction is in this third step, which checks that a univariate polynomial has low-degree. This task is referred to in the literature as Reed-Solomon testing, because codewords in the Reed-Solomo code consist of (evaluations of) low-degree univariate polynomials (cf. Remark 9.4).

The construction is recursive. The basic idea is to reduce the problem of checking that a *univariate* polynomial G_1 has degree at most d to the problem of checking that a related *bivariate* polynomial Q over $\mathbb{F}$ has degree at most $\sqrt{d}$ in each variable. It is known (cf. Lemma 9.5 below) how the latter problem can in turn be reduced back to a univariate problem, that is, to checking that a related univariate polynomial G_2 over $\mathbb{F}$ has degree at most $\sqrt{d}$. Recursing $\ell = O(\log \log n)$ times results in checking that a polynomial G_ℓ has *constant* degree, which can be done with a constant number of queries to the proof. We fill in some of the details of this outline below.

The precise soundness and completeness guarantees of this step are as follows. If G_1 indeed has degree at most d, then there is a proof π that is always accepted. Meanwhile, the soundness guarantee is that there is some universal constant k satisfying the following property: if a proof π is accepted with probability $1 - \varepsilon$, then there is a polynomial G of degree at most d such that G_1 agrees with G on at least a $1 - \varepsilon \cdot \log^k(S)$ fraction of points in $\mathbb{F}$ (we say that G and G_1 are at most δ-*far*, for $\delta = \varepsilon \cdot \log^k(S)$.)

The claimed polylogarithmic query complexity of the PCP as a whole comes by repeating the base protocol, say, $m = \log^{2k}(S)$ times and rejecting if any run of the protocol ever rejects. If a proof π is accepted by the m-fold repetition with probability $1 - \varepsilon$, then it is accepted by the base protocol with probability at least $1 - \varepsilon/\log^k m$, implying that G is ε-far from a degree d polynomial G_1.

Reducing Bivariate Low-Degree Testing on Product Sets to Univariate Testing.   The bivariate low-degree testing technique described here is due to Polishchuk and Spielman [212]. Assume that Q is a bivariate polynomial defined on a product set $A \times B \subseteq \mathbb{F} \times \mathbb{F}$, claimed to have degree d in each variable. (In all recursive calls of the protocol, A and B will in fact both be subspaces of $\mathbb{F}$). The goal is to reduce this claim to checking that a related univariate polynomial G_2 over $\mathbb{F}$ has degree at most d.

Definition 9.4. For a set $U \subseteq \mathbb{F} \times \mathbb{F}$, partial bivariate function $Q \colon U \to \mathbb{F}$, and nonnegative integers d_1, d_2, define $\delta^{d_1, d_2}(Q)$ to be the relative distance of Q from a polynomial of degree d_1 in its first variable and d_2 in its second variable.[7] Formally,

$$\delta^{d_1,d_2}(Q) := \min_{f(x,y)\colon U\to\mathbb{F},\deg_x(f)\leq d_1,\deg_y(f)\leq d_2} \delta(Q,f).$$

---

[7] By relative distance between Q and another polynomial P, we mean the fraction of inputs in $x \in U$ such that $Q(x) \neq P(x)$.

Let $\delta^{d_1,*}(Q)$ and $\delta^{*,d_2}(Q)$ denote the relative distances when the degree in one of the variables is unrestricted.

Lemma 9.5. (Bivariate test on a product set [212]). There exists a universal constant $c_0 \geq 1$ such that the following holds. For every $A, B \subseteq \mathbb{F}$ and integers $d_1 \leq |A|/4$, $d_2 \leq |B|/8$ and function $Q: A \times B \to \mathbb{F}$, it is the case that $\delta^{d_1,d_2}(Q) \leq c_0 \cdot \left(\delta^{d_1,*}(Q) + \delta^{*,d_2}(Q) \right)$.

The proof of Lemma 9.5 is not long, but we omit it from the survey for brevity.

Lemma 9.5 implies that, to test if a bivariate polynomial Q defined on a product set has degree at most d in each variable, it is sufficient to pick a variable $i \in \{1, 2\}$, then pick a random value $r \in \mathbb{F}$ and test whether the univariate polynomial $Q(r, \cdot)$ or $Q(\cdot, r)$ obtained by restricting the ith coordinate of Q to r has degree at most d.

To be precise, if the above test passes with probability $1 - \varepsilon$, then $\left(\delta^{d,*}(Q) + \delta^{*,d}(f) \right)/2 = \varepsilon$, and Lemma 9.5 implies that $\delta^{d,d}(Q) \leq 2 \cdot c_0 \cdot \varepsilon$. $Q(r, \cdot)$ and $Q(\cdot, r)$ are typically called a "random row" or "random column" of Q, respectively, and the above procedure is referred to as a "random row or column test".

Note that $\delta^{d,d}(f)$ may be larger than the acceptance probability ε by only a constant factor $c_1 = 2c_0$. Ultimately, the PCP will will recursively apply the "Reducing Bivariate Low-Degree Testing to Univariate Testing" technique $O(\log \log n)$ times, and each step may cause $\delta^{d_1,d_2}(Q)$ to blow up, relative to the rejection probability ε, by a factor of c_1. This is why the final soundness guarantee states that, if the recursive test as a whole accepts a proof with probability $1 - \varepsilon$, then the input polynomial G_1 is δ-close to a degree d polynomial, where $\delta = \varepsilon \cdot c_1^{O(\log \log S)} \leq \varepsilon \cdot \text{polylog}(S).^8$

Reducing Univariate Low-Degree Testing to Bivariate Testing on a Lower Degree Polynomial.
Let G_1 be a univariate polynomial defined

---

[8]This bound on δ is non-trivial only if ε is smaller than some inverse-polylogarithm in S. That is, the analysis only yields a non-trivial soundness guarantee if the prover convinces the verifier to accept with probability at least $1 - \varepsilon$, which is inverse-polylogarithmically close to 1. Accordingly, to achieve negligible soundness error, the PCP verifier's checks must be repeated polylogarithmically many times, leading to impractical verification costs.

on a linear subspace L of $\mathbb{F}$ (in all recursive calls of the protocol, the domain of G_1 will indeed be a linear subspace L of $\mathbb{F}$). Our goal in this step is to reduce testing that G_1 has degree at most d to testing that a related bivariate polynomial Q has degree at most $\sqrt{d}$ in each variable. It is okay to assume that the number of vectors in L is at most a constant factor larger than d, as this will be the case every time this step is applied.

Lemma 9.6. [50] Given any pair of polynomials $G_1(z)$, $q(z)$, there exists a unique bivariate polynomial $Q(x, y)$ with $\deg_x(Q) < \deg(G_1)$ and $\deg_y(Q) \le \lfloor \deg(G_1)/\deg(q) \rfloor$ such that $G_1(z) = Q(z, q(z))$.

Proof. Apply polynomial long-division to divide $G_1(z)$ by $(y - q(z))$, where throughout the long-division procedure, terms are ordered first by their degree in z and then by their degree in y.[9] This yields a representation of $G_1(z)$ as:

$$G_1(z) = Q_0(z, y) \cdot (y - q(z)) + Q(z, y). \tag{9.3}$$

By the basic properties of division in this ring, $\deg_y(Q) \le \lfloor \deg(G_1)/\deg(q) \rfloor$, and $\deg_z(Q) < \deg(q)$. To complete the proof, set $y = q(z)$ and notice that the first summand on the right-hand side of Equation (9.3) vanishes. $\qquad\square$

By Lemma 9.6, to establish that G_1 has degree at most d, it suffices for a PCP to establish that $G_1(z) = Q(z, q(z))$, where the degree of Q in each variable is at most $\sqrt{d}$. Thus, as a first (naive) attempt, the proof could specify Q's value on all points in $L \times \mathbb{F}$. Then $\mathcal{V}$ can check that $G_1(z) = Q(z, q(z))$, by picking a random $r \in L$ and checking that $G_1(r) = Q(r, q(r))$. If this check passes, it is safe for $\mathcal{V}$ to believe that

---

[9]Polynomial long division repeatedly divides the highest-degree term of the remainder polynomial by the highest-degree term of the divisor polynomial to determine a new term to add to the quotient, stopping when the remainder has lower degree than the divisor. See https://en.wikipedia.org/wiki/Polynomial_long_division for details of the univariate case. For division involving multivariate polynomials, the "term of highest degree" is not well-defined until we impose a total ordering on the degree of terms. Ordering terms by their degree in z and breaking ties by their degree in y ensures that the polynomial long division is guaranteed to output a representation satisfying the properties described immediately after Equation (9.3).

$G_1(z) = Q(z, q(z))$, as long as Q is indeed low-degree in each variable, and we have indeed reduced testing that G_1 has degree at most d to testing that Q has degree at most $\sqrt{d}$ in each variable.

The problem with the naive attempt is that the proof has length $|L| \cdot |\mathbb{F}|$, which is far too large; we need a proof of length $\tilde{O}(|L|)$. A second attempt might be to have the proof specify Q's value on all points in the set $\mathcal{T} := \{(z, q(z)) \colon z \in L\}$. This would allow $\mathcal{V}$ to check that $G_1(z) = Q(z, q(z))$ by picking a random $r \in L$ and checking that $G_1(r) = Q(r, q(r))$. While this shortens the proof to an appropriate size, the problem is that $\mathcal{T}$ is not a product set, so Lemma 9.5 cannot be applied to check that Q has low-degree in each variable.

To get around this issue, Ben-Sasson and Sudan ingeniously choose the polynomial $q(z)$ in such a way that there is a set $\mathcal{B}$ of points, of size $O(|L|)$, at which it suffices to specify Q's values. Specifically, they choose $q(z) = \prod_{\alpha \in L_0}(z - \alpha)$, where L_0 is a linear subspace of L containing $\sqrt{d}$ vectors. Then $q(z)$ is not just a polynomial of degree $\sqrt{d}$, it is also a *linear map* on L, with kernel equal to L_0. This has the effect of ensuring that $q(z)$ takes on just $|L|/|L_0|$ distinct values, as z ranges over L.

Ben-Sasson and Sudan use this property to show that, although $\mathcal{T}$ is not a product set, it is possible to add $O(L)$ additional points $\mathcal{S}$ to $\mathcal{T}$ to ensure that $\mathcal{B} := \mathcal{S} \cup \mathcal{T}$ contains within it a large subset that is product. So $\mathcal{P}$ need only provide Q's evaluation on the points in $\mathcal{B}$: since $\mathcal{T} \subseteq \mathcal{B}$, the verifier can check that $G_1(z) = Q(z, q(z))$ by picking a random $r \in L$ and checking that $G_1(r) = Q(r, q(r))$, and since there is a large product set within $\mathcal{S} \cup \mathcal{T}$, Lemma 9.5 can be applied.

10

Interactive Oracle Proofs

10.1 IOPs: Definition and Associated Succinct Arguments

The concrete costs of the PCP prover of the previous section are very large. In this section, we describe more efficient protocols that operate in a generalization of the PCP setting, called Interactive Oracle Proofs (IOPs). Introduced by [44], [214], IOPs in fact generalize both PCPs and IPs. An IOP is an IP where, in each round the verifier is not forced to read the prover's entire message, but rather is given query access to it, meaning it can choose to look at any desired symbol of the message at the "cost" of a single query. This enables the IOP verifier to run in time sub-linear in the total proof length (i.e., the sum of the lengths of all the messages sent by the prover during the IOP).

Ben-Sasson *et al.* [44] showed that any IOP can be transformed into a non-interactive argument in the random oracle model using Merkle-hashing and the Fiat-Shamir transformation, in a manner entirely analogous to the Kilian-Micali transformation from PCPs to succinct arguments of Section 9.2. Specifically, rather than sending the IOP prover's message in each round of the IOP, the argument system prover sends a Merkle-commitment to the IOP prover's message. The argument system verifier then simulates the IOP verifier to determine which elements of the message to query, and the argument system prover reveals the relevant symbols of the message by providing authentication paths in the Merkle tree. The interactive argument is then rendered non-interactive using the Fiat-Shamir transformation.[1]

The IOPs of This Section. In this section, we give an IOP for R1CS-satisfiability that is concretely much more efficient for the prover than the PCP of the previous section. The IOP can be understood as a combination of two constituent protocols. The first is a so-called *polynomial IOP* [83]; this is a variant of the IOP model described shortly. The specific polynomial IOP for R1CS that we cover, and optimizations thereof, was developed over a sequence of works [43], [98], [100].

The second is a *polynomial commitment scheme* (a notion introduced in Section 7.3) that is itself instantiated via an IOP. We give two such IOP-based polynomial commitment schemes in this section: one called FRI (short for Fast Reed-Solomon Interactive Oracle Proof of Proximity) with polylogarithmic proof length [34] (Section 10.4), and another implicit in a system called Ligero [7] with larger proofs but a concretely faster prover (Section 10.5). We also cover a generalization of Ligero with interesting performance characteristics, namely *asymptotically optimal* prover runtime, and no restrictions on the underlying field [67], [69], [137]. We refer to this as the Brakedown commitment, as that is the name of the first practical implementation of this variant [137].

10.2   Polynomial IOPs and Associated Succinct Arguments

As with standard IOPs introduced in Section 10.1 above, a polynomial IOP is an interactive proof, except that a subset of the prover's messages are not read in full by the verifier $\mathcal{V}$—let us call these messages "special". In a standard IOP, each special message is a string, and the verifier is given query access to individual symbols of the string. In a polynomial IOP, each special message i specifies a *polynomial* h_i over a finite field $\mathbb{F}$, with degree at most some specified upper bound d_i. In the IOPs of

---

[1] In the random oracle model, this IOP-to-SNARK transformation preserves both standard soundness and knowledge-soundness of the underlying IOP—see the end of Section 9.2.1 for details.

this section, h_i will always be a *univariate* polynomial, but in general h_i may be a multivariate polynomial.

Think of h_i as having a very large number of coefficients—in fact, in the polynomial IOP for R1CS given in this section, the degree d_i of h_i may be as large as the entire R1CS instance. This is why we do not want $\mathcal{V}$ to have to read a description of h_i in full, as that would require far more time than we'd like $\mathcal{V}$ to have to spend to check the proof. Rather, $\mathcal{V}$ is given query access to evaluations of h_i, meaning that $\mathcal{V}$ can choose any input r to h_i and learn $h_i(r)$.

Roughly speaking, the polynomial commitment schemes we cover in this section (Sections 10.4 and 10.5) allow the special messages themselves to be "implemented" via standard IOPs. That is, each polynomial h_i will be specified via a certain string m_i. An IOP will be given such that, when the verifier requests $h_i(r)$ and the prover sends back a claimed evaluation v_i, the verifier is able to confirm that m_i indeed specifies a polynomial h_i of the prescribed degree, with $v_i = h_i(r)$.

In summary, when one takes a polynomial IOP for R1CS-satisfiability, and replaces each "special message" and associated evaluation queries with a polynomial commitment scheme based on a standard IOP as above, the entire protocol is a standard IOP, which can then be transformed into a succinct argument via the transformation of [44].

Even if the polynomial commitment scheme is *not* implemented via a standard IOP (as with the schemes of Sections 14–16) one can still obtain a succinct argument via the following three-step design process.

- First, design a public-coin polynomial IOP for circuit- or R1CS-satisfiability.

- Obtain a public-coin, interactive succinct argument by replacing each "special" message h_i in the polynomial IOP with a polynomial commitment scheme.

- Remove interaction via Fiat-Shamir.

In fact, as explained next, all SNARKs covered in this survey are designed via this recipe, with the lone exception of those based on linear PCPs (Section 17).

Recasting Sections 7 and 8 as Polynomial IOPs. In Section 10.6, we recast the IP- and MIP-derived succinct arguments of Sections 7 and 8 as polynomial IOPs (in which there is a *single* special message, sent at the start of the protocol, which specifies a *multilinear* rather than univariate polynomial). This recasting provides a unified view of IP-, MIP-, and IOP-based SNARKs, and allows for a clean comparison of the pros and cons of the various approaches.

Relevant Costs of a Polynomial IOP. In a SNARK resulting from the above three-step design paradigm, the prover must (a) compute the polynomial h_i contained in each special message, and commit to it with the relevant polynomial commitment scheme (b) answer each evaluation query $h_i(r)$ made by the verifier and produce an associated evaluation-proof as per the polynomial commitment scheme (c) compute any non-special messages in the polynomial IOP. In practice, (a) and (b) are often the concrete bottlenecks for the prover. When h_i is a univariate polynomial, these costs grow at least linearly with the degree d_i of h_i, and hence a major goal when designing polynomial IOPs is to keep d_i linear in the size of the circuit or R1CS instance under consideration.

In terms of proof length and verifier time, verifying the evaluation-proofs sent in (b) above is often the concrete bottleneck. Hence, to minimize verification costs in the resulting SNARKs, a major goal is to minimize the number of evaluation queries that the polynomial IOP verifier makes to special messages.

10.3 A Polynomial IOP for R1CS-satisfiability

10.3.1 The Univariate Sum-Check Protocol

The key technical fact exploited in this section relates the sum of any low-degree polynomial over a potentially large subset of inputs H to the polynomial's evaluation at a *single* input, namely 0. Below, a non-empty subset $H \subseteq \mathbb{F}$ is said to be a multiplicative subgroup of field $\mathbb{F}$ if H is closed under multiplication and inverses, i.e., for any $a, b \in H$, $a \cdot b \in H$, and $a^{-1}, b^{-1} \in H$.

Fact 10.1. Let $\mathbb{F}$ be a finite field and suppose that H is a multiplicative subgroup of $\mathbb{F}$ of size n. Then for any polynomial q of degree less than $|H| = n$, $\sum_{a \in H} q(a) = q(0) \cdot |H|$. It follows that $\sum_{a \in H} q(a)$ is 0 if and only if $q(0) = 0$.

We provide a proof of this fact. Our proof assumes several basic results in group theory, and may be safely skipped with no loss of continuity.

Proof. When H is a multiplicative subgroup of order n, it follows from Lagrange's Theorem in group theory that $a^n = 1$ for any $a \in H$. Hence, H is precisely the set of n roots of the polynomial $X^n - 1$, i.e.,

$$\prod_{a \in H} (X - a) = X^n - 1. \tag{10.1}$$

We begin by proving the fact for $q(X) = X$, i.e., we show that $\sum_{a \in H} a = 0$. Indeed, it is easily seen that the coefficient of X^{n-1} when expanding out the left hand side of Equation (10.1) equals $-\sum_{a \in H} a$, and this must equal 0 because the coefficient of X^{n-1} on the right hand side of Equation (10.1) is 0.

Now let $q(X)$ be any monomial $X \mapsto X^m$ for $1 < m < n$. It is known that any multiplicative subgroup of a finite field $\mathbb{F}$ is cyclic, meaning there is some generator h such that $H = \{h, h^2, \ldots, h^n\}$. Then

$$\sum_{a \in H} q(a) = \sum_{a \in H} a^m = \sum_{j=1}^{n} h^{m \cdot j}. \tag{10.2}$$

Another application of Lagrange's theorem implies that if m and n are coprime, then h^m is also a generator of H, and hence $\sum_{j=1}^{n} h^{m \cdot j} = \sum_{j=1}^{n} h^j = \sum_{a \in H} a = 0$, where the final equality was established above.

If m and n are not coprime, then it is known that the order of h^m is $d := \gcd(m, n)$, and hence letting $H' := \{h^m, h^{2m}, \ldots, h^{(n/d)m}\}$, H is the disjoint union of the sets H', $h \cdot H'$, $h^2 \cdot H'$, $\ldots$, and $h^{d-1} \cdot H'$, where for any $a \in \mathbb{F}$, $a \cdot H'$ denotes the set $\{a \cdot b : b \in H'\}$.

Since H' is a multiplicative subgroup of order n/d, the reasoning in the first paragraph of the proof shows that $\sum_{a \in H'} a = 0$. Hence, the right hand size of Equation (10.2) equals $(1 + h + h^2 + \ldots + h^d) \cdot \sum_{a \in H'} a = 0$.

The lemma now follows for general polynomials $q(X) = \sum_{i=1}^{n-1} c_i X^i$ by linearity, combined with the fact that for any constant $c \in \mathbb{F}$, $\sum_{a \in H} c = |H| \cdot c$. $\qquad\square$

For the remainder of this section, let H be a multiplicative subgroup of $\mathbb{F}$ of size n as in Fact 10.1. Let p be any univariate polynomial of degree at most D, where D may be greater than $|H| = n$. Recall that

$$\mathbb{Z}_H(X) = \prod_{a \in H} (X - a)$$

denotes the vanishing polynomial of H. Note that Equation (10.1) implies that $\mathbb{Z}_H(X) = X^n - 1$, i.e., $\mathbb{Z}_H$ is sparse, and hence can be evaluated at any desired input r in time $O(\log n)$ via repeated squaring. We derive the following simple consequence of Fact 10.1.

Lemma 10.2. $\sum_{a \in H} p(a) = 0$ if and only if there exists polynomials h^*, f with $\deg(h^*) \leq D - n$ and $\deg(f) < n - 1$ satisfying:

$$p(X) = h^*(X) \cdot \mathbb{Z}_H(X) + X \cdot f(X). \tag{10.3}$$

Proof. Suppose first that Equation (10.3) holds. Then clearly

$$\sum_{a \in H} p(a) = \sum_{a \in H} (h^*(a) \cdot \mathbb{Z}_H(a) + a \cdot f(a)) = \sum_{a \in H} (h^*(a) \cdot 0 + a \cdot f(a))$$
$$= \sum_{a \in H} a \cdot f(a) = 0,$$

where the final equality holds by Fact 10.1 and the fact that $X \cdot f(X)$ evaluates to 0 on input 0.

Conversely, suppose that $\sum_{a \in H} p(a) = 0$. Dividing p by $\mathbb{Z}_H$ allows us to write $p(X) = h^*(X) \cdot \mathbb{Z}_H(x) + r(X)$ for some remainder polynomial r of degree less than n. Since $0 = \sum_{a \in H} p(a) = \sum_{a \in H} r(a)$, we conclude by Fact 10.1 that r has no constant term. That is, we can write $r(X)$ as $X \cdot f(X)$ for some f of degree less than $n - 1$. $\qquad\square$

The Univariate Sum-Check Protocol. Lemma 10.2 offers a polynomial IOP for verifiably computing sums of evaluations of univariate polynomials over multiplicative subgroup H (rather than sums of multivariate polynomial evaluations over the Boolean hypercube as considered in the sum-check protocol of Section 4.2). Specifically, in order to prove that a specified univariate polynomial p of degree D sums to 0 over a multiplicative subgroup H with $|H| = n$, Lemma 10.2 implies that it is sufficient for a prover to establish that there exists functions h^* and f of degrees at most $D - n$ and $n - 1$ such that h^* and f satisfy Equation (10.3).

The natural way to accomplish this is to have the prover send two special messages specifying f and h^* respectively. The verifier can then confirm (with high probability) that Equation (10.3) holds by evaluating the left hand side and right hand side of Equation (10.3) at a random point $r \in \mathbb{F}$ and checking that the two evaluations are equal. This requires the verifier to evaluate p, f, and h^* at a single point r. Since both the right hand side and left hand side of Equation (10.3) are polynomials of degree at most $\max\{D, n\}$, up to soundness error $\max\{D, n\}/|\mathbb{F}|$ over the choice of r, if Equation (10.3) holds at the randomly chosen point r, then it is safe for the verifier to believe that Equation (10.3) holds as an equality of formal polynomials.

Remark 10.1. It is also possible to give an analogous IOP for confirming that p sums to 0 over an *additive* rather than multiplicative subgroup H of $\mathbb{F}$. This can be useful when working over fields of characteristic 2 (i.e., of size equal to a power of 2), since if a field has size 2^k for positive integer k, then it has an additive subgroup H of size $2^{k'}$ for every positive integer $k' < k$; moreover the vanishing polynomial $\mathbb{Z}_H(Y) = \prod_{a \in H}(a - h)$ is sparse (just as in the PCP of Section 9.4.1).

10.3.2 A Polynomial IOP for R1CS-SAT via Univariate Sum-Check

Motivation.   In this section, we explain how to use the univariate sum-check protocol to give a polynomial IOP for R1CS-SAT. The reader may wonder, since IOPs are able to leverage interaction, why not just use the same techniques as in the MIP for R1CS-SAT of Section 8.4.2, which indeed we recast as a polynomial IOP in Section 10.6? The answer is that the MIP worked with multilinear polynomials over $O(\log n)$-variables, resulting in a protocol with at least $O(\log n)$ rounds. Here, we are seeking to have the prover only send univariate polynomials. This happens to result in a polynomial IOP with just constantly many rounds.[2,3] As we discuss in Section 10.6, this ultimately leads to SNARKs with a different cost profile than MIP-derived SNARKs.

In summary, in this section we wish for the prover to exclusively send univariate polynomials, and hence we have to "redo" the MIPs of Section 8, replacing each constituent multilinear polynomial appearing in that protocol with a univariate analog.

Protocol Description. Recall from Section 8.4 that an R1CS-SAT instance is specified by $m \times n$ matrices A, B, C, and the prover wishes to demonstrate that it knows a vector z such that $Az \circ Bz = Cz$, where $\circ$ denotes Hadamard (entrywise) product. For simplicity, we assume that $m = n$ and that there is a multiplicative subgroup H of $\mathbb{F}$ of size exactly n. Let us label the n entries of z with elements of H, and let $\hat{z}$ be the unique univariate polynomial of degree at most $n - 1$ over $\mathbb{F}$ that extends z in the sense that $\hat{z}(h) = z_h$ for all $h \in H$ (see Lemma 2.4). Similarly, let $z_A = Az$, $z_B = Bz$, and $z_C = Cz$ be vectors in $\mathbb{F}^n$, and let $\hat{z}_A, \hat{z}_B, \hat{z}_C$ extend z_A, z_B, z_C. To check that indeed $Az \circ Bz = Cz$, the verifier must confirm two properties. First:

$$\text{for all } h \in H, \ \hat{z}_A(h) \cdot \hat{z}_B(h) = \hat{z}_C(h). \tag{10.4}$$

Second:

$$\text{for all } h \in H, \text{ and } M \in \{A, B, C\}, \ \hat{z}_M(h) = \sum_{j \in H} M_{h,j} \cdot \hat{z}(j). \tag{10.5}$$

Equation (10.5) ensures that z_A, z_B, z_C are indeed equal to Az, Bz, and Cz. Assuming this to be so, Equation (10.4) confirms that $Az \circ Bz = Cz$.

The prover sends four special messages, respectively specifying the degree-n polynomials $\hat{z}$, $\hat{z}_A$, $\hat{z}_B$, and $\hat{z}_C$.

---

[2] Of course, if the polynomial IOP is combined with an IOP-based polynomial commitment scheme such as FRI that uses logarithmically many rounds, then the resulting (standard) IOP will have logarithmically many rounds.

[3] Another benefit of having the prover send only univariate polynomials is that one of the two polynomial commitment schemes considered in this section, namely FRI, directly applies only to univariate polynomials. Though we nonetheless explain in Section 10.4.5 how to build upon such a polynomial commitment in an indirect manner to obtain one for multilinear polynomials in the IOP model, albeit with additional overheads.

Checking Equation (10.4). By Lemma 9.3 from the previous section, the first check is equivalent to the existence of a polynomial h^* of degree at most n such that

$$\hat{z}_A(X) \cdot \hat{z}_B(X) - \hat{z}_C(X) = h^*(X) \cdot \mathbb{Z}_H(X). \tag{10.6}$$

The prover sends a special message specifying the polynomial h^*. The verifier probabilistically checks that Equation (10.6) holds by choosing a random $r \in \mathbb{F}$ and confirming that

$$\hat{z}_A(r) \cdot \hat{z}_B(r) - \hat{z}_C(r) = h^*(r) \cdot \mathbb{Z}_H(r). \tag{10.7}$$

This requires querying the committed polynomials $\hat{z}_A$, $\hat{z}_B$, $\hat{z}_C$, and h^* at r; the verifier can evaluate $\mathbb{Z}_H(r)$ on its own in logarithmic time because $\mathbb{Z}_H(r)$ is sparse. Since all of the special messages sent by the prover are polynomials of degree at most n, up to soundness error $2n/|\mathbb{F}|$ over the choice of r, if Equation (10.7) holds at r then it is safe for the verifier to believe that Equation (10.6) holds, and hence also Equation (10.4).

Checking Equation (10.5). To check that Expression (10.5) holds, we leverage interaction, a resource that was not available to the PCP of Section 9.4. Fix $M \in \{A, B, C\}$ for the remainder of the paragraph. Let $\hat{M}(X, Y)$ denote the bivariate low-degree extension of the matrix M, interpreted in the natural manner as a a function $M(x, y) \colon H \times H \to \mathbb{F}$ via $M(x, y) = M_{x,y}$ That is, $\hat{M}(x, y)$ is the unique bivariate polynomial of degree at most n in each variable that extends M. Since $\hat{z}_M$ is the *unique* extension of z_M of degree less than n, it is easily seen that Equation (10.5) holds for all $h \in H$ if and only if the following equality holds as formal polynomials:

$$\hat{z}_M(X) = \sum_{j \in H} \hat{M}(X, j)\hat{z}(j). \tag{10.8}$$

Since any two distinct polynomials of degree at most n can agree on at most n inputs, if the verifier chooses r' at random from $\mathbb{F}$, then up to soundness error $n/|\mathbb{F}|$ over the choice of r', Equation (10.5) holds if and only if

$$\hat{z}_M(r') = \sum_{j \in H} \hat{M}(r', j)\hat{z}(j). \tag{10.9}$$

The verifier checks Equation (10.9) by sending r' to the prover and proceeding as follows. Let

$$q(Y) = \hat{M}(r', Y)\hat{z}(Y) - \hat{z}_M(r') \cdot |H|^{-1},$$

so that the validity of Equation (10.9) is equivalent to $\sum_{j \in H} q(Y) = 0$. The verifier requests that the prover establish that $\sum_{j \in H} q(Y) = 0$ by applying the univariate sum-check protocol from Section 10.3.1.

At the end of the univariate sum-check protocol applied to q, the verifier needs to evaluate q at a randomly chosen point r''. Clearly this can be done in a constant number of field operations if the verifier is given $\hat{z}(r'')$, $\hat{z}_M(r')$, and $\hat{M}(r', r'')$. The first two evaluations, $\hat{z}(r'')$ and $\hat{z}_M(r')$, can be obtained with one query each to the special messages specifying the polynomials $\hat{z}$ and $\hat{z}_M$.

How the Verifier Computes $\hat{M}(r', r'')$. All that remains is to explain how and when the verifier can efficiently obtain $\hat{M}(r', r'')$. For some "structured" matrices M, it is possible that $\hat{M}$ may be evaluatable in time polylogarithmic in n. This is analogous to how the verifier in the GKR protocol or the MIP of Section 8.2 avoids pre-processing so long as the multilinear extensions of the wiring predicates of the circuit- or R1CS-satisfiability instance can be evaluated efficiently.

For unstructured matrices M, time linear in the number K of nonzero entries of M may be required to evaluate $\hat{M}(r', r'')$ (Equation (10.11) later in this section offers one way $\hat{M}(r', r'')$ can be evaluated in this time bound). If one is unhappy with this runtime for the verifier, one can seek to have a *trusted* party, in pre-processing, *commit* to $\hat{M}$, which then permits the *untrusted* prover to efficiently and verifiably reveal $\hat{M}(r', r'')$ to the verifier as needed during the polynomial IOP just described.[4] Ideally, the pre-processing time, and the runtime of the prover when revealing $\hat{M}(r', r'')$ to the verifier, will be just linear in

---

[4]As observed in [230], one can reduce the work done by the trusted party by orders of magnitude, by having an untrusted party commit to the $\hat{M}$, and the trusted party to merely evaluate $\hat{M}$ at a random point. The trusted party then asks the untrusted party to reveal the committed polynomial's evaluation at that same point. If the two evaluations are equal, then (up to some negligible soundness error) it is safe to believe that the committed polynomial is $\hat{M}$.

the number K of nonzero entries of M. This goal is sometimes called *holography* [98] or *computation commitments* [226].

If the matrix M were *dense* (i.e., with $K = \Omega(n^2)$), it would be straightforward to use polynomial commitment schemes such as those given in this section (Section 10.4.2 and 10.5) or Section 14 to accomplish this goal. But typically R1CS matrices are *sparse*, meaning K is $\Theta(n)$ (see for example Section 8.4.1). In this case, the goal is more challenging to achieve.

Chiesa *et al.* [98], [100] nonetheless give a way to achieve it. Their technique is analogous in many ways to the commitment scheme for sparse *multilinear* polynomials described later in this survey (Section 16.2), which can be used to commit to the sparse multilinear extensions $\widetilde{\text{add}}$ and $\widetilde{\text{mult}}$ of the wiring predicates used in the GKR protocol and the MIPs of Section 8, thereby achieving holography for those protocols. In both cases, the general idea is to express the "sparse" polynomial to be committed in terms of a constant number of *dense* polynomials, each of which can be straightforwardly committed in time linear in the sparsity K.[5]

Overview of Achieving Holography. The key to achieving this in the IOP setting is to give an explicit expression for $\hat{M}$, analogous to how Lemma 4.9 from Section 4.6.7.1 represents the *multilinear* extension of any function in terms of a higher-degree extension of the function. In more detail, recall that in Lemma 4.9, we defined $\widetilde{\beta}$ to be the unique multilinear extension of the "equality function" that takes two inputs from the Boolean hypercube and outputs 1 if and only if they are equal (see Equation (4.19)). In the setting of this section, the analog of the Boolean hypercube is the subgroup H, and the analog of $\widetilde{\beta}$ is the following bivariate polynomial: $u_H(X, Y) := \frac{\mathbb{Z}_H(X) - \mathbb{Z}_H(Y)}{X - Y}$. Though it is not immediately obvious, u_H is a polynomial of degree at most $|H| = n$

---

[5]Both here and in Section 16.2, K refers to the number of nonzero evaluations of the sparse polynomial over the relevant interpolating set defining the polynomial. In this section, that set is $H \times H$. In Section 16.2 and its application to the GKR protocols and the MIPs of Section 8, the relevant interpolating set is the Boolean hypercube.

in each variable.[6] For example, if $\mathbb{Z}_H(X) = X^n - 1$, then

$$u_H(X,Y) := \frac{X^n - Y^n}{X - Y} = X^{n-1} + X^{n-2}Y + X^{n-3}Y^2 + X^{n-4}Y^3 + \ldots$$
$$+ XY^{n-2} + Y^{n-1}. \tag{10.10}$$

It is easy to check that for $x, y \in H$ with $x \neq y$, $u_H(x, y) = 0$. While less obvious, it is also true that for all $x \in H$, $u_H(x, x) \neq 0$ (though unlike $\tilde{\beta}$, it is not necessarily the case that $u_H(x, x) = 1$ for all $x \in H$. For example, in Equation (10.10), $u_H(x, x) = nx^{n-1}$.).

Let $\mathcal{K}$ be a multiplicative subgroup of $\mathbb{F}$ of order K. Let us define three functions *val, row, col* mapping $\mathcal{K}$ to $\mathbb{F}$ as follows. We impose some canonical bijection between the nonzero entries of M and $\mathcal{K}$, and for $\kappa \in \mathcal{K}$, we define $row(\kappa)$ and $col(\kappa)$ to be the row index and column index of the κ'th nonzero entry of M, and define $val(\kappa)$ to be the value of this entry, divided by:

$$u_H(row(\kappa), row(\kappa)) \cdot u_H(col(\kappa), col(\kappa)).$$

Let $\hat{val}$, $\hat{row}$, and $\hat{col}$ be their unique extensions of degree at most K. Then we can express

$$\hat{M}(X, Y) = \sum_{\kappa \in \mathcal{K}} u_H(X, \hat{row}(\kappa)) \cdot u_H(Y, \hat{col}(\kappa)) \cdot \hat{val}(\kappa). \tag{10.11}$$

Indeed, it is easy to see that the right hand side of the above equation has degree at most $|H|$ in both X and Y, and agrees with $\hat{M}$ at all inputs in $H \times H$. Since $\hat{M}$ is the unique polynomial with these properties, the right hand side and left hand side are the same polynomial.

A First Attempt. Equation (10.11) expresses $\hat{M}$ in terms of degree-κ polynomials $\hat{row}$, $\hat{col}$, and $\hat{val}$, which suggests the following approach to permitting the verifier to efficiently learn $\hat{M}(r', r'')$ at the end of the polynomial IOP. The pre-processing phase can have a trusted party

---

[6]To see that $p_1(X, Y) := \mathbb{Z}_H(X) - \mathbb{Z}_H(Y)$ is divisible by $p_2 := X - Y$, observe that standard properties of polynomial division imply that when p_1 is divided by p_2, the remainder polynomial $r(X, Y)$ can be taken to have degree in X strictly less than that of p_2 in X, which is 1. Hence, $r(X, Y)$ has degree 0 in X. Since p_1 is symmetric, it can be seen that r is also symmetric, and hence $r(X, Y)$ is constant.

commit to the polynomials $\hat{val}$, $\hat{row}$, $\hat{col}$ (note that these are degree-K polynomials) and then when the verifier needs to know $\hat{M}(r', r'')$, the univariate sum-check protocol is invoked to establish that the polynomial

$$p(\kappa) := u_H(r', \hat{row}(\kappa)) \cdot u_H(r'', \hat{col}(\kappa)) \cdot \hat{val}(\kappa) \tag{10.12}$$

sums to the claimed value over inputs in $\mathcal{K}$.

This unfortunately does not yield the efficiency we desire, because $u_H(r', \hat{row}(\kappa))$ and $u_H(r'', \hat{col}(\kappa))$ have degree as large as $n \cdot K$, since u_H has degree n in both of its variables. This means that applying the univariate sum-check protocol to $p(\kappa)$ would require the prover to send a polynomial h^* of degree $\Theta(n \cdot K)$, when we are seeking a prover runtime (and hence degree bound on all special messages) proportional just to K.

The Actual Holography Protocol. In the actual protocol, the pre-processing phase still commits to the three degree-K polynomials $\hat{val}$, $\hat{row}$, and $\hat{col}$.

To address the issue with the first attempt, we have to modify the "online phase" of the protocol, whereby the prover reveals to the verifier $\hat{M}(r', r'')$ to reduce its cost for the prover. Let us define f to be the unique polynomial of degree at most K that agrees with p (Equation (10.12)) at all inputs in $\mathcal{K}$. We are going to have the prover commit to f, and in order for the verifier to be able to check that f and p agree at all inputs in $\mathcal{K}$, we will need to identify a new expression (simpler than Equation (10.12)) that describes p's values at inputs in $\mathcal{K}$.

Specifically, observe that for any $a \in \mathcal{K}$,

$$u_H(r', \hat{row}(a)) = \frac{\mathbb{Z}_H(r') - \mathbb{Z}_H(\hat{row}(a))}{(r' - \hat{row}(a))} = \frac{\mathbb{Z}_H(r')}{(r' - \hat{row}(a))},$$

where the final equality uses the fact that $\hat{row}(a) \in H$. Similarly, for any $a \in \mathcal{K}$,

$$u_H(r'', \hat{col}(a)) = \frac{\mathbb{Z}_H(r'')}{(r'' - \hat{col}(a))}.$$

Hence, for any $a \in \mathcal{K}$,

$$p(a) = \frac{\mathbb{Z}_H(r')\mathbb{Z}_H(r'') \cdot \hat{val}(a)}{(r' - \hat{row}(a)) \cdot (r'' - \hat{col}(a))}. \tag{10.13}$$

This discussion leads to the following protocol enabling the verifier to efficiently learn $\hat{M}(r', r'')$ following a pre-processing phase during which a trusted party commits to the degree-K polynomials $\hat{row}$, $\hat{col}$, and $\hat{val}$. First, the prover commits to the degree-K polynomial f defined above, and the prover and verifier apply the univariate sum-check protocol to compute $\sum_{a \in K} f(a)$. Recall from Equation (10.11) that if f is as claimed, then this quantity equals $\hat{M}(r', r'')$.

Second, observe that for all $a \in K$, $f(a)$ equals the expression in Equation (10.13) if and only if the following polynomial vanishes for all $a \in K$:

$$(r' - \hat{row}(a)) \cdot (r'' - \hat{col}(a)) \cdot f - \mathbb{Z}_H(r')\mathbb{Z}_H(r'') \cdot \hat{val}(a). \qquad (10.14)$$

By Lemma 9.3, Expression (10.14) vanishes for all $a \in K$ if and only if it is divisible by $\mathbb{Z}_K(Y) = \prod_{a \in K}(Y - a)$. The prover establishes this by committing to a polynomial q such that $q \cdot \mathbb{Z}_K$ equals Expression (10.14), and the verifier checks the claimed polynomial equality by confirming that it holds at a random input $r''' \in \mathbb{F}$. This does require the verifier to evaluate $\hat{row}$, $\hat{col}$, $\hat{val}$, f, q, and $\mathbb{Z}_K$ at r'''; the first three evaluations can be obtained from the pre-processing commitments to these polynomials, while $f(r''')$ and $q(r''')$ can be obtained from the prover's commitments to f and q, and $\mathbb{Z}_K(r)$ can be computed in logarithmic time because it is sparse.

The polynomials that the prover commits to in the univariate sum-check protocol and in verifier's second check (namely, f and q) have degree at most $2K$.

Costs of the Polynomial IOP.

Ignoring holography, the prover in the above polynomial IOP for R1CS-SAT sends five polynomials of degree at most n to check Equation (10.4): $\hat{z}$, $\hat{z}_A$, $\hat{z}_B$, $\hat{z}_C$, and h^*, each of which the verifier queries at a single point r. To check Equation (10.5) for each $M \in \{A, B, C\}$, the prover sends two polynomials of degree at most n as part of the sum-check protocol. During the univariate sum-check protocol, the verifier evaluates each of these polynomials at a random point r'' and also evaluates $\hat{z}$ at r'' and $\hat{z}_M$ at r'. In summary, if implemented naively, the prover in the polynomial IOP commits to 11 polynomials of degree at most n, and makes a total of 17 evaluation queries to the various polynomials. The number of evaluation queries can be reduced to 12 as follows: one can use the same random values r' and r'' for all three instances of Equation 10.5; also, by performing all evaluation queries at the end of the protocol, it is safe for the verifier to set $r = r''$.

[43], [98], [100] describe a number of additional optimizations that improve concrete efficiency of the polynomial IOP and/or the resulting SNARK when the polynomial IOP is combined with various polynomial commitment schemes. We briefly describe one of these optimizations for illustration. When evaluating multiple different committed polynomials at the same point r, as the verifier in the above polynomial IOP does, it is typically more efficient, at least for the proof length and verifier time, to "batch-verify" the claimed evaluations, rather than perform each verification independently.[7] Exactly how much more efficiently depends on the polynomial commitment scheme used—the IOP-based polynomial commitments covered in this section have worse amortization properties than the homomorphic commitments of Section 14. Section 16.1 has details in the homomorphic case.

This type of efficient batch-verification of multiple evaluations of committed polynomials will recur in Section 18.

10.4 FRI and Associated Polynomial Commitments

10.4.1 Overview

FRI was introduced by Ben-Sasson *et al.* [34], and its analysis has been improved over a sequence of works [36], [49], [221]. While we defer details of how FRI works until Section 10.4.4, it is useful now to precisely state the guarantee that it provides. Let d be a specified degree bound. The prover's first message in FRI specifies a function $g: L_0 \to \mathbb{F}$, where L_0 is carefully chosen subset of $\mathbb{F}$. The prover claims that g is a polynomial of degree at most d; an equivalent way of saying this is that g is a *codeword* in the *Reed-Solomon code* of degree d. L_0 is chosen to have size $\rho^{-1} \cdot d$, where $0 < \rho < 1$ is a specified constant that is referred

---

[7]Batching techniques are also known when evaluating multiple different committed polynomials at distinct points rather than the same point [64].

to as the *rate* of the Reed-Solomon code that the FRI prover claims g is a codeword in. In practice, protocols that use FRI choose $\mathbb{F}$ to be significantly bigger than L_0, because the message size (and hence prover runtime) is lower-bounded by $|L_0|$ (hence $|L_0|$ should be kept as small as possible) yet $|\mathbb{F}|$ should be large to ensure a strong soundness guarantee.

The "remainder" of the FRI protocol is an IOP with the following guarantee. For specified parameter $\delta \in (0, 1 - \sqrt{\rho})$, known analyses of FRI guarantee that if the verifier accepts, then with overwhelming probability (say, at least $1 - 2^{-128}$), g is within relative distance δ of some polynomial p of degree at most d. That is, the number of points $r \in L_0$ for which $g(r) \neq p(r)$ is at most $\delta \cdot |L_0|$.

The query complexity of the FRI IOP is the dominant factor determining the proof length in succinct argument systems derived thereof, as each IOP query translates into a Merkle-tree authentication path that must be sent in the resulting argument system (see Section 9.2). Meanwhile, the prover runtime in FRI is mainly determined by the rate parameter ρ. This is because the smaller ρ is chosen, the longer the prover's messages in the IOP, and hence the bigger the prover runtime to generate those messages. However, we will see that smaller choices of ρ potentially permit the FRI verifier to make fewer queries for a given security level, and hence keeps the proof shorter when the IOP is ultimately converted into an argument system. Argument system designers can choose ρ to obtain their preferred tradeoff between prover time and proof size.

10.4.2 Polynomial Commitments and Queries to Points Outside of L_0

We highlight the following subtlety of FRI. As we have seen (e.g., Section 10.2), the prevailing paradigm for SNARK design demands the functionality of a polynomial commitment scheme. That is, the prover in the IOP must somehow send or commit to a low-degree polynomial p and the verifier must be able to force the prover to later evaluate the committed polynomial p at any point $r \in \mathbb{F}$ of the verifier's choosing.

A natural attempt to use FRI to achieve this functionality is the following. To commit to a degree d polynomial p, the prover would send a function g (claimed to equal p) by specifying g's values over L_0 (a strict subset of $\mathbb{F}$). And the verifier can run FRI to confirm that (with overwhelming probability) g has relative distance at most δ from some degree d polynomial p. Note that if $\delta < \frac{1-d/|L_0|}{2} = \frac{1-\rho}{2}$, then p is unique, i.e., there can be only one degree d polynomial within relative distance δ of g. This is because any two distinct polynomials of degree at most d can agree on at most d points (Fact 2.1).

Already, there is the nuisance that g is only guaranteed to be *close* to p, not exactly equal to p. This is closely analogous to the "relaxed" nature of the polynomial commitment scheme arising in Section 7 and the MIPs of Section 8.

But there is an additional issue as well: since g is only specified via its evaluations at inputs in L_0, how can the verifier determine evaluations of p on inputs $r \in \mathbb{F} \setminus L_0$? The research literature posits two approaches to dealing with this. The first is to carefully design polynomial IOPs, so that the verifier need not ever evaluate a polynomial specified by the prover at an input outside of L_0 (for brevity, we do not cover this approach in this survey). The second approach utilizes an observation that will recur later in this survey when we cover pairing-based polynomial commitment schemes (Section 15.2). Specifically, for any degree-d univariate polynomial p, the assertion "$p(r) = v$" is equivalent to the assertion that there exists a polynomial w of degree at most $d - 1$ such that

$$p(X) - v = w(X) \cdot (X - r). \tag{10.15}$$

This is a special case of Lemma 9.3.

As observed in [240], the above observation means that in order to confirm that $p(r) = v$, the verifier can apply FRI to the function $X \mapsto (g(X) - v) \cdot (X - r)^{-1}$ using degree bound $d - 1$ (we define this function to be 0 at input r). Note that whenever the FRI verifier queries this function at a point in L_0, the evaluation can be obtained with one query to g at the same point. If the FRI verifier accepts, then with overwhelming probability this function is within distance δ of some polynomial q of degree at most $d-1$. Since g and p have relative distance at most δ over domain L_0, this means that the polynomials $q(X)(X - r)$ and $p(X) - v$ agree on at least $(1 - 2\delta) \cdot |L_0|$ inputs in L_0, and both have degree at most d.

Suppose that $\delta < \frac{1-\rho}{2}$, which guarantees that $(1 - 2\delta)|L_0| > d$. Since any two distinct polynomials of degree at most d can agree on at most d inputs, this implies that $q(X) \cdot (X - r)$ and $p(X) - v$ are the same polynomial, and this in turn implies by Equation (10.15) that $p(r) = v$.

In summary, if the prover sends a function $g \colon L_0 \to \mathbb{F}$ and convinces the FRI verifier that g has distance at most $\delta < \frac{1-\rho}{2}$ from some degree d polynomial p, and moreover the FRI verifier accepts when applied to $X \mapsto (g(X) - v) \cdot (X - r)^{-1}$ using degree bound $d - 1$, then with overwhelming probability, $p(r)$ indeed equals v. That is, the verifier can safely accept that the low-degree polynomial p committed to via g evaluates to v at input r.

Note that the prover in this polynomial commitment scheme is bound to an actual polynomial p of degree at most d, in the sense that the prover must answer any evaluation request at input $r \in \mathbb{F}$ with $p(r)$ in order to convince the verifier to accept with non-negligible probability. This is in contrast to FRI by itself, which only binds the prover to a function g over domain L_0 that is *close to p*.

In summary, the technique of this section addressed *both* issues that prevented FRI from giving a polynomial commitment scheme directly. As described, the technique introduces a concrete overhead for the verifier of a factor close to two. To commit to a degree-d polynomial p, the prover sends (a Merkle-hash of) all evaluations of p over domain L_0, and FRI is applied to confirm that the function g actually sent is indeed close to some degree d polynomial. But then when the verifier queries the committed polynomial p at a point r outside of L_0, FRI has to be applied a second time, to confirm that the function $(g(X) - v) \cdot (X - r)^{-1}$ is (close to) some polynomial of degree at most $d - 1$.

In fact, the first application of FRI can be omitted, thereby avoiding the overhead above. Indeed, since the second application of FRI guarantees that $(g(X) - v) \cdot (X - r)^{-1}$ has relative distance at most δ over L_0 from a polynomial $q(X)$ of degree $d - 1$, it follows that the degree-d polynomial $p(X) := q(X) \cdot (X - r) + v$ has relative distance at most δ over L_0. Guaranteeing the existence of such a polynomial p was the entire point of the first application of FRI.

10.4.3 Costs of FRI

Prover Time. In applications of FRI (e.g., transforming the polynomial IOP of Section 10.3 into a SNARK), the prover will know the coefficients of a degree-d polynomial p or its evaluations on a size-d subset of L_0. To apply FRI to p, the prover must evaluate p at the remaining points in L_0. This is the dominant cost in terms of prover runtime. The fastest known algorithms for this are essentially FFTs, and they require $\Theta(|L_0| \cdot \log |L_0|) = \Theta(\rho^{-1}d\log(\rho^{-1}d))$ field operations. For constant rate parameters ρ, this is $\Theta(d \log d)$ time. We remark that Ben-Sasson *et al.* [34] describe the prover time in FRI as $O(d)$ field operations, but this assumes that the prover already knows the evaluations of p at all inputs in L_0, which will not be the case in applications of FRI.

Proof Length. FRI can be broken into two phases: a *commitment phase* and a *query* phase. The commitment phase is when the prover sends all of its messages in the IOP phase (during this phase, the verifier need not actually query any of the prover's messages) and the verifier sends one random challenge to the prover in each of $\log_2 |L_0|$ rounds.

The query phase is when the verifier actually queries the prover's messages at the necessary points to check the prover's claims. The query phase in turn consists of a "basic protocol" that must be repeated many times to ensure good soundness error. Specifically, in the basic query protocol the verifier makes 2 queries to each each of the $\log_2 |L_0|$ messages sent by the prover. To ensure a $2^{-\lambda}$ upper bound on the probability that the FRI verifier accepts a function g of relative distance more than δ from any degree-d polynomial, the basic protocol must be repeated roughly $\lambda / \log_2 (1/(1 - \delta))$ times. This query phase is the dominant cost in the proof length of the argument systems obtained by combining FRI-based IOPs with Merkle-hashing. The argument system prover must send a Merkle-tree authentication path (consisting of $O(\log d)$ hash values) for each query in the IOP, the proof length of the resulting arguments is $O\left(\lambda \cdot \log^2(d)/\log_2\left(1/\left(1-\delta\right)\right)\right)$ hash values. For constant values of δ, this is $O(\lambda \cdot \log^2(d))$ hash values.

Remark 10.2. The FRI proof system is largely independent of the setting of the parameter δ. The only reason that the prover and verifier within FRI need to "know" what δ will be set to in the soundness analysis is to ensure that they repeat the query phase of FRI at least $\lambda/\log_2\left(1/(1-\delta)\right)$ times.

10.4.4 Details of FRI: Better Reed-Solomon Proximity Proofs via Interaction

Recall that the PCP for Reed-Solomon testing sketched in Section 9.4.3 worked by iteratively reducing the problem of testing a function G_i for proximity to a degree d_i polynomial to the problem of testing a related function G_{i+1} for proximity to a degree d_{i+1} polynomial where $d_{i+1} \ll d_i$ (more precisely, $d_{i+1} \approx \sqrt{d_i}$). A source of inefficiency in this construction was that each iterative reduction incurred a constant-factor loss in the distance from any low-degree polynomial of the function being analyzed. That is, if G_i is at least δ_i-far from every degree d_i polynomial, then G_{i+1} is only guaranteed to be at least (δ_i/c_0)-far from every polynomial of degree at most $\sqrt{d_i}$ for some universal constant $c_0 > 1$. This constant-factor loss in distance per iteration meant that we had to keep the number of iterations small if we wanted to maintain meaningful soundness guarantees. This in turn meant we needed to make sure that we made a *lot* of progress in reducing the degree parameter in each iteration. This is why we choose for d_{i+1} to be just $\sqrt{d_i}$—this ensured the d_i fell doubly-exponentially quickly in i, i.e., only $\Theta(\log \log d_0)$ iterations were required before the degree became 0, i.e., the function G_i became constant.

Unlike PCPs, IOPs such as FRI are allowed to be interactive, and FRI exploits interaction to ensure that the distance parameter δ_i does *not* fall by a constant factor in each round. This permits FRI to use exponentially more iterations—$\Theta(\log d_0)$ rather than $\Theta(\log \log d_0)$—while maintaining meaningful soundness guarantees, with corresponding efficiency benefits.

Recall from Section 10.4.1 that FRI proceeds in two phases, a *commitment phase* and a *query* phase. The commitment phase is when the prover sends all of its messages in the IOP (during this phase, the verifier need not actually query any of the prover's messages) and the verifier sends one random challenge to the prover in each round. The query phase is when the verifier queries the prover's messages at the necessary points to check the prover's claims.

Comparison of the IOP Commitment Phase to Section 9.4.3. For simplicity, let us suppose that in round i of the IOP, G_i is a function defined over a multiplicative subgroup L_i of $\mathbb{F}$, where $|L_i|$ is a power of 2, and the current degree bound d_i is also a power of 2. In round 0, G_0 is the evaluation table of the polynomial defined over domain L_0, for which we are testing proximity to univariate polynomials of degree d_0.

Recall that in Section 9.4.3, to show that G_i was a degree d_i polynomial, for any desired polynomial q_i of degree $\sqrt{d_i}$, it sufficed for the PCP to establish that $G_i(z) = Q_i(z, q_i(z))$ for some bivariate polynomial Q_i of degree at most $\sqrt{d_i}$ in each variable. When G_i indeed has degree at most d_i, the existence of such a polynomial Q_i was guaranteed by Lemma 9.6.

In the FRI IOP, $q_i(z)$ will simply be z^2 (since this choice of q_i does not depend on i, we omit the subscript i from q henceforth). When G_i indeed has degree at most d_i, Lemma 9.6 guarantees that there is a $Q_i(X, Y)$ of degree at most 1 in X and at most $d_i/2$ in Y such that $Q_i(z, z^2) = G_i(z)$. Under this setting of $q_i(z)$, this representation of G_i has an especially simple form. Let $P_{i,0}$ (respectively, $P_{i,1}$) consist of all monomials of G_i of even (respectively, odd) degree, but with all powers divided by two and then replaced by their integer floor. For example, if $G_i(z) = z^3 + 3z^2 + 2z + 1$, then $P_{i,0} = 3z + 1$ and $P_{i,1}(z) = z + 2$. When $q(z) = z^2$, Lemma 9.6 is simply observing that we can ensure that $G_i(z) = Q_i(z, z^2)$ by defining $Q_i(z, y) := P_{i,0}(y) + z \cdot P_{i,1}(y)$.

In the PCP for Reed-Solomon testing of Section 9.4.3, $q(z)$ was chosen to be a polynomial of degree $\sqrt{d_i}$ such that the size of the image $q(L_i)$ was much smaller than $|L_i|$ itself (smaller by a factor of $\sqrt{d_i}$). Similarly, when L_i is a multiplicative subgroup of $\mathbb{F}$, the map $z \to z^2$ is two-to-one on L_i,[8] so under our choice of $q(z) := z^2$, if we define

$$L_{i+1} = q(L_i), \tag{10.16}$$

then $|L_{i+1}| = |L_i|/2$.

Complete Description of the IOP Commitment Phase. After the IOP prover commits to the polynomial G_i defined over domain L_i, the IOP verifier chooses a random value $x_i \in \mathbb{F}$ and requests that the prover send it the univariate polynomial

$$G_{i+1}(Y) := Q_i(x_i, Y) = P_{i,0}(Y) + x_i \cdot P_{i,1}(Y), \tag{10.17}$$

defined over the domain L_{i+1} given in Equation (10.16).

This proceeds for rounds $i = 0, 1, \ldots, \log_2(d_0)$. Finally for $i^* = \log_2(d_0)$, $G_{i^*}(Y)$ is supposed to have degree 0 and hence be a constant function. In this round, the prover's message simply specifies the constant C, which the verifier interprets to specify that $G_{i^*}(Y) = C$.

Query Phase. The verifier $\mathcal{V}$ repeats the following ℓ times, for a parameter ℓ we set later. $\mathcal{V}$ picks an input $s_0 \in L_0$ at random, and for $i = 0, \ldots, i^* - 1$, $\mathcal{V}$ sets $s_{i+1} = q(s_i) = s_i^2$. The verifier then wishes to check that $G_{i+1}(s_{i+1})$ is consistent with Equation (10.17) at input s_{i+1}, i.e., that $G_{i+1}(s_{i+1})$ indeed equals $Q_i(x_i, s_{i+1})$. We now explain how this check can be performed with two queries to G_i.

Let $g(X) := Q_i(X, s_{i+1})$ and observe that $g(X)$ is a linear function in X. Hence the entire function g can be inferred from its evaluations at two inputs.

Specifically, let $s_i' \neq s_i$ denote the other element of L_i satisfying $(s_i')^2 = s_{i+1}$. Since we have assumed that L_i is a multiplicative subgroup of even order, L_i contains -1 (see Footnote 8), and hence $s_i' = -s_i$. We know that $g(s_i) = Q_i(s_i, s_{i+1}) = G_i(s_i)$, while $g(s_i') = Q_i(s_i', s_{i+1}) =$

---

[8]To see this, recall from the proof of Fact 10.1 that any multiplicative subgroup H of a finite field $\mathbb{F}$ is cyclic, meaning there is a $h \in H$ such that $H = \{h, h^2, \ldots, h^{|H|}\}$, where $h^{|H|} = 1$. If $|H|$ is even, this means that $H' := \{h^2, h^4, \ldots, h^{|H|}\}$ is also a multiplicative subgroup of $\mathbb{F}$, of order $|H|/2$, and H' consists of all perfect squares (also known as quadratic residues) in H. For each element h^{2i} in H', h^{2i} is the square of both h^i and $h^{i+|H|/2} = -h^i$.

$G_i(s_i')$. And since g is linear, these two evaluations are enough to infer the entire linear function g, and thereby evaluate $g(x_i)$. More concretely, it holds that

$$g(X) = (X - s_i) \cdot (s_i' - s_i)^{-1} \cdot G_i(s_i') + (X - s_i') \cdot (s_i - s_i')^{-1} \cdot G_i(s_i),$$

as this expression is a linear function of X that takes the appropriate values at $X = s_i$ and $X = s_i'$.

Accordingly, to check that $G_{i+1}(s_{i+1})$ indeed equals $Q_i(x_i, s_{i+1})$, the verifier queries G_i at s_i' and s_i, and checks that

$$G_{i+1}(s_{i+1}) = (x_i - s_i) \cdot (s_i' - s_i)^{-1} \cdot G_i(s_i') + (x_i - s_i') \cdot (s_i - s_i')^{-1} \cdot G_i(s_i).$$
(10.18)

Completeness and Soundness. Completeness of the protocol holds by design: it is clear that if G_0 is indeed a univariate polynomial of degree at most d_0 over domain L_0 and sends the prescribed messages, then all of the verifier's checks will pass. Indeed, all of the consistency checks will pass, and G_{i^*} will indeed be a constant function.

The state-of-the-art soundness guarantee for FRI is stated in Theorem 10.4 below. Its proof is quite technical and is omitted from the survey, but we sketch the main ideas in detail.

Worst-Case to Average-Case Reductions for Reed-Solomon Codes. The key technical notion in the analysis of FRI is the following statement. Let $f_1, \ldots, f_\ell$ be a collection of ℓ functions on domain L_i, and suppose that at least one of f_j has relative distance at least δ from every polynomial of degree at most d_i over L_i. Then if $f := \sum_{j=1}^{\ell} r_j f_j$ denotes a random linear combination of $f_1, \ldots, f_\ell$ (i.e., each r_j is chosen at random from $\mathbb{F}$), then with high probability over the random choices of $r_1, \ldots, r_\ell$, f also has distance at least δ from every polynomial of degree at most d_i over L_i. This statement is far from obvious, and to give a sense of why it is true, in Lemma 10.3 below we prove the following weaker statement that does *not* suffice to yield a tight analysis of FRI because it incurs a factor-of-2 loss in the distance parameter δ. Lemma 10.3 is due to Rothblum *et al.* [217]; our proof follows the presentation of Ames *et al.* [7, Proof of Case 1 of Lemma 4.2] almost verbatim.

Lemma 10.3. Let $f_1, \ldots, f_\ell$ be a collection of ℓ functions on domain L_i, and suppose that at least one of the functions, say f_{j^*}, has relative distance at least δ from every polynomial of degree at most d_i over L_i. If $f := \sum_{j=1}^{\ell} r_j \cdot f_j$ denotes a random linear combination of $f_1, \ldots, f_\ell$, then with probability at least $1 - 1/|\mathbb{F}|$, f has distance at least $\delta/2$ from every polynomial of degree at most d_i over L_i.

Proof. Let V denote the span of $f_1, \ldots, f_\ell$, i.e., V is the set of all functions obtained by taking arbitrary linear combinations of $f_1, \ldots, f_\ell$. Observe that a random element of V can be written as $\alpha \cdot f_{j^*} + x$ where α is a random field element and x is distributed independently of α. We argue that conditioned on any choice of x, there can be at most one choice of α such that $\alpha \cdot f_{j^*} + x$ has relative distance at most $\delta/2$ from some polynomial of degree at most d_i. To see this, suppose by way of contradiction that $\alpha \cdot f_{j^*} + x$ has relative distance less than $\delta/2$ from some polynomial p of degree d_i and $\alpha' \cdot f_{j^*} + x$ has relative distance less than $\delta/2$ from some polynomial q of degree d_i, where $\alpha \neq \alpha'$. Then by the triangle inequality, $(\alpha - \alpha')f_{j^*}$ has relative distance less than $\delta/2 + \delta/2 = \delta$ from $p - q$. This contradicts the assumption that f_{j^*} has distance at least δ from every polynomial of degree at most d_i. $\square$

A line of work [7], [36], [49], [217], [221] has improved Lemma 10.3 to avoid the factor-of-2 loss in the distance parameter δ. That is, rather than concluding that the random linear combination f has relative distance at most $\delta/2$ from every low-degree polynomial, these works show that f has relative distance at most δ from any low-degree polynomial. Two caveats are that these improvements do require δ to be "not too close to 1", and they also have worse failure probability than the $1/|\mathbb{F}|$ probability appearing in Lemma 10.3—see Theorem 10.4 for details on these caveats.

Detailed Soundness Analysis Sketch for FRI. The soundness analysis overview provided here below is merely a sketch, and we direct the interested reader to [49, Section 7] for a very readable presentation of the full details. Suppose that the function G_0 over domain L_0 has relative distance more than δ from every degree d_0 polynomial. We must show that for every prover strategy, with high probability the prover fails at least one of the FRI verifier's consistency checks during the Query Phase of FRI.

For any fixed value of x_0 chosen by the verifier, Equation (10.18) specifies a function G_1 over L_1 such that if the prover sends G_1 in round 1 of the Commitment Phase of FRI, then G_1 will always pass the verifier's consistency check. Namely if for any $s_1 \in L_1$ we let $s_0, s_0' \in L_0$ denote the two square roots of s_1, then

$$G_1(s_1) = (x_0 - s_0) \cdot (s_0' - s_0)^{-1} \cdot G_0(s_0') + (x_0 - s_0') \cdot (s_0 - s_0')^{-1} \cdot G_0(s_0).$$
$$(10.19)$$

Note that G_1 depends on x_0; when we need to make this dependence explicit, we will write G_{1,x_0} rather than G_1.

In round 1 of the Commitment Phase of FRI, a prover can hope to "luck out" in one of two ways. The first way is if the verifier happens to select a value $x_0 \in \mathbb{F}$ such that G_{1,x_0} has relative distance significantly less than δ from a polynomial of degree d_1. The second way is that the prover could send a message $G_1' \neq G_1$ such that G_1' is much closer to a low-degree polynomial than is G_1, and hope the verifier doesn't "detect" the deviation from G_1 via its consistency checks.

It turns out that the second approach, of sending $G_1' \neq G_1$, never increases the probability that the prover passes the verifier's checks. Roughly speaking, this is because any "distance improvement" that the prover achieves by sending a function G_1' that deviates from G_1 is compensated for by an increased probability that the prover fails the verifier's consistency checks.

Let us now explain why the probability that the prover lucks out in the first sense is at most some small quantity ε_1. The idea is that G_{1,x_0} is essentially a random linear combination of $G_{1,0}$ and $G_{1,1}$. Specifically, since G_{1,x_0} is a linear function in x_0 (see Equation (10.19)), we can write $G_{1,x_0} = G_{1,0} + x_0 \cdot G_{1,1}$. Since x_0 is chosen by the verifier uniformly at random from $\mathbb{F}$ this means G_{1,x_0} is essentially a random linear combination of $G_{1,0}$ and $G_{1,1}$ (not quite, because the coefficient of $G_{1,0}$ is fixed to 1 rather than a random field element, but let us ignore this complication). Moreover, it is possible to show (though we omit the derivation) that if $G_{1,0}$ and $G_{1,1}$ are each of relative distance at most δ over L_1 from some polynomials $p(X)$ and $q(X)$ of degree less than

$d_1 = d_0/2$, then G_0 is of relative distance at most δ over L_0 from the polynomial $p(X^2) + X \cdot q(X^2)$, which has degree less than $2d_1 = d_0$, contradicting our assumption. The strengthening of Lemma 10.3 discussed earlier in this section asserted that a random linear combination of two functions, at least one of which has relative distance at least δ from every polynomial of degree d_1, is very likely to itself have relative distance at least δ from every such polynomial. Hence we reach the desired conclusion that with high probability over the choice of x_0, G_{1,x_0} has relative distance at least δ from every polynomial of degree at most d_1.

The above analysis applies for every round i, not just to round $i = 1$. Specifically, the optimal prover strategy sends a specified function $G_{i,x_{i-1}}$ in each round i, and with high probability every $G_{i,x_{i-1}}$ has relative distance at least δ from a polynomial of degree at most d_i. If this holds for the final round i^*, then in each repetition of the Query Phase of FRI, the verifier's final consistency check will reject with probability at least $1 - \delta$. This is because $G_{i^*,x_{i^*-1}}$ will have relative distance δ from a constant function, and the prover in the final round of the commitment phase is forced to send a constant C with the verifier checking in each execution of the query phase whether $G_{i^*,x_{i^*-1}}(s_{i^*}) = C$ for a point s_{i^*} that is uniformly distributed in L_{i^*}.

In summary, conditioned on the optimal prover strategy not "lucking out" during the commitment phase (which happens with probability at most ε_1 by the analysis sketched above), each repetition of the query phase will reveal an inconsistency with probability at least $1 - \delta$. So the probability that all ℓ repetitions of the query phase fail to detect an inconsistency is $\varepsilon_2 = (1 - \delta)^\ell$. Hence, if G_0 has relative distance more than δ from any polynomial of degree at most d_0, then the FRI verifier rejects with probability at least $1 - \varepsilon_1 - \varepsilon_2$. This is formalized in the following theorem from [36].

Theorem 10.4 ([36]). Let $\rho = d_0/|L_0|$, $\eta \in (0, \sqrt{\rho}/20)$, and $\delta \in (0, 1 - \sqrt{\rho} - \eta)$. If FRI is applied to a function G_0 that has relative distance more than δ from any polynomial of degree at most d_0, then the verifier accepts with probability at most $\varepsilon_1 + \varepsilon_2$, where $\varepsilon_2 = (1 - \delta)^\ell$ and $\varepsilon_1 = \frac{(d_0+1)^2}{(2\eta)^7 \cdot |\mathbb{F}|}$.

To give a sense of how the parameters in Theorem 10.4 may be set, [36] work through a numerical example, setting ρ to $1/16$, $|\mathbb{F}|$ to be 2^{256}, η to 2^{-14}, and δ to $1 - \sqrt{\rho} - \eta = 3/4 - \eta$. They show that if d_0 is at most $2^{16} = 65536$, then with $\ell := 65$ invocations of the basic query phase, this leads to soundness error $\varepsilon_1 + \varepsilon_2 \leq 2^{-128}$.

If using FRI-based polynomial commitments to transform the polynomial IOP of Section 10.3.2 into a holographic SNARK, this setting of d_0 is only sufficient to capture R1CS instances $Az \circ Bz = Cz$ such that each matrix A, B, C, has at at most $d_0/2 = 32768$ nonzero entries. Handling significantly larger R1CS instances at the same security level would require a larger field, and either more repetitions (increasing proof length and verification costs), or lower rate (further increasing prover time).

Theorem 10.4 incentivizes protocol designers to set δ as large as possible, because larger values of δ lead to smaller values of ε_2. However, in the context of using FRI-based polynomial commitments to transform polynomial IOPs into SNARKs, there may be other issues that prevent setting δ as large as it is set in the above numerical example, at least according to known soundness analyses. For example, deriving an actual polynomial commitment scheme from FRI as in Section 10.4.2 requires $\delta < (1 - \rho)/2 < 1/2.$[9] As another example, some concrete optimizations to various polynomial IOP in the literature that have been combined with FRI, e.g., [100, Theorem 8.2], require the yet more stringent condition $\delta \leq (1 - \rho)/3 < 1/3$. Under such a restriction, FRI would require over 200 repetitions of the query phase to achieve soundness error less than 2^{-128}.

It is conjectured that an analog of Theorem 10.4 holds even for δ as large as roughly $1 - \rho$ (see for example [35], [36]) rather than the $1 - \sqrt{\rho} - \eta$ bound on δ assumed in Theorem 10.4.

---

[9]RedShift [165] uses FRI to construct a relaxation of a polynomial commitment called a *list polynomial commitment*, and shows this relaxed primitive suffices for transforming some polynomial IOPs into SNARKs (though it drastically increases the cost of holography). This relaxed primitive can be achieved with δ as large as roughly $1 - \sqrt{\rho}$.

10.4.5 From Univariate to Multilinear Polynomials

FRI can be used to give a polynomial commitment scheme for *univariate* polynomials (Section 10.4.2). Zhang *et al.* [256] observe that, given any such commitment scheme for univariate polynomials, it is possible to devise one for multilinear polynomials in the following manner. As observed in Lemma 3.8, evaluating an ℓ-variate multilinear polynomial q over $\mathbb{F}$ at an input $r \in \mathbb{F}^\ell$ is equivalent to computing the inner product of the following two (2^ℓ)-dimensional vectors $u_1, u_2 \in \mathbb{F}^{2^\ell}$. Associating $\{0,1\}^\ell$ with $\{0, \ldots, 2^\ell - 1\}$ in the natural way, the w'th entry of the first vector u_1 is $q(w)$ and the w'th entry of the second vector u_2 is $\chi_w(r)$, the w'th Lagrange basis polynomial evaluated at r. This simple observation, that one can view the task of evaluating a polynomial p at an input r as an inner product between the coefficient vector u_1 of the polynomial over the relevant basis (in this case, the Lagrange basis), and the vector u_2 of all basis functions evaluated at r, will recur over and over again in the many polynomial commitment schemes discussed in this text.

Let H be a multiplicative subgroup of $\mathbb{F}$ of size $n := 2^\ell$. (A multiplicative subgroup of exactly this size only exists if and only if 2^ℓ divides $|\mathbb{F}| - 1$, so let us assume this). Let $b \colon H \to \{0,1\}^\ell$ be a canonical bijection. To commit to a multilinear polynomial q, it suffices to commit to a *univariate* polynomial Q over $\mathbb{F}$ of degree $|H| = n$ such that for all $a \in H$, $Q(a) = q(b(a))$, as q is fully specified by its evaluations over $\{0,1\}^\ell$. To later reveal $q(z)$ at a point $z \in \mathbb{F}^\ell$ of the verifier's choosing, consider the vector u_2 containing all Lagrange basis polynomials evaluated at z. It suffices to confirm that

$$\sum_{a \in H} Q(a) \cdot u_2(a) = v, \tag{10.20}$$

where v is the claimed value of $q(z)$ and here we associate the $|H|$-dimensional vector u_2 with a function over H in the natural way.

Let $\hat{u}_2$ be the unique polynomial of degree at most $|H|$ extending u_2, and let

$$g(X) = Q(X) \cdot \hat{u}_2(X) - v \cdot |H|^{-1}.$$

Observe that Equation (10.20) holds if and only if $\sum_{a \in H} g(a) = 0$. Hence, Equation (10.20) can be checked by applying the univariate sum-check protocol described following Lemma 10.2 to the polynomial g. In more detail, in this protocol the prover sends a commitment to polynomials h^* and f such that

$$g(X) = h^*(X) \cdot \mathbb{Z}_H(X) + X \cdot f(X) \tag{10.21}$$

and f has degree at most $n - 1$. This requires the verifier to evaluate $g(r)$, $h^*(r)$, $\mathbb{Z}_H(r)$ and $f(r)$ for a randomly chosen $r \in \mathbb{F}$. As usual $\mathbb{Z}_H(r)$ is sparse so the verifier can compute this on its own in logarithmic time, and $h^*(r)$ and $f(r)$ can be obtained by querying the commitments to these polynomials.

Evaluating $g(r)$ requires evaluating $Q(r)$ and $\hat{u}_2(r)$. $Q(r)$ can be obtained by querying the commitment to Q. However, evaluating $\hat{u}_2(r)$ requires time linear in n (Lemma 3.8). Fortunately, the function $r \mapsto \hat{u}_2(r)$ is computed by a layered arithmetic circuit of size $O(n \log n)$, depth $O(\log n)$, and a wiring pattern for which $\widetilde{\text{add}}_i$ and $\widetilde{\text{mult}}_i$ can be evaluated in $O(\log n)$ time for each layer i. Hence, the verifier can outsource the evaluation of $\hat{u}_2(r)$ to the prover using the GKR protocol (Section 4.6), with the verifier running in $O(\log^2 n)$ time.

Note that this transformation introduces considerable overhead. In order to commit to a single multilinear polynomial with n coefficients and later produce a single evaluation-proof, the prover has to commit to 3 univariate polynomials of degree n rather than just one such polynomial. Moreover, the prover and verifier have to apply the GKR protocol to a circuit of size superlinear in the number n of coefficients of the polynomial being committed.

10.5 Ligero and Brakedown Polynomial Commitments

In this section, we describe IOP-based polynomial commitment schemes with a much faster prover than FRI but larger evaluation proofs. For simplicity, we describe the polynomial commitment scheme here in the context of univariate polynomials (expressed over the standard monomial basis), but in fact the scheme applies directly to multilinear polynomials as well (see Figure 14.2 in Section 14 for details).

10.5.1 Identifying Tensor Product Structure in Polynomial Evaluation Queries

Let q be a degree-$(n-1)$ univariate polynomial over field $\mathbb{F}_p$ that the prover wishes to commit to, and let u denote the vector of coefficients of u. Then, as observed in the previous section, we can express evaluations of q as inner products of u with appropriate "evaluation vectors". Specifically, if $q(X) = \sum_{i=0}^{n-1} u_i X^i$, then for $z \in \mathbb{F}_p$, $q(z) = \langle u, y \rangle$ where $y = (1, z, z^2, \ldots, z^{n-1})$ consists of powers of z, and $\langle u, y \rangle = \sum_{i=0}^{n-1} u_i v_i$ denotes the inner product of u and y.

Moreover, the vector y has a tensor-product structure in the following sense. Let us assume that $n = m^2$ is a perfect square, and define $a, b \in \mathbb{F}^m$ as $a := (1, z, z^2, \ldots, z^{m-1})$ and $b := (1, z^m, z^{2m}, \ldots, z^{m(m-1)})$. If we view y as an $m \times m$ matrix with entries indexed as $(y_{1,1}, \ldots, y_{m,m})$, then y is simply the outer product $b \cdot a^T$ of a and b. That is, $y_{i,j} = z^{i \cdot m + j} = b_i \cdot a_j$ for all $0 \le i, j \le m - 1$. Equivalently, we can write $q(z)$ as the vector-matrix-vector product $b^T \cdot u \cdot a$. This tensor structure is also exploited in several polynomial commitment schemes given in Section 14—Figure 14.1 in that section contains a pictorial example of this tensor structure.

10.5.2 Description of the Polynomial Commitment Scheme

Background on Error-Correcting Codes. To explain the commitment scheme, we need to introduce some terminology regarding error-correcting codes. An error-correcting code is specified by an encoding function E. E maps vectors in $\mathbb{F}^m$ to slightly longer vectors, in $\mathbb{F}^{\rho^{-1} \cdot m}$, where ρ is called the *rate* of the code (think of ρ as a constant such as $1/4$). E must be "distance-amplifying". This means that if messages $u_1, u_2 \in \mathbb{F}^m$ disagree in even a single coordinate, then $E(u_1)$ and $E(u_2)$ should disagree in a constant fraction of coordinates. The distance of the code is the minimum disagreement between any two codewords $E(u_1)$ and $E(u_2)$. The *relative distance* γ of the code is the distance divided by the codeword length.

The code is *linear* if E is a linear function. That is, $E(a \cdot u_1 + b \cdot u_2) = a \cdot E(u_1) + b \cdot E(u_2)$ for any messages $u_1, u_2 \in \mathbb{F}^m$ and scalars $a, b \in \mathbb{F}$.

A classic example of a linear code is the Reed-Solomon code. As we have seen throughout this survey, in this code a message $u_1 \in \mathbb{F}^m$ is interpreted as a degree-$m-1$ univariate polynomial p over $\mathbb{F}$. $E(u_1)$ is a list of $\rho^{-1}m$ evaluations of p. The distance of code is at least $(1-\rho) \cdot m$; this follows from the fact that any two distinct degree-$(m-1)$ polynomials can agree on at most $m-1$ inputs. For this code, $E(u_1)$ can be computed in time $O(\rho^{-1}m \log(\rho^{-1}m))$ using FFT-based multi-point evaluation algorithms.

For the rest of this section, let E denote the encoding function of a linear code with message length m, codeword length $\rho^{-1}m$, and constant relative distance $\gamma > 0$. Let us furthermore assume E is systematic, meaning for any message $u_1 \in \mathbb{F}^m$, the first m symbols of $E(u_1)$ are the entries of u_1 itself.

The commitment scheme described below is implicit in Ligero [7] in the case that E is the Reed-Solomon code (or, more precisely, its systematic variant, the univariate low-degree extension code, see Section 2.4). For general linear codes E, it is essentially implicit in work of Bootle *et al.* [67], see also [69]. Golovnev *et al.* [137] designed a concretely efficient error-correcting code E with a linear-time encoding procedure, and called the resulting implemented commitment scheme Brakedown (they also showed that the resulting polynomial commitment scheme is extractable). Xie *et al.* [253] refine the error-correcting code to improve performance, and use SNARK composition to reduce the length of the polynomial evaluation proofs in the resulting commitment scheme.

Commitment Phase. Recalling that $[m]$ denotes the set $\{1, 2, \ldots m\}$, let us view the coefficient vector u of q as an $m \times m$ matrix in the natural way (exactly as we viewed the vector y above as an $m \times m$ matrix). See Figure 14.1 in Section 14 for an example.

Let us denote the i'th row of u by u_i. Let $\hat{u}$ be the $m \times (\rho^{-1}m)$ matrix in which the i'th row is $E(u_i)$. In the IOP, the prover's commitment to u will simply be a message listing the entries of the matrix $\hat{u}$ (so in the final polynomial commitment scheme, the commitment to q will be the Merkle-hash of $\hat{u}$).

Let us denote the actual $m \times (\rho^{-1}m)$ matrix contained in the prover's commitment message by M. M is claimed to be $\hat{u}$, but if the prover is cheating, then M may differ from $\hat{u}$. Upon receiving M, the verifier's initial goal is to try to ascertain whether or not M is actually a "well-formed" commitment matrix, meaning that every row of M is a codeword in the error-correcting code specified by E. The verifier will probabilistically check this via a "random linear combination of rows" test.

Specifically, the verifier chooses a random vector $r \in \mathbb{F}^m$ and sends r to the prover. The prover responds with a vector $w \in \mathbb{F}^{\rho^{-1}m}$ claimed to equal $r^T \cdot M$, and the verifier confirms that w is a codeword. More precisely, the verifier can confirm this by having the prover not send w itself, but instead send a message $v \in \mathbb{F}^m$, and the verifier sets w to $E(v)$. This means that the verifier reads v in its entirety.

For some integer parameter $t = \Theta(\lambda)$ that we will specify later, the verifier then randomly selects t entries of w and confirms that those entries are "consistent" with the actual commitment matrix M. That is, the verifier picks a size-t subset Q of the $\rho^{-1}m$ entries of w at random. For each $i \in Q$, the verifier "opens" *all* m entries in the ith column of M, and confirms that these entries are consistent with w_i, i.e., that $w_i = r^T \cdot M_i$ where M_i denotes the ith column of M. Since the verifier "consistency checks" t entries of w and each check requires opening an entire column of M, the total number of queries the verifier makes to entries of M is $t \cdot m$.

Evaluation Phase.   Suppose the verifier requests that the prover reveal $q(z) = \langle u, y \rangle$ where u and y are defined as in Section 10.5.1. Recall that, viewing u as a matrix, $q(z) = b^T \cdot u \cdot a$, where $a, b \in \mathbb{F}^m$ are also as defined in Section 10.5.1. The evaluation phase is entirely analogous to the commitment phase, except that the random vector r used in the commitment phase is replaced with b.

In more detail, the prover first sends the verifier a vector v' claimed to equal $b^T \cdot u$, and analogous to the "random linear combination test", the verifier lets $w' := E(v')$. The verifier then picks a size-t subset Q' of columns of M and checks that for all $i \in Q'$, $w'_i = b^T \cdot M_i$, where M_i denotes the i'th column of M. If these checks all pass, then the verifier outputs $\langle w', a \rangle$ as its accepted value for $q(z)$.

This costs $t \cdot m$ queries to M. If the verifier's checks all pass, then the verifier outputs $\sum_{j=1}^{m} a_j \cdot v_i'$ as the evaluation $q(z)$ of the committed polynomial.

Intuition for Why This Scheme is Binding. If the prover is honest and every row of M is a codeword, then so will be any linear combination of the rows, by linearity of the code. Meanwhile, if M is "far" from having every row be a codeword (we make the relevant notion of "far" precise in the formal binding analysis), then it should be unlikely that the random linear combination $r^T M$ of the rows of M is close to any codeword z. In this event, since the verifier checks a large number of entries of z for consistency with the actual requested linear combination of the rows of M, the prover should fail one of the verifier's consistency checks with overwhelming probability.

So the "random linear combination" test roughly ensures that all rows of M are codewords, as claimed (this isn't quite true, but it is "close enough" to true for the remainder of the analysis to go through). If indeed all rows of M are codewords, let u_i be the message such that the i'th row of M equals $E(u_i)$, and let u denote the $m \times m$ matrix with i'th row equal to u_i. We claim that the prover is bound to answer any evaluation query $q(z)$ with $b^T \cdot ua$, meaning the prover is *bound* to the polynomial q whose coefficients are specified by the matrix u.

This holds because, by linearity of the code, the vector $b^T \cdot M$ requested in the evaluation phase is also a codeword. This means if the prover sends any codeword other than $b^T \cdot M$ in the evaluation phase, it will differ form $b^T \cdot M$ in many entries (by the distance properties of the code), and hence the verifier's consistency checks in that phase will detect the discrepancy with overwhelming probability. And because the code is systematic, if the prover indeed sends $b^T \cdot M$ in the evaluation phase, then the verifier outputs $b^T \cdot u \cdot a$ as the evaluation.

Details of Binding Analysis. For concreteness, we express the detailed binding analysis in the case that E is the Reed-Solomon encoding, but the analysis applies essentially unchanged to a general linear code E.

For the Reed-Solomon encoding of rate ρ, the relative distance of the code is greater than $1 - \rho$. This means that for any $\delta < (1 - \rho)/2$, and for any vector $w \in \mathbb{F}^{\rho^{-1}m}$, there is at most one codeword within relative distance δ of w.

In this code, there is some designated set $L_0 \subseteq \mathbb{F}$ of size $\rho^{-1}m$, a message $u_i \in \mathbb{F}^m$ is interpreted as the evaluations of a degree-m polynomial p_i over the first m points in L_0, and the encoding of u_i is the vector of all evaluations of p_i at points in L_0.

First Attempt at a Detailed Binding Analysis. Lemma 10.3, which states that when taking a random linear combination of functions, if even a single one of the functions is far from all codewords in the Reed-Solomon code of a given degree, then (with probability at least $1 - 1/|\mathbb{F}|$) so is the random linear combination. Quantitatively, for any parameter $\delta > 0$, if any row of M has relative distance more than δ from every codeword, then Lemma 10.3 guarantees that, with probability at least $1 - 1/|\mathbb{F}|$, $r^T M$ has relative distance at least $\delta/2$ from every polynomial of degree at most m. In this event, since the verifier knows that z is a codeword, $r^T M$ and z differ in at least a $\delta/2$ fraction of their entries. Hence, the probability that $z_i = r^T \cdot M_i$ for all $i \in Q$ is at most $(1 - \delta/2)^t$. We can set t to ensure that this probability is below some desired soundness level, e.g., to ensure that $(1 - \delta/2)^t \leq 2^{-\lambda}$. In summary, we have established the following.

Claim 10.5. If the verifier's checks in the Commitment Phase all pass with probability more than $1/|\mathbb{F}| + (1 - \delta/2)^t$, then each row i of M has relative distance at most δ from some codeword.

Henceforth, let us assume that $\delta < (1 - \rho)/2$. This assumption combined with Claim 10.5 ensures that if the prover passes the verifier's checks with probability more than $(1 - \delta/2)^t$, then for each row M_i of M, there is a *unique* codeword p_i of degree at most m at relative distance at most δ from the ith row of M.

Unfortunately, the above is not enough on its own to guarantee that the scheme is binding. The reason for this is the following.

Claim 10.5 asserts that the verifier can be confident that each row i of M has relative Hamming distance at most δ from some codeword $p_i \in \mathbb{F}^{|L_0|}$. Let $E_i = \{j : p_{i,j} \neq M_{i,j}\}$ denote the subset of entries on which p_i and row i of M differ, and let $E = \cup_{i=1}^m E_i$. That is, E is the set of columns such that at least one row i deviates from its closest polynomial p_i in that column. Claim 10.5 doesn't rule out the possibility $|E| = \sum_{i=1}^{m} |E_i|$. In other words, it leaves open the possibility that any two different rows i, i' of M deviate from the corresponding codewords $p_i, p_{i'}$ in different locations.

Full Binding Analysis. We need a refinement of Claim 10.5 that does rule out this possibility (this refinement also improves the the $\delta/2$ appearing in Claim 10.5 to δ). We do not prove this refinement—the interested reader can find the proof in [7, Lemma 4.2].

Claim 10.6. (Ames *et al.* [7, Lemma 4.2]) Suppose that $\delta < \frac{1-\rho}{3}$ and that the verifier's checks in the Commitment Phase all pass with probability more than $\varepsilon_1 := |L_0|/|\mathbb{F}| + (1-\delta)^t$. Let $E = \cup_{i=1}^{m} E_i$ be defined as above. Then $|E| \le \delta \cdot |L_0|$.

To argue binding, let $h' := \sum_{i=1}^{m} a_i \cdot p_i$. We claim that, if the prover passes the verifier's checks in the Commitment Phase with probability more than $\varepsilon_1 = |L_0|/|\mathbb{F}| + (1-\delta)^t$ and sends a codeword h in the Evaluation Phase such that $h \ne h'$, then the prover will pass the verifier's checks in the Evaluation Phase with probability at most $\varepsilon_2 := (\delta + \rho)^t$. To see this, observe that h and h' are two distinct codewords in the Reed-Solomon code with message length m, and hence they can agree on at most m inputs. Denote this agreement set by A. The verifier rejects in the Evaluation Phase if there is any $j \in Q'$ such that $j \notin A \cup E$, where E is as in Claim 10.6. $|A \cup E| \le |A| + |E| \le m + \delta \cdot |L_0|$, and hence a randomly chosen column j of M is in $A \cup E$ with probability at most $m/|L_0| + \delta \le \rho + \delta$. It follows that the verifier will reject with probability at least $1 - (\rho + \delta)^t$.

In summary, we have shown that for $\delta < (1 - \rho)/2$, if the prover passes the verifier's checks in the Commitment Phase with probability at least $|L_0|/|\mathbb{F}| + (1-\delta)^t$, then the prover is *bound* to the polynomial q^* whose coefficient matrix u has i'th row equal to the first m symbols of p_i. That is, on any evaluation query z, the verifier either outputs $q^*(z)$, or else rejects in the Evaluation Phase with probability at least $1 - (\rho + \delta)^t$.

10.5.3   Discussion of Costs

Let λ denote a security parameter defined as follows. Suppose we wish to guarantee that if the prover convinces the verifier not to reject in either the Commitment Phase or Query Phase with probability at least $\varepsilon_1 + \varepsilon_2 = 2^{-\lambda}$, then the prover is forced to answer any evaluation query consistent with a fixed polynomial q^* of degree at most $n - 1$. The costs of the polynomial commitment scheme are then as follows. Throughout, we suppress dependence on ρ^{-1} and δ, as we consider these parameters to be constants in $(0, 1)$.

Commitment and Evaluation Proof Sizes.   After some optimizations to the above commitment scheme (omitted from this survey for brevity), one can achieve a commitment that is just a single Merkle-hash, with evaluation proofs of size $O(\sqrt{n\lambda})$. The square root dependence on n arises because the vectors $v = r^T M$ and $v' = b^T \cdot u$ that the prover sends in response to the random linear combination test and evaluation query equals the number of columns of the matrices u and M, and because the verifier queries all entries of t columns of M, each of which has length equal to the number of rows of M. The matrix was chosen to have $\sqrt{n}$ rows and columns to balance these costs.

Prover Time.   The prover's runtime in the argument resulting from this IOP is dominated by two operations. The first is to encode each row of the matrix M. If the Reed-Solomon code is used as in Ligero, this requires one FFT operation per row, on vectors of length $\Theta(\sqrt{n})$. Since each such FFT requires $O(\sqrt{n} \log n)$ field operations, the total runtime for the FFTs is $O(n \log n)$ field operations.

If an error-correcting code with linear-time encoding is used (e.g., the one designed in [137]), then the encoding operations require only $O(n)$ time in total.

The second bottleneck is the need for the prover to compute a Merkle-hash of its first message, which has length $O(n)$. This requires $O(n)$ cryptographic hash evaluations. In practice, it is typically the encoding operations that dominate the prover's runtime, not the Merkle-hashing.

Verifier Time. After some concrete optimizations, the verifier's run-time in the argument system is dominated by the need to apply the error-correcting code's encoding procedure to two vectors v and v' of length $O(\sqrt{n\lambda})$. If using the Reed-Solomon code, this is $O(\sqrt{n\lambda}\log n)$ field operations; if using a linear-time encodable code, this is $O(\sqrt{n\lambda})$ field operations.

Comparison to FRI. The communication complexity and verifier run-time of the argument system are much larger than those of FRI, at least asymptotically. Whereas the FRI proof length and verifier time are polylogarithmic in n, these costs for the Ligero- and Brakedown-polynomial commitments are proportional to the square root of n.

The main benefit of Ligero- and Brakedown- polynomial commitments is a significantly faster prover—over an order of magnitude in practice for large enough values of n [137]. In the case of Brakedown, the prover time is asymptotically optimal $O(n)$ instead of $O(n \log n)$. Additionally, Brakedown works over any field of sufficient size, whereas FRI and Ligero's commitment require a field $\mathbb{F}$ that supports FFTs, meaning $\mathbb{F}$ must have a multiplicative or additive subgroup of appropriate size.[10]

Ligero++ [53] combines Ligero's commitment and FRI to obtain a polynomial commitment scheme with similar prover time to Ligero's commitment, and similar proof length to FRI's. However, this approach increases the verifier's runtime to close to linear in n.

10.6 Unifying IPs, MIPs, and IOPs via Polynomial IOPs

Sections 7–10 described succinct arguments for circuit- and R1CS-satisfiability obtained by combining an IP or MIP with a polynomial commitment scheme. We described the protocol of this section (Section 10.3) as a polynomial IOP. In this section, we recast the IPs and MIPs in the same framework. This permits shorter descriptions of the protocols and clarifies the pros and cons of the various approaches. To

---

[10]Recent work [37], [38] provides FFT-like algorithms and associated argument systems running in $O(n \log n)$ time in arbitrary fields, but a more expensive field-dependent pre-processing phase is required and at the time of writing the concrete costs of these algorithms are unclear.

avoid redundancy, our descriptions here are somewhat sketchy, as this section merely recasts protocols described in full detail earlier in this monograph.

Polynomial IOP from the GKR Protocol.   Here, we recast the IP-based succinct argument from Section 7 as a polynomial IOP. In this argument, the prover claims to know a witness $w \in \mathbb{F}^n$ such that $\mathcal{C}(w) = 1$, where $\mathcal{C}$ is a circuit known to both the prover and verifier. The one and only "special" message in this polynomial IOP is the first one. Specifically, the prover begins the protocol by sending the $(\log n)$-variate polynomial $\tilde{w}$, i.e., the multilinear extension of the witness w. The prover and verifier then apply the GKR protocol (Section 4.6) to the claim that $\mathcal{C}(w) = 1$. Note that the verifier in the GKR protocol does not need to know *anything* about w to execute its part of the protocol, until the very end of the protocol when it needs to know $\tilde{w}(r)$ for a randomly chosen $r \in \mathbb{F}^{\log n}$. This is why the verifier in this polynomial IOP does not need to learn the special message in full, but rather just a single evaluation of the polynomial $\tilde{w}$ described therein.

Polynomial IOP from Clover.   Here, we recast the MIP-based succinct argument from Section 8.2 as a polynomial IOP (the MIP for R1CS from Section 8.4 can be similarly recast). The section defined the notion of a *correct transcript* W for the claim that $\mathcal{C}(w) = 1$: a transcript W assigns a value to each of the S gates of $\mathcal{C}$, and W is *correct* if it assigns the output gate value 1, and actually corresponds to the gate-by-gate evaluation of $\mathcal{C}$ on some input w.

As with the GKR-based polynomial IOP, the one and only "special" message in this polynomial IOP is the first one. The prover begins the protocol by sending the $(\log S)$-variate polynomial $\tilde{W}$, i.e., the multilinear extension of the correct transcript W.

Equation (8.2) in Section 8.2 defines a *derived polynomial* $h_{\tilde{W}}$ such that the following two properties hold: (1) $\tilde{W}$ extends a correct transcript if and only if[11] $\sum_{u \in \{0,1\}^{3 \log S}} h_{\tilde{W}}(u) = 0$. (2) For any $r_1, r_2, r_3 \in \mathbb{F}^{\log S}$, $h_{\tilde{W}}(r_1, r_2, r_3)$ can be efficiently computed given $\tilde{W}(r_1)$, $\tilde{W}(r_2)$, $\tilde{W}(r_3)$.

Hence, the polynomial IOP simply applies the sum-check protocol to the polynomial $h_{\tilde{W}}$. Note that the verifier in the sum-check protocol does not need to know *anything* about $h_{\tilde{W}}$ to execute its part of the protocol, until the very end of the protocol when it needs to know $h_{\tilde{W}}(r_1, r_2, r_3)$ for a randomly chosen $(r_1, r_2, r_3) \in \mathbb{F}^{3 \log S}$. By the second property above, this evaluation can be efficiently obtained given $\tilde{W}(r_1)$, $\tilde{W}(r_2)$, $\tilde{W}(r_3)$.

Using the interactive proof of Section 4.5.2, the verifier can avoid making three evaluation-queries to $\tilde{W}$, instead making only a single evaluation query. Specifically, the verifier asks the prover to tell it (claimed values for) $\tilde{W}(r_1)$, $\tilde{W}(r_2)$, $\tilde{W}(r_3)$, and the technique of Section 4.5.2 allows the verifier to check this claim by evaluating $\tilde{W}(r_4)$ at a single randomly chosen point $r_4 \in \mathbb{F}^{\log S}$.

Remark 10.3. The above two protocol descriptions assume that the multilinear extensions of the "wiring predicates" of $\mathcal{C}$ used internally in the protocols can be evaluated quickly by the verifier. If not, holography can nonetheless be achieved via the commitment scheme for sparse multilinear polynomials given later, in Section 16.2.

Comparison of IP-, MIP-, and Constant-Round-Polynomial-IOP-Derived Arguments. The above recasting makes clear that in the arguments derived from IPs and MIPs above (which are both based on multilinear polynomials), the prover commits to only a *single* multilinear polynomial. In contrast, in the polynomial IOP of this section (Section 10.3), which exclusively uses univariate polynomials, the prover needs to commit to many polynomials, each at least as big as the polynomial committed from the IP- and MIP-derived arguments. Specifically, the prover from this section commits to 11 univariate polynomials, at least if naively implemented (and not counting the cost of holography). This is a major reason that arguments derived from constant-round

---

[11] More precisely, the definition of $h_{\tilde{W}}$ is randomized, with some small probability that $\tilde{W}$ does not extend a correct transcript, yet $h_{\tilde{W}}$'s evaluations over the Boolean hypercube do not sum to 0.

polynomial IOPs tend to be much more expensive for the prover in terms of both time and space requirements.[12, 13]

On the other hand, the fact that the univariate-polynomial-based IOP of this section is only a constant number of rounds is a significant benefit. This means that, if combined with a polynomial commitment scheme with constant-sized commitments and evaluation proofs (i.e., KZG commitments covered later in Section 15.2), it yields a SNARK with constant proof size.[14] In contrast, the use of multilinear polynomials and the sum-check protocol in the IP- and MIP-derived SNARKs results in at least logarithmically many rounds, and hence at least logarithmic proof size and verifier time.

In summary, the IP- and MIP-derived SNARKs tend to have much lower prover costs, but have higher verification costs than alternatives based on constant-round polynomial IOPs. The IP-based argument takes this to an extreme, because it applies the polynomial commitment scheme only to the circuit witness w; if w is smaller than the full circuit $\mathcal{C}$, this keeps prover costs low. But the resulting proofs can be quite large. Indeed, ignoring the cost of evaluation-proofs from the chosen polynomial scheme, the MIP-derived argument for circuit-satisfiability above has proofs that are shorter than the IP-based one by a factor roughly equal to the circuit depth. On the other hand, it applies the polynomial commitment scheme to the entire circuit transcript extension $\tilde{W}$ rather than just the witness extension $\tilde{w}$, which can lead to larger prover costs than the IP-derived arguments.

---

[12]The constant-round polynomial IOP described in this section underlies systems including Marlin [98] and Fractal [100]. Another popular constant-round polynomial IOP with a similar cost profile to Marlin is PlonK [123].

[13]There may be additional reasons constant-round polynomial IOPs are more expensive for the prover. For example, existing SNARKs derived from constant-round polynomial IOPs require the prover to perform FFTs, even when using a polynomial commitment scheme that does not require FFTs. This is not the case for the IP- and MIP-derived arguments above, which entirely avoid FFTs if they use a multilinear polynomial commitment scheme that does not require them.

[14]By constant proof size, we mean a constant number of elements of a cryptographic group $\mathbb{G}$.

11

Zero-Knowledge Proofs and Arguments

11.1 What is Zero-Knowledge?

The definition of a zero-knowledge proof or argument captures the notion that the verifier should learn nothing from the prover other than the validity of the statement being proven.[1] That is, any information the verifier learns by interacting with the honest prover could be learned by the verifier on its own without access to a prover. This is formalized via a simulation requirement, which demands that there be an efficient algorithm called the *simulator* that, given only as input the statement to be proved, produces a distribution over transcripts that is indistinguishable from the distribution over transcripts produced when the verifier interacts with an honest prover (recall from Section 3.1 that a transcript of an interactive protocol is a list of all messages exchanged by the prover and verifier during the execution of the protocol).

Definition 11.1 (Informal definition of zero-knowledge). A proof or argument system with prescribed prover $\mathcal{P}$ and prescribed verifier $\mathcal{V}$ for a language $\mathcal{L}$ is said to be zero-knowledge if for any probabilistic polynomial time verifier strategy $\hat{V}$, there exists a probabilistic polynomial time algorithm S (which can depend on $\hat{V}$), called the simulator, such

---

[1] Recall that a *proof* satisfies statistical soundness, while an argument satisfies computational soundness. See Definitions 3.1 and 3.2.

that for all $x \in \mathcal{L}$, the distribution of the output $S(x)$ of the simulator is "indistinguishable" from $\text{View}_{\hat{V}}(\mathcal{P}(x), \hat{V}(x))$. Here, $\text{View}_{\hat{V}}(\mathcal{P}(x), \hat{V}(x))$ denotes the distribution over transcripts generated by the interaction of prover strategy $\mathcal{P}$ and verifier strategy $\hat{V}$ within the proof or argument system.

Informally, the existence of the simulator means that, besides learning that $x \in \mathcal{L}$, the verifier $\mathcal{V}$ does not learn anything from the prover beyond what $\mathcal{V}$ could have efficiently computed herself. This is because, conditioned on x being in $\mathcal{L}$, $\mathcal{V}$ cannot tell the difference between generating a transcript by interacting with the honest prover versus generating the transcript by ignoring the prover and instead running the simulator. Accordingly, any information the verifier could have learned from the prover could also have been learned from the simulator (which is an efficient procedure, and hence the verifier can afford to run the simulator herself).

In Definition 11.1, there are three natural meanings of the term "indistinguishable".

- One possibility is to require that $S(x)$ and $\text{View}_{\hat{V}}(\mathcal{P}(x), \hat{V}(x))$ are literally the same distribution. In this case, the proof or argument system is said to be *perfect-zero knowledge*.[2]

- Another possibility is to require that the distributions $S(x)$ and $\text{View}_{\hat{V}}(\mathcal{P}(x), \hat{V}(x))$ have negligible *statistical distance*. In this case, the proof or argument system is said to be *statistical zero-knowledge*.

  Here, the statistical distance (also called total variation distance) between two distributions D_1 and D_2 is defined to be

  $$\frac{1}{2}\sum_y |\Pr[D_1(x) = y] - \Pr[D_2(x) = y]|,$$

---

[2]In the context of perfect zero-knowledge *proofs*, it is standard to allow the simulator to abort with probability up to $1/2$, and require $S(x)$ to be distributed identically to $\text{View}_{\hat{V}}(\mathcal{P}(x), \hat{V})$ conditioned on $S(x)$ not aborting. This is because, if the simulator is not permitted to abort, no perfect-zero knowledge proofs are known for any non-trivial problems (meaning problems not known to be in **BPP**, the class of problems solvable in randomized polynomial time). This subtlety will not be relevant to this survey.

and it equals the maximum over all algorithms $\mathcal{A}$ (including inefficient algorithms) of

$$| \Pr_{y \leftarrow D_1} [\mathcal{A}(y) = 1] - \Pr_{y \leftarrow D_2} [\mathcal{A}(y) = 1]|,$$

where $y \leftarrow D_i$ means that y is a random draw from the distribution D_i. Hence, if two distributions have negligible statistical distance, then no algorithm (regardless of its runtime) can distinguish the two distributions with non-negligible probability given a polynomial number of samples from the distributions.

- The third possibility is to require that all *polynomial time* algorithms $\mathcal{A}$ cannot distinguish the distributions $S(x)$ and $\text{View}_{\hat{V}}(\mathcal{P}(x), \hat{V}(x))$ except with negligible probability, when given as input a polynomial number of samples from the distributions. In this case, the proof or argument system is said to be *computational zero-knowledge*.

Accordingly, when someone refers to a "zero-knowledge protocol", there are actually *at least* 6 types of protocols they may be referring to. This is because soundness comes in two flavors—statistical (proofs) and computational (arguments)—and zero-knowledge comes in at least 3 flavors (perfect, statistical, and computational). In fact, there are even more subtleties to be aware of when considering how to define the notion of zero-knowledge.

- **(Honest vs. dishonest verifier zero-knowledge).** Definition 11.1 requires an efficient simulator for *every possible* probabilistic polynomial time verifier strategy $\hat{V}$. This is referred to as malicious- or dishonest-verifier- zero knowledge (though papers often omit the clarifying phrase malicious or dishonest-verifier). It is also interesting to consider only requiring an efficient simulator for the prescribed verifier strategy V. This is referred to as *honest-verifier* zero-knowledge.

- **(Plain zero-knowledge vs. auxiliary-input zero-knowledge).** Definition 11.1 considers the verifier $\hat{V}$ to have only one input, namely the public input x. This is referred to as *plain* zero-knowledge, and was the original definition given in the conference paper of Goldwasser *et al.* [133] that introduced the notion of zero-knowledge (along with the notion of interactive proofs). However, when zero-knowledge proofs and arguments are used as subroutines within larger cryptographic protocols, one is typically concerned about dishonest verifiers that may compute their messages to the prover based on information acquired from the larger protocol prior to executing the zero-knowledge protocol. To capture such a setting, one must modify Definition 11.1 to refer to verifier strategies $\hat{V}$ that take two inputs: the public input x known to both the prover and verifier, and an *auxiliary input* z known only to the verifier and simulator, and insist that the output $S(x, z)$ of the simulator is "indistinguishable" from $\text{View}_{\hat{V}}(\mathcal{P}(x), \hat{V}(x, z))$. This modified definition is referred to as *auxiliary-input* zero-knowledge. Of course, the distinction between auxiliary-input and plain zero-knowledge is only relevant when considering dishonest verifiers.

An added benefit of considering auxiliary-input computational zero-knowledge is that this notion is closed under sequential composition. This means that if one runs several protocols satisfying auxiliary-input computational zero-knowledge, one after the other, the resulting protocol remains auxiliary-input computational zero-knowledge. This is actually not true for plain computational zero-knowledge, though known counterexamples are somewhat contrived. The interested reader is directed to [54] and the references therein for a relatively recent study of the composition properties of zero-knowledge proofs and arguments.

The reader may be momentarily panicked at the fact that we have now roughly 24 notions of zero-knowledge protocols, one for every possible combination of (statistical vs. computational soundness), (perfect vs. statistical vs. computational zero-knowledge), (honest-verifier vs. dishonest-verifier zero-knowledge), and (plain vs. auxiliary input zero-knowledge). That's $2 \cdot 3 \cdot 2 \cdot 2$ combinations in total, though for honest-verifier notions of zero-knowledge the difference between auxiliary-input and plain zero-knowledge is irrelevant. Fortunately for us, there are only a handful of variants that we will have reason to study in this monograph, summarized below.

In Sections 11.2–11.4, we briefly discuss statistical zero-knowledge proofs. Our discussion is short because, as we explain, statistical zero-knowledge proofs are not very powerful (e.g., while they are capable of solving some problems believed to be outside of **BPP**, they are not believed to be able to solve **NP**-complete problems). Roughly all we do is describe what is known about their limitations, and then give a sense of what they are capable of computing by presenting two simple examples: a classic zero-knowledge proof system for graph non-isomorphism due to [131] (Section 11.3), and a particularly elegant protocol for a problem called the Collision Problem (this problem is somewhat contrived, but the protocol is an instructive example of the power of zero-knowledge).

In subsequent sections, we present a variety of perfect zero-knowledge arguments. All are non-interactive (possibly after applying the Fiat-Shamir transformation), rendering the distinction between malicious- and honest-verifier (and auxiliary-input vs. plain) zero-knowledge irrelevant.[3, 4, 5]

---

[3]More precisely, when the Fiat-Shamir transformation is applied to an honest-verifier zero-knowledge proof or argument and is instantiated in the plain model (by replacing the random oracle with a concrete hash function), the resulting non-interactive argument is zero-knowledge so long as the hash family used to instantiate the random oracle satisfies a property called programmability. The result applies even to dishonest verifiers, since non-interactive protocols leave no room for misbehavior on the part of the verifier. Roughly speaking, the simulator for the non-interactive argument obtains a transcript by running the simulator for the interactive argument, and then samples the hash function h used in the Fiat-Shamir transformation at random conditioned on it producing the verifier challenges in the transcript (this ability to perform such conditional sampling of h is what is referred to by programmability). This produces the same distribution over (hash function, transcript) pairs as first selecting h at random, and then having the honest prover use h when applying the Fiat-Shamir transformation to the interactive protocol. See [218] for additional details.

[4] When working in the random oracle model instead of the plain model, there are some subtleties regarding how to formalize zero-knowledge that we elide in this survey (the interested reader can find a discussion of these subtleties in [204], [247]).

[5]For non-interactive arguments that use a structured reference string (SRS), such as the one we describe later in Section 17.5.6, one may consider (as an analog of malicious-verifier zero-knowledge) settings in which the SRS is not generated

Remarks on Simulation.   A common source of confusion for those first encountering zero-knowledge is to wonder whether an efficient simulator for the honest verifier's view in a zero-knowledge proof or argument for a language $\mathcal{L}$ implies that the problem can be solved by an efficient algorithm (with no prover). That is, given input x, why can't one run the simulator S on x several times and try to discern from the transcripts output by S whether or not $x \in \mathcal{L}$? The answer is that this would require that for every pair of inputs (x, x') with $x \in \mathcal{L}$ and $x' \notin \mathcal{L}$, the distributions $S(x)$ and $S(x')$ are efficiently distinguishable. Nothing in the definition of zero-knowledge guarantees this. In fact, the definition of zero-knowledge says nothing about how the simulator S behaves on inputs x' that are not in $\mathcal{L}$.

Indeed, it is entirely possible that an efficient simulator S can produce accepting transcripts for a zero-knowledge protocol even when run on inputs $x' \notin \mathcal{L}$. Similarly, in the context of zero-knowledge proofs *of knowledge*, where the prover is claiming to *know* a witness w satisfying some property, the simulator will be able to produce accepting transcripts *without* knowing a witness.

One may initially wonder whether the preceding paragraph contradicts soundness of the protocol: if the simulator can find accepting transcripts for false claims, can't a cheating prover somehow use those transcripts to convince the verifier to accept false claims as valid? The answer is no. One reason for this is that a zero-knowledge protocol may be interactive, yet the simulator only needs to produce convincing *transcripts* of the interaction. This means that the simulator is able to do things like first choose all of the verifier's challenges, and then choose all of the prover's messages in a manner that depends on those challenges. In contrast, a cheating prover must send its message in each round prior to learning the verifier's challenge in that round. So even if the simulator can find accepting transcripts for inputs $x \notin \mathcal{L}$, it will be

---

properly. For example, the notion of *subversion zero knowledge* demands that zero-knowledge be maintained even when the SRS is chosen maliciously. SNARKs that we describe in this survey that use an SRS can be tweaked to satisfy subversion zero-knowledge [1], [28], [116]. On the other hand, it is not possible for a SNARK for circuit satisfiability to be sound in the presence of a maliciously chosen SRS if the SNARK is zero-knowledge [28].

of no help to a dishonest prover trying to convince $\mathcal{V}$ that $x \in \mathcal{L}$. This will be the situation for the simulators we construct in Section 11.4 for the Collision Problem, and the zero-knowledge proofs of knowledge that we develop in Section 12.2 (e.g., in Schnorr's protocol for establishing knowledge of a discrete logarithm).[6]

Some Final Intuition. Another way of thinking about a zero-knowledge protocol is as follows. If the prover $\mathcal{P}$ convinces the verifier $\mathcal{V}$ to accept, then $\mathcal{V}$ can infer (unless $\mathcal{P}$ got very lucky in terms of the random challenges the verifier happened to send to the prover during the interaction) that $\mathcal{P}$ must have had an effective *strategy* for answering verifier challenges. That is, $\mathcal{P}$ must have been prepared to successfully answer many different challenges that $\mathcal{V}$ *might have* asked (but did not actually ask) during the protocol's execution. If the protocol has low soundness error, this implies that $\mathcal{P}$'s claim is accurate, i.e., that $x \in \mathcal{L}$.

Meanwhile, zero-knowledge guarantees that $\mathcal{P}$'s answers to the *actual* challenges asked by $\mathcal{V}$ during the protocol reveal no other information whatsoever. Put another way, $\mathcal{P}$'s answers to the challenges sent during the zero-knowledge protocol are only useful for convincing $\mathcal{V}$ that $\mathcal{P}$ was prepared to answer other challenges that were not actually asked. $\mathcal{P}$'s preparation reveals to $\mathcal{V}$ that $\mathcal{P}$'s claim is accurate, but reveals nothing else.

This intuition will become clearer in Section 12.2, when we cover so-called special-sound protocols. These are three-message protocols in which the verifier $\mathcal{V}$ sends a single random challenge to the prover (this challenge is the protocol's second message). Following the prover's first message, if $\mathcal{V}$ were somehow able to obtain the prover's answers to *two* different challenges, then $\mathcal{V}$ would indeed learn information from the two responses. This does not violate zero-knowledge because the verifier

---

[6]A second possible reason that the existence of a simulator may not help a cheating prover is that, if the protocol is private coin, then the simulator can choose the verifier's private coins and use its knowledge of the private coins to produce accepting transcripts, while a cheating prover does not have access to the verifier's private coins. We only cover one such example of a private-coin zero-knowledge protocol: the graph non-isomorphism protocol given in Section 11.3.

in the protocol only interacts with $\mathcal{P}$ once, and can only send a single challenge during that interaction.

11.2   The Limits of Statistical Zero Knowledge Proofs

It is known that any language solvable by a statistical zero-knowledge proof with a polynomial time verifier is in the complexity class $\mathbf{AM} \cap \mathbf{coAM}$ [3], [112].[7] This means that such proof systems are certainly no more powerful than *constant-round* (non-zero-knowledge) interactive proofs, and such proof systems are unlikely to exist for any $\mathbf{NP}$-complete problems.[8] In contrast, the SNARKs we give in this survey with polynomial time verifiers are capable of solving problems in $\mathbf{NEXP}$, a vastly bigger class than $\mathbf{NP}$ (and with linear-time verifiers and logarithmic proof length, the SNARKs in this survey can solve $\mathbf{NP}$-complete problems). The upshot is that statistical zero-knowledge proof systems are simply not powerful enough to yield efficient general-purpose protocols (i.e., to verifiably outsource arbitrary witness-checking procedures in zero-knowledge). Accordingly, we will discuss statistical zero-knowledge proofs only briefly in this survey. The reason we discuss them at all is because they do convey some intuition about the power of zero-knowledge that is useful even once we turn to the more powerful setting of (perfect honest-verifier) zero-knowledge *arguments*.

11.3   Honest-Verifier SZK Protocol for Graph Non-Isomorphism

Two graphs G_1, G_2 on n vertices are said to be isomorphic if they are the same graph up to labelling of vertices. Formally, for a permutation $\pi \colon \{1, \ldots, n\} \to \{1, \ldots, n\}$, let $\pi(G_i)$ denote the graph obtained by

---

[7] $\mathbf{AM}$ (respectively, $\mathbf{coAM}$) is the class of languages, membership (respectively, *non*-membership) in which can be established via a 2-message interactive proofs with a polynomial time verifier. Intuitively, $\mathbf{AM}$ captures "minimally interactive" proofs. There is evidence that such proof systems are no more powerful than non-interactive proofs [169], [193].

[8] If $\mathbf{AM} \cap \mathbf{coAM}$ contains $\mathbf{NP}$-complete problems, then $\mathbf{AM} = \mathbf{coAM}$, which many people believe to be false. That is, the existence of efficient one-round proofs of membership in a language does not seem like it should necessarily imply the existence of efficient one-round proofs of *non*-membership in the same language.

replacing each edge (u, v) with $(\pi(u), \pi(v))$. Then G_1 is isomorphic to G_2 if there exists a permutation π such that $\pi(G_1) = G_2$. That is, π is an isomorphism between G_1 and G_2 so long as $(i, j) \in G_1$ if and only if $(\pi(i), \pi(j))$ is an edge of G_2.

There is no known polynomial time algorithm for the problem of determining whether two graphs are isomorphic (though a celebrated recent result of Babai [16] has given a *quasipolynomial* time algorithm for the problem). In Protocol 2, we give a perfect honest-verifier zero-knowledge protocol for demonstrating that two graphs are *not* isomorphic, due to seminal work of Goldreich *et al.* [131]. Note that it is not even obvious how to obtain a protocol for this problem that is not zero-knowledge. While a (non-zero-knowledge) proof that two graphs *are* isomorphic can simply specify the isomorphism π,[9] it is not clear that there is a similar witness for the *non-existence* of any isomorphism.

Protocol 2 Honest-verifier perfect zero-knowledge protocol for graph non-isomorphism

---

Verifier picks $b \in \{1, 2\}$ at random, and chooses a random permutation $\pi \colon \{1, \ldots, n\} \to \{1, \ldots, n\}$.
Verifier sends $\pi(G_b)$ to prover.
Prover responds with b'.
Verifier accepts if $b' = b$ and rejects otherwise.

We now explain that the protocol in Protocol 2 is perfectly complete, has soundness error at most $1/2$, and is honest-verifier perfect zero-knowledge.

Perfect Completeness. If G_1 and G_2 are not isomorphic, then $\pi(G_i)$ is isomorphic to G_i but not to G_{3-i}. Hence, the prover can identify b from $\pi(G_b)$ by determining which of G_1, G_2 it is that $\pi(G)$ is isomomorphic to.

Soundness. If G_1 and G_2 are isomorphic, then $\pi(G_1)$ and $\pi(G_2)$ are identically distributed when π is a permutation chosen uniformly at random over the set of all $n!$ permutations over $\{1, \ldots, n\}$. Hence, statistically speaking, the graph $\pi(G_b)$ provides no information as to the

---

[9]A perfect zero-knowledge proof for graph isomorphism is also known, an exposition of which can be found in [130, Section 4.3.2].

value of b, which means regardless of the prover's strategy for selecting b', b' will equal b with probability exactly $1/2$. The soundness error can be reduced to 2^{-k} by repeating the protocol k times sequentially.

Perfect honest-verifier zero-knowledge. Intuitively, when the graphs are not isomorphic, the honest verifier cannot possibly learn anything from the prover because the prover just sends the verifier a bit b' equal to the bit b that the verifier selected on its own. Formally, consider the simulator that on input (G_1, G_2), simply chooses b at random from $\{1, 2\}$ and chooses a random permutation π, and outputs the transcript $(\pi(G_b), b)$. This transcript is distributed identically to the honest verifier's view when interacting with the prescribed prover.

Discussion of zero-knowledge. We remark that the protocol is not zero-knowledge against malicious verifiers (assuming there is no polynomial time algorithm for graph isomorphism[10]). Imagine a dishonest verifier that somehow knows a graph H that is isomorphic to one of G_1, G_2, but the verifier does not know which. If the verifier replaces its prescribed message $\pi(G_b)$ in the protocol with the graph H, then the honest prover will reply with the value b' such that H is isomorphic to $G_{b'}$. Hence, this dishonest verifier learns which of the two input graphs H is isomorphic to, and if there is no efficient algorithm for graph isomorphism, then this is information that the verifier could not have computed efficiently on its own.

It is possible to transform this protocol into a proof that is zero-knowledge even against dishonest verifiers. Our sketch of this result follows [130, Section 4.7.4.3]. The rough idea is that if the verifier only sends query graphs H to the prover such that the verifier *already knows* which of G_1, G_2 it is that H is isomorphic to, then the verifier cannot possibly learn anything from the prover's response (as the prover's response is simply a bit b' such that H is isomorphic to $G_{b'}$). Hence, we can insist that the verifier first *prove to the prover* that the verifier knows a bit b such that H is isomorphic to G_b.

For this approach to preserve soundness, it is essential that the verifier's proof not leak any information to the prover about b (i.e.,

---

[10]Though it may not be terribly surprising if this assumption turns out to be false, in light of the recent result of Babai [16].

the verifier's proof to the prover should itself be zero-knowledge, or at least satisfy a weaker property called witness-independence (see [130, Section 4.6])). This is because, if G_1 and G_2 are isomorphic (i.e., the prover is lying when it claims that G_1 and G_2 are not isomorphic), a cheating prover could use information leaked from the verifier's proof about bit b in order to guess the value of b with probability more than $1/2$.

Of course, we are omitting many details of how the verifier might prove to the prover in zero-knowledge that it knows a b such that H is isomorphic to G_b. But hopefully this gives some sense of how one might transform honest-verifier zero-knowledge proofs into dishonest-verifier proofs. Clearly, the resulting dishonest-verifier zero-knowledge protocol is more expensive than the honest-verifier zero-knowledge one, because achieving zero-knowledge against dishonest verifiers requires the execution of a second zero-knowledge proof (with the role of prover and verifier reversed).

11.4 Honest-Verifier SZK Protocol for the Collision Problem

In the Collision Problem, the input is a list $(x_1, \ldots, x_N)$ of N numbers from a range of size $R = N$ (while the list length and the range size are equal, it is helpful to distinguish the two quantities, with N referring to the former and R referring to the latter). The goal of the problem is to determine whether every range element appears in the list. Since $R = N$, this holds if and only if every range element appears *exactly* once in the list. However, there is a twist to make the problem easier: it is assumed that *either* every range element appears exactly once in the list (call such inputs YES instances), *or* exactly $R/2$ range elements appear twice in the list (this means, of course, that the other $R/2$ range elements do not appear in the list at all). Call such inputs NO instances. Algorithms for the Collision Problem are allowed to behave arbitrarily on inputs that fail to satisfy the above assumption.

The name Collision Problem refers to the fact that if the input list is interpreted as the evaluation table of a function h mapping domain $\{1, \ldots, N\}$ to range $\{1, \ldots, R\}$, then YES instances have no collisions (i.e., $h(i) \neq h(j)$ unless $i = j$), while NO instances have many collisions (there are $N/2$ pairs (i, j) such that $h(i) = h(j)$ yet $i \neq j$). This problem was originally introduced as a loose and idealized model of the task of finding collisions in a cryptographic hash function h.[11] With this interpretation as motivation, for each range element $k \in \{1, \ldots, R\}$, we refer to any i with $x_i = k$ as a *pre-image* of k.

In the Collision Problem, since N is thought of as modeling the domain size and range size of a cryptographic hash function, we consider N to be "exponentially large".[12] Accordingly, for this problem, an algorithm should be considered "efficient" (i.e., "polynomial time") only if it runs in time $\text{polylog}(N)$.

Fastest Algorithm with no Prover. It is known that the fastest possible algorithm for the Collision problem runs in time $\Theta(\sqrt{N})$ (see Footnote 7 in Section 7.3.2.2), i.e., there is no "efficient" algorithm for the Collision Problem. We briefly sketch how to show this. The best algorithm simply inspects $c \cdot \sqrt{N}$ randomly chosen list elements for a sufficiently large constant $c > 0$, and outputs 1 if they are all distinct, and outputs 0 otherwise. Clearly, when run on a YES instance, the algorithm outputs 1 with probability 1, since for YES instances every list element is distinct. Whereas when run on a NO instance, the birthday paradox implies that for a large enough constant $c > 0$, there will be a "collision" in the sampled list elements with probability at least $1/2$.[13] This runtime is optimal up to a constant factor, because it is known that any algorithm that "inspects" $\ll \sqrt{N}$ list elements cannot effectively distinguish YES instances from NO instances (intuitively, this

---

[11] A key difference between finding collisions in a real-world cryptographic hash function h and the Collision Problem is that in the former task, h will have a succinct implicit description (e.g., via a computer program or circuit that on input i quickly outputs $h(i)$), while in the Collision Problem h does not necessarily have a description that is shorter than the list of all of its evaluations.

[12] Strictly speaking, this is a misnomer, because the size of the input to the Collision Problem is N. But the Collision Problem is modeling a setting where the size of the input (namely, the description of a cryptographic hash function h with domain size and range size N) is really $\text{polylog}(N)$.

[13] Let $c = 2$. If there is a collision within the first $\sqrt{N}$ samples, we are done. Otherwise, the probability that none of the first $\sqrt{N}$ sampled range elements appear within the second $\sqrt{N}$ sampled range elements is at most $(1 - \sqrt{N}/N)^{\sqrt{N}} = (1 - 1/\sqrt{N})^{\sqrt{N}} \approx 1/e < 1/2$.

is because any algorithm that inspects fewer than $\Theta(\sqrt{N})$ list elements of a random NO instance will with probability $1 - o(1)$ fail to find a collision, and in this case the algorithm has no way to tell the input apart from a random YES instance).[14]

HVSZK Protocol with Efficient Verifier. Here is an honest-verifier statistical zero-knowledge proof for the Collision Problem. The protocol consists of just one round (one message from verifier to prover and one reply from prover to verifier), and the verifier runs in time just $O(\log N)$ (both messages consist of $\log N$ bits, and to check the proof the verifier inspects only *one* element of the input list).

The first message of the protocol, from verifier to prover, consists of a random range element $k \in \{1, \ldots, R\}$. The prover responds with a pre-image i of k. The verifier simply checks that indeed $x_i = k$, outputting ACCEPT if so and REJECT otherwise.

We now explain that the protocol is complete, sound, and honest-verifier perfect zero-knowledge. Recall that this means there is a simulator running in time $\text{polylog}(N)$ that, on any YES instance, produces a distribution over transcripts identical to that of that of the honest verifier interacting with the honest prover.

Completeness is clear because for YES instances, each range element appears once in the input list, and hence regardless of which range element $k \in \{1, \ldots, R\}$ is selected by the verifier, the prover can provide a pre-image of k. Soundness holds because for NO instances, $R/2$ range elements do not appear at all in the input list, and hence with probability $1/2$ over the random choice of $k \in \{1, \ldots, R\}$, it will be impossible for the prover to provide a pre-image of k.

To establish honest-verifier perfect zero-knowledge, for any YES instance $(x_1, \ldots, x_N)$, we have to give an efficient simulator that generates transcripts distributed identically to those generated by the honest verifier interacting with the honest prover. The simulator picks a random domain item $i \in \{1, \ldots, N\}$, and outputs the transcript (x_i, i). Clearly,

---

[14]The expected number of collisions observed on a random NO instance after inspecting at most T items of the input list is $O(T^2/N)$, so if $T \leq o(\sqrt{N})$ this expectation is $o(1)$. Markov's inequality then implies that with probability $1 - o(1)$, no collision is observed by the algorithm.

the simulator runs in logarithmic time (it simply chooses i, which consists of $\log N$ bits, and inspects one element of the input list, namely x_i). Since in any YES instance, each range element appears exactly once in the input list, picking a random domain item $i \in \{1, \ldots, N\}$ and outputting the transcript (x_i, i) yields the same distribution over transcripts as picking a random range element k and outputting (x_i, i) where i is the unique pre-image of k. Hence, on YES instances, the simulator's output is distributed identically to the view of the honest verifier interacting with the honest prover. Put more intuitively, the honest verifier in this protocol, when run on a YES instance, simply learns a random pair (x_i, i) where i is chosen at random from $\{1, \ldots, N\}$, and this is clearly information the verifier could have efficiently computed on its own, by choosing i at random and inspecting x_i.

Discussion.   This protocol is included in this survey because it cleanly elucidates some of the counter-intuitive features of zero-knowledge protocols.

- The simulator, even if run on a NO instance, will always output an accepting transcript (x_i, i). This fact may initially feel like it contradicts soundness of the protocol. However, it does not. This is because, if run on a NO instance, the simulator picks the verifier challenge x_i specifically to be an "answerable" challenge, i.e., a range element that appears in the input list. The actual verifier would have chosen a *random* range element as a challenge, which on a NO instance will, with probability $1/2$, have no pre-image and hence not be answerable.

- The existence of an efficient simulator is no barrier to intractability of the problem. While the simulator runs in time $O(\log N)$, the fastest algorithm for the problem requires time $\Theta(\sqrt{N})$.

- While the protocol is honest-verifier zero-knowledge, it is not dishonest-verifier zero-knowledge. Indeed, a dishonest verifier can "use" the honest prover to solve the problem of finding a pre-image of a specific range element of the verifier's choosing (a problem that would require $\Theta(N)$ queries without access to a prover). That is, on a YES instance, if the dishonest verifier sent to the prover a range element k of its choosing (rather than a uniform random range element as the honest verifier does), then the prover will reply with a pre-image of k. The verifier would not have been able to compute such a pre-image on its own in $o(N)$ time, except with probability $o(1)$.

12

Σ-Protocols and Commitments from Hardness
of Discrete Logarithm

12.1   Cryptographic Background

12.1.1   A Brief Introduction to Groups

Informally, a group $\mathbb{G}$ is any set equipped with an operation that behaves like multiplication. To be more precise, a group is a collection of elements equipped with a binary operation (which we denote by $\cdot$ and refer to in this monograph as multiplication) that satisfies the following four properties.

- Closure: the product of two elements in $\mathbb{G}$ are also in $\mathbb{G}$, i.e., for all $a, b \in \mathbb{G}$, $a \cdot b$ is also in $\mathbb{G}$.

- Associativity: for all $a, b, c \in \mathbb{G}$, $a \cdot (b \cdot c) = (a \cdot b) \cdot c$.

- Identity: there an element denoted $1_{\mathbb{G}} \in \mathbb{G}$ such that $1_{\mathbb{G}} \cdot g = g \cdot 1_{\mathbb{G}} = g$ for all $g \in \mathbb{G}$.

- Invertibility: For each $g \in \mathbb{G}$, there is an element h in $\mathbb{G}$ such that $g \cdot h = 1_{\mathbb{G}}$. This element h is denoted g^{-1}.

One important example of a group is the set of nonzero elements of any field, which forms a group under the field multiplication operation.

This is referred to as the multiplicative group of the field. Another is the the set of invertible matrices, which forms a group under the matrix multiplication operation. Note that matrix multiplication is not commutative. In cases where the group operation *is* commutative, the group is called abelian.

Sometimes it is convenient to think of the group operation as addition rather than multiplication, in which case the operation is denoted with a + symbol instead of ·. Whether a group is considered additive or multiplicative is a matter of context, convenience, and convention. As an example, any field is a group under the field's addition operation, and the set of all $n \times n$ matrices over the field form a group under the matrix addition operation. For these groups it is of course natural to denote the group operation with + rather than ·. Henceforth in this monograph, *with the lone exception of two subsections in the Section 14 and 15 (Sections 14.4 and 15.4)*, we will exclusively refer to multiplicative groups, using · to denote the group operation.

A group $\mathbb{G}$ is said to be *cyclic* if there is some group element g such that all group elements can be generated by repeatedly multiplying g with itself, i.e., if every element of $\mathbb{G}$ can be written as g^i for some positive integer i. Here, in analogy to how exponentiation refers to repeated multiplication in standard arithmetic, g^i denotes $\underbrace{g \cdot g \cdots \cdots g}_{i \text{ copies of } g}$.[1]

Such an element of g is called a generator for $\mathbb{G}$. Any cyclic group is abelian.

The cardinality $|\mathbb{G}|$ is called the *order* of $\mathbb{G}$. A basic fact from group theory is that for any element $g \in \mathbb{G}$, $g^{|\mathbb{G}|} = 1_{\mathbb{G}}$. This implies that when considering any group exponentiation, i.e., g^ℓ for some integer ℓ, reducing the exponent ℓ modulo the group size $|\mathbb{G}|$ does not change anything: for any integer ℓ, if $z \equiv \ell \mod |\mathbb{G}|$, then $g^\ell = g^z$.

A *subgroup* of a group $\mathbb{G}$ is a subset $\mathbb{H}$ of $\mathbb{G}$ that itself forms a group under the same binary operation as $\mathbb{G}$ itself. Another basic fact from group theory states that the order of any subgroup $\mathbb{H}$ of $\mathbb{G}$ divides the order of $\mathbb{G}$ itself. A consequence is that any prime-order group $\mathbb{G}$ is cyclic: in fact, each non-identity element $g \in \mathbb{G}$ is a group generator.

---

[1] Similarly, g^{-i} denotes the ith power of the inverse of g, i.e, $\left(g^{-1}\right)^i$.

This is because the set $\{g, g^2, g^3, \ldots, \}$ of powers of g is easily seen to be a subgroup of $\mathbb{G}$, referred to as the subgroup *generated by* g. Since $g \geq 1_{\mathbb{G}}$, its order is an integer strictly between 1 and $|\mathbb{G}|$, and since $|\mathbb{G}|$ is prime, the order must equal $|\mathbb{G}|$. Hence, the subgroup generated by g in fact equals the entire group $\mathbb{G}$.

12.1.2 The Discrete Logarithm Problem and Background on Elliptic Curves

12.1.2.1 *Discrete Log Problem*

For a specified group $\mathbb{G}$ the discrete logarithm problem takes as input two group elements g and h, and the goal is to output a positive integer i such that $g^i = h$ (if $\mathbb{G}$ is of prime order then such an i is guaranteed to exist).

The discrete logarithm problem is believed to be computationally intractable in certain groups $\mathbb{G}$. In modern cryptography, the groups used are typically cyclic subgroups of groups defined via elliptic curves over finite fields, or the multiplicative group of integers modulo a very large prime p. An important caveat is that quantum computers can solve the discrete logarithm problem in polynomial time via Shor's algorithm [233]. Hence, cryptosystems whose security is based on the assumed hardness of the discrete logarithm problem are not post-quantum secure.

12.1.2.2 *Elliptic Curve Groups*

Though it is a fascinating and important topic, we will not go into great detail on elliptic curve cryptography in this monograph, and restrict ourselves to the following comments. Any elliptic curve group is defined with respect to a (finite) field $\mathbb{F}$, called the *base field* of the curve. Group elements correspond to pairs of points $(x, y) \in \mathbb{F} \times \mathbb{F}$ that satisfy an equation of the form $y^2 = x^3 + ax + b$ for designated field elements a and b.[2] Given two elements P and Q of the group, the precise definition of the group product $P \cdot Q$ will not be important in this monograph, but for the interested reader, here is a rough sketch.

---

[2]The group also contains one extra element known as the *point at infinity*; this detail will not be relevant to this monograph.

Sketch of the Group Operation. Recalling that P and Q each consist of a *pair* of elements of the base field $\mathbb{F}$ satisfying the curve equation, we can visualize P and Q as two points in the two-dimensional plane. Draw a line through these two points. This line typically turns out to intersect the elliptic curve at a third point $R = (x, y)$. The group product $P \cdot Q$ is defined to equal $(x, -y)$. Here, if $R = (x, y)$ is on the curve $y^2 = x^3 + ax + b$, then so is $(x, -y)$, owing to the fact that $y^2 = (-y)^2$.

Algorithms for Computing Discrete Logarithms. The fastest known classical algorithm to solve the Discrete Logarithm problem over most elliptic curve groups used in practice runs in time $O(\sqrt{|\mathbb{G}|})$.[3] Under the assumption that these are in fact the fastest attacks possible, this means that to obtain "λ bits of security" (meaning security against attackers running in time 2^λ, see Footnote 7 in Section 7.3.2.2), one should use an elliptic curve group of order $2^{2\lambda}$. For example, a popular elliptic curve called Curve25519, which is defined over base field $\mathbb{F}$ of size $2^{255} - 19$, defines a cyclic group of order close to 2^{252}; hence, this group provides slightly less than 128 bits of security [52].

One reason Curve25519 is popular is efficiency of group operations: the computational bottleneck in multiplying elliptic curve group elements turns out to be performing multiplications in the base field $\mathbb{F}$. Because $p = 2^{255} - 19$ is a power of two minus a small constant, multiplication in $\mathbb{F}$ can be implemented more efficiently than if p did not have this form. As general (rough) guidance, the time cost of performing one group multiplication in an elliptic curve group defined over field $\mathbb{F}$ is typically about 10 times as expensive as performing one multiplication in $\mathbb{F}$.

Scalar Field vs. Base Field. Elliptic curve groups used in practice are chosen to have large prime order.[4] This is because there are known

---

[3]See, for example, the wikipedia article on Pollard's rho algorithm https://en.wikipedia.org/wiki/Pollard%27s_rho_algorithm_for_logarithms, introduced in [213].

[4]A subtlety arising in modern elliptic curves used in cryptography is that the group order is typically a small constant—typically 4 or 8—times a prime. For

algorithms, such as the Pohlig-Hellman algorithm [210], that can compute discrete logarithms in group $\mathbb{G}$ in time proportional to the largest prime-order subgroup of $\mathbb{G}$, The field of size equal to the (prime) order of the elliptic curve group $\mathbb{G}$ is typically referred to as the *scalar field* of $\mathbb{G}$.

Recall that prime-order groups $\mathbb{G}$ are cyclic: for any group element $g \neq 1_{\mathbb{G}}$, we can write $\mathbb{G} = \{g^x : x = 0, 1, \ldots, |\mathbb{G}| - 1\}$. Hence, we can think of elements x of the scalar field of $\mathbb{G}$ as *exponents*, when expressing $\mathbb{G}$ as powers of a generator g.

Note that the scalar field of the elliptic curve group is *not* the same as the base field $\mathbb{F}$ over which the curve is defined.[5, 6] This is particularly relevant to the concrete performance of "SNARK composition", a topic discussed at length later in this survey (Section 18.2).

Readers interested in more detailed (and illustrated) introductions to elliptic curve groups are directed to [73], [109].

12.2 Schnorr's Σ-Protocol for Knowledge of Discrete Logarithms

In this section, we describe several perfect honest-verifier zero-knowledge proof systems. These proof systems have a very simple structure, involving only three messages exchanged between prover and verifier. They are *special-purpose*, meaning that, as standalone objects, they do not solve **NP**-complete problems such as circuit satisfiability. Rather, they solve specific problems including (a) establishing that the prover has knowledge of a discrete logarithm of some group element (Section 12.2.2); (b) allowing the prover to cryptographically commit to group elements without revealing the committed group element to the verifier until

---

example, the order of Curve25519 is 8 times a prime. For this reason, implementations typically work over the prime-order subgroup of the full elliptic curve group, or they add a layer of abstraction that exposes a prime-order interface. The interested reader is directed to [147] and https://ristretto.group/why_ristretto.html for an overview of these details.

[5]However, the sizes of the two fields cannot be too far apart: a result known as Hasse's theorem [148] states that for all elliptic curve groups $\mathbb{G}$ over field $\mathbb{F}$, $|\mathbb{G}| - (|\mathbb{F}| + 1) \leq 2\sqrt{|\mathbb{F}|}$.

[6]The discrete logarithm problem is easy in elliptic curve groups for which the base field and scalar field are the same. So for all curves used in cryptography, the two fields are different.

later (Section 12.3); and (c) establishing product relationships between committed values (Section 12.3.2).

While the protocols covered in this section are special-purpose, we will see (e.g., Section 13.1) that they can be *combined* with general-purpose protocols such as IPs, IOPs, and MIPs to obtain general-purpose zk-SNARKs.

12.2.1 Σ-Protocols

The presentation in this section closely follows other authors [85]. A relation $\mathcal{R}$ specifies a collection of "valid" instance-witness pairs (h, w). For example, given a group $\mathbb{G}$ and a generator g, the discrete logarithm relation $\mathcal{R}_{\mathsf{DL}}(\mathbb{G}, g)$ is the collection of pairs $(h, w) \in \mathbb{G} \times \mathbb{Z}$ such that $h = g^w$.

A Σ-protocol for a relation $\mathcal{R}$ is a 3-message public coin protocol between prover and verifier in which both prover and verifier know a public input h, and the prover knows a witness w such that $(h, w) \in \mathcal{R}$.[7] Let us denote the three messages by (a, e, z), with the prover first sending a, the verifier responding with a challenge e (chosen via public random coin tosses), and the prover replying with z. A Σ-protocol is required to satisfy perfect completeness, i.e., if the prover follows the prescribed protocol then the verifier will accept with probability 1. It is also required to satisfy two additional properties.

Special Soundness: There exists a polynomial time algorithm $\mathcal{Q}$ such that, when given as input a pair of accepting transcripts (a, e, z) and (a, e', z') with $e \neq e'$, $\mathcal{Q}$ outputs a witness w such that $(h, w) \in \mathcal{R}$.

Intuitively, special soundness guarantees that if, after sending its first message in the Σ-protocol, the prover is prepared to answer more than one challenge from the verifier, then the prover much *know* a witness w such that $(h, w) \in \mathcal{R}$.

Honest Verifier Perfect Zero-Knowledge.   There must be a randomized polynomial time simulator that takes as input the public input h

---

[7]The term Σ-protocol was coined because pictorial diagrams of 3-message protocols are vaguely reminiscent of the Greek letter Σ.

from the Σ-protocol, and outputs a transcript (a, e, z) such that the distribution over transcripts output by the simulator is *identical* to the distribution over transcripts produced by the honest verifier in the Σ-protocol interacting with the honest prover.

Remark 12.1. Special soundness implies that, if the verifier in the Σ-protocol were to be given "rewinding access" to the prover, then the Σ-protocol would *not* be zero-knowledge. That is, special soundness says that if the verifier could run the protocol to completion to obtain the transcript (a, e, z), then "rewind" to just after the prover sent its first message a, and restart the protocol with a new challenge e', then, assuming both transcripts lead to acceptance, the verifier would learn a witness (see Section 12.2.3 for additional discussion of this witness-extraction procedure). This clearly violates zero-knowledge if witnesses are assumed to be intractable to compute. Hence, the honest-verifier zero-knowledge property of Σ-protocols only holds if the verifier is never allowed to run the prover more than once with the same first prover message a.

12.2.2 Schnorr's Σ-Protocol for the Discrete Logarithm Relation

Let $\mathbb{G}$ be a cyclic group of prime order generated by g. Recall that in any Σ-protocol for the discrete logarithm relation, $\mathcal{P}$ holds (h, w) such that $h = g^w$ in $\mathbb{G}$, while $\mathcal{V}$ knows h and g.[8]

To convey the intuition behind Schnorr's [223] protocol, we describe a number of progressively more sophisticated attempts at designing a proof of knowledge for the discrete logarithm relation.

Attempt 1. The most straightforward possible proof of knowledge for any relation is to simply have the prover $\mathcal{P}$ send the witness w for the public input h, so the verifier $\mathcal{V}$ can check that $(h, w) \in \mathcal{R}$. However, this reveals w to the verifier, violating zero-knowledge (assuming the verifier could not efficiently compute the witness on her own).

---

[8]In this monograph we only consider Σ-protocols for groups of prime order. Σ-protocols (and related proof systems) for problems over composite and hidden-order groups have also been studied, see for example [18], [63], [118].

Attempt 2. $\mathcal{P}$ could pick a random value $r \in \{0, \ldots, |\mathbb{G}| - 1\}$ and send $(w + r) \bmod |\mathbb{G}|$ to $\mathcal{V}$. This totally "hides" w in that $(w + r) \bmod |\mathbb{G}|$ is a uniform random element of the set $\{0, \ldots, |\mathbb{G}| - 1\}$, and hence this message does not violate zero-knowledge. But for the same reason, $(w + r) \bmod |\mathbb{G}|$ is useless to $\mathcal{V}$ as far as ensuring soundness goes. It is simply a random number, which $\mathcal{V}$ could have generated on her own.

Attempt 3. To address the issue in Attempt 2 that $(w + r) \bmod |\mathbb{G}|$ is useless on its own, $\mathcal{P}$ could first send r, followed by a value z claimed to equal $(w + r) \bmod |\mathbb{G}|$. $\mathcal{V}$ checks that $g^r \cdot h = g^z$.

This protocol is complete and sound, but it is not zero-knowledge. Completeness is easy to check, while special soundness holds because if $g^r \cdot h = g^z$, then $g^{z-r} = h$, i.e., $z - r$ is a witness. That is, a witness can be extracted from even a single accepting transcript. Of course, for the same reason, this protocol is not zero-knowledge.

Effectively, Attempt 3 broke w into two pieces, $z := w + r \bmod |\mathbb{G}|$ and r, such that each piece individually reveals no information to $\mathcal{V}$ (because each is simply a random element of $\{0, 1, \ldots |\mathbb{G}|\}$). But together, the pieces reveal the witness w to the verifier (since $z - r = w$). Hence, this attempt is no closer to satisfying zero-knowledge than Attempt 1.

Attempt 4. We could modify Attempt 3 above so that, rather than $\mathcal{P}$ sending r to $\mathcal{V}$, $\mathcal{P}$ instead sends a group element a claimed to equal g^r, followed by a number z exactly as in Attempt 3, i.e., z is claimed to equal $(w + r) \bmod |\mathbb{G}|$. $\mathcal{V}$ checks that $a \cdot h = g^z$.

This attempt turns out to be complete and zero-knowledge, but not special sound. Completeness is easy to verify: if the prover is honest, then $a \cdot h = g^r \cdot h = g^{r+w} = g^z$. It is zero-knowledge because a simulator can choose an element $z \in \{0, 1, \ldots, |\mathbb{G}| - 1\}$ at random, and then set a to be $g^z \cdot h^{-1}$, and output the transcript (a, z). This generates a transcript distributed identically to that generated by the honest prover.

Conceptually, while the honest prover in Attempt 4 chooses a random group element $a = g^r$ and then chooses z to be the unique number such that the verifier accepts (a, z), the simulator chooses z first at random and then chooses a to be the unique group element causing the verifier to accept (a, z). The two distributions are identical—in both cases, a and z are individually uniformly distributed (a from $\mathbb{G}$ and z from $\{0, 1, \ldots, |\mathbb{G}| - 1\}$), with the value of a determining the value of z and vice versa.

Sadly, Attempt 4 is not special sound for the same reason it is zero-knowledge. The simulator is able to generate accepting transcripts, and since the protocol is totally non-interactive (there is no challenge sent by verifier to prover), the simulator itself acts as a "cheating" prover capable of convincing the verifier to accept despite not knowing a witness.

Comparison of Attempts 3 and 4. The reason Attempt 4 is zero-knowledge while Attempt 3 is not is that whereas Attempt 3 has $\mathcal{P}$ send r "in the clear", Attempt 4 "hides" r in the exponent of g, and accordingly the subtraction of r from z by the verifier in Attempt 4 happens "in the exponent" of g rather than in the clear.

The fact that Attempt 4 is zero-knowledge may seem surprising at first. After all, on an information-theoretic level, r can be derived from g^r, and then the witness $z - r$ can be computed, and this may seem like a violation of zero-knowledge. But the derivation of r requires finding the discrete logarithm of g^r, which is just as hard as deriving a witness w (i.e., a discrete logarithm of h). In summary, the fact that Attempt 4 reveals r to the verifier in an information-theoretic sense does not contradict zero-knowledge, because the public input $h = g^w$ itself information-theoretically specifies w in the same way that $a = g^r$ information-theoretically specifies r. In fact, g^r combined with $(w + r)$ mod $|\mathbb{G}|$ does not actually reveal any new information to the verifier beyond what was already revealed by h itself.

Schnorr's Σ-Protocol. Protocol 3 describes Schnorr's Σ-protocol. Essentially, Schnorr's protocol modifies Attempt 4 so that, after $\mathcal{P}$ sends a but before $\mathcal{P}$ sends z, the verifier sends a random challenge e drawn from $\{0, 1, \ldots, |\mathbb{G}| - 1\}$. Compared to Attempt 4, the verifier's check is modified so that it will pass if $z = w \cdot e + r$ (Attempt 4 above is identical to Schnorr's protocol with the verifier's challenge e fixed to 1).

These modifications to Attempt 4 do not alter the completeness or zero-knowledge properties of the protocol. The intuition for why Schnorr's protocol is special sound is that if $\mathcal{P}$'s first message is $a = g^r$ and $\mathcal{P}$ can produce accepting transcripts (a, e, z) and (a, e', z') with $e \neq e'$, then $\mathcal{V}$'s acceptance criterion implies that $z = w \cdot e + r$ and $z' = w \cdot e' + r$.[9] These are two linearly independent equations in two unknowns, namely w and r. Hence, one can take these two transcripts and efficiently solve for both w and r.

Protocol 3 Schnorr's Σ-protocol for the Discrete Logarithm Relation

---
1: Let $\mathbb{G}$ be a (multiplicative) cyclic group of prime order with generator g.
2: Public input is $h = g^w$, where only prover knows w.
3: $\mathcal{P}$ picks a random number r in $\{0, \ldots, |\mathbb{G}| - 1\}$ and sends $a \leftarrow g^r$ to the verifier.
4: Verifier responds with a random element $e \in \{0, \ldots, |\mathbb{G}| - 1\}$.
5: Prover responds with $z \leftarrow (we + r) \mod |\mathbb{G}|$.
6: Verifier checks that $a \cdot h^e = g^z$.

We now turn to formally proving that Schnorr's protocol satisfies perfect completeness, special soundness, and honest-verifier zero-knowledge.

Perfect completeness is easy to establish: if $a \leftarrow g^r$ and $z \leftarrow (we + r) \mod |\mathbb{G}|$, then

$$a \cdot h^e = g^r \cdot h^e = g^r \cdot (g^w)^e = g^{r+we} = g^z,$$

so the verifier accepts transcript (a, e, z).

Special soundness: Suppose we are given two accepting transcripts (a, e, z) and (a, e', z') with $e \neq e'$. We must show that a witness w^* can be extracted in polynomial time from these two transcripts.

---

[9]Similar to Attempt 4, note that $\mathcal{V}$'s check on transcript (a, e, z) in Schnorr's protocol confirms "in the exponent" that $z = w \cdot e + r$. $\mathcal{V}$ is able to perform this check in the exponent despite only knowing z, g^r, and h (in particular, without knowing r and w, which are the discrete logarithms of g^r and h).

Let $(e - e')^{-1}$ denote the multiplicative inverse of $e - e'$ modulo $|\mathbb{G}|$, i.e., $(e - e')^{-1}$ denotes a number ℓ such that $\ell \cdot (e - e') \equiv 1 \mod |\mathbb{G}|$. Since $e \neq e'$, such a multiplicative inverse is guaranteed to exist because $|\mathbb{G}|$ is prime and every nonzero number has a multiplicative inverse modulo any prime, and in fact ℓ can be computed efficiently via the Extended Euclidean algorithm.

Let $w^* = ((z - z') \cdot (e - e')^{-1}) \mod |\mathbb{G}|$. To see that w^* is a witness, observe that since (a, e, z) and (a, e', z') are both accepting transcripts, it holds that $a \cdot h^e = g^z$ and $a \cdot h^{e'} = g^{z'}$. Since $\mathbb{G}$ is cyclic and g is a generator of $\mathbb{G}$, both a and h are powers of g, say, $a = g^j$ and $h = g^w$ for integers j, w. Then the preceding two equations imply that

$$g^{j+we} = g^z$$

$$g^{j+we'} = g^{z'}.$$

Together, these two equations imply that

$$g^{w(e-e')} = g^{z-z'}.$$

Hence, $w(e - e') \equiv z - z' \mod |\mathbb{G}|$, i.e., $w \equiv (z - z') \cdot (e - e')^{-1} \mod |\mathbb{G}| = w^*$. That is, $h^w = h^{w^*}$, meaning that w^* is a witness.

Honest-Verifier Perfect Zero Knowledge. We need to construct a polynomial time simulator that produces a distribution over transcripts (a, e, z) identical to the distribution produced by the honest verifier and prover. The simulator selects e uniformly at random from $\{0, \ldots, |\mathbb{G}|-1\}$ and samples z uniformly at random from $\{0, \ldots, |\mathbb{G}| - 1\}$. Finally, the simulator sets $a \leftarrow g^z \cdot (h^e)^{-1}$.

The distribution over transcripts produced by the simulator is identical to that produced by the honest verifier interacting with the prescribed prover. In both cases, the distribution produces a random $e \in \{0, \ldots, |\mathbb{G}|-1\}$, and then chooses a pair (a, z) such that a is chosen uniformly random from $\mathbb{G}$ and z from $\{0, \ldots, |\mathbb{G}| - 1\}$, subject to the constraint that $a \cdot h^e = g^z$ (the key observation from which this follows is that, for fixed e, for any $a \in \mathbb{G}$ there is exactly one $z \in \{0, \ldots, |\mathbb{G}| - 1\}$ satisfying this equality, and vice versa).

Remark 12.2. Schnorr's protocol is only *honest-verifier* zero knowledge (HVZK) because the simulated distribution over transcripts is identical to the verifier's view in the actual protocol only if the verifier's message e is a uniformly random element from $\{0, \ldots, |\mathbb{G}| - 1\}$. Two remarks are in order. First, if we render the protocol non-interactive using the Fiat-Shamir transformation (see Section 12.2.3), the distinction between honest-verifier and dishonest-verifier zero-knowledge is eliminated (see Footnote 4 for a brief discussion of this point). Second, it turns out that Schnorr's protocol actually *is* dishonest-verifier zero-knowledge, with the following caveat: the simulation is efficient only if the challenge e is not selected at random from $\{0, \ldots, |\mathbb{G}| - 1\}$, but rather is only permitted to be selected from a designated polynomial-size subset S of $\mathbb{G}$ (this is because the known simulator for an arbitrary dishonest verifier's view has a runtime that grows with $|S|$). To obtain negligible soundness error from such a protocol, one must repeat it $\omega(1)$ many times sequentially, adding additional communication and computation costs. The interested reader is directed to [189, Section 4] for details.

12.2.3 Fiat-Shamir Applied to Σ-Protocols

In this section, we explain that applying the Fiat-Shamir transformation (Section 5.2) to any Σ-protocol (such as Schnorr's) yields a non-interactive argument of knowledge in the random oracle model. This result is originally due to Pointcheval and Stern [211].

For concreteness, we couch the presentation in the context of Schnorr's protocol, where the input is a group element h, and the prover claims to know a witness w such that $h = g^w$, where g is a specified group generator. Recall that in the resulting non-interactive argument, the honest prover aims to produce an accepting transcript (a, e, z) for the Σ-protocol, where $e = R(h, a)$ and R denotes the random oracle.

Let $\mathcal{I}$ refer to the Σ-protocol and $\mathcal{Q}$ refer to the non-interactive argument obtained by applying the Fiat-Shamir transformation to $\mathcal{I}$. Let $\mathcal{P}_{\mathcal{FS}}$ be a prover for $\mathcal{Q}$ that produces a convincing proof on input h with probability at least ε. That is, when $\mathcal{P}_{\mathcal{FS}}$ is run on input h, it outputs a transcript (a, e, z) that, with probability at least ε, is an accepting transcript for $\mathcal{I}$ and satisfies $e = R(h, a)$ (here, the probability is over the choice of random oracle and any internal randomness used by $\mathcal{P}_{\mathcal{FS}}$).

We show that by running $\mathcal{P}_{\mathcal{FS}}$ at most twice, we can, with probability at least $\Omega(\varepsilon^4/T^3)$, "extract" from $\mathcal{P}_{\mathcal{FS}}$ two accepting transcripts for $\mathcal{I}$ of the form (a, e, z) and (a, e', z') with $e \neq e'$.[10] By special soundness of $\mathcal{I}$, these two transcripts can in turn be efficiently transformed into a witness w. If T is polynomial and ε is non-negligible, then $\Omega(\varepsilon^4/T^3)$ is non-negligible, contradicting the assumed intractability of finding a witness.[11]

What We Can Assume About $\mathcal{P}_{\mathcal{FS}}$ Without Loss of Generality. As in the proof of Theorem 5.1, we will assume that $\mathcal{P}_{\mathcal{FS}}$ always makes exactly T queries to the random oracle R, that all queries $\mathcal{P}_{\mathcal{FS}}$ makes are distinct, and that $\mathcal{P}_{\mathcal{FS}}$ always outputs a transcript of the form (a, e, z) with $e = (h, a)$, such that at least one of $\mathcal{P}_{\mathcal{FS}}$'s T queries to R was at point (h, a). See the proof of Theorem 5.1 for an explanation of why these assumptions are without loss of generality.

The Witness Extraction Procedure. There is a natural way to extract from $\mathcal{P}_{\mathcal{FS}}$ two accepting transcripts (a, e, z) and (a, e', z). First, fix the value of any internal randomness used by $\mathcal{P}_{\mathcal{FS}}$. The first transcript is obtained by simply running $\mathcal{P}_{\mathcal{FS}}$ once, generating a random value for R's response to each query $\mathcal{P}_{\mathcal{FS}}$ makes to the random oracle. This yields a transcript (a, e, z) satisfying $e = R(h, a)$ such that with probability at least ε the transcript is an accepting one for $\mathcal{I}$. By assumption, during this execution of $\mathcal{P}_{\mathcal{FS}}$, exactly one of the T queries to R was equal to (h, a). Rewind $\mathcal{P}_{\mathcal{FS}}$ to just before it queries R at (h, a), and change R's response to this query from e to a fresh randomly chosen value e'. Then run $\mathcal{P}_{\mathcal{FS}}$ once again to completion (again generating a random value from R's response to each query made by $\mathcal{P}_{\mathcal{FS}}$), and hope that $\mathcal{P}_{\mathcal{FS}}$ outputs an accepting transcript of the from (a, e', z').

---

[10]For simplicity, we do not provide a quantitatively tight analysis of the witness extraction procedure.

[11]One can find a witness with constant probability instead of just with non-negligible probability by running the witness-finding procedure $\ell = O(T^3/\varepsilon^4)$ times. The probability that all ℓ invocations of the procedure fail to find a witness is at most $(1 - 1/\ell)^\ell \leq 1/e < 1/2$.

Analysis of the Witness Extraction Procedure. We must show that the probability this procedure outputs two accepting transcripts of the form (a, e, z) and (a, e', z') with $e \neq e'$ is at least $\Omega(\varepsilon^3/T^2)$. Note that e will not equal e' with probability $1 - 1/2^\lambda$, where λ denotes the number of bits output by R on any query. For simplicity, let us assume henceforth that $e \neq e'$, as this will affect the success probability of the extraction procedure by at most $1/2^\lambda$.

Key to the analysis is the following basic result in probability theory.

Claim 12.1. Suppose (X, Y) are jointly distributed random variables and let $A(X, Y)$ be any event such that $\Pr[A(X, Y)] \geq \varepsilon$. Let μ_X be the marginal distribution of X, and for x in the support of μ_X, call x *good* if the conditional probability $\Pr[A(X, Y)|X = x]$ is at least $\varepsilon/2$. Let $p = \Pr_{x \sim \mu_X}[x \text{ is good}]$ denote the probability that an x drawn at random from the distribution μ_X is good. Then $p \geq \varepsilon/2$.

Proof. If x is not good, let us call x bad. We can write:

$$
\begin{aligned}
\Pr[A(X, Y)] &= \Pr[A(X, Y)|X \text{ is good}] \cdot \Pr[X \text{ is good}] \\
&\quad + \Pr[A(X, Y)|X \text{ is bad}] \cdot \Pr[X \text{ is bad}] \\
&= \Pr[A(X, Y)|X \text{ is good}] \cdot p + \Pr[A(X, Y)|X \text{ is bad}] \\
&\quad \times (1 - p) \leq 1 \cdot p + \varepsilon/2,
\end{aligned}
$$

where the final inequality holds by the definition of "bad" outcomes x of X. Since $\Pr[A(X, Y)] \geq \varepsilon$, we conclude that $p \geq \varepsilon/2$. □

Say that $\mathcal{P}_{\mathcal{FS}}$ *wins* if the transcript (a, e, z) that $\mathcal{P}_{\mathcal{FS}}$ produces is an accepting one satisfying $e = R(h, a)$. Consider applying Claim 12.1, with X equal to $\mathcal{P}_{\mathcal{FS}}$'s internal randomness, Y equal to the evaluations of the random oracle R, and $A(X, Y)$ equal to the event that $\mathcal{P}_{\mathcal{FS}}$ wins when run with internal randomness X and random oracle Y. Claim 12.1 implies that with probability at least $\varepsilon/2$, $\mathcal{P}_{\mathcal{FS}}$'s internal randomness is "good", which in this context means that when the internal randomness is set to X, the probability over the random oracle R that $\mathcal{P}_{\mathcal{FS}}$ produces an accepting transcript (a, e, z) with $e = R(h, a)$ is at least $\varepsilon/2$. Let E be the event that $\mathcal{P}_{\mathcal{FS}}$'s internal randomness is good. We can write the probability that the witness extraction procedure succeeds as

$$\Pr[E] \cdot \Pr[\text{witness extraction succeeds}|E]$$
$$\geq (\varepsilon/2) \cdot \Pr_R[\text{witness extraction succeeds}|E].$$

Here, the subscript R indicates that the probability is over the randomness in the random oracle R.

For the remainder of the proof, we bound $\Pr_R[\text{witness extraction succeeds}|E]$. For notational brevity, we will leave the conditioning on E implicit when writing out the probabilities of various events. By conditioning on E, we may henceforth consider $\mathcal{P}_{\mathcal{FS}}$ to be a *deterministic* algorithm (i.e., no internal randomness), that wins with probability at least $\varepsilon/2$ over the random choice of the random oracle R.

Let $Q_1, \ldots, Q_T$ denote the T queries that $\mathcal{P}_{\mathcal{FS}}$ makes to the random oracle (note that these are random variables that depend on R). Next, we claim that there is at least one integer $i^* \in \{1, \ldots, T\}$ such that

$$\Pr_R[\mathcal{P}_{\mathcal{FS}} \text{ wins} \cap Q_{i^*} = (h, a)] \geq \varepsilon/(2T). \tag{12.1}$$

Indeed, if $\Pr_R[\mathcal{P}_{\mathcal{FS}} \text{ wins} \cap Q_i = (h, a)] < \varepsilon/(2T)$ for all $i = 1, \ldots, T$, then since we have assumed that for any transcript (a, e, z) output by $\mathcal{P}_{\mathcal{FS}}$ there is some $i \in \{1, \ldots, T\}$ such that $Q_i = (h, a)$,

$$\Pr_R[\mathcal{P}_{\mathcal{FS}} \text{ wins}] \leq \sum_{i=1}^{T} \Pr_R[\mathcal{P}_{\mathcal{FS}} \text{ wins} \cap Q_i = (h, a)] < T \cdot (\varepsilon/2) = \varepsilon/2,$$

a contradiction.

Let i^* satisfy Equation (12.1). Consider applying Claim 12.1, now with X equal to R's responses to the first $i^* - 1$ queries, and Y equal to R's responses to the remaining $T - i^* + 1$ queries. And now let A be the event that $\mathcal{P}_{\mathcal{FS}}$, when run with random oracle R, produces a winning transcript (a, e, z) with (h, a) equal to $\mathcal{P}_{\mathcal{FS}}$'s (i^*)'th query, namely Q_{i^*}.

For a value of x in the support of X, call x good if $\Pr[A(X, Y)|X = x] \geq \varepsilon/(4T)$. Equation (12.1) asserts that $\Pr[A(X, Y)] \geq \varepsilon/(2T)$. Hence, Claim 12.1 asserts that X is good with probability at least $\varepsilon/(4T)$.

We can think of the process of generating the two transcripts (a, e, z) and (a', e', z') as first selecting X (thereby determining the first i^* queries

$Q_1, \ldots, Q_{i^*}$ made by $\mathcal{P}_{\mathcal{FS}}$), then drawing two independent copies Y' and Y'' of Y. Both (a, e, z) and (a', e', z') are accepting transcripts with $Q_{i^*} = (h, a) = (h, a')$ if (X, Y') and (X, Y'') both satisfy event A. This probability is at least

$$\Pr[X \text{ is good}] \cdot \Pr[A(X, Y')|X \text{ is good}] \cdot \Pr[A(X, Y'')|X \text{ is good}]$$
$$\geq (\varepsilon/(4T))^3.$$

In conclusion (taking into account that the argument above has conditioned on the event E that the choice of $\mathcal{P}_{\mathcal{FS}}$'s internal randomness is good, an event that happens with probability at least $\varepsilon/2$), we have shown our witness-extraction procedure succeeds with probability at least $\Omega(\varepsilon^4/T^3)$ as claimed.

Remark 12.3. Results lower bounding the success probability of witness extraction procedures related to the one in this section are called *forking lemmas*. The terminology highlights the fact that the witness extraction procedure runs $\mathcal{P}_{\mathcal{FS}}$ twice, once using random oracle responses (X, Y') and once using (X, Y''), where X captures the random oracle's responses to the first i^* queries made by $\mathcal{P}_{\mathcal{FS}}$ and Y' and Y'' capture responses to the remaining queries. One thinks of the random oracle generation process as "forking" into two different paths after the first i^* responses are generated.

Knowledge-Soundness of the Σ-Protocol Itself. We have just seen how to generate a 2-transcript-tree given a convincing prover for any Σ-protocol that has been rendered non-interactive via the Fiat-Shamir transformation. If the Fiat-Shamir transformation has not been applied, generating a 2-transcript-tree for a Σ-protocol is even simpler: run $(\mathcal{P}, \mathcal{V})$ once to generate an accepting transcript for the Σ-protocol, then rewind the Σ-protocol to just after $\mathcal{P}$ sent its first message, and restart the Σ-protocol with a fresh random challenge to generate a new transcript (see Remark 12.1). A similar analysis to the above shows that both generated transcripts will be accepting with probability at least $\Omega(\varepsilon^3)$ where ε is the probability $\mathcal{P}$ passes $\mathcal{V}$'s checks in the Σ-protocol. And with overwhelming probability the two verifier challenges in the two transcripts will be distinct—specifically, with probability at least $1 - 1/2^\lambda$, where 2^λ is the size of the set from which the verifier's challenge is chosen. In this event, the two transcripts form a 2-transcript tree. This procedure can be repeated $O(1/\varepsilon^3)$ times to ensure that the probability of successfully generating at least one 2-transcript-tree is at least, say, $9/10$.

12.3 A Homomorphic Commitment Scheme

Commitment Schemes. In a commitment scheme, there are two parties, a committer and a verifier. The committer wishes to bind itself to a message without revealing the message to the verifier. That is, once the committer sends a commitment to some message m, it should be unable to "open" to the commitment to any value other than m (this property is called binding). But at the same time the commitment itself should not reveal information about m to the verifier (this is called hiding).

Most properties come in statistical and computational flavors, just like soundness in interactive proofs and arguments. That is, binding can hold statistically, meaning that even computationally unbounded committers are unable to open a commitment to two different messages except with negligible probability of success. Or it can hold only computationally: polynomial-time committers are unable to open commitments to two different messages. Similarly, hiding may be statistical: even computationally unbounded verifiers cannot extract any information about m from the commitment to m. Or it may be computational: polynomial time verifiers are unable to extract information about m from the commitment.

A commitment can be statistically binding and computationally hiding or vice versa, but it cannot be simultaneously statistically hiding and binding. This is because any commitment that statistically binds the committer to a message must by definition reveal the message in a statistical sense.[12] In this monograph, we will only consider commitment schemes that are computationally binding and perfectly hiding.

Formally, a commitment scheme is specified by three algorithms, KeyGen, Commit, and Verify. KeyGen is a randomized algorithm that generates a commitment key ck and verification key vk that are available to the committer and the verifier respectively (if all keys are public then ck = vk), while Commit is a randomized algorithm that takes as input the committing key ck and the message m to be committed and outputs the commitment c, as well as possibly extra "opening information" d that the committer may hold onto and only reveal during the verification procedure. Verify takes as input the commitment, the verification key, and a claimed message m' provided by the committer, and any opening information d and decides whether to accept m' as a valid opening of the commitment.

A commitment scheme is *correct* if Verify(vk, Commit(m, ck), m) accepts with probability 1, for any m (i.e., an honest committer can always successfully open the commitment to the value that was committed). A commitment scheme is perfectly hiding if the distribution of the commitment Commit(m, ck) is independent of m. Finally, a commitment scheme is computationally binding if for every polynomial time algorithm $\mathcal{Q}$, the probability of winning the game depicted in Protocol 4 is negligible (i.e., inverse-superpolynomial in the security parameter).

Protocol 4 Binding Game for Commitment Schemes

1: (vk, ck) ← KeyGen()
2: (c, d, m, d', m') ← $\mathcal{Q}$(ck)
  ▷ c should be thought of as a commitment.
  ▷ d and d' should be thought of as opening information, to open c to messages m and m' respectively.
3: $\mathcal{Q}$ wins if Verify(vk, $(c, d), m$) = Verify(vk, $(c, d'), m'$) = 1 and $m \neq m'$

---

[12]A computationally unbounded verifier could simulate a computationally unbounded cheating prover's efforts to open the commitment to multiple messages; statistical binding guarantees that these efforts will succeed for only one message except with negligible probability.

A Perfectly Hiding Commitment Scheme from any Σ-Protocol. Informally, a relation $\mathcal{R}$ is said to be hard if there is no efficient algorithm for identifying a witness w such that $(h, w) \in \mathcal{R}$. More precisely, a *hard relation* is one for which there is some efficient randomized algorithm Gen that generates "hard instances" of the relation in the following sense. Gen outputs pairs (h, w), and there is no polynomial time algorithm that, when fed the value h output by Gen, can find a witness w' such that $(h, w') \in \mathcal{R}$ except with negligible probability. For example, for the discrete logarithm relation in prime order groups $\mathbb{G}$ with generator g for which the discrete logarithm problem is believed to be intractable, Gen would pick a random integer $r \in \{0, \ldots, |\mathbb{G}| - 1\}$ and output (h, r) where $h = g^r$.

Damgård [105] showed how to use any Σ-protocol for any hard relation to obtain a perfectly hiding, computationally binding commitment scheme. By instantiating Damgård's construction with Schnorr's Σ-protocol [223] for the discrete logarithm relation, one recovers a well-known commitment scheme due to Pedersen [206] that will play an important role in this monograph. (The typical presentation of Pedersen's commitment scheme differs slightly, in an entirely cosmetic manner, from the version recovered here. See Protocols 5 and 6 for details.)

Actually, to ensure hiding, Damgård's transformation does require the Σ-protocol to satisfy one property that was not mentioned above. The simulator used to establish HVZK must be able to take as input not only the public input h, but also a challenge e^*, and output a transcript (a, e^*, z) such that the distribution over transcripts produced by the simulator is identical to the distribution over transcripts produced by the interaction of the verifier and prescribed prover when the verifier's challenge is fixed to e^*. This property is called *special* honest-verifier perfect zero-knowledge. The simulator for Schnorr's Σ-protocol satisfies this property simply by fixing the challenge chosen by the simulator to e^*, rather than having the simulator choose the challenge at random from the challenge space.

Here is how Damgård's commitment scheme works. The key generation procedure runs the generation algorithm for the hard relation $\mathcal{R}$ to obtain an (instance, witness) pair $(h, w) \leftarrow$ Gen, and declares h to be both the committing key ck and the verification key vk. Note that the witness w represents "toxic waste" that must be discarded, in the sense that anyone who knows w may be able to break binding of the commitment scheme. To commit to a message m, the committer runs the simulator from the Σ-protocol for $\mathcal{R}$ (whose existence is guaranteed by the special HVZK property of the Σ-protocol) on public input h to generate a transcript in which the challenge is the message m (this is where the property of the simulator described in the previous paragraph is exploited). Let (a, e, z) be the output of the simulator. The committer sends a as the commitment, and keeps $e = m$ and z as opening information. In the verification stage for the commitment scheme, the committer sends the opening information $e = m$ and z to the verifier, who uses the verification procedure of the Σ-protocol to confirm that (a, e, z) is an accepting transcript for public input h.[13]

We need to show that the commitment scheme satisfies correctness, computational binding, and perfect hiding. Correctness is immediate from the fact that the HVZK property of the Σ-protocol guarantees that the simulator only outputs accepting transcripts. Perfect hiding follows from the fact that in any Σ-protocol, the first message a sent by the prover is independent of the verifier's challenge in the Σ-protocol (which equals the message being committed to in the commitment scheme). Computational binding follows from special soundness of the Σ-protocol: if the committer could output a commitment a and two sets of "opening information" (e, z) and (e', z') that both cause the commitment verifier to accept, then (a, e, z) and (a, e', z') must be accepting transcripts for the Σ-protocol, and there is an efficient procedure to take two such transcripts and produce a witness w such that $(h, w) \in \mathcal{R}$. The fact that $\mathcal{R}$ is hard means that this can only be done with non-negligible probability if the committer runs in superpolynomial time.

Note that when applying the transformation to Schnorr's protocol for the discrete logarithm relation, the key generation procedure produces a random power of generator g, which is simply a random group element

---

[13]If the committed message m contains data that the verifier couldn't compute on its own, then revealing m to the verifier violates zero-knowledge. In our actual zero-knowledge arguments that make use of Pedersen commitments, the prover will never actually open any commitment, but rather will prove in zero-knowledge that it *could* open the commitment if it wanted to. See Protocol 7.

h. Hence, the commitment key and verification key in the resulting commitment scheme can be generated *transparently* (meaning no toxic waste produced). That is, rather than choosing a witness r at random and letting $h = g^r$, thereby producing toxic waste r that could be used to break binding of the commitment scheme, h can be directly chosen to be a random group element. In this way, no one knows the discrete logarithm of h to base g (and by assumption, computing this discrete logarithm given h and g is intractable).

The resulting commitment scheme is displayed in Protocol 6. The traditional (and equivalent, up to cosmetic differences) presentation of Pedersen commitments is given in Protocol 5 for comparison. To maintain consistency with the literature, for the remainder of this monograph we follow the traditional presentation of Pedersen commitments (Protocol 5). In the traditional presentation, to commit to a message m, the committer picks a random exponent z in $\{0, \ldots, |\mathbb{G}| - 1\}$ and the commitment is $g^m \cdot h^z$. One thinks of h^z as a random group element that operates as a "blinding factor": by multiplying g^m by h^z, one ensures that the commitment is a random group element, statistically independent of m.[14]

Protocol 5 Standard presentation of Pedersen commitments in a cyclic group $\mathbb{G}$ for which the Discrete Logarithm problem is intractable.

1: Let $\mathbb{G}$ be a (multiplicative) cyclic group of prime order. The key generation procedure publishes randomly chosen generators $g, h \in \mathbb{G}$, which serve as both the commitment key and verification key.
2: To commit to a number $m \in \{0, \ldots, |\mathbb{G}| - 1\}$, committer picks a random $z \in \{0, \ldots, |\mathbb{G}| - 1\}$ and sends $c \leftarrow g^m \cdot h^z$.
3: To open a commitment c, committer sends (m, z). Verifier checks that $c = g^m \cdot h^z$.

---

[14]The blinding factor h^z ensures that the Pedersen commitment is *perfectly* (i.e., statistically) hiding. Even if the blinding factor is omitted, the commitment may not reveal m to a polynomial-time receiver. This is because computing m from the "unblinded" commitment g^m requires solving the discrete logarithm problem to base g. If m is itself uniformly distributed, the binding analysis already assumes this is intractable. Intuitively, m is "hidden in the exponent" of g.

Protocol 6 Commitment scheme obtained from Schnorr's protocol via Damgård's transformation. This is the same as Protocol 5 except for the cosmetic difference that the commitment is taken to be $h^{-m} \cdot g^z$ instead of $g^m \cdot h^z$, with the verification procedure modified accordingly (i.e., the roles of g and h are reversed, and m is replaced with $-m$).

1: Let $\mathbb{G}$ be a (multiplicative) cyclic group of prime order.

2: The key generation procedure publishes randomly chosen generators $g, h \in \mathbb{G}$, which serve as both the commitment key and verification key.

3: To commit to a number $m \in \{0, \ldots, |\mathbb{G}| - 1\}$, committer picks a random $z \in \{0, \ldots, |\mathbb{G}| - 1\}$ and sends

$$c \leftarrow h^{-m} \cdot g^z.$$

4: To open a commitment c, committer sends (m, z). Verifier checks that $c \cdot h^m = g^z$.

12.3.1   Important Properties of Pedersen Commitments

Additive Homorphism.   One important property of Pedersen commitments is that they are *additively homomorphic*. This means that the verifier can take two commitments c_1 and c_2, to values $m_1, m_2 \in \{0, \ldots, |\mathbb{G}| - 1\}$ (with m_1, m_2 known to the committer but not to the verifier), and the verifier on its own can derive a commitment c_3 to $m_3 := m_1 + m_2$, such that the prover is able to open c_3 to m_3. This is done by simply letting $c_3 \leftarrow c_1 \cdot c_2$. As for "opening information" provided by the prover, if $c_1 = h^{m_1} \cdot g^{z_1}$ and $c_2 = h^{m_2} \cdot g^{z_2}$, then $c_3 = h^{m_1 + m_2} \cdot g^{z_1 + z_2}$, so the opening information for c_3 is simply $(m_1 + m_2, z_1 + z_2)$. In summary, Pedersen commitments over a multiplicative group $\mathbb{G}$ are additively homomorphic, with addition of messages corresponds to group-multiplication of commitments.

Perfect HVZK Proof of Knowledge of Opening.   We will see that in the design of general-purpose zero-knowledge arguments, it will occasionally be useful for the prover to prove that it knows how to open a commitment c to some value, *without* actually opening the commitment. As observed by Schnorr, Pedersen commitments have this property, using similar techniques to his Σ-protocol for the Discrete Logarithm relation. See Protocol 7.

The idea is that, for $\mathcal{P}$ to prove it knows m, z such that $c = g^m h^z$, in the first round of the proof, the prover sends a group element $a \leftarrow g^d \cdot h^r$ for a random pair of exponents d, r. One should think of a as $\mathsf{Com}(d, r)$, i.e., a commitment to d using randomness r. Then the verifier sends a random challenge e, and the verifier on its own can derive a commitment to $me + d$ via additive homomorphism, and the prover can derive an opening for this commitment. Specifically, $g^{me+d} \cdot h^{ze+r}$ commits to $me + d$, using randomness $ze + r$. Finally, the prover responds with opening information $(me + d, ze + r)$ for this derived commitment. An equivalent description of the protocol using this perspective is given in Protocol 8.

The idea for why the protocol is zero-knowledge is that since the verifier never learns d or r, the quantities $me + d$ and $ze + r$ that the prover sends to the verifier simply appear to be random elements modulo $|\mathbb{G}|$ from the verifier's perspective. The intuition for why this is special sound is that since the committer does not know e before choosing d, there is no way for the prover to open the commitment to $me + d$ unless it knows how to open the commitment to m. In more detail, if the input commitment is $\mathsf{Com}(m, z) = g^m h^z$, and $\mathcal{P}$'s first message in the protocol is $a = g^d h^r$, then if $\mathcal{P}$ can produce two accepting transcripts $(a, e, (m', z'))$ and $(a, e', (m'', z''))$ with $e \neq e'$, $\mathcal{V}$'s acceptance criterion roughly implies that $m' = m \cdot e + d$ and $z' = z \cdot e + r$ while $m'' = m \cdot e' + d$ and $z'' = z \cdot e' + r$. These are four linearly independent equations in four unknowns, namely m, z, d, and r. Hence, one can take these two transcripts and efficiently solve for both m and z, as $m = (m' - m'')/(e - e')$ and $z = (z' - z'')/(e - e')$.

These intuitions are made formal below.

Perfect Completeness. If prover follows the prescribed protocol in Protocol 7 then

$$g^{m'} \cdot h^{z'} = g^{me+r} \cdot h^{ze+r} = c^e \cdot a.$$

Protocol 7 Zero-Knowledge Proof of Knowledge of Opening of Pedersen Commitment

---

1: Let $\mathbb{G}$ be a (multiplicative) cyclic group of prime order over which the Discrete Logarithm relation is hard, with randomly chosen generators g and h.
2: Input is $c = g^m \cdot h^z$. Prover knows m and z, Verifier only knows c, g, h.
3: Prover picks $d, r \in \{0, \ldots, |\mathbb{G}| - 1\}$ and sends to verifier $a \leftarrow g^d \cdot h^r$.
4: Verifier sends challenge e chosen at random from $\{0, \ldots, |\mathbb{G}| - 1\}$.
5: Prover sends $m' \leftarrow me + d$ and $z' \leftarrow ze + r$.
6: Verifier checks that $g^{m'} \cdot h^{z'} = c^e \cdot a$.

Protocol 8 Equivalent Exposition of Protocol 7 in terms of commitments and additive homomorphism.

1: Let $\mathbb{G}$ be a (multiplicative) cyclic group of prime order over which the Discrete Logarithm relation is hard, with randomly chosen generators g and h.
2: Let $\mathsf{Com}(m, z)$ denote the Pedersen commitment $g^m \cdot h^z$. Prover knows m and z, Verifier only knows $\mathsf{Com}(m, z), g, h$.
3: Prover picks $d, r \in \{0, \ldots, |\mathbb{G}| - 1\}$ and sends to verifier $a \leftarrow \mathsf{Com}(d, r)$.
4: Verifier sends challenge e chosen at random from $\{0, \ldots, |\mathbb{G}| - 1\}$.
5: Let $m' \leftarrow me + d$ and $z' \leftarrow ze + r$, and let $c' \leftarrow \mathsf{Com}(m', z')$. While Verifier does not know m' and z', Verifier can derive c' unaided from $\mathsf{Com}(m, z)$ and $\mathsf{Com}(d, r)$ using additive homomorphism.
6: Prover sends (m', z').
7: Verifier checks that m', z' is valid opening information for c', i.e., that $g^{m'} \cdot h^{z'} = c'$.

Special Soundness. Given two accepting transcripts $(a, e, (m'_1, z'_1))$ and $(a, e', (m'_2, z'_2))$ with $e \neq e'$, we have to extract a valid opening (m, z) for the commitment c, i.e., $g^m \cdot h^z = c$. As in the analysis of the Σ-protocol for the Discrete Logarithm relation, let $(e - e')^{-1}$ denote the multiplicative inverse of $e - e'$ modulo $|\mathbb{G}|$, and define

$$m^* = (m'_1 - m'_2) \cdot (e - e')^{-1} \mod |\mathbb{G}|,$$

$$z^* = (z_1' - z_2') \cdot (e - e')^{-1} \mod |\mathbb{G}|.$$

Then

$$g^{m^*} \cdot h^{z^*} = \left(g^{(m_1' - m_2')} h^{(z_1' - z_2')}\right)^{(e - e')^{-1}}$$

$$= \left(c^e \cdot a \cdot \left(c^{e'} \cdot a\right)^{-1}\right)^{(e - e')^{-1}} = c,$$

where the penultimate equality follows from the fact that $(a, e, (m_1', z_1'))$ and $(a, e', (m_2', z_2'))$ are accepting transcripts. That is, (m^*, z^*) is a valid (message, opening information) pair for the commitment c.

Perfect HVZK. The simulator samples e, m', z' uniformly at random from $\{0, \ldots, |\mathbb{G}| - 1\}$ and then sets

$$a \leftarrow g^{m'} \cdot h^{e'} \cdot c^{-e},$$

and outputs

$$(a, e, (m', z')).$$

This ensures that e is uniformly distributed, and a, and (m', z') are also uniformly distributed over $\mathbb{G}$ and $\{0, \ldots, |\mathbb{G}| - 1\}^2$ under the constraint that $g^{m'} \cdot h^{e'} = c^e \cdot a$. This is the same distribution as that generated by the honest verifier interacting with the prescribed prover.

Perfect HVZK Proof of Knowledge of Opening to A Specific Value.
The above protocol allows the prover to establish it knows how to open a Pedersen commitment c to *some* value. A variant we will also find useful allows the prover to establish in zero-knowledge that it knows how to open c to a specific public value y. Since a Pedersen commitment c to public value y is of the form $g^y h^r$ for a random $r \in \mathbb{G}$, proving that knowledge of how to open c to y is equivalent to proving knowledge of a value r such that $h^r = c \cdot g^{-y}$. This amounts to proving knowledge of the discrete logarithm of $c \cdot g^{-y}$ in base h, which can be done using Protocol 3.

A Final Perspective on Protocol 7. Protocol 7 asks the prover *not* to open c itself (which would violate zero-knowledge), but instead to open a different commitment c', to random group element that is derived homomorphically from both c and a commitment to random value d that the prover sends via its first message. Both the prover and verifier "contribute randomness" to the value $m' = me + d$ committed by c'. The randomness contributed by the prover (namely d) is used to ensure that m' is statistically independent of m, which ensures that the opening m' for c' reveals no information about m. The verifier's contribution e to m' is used to ensure special soundness: the prover cannot open c' for more than one value of the verifier's challenge e unless the prover knows how to open c.

We will see more twists on this paradigm (in Sections 12.3.2 and 14.2), in contexts where the prover wants to establish in zero-knowledge that various committed values satisfy certain relationships. Directly opening the commitments would enable to verifier to easily check the claimed relationship, but violate zero-knowledge. So instead the prover opens *derived* commitments, with both the prover and verifier contributing randomness to the derived commitments in a manner such that the derived commitments satisfy the same property that the prover claims is satisfied by the original commitments.

12.3.2 Establishing A Product Relationship Between Committed Values

We have already seen the Pedersen commitments are additively homomorphic, meaning the verifier can take two commitments c_1 and c_2 to values m_1 and m_2 in $\{0, \ldots, |\mathbb{G}| - 1\}$, and without any help from the committer, the verifier can derive a commitment to $m_1 + m_2$ (despite the fact that the verifier has no idea what m_1 and m_2 are, owing to the hiding property of the commitments).

Unfortunately, Pedersen commitments are not *multiplicatively* homomorphic: there is no way for the verifier to derive a commitment to $m_1 \cdot m_2$ without help from the committer. But suppose the committer *sends* a commitment c_3 that is claimed to be a commitment to value $m_1 \cdot m_2$ (meaning that the prover knows how to open up c_3 to the value $m_1 \cdot m_2$). Is it possible for the prover to prove to the verifier that c_3 indeed commits to $m_1 \cdot m_2$, without actually opening up c_3 and thereby

revealing $m_1 \cdot m_2$? The answer is yes, using a somewhat more complicated variant of the Σ-protocols we have already seen. The Σ-protocol
is depicted in Protocol 9, with an equivalent formulation in terms of
commitments and additive homomorphism given in Protocol 10.

The rough idea of the protocol is that if m_3 indeed equals $m_1 \cdot m_2$,
then c_3 can be thought of not only as a Pedersen commitment to $m_1 \cdot m_2$
using group generators g and h, i.e., $c_3 = \mathsf{Com}_{g,h}(m_1 \cdot m_2, r_3)$, but also
as a Pedersen commitment to m_2 using group generators $c_1 = g^{m_1} h^{r_1}$
and h. That is, if $m_3 = m_1 \cdot m_2$, it can be checked that

$$c_3 = \mathsf{Com}_{c_1,h}(m_2, r_3 - r_1 m_2).$$

Equivalently, c_3 is a commitment to the same message m_2 as c_2, just
using a different generator (c_1 in place of g) and a different blinding
factor ($r_3 - r_1 m_2$ in place of r_2). The protocol roughly enables the
prover to establish in zero-knowledge that it knows how to open c_3 as a
commitment of this form.

Similar to Protocol 7, the idea is to have the prover send commitments to random values b_1 and b_3, the latter being committed twice,
once using generators (g, h) and once using generators (c_1, h). The verifier then derives commitments to $em_1 + b_1$ and $em_2 + b_3$ using additive
homomorphism (with two commitments derived for the latter quantity,
one under the pair of generators (g, h) and the other under (c_1, h)), and
then the prover opens these derived commitments. Roughly speaking,
the protocol is zero-knowledge since the random choice of b_1 and b_3 ensures that the revealed opening is a random group element independent
of m_1 and m_2.

In more detail, the prover first sends three values α, β, γ, where
$\alpha = \mathsf{Com}_{g,h}(b_1, b_2)$ and $\beta = \mathsf{Com}_{g,h}(b_3, b_4)$ are commitments to random
values $b_1, b_3 \in \{0, \ldots, |\mathbb{G}| - 1\}$ using random blinding factors $b_2, b_4 \in
\{0, \ldots, |\mathbb{G}| - 1\}$. Here, the group generators used to produce the two
commitments are g and h. γ on the other hand is *another* commitment
to b_3 (just as β is), but using group generators c_1 and h rather than g
and h. That is, γ is set to $\mathsf{Com}_{c_1,h}(b_3, b_5)$ for a randomly chosen b_5.

From these three values, and despite not knowing $m_1, m_2, r_1, r_2,$
r_3, or $b_1, \ldots, b_5$, the verifier can, for any value $e \in \mathbb{G}$, use additive
homomorphism to derive commitments $c'_1 = \mathsf{Com}_{g,h}(b_1 + em_1, b_2 +$

er_1), $c_2' = \mathsf{Com}_{g,h}(b_3 + em_2, b_4 + er_2)$, and $c_3' = \mathsf{Com}_{c_1,h}(b_3 + em_2, b_5 + e(r_3 - r_1 m_2))$. After the verifier sends a random challenge e, the prover responds with five values $z_1, \ldots, z_5$ such that (z_1, z_2), (z_3, z_4) and (z_3, z_5) are opening information for c_1', c_2' and c_3' respectively.

Completeness, Special Soundness, and Honest-Verifier Zero-Knowledge. Completeness holds by design. For brevity, we merely sketch the intuition for why special soundness and zero-knowledge hold (though the formal proofs are not difficult and can be found in [189] or [244, Appendix A]).

The intuition for why the protocol is honest-verifier zero-knowledge is that the blinding factors b_2, b_4, b_5 ensure that the prover's first message (α, β, γ) leaks no information about the random committed values b_1, b_3, and this in turn ensures that the prover's second message $(z_1, \ldots, z_5)$ reveal no information about m_1 and m_2.

The intuition for why the protocol is special-sound is that if (a, e, z) and (a, e', z') are two accepting transcripts, where $a = (\alpha, \beta, \gamma)$, $z = (z_1, \ldots, z_5)$, and $z' = (z_1', \ldots, z_5')$ then the verifier's checks roughly ensure that:

- $b_1 + em_1 = z_1$ and $b_1 + e'm_1 = z_1'$.

- $b_2 + er_1 = z_2$ and $b_2 + e'r_1 = z_2'$.

- $b_3 + em_2 = z_3$ and $b_3 + e'm_2 = z_3'$.

- $b_4 + er_2 = z_4$ and $b_4 + e'r_2 = z_4'$.

- $b_5 + e(r_3 - r_1 m_2) = z_5$ and $b_5 + e'(r_3 - r_1 m_2) = z_5'$

The first two bullet points refer to the fact that (z_1, z_2) opens $\mathsf{Com}_{g,h}(b_1 + em_1, b_2 + er_1)$ and (z_1', z_2') open $\mathsf{Com}_{g,h}(b_1 + e'm_1, b_2 + e'r_1)$. As in the special soundness analysis of Protocol 7, if $e \neq e'$ then the first bullet point represents two linearly independent equations in the unknown m_1 and hence enables solving for m_1 as $(z_1 - z_1') \cdot (e - e')^{-1}$. Similarly, the second bullet point enables solving for r_1 as $(z_2 - z_2') \cdot (e - e')^{-1}$. Formally, one can show that $((z_1 - z_1') \cdot (e - e')^{-1}, (z_2 - z_2') \cdot (e - e')^{-1})$ is a valid opening for c_1 using generators g and h.

The next two bullet points refer to the fact that (z_3, z_4) opens $\mathsf{Com}_{g,h}(b_3 + em_2, b_4 + er_2)$ and (z'_3, z'_4) open $\mathsf{Com}_{g,h}(b_3 + e'm_2, b_4 + e'r_2)$, and enable solving for m_2 and r_2 as $(z_3 - z'_3) \cdot (e - e')^{-1}$ and $(z_4 - z'_4) \cdot (e - e')^{-1}$. Formally, one can show that $((z_3 - z'_3) \cdot (e - e')^{-1}, (z_4 - z'_4) \cdot (e - e')^{-1})$ is a valid opening for c_2 using generators g and h.

The final bullet point refers to the fact that (z_3, z_5) opens $\mathsf{Com}_{c_1,h}(b_3 + em_2, b_5 + e(r_3 - r_1 m_2))$ and (z'_3, z'_5) opens $\mathsf{Com}_{c_1,h}(b_3 + e'm_2, b_5 + e'(r_3 - r_1 m_2))$. Since r_1 and m_2 have already been derived from the preceding bullet points, the two equations in the final bullet point enable solving for r_3 as $(z_5 - z'_5) \cdot (e - e')^{-1} + r_1 m_2$. Formally, one can show that $(m_1 \cdot m_2, (z_5 - z'_5) \cdot (e - e')^{-1} + r_1 m_2)$ is a valid opening for c_3 using generators g and h.

Protocol 9 Zero-Knowledge PoK of Opening of Pedersen Commitments Satisfying Product Relationship

---

1: Let $\mathbb{G}$ be a (multiplicative) cyclic group of prime order over which the Discrete Logarithm relation is hard.

2: Input is $c_i = g^{m_i} \cdot h^{r_i}$ for $i \in \{1, 2, 3\}$ such that $m_3 = m_1 \cdot m_2$ mod $|\mathbb{G}|$.

3: Prover knows m_i and r_i for all $i \in \{1, 2, 3\}$, Verifier only knows c_1, c_2, c_3, g, h.

4: Prover picks $b_1, \ldots, b_5 \in \{0, \ldots, |\mathbb{G}| - 1\}$ and sends to verifier three values:

$$\alpha \leftarrow g^{b_1} \cdot h^{b_2}, \ \beta \leftarrow g^{b_3} \cdot h^{b_4}, \ \gamma \leftarrow c_1^{b_3} \cdot h^{b_5}.$$

5: Verifier sends challenge e chosen at random from $\{0, \ldots, |\mathbb{G}| - 1\}$.

6: Prover sends $z_1 \leftarrow b_1 + e \cdot m_1$, $z_2 \leftarrow b_2 + e \cdot r_1$, $z_3 \leftarrow b_3 + e \cdot m_2$, $z_4 \leftarrow b_4 + e \cdot r_2$, $z_5 \leftarrow b_5 + e \cdot (r_3 - r_1 m_2)$.

7: Verifier checks that the following three equalities hold:

$$g^{z_1} \cdot h^{z_2} = \alpha \cdot c_1^e,$$

$$g^{z_3} \cdot h^{z_4} = \beta \cdot c_2^e,$$

and

$$c_1^{z_3} \cdot h^{z_5} = \gamma \cdot c_3^e.$$

Protocol 10 Equivalent description of Protocol 9 in terms of commitments and additive homomorphism. The notation $\mathsf{Com}_{g,h}(m, z) := g^m h^z$ indicates that the group generators used to produce the Pedersen commitment to m with blinding factor z are g and h.

1: Let $\mathbb{G}$ be a (multiplicative) cyclic group of prime order over which the Discrete Logarithm relation is hard.
2: Input is $c_i = g^{m_i} \cdot h^{r_i} = \mathsf{Com}_{g,h}(m_i, r_i)$ for $i \in \{1, 2, 3\}$ such that $m_3 = m_1 \cdot m_2 \mod |\mathbb{G}|$.
3: Prover knows m_i and r_i for all $i \in \{1, 2, 3\}$, Verifier only knows c_1, c_2, c_3, g, h.
4: Prover picks $b_1, \ldots, b_5 \in \{0, \ldots, |\mathbb{G}| - 1\}$ and sends to verifier three values:

$$\alpha \leftarrow \mathsf{Com}_{g,h}(b_1, b_2), \quad \beta \leftarrow \mathsf{Com}_{g,h}(b_3, b_4), \quad \gamma \leftarrow \mathsf{Com}_{c_1,h}(b_3, b_5).$$

5: Verifier sends challenge e chosen at random from $\{0, \ldots, |\mathbb{G}| - 1\}$.
6: Let $z_1 \leftarrow b_1 + e \cdot m_1$, $z_2 \leftarrow b_2 + e \cdot r_1$, $z_3 \leftarrow b_3 + e \cdot m_2$, $z_4 \leftarrow b_4 + e \cdot r_2$, $z_5 \leftarrow b_5 + e \cdot (r_3 - r_1 m_2)$.
7: While Verifier does not know $z_1, \ldots, z_5$, using additive homomorphism Verifier can derive the following three commitments unaided using additive homomorphism:

$$c_1' = \mathsf{Com}_{g,h}(z_1, z_2) = \alpha \cdot c_1^e,$$
$$c_2' = \mathsf{Com}_{g,h}(z_3, z_4) = \beta \cdot c_2^e,$$
$$c_3' = \mathsf{Com}_{c_1,h}(z_3, z_5) = \gamma \cdot c_3^e.$$

This final equality for c_3' exploits that

$$c_3^e = g^{em_1 m_2} h^{er_3} = c_1^{em_2} h^{er_3 - er_1 m_2} = \mathsf{Com}_{c_1,h}(em_2, er_3 - er_1 m_2).$$

8: Prover sends $z_1, \ldots, z_5$.
9: Verifier checks that:

- (z_1, z_2) is valid opening information for c_1' using generators g, h.
- (z_3, z_4) is valid opening information for c_2' using generators g, h.
- (z_3, z_5) is valid opening information for c_3' using generators c_1, h.

13

Zero-Knowledge via Commit-And-Prove and Masking Polynomials

Historically, the first zero-knowledge argument for an **NP**-complete problem was given by Goldreich, Micali, and Wigderson (GMW) [131]. GMW designed a zero-knowledge argument with a polynomial-time verifier for the Graph 3-Coloring problem. This yields a zero-knowledge argument with a polynomial time verifier for any language $\mathcal{L}$ in **NP** (including arithmetic circuit satisfiability), because any instance of $\mathcal{L}$ can first be transformed into an equivalent instance of Graph 3-Coloring with a polynomial blowup in instance size, and then GMW's zero-knowledge argument for Graph 3-Coloring can be applied. However, this does not yield a practical protocol for two reasons. First, GMW's construction works by first designing a "basic" protocol that has large soundness error $(1 - 1/|E|$, where $|E|$ denotes the number of edges in the graph) and hence needs to be repeated a polynomial number of times to ensure negligible soundness error. Second, for problems in **NP** that are relevant in practice, reductions to Graph 3-Coloring can introduce large (polynomial) overheads. That is, we saw in Section 6 that arbitrary non-deterministic RAMs running in time T can be transformed into equivalent circuit satisfiability instances of size $\tilde{O}(T)$, but an analogous result is not known for Graph 3-Coloring. For this

331

reason, our focus in this monograph is on directly giving zero-knowledge arguments for circuit satisfiability and related problems, rather than for other **NP**-complete problems. The interested reader can learn more about GMW's seminal zero-knowledge argument from any standard text on zero-knowledge (e.g., [130, Section 4.4.2]).

Commit-and-Prove Zero-Knowledge Arguments.   In this section, we describe our first zero-knowledge arguments for circuit satisfiability. These are based on a technique often called *commit-and-prove*.[1] The idea is as follows. Suppose that for some agreed-upon circuit $\mathcal{C}$, the prover wants to establish that it knows a witness w such that $\mathcal{C}(w) = 1$,[2] and consider the following naive, information-theoretically secure and non-interactive proof system, which is (perfectly) sound but not zero-knowledge. The prover sends w to the verifier, along with the value of every gate of $\mathcal{C}$ when $\mathcal{C}$ is evaluated on input w. The verifier simply checks that the claimed value of the output gate is 1, and checks gate-by-gate that the claimed value of the gate is accurate (i.e., for any multiplication (respectively, addition) gate, the value the prover sends for that gate is indeed the product (respectively, sum) of the two in-neighbors of the gate). Clearly, this proof system is information-theoretically sound, but is not zero-knowledge because the verifier learns the witness w.

To obtain a zero-knowledge argument, the prover will instead send a hiding commitment to each gate, and prove in zero-knowledge that the

---

[1]An important warning: some papers use the phrase "commit-and-prove SNARKs", e.g., [87], which is related to but different than our use of the term commit-and-prove in this survey. Commit-and-prove SNARKs are SNARKs in which the verifier is given a compressing commitment to an input vector (e.g., using the generalized Pedersen commitment we describe later in Section 14.2), and the SNARK is capable of establishing that the prover knows an opening w for the commitment such that w satisfies a property of interest. Hence, commit-and-prove SNARKs are SNARKs for a particular type of statement. In contrast, we use commit-and-prove to refer to a particular *design approach* for zero-knowledge arguments.

[2]In previous sections of this survey, we have considered arithmetic circuits that take as input a public input x and witness w, and the prover wants to establish knowledge of a w such that $\mathcal{C}(x, w) = 1$. In this section we omit the public input x for brevity. It is easy to modify the arguments given here to support a public input x in addition to a witness w.

committed values satisfy the checks that the verifier in the naive (non-zero-knowledge) proof system performs. This way the argument system verifier learns nothing about the committed values, but nonetheless confirms that the committed values would have satisfied the verifier within the information-theoretically secure protocol.

The next section contains additional details of this approach when the commitment scheme used is Pedersen commitments.

13.1   Proof Length of Witness Size Plus Multiplicative Complexity

Section 12.3.2 explained that Pedersen commitments satisfy the following properties: (a) they are additively homomorphic, meaning that given commitments c_1, c_2 to values m_1, m_2, the verifier can compute a commitment to $m_1 + m_2 \mod |\mathbb{G}|$ directly from c_1, c_2, even though the verifier does not know m_1 or m_2 (b) given commitments c_1, c_2, c_3 to values m_1, m_2, m_3 there is a Σ-protocol (Protocol 9) for which the prover can establish in (honest verifier) zero-knowledge that c_3 is a commitment to $m_1 \cdot m_2 \mod |\mathbb{G}|$.

Addition and multiplication are a universal basis, meaning that with these two operations alone, one can compute *arbitrary* functions of any input. Hence, properties (a) and (b) together effectively mean that a verifier is able to do arbitrary computation over committed values, without making the prover ever reveal the committed values.

In more detail, we have the following zero-knowledge argument for arithmetic circuit satisfiability. While conceptually appealing, this argument is not succinct—the communication complexity is linear in the witness size $|w|$ plus the number M of multiplication gates of the circuit, leading to very large proofs.

Let $\mathcal{C}$ be an arithmetic circuit over $\mathbb{F}$ of prime order, and let $\mathbb{G}$ be a cyclic group of the same order as $\mathbb{F}$ in which the Discrete Logarithm relation is assumed to be hard. Let us suppose that multiplication gates in $\mathcal{C}$ have fan-in 2 (the zero-knowledge argument in this section naturally supports addition gates of unbounded fan-in, in which case we can assume without loss of generality that the in-neighbors of any addition gate consist entirely of multiplication gates). Suppose the prover claims that it knows a w such that $\mathcal{C}(w) = 1$.

At the start of the protocol, the prover sends Pedersen commitments to each entry of w, as well as Pedersen commitments to the value of every multiplication gate in C. Then, for each entry of witness w, the prover proves via Protocol 7 that the prover knows an opening of the commitment to that entry. Next, for each multiplication gate in the circuit, the prover uses Protocol 9 to prove that the committed values respect the operations of the multiplication gates. That is, if a multiplication gate g_1 computes the product of gates g_2 and g_3, the verifier can demand that the prover prove in zero-knowledge that the commitment c_1 to the value of gate g_1 equals the product of the commitments c_2 and c_3 to the value of gates g_2 and g_3. Addition gates are handled within the protocol without any communication between prover and verifier by using the additive homomorphism property of Pedersen commitments: if an addition gate g_1 computes the sum of gates g_2 and g_3, the verifier can on its own, via Property (a), compute a commitment to the value of g_1 given commitments to the values of gates g_2 and g_3. Finally, at the end of the protocol, the prover uses Protocol 3 to prove knowledge of how to open the commitment to the value of the output gate of C to value $y = 1$.

The resulting proof system is clearly complete because each of the subroutines (Protocols 3, 7, and 9) is complete. To show it is perfect honest-verifier zero-knowledge, one must construct an efficient simulator whose output is distributed identically to the honest verifier's view in the protocol. The idea of the construction is simply that the protocol is comprised entirely of $|w| + M + 1$ sequential invocations of Σ-protocols that are themselves perfect honest-verifier zero-knowledge. The simulator for the entire protocol can simply run the simulator for each of these subroutines in sequence and concatenate the transcripts that it generates.

13.1.1   Establishing Knowledge-Soundness

To establish our argument system is an argument of knowledge for arithmetic circuit satisfiability, we need to show that if the prover convinces the verifier to accept with non-negligible probability, then it is possible to efficiently extract from the prover a witness w such that $C(w) = 1$. Formally, we must show that for any prover $\mathcal{P}$ that convinces the argument system verifier to accept with non-negligible probability, there is a polynomial-time algorithm $\mathcal{E}$ that, given access to a rewindable transcript generator for the prover-verifier pair $(\mathcal{P}, \mathcal{V})$ for the argument system, outputs a w such that $C(w) = 1$.

Naturally, the procedure to extract the witness w relies on the fact that each of the $|w| + M + 1$ subroutines used in the argument system protocol themselves satisfies special soundness. Recall that this means the protocols consist of three messages, and given access to two accepting transcripts that share a first message and differ in their second message, there is an efficient procedure to extract a witness for the statement being proven. We call such a set of transcripts a 2-transcript-tree for the subroutine.

Using its access to a rewindable transcript generator for $(\mathcal{P}, \mathcal{V})$, $\mathcal{E}$ can in polynomial time identify a 2-transcript-tree for each subroutine with high probability.

By special soundness of Protocol 7, given such a set of 2-transcript-trees for all of the subroutines of the argument system, $\mathcal{E}$ can extract an opening of the commitment to each entry i of the witness, and output the vector w of extracted values. We now explain that the vector w that is output in this manner indeed satisfies $C(w) = 1$.

Just as $\mathcal{E}$ extracted an opening for each entry of w from the 2-transcript-trees for each invocation of Protocol 7, given the 2-transcript-trees for the invocation of Protocol 9 to the ith multiplication gate of $\mathcal{C}$, there is an efficient procedure to extract openings to the commitment for multiplication gate i and the commitments to its two in-neighbor gates such that the values opened respect the multiplication operation (one or both of these in-neighbors may be addition gates, the commitments for which are derived via additive homomorphism from the commitments to multiplication gates sent by the prover). Similarly, given the 2-transcript-tree for the lone invocation of Protocol 3, there is an efficient procedure to extract an opening of the commitment to the output gate value to 1.

Observe that a value for any particular gate g in $\mathcal{C}$ may be extracted multiple times by these extraction procedures. For example, the value of a gate g will be extracted via the 2-transcript-tree for any invocation of Protocol 9 to a gate g' for which g is an in-neighbor. And if g is itself a multiplication gate, its value will be extracted an additional time from the application of Protocol 9 to g itself. And the output gate of $\mathcal{C}$ will have an opening of its commitment to value 1 extracted due to the invocation of Protocol 3.

For any gate whose value is extracted multiple times, the extracted values must all be the same, for if this were not the case, the extraction procedure would have identified two different openings of the same commitment. This would violate the binding property of the commitment scheme, since all the 2-transcript-trees were constructed in polynomial time and the extraction procedure from each 2-transcript-tree is also efficient.

In summary, we have established the following properties of the extracted values:

- A unique value is extracted for every gate of $\mathcal{C}$ and entry of the witness w.

- The extracted values for all multiplication gates respect the multiplication operation of the gate (this holds by the special soundness of Protocol 9).

- The extracted values of the gates also respect the addition operations computed by all addition gates of $\mathcal{C}$ (this holds by the additive homomorphism of the commitment scheme).

- The extracted value for the output gate is 1.

This four properties together imply that $\mathcal{C}(w) = 1$ where w is the extracted witness.

13.1.2   A Final Perspective on Commit-and-Prove

The commit-and-prove argument described above is conceptually related to *fully homomorphic encryption* (FHE). An FHE scheme allows for computation over encrypted data. Specifically, let c_1 and c_2 by ciphertexts with corresponding plaintexts m_1 and m_2. An FHE scheme allows anyone given c_1 and c_2 (but not the corresponding plaintexts) to compute encryptions of $m_1 \cdot m_2$ and $m_1 + m_2$. This allows any arithmetic circuit to be evaluated gate-by-gate over encrypted data.

For example, a computationally limited user can offload sensitive computation to a cloud computing service by encrypting their data with an FHE scheme, and asking the cloud computing service to evaluate an arithmetic circuit over their encrypted data. The cloud service can proceed gate-by-gate through the circuit. For each addition gate and multiplication gate in the circuit, the service can apply the addition or multiplication operation to the plaintexts "inside" the ciphertexts of the gate's in-neighbors, without ever "opening" the ciphertexts. In this way, the cloud service obtains an encryption of the circuit output, which it can send to the user, who decrypts it. The use of FHE here avoids leaking the user's information to the cloud.[3]

The commit-and-prove zero-knowledge argument is conceptually similar, with the argument *prover* playing the role of user, and the *verifier* playing the role of the cloud service. To preserve zero-knowledge, the prover wishes to keep the elements of the witness hidden from the verifier. So the prover *commits* to the witness elements using an additively homomorphic commitment scheme (Pedersen commitments)–these commitments are analogs of the ciphertexts in the FHE scenario above. The verifier seeks to obtain a commitment to the output of the circuit, analogously to how the cloud server seeks to obtain an encryption of the output. The key difference in the commit-and-prove argument is that the commitment scheme is only additively homomorphic rather than fully homomorphic. This means that the verifier on its own can "add two committed values" without ever opening the commitments, but cannot multiply them. So for every multiplication gate in the circuit, the prover in the commit-and-prove argument *helps* the verifier compute the multiplication, by sending a commitment to the product and proving in zero-knowledge that indeed it can open that commitment to the appropriate product of committed values. This is why the proof length grows linearly with the number of multiplication gates in the circuit, but has no dependence on the number of addition gates.

---

[3]Note that FHE does not provide a guarantee that the cloud correctly evaluated the designated arithmetic circuit on the user's data. One would need to combine FHE with a proof or argument system to obtain such a guarantee.

13.1.3   Commit-and-Prove with Other Commitment Schemes

We used Pedersen commitments in the commit-and-prove zero-knowledge argument system above. However, the only properties of Pedersen commitments we needed were: perfect hiding, computational binding, additive homomorphism, and zero-knowledge arguments of knowledge for opening information and product relationships. One can replace Pedersen commitments with any other commitment scheme satisfying these properties. To this end, several works [23], [107], [248] essentially replace Pedersen commitments with a commitment scheme derived from a primitive called *vector oblivious linear evaluation* (VOLE) [8]. This has the following benefits over Pedersen commitments. First, using Pedersen commitments to implement commit-and-prove leads to proofs containing 10 elements of a cryptographic group per multiplication gate. The use of VOLE-based commitments can reduce this communication to as low as 1 or 2 field elements per multiplication gate. Second, the computational binding property of Pedersen commitments is based on the intractability of the discrete logarithm problem, and since quantum computers can efficiently compute discrete logarithms, the resulting commit-and-prove arguments are not quantum-sound. In contrast, VOLE-based commitments are believed to be quantum-sound (they are based on variants of the so-called Learning Parity with Noise (LPN) assumption).

However, the use of VOLE-based commitments comes with significant downsides as well. Specifically, these commitments currently require an interactive pre-processing phase Unlike commit-and-prove with Pedersen-based commitments, the interaction cannot be fully removed with the Fiat-Shamir transformation, and accordingly the resulting arguments for circuit satisfiability are not publicly verifiable.

13.2   Avoiding Linear Dependence on Multiplicative Complexity: zk-Arguments from IPs

The proof length in the zero-knowledge argument of the previous section is linear in the witness length and number of multiplication gates of $\mathcal{C}$. Moreover, the verifier's runtime is linear in the size of $\mathcal{C}$ (witness length plus number of addition and multiplication gates), as the verifier effectively applies every gate operation in $\mathcal{C}$ "underneath the commitments" (i.e., the verifier evaluates every gate on committed values, without ever asking the prover to open any commitments).

It is possible to reduce the communication complexity and verifier runtime to $O(|w| + d \cdot \text{polylog}(|\mathcal{C}|))$, where d is the depth of $|\mathcal{C}|$, by combining the ideas of the previous section with the GKR protocol. The idea is to start with our first, naive protocol for circuit satisfiability, (Section 7.1), which is not zero-knowledge, and combine it with the ideas of the previous section to render it zero-knowledge without substantially increasing any of its costs (communication, prover runtime, or verifier runtime). Specifically, recall that in the naive protocol of Section 7.1 we had the prover explicitly send w to the verifier, and then applied the GKR protocol to prove that $\mathcal{C}(w) = 1$. This was not zero-knowledge because the verifier learns the witness w.

To render it zero-knowledge, we can have the prover send Pedersen commitments to each element of w and use Protocol 7 to prove knowledge of openings of each commitment, exactly as the prover did at the start of the zero-knowledge argument from the previous section. Then we can apply the GKR protocol to the claim that $\mathcal{C}(w) = 1$. However, the prover's messages within the GKR protocol also leak information about the witness w to the verifier, as the prover's messages all consist of low-degree univariate polynomials whose coefficients are derived from $\mathcal{C}$'s gate values when evaluated on w. To address this issue, we do not have the prover send the coefficients of these polynomials to the verifier "in the clear", but rather have the prover $\mathcal{P}$ send Pedersen commitments to these coefficients and engage for each one in an invocation of Protocol 7 to prove that $\mathcal{P}$ knows an opening of the commitment. In sum, when the argument system prover and verifier have finished simulating the GKR protocol, the argument system prover has sent Pedersen commitments to all entries of the witness w and all entries of the GKR prover's messages.

We now have to explain how the argument system verifier can confirm in zero-knowledge that the values inside these commitments would have convinced the GKR verifier to accept the claim that $\mathcal{C}(w) = 1$. The idea is roughly that there is a circuit $\mathcal{C}'$ that takes as input the prover's messages in the GKR protocol (including the witness w), and such that (1) all of $\mathcal{C}'$ outputs are 1 if and only if the prover's messages would convince the GKR verifier to accept, and (2) $\mathcal{C}'$ contains $O(d \log |\mathcal{C}| + |w|)$ addition and multiplication gates. Hence, we can apply the zero-knowledge argument of the previous section to the claim that $\mathcal{C}'$ outputs the all-1s vector. Recall that at the start of the argument system of the previous section applied to the claim $\mathcal{C}'(w') = 1$, the prover sent commitments to each entry of w'. In this case, w' consists of the witness w for $\mathcal{C}$ and the prover's messages within the GKR protocol, and the argument system has already committed to these values (via the last sentence of the previous paragraph). By Property (2) of $\mathcal{C}'$, the total communication cost and verifier runtime of the zero-knowledge argument applied to $\mathcal{C}'$ is $O(|w| + d \log |\mathcal{C}|)$.

The argument for $\mathcal{C}$ is easily seen to be complete and honest-verifier zero-knowledge (since it consists of the sequential application of honest-verifier zero-knowledge argument systems). To formally prove that it is knowledge sound, one needs to show that, given any argument system prover $\mathcal{P}$ that runs in polynomial time and causes the argument system verifier to accept with non-negligible probability, one can extract a witness w and a prover strategy $\mathcal{P}'$ for the GKR protocol applied to the claim $\mathcal{C}(w) = 1$ that causes the GKR verifier to accept with high probability. Soundness of the GKR protocol then implies that $\mathcal{C}(w) = 1$. The witness w can be extracted from $\mathcal{P}$ as in the previous section via the special soundness of Protocol 7. In each round of the GKR protocol, the message to be sent by the GKR prover $\mathcal{P}'$ in response to the GKR verifier's challenge can also be extracted from the commitments sent by the argument system prover $\mathcal{P}$ in response to the same challenge, because Protocol 7 was invoked in each round of the argument system to prove that $\mathcal{P}'$ knows openings to every commitment sent.

The probability that the GKR verifier accepts when interacting with $\mathcal{P}'$ is analyzed by exploiting the fact that the GKR verifier's checks on the committed messages sent by $\mathcal{P}'$ are performed by applying the zero-knowledge proof of knowledge of the previous section to $\mathcal{C}'$. Specifically, soundness of the argument system applied to $\mathcal{C}'$ ensures that whenever $\mathcal{P}$ convinces the argument system verifier to accept, $\mathcal{P}'$ convinces the GKR verifier to accept (up to the negligible probability with which a polynomial time adversary is able to break binding property of the commitment scheme).

To summarize, in the above argument system, we essentially applied the commit-and-prove zero-knowledge argument of Section 13.1 not to $\mathcal{C}$ itself, but rather to the verifier in the GKR protocol applied to check the claim that $\mathcal{C}(w) = 1$.

Reducing the Dependence on Witness Size Below Linear. The argument system just described has communication complexity that grows linearly with $|w|$, because the prover sends a hiding commitment to each entry of w and proves in zero-knowledge that it knows openings to each commitment. The next section describes several practical polynomial commitment schemes. Rather than committing to each entry of w individually, the prover could commit to the multilinear extension $\tilde{w}$ of w using an extractable polynomial commitment scheme as outlined in Section 7.3, and thereby reduce the dependence on the proof length on $|w|$ from linear to sublinear or even logarithmic. (More precisely, to ensure zero-knowledge, the polynomial commitment scheme should be hiding, and during its evaluation phase it should reveal to the verifier a hiding *commitment* to $\tilde{w}(z)$ for any point z chosen by the verifier. See for example the multilinear polynomial commitment scheme in Section 14.3.)

This same approach also transforms the succinct MIP-derived argument of Section 8.3 into a zero-knowledge one. Specifically, after having the argument system prover first commit to the multilinear polynomial Z claimed to extend a valid circuit transcript (with a hiding commitment scheme), the prover and verifier then simulate the MIP verifier's interactions with the first MIP prover, but with the prover sending Pedersen commitments to the MIP prover's messages rather than the messages themselves, and proves in zero-knowledge that it knows openings for the commitments. The argument system verifier then confirms in zero-knowledge that the values inside these commitments would have convinced the MIP verifier to accept the claim.

The ideas in this section and the previous section were introduced by Cramer and Damgård [104] and first implemented and rendered practical via optimizations in [226], [244], [257].

13.3 Zero-Knowledge via Masking Polynomials

The preceding section (Section 13.2) gave a generic technique for transforming any IP into a zero-knowledge argument: the argument system prover mimics the IP prover, but rather than sending the IP prover's messages in the clear, it sends hiding commitments to those messages, and proves in zero-knowledge that it knows how to open the commitments. At the end of the protocol, the argument system prover establishes in zero-knowledge that the committed messages would have caused the IP verifier to accept; this is done efficiently by exploiting homomorphism properties of the commitments.

In this section, we discuss another technique for transforming any IP into a zero-knowledge argument. The technique makes use of any extractable polynomial commitment scheme, meaning that we assume the prover is able to cryptographically bind itself to a desired polynomial p, and later the verifier can force the prover to reveal the evaluation $p(r)$ for a random input r to p of the verifier's choosing. Suppose further that the polynomial commitment scheme is zero-knowledge, meaning that the verifier learns nothing about p from the commitment, and the evaluation phase reveals no information about p to the verifier other than the evaluation $p(r)$. One benefit of this technique is that if the polynomial commitment scheme is binding even against quantum cheating provers, then the resulting zero-knowledge argument is also plausibly post-quantum sound. For example, the FRI-based polynomial commitment scheme of Section 10.4.2 is plausibly sound against cheating provers that can run polynomial time quantum algorithms.[4] In contrast, any protocol (such as that of the last section) that makes use of Pedersen commitments is not post-quantum sound, because Pedersen commitments are only binding if the discrete logarithm problem is intractable, and quantum computers can compute discrete logarithms in polynomial time.

---

[4]FRI-derived polynomial commitments are not zero-knowledge, but can be rendered zero-knowledge using techniques similar to those in this section.

Another Zero-Knowledge Sum-Check Protocol. Consider applying the sum-check protocol to an ℓ-variate polynomial g over $\mathbb{F}$ to check the prover's claim that $\sum_{x \in \{0,1\}^\ell} g(x)$ equals some value G. Let us assume that the verifier has oracle access to g, in the sense that for any point $r \in \mathbb{F}^\ell$, the verifier can obtain $g(r)$ with one query to the oracle. Recall (Section 4.1) that the sum-check protocol consists of ℓ rounds, where the honest prover's message in each round i is a univariate polynomial of degree $\deg_i(g)$ derived from g, namely

$$\sum_{b_{i+1},\ldots,b_\ell \in \{0,1\}} g(r_1, \ldots, r_{i-1}, X_i, b_{i+1}, \ldots, b_\ell).$$

Here, $\deg_i(g)$ is the degree of g in variable i and is assumed known to the verifier, and $r_1, \ldots, r_{i-1}$ are random field elements chosen by the verifier in rounds $1, 2, \ldots, i-1$.

There are three ways in which the verifier "learns" information about g in the sum-check protocol. First, the verifier learns that $\sum_{x \in \{0,1\}^\ell} g(x) = G$, but this information is not meant to be "protected" as the entire point of the sum-check protocol is to ensure that the verifier learns this value. Second, the prover's messages leak information about g to the verifier that the verifier may not be able to compute on her own. Third, the verifier learns the value $g(r)$ via the oracle query at the end of the protocol.

In the preceding section, we addressed the second source of information leakage by having the prover send hiding commitments to the messages rather than the messages themselves. Here is a different technique for ensuring that the prover's messages do not leak any information about g to the verifier; this approach originated in [39], [97].

To ensure that the prover's messages in the sum-check protocol reveal no information about g, the prover can at the very start of the protocol choose a random polynomial p with the same degree as g in each variable, commit to p, and send to the verifier a value P claimed to equal $\sum_{x \in \{0,1\}^\ell} p(x)$. The verifier then picks a random $\rho \in \mathbb{F} \setminus \{0\}$ and sends it to the prover, and the prover and verifier apply the sum-check protocol not to g itself but rather to $g + \rho \cdot p$, to check that $\sum_{x \in \{0,1\}^\ell} (g + \rho \cdot p)(x) = G + \rho \cdot P$.

At the end of the sum-check protocol, the verifier needs to evaluate $g + \rho \cdot p$ at a random input $r \in \mathbb{F}^{\ell}$. The value $p(r)$ can be obtained via the evaluation phase of the commitment scheme that was applied to p, while $g(r)$ is obtained by the verifier with a single oracle query.

Completeness and soundness. The protocol clearly satisfies completeness. To see that it is sound, consider any prover strategy $\mathcal{P}$ capable of convincing the verifier to accept with non-negligible probability. By extractability of the polynomial commitment scheme, it is possible to efficiently extract from $\mathcal{P}$ a polynomial p such that the prover is bound to p, in the sense that any value revealed by the prover in the evaluation phase of the commitment scheme is consistent with p. Letting P be the claimed value of $\sum_{x \in \{0,1\}^{\ell}} p(x)$ sent by $\mathcal{P}$, consider the two functions $\pi_1(\rho) = G + \rho P$ and $\pi_2(\rho) = \sum_{x \in \{0,1\}^{\ell}} (g + \rho \cdot p)(x)$. Both are linear functions in ρ. If either $G \neq \sum_{x \in \{0,1\}^{\ell}} g(x)$ or $P \neq \sum_{x \in \{0,1\}^{\ell}} \rho \cdot p(x)$ then $\pi_1 \neq \pi_2$, and hence the two linear functions can agree on at most one value of ρ. This means that with probability at least $1 - \frac{1}{|\mathbb{F}|-1}$ over the random choice of ρ, $G + \rho P \neq \sum_{x \in \{0,1\}^{\ell}} (g + \rho \cdot p)(x)$. In this event, the sum-check protocol is applied to a false claim, and we conclude that the verifier will reject with high probability because the sum-check protocol is sound.

Honest-Verifier Zero-Knowledge. We claim that the honest verifier in this protocol learns nothing about g other than G and $g(r)$. This is formalized by giving an efficient simulator that, given G and the ability to query g at a single input r, produces a distribution identical to that of the prover's messages in the above protocol.

The intuition is that, since p is random, adding $\rho \cdot p$ to g yields a random polynomial satisfying the same degree bounds as g, and hence the prover's messages in the sum-check protocol applied to $g + \rho \cdot p$ are indistinguishable from those obtained by applying the sum-check protocol to a randomly chosen polynomial. Formally, the simulator selects a random polynomial p subject to the appropriate degree bounds (i.e., $\deg_i(p) = \deg_i(g)$ for all i), commits to p exactly as does the honest prover in the protocol above (here, we are using the fact that p is chosen totally independent of g and hence the simulator can commit to p even though the simulator has no knowledge of g), and sets

$P \leftarrow \sum_{x \in \{0,1\}^{\ell}} p(x)$. The simulator then chooses ρ at random from $\mathbb{F} \setminus \{0\}$, and chooses a random value $r = (r_1, \ldots, r_\ell) \in \mathbb{F}^\ell$. The simulator queries the oracle for g at r to obtain $g(r)$ and then chooses a random polynomial f subject to the constraint that f sums to G over inputs in $\{0,1\}^\ell$ and $f(r) = g(r)$ (this can be done in time $O(2^\ell)$, which is polynomial in n if $\ell = O(\log n)$). The simulator then computes the honest prover's messages in the sum-check protocol applied to $f + \rho p$ when the sum-check verifier's randomness is r. At the end of the sum-check protocol, when the verifier needs to learn $p(r)$, the simulator simulates the honest prover and verifier in the evaluation phase of the polynomial commitment scheme applied to reveal $p(r)$ to the verifier. This completes the description of how the simulator produces a simulated transcript of the verifier's interaction with the prover in the zero-knowledge sum-check protocol. We now explain why the simulated prover messages are distributed identically to those sent by the honest prover in response to the honest verifier.

By the zero-knowledge property of the polynomial commitment scheme, the evaluation proof of the commitment scheme can itself be simulated given $p(r)$ alone, and in particular does not depend on p's evaluations at any points other than r. This ensures that, conditioned on the values of $g(r)$, ρ, and the prover's messages during the evaluation phase of the polynomial commitment scheme, $q := g + \rho p$ is a random polynomial with the same variable degrees as g, subject to the constraints that $q(r) = g(r) + \rho \cdot p(r)$ and $\sum_{x \in \{0,1\}^\ell} q(x) = G + \rho \cdot P$. Since $f + \rho p$ is a random polynomial subject to the same constraints, the prover messages generated by the simulator are distributed identically to the honest prover's messages in the actual protocol (we omit details of how this assertion is achieved, as it does require modest modifications to the univariate and multilinear polynomial commitment schemes, because p is neither a univariate polynomial nor multilinear).

Costs. When the sum-check protocol is applied in an IP or MIP for circuit-satisfiability, the polynomial g to which it is applied has $\ell \approx 2 \log S$ or $\ell \approx 3 \log S$, where S is either the size of the circuit $\mathcal{C}$ or a the number of gates at a single layer of $\mathcal{C}$ (see Sections 4.6 and 8.2). This means that a random polynomial p with the same variable degree as g has at least S^2 coefficients, so even writing p down takes time at least quadratic in S, which is totally impractical. Fortunately, Xie *et al.* [251] show that p does not actually need to be a random polynomial of the appropriate variable degrees. Rather, it suffices for p to be a sum of ℓ randomly chosen univariate polynomials $s_1, \ldots, s_\ell$, one for each of the ℓ variables of g, where the degree of s_i equals $\deg_i(g)$. This ensures that p can be committed to in time $\tilde{O}(\ell)$ using (zero-knowledge variants of) any of the polynomial commitment schemes discussed in this monograph.

Masking $g(r)$. When the sum-check protocol is applied to a polynomial g in an IP or MIP for circuit- or R1CS-satisfiability, allowing the verifier to learn even a single evaluation $g(r)$ of g will violate zero-knowledge, because g itself depends on the witness.

For example, recall that in the MIP for circuit satisfiability of Section 8.2, to check the claim that $\mathcal{C}(x, w) = y$, the prover applies the sum-check protocol exactly once, to the polynomial

$$h_{x,y,Z}(Y) := \tilde{\beta}_{3k}(r, Y) \cdot g_{x,y,Z}(Y).$$

(See Equation (8.2)). Here, Z denotes some polynomial mapping $\{0, 1\}^{\log S}$ to $\mathbb{F}$, and

$$g_{x,y,Z}(a, b, c) := \widetilde{\text{io}}(a, b, c) \cdot (\tilde{I}_{x,y}(a) - Z(a)) + \widetilde{\text{add}}(a, b, c) \cdot (Z(a)$$
$$- Z(b) + Z(c)) + \widetilde{\text{mult}}(a, b, c) \cdot (Z(a) - Z(b) \cdot Z(c)).$$

The honest prover in the MIP sets Z to the multilinear extension $\widetilde{W}$ of a correct transcript W for the claim that $\mathcal{C}(x, w) = y$ (where W is viewed as a function mapping $\{0, 1\}^{\log S} \to \mathbb{F}$).

The key point above is that, since the correct transcript W fully determines the multilinear extension $\widetilde{W}$, and W depends on the witness w, even a single evaluation of $\widetilde{W}$ leaks information about w to the verifier. Hence, any zero-knowledge argument system cannot reveal $\widetilde{W}(r)$ to the verifier for even a single point r.

Here is a technique for addressing this issue. In a sentence, the idea is to replace $\widetilde{W}(r)$ with a slightly higher-degree (randomly chosen) extension polynomial Z of W. This ensures that if the verifier learns a couple of evaluations $Z(r_1)$, $Z(r_2)$ of Z, so long as $r_1, r_2 \notin \{0, 1\}^\ell$, these evaluations are simply independent random field elements and in particular are totally independent of the transcript W.

In more detail, recall further that in argument systems derived from the MIP, the prover uses a polynomial commitment scheme to commit to an extension Z of a correct transcript W. The verifier ignores the commitment until the very end of the sum-check protocol applied to $h_{x,y,Z}$, at which time the verifier needs to evaluate $h_{x,y,Z}$ at a random input $r = (r_1, r_2) \in \mathbb{F}^{\log S} \times \mathbb{F}^{\log S}$. Assuming the verifier can efficiently evaluate $\widetilde{\text{io}}$, $\widetilde{I}$, $\widetilde{\text{add}}$, and $\widetilde{\text{mult}}$ on its own, $h_{x,y,Z}(r)$ can be easily computed given $Z(r_1)$ and $Z(r_2)$. The verifier obtains these two values using the evaluation phase of the polynomial commitment scheme.

As discussed above, in the MIP of Section 8.2, the prover sets Z to $\widetilde{W}$, but this does not yield a zero-knowledge argument. Instead, let us modify the protocol as follows to achieve perfect zero-knowledge. First, we insist that the verifier choose the coordinates of r from $\mathbb{F} \setminus \{0, 1\}$ rather than from $\mathbb{F}$ (this has a negligible effect on soundness). Second, we prescribe that the honest prover chooses Z to be a random extension polynomial of the correct transcript W where Z has at least two more coefficients than a multilinear polynomial. For example, we can prescribe that the prover set

$$Z(X_1, \ldots, X_{\log S}) := \widetilde{W}(X_1, \ldots, X_{\log S}) + c_1 X_1 (1 - X_1) + c_2 X_2 (1 - X_2),$$

where the prover chooses c_1 and c_2 at random. Since $X_1(1 - X_1)$ and $X_2(1 - X_2)$ vanish on inputs in $\{0, 1\}^2$, it is clear that Z extends W. Basic linear algebra implies that for any two points $r_1, r_2 \in \mathbb{F}^{\log S} \setminus \{0, 1\}^{\log S}$, $Z(r_1)$ and $Z(r_2)$ are uniform random field elements, independent of each other and of W. Third, as in the zero-knowledge sum-check protocol described earlier in this section, we insist that the polynomial commitment scheme used to commit to Z is zero-knowledge, meaning that the verifier learns nothing from the commitment or the prover's messages in the evaluation phase of the protocol other than the requested evaluations $Z(r_1)$ and $Z(r_2)$. Fourth, rather than directly applying the sum-check protocol to $h_{x,y,Z}$, we apply the zero-knowledge variant of the sum-check protocol described earlier in this section (with g set to $h_{x,y,Z}$).

The modified argument system clearly remains complete, and it is sound, as the (zero-knowledge) sum-check protocol applied to $h_{x,y,Z}$ confirms with high probability that Z is an extension polynomial of a valid transcript W. It is also perfect zero-knowledge. The simulator is essentially the same as that for the zero-knowledge sum-check protocol. The primary modification of the simulator is that, for $r = (r_1, r_2)$, the simulator's oracle query to obtain $g(r)$ is replaced with the following procedure. First, the simulator chooses values $Z(r_1)$ and $Z(r_2)$ to be random field elements, and then derives $g(r)$ based on these values, according to the definition of $g = h_{x,y,Z}$ in Equation (8.2). Second, the simulator simulates the evaluation proof from the polynomial commitment scheme for the evaluations $Z(r_1)$, $Z(r_2)$ using the zero-knowledge property of the commitment scheme.

Costs. The argument system above is essentially the same as the nonzero-knowledge argument system derived from the MIP of Section 8.2, since all we did was replace the multilinear extension $\widetilde{W}$ with a slightly higher-degree extension Z. Committing to the extension Z as above does require minor modification of the polynomial commitment schemes covered in this survey, as Z is not multilinear (we omit these details for brevity). However, the modifications add very little cost to the commitment protocol, since Z has only two more coefficients than $\widetilde{W}$.

13.4 Discussion and Comparison

This section provided two quite general techniques for transforming a non-zero-knowledge protocol $\mathcal{Q}$ into zero-knowledge one $\mathcal{Z}$. This allows protocol designers to first design an efficient protocol $\mathcal{Q}$ without having to worry about zero-knowledge, and then apply one of the two transformations to "add" zero-knowledge (hopefully, with minimal concrete overhead or additional cognitive load).

Here is a recap of the first transformation. Suppose in the non-zero-knowledge protocol $\mathcal{Q}$, all messages from prover to verifier consist of elements of some field $\mathbb{F}$. Section 13.2 would render the protocol zero-knowledge via the "commit-and-prove" approach as follows: for every field element sent by the prover in $\mathcal{Q}$, the prover in $\mathcal{Z}$ would instead send a *hiding commitment* to that field element, and then at the end of the protocol the prover in $\mathcal{Z}$ would prove in zero-knowledge (via the proof system of Section 13.1) that the committed values would have caused the $\mathcal{Q}$ verifier to accept.

The downsides of this first transformation are two-fold: first, if (as with Pedersen commitments) the commitment scheme is not binding against quantum adversaries, then $\mathcal{Z}$ will not be post-quantum-sound even if $\mathcal{Q}$ is. Second, as discussed already in Section 13.1.3, verification costs are higher in $\mathcal{Z}$ than in $\mathcal{Q}$, first because commitments to field elements may be larger than the field elements themselves (thereby increasing proof length) and second because the $\mathcal{Z}$ verifier must effectively run the $\mathcal{Q}$ verifier "on the committed values", without opening the commitments, and this will further increase proof size and verifier time. For example, each field multiplication that the $\mathcal{Q}$ verifier does may turn into an invocation of Protocol 9 from Section 12.3.2, which requires the prover to send at least 9 extra group elements and the verifier to perform at least nine group exponentiations and several group multiplications, rather than one field multiplication.

While this may appear to be a massive overhead in verifier time and proof length, many non-zero-knowledge protocols $\mathcal{Q}$ will make use of a polynomial commitment scheme. If the commitment scheme is hiding, i.e., it reveals no information to the verifier about the committed polynomial, then the messages sent by the prover of $\mathcal{Q}$ within the scheme do not need to be fed through the commit-and-prove transformation (see the paragraph "Reducing the dependence on witness size below linear" in Section 13.2 for further discussion). In these settings, the verification overhead introduced by the commit-and-prove transformation may be a low-order cost relative to that of the polynomial commitment.

Similarly, from the perspective of the prover's runtime, the transformation from $\mathcal{Q}$ to $\mathcal{Z}$ does not add much overhead so long as $\mathcal{Q}$ is succinct (i.e., the proof length in $\mathcal{Q}$ is much smaller than the size of the statement being proven). This is because, from the prover's perspective, all of the cryptographic overhead of the transformation (namely sending commitments to field elements rather than the field elements themselves, and proving in zero-knowledge that the committed values would have caused the $\mathcal{Q}$ verifier to accept) is applied only to the *verification procedure* in $\mathcal{Q}$. If this verification procedure is much simpler than statement being proven, this computational overhead should be dwarfed by the cost of simply processing the statement itself, which is a lower bound on the prover's runtime in $\mathcal{Q}$.

If $\mathcal{Q}$ is based on the sum-check protocol (Section 4.2), then the second transformation of this section, based on masking-polynomials (Section 13.3) can be applied. This has the dual benefits of plausibly preserving post-quantum soundness, and typically adding less overhead than the commit-and-prove-based transformation. With masking polynomials, the main extra cost in the resulting zero-knowledge protocol $\mathcal{Z}$ compared to the non-zero-knowledge protocol $\mathcal{Q}$ is that the prover has to commit to one masking polynomial for each invocation of the sum-check protocol in $\mathcal{Q}$, and the verifier has to obtain an evaluation of the committed masking polynomial. As described in Section 13.3, these masking polynomials can typically be made very small (of size linear in communication cost of the sum-check protocol, which is typically just logarithmic in the size of the statement being proven).

On the other hand, the masking-polynomial-based transformation is conceptually more complicated and ad hoc than the "commit-and-prove" approach, and accordingly is not as general: it applies only to sum-check-based protocols $\mathcal{Q}$ (though related techniques typically can be used to render other polynomial-based protocols zero-knowledge, such as those in Section 10.3).

14

Polynomial Commitments from Hardness of Discrete Logarithm

Polynomial Commitments Schemes and a Trivial Solution. Recall that polynomial commitment scheme is meant to simulate the following idealized process. An untrusted prover $\mathcal{P}$ has in its head a polynomial q (for applications to succinct arguments, we are primarily interested in the cases the q is a univariate polynomial, or a multilinear polynomial). $\mathcal{P}$ sends a complete description of q to the verifier $\mathcal{V}$ (say, a list of all of q's coefficients over an appropriate basis). $\mathcal{V}$, having learned q, can evaluate q at any point z of its choosing. In particular, once $\mathcal{P}$ sends the polynomial q to $\mathcal{V}$, $\mathcal{P}$ cannot go and "change" q based on the point z at which $\mathcal{V}$ wishes to evaluate it. Let us call this procedure, in which $\mathcal{P}$ explicitly sends q to $\mathcal{V}$, the *trivial polynomial commitment scheme*.

There are three potential issues with the trivial polynomial commitment scheme, two of which involve efficiency considerations.

- In our applications to SNARKs (Sections 7–10), q may be very large—often as large as the entire statement being proved. So having $\mathcal{P}$ send all coefficients of q to $\mathcal{V}$ will require a huge amount of communication. Hence, using the trivial polynomial commitment does not yield *succinct* arguments.

- $\mathcal{V}$ has to spend time linear in the number of coefficients to compute $q(z)$ (i.e., the trivial polynomial commitment would not yield a *work-saving* argument, meaning one whose verifier is faster than the trivial one that is sent a witness and checks its correctness).

- $\mathcal{V}$ learns the entire polynomial q. This may be incompatible with zero-knowledge (in applications to SNARKs, q typically "encodes" a witness, and hence sending q to $\mathcal{V}$ leaks the entire witness).

Using cryptography, one can hope to address all three issues while achieving the same functionality as the trivial polynomial commitment scheme. Specifically, $\mathcal{P}$ can compute a "compressing" commitment c to q and send only c to the verifier. Compressing means that c is much smaller than q, addressing the first issue above regarding succinctness. Because c is smaller than p itself, c does not bind $\mathcal{P}$ to q in a statistical sense. That is, there will *exist* many different polynomials for which c is a valid commitment, and when the verifier asks $\mathcal{P}$ the evaluation $q(z)$, $\mathcal{P}$ will be able to respond with $p(z)$ for any valid "opening" polynomial p of c. However, it is possible to design polynomial commitment schemes that are *computationally binding*, meaning that any efficient prover (e.g., one unable to solve the discrete logarithm problem, or find a collision in a cryptograph hash function) is unable to respond to any evaluation query z with a quantity other than $q(z)$. More precisely, along with a claimed value v for $q(z)$, the prover will send an *evaluation proof* π. Computational binding guarantees that any efficient prover will be unable to generate a convincing π unless indeed $v = q(z)$.

We have already covered some polynomial commitment schemes in earlier sections (e.g., Sections 10.4.2 and 10.5). As with those earlier schemes, in this section we will see polynomial commitment schemes in which π can be checked far faster than what would be required just to read an explicit description of q. This addresses the first two issues of the trivial scheme (succinctness and verifier time). We will also see schemes where π reveals nothing about q, and even schemes where, if desired, the verifier does not actually learn the requested evaluation $q(z)$ but rather a *hiding commitment* to $q(z)$. In this manner, the polynomial commitment schemes can support zero-knowledge, leaking no information about q (and the witness it encodes) to the verifier.

Revealing $q(z)$ Itself vs. a Commitment to $q(z)$. The polynomial commitment schemes we describe in Section 14 reveal to the verifier (Pedersen) commitments to the value $v = q(z)$, because this is what is required for their use in the zero-knowledge arguments of Section 13.2. Other zero-knowledge arguments (such as those in Section 13.3) call for v to be revealed explicitly to the verifier. Fortunately, it is easy to modify the commitment schemes of Section 14 to reveal v to the verifier, for example by having the prover use Protocol 3 to establish in zero-knowledge that it knows how to open the commitment to value v (see the final paragraph of Section 12.3.1 for details). The pairing-based polynomial commitment scheme in Section 15 is described in the setting where the evaluation $v = q(z)$ is revealed explicitly to the verifier.

Polynomial Commitments from Earlier Sections and How they Compare to this Section. We have previously seen that one way to obtain a polynomial commitment scheme is to combine an appropriate PCP or IOP with Merkle-hashing (Sections 10.4.2 and 10.5). Whereas the Merkle-hashing approach only exploited "symmetric key" cryptographic primitives (namely collision-resistant hash functions, combined with the random oracle model to remove interaction), the approaches in this section are based on "public key" cryptographic primitives. Such primitives require stronger cryptographic assumptions such as hardness of the discrete logarithm problem in elliptic curve groups. Discussion of the pros and cons of IOP-based polynomial commitments vs. the commitments of this section can be found in Section 16.3.

Overview of this Section's Schemes. Known polynomial commitment schemes tend to be somewhat more general: they enable a prover to commit to any *vector* $u \in \mathbb{F}^n$, and then later prove statements about the inner product of u with any vector $y \in \mathbb{F}^n$ requested by the verifier. In the polynomial commitment scheme, u will be the coefficients of the polynomial q to be committed over an appropriate basis (e.g., the standard monomial basis for univariate polynomial, or the Lagrange basis for multilinear polynomials). Evaluating $q(z)$ is then equivalent to computing the inner product of u with the vector y obtained by evaluating each basis polynomial at z.

For example, if q is univariate, say, $q(X) = \sum_{i=0}^{n-1} u_i X^i$, then for any input z to q $q(z) = \langle u, y \rangle$ where $y = (1, z, z^2, \ldots, z^{n-1})$ consists of powers of z, and $\langle u, y \rangle = \sum_{i=0}^{n-1} u_i y_i$ denotes the inner product of u and y. Similarly, if q is multilinear, say $q(X) = \sum_{i=0}^{2^\ell} u_i \chi_i(X)$, where $\chi_1, \ldots, \chi_{2^\ell}$ denotes the natural enumeration of the Lagrange basis polynomials,[1] then for $z \in \mathbb{F}_p^\ell$, $q(r) = \langle u, y \rangle$ where $y = (\chi_1(z), \ldots, \chi_{2^\ell}(z))$ is the vector of all Lagrange basis polynomials evaluated at z.

Hence, to commit to q, it suffices to commit to the *vector u of coefficients* of q. Then to later reveal (a commitment to) $q(z)$, it suffices to reveal (a commitment to) the inner product of u with the vector y.

Tensor Structure in the Evaluation Vector.   Exactly as in Section 10.5.1, in both the univariate and multilinear cases above, the vector y has a tensor-product structure. Some, but not all, of the polynomial commitment schemes covered in this section will exploit this tensor structure (specifically, the schemes in Sections 14.3 and 15.4); the others support inner products of a committed vector with an *arbitrary* vector y.

What we mean by tensor structure is the following. In the univariate case, let $n - 1$ equal the degree of q and let us assume $n = m^2$ is a perfect square, and define $a, b \in \mathbb{F}^m$ as $a := (1, z, z^2, \ldots, z^{m-1})$ and $b := (1, z^m, z^{2m}, \ldots, z^{m(m-1)})$. If we view y as an $m \times m$ matrix with entries indexed as $(y_{1,1}, \ldots, y_{m,m})$, then y is simply the outer product $b \cdot a^T$ of a and b. That is, $y_{i,j} = z^{i \cdot m + j} = b_i \cdot a_j$. Similarly, if q is an ℓ-variate multilinear polynomial, suppose that $2^\ell = m^2$, and let $z_1, z_2 \in \mathbb{F}^{\ell/2}$ denote the first half and second half of $z \in \mathbb{F}^\ell$. Then let $\chi_1', \ldots, \chi_m'$ denote the natural enumeration of the $(\ell/2)$-variate Lagrange basis polynomials, and define $a, b \in \mathbb{F}^m$ as $a := (\chi_1'(z_1), \ldots, \chi_m'(z_1))$ and $b := (\chi_1'(z_2), \ldots, \chi_m'(z_2))$. Then $y = b \cdot a^T$. That is, $y_{i,j} = \chi_{i \cdot m + j}(z) = \chi_i'(z_1) \cdot \chi_j'(z_2) = b_i \cdot a_j$.

In summary, for both univariate and multilinear polynomials q, once the coefficient vector u of q is committed, computing $q(z)$ is equivalent to evaluating the inner product of u with a vector y satisfying $y_{i,j} = b_i \cdot a_j$

---

[1]See Lemma 3.7 for a definition of the Lagrange basis polynomials. In the natural enumeration, if i has binary representation $i_1, \ldots, i_\ell \in \{0, 1\}^\ell$, then $\chi_i(X_1, \ldots, X_\ell) = \prod_{j=1}^\ell (X_i i_j + (1 - X_i)(1 - i_j)) = \left(\prod_{j: \, i_j = 1} X_j \right) \left(\prod_{j: \, i_j = 0} (1 - X_j) \right)$.

for some m-dimensional vectors a, b, where m is the square root of the number of coefficients of q. Equivalently, we can express the inner product of u and y as a vector-matrix-vector product:

$$\langle u, y \rangle = \sum_{i,j=1,\ldots,m} u_{i,j} b_i a_j = b^T \cdot u \cdot a, \tag{14.1}$$

where on the right hand side we are viewing u as an $m \times m$ matrix. See Figures 14.1 and 14.2 for examples in both the univariate and multilinear cases.

14.1 A Zero-Knowledge Scheme with Linear Size Commitments

We begin by describing a scheme that does not improve over the costs of the trivial polynomial commitment scheme, but does render it zero-knowledge. That is, is the prover's commitment to q is as large of q itself, and given the commitment to q, the verifier on its own can derive a commitment to $q(z)$ for any input z of the verifier's choosing.

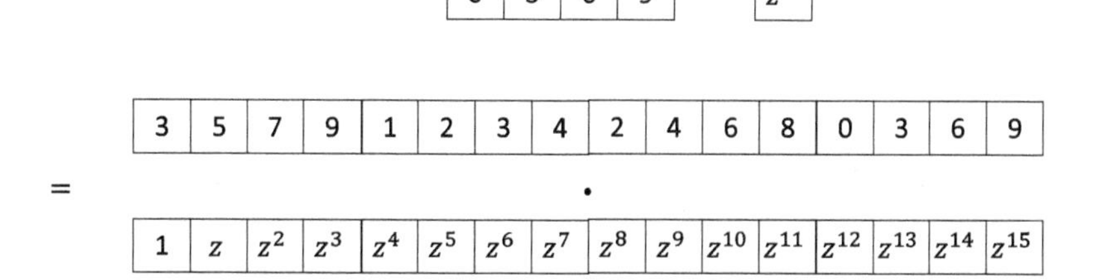

$q(z) = 3 + 5z + 7z^2 + 9z^3 + z^4 + 2z^5 + 3z^6 + 4z^7 + 2z^8 + 4z^9 + 6z^{10} + 8z^{11} + 3z^{13} + 6z^{14} + 9z^{15}$

Figure 14.1: Example of a degree-15 univariate polynomial q expressed via its coefficients over the standard monomial basis. The second line shows that the evaluation $q(z)$ for any input z can be expressed as a vector-matrix-vector product, where the matrix is specified by the coefficients of q, and the two vectors by the evaluation point r. The third line shows $q(z)$ can be equivalently be expressed as an inner product between the coefficient vector of q and an "evaluation vector" consisting of powers of z.

$$q(r_1, r_2, r_3, r_4) =$$
$$3(1-r_1)(1-r_2)(1-r_3)(1-r_4) + 5(1-r_1)(1-r_2)(1-r_3)r_4 + 7(1-r_1)(1-r_2)r_3(1-r_4) + 9(1-r_1)(1-r_2)r_3r_4$$
$$+(1-r_1)r_2(1-r_3)(1-r_4) + 2(1-r_1)r_2(1-r_3)r_4 + 3(1-r_1)r_2r_3(1-r_4) + 4(1-r_1)r_2r_3r_4$$
$$+2r_1(1-r_2)(1-r_3)(1-r_4) + 4r_1(1-r_2)(1-r_3)r_4 + 6r_1(1-r_2)r_3(1-r_4) + 8r_1(1-r_2)r_3r_4$$
$$+3r_1r_2(1-r_3)r_4 + 6r_1r_2r_3(1-r_4) + 9r_1r_2r_3r_4$$

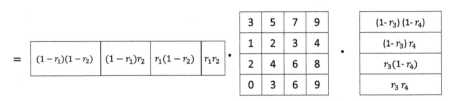

Figure 14.2: Example of a 4-variate multilinear polynomial q expressed via its coefficients over the Lagrange basis (see Lemma 3.7). The evaluation $q(r)$ for any input $r = (r_1, r_2, r_3, r_4) \in \mathbb{F}^4$ can be expressed as a vector-matrix-vector product, where the matrix is specified by the coefficients of q, and the two vectors by the evaluation point r.

Recall that in a Pedersen commitment (Section 12.3) over group $\mathbb{G}$ of prime order p with generators g, h, a commitment to a value $m \in \mathbb{F}_p$ is $c \leftarrow h^m \cdot g^r$ for a value $r \in \{0, \ldots, p-1\}$ randomly chosen by the committer. Pedersen commitments are perfectly hiding and computationally binding.

Commitment Phase. To commit to q, rather than the prover sending each entry of the coefficient vector u to the verifier "in the clear" as in the trivial scheme, $\mathcal{P}$ sends a Pedersen commitment c_i to each entry u_i of u. Pedersen commitments are hiding, so this reveals to the receiver nothing at all about u.

Evaluation Phase. Let y be the vector such that $q(z) = \langle u, y \rangle = \sum_i u_i y_i$. Since the verifier knows y and has a commitment to each entry u_i of u, using the homomorphism property of Pedersen commitments, the verifier can on its own derive a commitment c to $\sum_i u_i y_i$. $\mathcal{P}$ can prove in zero-knowledge that it knows how to open the commitment c via Protocol 7 (Section 12.3.1).

Extractability. In the above scheme, suppose that the committer, before sending the commitment, knows what the evaluation query z will be. As we now explain, the committer can arrange to be able to open the commitment c derived by the verifier in the evaluation phase to a value $a \in \mathbb{F}_p$ of the committer's choosing, *without* being able to open any of the commitments c_i sent during the commit phase. Put another way, the commitment scheme is not extractable in this setting (see Section 7.4): the prover may not "know" a polynomial p of the claimed degree that explains its answers to all evaluation queries for which it is capable of passing the verifier's checks.

For example, suppose that $n = 2$, so the polynomial commitment consists of two Pedersen commitments, c_0 and c_1, each ostensibly a Pedersen commitment to one of the two coefficients of the polynomial. For simplicity, assume and the group generator h used as a blinding factor in the Pedersen commitment scheme is the identity element in $\mathbb{G}$ (equivalently, the blinding factor is simply omitted from the Pedersen commitment scheme).

Then a committer could choose c_0 to be a random group element, meaning the committer is unable to open c_0, and also set c_1 to $\left(g^a \cdot c_0^{-1}\right)^{z^{-1}}$ where z^{-1} denotes the multiplicative inverse of z modulo p. This ensures that the commitment c derived by the verifier during the evaluation phase above is $c_0 \cdot c_1^z = g^a$, which the committer can open to a, despite not knowing how to open the commitments c_0 and c_1.

One way to address the above issue and thereby achieve extractability is to modify the commitment phase to require the committer to prove in zero-knowledge, via Protocol 7, that it can open each Pedersen commitment c_i. Of course, this concretely increases the costs of the commitment phase.

In applications of polynomial commitment schemes to succinct arguments, the evaluation point z is chosen at random by the verifier and not known to the prover at the time the polynomial commitment is sent. In this setting, the above polynomial commitment scheme *is* extractable (without modifying the commitment phase). Specifically, by randomly choosing many different evaluation points, the extraction procedure can find n evaluation points $z^{(1)}, \ldots, z^{(i)}$ for which the committer is able to pass the verifier's checks. If $y^{(i)}$ denotes the vector such that

$q(z^{(i)}) = \langle u, y^{(i)} \rangle$, and the committer claims that $q(z^{(i)}) = v^{(i)}$,[2] then this yields n linearly independent equations in the n unknown entries of u, with the i'th equation being

$$\langle u, y^{(i)} \rangle = v^{(i)}.$$

The extractor then uses Gaussian elimination to efficiently solve these n equations for the entries of u, i.e., for the coefficients of the committed polynomial q.

Similar remarks apply to the polynomial commitment scheme with square-root verification costs given later, in Section 14.3.

14.2   Constant Size Commitments But Linear Size Evaluation Proofs

In the commitment scheme of Section 14.1, the commitment was as big as the polynomial being committed. In this section, we give a scheme that reduces the commitment size to constant (one group element). However, evaluation proofs (and hence also verification time) will become very large—as big as the polynomial being committed.[3]

Commitment Phase.   Assume that n generators $g_1, \ldots, g_n$ for $\mathbb{G}$ are chosen at random from $\mathbb{G}$. To commit to $u \in \mathbb{F}_p^n$, committer will pick a random value $r_u \in \{0, 1, \ldots, |\mathbb{G}| - 1\}$ and send the value $\mathsf{Com}(u; r_u) := h^{r_u} \cdot \prod_{i=1}^n g_i^{u_i}$. This quantity is often referred to as a *generalized Pedersen commitment*, or a *Pedersen vector commitment* (a standard Pedersen commitment is equivalent to a generalized Pedersen commitment when $n = 1$). Note that Pedersen vector commitments are homomorphic: given two commitments c_u, c_w to two vectors u and w in $\mathbb{F}_p^n$, and any

---

[2]More precisely, the evaluation $v^{(i)}$ is not explicitly revealed by the committer in the scheme of this section. Rather, the committer proves knowledge of $v^{(i)}$ using Protocol 7. But $v^{(i)}$ can be efficiently extracted from the committer owing to the knowledge-soundness of Protocol 7.

[3]The number of public parameters for the scheme of this section is also very large, consisting of n randomly chosen group elements $g_1, \ldots, g_n$, where n is the length of the coefficient vector u. But in the random oracle model g_i can be chosen via a random oracle by evaluating the random oracle at input i, in which case the public parameter size is constant.

two scalars $a_1, a_2 \in \mathbb{F}_p$, one can compute a commitment to the linear combination $a_1 u + a_2 w$, as $c_u^{a_1} \cdot c_w^{a_2}$.

Pedersen *vector* commitments should contrasted with the scheme of Section 14.1, which committed to the vector $u \in \mathbb{F}_p^n$ by sending a different Pedersen commitment for each entry of u (using the same public group generator g for all n commitments). This was not a compressing commitment. Pedersen vector commitments compute a different Pedersen commitment $g_i^{u_i}$ for each entry u_i of u (but without a blinding factor, see Footnote 14), with each commitment using a different group generator $g_i \in \mathbb{G}$.[4] But rather than sending all n commitments to the verifier, they are all "compressed" into a single commitment using the group operation of $\mathbb{G}$ (and then the result is blinded by the factor h^{r_u}).

Evaluation Phase. Recall that evaluating a committed polynomial q at input z is equivalent to computing $\langle u, y \rangle$ for the coefficient vector u and a vector y derived from z. Suppose we are given a commitment $c_u = \mathsf{Com}(u, r_u)$, a public query vector y, and a commitment $c_v = \mathsf{Com}(v, r_v) = g_1^v \cdot h^{r_v}$ where $v = \langle u, y \rangle$, and the committer knows r_u and r_v but the verifier does not. The committer wishes to prove in zero-knowledge that it knows an openings u of c_u and v of c_v such that $\langle u, y \rangle = v$, as unless the prover can break the binding property of the commitments, this is equivalent to establishing that $q(z) = v$.

As with Protocol 7 (see the end of Section 12.3.1), directly opening the commitments to u and v would enable to verifier to easily check that $v = \langle u, y \rangle$, but would violate zero-knowledge. So instead the prover opens *derived* commitments, with both the prover and verifier contributing randomness to the derived commitments in a manner such that the derived commitments satisfy the same property that the prover claims is satisfied by the original commitments.

In more detail, first the committer samples a random n-dimensional vector d with entries in $\{0, \ldots, p-1\}$ and two random values $r_1, r_2 \in$

---

[4]If the same group generator g were used for all i, the commitment $\prod_{i=1}^{n} g^{u_i}$ would not bind the committer to the vector u, but rather only to some permutation of u. For example, if $n = 2$, then $u = (1, 2)$ would produce the same commitment as $u = (2, 1)$: in the first case the commitment would be $g^2 \cdot g = g^3$ and in the second case it would be $g \cdot g^2$, which also equals g^3.

$\{0, \ldots, p-1\}$. The committer sends two values $c_1, c_2 \in \mathbb{G}$ claimed to equal $\mathsf{Com}(d, r_1)$ and $\mathsf{Com}(\langle d, y \rangle, r_2)$. The verifier responds with a random challenge $e \in \{0, \ldots, p-1\}$. The prover responds with three quantities $u', r_{u'}, r_{v'} \in \{0, \ldots, p-1\}$ claimed to respectively equal the following (with all arithmetic done modulo p):

$$e \cdot u + d \in \{0, \ldots, p-1\}^n, \tag{14.2}$$

$$e \cdot r_u + r_1 \in \{0, \ldots, p-1\}, \tag{14.3}$$

$$e \cdot r_v + r_2 \in \{0, \ldots, p-1\}. \tag{14.4}$$

Finally, the verifier checks that $c_u^e \cdot c_1 = \mathsf{Com}(u', r_{u'})$ and $c_v^e \cdot c_2 = \mathsf{Com}(\langle u', y \rangle, r_{v'})$.

This protocol can be proved complete, special-sound, and perfect honest-verifier zero knowledge in a manner very similar to Protocol 7. Before writing out the formal analysis, we explain how each step of the protocol here is in direct analogy with each step of Protocol 7.

In Protocol 7, the prover's first message contained a commitment to a random value $d \in \{0, \ldots, p-1\}$. Here, since we are dealing with vector commitments, the prover's first message contains a commitment to a random *vector* d with entries in $\{0, \ldots, p-1\}$. Since this protocol is meant to establish not only that the prover knows how to open the commitment to vector u, but also that the prover knows how to open the second commitment to $\langle u, y \rangle$, the protocol here also has the prover send a second commitment, to $\langle d, y \rangle$.

In Protocol 7, after the verifier sent a random challenge e, the prover responded with an opening of the commitment to $e \cdot m + r_1$ that can be derived homomorphically from the commitments to m and d. Analogously, here the prover responds with opening information for the derived commitments to the vector $e \cdot u + d$ (that opening information is specified via Equations (14.2) and (14.3)) and to the value $\langle eu + d, y \rangle$ (the opening information is $(\langle u', y \rangle, r_{v'})$, where if the prover is honest, u' is specified as per Equation (14.2) and $r_{v'}$ is specified as per Equation (14.4)). In both protocols, the verifier simply checks that the opening information for both commitment(s) is valid. Effectively, the verifier confirms that the derived commitments, to vector $u' = eu + d$ and to value $\langle u', y \rangle$, satisfy the same relationship that the prover claims holds

---

Protocol 11 Evaluation phase of the polynomial commitment scheme of Section 14.2. If the committed polynomial is q and the evaluation point is z, $u \in \mathbb{F}_p^n$ denotes the coefficient vector of q (which is assumed to be defined over field $\mathbb{F}_p$ for prime p) and $y \in \mathbb{F}_p^n$ is a vector such that $q(z) = \langle u, y \rangle = \sum_{i=1}^n u_i \cdot y_i$.

1: Let $\mathbb{G}$ be a (multiplicative) cyclic group of prime order p over which the Discrete Logarithm relation is hard, with randomly chosen generators $h, g_1, \ldots, g_n$ and g.

2: Let $c_u = \mathsf{Com}(u; r_u) := h^{r_u} \cdot \prod_{i=1}^n g_i^{u_i}$ and $c_v = \mathsf{Com}(v, r_v) = g^v h^{r_v}$. Prover knows u, r_u, v, and r_v. Verifier only knows c_u, c_v, h, $g_1, \ldots, g_n$, and g.

3: Prover picks $d \in \{0, \ldots, p-1\}^n$ and $r_1, r_2 \in \{0, \ldots, p-1\}$ and sends to verifier $c_d := \mathsf{Com}(d, r_1)$ and $c_{\langle d, y \rangle} := \mathsf{Com}(\langle d, y \rangle, r_2)$.

4: Verifier sends challenge e chosen at random from $\{0, \ldots, |\mathbb{G}| - 1\}$.

5: Let $u' \leftarrow u \cdot e + d$ and $r_{u'} \leftarrow r_u \cdot e + r_1$, and let $c_{u'} \leftarrow \mathsf{Com}(u', r_u')$. While Verifier does not know u' and $r_{u'}$, Verifier can derive $c_{u'}$ unaided from c_u and c_d using additive homomorphism, as $c_u^e \cdot c_d$.

6: Similarly, let $v' \leftarrow v \cdot e + \langle d, y \rangle = \langle u', y \rangle$ and $r_{v'} \leftarrow r_v \cdot e + r_2$, and let $c_{v'} \leftarrow \mathsf{Com}(v', r_{v'})$. While Verifier does not know v' and $r_{v'}$, Verifier can derive $c_{v'}$ unaided from c_v and $c_{\langle d, y \rangle}$ using additive homomorphism, as $c_v^e \cdot c_{\langle d, y \rangle}$.

7: Prover sends $(u', r_{u'})$ and $r_{v'}$ to Verifier.

8: Verifier checks that $(u', r_{u'})$ is valid opening information for $c_{u'}$, and that $(\langle u', y \rangle, r_{v'})$ is valid opening information for $c_{v'}$. Equivalently, Verifier checks that:

$$h^{r_{u'}} \cdot \prod_{i=1}^n g_i^{u'_i} = c_{u'}$$

and

$$h^{r_{v'}} \cdot g^{\langle u', y \rangle} = c_{v'}.$$

---

between the original committed vector u and value v, namely that the latter equals the inner product of the former with vector y.

Completeness, Special Soundness, and Zero-Knowledge.
Completeness is clear by inspection of Protocol 11. For special soundness, let

$(c_d, c_{\langle d,y \rangle})$ be the first message sent by the prover, and let $((c_d, c_{\langle d,y \rangle}), e,$ $(u^*, c_{u^*}, r^*))$ and $((c_d, c_{\langle d,y \rangle}), e', (\hat{u}, c_{\hat{u}}, \hat{r}))$ be two accepting transcripts. Owing to the transcripts passing the two tests performed by the verifier in Step 8 of Protocol 11, this means that:

$$h^{r_{u^*}} \cdot \prod_{i=1}^{n} g_i^{u_i^*} = c_u^e \cdot c_d, \tag{14.5}$$

$$h^{r_{\hat{u}}} \cdot \prod_{i=1}^{n} g_i^{\hat{u}_i} = c_u^{e'} \cdot c_d, \tag{14.6}$$

$$h^{r^*} \cdot g^{\langle u^*, y \rangle} = c_v^e \cdot c_{\langle d,y \rangle}. \tag{14.7}$$

$$h^{\hat{r}} \cdot g^{\langle \hat{u}, y \rangle} = c_v^{e'} \cdot c_{\langle d,y \rangle}. \tag{14.8}$$

Let

$$\bar{u} := (u^* - \hat{u}) \cdot (e - e')^{-1} \quad \mathrm{mod}\ |\mathbb{G}|,$$

$$r_{\bar{u}} := (r_{u^*} - r_{\hat{u}}) \cdot (e - e')^{-1} \quad \mathrm{mod}\ |\mathbb{G}|,$$

and

$$r_{\bar{v}} := (r^* - \hat{r}) \cdot (e - e')^{-1} \quad \mathrm{mod}\ |\mathbb{G}|$$

Dividing Equation (14.5) by Equation (14.6) implies that

$$h^{\bar{v}} \cdot \prod_{i=1}^{n} g_i^{\bar{u}_i} = c_u,$$

and dividing Equation (14.7) by Equation (14.8) implies that:

$$h^{\bar{r}} \cdot g^{\langle \bar{u}, y \rangle} = c_v.$$

That is, $(\bar{u}, r_{\bar{u}})$ is an opening of c_u and $(\langle \bar{u}, y \rangle, r_{\bar{v}})$ is an opening of c_v, and the two openings satisfy the claimed relationship that the value committed by c_v is the inner product of the vector committed by c_u with y.

To establish honest-verifier perfect zero-knowledge, consider the following simulator. To generate an accepting transcript $((c_d, c_{\langle d,y \rangle}),$ $e, (u', r_{u'}, r_{v'}))$, the simulator proceeds as follows. First, it selects the verifier's challenge e at random from $\{0, \ldots, p - 1\}$, and then picks a vector u' at random from $\{0, 1, \ldots, p - 1\}^n$ and $r_{u'}, r_{v'}$ at random from

$\{0, 1, \ldots, p-1\}$. Finally, it chooses c_d and $c_{\langle d,y \rangle}$ to be the unique values that yield an accepting transcript, i.e., c_d is set to $c_u^{-e} \cdot h^{r_{u'}} \cdot \prod_{i=1}^n g_i^{u'_i}$ and $c_{\langle d,y \rangle}$ is set to $c_v^{-e} \cdot h^{r_{v'}} \cdot g^{\langle u',y \rangle}$. These choices of c_d and c_v are specifically chosen to ensure that the generated transcript is an accepting one. One can show that the distribution over accepting transcripts generated by this simulator is equal to the distribution generated by the honest verifier interacting with the honest prover by establishing a one-to-one correspondence between transcripts that the simulator outputs with transcripts generated by the honest verifier interacting with the honest prover (details omitted for brevity).

Costs. The commitment consists of a single group element. The computational cost of computing the commitment is performing n group exponentiations. Naively performing each exponentiation independently using repeated squaring requires $O(\log |\mathbb{G}|)$ group multiplications per exponentiation, which implies $\Theta(n \log |\mathbb{G}|)$ group multiplications in total. However, Pippenger's multi-exponentiation algorithm [209] can reduce this quantity by a factor of $(\log(n) + \log\log |\mathbb{G}|)$.[5]

In the evaluation phase, the proof consists of $n + 2$ numbers in $\{0, \ldots, p-1\}$ that can be computed with $O(n)$ field operations in $\mathbb{F}_p$ in total. The verification procedure requires the verifier to perform $O(n)$ group exponentiations, which can be performed using Pippenger's algorithm in the time bound described in the previous paragraph.

14.3 Trading Off Commitment Size and Verification Costs

Recall that the polynomial commitment scheme of the previous section had very small commitments (1 group element), but large proofs-of-evaluation ($\Theta(n)$ group elements).

In this section, we show how to exploit tensor-structure in the vector y (captured in Equation (14.1)) to reduce the size of the proof in the evaluation phase of the polynomial commitment scheme of the previous section, at the cost of increasing the commitment size. For example,

---

[5]A *multi-exponentiation* in a multiplicative group is a product of powers of elements of the group.

we can set both the commitment size and the evaluation proof size to $\Theta(\sqrt{n})$ group elements. This technique was presented in the context of multilinear polynomials in a system called Hyrax [244], building directly on a univariate polynomial commitment scheme given in [66].

Commitment Phase. Recall that u denotes the coefficient vector of the polynomial q to which the committer wishes to commit, and as per Equation (14.1), we view u as an $m \times m$ matrix. Letting $u_j \in \mathbb{F}^m$ denote the jth column of u, the committer picks random numbers $r_1, \ldots, r_m \in \{0, \ldots, p-1\}$ and sends a set of vector commitments $c_1 = \mathsf{Com}(u_1, r_1), \ldots, c_m = \mathsf{Com}(u_m, r_m)$, one for each column. Here,

$$\mathsf{Com}(u_j, r_j) = h^{r_j} \cdot \prod_{k=1}^{m} g_k^{u_{j,k}}$$

for public parameters $g_1, \ldots, g_m \in \mathbb{G}$. Hence, compared to the previous section, we have increased the size of the commitment for u from 1 group element to m group elements. Rather than applying the vector-commitment scheme of the previous section to one vector of length m^2, we applied it m times, to vectors of length m.

Evaluation Phase. When the verifier asks the committer to provide a commitment to $q(z)$ for a verifier-selected input z, the prover sends a commitment c^* to $q(z) = \langle u, y \rangle = b^T \cdot u \cdot a$, where the m-dimensional vectors b and a are as in Equation (14.1) and are known to both the prover and verifier. Using the additive homomorphism of the commitment scheme, the verifier can on its own compute a commitment to the vector $u \cdot a$, namely $\prod_{j=1}^{m} \mathsf{Com}(u_j)^{a_j}$. At this point, the prover needs to prove that c^* is a commitment to $b^T \cdot (u \cdot a) = \langle b, u \cdot a \rangle$. Since the verifier has derived a commitment to the vector $u \cdot a$, this is exactly an instance of the problem that the protocol of the previous section was designed to solve, using a proof of size m.[6]

---

[6]A subtlety of this polynomial commitment scheme's security guarantee is that the protocol establishes only that the prover knows a z-dependent linear combination of the column commitments, where z is the evaluation point. This means that if the committer can choose z, the committer may be able to pass the evaluation phase

In summary, we have given a (public-coin) commitment scheme for univariate and multilinear polynomials in which the commitment size proof length in the evaluation phase, and total verifier time are equal to the square root of the number of coefficients of the polynomial.

14.4 Bulletproofs

In this section, we give a scheme in which the commitment size is constant and the proof length in the evaluation phase is *logarithmic* in the number of coefficients of the polynomial. However, the verifier's runtime to process the proof is *linear* in the number of coefficients. Compared to the commitment scheme of Section 14.2, this is a strict improvement because the proof length in the evaluation phase is logarithmic as opposed to linear in the length of the coefficient vector. Compared to the scheme of Section 14.3, the verifier's runtime is worse (linear rather than proportional to the square root of the number of coefficients), but the communication cost is much better (logarithmic as opposed to square root).

The scheme of this section is a variant of a system called Bulletproofs [80], which itself directly builds on a univariate polynomial commitment scheme given in [66]. Our presentation draws substantially on a perspective developed in [64].

14.4.1 Warm-up: Proof of Knowledge for Opening of Vector Commitment

Before presenting the polynomial commitment in full, we start with a warmup that illustrates the key ideas of the full Bulletproofs polynomial commitment scheme. Specifically, the warmup is a protocol enabling the prover to establish that it knows how to open a generalized Pedersen commitment to a vector $u \in \mathbb{F}_p^n$.

---

without knowing how to open every column commitment [179]. This weakened guarantee is nonetheless sufficient for the scheme's use in succinct interactive arguments and SNARKs derived thereof, where z is chosen at random by the SNARK verifier or via the Fiat-Shamir transformation.

Notational Changes for this Section. Recall that a generalized Pedersen commitment to u is $\mathsf{Com}(u; r_u) := h^{r_u} \cdot \prod_{i=1}^{n} g_i^{u_i}$ where r_u is chosen at random by the committer, and the g_i's are public generators in $\mathbb{G}$. To further simplify the presentation, let us omit the blinding factor h^{r_u} from the vector commitment, so that we now define $\mathsf{Com}(u) := \prod_{i=1}^{n} g_i^{u_i}$ (the resulting commitment scheme without the blinding factor is still computationally binding, but it is not perfectly hiding, see Footnote 14 in Section 12.3).

For the remainder of this section, we write $\mathbb{G}$ as an additive rather than multiplicative group. This is because, by doing so, we can think of $\mathsf{Com}(u) = \sum_{i=1}^{n} u_i \cdot g_i$ as the inner product between u and the vector $\mathbf{g} = (g_1, \ldots, g_n)$ of public group generators, and hence we denote $\sum_{i=1}^{n} u_i \cdot g_i$ as $\langle u, \mathbf{g} \rangle$.[7] Under this notation, the prover is claiming to know a vector u such that

$$\langle u, \mathbf{g} \rangle = c_u. \tag{14.9}$$

Overview of the Protocol. The protocol is vaguely reminiscent of the IOP-based polynomial commitment scheme FRI (Section 10.4.4), in the following sense. At the start of the protocol, the prover has sent a commitment c_u to a vector u of length n. The protocol proceeds in $\log_2 n$ rounds, where in each round i the verifier sends the prover a random field $\alpha_i \in \mathbb{F}_p$, and α_i is used to "halve the length of the committed vector". After $\log_2 n$ rounds, the prover is left with a claim that it knows a vector u of length 1 satisfy a certain inner product relationship. In this case, u is so short that the prover can succinctly prove the claim by simply sending u to the verifier.

In more detail, at the start of each round $i = 1, 2, \ldots, \log_2 n$, the prover has sent a commitment $c_{u^{(i)}}$ to some vector $u^{(i)}$ of length $n \cdot 2^{-(i-1)}$, and the prover must establish that it knows a vector $u^{(i)}$ such that $\langle u^{(i)}, \mathbf{g}^{(i)} \rangle = c_{u^{(i)}}$ (when $i = 1$, $u^{(i)} = u$ and $\mathbf{g}^{(i)} = \mathbf{g}$). The goal of round i is to reduce the claim that $\langle u^{(i)}, \mathbf{g}^{(i)} \rangle = c_{u^{(i)}}$ to a claim of the

---

[7]Strictly speaking, referring to $\sum_{i=1}^{n} u_i g_i$ as an inner product is a misnomer because the u_i's are integers in $\{0, 1, \ldots, p - 1\}$ while the g_i's are elements of the group $\mathbb{G}$ of size p, but we ignore this and write $\mathsf{Com}(u) = \langle u, \mathbf{g} \rangle$ for the remainder of this section.

same form, namely that the prover knows a vector $\langle u^{(i+1)}, \mathbf{g}^{(i+1)} \rangle = c_{u^{(i+1)}}$ for some vector of group generators $\mathbf{g}^{(i+1)}$ that is known to the verifier, but where $u^{(i+1)}$ and $\mathbf{g}^{(i+1)}$ each have half the length of $u^{(i)}$ and $\mathbf{g}^{(i)}$. For notational brevity let us fix a round i and accordingly drop the superscript (i), simply writing u, $\mathbf{g}$, and c_u.

A First Attempt that Does Not Work. The idea of the protocol is to break u and $\mathbf{g}$ into two halves, writing $u = u_L \circ u_R$ and $\mathbf{g} = \mathbf{g}_L \circ \mathbf{g}_R$, where $\circ$ denotes concatenation. Then

$$\langle u, \mathbf{g} \rangle = \langle u_L, \mathbf{g}_L \rangle + \langle u_R, \mathbf{g}_R \rangle. \tag{14.10}$$

Suppose the verifier chooses a random $\alpha \in \mathbb{F}_p$ and define

$$u' = \alpha u_L + \alpha^{-1} u_R \tag{14.11}$$

and

$$\mathbf{g}' = \alpha^{-1} \mathbf{g}_L + \alpha \mathbf{g}_R. \tag{14.12}$$

Note that the verifier $\mathcal{V}$ can compute $\mathbf{g}'$ on its own since it knows $\mathbf{g}_L$ and $\mathbf{g}_R$ (but just as $\mathcal{V}$ does not know u, $\mathcal{V}$ also does not know u'). One might hope that for any choice of $\alpha \in \mathbb{F}_p$,

$$\langle u', \mathbf{g}' \rangle = \langle u, \mathbf{g} \rangle, \tag{14.13}$$

and moreover that the only way an efficient party can compute a u' satisfying Equation (14.13) is to know a u satisfying Equation (14.9) and then set $u' = \alpha u_L + \alpha^{-1} u_R$ as per Equation (14.11). If this were the case, then the prover's original claim, to know a u such that $\langle u, \mathbf{g} \rangle = c_u$, would be *equivalent* to the claim of knowing a u' such that $\langle u', \mathbf{g}' \rangle = c_u$. This would mean that the verifier would have (with no help whatsoever from the prover) successfully reduced the prover's original claim about knowing u to an equivalent claim of the same form, but about vectors of half the length.

The Actual Equality. Unfortunately, Equation (14.13) does not hold. But the following modification does, for any $\alpha \in \mathbb{F}_p$:

$$\langle u', \mathbf{g}' \rangle = \langle \alpha u_L + \alpha^{-1} u_R, \alpha^{-1} \mathbf{g}_L + \alpha \mathbf{g}_R \rangle$$
$$= \langle \alpha u_L, \alpha^{-1} \mathbf{g}_L \rangle + \langle \alpha^{-1} u_R, \alpha \mathbf{g}_R \rangle + \langle \alpha u_L, \alpha \mathbf{g}_R \rangle$$
$$+ \langle \alpha^{-1} u_R, \alpha^{-1} \mathbf{g}_L \rangle$$
$$= (\langle u_L, \mathbf{g}_L \rangle + \langle u_R, \mathbf{g}_R \rangle) + \alpha^2 \langle u_L, \mathbf{g}_R \rangle + \alpha^{-2} \langle u_R, \mathbf{g}_L \rangle$$
$$= \langle u, \mathbf{g} \rangle + \alpha^2 \langle u_L, \mathbf{g}_R \rangle + \alpha^{-2} \langle u_R, \mathbf{g}_L \rangle. \tag{14.14}$$

Here, the first equality uses the definitions of u' and $\mathbf{g}'$ (Equations (14.11) and (14.12)) and the final equality uses Equation (14.10). Relative to the hoped-for Equation (14.13) (which does not actually hold), Expression (14.14) involves "cross terms" $\alpha^2 \langle u_L, \mathbf{g}_R \rangle + \alpha^{-2} \langle u_R, \mathbf{g}_L \rangle$. The verifier $\mathcal{V}$ does not know these cross-terms, since they depend on the vectors u_L and u_R that are unknown to $\mathcal{V}$. In the actual protocol, $\mathcal{P}$ will simply send values v_L and v_R to $\mathcal{V}$ claimed to equal $\langle u_L, \mathbf{g}_R \rangle$ and $\langle u_R, \mathbf{g}_L \rangle$ *before learning the random value α chosen by the verifier.* If v_L and v_R are as claimed, then this allows $\mathcal{V}$ to compute the right hand side of Equation (14.14) (let's call it $c_{u'}$), and the prover can, in the next round, turn to proving knowledge of a u' such that $\langle u', \mathbf{g}' \rangle$ equals $c_{u'}$.

Self-Contained Protocol Description.   Recall that at the start of the round, the prover has already sent a value c_u claimed to equal $\langle u, \mathbf{g} \rangle$. If u and $\mathbf{g}$ both have length 1, then establishing that the prover knows a u such that $\langle u, \mathbf{g} \rangle = c_u$ is equivalent to establishing knowledge of a discrete logarithm of c_u to base $\mathbf{g}$, which the prover can achieve by simply sending u to $\mathcal{V}$.[8] Otherwise, the protocol proceeds of follows: The prover starts by sending values v_L, v_R claimed to equal the cross terms $\langle u_L, \mathbf{g}_R \rangle$ and $\langle u_R, \mathbf{g}_L \rangle$. At that point the verifier chooses $\alpha \in \mathbb{F}_p$ at random and sends it to the prover.

Let $c_{u'} = c_u + \alpha^2 v_L + \alpha^{-2} v_R$. This value is specifically defined so that if v_L and v_R are as claimed, then $\langle u', \mathbf{g}' \rangle = c_{u'}$. Furthermore, the verifier can compute $\mathbf{g}'$ and $c_{u'}$ given c_u, α, v_L, and v_R. Accordingly, the

---

[8]For simplicity, we do not concern ourselves during this warmup with designing a zero-knowledge protocol; if we did want to achieve zero-knowledge, we would use Schnorr's protocol (Section 12.2.2) for the prover to establish knowledge of the discrete logarithm of c_u. See Section 14.4.2 for details.

next round of the protocol is then meant to establish that the prover
indeed knows a vector u' such that

$$\langle u', \mathbf{g}' \rangle = c_{u'}. \tag{14.15}$$

This is exactly the type of claim that the protocol was meant to establish,
but on vectors of length $n/2$ rather than n, so the protocol verifies this
claim recursively. See Protocol 12 for pseudocode.

Protocol 12 A public-coin zero-knowledge argument of knowledge of
an opening for a generalized Pedersen commitment c_u to a vector u of
length n. The protocol consists of $\log_2 n$ rounds and 2 group elements
communicated from prover to verifier per round, and satisfies knowledge-
soundness assuming hardness of the discrete logarithm problem. For
simplicity, we omit the blinding factor from the Pedersen commitment
to u and treat the group $\mathbb{G}$ over which the commitments are defined as
an additive group.

1: Let $\mathbb{G}$ be an *additive* cyclic group of prime order p over which
   the Discrete Logarithm relation is hard, with vector of generators
   $\mathbf{g} = (g_1, \ldots, g_n)$.
2: Input is $c_u = \mathsf{Com}(u) := \sum_{i=1}^{n} u_i g_i$. Prover knows u, Verifier only
   knows $c_u, g_1, \ldots, g_n$.
3: If $n = 1$, Prover sends u to the verifier and the verifier checks that
   $ug_1 = c_u$.
4: Otherwise, write $u = u_L \circ u_R$ and $\mathbf{g} = \mathbf{g}_L \circ \mathbf{g}_R$. Prover sends v_L, v_R
   claimed to equal $\langle u_L, g_R \rangle$ and $\langle u_R, g_L \rangle$.
5: Verifier responds with a randomly chosen $\alpha \in \mathbb{F}_p$.
6: Recurse on commitment $c_{u'} := c_u + \alpha^2 v_L + \alpha^{-2} v_R$ to vector $u' = \alpha u_L + \alpha^{-1} u_R$ of length $n/2$, using the vector of group generators
   $\mathbf{g}' := \alpha^{-1} \mathbf{g}_L + \alpha \mathbf{g}_R$.

Costs. It is easy to see that u' and $\mathbf{g}'$ have half the length of u and
$\mathbf{g}$, and hence the protocol terminates after $\log_2 n$ rounds, with only
two group elements sent by the prover to the verifier in each round.
Both the prover and verifier's runtimes are dominated by the time
required to update the generator vector in each round. Specifically, to

compute $\mathbf{g}'$ from $\mathbf{g}$ in each round, the verifier performs a number of group exponentiations proportional to the length of $\mathbf{g}$, which means the total number of group exponentiations is $O(n + n/2 + n/4 + \cdots + 1) = O(n)$.[9] Hence's the prover and verifier's runtime over the entire protocol is proportional to the time required to perform $O(n)$ group exponentiations.[10]

Completeness and Intuition for Knowledge-Soundness. The protocol is clearly complete, i.e., if the prover is honest (meaning that c_u indeed equals $\langle u, \mathbf{g} \rangle$ and v_L and v_R are as claimed), then indeed Equation (14.15) holds.

To explain the intuition for why knowledge-soundness holds, let us assume for the moment that the prover *does* know a vector u such that $c_u = \langle u, \mathbf{g} \rangle$, but the prover sends values v_L and v_R that are *not* equal to $\langle u_L, \mathbf{g}_R \rangle$ and $\langle u_R, \mathbf{g}_L \rangle$. Then, as we explain in the following paragraph, with high probability over the choice of α, Equation (14.15) will fail to hold. In this event, it is not clear how the prover will find a vector whose inner product with $\mathbf{g}'$ equals $c_{u'}$.

That Equation (14.15) fails to hold with high probability over the choice of α follows by the following reasoning. Let Q be the degree-4 polynomial

$$Q(\alpha) = \alpha^2 c_{u'} = \alpha^2 c_u + \alpha^4 v_L + v_R$$

and

$$P(\alpha) = \alpha^2 \cdot \langle u', \mathbf{g}' \rangle = \alpha^2 c_u + \alpha^4 \langle u_L, \mathbf{g}_R \rangle + \langle u_R, \mathbf{g}_L \rangle.$$

If v_L and v_R are not equal to $\langle u_L, \mathbf{g}_R \rangle$ and $\langle u_R, \mathbf{g}_L \rangle$, then Q and P are not the same polynomial. Since they both have degree at most 4, with probability at least $1 - 4/p$ over the random choice of α, $Q(\alpha) \neq P(\alpha)$.

---

[9] The terminology "group exponentiation" here, while standard, may be confusing because in this section we are referring to $\mathbb{G}$ as an additive group, while the terminology refers to a multiplicative group. In the additive group notation of this section, we are referring to taking a group element and multiplying it by α or α^{-1}. The same operation in multiplicative group notation would be denoted by raising the group element to the power α or α^{-1}, hence our use of the term group exponentiation.

[10] Actually, it is possible to optimize the verifier's computation in Bulletproofs to perform one multi-exponentiation of length $O(n)$ rather than $O(n)$ independent group exponentiations, enabling a speedup due to Pippenger's algorithm (Section 14.2) of roughly a factor of $O(\log n)$ group operations.

In this event, $c_{u'} \neq \langle u', \mathbf{g}' \rangle$, and hence the prover is left to prove a false claim in the next round.

The above line of reasoning suggests that a prover who knows an opening u of c_u should not be able to convince the verifier to accept with non-negligible probability if the prover does not behave as prescribed in each round (i.e., if sending commitments to values v_L and v_R not equal to $\langle u_L, \mathbf{g}_R \rangle$ and $\langle u_R, \mathbf{g}_L \rangle$). And if the prover does *not* know a u such that $\langle u, \mathbf{g} \rangle$, then, intuitively, the prover should be even worse off than knowing such a u but attempting to deviate from the prescribed protocol.

However, to formally establish knowledge-soundness, we must show that given any prover $\mathcal{P}$ that convinces the verifier to accept with non-negligible probability, there is an efficient algorithm to extract an opening u of c_u from $\mathcal{P}$. This requires a more involved analysis.

Proof of Knowledge-Soundness. Recall that in Section 12.2.3, we established the knowledge-soundness of any Σ-protocol via a two-step analysis. First, we showed that from any convincing prover for the Σ-protocol, one can efficiently extract a pair of accepting transcripts (a, e, z) and (a, e', z') that share the same first message a, but for which the verifier's challenges e and e' differ. Second, by special soundness of any Σ-protocol, there is an efficient procedure to extract a witness from any such pair of transcripts.

The first step of this analysis is called a *forking lemma*. This name comes from the procedure to obtain the pair of transcripts: one runs the prover once to (hopefully) produce an accepting transcript (a, e, z), then rewinds the prover to immediately after it sent its first message a, and "restarts it" with a different verifier challenge e'. This (hopefully) yields a second accepting transcript (a, e', z). One thinks of this as "forking" the protocol into two different executions after the prover's first message a is sent.

The analysis establishing knowledge-soundness of Protocol 12 follows a similar two-step paradigm. In the first step, a generalized forking lemma is proved for multi-round protocols such as Protocol 12. The lemma shows that given any convincing prover for the protocol, one can extract a collection of accepting transcripts whose messages overlap in a manner analogous to how (a, e, z) and (a, e', z) above share the same first message, a. In the second step, an efficient procedure is given to extract a witness from any such tree of transcripts.

Step 1: A Forking Lemma for Multi-Round Protocols. First, we argue that there is a polynomial-time extraction algorithm $\mathcal{E}$ that, given any prover $\mathcal{P}$ for Protocol 12 that convinces the verifier to accept with non-negligible probability, constructs a 3-transcript-tree $\mathcal{T}$ for the protocol with non-negligible probability. Here, a 3-transcript tree is a collection of $|\mathcal{T}| = 3^{\log_2 n} \leq n^{1.585}$ accepting transcripts for the protocol, with the following relationship between the prover messages and verifier challenges in each transcript.

The transcripts correspond to the leaves of a complete tree where each non-leaf node has 3 children. The depth of the tree equals the number of verifier challenges sent in Protocol 12, which is $\log_2 n$. Each edge of the tree is labeled by a verifier challenge, and each non-leaf node is associated with a prover message (v_L, v_R). That is, if an edge of the tree connects a node at distance i from the root to a node at distance $i + 1$, then the edge is labelled by a value for the ith message that the verifier sends to the prover in Protocol 12. It is required that (a) no two edges of the tree are assigned the same label and (b) for each transcript at a leaf of the tree, the verifier's challenges in that transcript are given by the labels assigned to the edges of the root-to-leaf path for that leaf, and the prover's messages in the transcript are given by the prover responses associated with the nodes along the path.[11]

The idea is to generate the first leaf of the tree by running the prover and verifier once to (hopefully) generate an accepting transcript. Then generate that leaf's sibling by rewinding the prover until just before the verifier sends its last challenge, and restart the protocol with a fresh random value for the verifier's final challenge. Then to generate the next leaf, rewind the prover again until just before the verifier sends its second to last challenge, and restart the protocol from that point with a fresh random value for the verifier's second to last challenge.

---

[11]For comparison, recall that special soundness of Σ-protocols refers to a pair of accepting transcript (a, e, z) and (a, e', z) with $e \neq e'$. Such a pair of transcripts forms a "2-transcript tree" for a protocol consisting of a single verifier challenge.

And so on. Some complications arise to account for the possibility that the prover sometimes fails to convince the verifier to accept, and the (unlikely) possibility that this process leads to two edges labeled with the same value.

We provide a formal statement and proof of this result below; our presentation follows [66, Lemma 1].

Theorem 14.1. There is a probabilistic extractor algorithm $\mathcal{E}$ satisfying the following property. Given the ability to repeatedly run and rewind a prover $\mathcal{P}$ for Protocol 12 that causes the verifier to accept with probability at least ε for some non-negligible quantity ε, $\mathcal{E}$ runs in expected time at most $\text{poly}(n)$, and $\mathcal{E}$ outputs a 3-transcript tree $\mathcal{T}$ for Protocol 12 with probability at least $\varepsilon/2$.

Proof. $\mathcal{E}$ is a recursive procedure that constructs $\mathcal{T}$ in depth-first fashion. Specifically, $\mathcal{E}$ takes as input the identity of a node j in $\mathcal{T}$, as well as the verifier challenges associated with the edges along the path in $\mathcal{T}$ connecting j to the root, and the prover messages associated with the nodes along that path. $\mathcal{E}$ then (attempts to) produce the subtree of $\mathcal{T}$ rooted at j. (In the very first call to $\mathcal{E}$, j is the root node of $\mathcal{T}$, so in this case there are no edges or nodes along the path of the j to the root, i.e., itself).

If j is a leaf node, the input to $\mathcal{E}$ specifies a complete transcript for Protocol 12, so $\mathcal{E}$ simply outputs the transcript if it is an accepting transcript, and otherwise it outputs "fail".

If j is not a leaf node of $\mathcal{T}$, then the input to $\mathcal{E}$ specifies a partial transcript for Protocol 12 (if j has distance ℓ from the root, then the partial transcript specifies the prover messages and verifier challenges from the first ℓ rounds of Protocol 12). The first thing $\mathcal{E}$ does is associate a prover message with j by "running" $\mathcal{P}$ on the partial transcript to see how $\mathcal{P}$ would respond to the most recent verifier challenge in this partial transcript.

Second, $\mathcal{E}$ attempts to construct the subtree rooted at the left-most subchild of j, which we denote by j'. Specifically, $\mathcal{E}$ chooses a random verifier challenge to assign the edge (j, j') of $\mathcal{T}$, and then calls itself recursively on j'. If $\mathcal{E}$'s recursive call on j' returns "fail" (i.e., it fails to generate the subtree of $\mathcal{T}$ rooted at j'), then $\mathcal{E}$ halts and outputs "fail".

Otherwise, $\mathcal{E}$ proceeds to generate the subtrees of the remaining two children j'' and j''' of j by assigning fresh random verifier challenges to the edges connecting j to those nodes and calling itself recursively on j'' and j''' until it successfully generates these two subtrees (this may require many repetitions of the recursive calls, as $\mathcal{E}$ will simply keep calling itself on j'' and j''' until it finally succeeds in generating these two subtrees).

Expected Running Time of $\mathcal{E}$. Recall that when $\mathcal{E}$ is called on a non-leaf node j, it recursively calls itself once on the first child j' of j in an attempt to construct the subtree rooted at j', and then continues to construct the subtrees rooted at its other two children only if the recursive call on j' succeeds. Let ε' denote this probability. Then the expected number of recursive calls is $1 + \varepsilon' \cdot 2/\varepsilon' = 3$. Here, the first term, 1, comes from the first recursive call, on j'. The first factor of ε' in the second term denotes the probability that $\mathcal{E}$ does not halt after the first recursive call. Finally, the factor $2/\varepsilon'$ captures the expected number of times $\mathcal{E}$ must be called on j'' and j''' before it succeeds in constructing the subtree rooted at these nodes (as $1/\varepsilon'$ is the expected value of a geometric random variable with success probability ε'). Meanwhile, when $\mathcal{E}$ is called on a leaf node, it simply checks whether or not the associated transcript is an accepting transcript, which requires $\mathrm{poly}(n)$ time. We conclude that the total runtime of $\mathcal{E}$ is proportional to the number of leaves (which is $3^{\log_2 n} \le O(n^{1.585})$), times the runtime of the verifier in Protocol 12, which is clearly $\mathrm{poly}(n)$.

Success Probability of $\mathcal{E}$. The initial call to $\mathcal{E}$ on the root of $\mathcal{T}$ returns "fail" if and only if the very first recursive call made by *every* invocation of $\mathcal{E}$ in the call stack returns "fail". That is, $\mathcal{E}$ succeeds in outputting a tree of accepting transcripts when called on the root whenever its recursive call on the first child j of the root succeeds, which itself succeeds whenever its recursive call on the first child of j succeeds, and so forth. This probability is exactly the probability $\mathcal{P}$ succeeds in convincing the verifier to accept, namely ϵ.

We still need to argue that the probability that conditioned on $\mathcal{E}$ successfully outputting a tree, the probability that $\mathcal{E}$ assigns any two edges in the graph the same challenge by $\mathcal{E}$ is negligible. To argue this, let us assume that $\mathcal{E}$ never runs for more than T time steps, for $T = p^{1/3}$. Here, p denotes the order of $\mathbb{G}$, and hence the size of the verifier's challenge space. We can ensure this by having $\mathcal{E}$ halt and output "fail" if it surpasses T time steps—by Markov's inequality, since $\mathcal{E}$ runs in expected time $\text{poly}(n)$, the probability $\mathcal{E}$ exceeds T timesteps is at most $\text{poly}(n)/T$, which is negligible assuming p is superpolynomially large in n. Hence, after ensuring this assumption holds, the probability $\mathcal{E}$ succeeds in outputting a tree of accepting transcripts is still at most ε minus a negligible quantity. If $\mathcal{E}$ never runs for more than T timesteps, then it only can only generate at most T random challenges of the verifier over the course of its execution. The probability of a collision amongst these at most T challenges is bounded above by $T^2/p \leq 1/p^{1/3}$, which is negligible. We conclude as desired that the probability $\mathcal{E}$ output a 3-transcript tree is at least ε minus a negligible quantity, which is at least $\varepsilon/2$ if ε is non-negligible. $\qquad\square$

Step 2: Extracting a Witness from Any 3-Transcript Tree. Second, we must give a polynomial time algorithm that takes as input a 3-transcript tree for Protocol 12 and outputs a vector u such that $c_u = \sum_{i=1}^{n} u_i g_i$. The idea for how this is done is to iteratively compute a label u for each node in the tree, starting with the leaves and working layer-by-layer towards the root. For each node in the tree, the procedure will essentially reconstruct the vector u that the prover must have "had in its head" at that stage of the protocol's execution. That is, each node in the tree is associated with a vector of generators $\mathbf{g}'$ and a commitment c, and the extractor will identify a vector u' such that $\langle u', \mathbf{g}' \rangle = c$.

Associating a Generator Vector and Commitment with Each Node in the Tree. For any node in the tree, we may associate with that node a generator vector and commitment in the natural way. That is, Protocol 12 is recursive, and each node in the tree at distance i from the root corresponds to a call to Protocol 12 at depth i of the call stack. As per Line 2, the verifier in each recursive call to Protocol 12 is aware of a generator vector and a commitment c (supposedly a commitment to some vector known to the prover, using the generator vector).

For example, the root of the tree is associated with $\mathbf{g} = \mathbf{g}_L \circ \mathbf{g}_R$ and commitment $c = c_u$ that is input to the original call to Protocol 12. If the root is associated with prover message (v_L, v_R), then a child connected to the root by an edge of label α is associated with vector $\mathbf{g}' = \alpha^{-1}\mathbf{g}_L + \alpha\mathbf{g}_R$ and commitment $c' = c_u + \alpha^2 v_L + \alpha^{-2} v_R$, where v_L and v_R denote the prover messages associated with the edge. And so on down the tree.

Assigning a Label to Each Node of the Tree, Starting with the Leaves and Working Toward the Root.

Given a 3-transcript tree, begin by labelling each leaf with the prover's final message in the protocol. Because every leaf transcript is accepting, if a leaf is assigned label u, generator g, and commitment c, then we know that $g^u = c$.

Now assume by way of induction that, for each node at distance at most $\ell \geq 0$ from the leaves, if the node is associated with generator vector $\mathbf{g}$ and commitment c, the label-assigning procedure has successfully assigned a label vector u to the node such that $\langle u, \mathbf{g} \rangle = c$. We explain how to extend the procedure to assign such labels to nodes at distance $\ell + 1$ from the leaves.

To this end, consider such a node j and let the associated generator vector be $\mathbf{g} = \mathbf{g}_L \circ \mathbf{g}_R$ and associated commitment be c. For $i = 1, 2, 3$, let $\mathbf{g}_i$ and c_i denote the generator vector and commitment associated with j's ith child, u_i denote the label that has already been assigned to the ith child, and α_i denote the verifier challenge associated with the edge connecting j to its ith child. By construction of the generators and commitment associated with each node in the tree, for each i, the following two equations hold, relating the generators and commitment for node j to those of its children:

$$\mathbf{g}_i = \alpha_i^{-1}\mathbf{g}_L + \alpha_i\mathbf{g}_R \tag{14.16}$$

and

$$c_i = c + \alpha_i^2 v_L + \alpha_i^{-2} v_R. \tag{14.17}$$

Moreover, by the inductive hypothesis, the label-assigning algorithm has ensured that

$$\langle u_i, \mathbf{g}_i \rangle = c_i. \tag{14.18}$$

At an intuitive level, Equation (14.18) identifies a vector u_i "explaining" the commitment c_i of child i in terms of the generator vector $\mathbf{g}_i$, while Equations (14.16) and (14.17) relate c_i and $\mathbf{g}_i$ to c and $\mathbf{g}$. We would like to put all of this information together to identify a vector u "explaining" c in terms of $\mathbf{g}$.

To this end, combining Equations (14.16)–(14.18), we conclude that

$$\langle u_i, \alpha_i^{-1}\mathbf{g}_L + \alpha_i\mathbf{g}_R\rangle = c + \alpha_i^2 v_L + \alpha_i^{-2}v_R,$$

and by applying the distributive law to the left hand side, we finally conclude that:

$$\langle \alpha_i^{-1}u_i, \mathbf{g}_L\rangle + \langle \alpha_i u_i, \mathbf{g}_R\rangle = c + \alpha_i^2 v_L + \alpha_i^{-2}v_R. \tag{14.19}$$

Equation (14.19) "almost" achieves our goal of identify a vector u such that $\langle u, \mathbf{g}\rangle = c$, in the sense that if the "cross terms" $\alpha_i^2 v_L + \alpha_i^{-2}v_R$ did not appear in Equation (14.19) for, say, $i = 1$, then the vector $u = \alpha_1^{-1}u_1 \circ \alpha_1 u_1$ would satisfy $\langle u, \mathbf{g}\rangle = c$. The point of deriving Equation (14.19) not only for $i = 1$, but also for $i = 2$ and $i = 3$ is that we can use the latter two equations to "cancel out the cross terms" from the right hand side of the equation for $i = 1$. Specifically, there exists some coefficients $\beta_1, \beta_2, \beta_3 \in \mathbb{F}_p$ such that

$$\sum_{i=1}^{3} \beta_i \cdot \left(c + \alpha_i^2 v_L + \alpha_i^{-2}v_R\right) = c. \tag{14.20}$$

This follows from the fact that the following matrix is full rank, and hence has the vector $(1, 0, 0)$ in its row-span:

$$A = \begin{bmatrix} 1 & \alpha_1^2 & \alpha_1^{-2} \\ 1 & \alpha_2^2 & \alpha_2^{-2} \\ 1 & \alpha_3^2 & \alpha_3^{-2} \end{bmatrix}. \tag{14.21}$$

One way to see that A is invertible is to directly compute the determinant as $-\frac{(\alpha_1^2-\alpha_2^2)(\alpha_1^2-\alpha_3^2)(\alpha_2^2-\alpha_3^2)}{\alpha_1^2\alpha_2^2\alpha_3^2}$, which is clearly nonzero so long as α_1, α_2, and α_3 are all distinct. Moreover, $(\beta_1, \beta_2, \beta_3)$ can be computed efficiently–in fact, it equals the first row of A^{-1}.

Equation (14.20) combined with Equation (14.19) implies that

$$u = \sum_{i=1}^{3} (\beta_i \cdot \alpha_i^{-1} \cdot u_i) \circ (\beta_i \cdot \alpha_i \cdot u_i) \tag{14.22}$$

satisfies $\langle u, \mathbf{g} \rangle = c$, where $\circ$ denotes concatenation.

In this manner, labels can be assigned to each node in the tree, starting with the leaves and proceeding layer-by-layer towards the root. The label u assigned to the root satisfies $\langle u, \mathbf{g} \rangle = c_u$ as desired.

Example of the knowledge extractor. Although in Protocol 12, $\mathbf{g} \in \mathbb{G}^n$ will be a vector of elements of the elliptic curve group $\mathbb{G}$, and $\langle u, \mathbf{g} \rangle$ will also be a group element, for illustration we give an example of the extraction procedure with group elements replaced by integers.

Suppose that $n = 2$, and the committed vector $u = (u_1, u_2)$ is $(1, 6)$ while the commitment key $\mathbf{g} = (g_1, g_2)$ is $(12, 1)$. Then the commitment c to u is $\langle u, \mathbf{g} \rangle = 1 \cdot 12 + 6 \cdot 1 = 18$. The prescribed prover begins Protocol 12 by sending the cross terms $v_L = 1 \cdot 1 = 1$ and $v_R = 6 \cdot 12 = 72$.

The knowledge extraction procedure is not given the vector u that the prover "had in its head" when producing the commitment c or the cross-terms v_L and v_R. Nonetheless, it needs to identify a vector u such that $\langle u, \mathbf{g} \rangle = 18$. To do so, it first generates a (depth-1) 3-transcript tree for Protocol 12. Suppose the three produced accepting transcripts respectively have verifier challenge $\alpha_1 = 1$, $\alpha_2 = 2$, and $\alpha_3 = 3$. Then the three transcripts (one per leaf of the tree) are respectively associated with the following values:

- For leaf $i = 1$, the verifier computes:

  - $\mathbf{g}' = \alpha_1^{-1} \cdot g_1 + \alpha_1 \cdot g_2 = 1^{-1} \cdot 12 + 1 \cdot 1 = 13$.
  - $c' = c + \alpha_1^2 v_L + \alpha_1^{-2} v_R = 18 + 1 \cdot 1 + 1^{-1} \cdot 72 = 91$.

  Since the leaf captures an accepting transcript, the prover in the final round of the protocol must provide a value u' such that $\langle u', \mathbf{g}' \rangle = 91$, and hence $u' = 91/13 = 7$.

- For leaf $i = 2$, the verifier computes:

    - $\mathbf{g}' = \alpha_2^{-1} \cdot g_1 + \alpha_2 \cdot g_2 = 2^{-1} \cdot 12 + 2 \cdot 1 = 8$.
    - $c' = c + \alpha_2^2 v_L + \alpha_2^{-2} v_R = 18 + 4 \cdot 1 + 4^{-1} \cdot 72 = 40$.

    The prover in the final round of the protocol must provide a value u' such that $\langle u', \mathbf{g}' \rangle = 40$, and hence $u' = 40/8 = 5$.

- For leaf $i = 3$, the verifier computes:

    - $\mathbf{g}' = \alpha_3^{-1} \cdot g_1 + \alpha_3 \cdot g_2 = 3^{-1} \cdot 12 + 3 \cdot 1 = 7$.
    - $c' = c + \alpha_3^2 v_L + \alpha_3^{-2} v_R = 18 + 9 \cdot 1 + 9^{-1} \cdot 72 = 35$.

    The prover in the final round of the protocol must provide a value u' such that $\langle u', \mathbf{g}' \rangle = 35$, and hence $u' = 35/7 = 5$.

For the matrix A defined as per Equation (14.21), the first row of A^{-1} is $(\beta_1, \beta_2, \beta_3)$ where $\beta_1 = -\frac{13}{24}$, $\beta_2 = \frac{8}{3}$, and $\beta_3 = -\frac{9}{8}$. Then given the three values of u' constructed above, the reconstructed vector u from Equation (14.22) has first entry equal to

$$-\frac{13}{24} \cdot 1^{-1} \cdot 7 + \frac{8}{3} \cdot 2^{-1} \cdot 5 - \frac{9}{8} \cdot 3^{-1} \cdot 5 = 1$$

and second entry equal to

$$-\frac{13}{24} \cdot 1 \cdot 7 + \frac{8}{3} \cdot 2 \cdot 5 - \frac{9}{8} \cdot 3 \cdot 5 = 6.$$

Hence, in this example, the extractor successfully reconstructed the vector $u = (1, 6)$ such that $\langle u, \mathbf{g} \rangle = c$.

14.4.2 The Polynomial Commitment Scheme

The preceding section describes a (non-zero-knowledge) argument of knowledge of an opening $u \in \mathbb{F}_p^n$ of a generalized Pedersen commitment c_u, i.e., a u such that $\sum_{i=1}^n u_i \cdot g_i = c_u$. To obtain a (non-zero-knowledge) polynomial commitment scheme, we need to modify this argument of knowledge to establish not only that

$$\sum_{i=1}^{n} u_i \cdot g_i = c_u, \tag{14.23}$$

but also that

$$\sum_{i=1}^{n} u_i \cdot y_i = v \tag{14.24}$$

for some public vector $y \in \mathbb{F}_p^n$ and $v \in \mathbb{F}_p$ (recall from Section 14.2 that u will be the coefficient vector of the committed polynomial, y will be a vector derived from the point at which the verifier requests to evaluate the committed polynomial, and v will be the claimed evaluation of the polynomial).

The idea is that Equations (14.23) and (14.24) are of exactly the same form, namely they both involve computing the inner product of u with another vector (though each g_i is a group element in $\mathbb{G}$, while each y_i is a field element in $\mathbb{F}_p$). So one can simply run two parallel invocations of Protocol 12, using the same verifier challenges in both, but with the second instance replacing the vector of group generators $\mathbf{g}$ with the vector y, and the group element c_u with the field element v. See Figure 13 for a complete description of the protocol.

Sketch of How to Achieve Zero-Knowledge.   To render Protocol 13 zero-knowledge, one can apply commit-and-prove style techniques. This means that in every round, the prover does not send v'_L and v'_R to the verifier in the clear, but rather sends Pedersen commitments to these quantities (if one wants perfect rather than computational zero-knowledge, then a blinding factor h^z for randomly chosen z should be included in the Pedersen commitments as per Protocol 5; likewise, the group elements v_L and v_R sent in each round should be blinded as well). At the very end of the protocol, the prover proves in zero-knowledge that the committed values sent over the course of the $\log_2 n$ rounds of the protocol would have passed the check performed by the verifier in the final round of Protocol 13 (Line 3).[12]

---

[12]Bulletproofs [80] contains an optimization that reduces the number of commitments sent by the prover in each round from 4 to 2, by effectively compressing the

Protocol 13 Extending Protocol 12 to an evaluation-proof for a polynomial commitment scheme, where u is the coefficient vector of the
committed polynomial q, and c_u is the commitment to the polynomial.
If the verifier requests the evaluation $q(z)$, then v denotes the claimed
evaluation and y denotes the vector such that $q(z) = \langle u, y \rangle$. Note that in
applications of polynomial commitment schemes to succinct arguments,
the evaluation point z, and hence y and v, are typically not chosen by
the verifier until after the prover sends the commitment c_u.

1: Let $\mathbb{G}$ be an *additive* cyclic group of prime order p over which
   the Discrete Logarithm relation is hard, with vector of generators
   $\mathbf{g} = (g_1, \ldots, g_n)$. Let $y \in \mathbb{F}_p^n$ be a public vector and public value
   $v \in \mathbb{F}_p$.
2: Input is $c_u = \mathsf{Com}(u) := \sum_{i=1}^n u_i g_i$. Prover knows u, Verifier only
   knows c_u, $\mathbf{g}$, y, and v.
3: If $n = 1$, the prover sends u to the verifier and the verifier checks
   that $u g_1 = c_u$ and that $u y_1 = v$.
4: Otherwise, write $u = u_L \circ u_R$, $\mathbf{g} = \mathbf{g}_L \circ \mathbf{g}_R$, and $y = y_L \circ y_R$. Prover
   sends v_L, v_R claimed to equal $\langle u_L, g_R \rangle$ and $\langle u_R, g_L \rangle$, as well as v'_L, v'_R
   claimed to equal $\langle u_L, y_R \rangle$ and $\langle u_R, y_L \rangle$.
5: Verifier responds with a randomly chosen $\alpha \in \mathbb{F}_p$.
6: Recurse on commitment $c_{u'} := c_u + \alpha^2 v_L + \alpha^{-2} v_R$ to vector $u' = \alpha u_L + \alpha^{-1} u_R$ of length $n/2$, using the vector of group generators
   $\mathbf{g}' := \alpha^{-1} \mathbf{g}_L + \alpha \mathbf{g}_R$, and using public vector $y' := \alpha^{-1} y_L + \alpha y_R$ and
   public value $v' = v + \alpha^2 v'_L + \alpha^{-2} v'_R$.

Non-interactive protocol via Fiat-Shamir. Protocols 12 and 13 are
public coin, and hence can be rendered non-interactive using the Fiat-
Shamir transformation. Despite Bulletproofs being a super-constant
round protocol, recent work has placed tight bounds on the concrete
knowledge-soundness of the resulting non-interactive protocol in the
random oracle model [14], [249] (these analyses apply more generally to
any protocol satisfying a generalization of special-soundness (Section
12.2.1) to multi-round settings, namely that a valid witness can be

---

two commitments v_L and v'_L into a single commitment, and similarly for v_R and v'_R.
This is the primary optimization in Bulletproofs [80] over earlier work [66].

extracted from an appropriate transcript tree). This yields an extractable polynomial commitment scheme in which evaluation proofs are non-interactive.

Dory: Reducing Verifier Time To Logarithmic.   Recall that the Bulletproofs polynomial commitment scheme achieves constant commitment size, and evaluation proofs consisting of $O(\log n)$ group elements, but both the prover and verifier had to perform $\Theta(n)$ exponentiations in the group $\mathbb{G}$. Lee [179] showed how to reduce the verifier's runtime to $O(\log n)$ group exponentiations, following a one-time setup phase costing $O(n)$ group exponentiations. Lee naming the resulting commit scheme Dory.

More precisely, the setup phase in Dory produces a logarithmic-sized "verification key" derived from the length-n public vector of group generators **g** such that any party with the verification key can implement the verifier's checks in only $O(\log n)$ rather than $O(n)$ group exponentiations. One can think of the verification key as a small "summary" of the public vector **g** that suffices to implement the verifier's check in $O(\log n)$ time, in the sense that once the verifier knows the verification key, it can forget the actual generators that the key summarizes.

Note that, unlike the KZG polynomial commitments that we cover in Section 15.2, this pre-processing phase is *not* what is called a *trusted setup*, which refers to a pre-processing phase that produces "toxic waste" (also called a trapdoor) such that any party with the trapdoor can break binding of the polynomial commitment scheme. That is, while the setup phase in Dory produces a structured verification key (meaning the key does not consist of randomly chosen group elements), there is no trapdoor, and anyone willing to invest the computational effort can derive the key. Protocols such as Dory that do not require a trusted setup are often called *transparent*. We defer detailed coverage of Dory to Section 15.4 because it uses pairing-based cryptography, a topic we introduce in Section 15.

Combining Techniques.   The protocol of Section 14.3 that leveraged the polynomial commitment scheme of Section 14.2 as a subroutine can replace the subroutine with any extractable additively-homomorphic vector-commitment scheme supporting inner product queries, including Bulletproofs or Dory. If combined with Bulletproofs, the resulting scheme reduces the public parameter size of Bulletproofs from n to $\Theta(\sqrt{n})$, maintains an evaluation-proof size of $O(\log n)$ group elements, and reduces the number of group exponentiations the verifier has to perform at the end of the protocol from n to $\Theta(\sqrt{n})$. The downside relative to vanilla Bulletproofs is that the size of the commitment increases from one group element to $\Theta(\sqrt{n})$ group elements.

If combined with Dory, the resulting scheme does not asymptotically reduce any costs relative to Dory alone, but does reduce constant factors in the prover's runtime and the runtime of the pre-processing phase [179], [230]. It is actually possible to combine the idea of Section 14.3 with techniques from Dory in a way that keeps the commitment size one group element instead of $O(\sqrt{N})$ group elements, see Section 15.4.5—this combination is what we refer to as Dory in Table 16.1, which summarizes the costs of the transparent polynomial commitments that we have covered.

In Section 16.4, we briefly describe additional polynomial commitment schemes inspired by similar techniques, but based on cryptographic assumptions other than hardness of the discrete logarithm problem.

15

Polynomial Commitments from Pairings

This section explains how to use a cryptographic primitive called pairings (also referred to as bilinear maps) to give polynomial commitment schemes with different cost profiles that those of the previous section. The two major pairing-based schemes that we cover are called KZG commitments and Dory.

KZG commitments are named after Kate *et al.* [164], the authors of the work in which they were introduced. A major benefit of them is that commitments and openings consist of only a constant number of group elements. A downside is that it requires a *structured reference string* (SRS) that is as long as the number of coefficients in the polynomial being committed to. This string must be generated in a specified manner and made available to any party that wishes to commit to a polynomial. The generation procedure produces "toxic waste" (also called a trapdoor) that must be discarded. That is, whatever party generates the reference string knows a piece of information that would let the party break the binding property of the polynomial commitment scheme, and thereby destroy soundness of any argument system that uses the commitment scheme. The generation of such an SRS is also called a *trusted setup*.

As discussed in Section 14.4.2, Dory is transparent. This means that, although there is a pre-processing phase that takes time linear in the number of coefficients of the polynomial to be committed, there is no toxic waste produced. However, Dory's proof size and verification time are logarithmic in the number of coefficients, rather than constant.

15.1   Cryptographic Background

The following background material on pairings builds on Section 12.1, which introduced cryptographic groups and the discrete logarithm problem.

The Decisional Diffie-Helman Assumption.   The Decisional Diffie-Helman (DDH) assumption in a cyclic group $\mathbb{G}$ with generator g states that, given g^a and g^b for a, b chosen uniformly and independently from $|\mathbb{G}|$, the value g^{ab} is computationally indistinguishable from a random group element. Formally, the assumption is that the following two distributions cannot be distinguished, except for negligible advantage over random guessing, by any efficient algorithm:

- (g, g^a, g^b, g^{ab}) where a and b are chosen uniformly at random from $\{0, \ldots, |\mathbb{G}| - 1\}$ and g from $\mathbb{G}$.

- (g, g^a, g^b, g^c) where a, b, and c are chosen uniformly at random from $\{0, \ldots, |\mathbb{G}| - 1\}$ and g from $\mathbb{G}$.

If one could compute discrete logarithms efficiently in $\mathbb{G}$, then one could break the DDH assumption in that group: given as input a triple of group elements (g, g_1, g_2, g_3), one could compute the discrete logarithms a, b, c of g_1, g_2, g_3 in base g, and check whether $c = a \cdot b$, outputting "yes" if so. This algorithm would always output yes under draws from the first distribution above, and output yes with probability just $1/|\mathbb{G}|$ under draws from the second distribution.

Hence, the DDH assumption is a stronger assumption than hardness of the Discrete Logarithm problem. In fact, there are groups in which the DDH assumption is false, yet the discrete logarithm problem is nonetheless believed to be hard.

A close relative of DDH is the *computational Diffie-Helman* (CDH) assumption, which states that given g, g^a, and g^b, no efficient algorithm can compute g^{ab}. CDH is a weaker assumption than DDH in the sense that if one can compute g^{ab} given g, g^a and g^b, then one can also solve the DDH problem of distinguishing (g, g^a, g^b, g^{ab}) from (g, g^a, g^b, g^c) for random $a, b, c \in \mathbb{F}_p$. Given a tuple (g, g^a, g^b, g^c), one simply computes g^{ab} and outputs 1 if and only if $g^c = g^{ab}$.

As we will see, there are groups in which CDH is believed to hold but DDH does not.

Pairing-Friendly Groups and Bilinear Maps. Let $\mathbb{G}$ and $\mathbb{G}_t$ be two cyclic groups of the same order. A map $e\colon \mathbb{G} \times \mathbb{G} \to \mathbb{G}_t$ is said to be bilinear if for all $u, v \in \mathbb{G}$ and $a, b \in \{0, \ldots, |\mathbb{G}| - 1\}$, $e(u^a, v^b) = e(u, v)^{ab}$.[1] If a bilinear map e is also non-degenerate (meaning, it does not map all pairs in $\mathbb{G} \times \mathbb{G}$ to the identity element 1_{G_t}) and e is efficiently computable, then e is called a pairing. This terminology refers to the fact that e associates each pair of elements in $\mathbb{G}$ to an element of $\mathbb{G}_t$.

Note that any two cyclic groups $\mathbb{G}$ and $\mathbb{G}_t$ of the same order are in fact isomorphic, meaning there is a bijective mapping $\pi\colon \mathbb{G} \mapsto \mathbb{G}_t$ that preserves group operations, i.e., $\pi(a \cdot b) = \pi(a) \cdot \pi(b)$ for all $a, b \in \mathbb{G}$. But just because $\mathbb{G}$ and $\mathbb{G}_t$ are isomorphic does not mean they are equivalent from a computational perspective; elements of $\mathbb{G}$ and $\mathbb{G}_t$ and the respective group operations can be represented and computed in very different ways.

Not all cyclic groups $\mathbb{G}$ for which the discrete logarithm problem is believed to be hard are "pairing-friendly", i.e., come with a bilinear map e mapping $\mathbb{G} \times \mathbb{G}$ to $\mathbb{G}_t$. For example, as elaborated upon shortly, the popular Curve25519, which is believed to yield an elliptic curve group in which the discrete logarithm problem is hard, is not pairing-friendly. As a result, group operations of pairing-friendly elliptic curves

---

[1] In general, the domain of a bilinear map typically consists of pairs of elements from two different cyclic groups $\mathbb{G}_1, \mathbb{G}_2$ of the same order as $\mathbb{G}_t$, rather than pairs of elements from the same cyclic group $\mathbb{G}$. In the general case that $\mathbb{G}_1 \neq \mathbb{G}_2$, the pairing is said to be *asymmetric*, while the case that $\mathbb{G}_1 = \mathbb{G}_2$ is called *symmetric*. Asymmetric pairings are much more efficient in practice than symmetric pairings. But for simplicity in this monograph we will primarily consider the symmetric case in which $\mathbb{G}_1 = \mathbb{G}_2$.

tend to be concretely slower than preferred groups that need not be pairing-friendly.

In more detail, in practice, if $\mathbb{G}$ is an elliptic curve group defined over field $\mathbb{F}_p$, then $\mathbb{G}_t$ is typically a multiplicative subgroup of an extension field $\mathbb{F}_{p^k}$ for some positive integer k (recall from Section 2.1.5 that $\mathbb{F}_{p^k}$ denotes the finite field of size p^k). That is, $\mathbb{G}_t$ consists of (a subgroup of) the nonzero elements of $\mathbb{F}_{p^k}$, with the group operation being field multiplication. As the multiplicative subgroup of $\mathbb{F}_{p^k}$ has size $p^k - 1$, and the order $|\mathbb{H}|$ of any subgroup $\mathbb{H}$ of a group $\mathbb{G}'$ divides $|\mathbb{G}'|$, k is chosen to be the smallest integer such that $|\mathbb{G}|$ divides $p^k - 1$; this value of k is called the *embedding degree* of $\mathbb{G}$. To efficiently implement pairings in this manner, $\mathbb{G}$ must have low embedding degree. This is because elements of $\mathbb{F}_{p^k}$ are k times bigger than elements of the field $\mathbb{F}_p$ over which $\mathbb{G}$ is defined, and multiplication within $\mathbb{F}_{p^k}$ is at least k times slower than within $\mathbb{F}_p$. So if k is large, $\mathbb{G}_t$ elements will be much more expensive to write down and operate on than elements of $\mathbb{G}$.[2] There are often ways of reducing this naive representation size of $\mathbb{G}_t$ elements by a constant factor such as 3, with corresponding speed improvements when multiplying two $\mathbb{G}_t$ elements (see, e.g., [196]), but this will not help much if the embedding degree k is enormous.

Unfortunately, popular groups in which the Discrete Logarithm problem is believed intractable, such as Curve25519, have enormous embedding degree. This is why arithmetic in pairing-friendly groups tends to be concretely slower then in non-pairing-friendly groups. At the time a writing, a popular pairing-friendly curve for use in SNARKs is called BLS12-381, which has embedding degree 12 and targets roughly 120 bits of security.[3]

---

[2]Since $\mathbb{G}_t$ is a subgroup of $\mathbb{F}_{p^k}$ of size only p, information-theoretically speaking each element of $\mathbb{G}_t$ can be uniquely represented with only $\log_2 p$ bits. But there will likely not be an efficient algorithm for performing $\mathbb{G}_t$ operations if using such a space-optimal representation of the $\mathbb{G}_t$ elements.

[3]See https://electriccoin.co/blog/new-snark-curve/ and https://hackmd.io/@benjaminion/bls12-381 for discussion of BLS12-381. As a general ballpark, operations in this pairing-friendly group may be about 4× slower than in Curve25519—of course, a precise comparison will depend on implementation details and the hardware on which a comparison is performed. BLS12-381 was designed to work over a field

Note that in any group $\mathbb{G}$ equipped with a symmetric pairing, the Decisional Diffie-Hellman assumption does not hold. This is because one can distinguish triples (g, g_1, g_2, g_3) of the form $(g, g_1 = g^a, g_2 = g^b, g_3 = g^{ab})$ from $(g, g_1 = g^a, g_2 = g^b, g_3 = g^c)$ for randomly chosen $c \in \{0, \ldots, |\mathbb{G}| - 1\}$ by checking whether $e(g, g_3) = e(g_1, g_2)$. In the case where $g_3 = g^{ab}$, this check will always pass by bilinearity of e, while if e is non-degenerate, this check will fail with overwhelming probability if g_3 is a random group element in $\mathbb{G}$. Nonetheless, even in groups equipped with a symmetric pairing, it is often assumed that the *computational* Diffie-Hellman assumption holds.

Intuition for Why Bilinear Maps are Useful. Recall that an additively homomorphic commitment scheme such as Pedersen commitments allows any party to perform addition "underneath commitments". That is, despite the fact that the commitments perfectly hide the value that is committed, it is possible for anyone to take two commitments c_1, c_2 to values m_1, m_2, and compute a commitment c_3 to $m_1 + m_2$, despite not actually knowing anything about m_1 or m_2. However, Pedersen commitments are not multiplicatively homomorphic: while we gave an efficient interactive protocol (Protocol 9) for a prover (that knows how to open c_1 and c_2) to prove that c_3 commits to $m_1 \cdot m_2$, it is not possible for a party that does not know m_1 or m_2 to compute a commitment to $m_1 \cdot m_2$ on its own.

Bilinear maps effectively convey the power of multiplicative-homomorphism, but only for *one* multiplication operation. To be more concrete, let us think of a group element $g^{m_i} \in \mathbb{G}$ as a commitment to m_i (if m_i is chosen at random, the commitment is computationally hiding if the discrete logarithm problem is hard in $\mathbb{G}$, meaning it is hard to determine m_i from g^{m_i}). Then bilinear maps allow any party, given commitments c_1, c_2, c_3 to check whether the values m_1, m_2, m_3 inside the commitments satisfy $m_3 = m_1 \cdot m_2$. This is because by bilinearity of the map $e \colon \mathbb{G} \times \mathbb{G} \to \mathbb{G}_t$, $e(g^{m_1}, g^{m_2}) = e(g^{m_3}, g)$ if and only if $m_3 = m_1 \cdot m_2$.

---

that supports efficient FFT algorithms, so that its use is compatible with SNARKs in which the prover must perform an FFT (see Section 19.3.1 for further dicussion).

It turns out that the power to perform a single "multiplication check" of committed values is enough to obtain a polynomial commitment scheme. This is because Lemma 9.3 implies that for any degree-D univariate polynomial p, the assertion "$p(z) = v$" is equivalent to the assertion that there exists a polynomial w of degree at most $D - 1$ such that

$$p(X) - v = w(X) \cdot (X - z). \tag{15.1}$$

Equation (15.1) can be probabilistically verified by evaluating the two polynomials on the left hand side and right hand side at a randomly chosen point τ. This intuitively means that the committer can commit to p by sending a commitment c_3 to $m_3 := p(\tau)$, and then convince a verifier that Equation (15.1) holds by sending a commitment c_2 to $m_2 := w(\tau)$. If the verifier can compute a commitment c_1 to $m_1 := \tau - z$ on its own, then the verifier can use the bilinear map to check that indeed the $m_3 = m_1 \cdot m_2$ (i.e., Equation (15.1) holds at input τ). This entire approach assumes that the committer does not know τ, since if it did, it could choose the polynomial w so that Equation (15.1) does not hold as an equality of polynomials, but does hold at τ.[4]

The following section makes the above high-level outline formal.

15.2   KZG: Univariate Polynomial Commitments from Pairings and a Trusted Setup

A Binding Scheme.   Let e be a bilinear map pairing groups $\mathbb{G}, \mathbb{G}_t$ of prime order p, and $g \in \mathbb{G}$ be a generator, and D be an upper bound on the degree of the polynomials we would like to support commitments to. The structured reference string consists of encodings in $\mathbb{G}$ of all powers of a random nonzero field element $\tau \in \mathbb{F}_p$. That is, τ is an integer chosen at random from $\{1, \ldots, p - 1\}$, and the SRS equals $(g, g^\tau, g^{\tau^2}, \ldots, g^{\tau^D})$.

---

[4]One may wonder if one can instead use a non-pairing-friendly group, and use Protocol 9 rather than the bilinear map to check that $m_3 = m_1 \cdot m_2$. This would work, but the proofs would be considerably longer, though still a constant number of group elements. Also, to render the argument system non-interactive, one would need to apply the Fiat-Shamir transformation, forcing the verifier to perform hashing operations. All told, this yields more expensive verification than KZG commitments. The raison d'être of KZG commitments is the remarkable efficiency of evaluation-proof verification.

The value τ is toxic waste that must be discarded because it can be used to destroy binding.

To commit to a polynomial q over $\mathbb{F}_p$, the committer sends a value c claimed to equal $g^{q(\tau)}$. Note that while the committer does not know τ, it is still able to compute $g^{q(\tau)}$ using the SRS and additive homomorphism: if $q(Z) = \sum_{i=0}^{D} c_i Z^i$, then $g^{q(\tau)} = \prod_{i=0}^{D} (g^{\tau^i})^{c_i}$, which can be computed given the values g^{τ^i} for all $i = 0, \ldots, D$ even without knowing τ.[5]

To open the commitment at input $z \in \{0, \ldots, p-1\}$ to some value v, i.e., to prove that $q(z) = v$, the committer computes a "witness polynomial"

$$w(X) := (q(X) - v)/(X - z),$$

and sends a value y claimed to equal $g^{w(\tau)}$ to the verifier. Again, since w has degree at most D, $g^{w(\tau)}$ can be computed from the SRS despite the fact that the prover does not know τ. The verifier checks that

$$e(c \cdot g^{-v}, g) = e(y, g^{\tau} \cdot g^{-z}). \tag{15.2}$$

Note that this requires the verifier to know c, v, y, z, and g^{τ}. The first three values are provided by the prover, the opening query z is determined by the verifier itself, and g^{τ} is an entry of the SRS. Note that g^{τ} and g are the only entries of the SRS needed for verification. For this reason, some works refer to the entire SRS as the *proving key* and (g, g^{τ}) as the *verification key*, and think of the verifier as only downloading the verification key, not the entire proving key.

Analysis of Correctness and Binding. Correctness is easy to establish: if $c = g^{q(\tau)}$ and $y = g^{w(\tau)}$ then

$$e(c \cdot g^{-v}, g) = e(g^{q(\tau)-v}, g) = e(g^{w(\tau)\cdot(\tau-z)}, g) = e(g^{w(\tau)}, g^{\tau-z})$$
$$= e(y, g^{\tau} \cdot g^{-z}).$$

---

[5]As in Section 14.4, one can think of g^{τ^i} as a Pedersen commitment to τ^i (Protocol 5), but without the blinding factor h^z. This yields a commitment that is perfectly binding but at best computationally hiding: g^{τ^i} information-theoretically specifies τ^i, but deriving τ^i from g^{τ^i} requires computing the discrete logarithm of g^{τ^i} to base g. The ability of the committer to compute $g^{q(\tau)}$ from the SRS without knowing τ follows from the fact that this modified Pedersen commitment is additively homomorphic.

Here, the first inequality holds because $c = g^{q(\tau)}$, the second holds by definition of w as $(q(X) - v)/(X - z)$, the third holds by bilinearity of e, and the fourth holds because $y = g^{w(\tau)}$.

The intuition for why binding holds is as follows. If $q(z) \neq v$, then passing the verifier's check (Equation (15.2)) requires computing $g^{w(\tau)}$, where $w(X) = (q(X) - v)/(X - z)$ is *not* a polynomial in X. Rather, it is a polynomial in X, multiplied by the rational function $1/(X - z)$. The SRS, by containing g raised to all positive powers of τ, provides enough information for the prover to evaluate "in the exponent of g" any desired degree-D polynomial at τ, despite not knowing τ. But, intuitively, this information should not be enough to allow the prover to then "divide in the exponent" by $\tau - z$, as appears to be required to compute $g^{w(\tau)} = g^{(q(\tau)-v)/(\tau-z)}$.

To make this intuition precise, we show that binding follows from a cryptographic assumption, called the *D-strong Diffie-Hellman (SDH) assumption*, that essentially just asserts that "dividing in the exponent" by $\tau - z$ is intractable, even for an adversary given the SRS used by the KZG commitment scheme. That is, SDH assumes that, given the SRS that consists of the generator g raised to all powers of τ up to power-D, there is no efficient algorithm $\mathcal{A}$ that outputs a pair $(z, g^{1/(\tau-z)})$ except with negligible probability. The SDH assumption was introduced by Boneh and Boyen [62]. It is closely related to an earlier assumption called the Strong RSA assumption [20], the main difference being that SDH refers to (pairing-friendly) cyclic groups while the Strong RSA assumption refers to the (non-cyclic) groups arising in the RSA cryptosystem.

Note that the SDH assumption in $\mathbb{G}$ implies that the Discrete Logarithm problem is hard in $\mathbb{G}$, because if discrete logarithms are easy to compute, then τ can be efficiently computed from g^τ, and given τ and z it is easy to compute $g^{1/(\tau-z)}$. Indeed, this can be done by computing the multiplicative inverse ℓ modulo p of $\tau - z$ using the Extended Euclidean algorithm. Since $\mathbb{G}$ has order p, and hence $g^{ip} = 1_\mathbb{G}$ for all integers i, $g^\ell = g^{1/(\tau-z)}$.[6]

---

[6]There are known algorithms that use the group elements g^{τ^i} for $i > 1$ given in the SRS to speed up the computation of τ, relative to the fastest known algorithms that

Formally, to establish binding of KZG commitments assuming SDH, one must show that if one can open a commitment c at point $z \neq \tau$ to two different values v, v', then one can efficiently compute $g^{1/(\tau - z)}$, thereby violating the SDH assumption.

Some More Intuition. Recall that, if $c = g^{q(\tau)}$ and $y = g^{w(\tau)}$, then the verifier's check in Equation (15.2) confirms "in the exponent of g" that $q(\tau) - v = w(\tau) \cdot (\tau - z)$. So opening $c = g^{q(\tau)}$ to two different values v, v' intuitively requires identifying two different exponents $w(\tau)$ and $w'(\tau)$ such that

$$q(\tau) - v = w(\tau) \cdot (\tau - z)$$

and

$$q(\tau) - v' = w'(\tau) \cdot (\tau - z).$$

Subtracting these two equations from each other implies that

$$v' - v = (w(\tau) - w'(\tau))(\tau - z).$$

Since $v - v' \neq 0$, and assuming $\tau \neq z$, one can divide both sides by $(v - v') \cdot (\tau - z)$ to conclude that

$$1/(\tau - z) = (w(\tau) - w'(\tau))/(v - v').$$

Thus, one has solved for $1/(\tau - z)$ "in the exponent" of g, contradicting the SDH assumption. The following analysis makes this formal.

Formal Binding Analysis. To open c to values v and v' the committer must identify values $y, y' \in \mathbb{G}$ such that:

$$e(c \cdot g^{-v}, g) = e(y, g^{\tau - z})$$

and

$$e(c \cdot g^{-v'}, g) = e(y', g^{\tau - z}).$$

For simplicity, let us write $c = g^{r_1}$, $y = g^{r_2}$, and $y' = g^{r_3}$ (although the committer may not know r_1, r_2, or r_3). By bilinearity of e, these

---

solve for τ given only g and g^{τ}. However, the speedups are modest, i.e., solving for τ given $g, g^{\tau}, g^{\tau^2}, \ldots, g^{\tau^D}$ is believed to require super-polynomial time for appropriately chosen cryptographic groups. See [98, Appendix A.5] for details.

two equations imply that

$$g^{r_1} \cdot g^{-v} = g^{r_2 \cdot (\tau - z)}$$

and

$$g^{r_1} \cdot g^{-v'} = g^{r_3 \cdot (\tau - z)}.$$

Together, these two equations imply that:

$$g^{v - v'} = g^{(r_3 - r_2)(\tau - z)}.$$

In other words,

$$\left((y' \cdot y^{-1})^{1/(v - v')} \right)^{(\tau - z)} = g. \tag{15.3}$$

Here, $(y' \cdot y^{-1})^{1/(v - v')}$ denotes the value obtained raising the group element $y' \cdot y^{-1} \in \mathbb{G}$ to the power x, where x is the multiplicative inverse of $v - v'$ modulo p; note that x can be computed efficiently (in time $\tilde{O}(\log p)$) via the Extended Euclidean algorithm. Equation (15.3) states that $\left((y' \cdot y^{-1})^{1/(v - v')} \right)$ equals $g^{1/(\tau - z)}$. Since this value can be computed efficiently given v, v', y, y' provided by the committer, the committer must have broken the SDH assumption.

An Extractable Scheme. Recall (Section 7.4) that an extractable polynomial commitment scheme guarantees that for every "efficient committer adversary $\mathcal{A}$" that takes as input the public parameters of the commitment scheme and a degree bound D and outputs a polynomial commitment c, there is an efficient algorithm E (which depends on $\mathcal{A}$) that produces a degree-D polynomial p explaining all of $\mathcal{A}$'s answers to evaluation queries. That is, if $\mathcal{A}$ is able to successfully answer evaluation query z with value v, then $p(z) = v$. Since E is efficient, it cannot know anything more than $\mathcal{A}$ does (since $\mathcal{A}$ can afford to run E), and E clearly knows p by virtue of outputting it. This captures the intuition that $\mathcal{A}$ must "know" a polynomial p that $\mathcal{A}$ is using to answer evaluation queries.

The binding analysis above shows that, once the prover sends a KZG commitment, it is bound to some function. This means that for each possible evaluation query z, there is at most one value v

that the committer can successfully answer the query with. But it
doesn't establish that the function the prover is bound to is a degree-D
polynomial. To make this polynomial commitment scheme extractable
rather than simply binding, it must be modified and/or additional
cryptographic assumptions are required (see for example the discussion
of the Generic Group Model later in this section).

Here is one method of achieving extractability that does require
modifying the scheme, as well as an additional cryptographic assumption.
Recall that $\mathbb{G}$ is a cyclic group of order p with public generator g. In
the modified scheme, the SRS doubles in size. Specifically, for τ and α
chosen at random from $\mathbb{F}_p$, the modified SRS consists of the pairs

$$\{(g, g^\alpha), (g^\tau, g^{\alpha\tau}), (g^{\tau^2}, g^{\alpha\tau^2}), \ldots, (g^{\tau^D}, g^{\alpha\tau^D})\}.$$

That is, the SRS consists not only of powers of τ in the exponent
of g, but also the same quantities raised to the power α. Note that
neither τ nor α are included in the SRS—they are "toxic waste" that
must be discarded after the SRS is generated, as any party that knows
these quantities can break extractability or binding of the polynomial
commitment scheme.

The Power Knowledge of Exponent (PKoE) assumption [141] posits,
roughly, that for any polynomial time algorithm $\mathcal{A}$ given access to the
SRS, whenever the algorithm outputs any two group elements $g_1, g_2 \in \mathbb{G}$
such that $g_2 = g_1^\alpha$, the algorithm must "know" coefficients $c_1, \ldots, c_D$
that "explain" g_2, in the sense that $g_2 = \prod_{i=1}^{D} g^{c_i \cdot \tau^i}$. The idea is that,
given access to the SRS, it is easy to compute a pair (g_1, g_2) with
$g_2 = g_1^\alpha$ in the following manner: let g_1 equal any product of quantities
in the first half of the SRS raised to constant powers, e.g.,

$$g_1 := \prod_{i=0}^{D} g^{c_i \tau^i},$$

and let g_2 be the result of applying the same operations to the second
half of the SRS, i.e., $g_2 := \prod_{i=0}^{D} g^{c_i \alpha \tau^i}$. The PKoE essentially assumes
that this is the *only way* that an efficient party is capable of computing
two group elements with this relationship to each other. It formalizes
this by assuming that, for any efficient adversary $\mathcal{A}$ that takes as input
the SRS and produces such pairs of group elements, there is an efficient

procedure E (which can depend on $\mathcal{A}$) that actually produces such c_i values. Since E is efficient, it cannot "know" anymore than $\mathcal{A}$ does, and E obviously knows the c_i values.

Whereas in the original commitment scheme, which was binding but not necessarily extractable, the commitment to polynomial q was $g^{q(\tau)}$, in the modified scheme the commitment is the pair $(g^{q(\tau)}, g^{\alpha q(\tau)})$. The committer can compute this pair using the modified SRS. To open a commitment $c = (U, V)$ at $z \in \mathbb{F}_p$ to value y, the committer computes the degree-$(D - 1)$ polynomial $w(X) := (q(X) - v)/(X - z)$ and sends a value y claimed to equal $w(\tau)$ exactly as in the original scheme. The verifier checks not only that

$$e(U \cdot g^{-v}, g) = e(y, g^\tau \cdot g^{-z}),$$

but also that $e(U, g^\alpha) = e(V, g)$.

Completeness for the first check holds exactly as in the unmodified scheme. Completeness for the verifier's second check holds because if U and V are provided honestly then $V = U^\alpha$ (despite the fact that neither the prover nor the verifier know α), and hence by bilinearity of e, $e(U, g^\alpha) = e(V, g)$.

To prove that the modified scheme is extractable, we use the extractor E whose existence is asserted by the PKoE assumption to construct an extractor $\mathcal{E}$ for the polynomial commitment scheme. Specifically, the second check made by the verifier during opening ensures that $V = U^\alpha$, despite the fact that the verifier does not know α. The PKoE assumption therefore asserts the existence of an efficient extraction procedure E that outputs quantities $c_1, \ldots, c_D$ such that $U = \prod_{i=1}^{D} g^{c_i \cdot \tau^i}$. We define the extractor $\mathcal{E}$ to run E to produce these $c_1, \ldots, c_D$ values, and then output the polynomial $s(X) = \sum_{i=1}^{D} c_i X^i$.

Clearly, $g^{s(\tau)} = U$, so (U, V) is indeed a commitment to the polynomial s. In particular, U is a commitment to s under the original unmodified commitment scheme. Since we showed that the original scheme is binding under the SDH assumption, this means that the committer is bound to s in the modified scheme.[7]

---

[7]The SRS of the modified commitment scheme contains additional group elements $g^{\alpha\tau}, g^{\alpha\tau^2}, \ldots, g^{\alpha\tau^D}$ for a random $\alpha \in \mathbb{F}$. Any adversary $\mathcal{A}$ for the SDH assumption

In more detail, suppose that the committer in the modified scheme is able to open $c = (U, V)$ to value v at point z, and $v \neq s(z)$. Then the committer in the unmodified scheme can in fact open U to both v and $s(z)$. For example, to open U to $s(z)$, the committer can let $w'(X) = (s(X) - s(z))/(X - z)$, which is a polynomial of degree at most $D - 1$, and send $g^{w'(\tau)}$ during the opening procedure. This quantity will pass the verifier's first check by the completeness analysis of the unmodified commitment scheme.

Discussion of the PKoE Assumption. The PKoE assumption is qualitatively different from all other cryptographic assumptions that we have discussed thus far in this monograph, including the DDH and CDH assumptions, the discrete logarithm assumption, and the existence of collision-resistant families of hash functions. Specifically, all of these other assumptions satisfy a property called *falsifiability*. Falsifiability is a technical notion formalized by Naor [197]: a cryptographic assumption is said to be falsifiable if it can be captured by defining an interactive game between a polynomial-time challenger and an adversary, at the conclusion of which the challenger can decide in polynomial-time whether the adversary won the game. A falsifiable assumption must be of the form "every efficient adversary has a negligible probability of winning the game".

For example, the assumption that a hash family is collision-resistant can be modeled by having the challenger send the adversary a hash function h chosen at random from the family, and challenging the adversary to find a collision, i.e., two distinct strings x, y such that $h(x) = h(y)$. Clearly, the challenger can efficiently check whether the adversary won the game, by evaluating h at x and y and confirming that indeed $h(x) = h(y)$. In contrast, a knowledge-of-exponent assumption such as PKoE is not falsifiable: if the adversary computes a pair (g_1, g_1^α), it is not clear how the challenger could determine whether the adversary broke the assumption. That is, since the challenger does not have access to

---

that is given access to the original SRS can efficiently simulate these extra group elements itself by picking α at random and raising every element of the unmodified SRS to the power α. Hence, these extra group elements do not give the SDH adversary any extra power.

the internal workings of the adversary, it is not clear how the challenger could determine whether or not the adversary computed (g_1, g_1^α) without the adversary "knowing in its own head" coefficients $c_1, \ldots, c_D$ such that $g_1 = \prod_{i=1}^{D} g^{c_i \cdot \tau^i}$. The issue is that in claiming to have broken the assumption, the adversary is claiming to *not know* certain information, namely, the coefficients $c_1, \ldots, c_D$ of the previous sentence. This entire manuscript is devoted to efficiently proving knowledge to an untrusting party, but there is no way to prove *lack* of knowledge.

Theoretical cryptographers generally prefer falsfiable assumptions because they seem easier to reason about and are arguably more concrete, as there is an efficient process to check whether an adversarial strategy falsifies the assumption. That said, not all falsifiable assumptions are "superior" to all non-falsifiable ones: indeed, some falsifiable assumptions proposed in the research literature have turned out to be false! And cryptographers certainly do believe that the PKoE assumption holds in many groups.

We have presented some succinct *interactive* arguments for circuit satisfiability in this monograph that are based on falsifiable assumptions (e.g., the 4-message argument argument obtained by combining PCPs with Merkle trees from Section 9.2). But none of the *non-interactive* succinct arguments of knowledge (SNARKs) for circuit satisfiability that we present are based on falsifiable assumptions; they are either based on knowledge-of-exponent assumptions such as PKoE, or they are sound in the random oracle model.[8] This is because it is not known how to base a SNARK for circuit satisfiability on a falsifiable assumption, and indeed barriers to achieving this are known [126].

In summary, while assumptions like PKoE are slightly controversial in the theoretical cryptography community, many researchers and practitioners are nonetheless confident in their veracity. It is perhaps reasonable to expect that any given deployed SNARK is more likely

---

[8]We did explain a succinct non-interactive argument for circuit *evaluation* based on falsifiable assumptions in Section 5.2, by instantiating the Fiat-Shamir transformation of the GKR protocol with a correlation-intractable hash family in place of the random oracle.

to be broken for mundane reasons such as unnoticed flaws in the security proofs or bugs in the implementation, than because the PKoE assumption turns out to be false in the group used by the SNARK.

Generic Group Model and Algebraic Group Model. The unmodified polynomial commitment scheme covered in this section is also known to be extractable in the so-called *Generic Group model* (GGM), as well as in a variant model called the *Algebraic Group model* (AGM) [117]. The Generic Group model is similar in spirit to the random oracle model (see Section 5.1). Recall that the random oracle model models cryptographic hash functions as truly random functions. In contrast, "real-world" implementations of protocols in the random oracle model must instantiate the random oracle with concrete hash functions, and real-world attackers trying to "break" the protocol can try to exploit properties of the concrete hash function. Accordingly, the random oracle model only captures "attacks" that do not exploit any structure in the concrete hash functions. The rationale for why this is reasonable is that real-world cryptographic hash functions are designed to (hopefully) "look random to efficient adversaries"; hence we generally do not know real-world attacks that exploit structure in concrete hash functions, though contrived protocols are known for which no real-world instantiation of the protocol with a concrete hash function is secure.

Similarly, the GGM considers adversaries that are only given access to cryptographic groups $\mathbb{G}, \mathbb{G}_t$ via an oracle that computes the group multiplication operation. The pairing operation $e \colon \mathbb{G} \times \mathbb{G} \to \mathbb{G}_t$ is modeled as an additional oracle. In the real-world, attackers are actually given explicit representations of group elements, as well as efficient computer code that, given the representation of two group elements, computes the representation of the product of those two elements. But we generally do not know of attacks on real-world protocols that exploit these explicit representations.

The AGM is a model that lies in between the GGM and the real world. The AGM has a similar flavor to knowledge-of-exponent assumptions like PKoE, in that it assumes whenever an efficient algorithm $\mathcal{A}$ outputs a "new" group element $g \in \mathbb{G}$, it also outputs an "explanation" of g as a combination of "known" group elements $L = (L_1, \ldots, L_t)$

that were previously given to $\mathcal{A}$, i.e., numbers $c_1, \ldots, c_t$ such that $g = \prod_{i=1}^{t} L_i^{c_i}$. Any attacker operating in the GGM can also be implemented in the AGM [201], so the known extractability of the KZG polynomial commitment in the AGM [98] is a strictly stronger result than security in the GGM.[9]

15.3 Extension of KZG to Multilinear Polynomials

The previous section gave a polynomial commitment scheme based on pairings, for univariate polynomials over the field $\mathbb{F}_p$ where p is the order of the groups involved in the pairing. In this section, we wish to give a similar commitment scheme for *multilinear* polynomials q over $\mathbb{F}_p$, proposed by Papamanthou *et al.* [202]. Let ℓ denote the number of variables of q, so $q \colon \mathbb{F}_p^{\ell} \to \mathbb{F}_p$. In applications of multilinear polynomial commitment schemes (namely, to transforming IPs and MIPs to succinct arguments for circuit satisfiability), it is convenient to work with polynomials specified over the Lagrange basis (see Lemma 3.8 for a definition of the Lagrange basis polynomials), so we present the commitment scheme in this setting, though the scheme works just as well over any basis of multilinear polynomials.

The structured reference string (SRS) now consists of encodings in $\mathbb{G}$ of all powers of all Lagrange basis polynomials evaluated at a randomly chosen input $r \in \mathbb{F}^{\ell}$. That is, if $\chi_1, \ldots, \chi_{2^{\ell}}$ denotes an enumeration of the 2^{ℓ} Lagrange basis polynomials, the SRS equals $(g^{\chi_1(r)}, \ldots, g^{\chi_{2^{\ell}}(r)})$. Once again, the toxic waste that must be discarded because it can be used to destroy binding is the value r.

As in the univariate commitment scheme, to commit to a multilinear polynomial q over $\mathbb{F}_p$, the committer sends a value c claimed to equal $g^{q(r)}$. Note that while the committer does not know r, it is still able to compute $g^{q(r)}$ using the SRS: if $q(X) = \sum_{i=0}^{2^{\ell}} c_i \chi_i(X)$, then $g^{q(r)} = \prod_{i=0}^{2^{\ell}} (g^{\chi_i(r)})^{c_i}$, which can be computed given the values $g^{\chi_i(r)}$ for all $i = 0, \ldots, 2^{\ell}$ even without knowing r.

---

[9]To be precise, there are a couple of variants of the GGM considered in the literature [188], [234]. See [167] for a discussion of subtleties regarding the relationship between these different versions of the GGM and the AGM.

To open the commitment at input $z \in \mathbb{F}_p^\ell$ to some value v, i.e., to prove that $q(z) = v$, the committer computes a series of ℓ "witness polynomials" $w_1, \ldots, w_\ell$, defined in the following fact.

Fact 15.1 (Papamanthou *et al.* [202]). For any fixed $z = (z_1, \ldots, z_\ell) \in \mathbb{F}_p^\ell$ and any multilinear polynomial q, $q(z) = v$ if and only if there is a unique set of ℓ multilinear polynomials $w_1, \ldots, w_\ell$ such that

$$q(X) - v = \sum_{i=1}^{\ell} (X_i - z_i) w_i(X). \tag{15.4}$$

Proof. If $q(X) - v$ can be expressed as the right hand side of Equation (15.4), then clearly $q(z) - v = 0$, and hence $q(z) = v$.

On the other hand, suppose that $q(z) = v$. Then by dividing the polynomial $q(X) - v$ by the polynomial $(X_1 - z_1)$, we can identify multilinear polynomials w_1 and s_1 such that

$$q(X) - v = (X_1 - z_1) \cdot w_1(X_1, X_2, \ldots, X_\ell) + s_1(X_2, X_3, \ldots, X_\ell),$$

where $s_1(X_2, X_3, \ldots, X_\ell)$ is the remainder term, and does not depend on variable X_1. Iterating this process, we can divide s_1 by the polynomial $(X_2 - Z_2)$ to write

$$q(X) - v = (X_1 - z_1) \cdot w_1(X_1, X_2, \ldots, X_\ell) + (X_2 - z_2) \cdot w_2(X_2, \ldots, X_\ell)$$
$$+ s_2(X_3, X_4, \ldots, X_\ell)$$

and so forth until we have written

$$q(X) - v = \sum_{i=1}^{\ell} (X_i - z_i) \cdot w_i(X_1, X_2, \ldots, X_\ell) + s_\ell,$$

where s_ℓ depends on no variables, i.e., s_ℓ is simply an element in $\mathbb{F}_p$. Since $q(z) - v = 0$, it must hold that $s_\ell = 0$, completing the proof. □

To open the commitment at input $z \in \mathbb{F}_p^\ell$ to value v, the prover computes $w_1, \ldots, w_\ell$ as per Fact 15.1 and sends to the verifier values $y_1, \ldots, y_\ell$ claimed to equal $g^{w_i(r)}$ for $i = 1, \ldots, \ell$. Again, since each w_i is multilinear, $g^{w_i(r)}$ can be computed from the SRS despite the fact that the prover does not know r. The verifier checks that

$$e(c \cdot g^{-v}, g) = \prod_{i=1}^{\ell} e(y_i, g^{r_i} \cdot g^{-z_i}).$$

Note that the verifier is able to perform this check so long as the verification key includes g^{r_i} for each i (the verification key is a subset of the SRS, as each dictator function $(X_1, \ldots, X_\ell) \mapsto X_i$ is a Lagrange basis polynomial).

Correctness is clear: if $c = g^{q(r)}$ and $y_i = g^{w(r_i)}$ for $i = 1, \ldots, \ell$, then

$$e(c \cdot g^{-v}, g) = e(g^{q(r)-v}, g) = e(g^{\sum_{i=1}^{\ell} w_i(r) \cdot (r_i - z_i)}, g)$$

$$= \prod_{i=1}^{\ell} e(g^{w_i(r)}, g^{r_i - z_i}) = e(y_i, g^{r_i} \cdot g^{-z_i}).$$

Here, the first inequality holds because $c = g^{q(r)}$, the second holds by Equation (15.4), the third holds by bilinearity of e, and the fourth holds because $y_i = g^{w_i(r)}$.

The proof of binding and techniques to achieve extractability are similar to the previous section and we omit them for brevity.

Costs. Like the univariate pairing-based polynomial commitment scheme of the previous section (Section 15.2), the ℓ-variate multilinear polynomial commitment consists of a constant number of group elements. However, whereas evaluation proofs for the univariate protocol also consisted of a constant number of group elements, evaluation proofs for the multilinear polynomial protocol are ℓ group elements rather than $O(1)$, with a corresponding increase in verification time from $O(1)$ group operations and bilinear map evaluations, to $O(\ell)$.

In terms of committer runtime, Zhang *et al.* [259, Appendix G] show that the committer in the protocol for multilinear polynomials can compute the polynomials $w_1, \ldots, w_\ell$ with just $O(2^\ell)$ field operations in total. And once these polynomials are computed, the prover can compute all ℓ necessary values $g^{w_i(r)}$ with $O(2^\ell)$ many group exponentiations in total.

15.4　Dory: Transparent Scheme with Logarithmic Verification Costs

This section describes a polynomial commitment scheme called Dory with similar (logarithmic) verification costs to the polynomial commitment scheme of the previous section, but that does not rely on a trusted setup. It does require a pre-processing phase that requires time square root in the size of the polynomial to be committed, but this pre-processing phase does not produce any "toxic waste" that must be discarded to guarantee no one can break the scheme's binding property. Asymptotically, its verifier costs compare favorably to Bulletproofs (Section 14.4): like Bulletproofs, it is transparent with logarithmic-sized proofs, but unlike Bulletproofs it has logarithmic rather than linear verifier time. However, concretely its proofs are larger than Bulletproofs by a significant constant factor.

Dory builds on beautiful ideas and building blocks developed over a variety of works [2], [75], [84], especially so-called AFGHO commitments [2]. While Dory itself is arguably somewhat complicated, the building blocks that comprise it are simpler and useful in their own right.

15.4.1 Commitments to Vectors of Group Elements via Inner Pairing Products

Let $\mathbb{F}_p$ be the field of prime order p and $\mathbb{G}$ be a multiplicative cyclic group of order p. Let $\mathbf{h} = (h_1, \ldots, h_n)$ be a public vector of (randomly chosen) generators of $\mathbb{G}$. Recall that an (unblinded) Pedersen vector commitment is a compressing commitment to a vector of field elements $v \in \mathbb{F}_p^n$, given by $\mathsf{Com}(v) = \prod_{i=1}^n h_i^{v_i}$ (see Section 14.2). In other words, this commitment takes (unblinded) Pedersen commitments to each entry of v, and multiplies them together to get a single commitment to the whole vector. The commitment is a single element of the group $\mathbb{G}$.

Now let $\mathbb{G}_1, \mathbb{G}_2, \mathbb{G}_t$ be a pairing-friendly triple of groups of order p. In the previous paragraph, we expressed $\mathbb{G}$ as a multiplicative group, but for the remainder of this section, we will express $\mathbb{G}_1, \mathbb{G}_2, \mathbb{G}_t$ as *additive* groups. As in Section 14.4 where we described Bulletproofs, this allows us to express commitments as an inner product between the vector to be committed and the commitment key.

Using pairings, one can define an analog of Pedersen vector commitments that allows one to commit to vectors of *group elements*, i.e., vectors in $\mathbb{G}_1^n$, rather than vectors of field elements. Specifically, for $w \in \mathbb{G}_1^n$, and for a fixed vector $\mathbf{g} = (g_1, \ldots, g_n) \in \mathbb{G}_2^n$ of public, randomly chosen group elements, define

$$\text{IPPCom}(w) = \sum_{i=1}^{n} e(w_i, g_i). \tag{15.5}$$

Note that $\text{IPPCom}(w)$ is a single element of the target group $\mathbb{G}_t$. We use the notation IPPCom as short-hand for the term *inner-pairing-product commitment*. This refers to the fact that $\text{IPPCom}(w)$ can be thought of as the inner product $\langle w, \mathbf{g} \rangle = \sum_{i=1}^{n} w_i \cdot g_i$, where the "multiplication" of w_i and g_i is defined via the pairing $e(w_i, g_i)$. From now on, for $w \in \mathbb{G}_1^n, \mathbf{g} \in \mathbb{G}_2^n$, we use $\langle w, \mathbf{g} \rangle$ to denote the inner-pairing-product $\sum_{i=1}^{n} e(w_i, g_i)$.

Intuitively, $e(w_i, g_i)$ acts as a Pedersen commitment to w_i despite the fact that w_i is a group element in $\mathbb{G}_1$ rather than a field element in $\mathbb{F}_p$. The sum $\sum_{i=1}^{n} e(w_i, g_i)$ of all such entry-wise Pedersen commitments is the natural compressing commitment to the vector w.

The above commitment scheme for vectors of group elements originated in work of Abe *et al.* [2], [143] and are often called AFGHO-commitments. We use the terms AFGHO-commitments and inner-pairing-product commitments interchangeably.

Rendering the Commitment Perfectly Hiding. Recall that a Pedersen vector commitment in group $\mathbb{G}_1$ can be made perfectly hiding by having an extra randomly chosen public parameter $g \in \mathbb{G}_1$, and having the committer pick a random $r \in \mathbb{F}_p$ and include a blinding factor g^r in the commitment. Analogously, $\text{IPPCom}(w)$ can be made perfectly hiding by having the committer pick a random $r \in \mathbb{G}_1$ and including a blinding term $e(r, g)$ in the commitment, i.e., defining

$$\text{IPPCom}(w) = e(r, g) + \sum_{i=1}^{n} e(w_i, g_i).$$

For simplicity, we omit this blinding factor from the remainder of our treatment.

Computational Binding. Recall from Section 15.1 that the Decisional Diffie-Hellman (DDH) assumption for an additive group $\mathbb{G}_1$ states that no efficient algorithm can meaningfully distinguish between a random tuple of the form

$$(g, a \cdot g, b \cdot g, c \cdot g)$$

with a, b, c chosen at random from $\mathbb{F}_p$ versus one of the form

$$(g, a \cdot g, b \cdot g, (ab) \cdot g).$$

We show that assuming DDH holds in $\mathbb{G}_1$, $\text{IPPCom}(w)$ is a computationally binding commitment to $w \in \mathbb{G}_1^n$. For expository clarity, our presentation assumes that $n = 2$.

Given a DDH challenge $(g, a \cdot g, b \cdot g, c \cdot g)$ in $\mathbb{G}_1$, we must explain how to use an efficient prover $\mathcal{P}$ that breaks binding of the commitment scheme to give an efficient algorithm $\mathcal{A}$ that breaks the DDH assumption. $\mathcal{A}$ sets $\mathbf{g} = (g, a \cdot g) \in \mathbb{G}_1 \times \mathbb{G}_1$; note that by definition of the DDH challenge distributions, both entries of $\mathbf{g}$ are uniform random group elements. $\mathcal{A}$ then runs $\mathcal{P}$ to identify a nonzero commitment $c^* \in \mathbb{G}_t$ and two openings $u = (u_1, u_2), w = (w_1, w_2)$ of c^*, meaning that

$$c^* = e(u_1, g) + e(u_2, a \cdot g) = e(w_1, g) + e(w_2, a \cdot g).$$

Let $v = u - w$, and write $v = (v_1, v_2) \in \mathbb{G}_1 \times \mathbb{G}_1$. Since $c^* \neq 0$, it follows that v is not the zero-vector. Moreover, by bilinearity of e,

$$e(v_1, g) + e(v_2, a \cdot g) = 0. \tag{15.6}$$

The DDH adversary $\mathcal{A}$ then outputs 1 if and only if

$$e(v_1, b \cdot g) + e(v_2, c \cdot g) = 0. \tag{15.7}$$

That $\mathcal{A}$ breaks the DDH assumption in $\mathbb{G}_1$ can be seen as follows. First, if $c = a \cdot b$, then the left hand side of Equation (15.7) equals:

$$e(v_1, b \cdot g) + e(v_2, (a \cdot b) \cdot g) = e(v_1, b \cdot g) + e(v_2, b \cdot (a \cdot g))$$
$$= b \cdot (e(v_1, b \cdot g) + e(v_2, c \cdot g)).$$

This last expression equals 0 by Equation (15.6). Hence, in this case $\mathcal{A}$ outputs 1. Meanwhile, if c is chosen at random from $\mathbb{F}_p$, then since v is not the zero-vector, Equation (15.7) holds with probability just $1/p$.

Hence, $\mathcal{A}$ succeeds in distinguishing tuples of the form $(g, a \cdot g, b \cdot g, c \cdot g)$, with a, b, c chosen at random from $\mathbb{F}_p$, from those of the form $(g, a \cdot g, b \cdot g, (ab) \cdot g)$.

15.4.2   Committing to Field Elements Using Pairings

One can also use inner-pairing-product commitments in place of Pedersen-vector commitments to commit to vectors of field elements. Let h be any element of $\mathbb{G}_1$ and $\mathbf{g} = (g_1, \ldots, g_n) \in \mathbb{G}_2^n$ be a random vector of $\mathbb{G}_2$ elements. For a vector $v \in \mathbb{F}_p^n$, consider the vector $w(v)$ of entry-wise (unblinded) Pedersen commitments to v in $\mathbb{G}_1$ with commitment key h, i.e., $w(v)_i = v_i \cdot h$, and define IPPCom(v) as

$$\text{IPPCom}(v) = \text{IPPCom}(w(v)) = \langle w(v), \mathbf{g} \rangle = \sum_{i=1}^{n} e(v_i \cdot h, g_i). \quad (15.8)$$

Since IPPCom($w(v)$) is a binding commitment to $w(v)$, and the map $v \mapsto w(v)$ is bijective, IPPCom(v) is a binding commitment to $v \in \mathbb{F}_p^n$. It will be important both for concrete efficiency of computing commitments, and for the polynomial commitment scheme that we develop (Sections 15.4.4 and 15.4.5), that the *same* group element h is used to compute every entry of $w(v)$.

Efficiency Comparison.   There are two natural ways to compute IPPCom(v). One is by computing the right hand side of Expression (15.8) directly, which requires n evaluations of the bilinear map e and n group operations in the target group $\mathbb{G}_t$. The other (faster) way is by computing a Pedersen-vector commitment $c = \sum_{i=1}^{n} v_i g_i$ in $\mathbb{G}_2$, and then applying the bilinear map just once to compute $e(h, c)$. By bilinearity of e,

$$e(h, c) = e(h, \sum_{i=1}^{n} v_i \cdot g_i) = \sum_{i=1}^{n} e(h, v_i \cdot g_i) = \sum_{i=1}^{n} e(v_i \cdot h, g_i) = \text{IPPCom}(v).$$

Both methods of computing IPPCom(v) are concretely slower than computing a Pedersen vector commitment to v in $\mathbb{G}_1$. This is because group operations in $\mathbb{G}_2$ and $\mathbb{G}_t$ are typically slower than group operations in $\mathbb{G}_1$, and computing an evaluation of the bilinear map e is slower still. For example, according to microbenchmarks in [179], if using the popular pairing-friendly curve BLS12-381, a $\mathbb{G}_t$ operation is about 4 times slower than one in $\mathbb{G}_1$ while a $\mathbb{G}_2$ operation is about 2 times slower than one in $\mathbb{G}_1$. Moreover, operations in a pairing-friendly group

$\mathbb{G}_1$ such as BLS12-381 are perhaps 2-3 times slower than operations in the fastest non-pairing-friendly groups.

On top of this slow commitment computation, the commitment size IPPCom(v) is concretely larger—for BLS12-381, representations of elements of the target group $\mathbb{G}_t$ are four times bigger than those of elements of $\mathbb{G}_1$. In summary, while the asymptotic costs of computing and sending IPPCom(w) are similar to Pedersen vector commitments, the concrete costs are worse.

A Simplification in the Remainder of the Presentation. As discussed in Section 15.1, the DDH assumption *cannot* hold in $\mathbb{G}_1$ if $\mathbb{G}_1 = \mathbb{G}_2$, i.e., if the pairing is a symmetric pairing. This is because, given tuple (g, ag, bg, cg), one can check whether $c = a \cdot b$ by checking whether $e(g, c \cdot g) = e(a \cdot g, b \cdot g)$.

However, the DDH assumption can hold in $\mathbb{G}_1$ and $\mathbb{G}_2$ if the two groups are not equal, i.e., if there is no efficiently computable mapping ϕ group $\mathbb{G}_1$ to $\mathbb{G}_2$ or vice versa that preserves group structure in the sense that $\phi(a+b) = \phi(a) + \phi(b)$. This is (believed to be) the case for pairings used in practice, such as BLS12-381. The assumption that DDH holds in both $\mathbb{G}_1$ and $\mathbb{G}_2$ is called the *symmetric external Diffie-Hellman assumption*, abbreviated SXDH.

Despite the fact that IPPCom(w) is *not* necessarily a binding commitment to w if $\mathbb{G}_1 = \mathbb{G}_2$, we will nonetheless assume for the remainder of our presentation of Dory that $\mathbb{G}_1 = \mathbb{G}_2$, denoting both groups by $\mathbb{G}$.[10] This simplifies the presentation of the Dory protocol. The changes required to the protocol in the case where $\mathbb{G}_1 \neq \mathbb{G}_2$ are straightforward, but they introduce a notational burden that we prefer to avoid.

Outline for the Remainder of the Presentation. In order to highlight in a modular fashion the main ideas that go into the Dory polynomial commitment scheme, we describe progressively more sophisticated protocols. First, in Section 15.4.3, we explain how a prover $\mathcal{P}$ can convince

---

[10]See [143] for a modification of the commitment scheme that is binding under a plausible assumption for symmetric pairings.

a verifier that $\mathcal{P}$ knows how to open some inner-pairing-product commitment $c_u = \text{IPPCom}(u)$ to some vector $u \in \mathbb{G}^n$. The proof size and verification cost of this protocol are $O(\log^2 n)$, after a transparent linear-time pre-processing phase. Second, in Section 15.4.4 we explain how to extend this protocol to give a transparent polynomial commitment scheme in which the verifier's runtime is $O(\log^2 n)$. Third, in Section 15.4.5, we explain a modification of the protocol of Section 15.4.3 that reduces the runtime of the pre-processing phase from linear in n to $O(n^{1/2})$. Finally, in Section 15.4.6, we present a more complicated variant of the protocol of Section 15.4.3 that reduces verification costs from $O(\log^2 n)$ to $O(\log n)$.

15.4.3   Proving Knowledge of Opening with $O(\log^2 n)$ Verification Cost

Let $u \in \mathbb{G}^n$, and assume for simplicity that n is a power of 2. Given public input $c_u = \text{IPPCom}(u)$, the following protocol is transparent and allows the prover to prove knowledge of an opening u of c_u. The verifier runs in $O(\log^2 n)$ time, after a transparent pre-processing phase that is independent of u.

Recap of Bulletproofs. Let us briefly recall the Bulletproofs (Section 14.4) protocol for establishing knowledge of an opening $u^{(0)} \in \mathbb{F}_p^n$ of a *Pedersen* vector commitment

$$c_{u^{(0)}} = \langle u^{(0)}, \mathbf{g}^{(0)} \rangle = \sum_{i=1}^{n} u_i \cdot g_i.$$

Conceptually, $\mathbf{g}^{(0)}$ is broken into two halves $\mathbf{g}_L^{(0)}$ and $\mathbf{g}_R^{(0)}$, and likewise $u^{(0)}$ is written as $(u_L^{(0)}, u_R^{(0)})$. The prover sends two commitments v_L and v_R claimed to equal $\langle u_L^{(0)}, \mathbf{g}_R^{(0)} \rangle$ and $\langle u_R^{(0)}, \mathbf{g}_L^{(0)} \rangle$. The verifier picks a random $\alpha_1 \in \mathbb{F}_p$ and sends it to $\mathcal{P}$, and uses v_L and v_R to homomorphically update the commitment $c_{u^{(0)}}$ to

$$c_{u^{(1)}} := c_{u^{(0)}} + \alpha_1^2 v_L + \alpha_1^{-2} v_R.$$

If the prover is honest, $c_{u^{(1)}}$ is a commitment to the to length-$(n/2)$ vector

$$u^{(1)} = \alpha_1 u_L^{(0)} + \alpha_1^{-1} u_R^{(0)}.$$

using the commitment key

$$\mathbf{g}^{(1)} := \alpha_1^{-1} \mathbf{g}_L^{(0)} + \alpha_1 \mathbf{g}_R^{(0)}. \tag{15.9}$$

$\mathcal{P}$ and $\mathcal{V}$ then proceed to the next round, in which $\mathcal{P}$ recursively establishes knowledge of an opening $u^{(1)}$ to $c_{u^{(1)}}$. This continues for $\log n$ rounds, at which point the recursion bottoms out: $u^{(\log n)}$ and $\mathbf{g}^{(\log n)}$ have length 1, and hence (if zero-knowledge is not a consideration) $\mathcal{P}$ can afford to prove knowledge of $u^{(\log n)}$ by sending it explicitly to $\mathcal{V}$, who can check that $u^{(\log n)} \cdot \mathbf{g}^{(\log n)} = c_{u^{(\log n)}}$.

Why is the verifier runtime in the above protocol linear rather than logarithmic? The answer is: in each round, the verifier needs to update the commitment key from $\mathbf{g}^{(i-1)}$ to $\mathbf{g}^{(i)} = \alpha_i^{-1} \mathbf{g}_L^{(i-1)} + \alpha \mathbf{g}_R^{(i-1)}$. This takes time at least $O(n/2^i)$.

The Pre-Processing Procedure. Now let $u^{(0)}$ be a vector in $\mathbb{G}^n$, and let $c_{u^{(0)}} = \text{IPPCom}(u^{(0)})$. To avoid linear verifier time in our protocol for establishing knowledge of an opening $u^{(0)} \in \mathbb{G}^n$ for $c_{u^{(0)}}$, we rely on a pre-processing phase that is independent of $u^{(0)}$, depending only on the public commitment key $\mathbf{g}$. For exposition, we describe the preprocessing as occurring over $\log n$ iterations, with two inner-pairing-product commitments (i.e., elements of $\mathbb{G}_t$) produced per iteration. We refer to the party doing the pre-processing as the verifier—in fact, any entity willing to invest the effort can perform the pre-processing and distribute the resulting (logarithmically-many) commitments to the world. Any entity willing to invest the effort can also validate the distributed commitments, raising an alarm if a discrepancy is found.

- (First iteration of pre-processing): Let $\mathbf{g}^{(0)} = (\mathbf{g}_L^{(0)}, \mathbf{g}_R^{(0)}) \in \mathbb{G}^{n/2} \times \mathbb{G}^{n/2}$ be the commitment key used to compute the initial commitment $c_{u^{(0)}} = \langle u^{(0)}, \mathbf{g}^{(0)} \rangle$. The first pre-processing iteration outputs inner-pairing-product commitments $\Delta_L^{(1)}$ and $\Delta_R^{(1)}$ to $\mathbf{g}_L^{(0)}$ and to $\mathbf{g}_R^{(0)}$ respectively, using public, randomly chosen commitment key $\Gamma^{(1)} \in \mathbb{G}^{n/2}$.[11] That is, $\Delta_L^{(1)} = \langle \mathbf{g}_L^{(0)}, \Gamma^{(1)} \rangle$ and $\Delta_R^{(1)} = \langle \mathbf{g}_R^{(0)}, \Gamma^{(1)} \rangle$.

---

[11] $\Gamma^{(1)}$ need not be independent of $\mathbf{g}^{(0)}$, e.g., it is fine for $\Gamma^{(0)}$ to equal $\mathbf{g}_L^{(0)}$.

- (Second iteration): Write $\Gamma^{(1)}$ itself as $(\Gamma_L^{(1)}, \Gamma_R^{(1)}) \in \mathbb{G}^{n/4} \times \mathbb{G}^{n/4}$. The second iteration computes commitments $\Delta_L^{(2)}$ and $\Delta_R^{(2)}$ to $\Gamma_L^{(1)}$ and to $\Gamma_R^{(1)}$ respectively, using public, randomly chosen commitment key $\Gamma^{(2)} \in \mathbb{G}^{n/4}$.[12]

- In general, in iteration $i > 1$: compute commitments $\Delta_L^{(i)}$ and $\Delta_R^{(i)}$ to the left and right halves of the commitment key $\Gamma^{(i-1)}$ that was used to compute the previous iteration's commitments $\Delta_L^{(i-1)}$ and $\Delta_R^{(i-1)}$.

The pre-processing ends after iteration $i = \log(n)$. At that point, $\Gamma^{(i)}$ has length 1, so the pre-processing just outputs $\Gamma^{(i)}$ explicitly. Note that after the pre-processing is done, a logarithmic-time verifier does have time to read and store the two commitments $\Delta_L^{(i)}$ and $\Delta_R^{(i)}$ output by each iteration of pre-processing, but does *not* have the time to read or store the corresponding *commitment key* $\Gamma^{(i)}$ used to produce $\Delta_L^{(i)}$ and $\Delta_R^{(i)}$. This is because $\Gamma^{(i)}$ has size $n/2^i$ and hence is super-logarithmic for all $i \leq \log(n) - \log\log(n)$. As we will see, this means the verifier in the knowledge-of-opening protocol described below will have to somehow "check" that the prover knows how to open many different commitments $\Delta_L^{(i)}$ and $\Delta_R^{(i)}$ *without the verifier even knowing the keys* used to produce those commitments.

The Knowledge of Opening Protocol. Let $u^{(0)}$ be a vector in $\mathbb{G}^n$. The verifier begins the protocol knowing a commitment $c_{u^{(0)}}$. If the prover is honest,

$$c_{u^{(0)}} = \langle u^{(0)}, \mathbf{g}^{(0)} \rangle, \tag{15.10}$$

and the prover needs to prove that it knows a vector $u^{(0)}$ satisfying Equation (15.10). Recall that a core difficulty here is that the verifier doesn't know $\mathbf{g}^{(0)}$ as in Bulletproofs, but rather only some "pre-processed" information about $\mathbf{g}^{(0)}$, namely commitments to $\mathbf{g}_L^{(0)}$ and $\mathbf{g}_R^{(0)}$ under some different commitment key $\Gamma^{(1)}$.

The key idea is that, in each round i, rather than explicitly computing $\mathbf{g}^{(i)}$ from $\mathbf{g}^{(i-1)}$ as per Equation (15.9), $\mathcal{V}$ instead uses homomorphism

---

[12]As in Footnote 11, $\Gamma^{(2)}$ need not be independent of $\Gamma^{(1)}$, e.g., it is fine for $\Gamma^{(2)}$ to equal $\Gamma_L^{(1)}$.

of the commitments output by the pre-processing procedure to compute in constant time a *commitment* to $\mathbf{g}^{(i)}$ under a suitable commitment key. Roughly speaking, the verifier can use this commitment to force the prover to do the hard work of computing $\mathbf{g}^{(i)}$ explicitly. The prover will only ever explicitly reveal to the verifier the final "fully collapsed" commitment key $\mathbf{g}^{(\log n)}$, which consists of a single group element. Protocol details follow.

Round 1 procedure: As in Bulletproofs, the prover begins by sending two commitments v_L and v_R claimed to equal $\langle u_L^{(0)}, \mathbf{g}_R^{(0)} \rangle$ and $\langle u_R^{(0)}, \mathbf{g}_L^{(0)} \rangle$. The verifier picks a random $\alpha_1 \in \mathbb{F}_p$ and sends it to $\mathcal{P}$. The verifier uses v_L and v_R to homomorphically update the commitment $c_{u^{(0)}}$ to

$$c_{u^{(1)}} := c_{u^{(0)}} + \alpha_1^2 v_L + \alpha_1^{-2} v_R.$$

Recall that unlike in Bulletproofs, our $\mathcal{V}$ does not know $\mathbf{g}^{(0)}$, but does know pre-processing commitments $\Delta_L^{(1)} = \langle g_L^{(0)}, \Gamma^{(1)} \rangle$ and $\Delta_R^{(1)} = \langle g_R^{(0)}, \Gamma^{(1)} \rangle$. Via homomorphism, $\mathcal{V}$ can compute a commitment

$$c_{\mathbf{g}^{(1)}} = \alpha_1^{-1} \Delta_L^{(1)} + \alpha_1 \Delta_R^{(1)}$$

to $\mathbf{g}^{(1)} = \alpha_1^{-1} \mathbf{g}_L^{(0)} + \alpha_1 \mathbf{g}_R^{(0)}$ under commitment key $\Gamma^{(1)}$.

The above Round 1 leaves the prover and verifier in the following situation. Unlike in Bulletproofs, at the start of Round 2, our verifier does not know $\mathbf{g}^{(1)}$. All that our verifier knows is a *commitment* $c_{\mathbf{g}^{(1)}}$ to $\mathbf{g}^{(1)}$ under commitment key $\Gamma^{(1)} = (\Gamma_L^{(1)}, \Gamma_R^{(1)}) \in \mathbb{G}^{n/4} \times \mathbb{G}^{n/4}$.

Because the information known to $\mathcal{V}$ is so limited, at the start of Round 2, $\mathcal{P}$ needs to prove that it knows vectors $u^{(1)}$ and $\mathbf{g}^{(1)}$ in $\mathbb{G}^{n/2}$ such that

$$c_{u^{(1)}} = \langle u^{(1)}, \mathbf{g}^{(1)} \rangle \tag{15.11}$$

and

$$c_{\mathbf{g}^{(1)}} = \langle \mathbf{g}^{(1)}, \Gamma^{(1)} \rangle. \tag{15.12}$$

In summary, the first round of our protocol started with a claim about *one* inner product equation involving two vectors $u^{(0)}$ and $\mathbf{g}^{(0)}$ of length n (Equation (15.10)), in which $\mathcal{V}$ only knew "pre-computed commitments" $\Delta_L^{(1)}, \Delta_R^{(1)}$ to $\mathbf{g}^{(0)}$. And it reduced it to a claim about *two* inner product equations involving *three* vectors of length $n/2$, namely $u^{(1)}$, $\mathbf{g}^{(1)}$, and $\Gamma^{(1)}$, in which $\mathcal{V}$ only knows pre-computed commitments $\Delta_L^{(2)}, \Delta_R^{(2)}$ to $\Gamma_L^{(1)}$ and $\Gamma_R^{(1)}$.

Round 2 Procedure.

- *A trivial case:* If $n = 2$, so the pre-processing phase output $\Gamma^{(1)}$ explicitly, then a trivial way for the prover to establish both of these claims is to explicitly reveal $u^{(1)}$ and $\mathbf{g}^{(1)}$ to $\mathcal{V}$, who can then check Equations (15.11) and (15.12) explicitly. But this does not work if $n \geq 4$.

- *What to do if $n \geq 4$.* Fortunately, Equations (15.11) and (15.12) are both of a form that Bulletproofs was designed to handle. Namely, $\mathcal{P}$ is claiming to know some vector satisfying an inner-product relation with some other vector ($u^{(1)}$ with $\mathbf{g}^{(1)}$ in Equation (15.11) and $\mathbf{g}^{(1)}$ with $\Gamma^{(1)}$ in Equation (15.12)). So $\mathcal{P}$ and $\mathcal{V}$ can apply the Bulletproofs scheme in parallel to both claims, using the same random verifier-chosen $\alpha_2 \in \mathbb{F}_p$ for both, to reduce each claim to an equivalent one involving vectors of half the length.

  That is, $\mathcal{P}$ sends commitments $v_L, v_R, w_L, w_R \in \mathbb{G}_t$ claimed to equal $\langle u_L^{(1)}, \mathbf{g}_R^{(1)} \rangle$, $\langle u_R^{(1)}, \mathbf{g}_L^{(1)} \rangle$, $\langle \mathbf{g}_L^{(1)}, \Gamma_R^{(2)} \rangle$ and $\langle \mathbf{g}_R^{(1)}, \Gamma_L^{(2)} \rangle$. $\mathcal{V}$ then sends $\alpha_2 \in \mathbb{F}$ to $\mathcal{P}$. $\mathcal{V}$ sets

$$c_{u^{(2)}} := c_{u^{(1)}} + \alpha_2^2 v_L + \alpha_2^{-2} v_R.$$

If $\mathcal{P}$ is honest, then

$$c_{u^{(2)}} = \langle u^{(2)}, \mathbf{g}^{(2)} \rangle,$$

where

$$u^{(2)} = \alpha_2 u_L^{(1)} + \alpha_2^{-1} u_R^{(1)},$$

and

$$\mathbf{g}^{(2)} := \alpha_2^{-1} \mathbf{g}_L^{(1)} + \alpha_2 \mathbf{g}_R^{(1)}.$$

Likewise, $\mathcal{V}$ sets

$$c_{\mathbf{g}^{(2)}} := c_{\mathbf{g}^{(1)}} + \alpha_2^{-2} w_L + \alpha_2^2 w_R.$$

If $\mathcal{P}$ is honest, then $c_{\mathbf{g}^{(2)}}$ is a commitment to $\mathbf{g}^{(2)}$ under commitment key $\Gamma' = \alpha_2 \Gamma_L^{(1)} + \alpha_2^{-1} \Gamma_R^{(1)}$, i.e.,

$$c_{\mathbf{g}^{(2)}} = \langle \alpha_2^{-1} \mathbf{g}_L^{(1)} + \alpha_2 \mathbf{g}_R^{(1)}, \alpha_2 \Gamma_L^{(1)} + \alpha_2^{-1} \Gamma_R^{(1)} \rangle.$$

Finally, $\mathcal{V}$ computes a commitment $c_{\Gamma'}$ to Γ' under commitment key $\Gamma^{(2)}$ homomorphically given the pre-processing commitments $\Delta_L^{(2)}$ and $\Delta_R^{(2)}$, via $c_{\Gamma'} = \alpha_2 \Delta_L^{(2)} + \alpha_2^{-1} \Delta_R^{(2)}$.

The above Round 2 procedure reduces the task of proving knowledge of $u^{(1)}, \mathbf{g}^{(1)} \in \mathbb{G}^{n/2}$ satisfying Equations (15.11) and (15.12) to proving knowledge of $u^{(2)}, \mathbf{g}^{(2)}, \Gamma' \in \mathbb{G}^{n/4}$ satisfying:

$$c_{u^{(2)}} = \langle u^{(2)}, \mathbf{g}^{(2)} \rangle, \tag{15.13}$$

$$c_{\mathbf{g}^{(2)}} = \langle \mathbf{g}^{(2)}, \Gamma' \rangle, \tag{15.14}$$

$$c_{\Gamma'} = \langle \Gamma', \Gamma^{(2)} \rangle. \tag{15.15}$$

That is, as discussed in the "sketch of the knowledge extractor" several paragraphs hence, $\mathcal{P}$'s knowledge of $u^{(2)}, g^{(2)}, \Gamma' \in \mathbb{G}^{n/4}$ satisfying Equations (15.13)–(15.15) (for at least 3 values of $\alpha_2 \in \mathbb{F}_p$) implies knowledge of $u^{(1)}$ and $\mathbf{g}^{(1)}$ satisfying Equations (15.11) and (15.12).

In summary, Round 2 started with a claim about *two* inner product equations involving *three* vectors of length $n/2$, namely $u^{(1)}, \mathbf{g}^{(1)}, \Gamma^{(1)}$, in which $\mathcal{V}$ only knows pre-computed commitments $\Delta_L^{(2)}, \Delta_R^{(2)}$ to $\Gamma^{(1)}$. And it reduced it to a claim about *three* inner product equations involving *four* vectors of length $n/4$, in which $\mathcal{V}$ only knows pre-computed commitments to the fourth vector $\Gamma^{(2)}$.

Round $i > 2$. The above Round-2 procedure can be iterated, to ensure that at the start of Round i, the prover has to establish knowledge of $i+1$ vectors, each of length $n/2^i$, satisfying i inner product equations. In more detail, denote the $i + 1$ vectors $\mathcal{P}$ claims to know at the start of round i by $v_1, \ldots, v_{i+1}$. Then $v_1 = u^{(i-1)}$, $v_2 = \mathbf{g}^{(i-1)}$, and $v_{i+1} = \Gamma^{(i-1)}$. And the j'th equation at the start of Round i is of the form $\langle v_j, v_{j+1} \rangle = c_j$ for some commitment c_j.

The prover operates analogously to Round 2, sending commitments to two cross-terms per equation, with the verifier then picking a random

$\alpha_i \in \mathbb{F}_p^n$ and sending it to $\mathcal{P}$. For each odd $j \in \{1, \ldots i+1\}$, the verifier uses homomorphism to derive a commitment to $\alpha_i \cdot v_{j,L} + \alpha_i^{-1} \cdot v_{j,R}$. Likewise, for each even j, $\mathcal{V}$ derives a commitment to $\alpha_i^{-1} \cdot v_{j,L} + \alpha_i \cdot v_{j,R}$. For $v_{i+1} = \Gamma^{(i-1)}$, the appropriate commitment is derived homomorphically from the pre-processing commitments $\Delta_L^{(i)}$ and $\Delta_R^{(i)}$. Round $i+1$ is then devoted to proving that the prover indeed knows how to open each of the $i+1$ derived commitments, which entails $i+1$ inner-product equations involving $i+2$ vectors.

The iterations stop after round $\log(n)$; at that point, the vectors involved in each of the $\log(n) + 1$ equations have length just 1. If zero-knowledge is not a consideration, the prover can establish that it knows such vectors by simply sending them explicitly to $\mathcal{V}$, and $\mathcal{V}$ can directly check that the received values indeed satisfy all the equations claimed.

Verification Costs. The total number of commitments sent by the prover in Round i is $O(i)$, leading to a communication cost $O(\sum_{i=1}^{\log(n)} i) = O(\log^2 n)$. The verifier's total runtime is also $O(\log^2 n)$ scalar multiplications in $\mathbb{G}_t$.

Sketch of the Knowledge Extractor. The knowledge extractor for the above protocol proceeds similarly to that for Bulletproofs (Section 14.4). After first generating a 3-transcript tree via the forking lemma (Theorem 14.1), the extractor proceeds from the leaves toward the root, and at each vertex i layers below the root it constructs the $i+1$ vectors satisfying the i inner-product equations that the prover claims to know at the point in the protocol corresponding to that vertex. For example, when the extractor comes to the root itself, the extractor has already constructed, for each child of the root, vectors $u^{(1)}$ and $\mathbf{g}^{(1)}$ such that Equations (15.11) and (15.12) hold, i.e., $\langle u^{(1)}, \mathbf{g}^{(1)} \rangle = c_{u^{(1)}}$ and $\langle \mathbf{g}^{(1)}, \Gamma^{(1)} \rangle = c_{\mathbf{g}^{(1)}}$. Note the extractor knows $\Gamma^{(1)}$, because $\Gamma^{(1)}$ is public and, unlike the verifier, the extractor need only run in polynomial time, not logarithmic time.

The Bulletproofs extractor (Section 14.4) gives a procedure to take the $\mathbf{g}^{(1)}$ vectors for all three children of the root and reconstruct a $\mathbf{g}^{(0)}$ that "explains" all three children's $\mathbf{g}^{(1)}$ vectors, in the sense that for each child of the root, $\mathbf{g}^{(1)} = \alpha_1^{-1}\mathbf{g}_L^{(0)} + \alpha_1\mathbf{g}_R^{(0)}$, where α_1 is label of the edge connecting the root to the child under consideration. Once $\mathbf{g}^{(0)}$ is identified, the same Bulletproofs extraction procedure identifies a vector $u^{(0)}$ that explains all three children's $u^{(1)}$ vectors, i.e., such that at each child of the root, $u^{(1)} = \alpha_1 u_L^{(0)} + \alpha_1^{-1}u_R^{(0)}$, and moreover $c_{u^{(0)}} = \langle u^{(0)}, \mathbf{g}^{(0)} \rangle$.

15.4.4 Extending to a Polynomial Commitment

Extending the knowledge-of-opening protocol of Section 15.4.3 to a polynomial commitment scheme follows the outline provided at the start of the section: let $a \in \mathbb{F}_p^n$ be the coefficient vector of the polynomial $q(X) = \sum_{i=0}^{n-1} a_i X^i$ to be committed, of degree $n-1$. Then the commitment to q is just an AFGHO-commitment to a (Section 15.4.2).[13]

Recall this means the following. If $\mathbf{g} = (g_1, \ldots, g_n) \in \mathbb{G}^n$ and $h \in \mathbb{G}$ are public commitment keys, and $w(a) \in \mathbb{G}^n = (a_1 \cdot h, \ldots, a_n \cdot h)$ is the vector of Pedersen commitments to a with key $h \in \mathbb{G}$, then the commitment to the polynomial is $c_q := \text{IPPCom}(w(a)) = \prod_{i=1}^n e(a_i \cdot h, g_i)$.

Suppose the verifier then requests to evaluate the committed polynomial at input $z \in \mathbb{F}_p$, and the prover claims that $q(z) = v$. Then the prover has to establish that it knows a vector a such that two equalities hold: (1) $c_q = \text{IPPCom}(w(a))$, and (2) $q(r) = v$. Recall that the latter claim is equivalent to $\langle a, y \rangle = v$ where $y = (1, r, r^2, \ldots, r^{n-1})$.

Claim (1) is established by applying the protocol of Section 15.4.3 establish that $\mathcal{P}$ knows $u := w(a)$ opening c_q. Claim (2) is established in parallel with this protocol, in close analogy to the Bulletproofs polynomial commitment scheme (Protocol 13). In slightly more detail, there are two differences from Protocol 13, aside from using the protocol of Section 15.4.3 in place of Protocol 12 to establish that $\mathcal{P}$ knows an opening of c_q:

- In Protocol 13, the verifier explicitly computes the vector $y^{(i)}$ in each round. This requires time $O(n/2^i)$ in round i, which is

---

[13]Recall that the same approach applies to multilinear polynomials; we restrict our attention to univariate polynomials in this section for brevity.

far too large for the polylogarithmic time verifier we set out to achieve in this section. To address this, the key observation is that $\mathcal{V}$ does not actually need to know $y^{(i)}$ for $i < \log n$. The only information the verifier actually needs to perform its checks in the protocol is the final-round value $y^{(\log n)}$. Moreover, not only does $y = (1, r, \ldots, r^{n-1})$ have "tensor structure", but so do the round-by-round updates to y. This enables $\mathcal{V}$ to compute $y^{(\log n)}$ in logarithmic time.

Specifically, for $(a, b) \in \mathbb{F}_p^2$ and a vector $v \in \mathbb{F}_p^n$, define the vector $v \otimes (a, b)$ to be $(a \cdot v, b \cdot v) \in \mathbb{F}_p^{2n}$. Then it can be checked that $y = \otimes_{i=0}^{\log(n)-1}(1, r^{2^i})$. For example,

$$(1, r) \otimes (1, r^2) = (1, r, r^2, r^3)$$

and

$$(1, r) \otimes (1, r^2) \otimes (1, r^4) = (1, r, r^2, \ldots, r^7).$$

For $i \in \{1, \ldots, \log n\}$, let $\bar{i} = \log(n) - i$. It can be checked that the above tensor structure in the vector y leads to the following equality:

$$y^{(\log n)} = \prod_{i=1}^{\log n} (\alpha_i + \alpha_i^{-1} r^{2^{\bar{i}}}). \tag{15.16}$$

Clearly, the right hand side of Equation (15.16) can be computed in $O(\log n)$ time.

For example, if $n = 4$, then

$$y^{(1)} = (1, r, r^2, r^3),$$
$$y^{(2)} = (\alpha_1 \cdot 1 + \alpha_1^{-1} \cdot r^2, \alpha_1 r + \alpha_1^{-1} r^3),$$

and

$$y^{(3)} = \alpha_2 y_L^{(2)} + \alpha_2^{-1} y_R^{(2)} = \alpha_2 \cdot \alpha_1 \cdot 1 + \alpha_2^{-1} \cdot \alpha_1 \cdot r + \alpha_2 \cdot \alpha_1^{-1} r^2$$
$$+ \alpha_2^{-1} \alpha_1^{-1} r^3 = \left(\alpha_1 + \alpha_1^{-1} r^2\right) \left(\alpha_2 + \alpha_2^{-1} r\right).$$

- In the final round, round $\log n$, of the protocol of Section 15.4.3, the prover should reveal not only the group element $u^{(\log n)}$ such that $e(u^{(\log n)}, \mathbf{g}^{(\log n)}) = c_{u^{(\log n)}}$, but also the discrete logarithm $a^* \in \mathbb{F}_p$ to base h, i.e., the field element to which $u^{(\log n)}$ is a Pedersen commitment. This enables the verifier to confirm that indeed $\langle a^*, y^{(\log n)} \rangle = a^* \cdot y^{(\log n)} = v^{(\log n)}$, where $y^{(i)}$ and $v^{(i)}$ denote the round-i values of the vectors y and v from Protocol 13.

15.4.5 Reducing Pre-Processing Time to $O(\sqrt{n})$ via Matrix Commitments

Analogy to Hyrax Polynomial Commitment. Recall that Section 14.2 used Pedersen vector commitments to give a constant-size polynomial commitment, but with linear-size evaluation proofs and verification time. Section 14.3 reduced the evaluation proof size and verification time to square root, but at the cost of increasing commitment size from constant to square root. It worked by expressing any polynomial evaluation query $q(z)$ as a vector-matrix-vector product $b^T \cdot u \cdot a$ and having the prover commit to each column of the matrix u separately. The verifier could then use homomorphism of the column commitments to compute a commitment to $u \cdot a$, and the prover could then invoke the evaluation procedure of the commitment scheme to reveal $b^T \cdot (u \cdot a)$.

Unlike the commitment scheme of Section 14.2, the schemes of this section *already* have (poly)logarithmic verification costs, following a linear-time pre-processing phase. It is nonetheless possible to combine this section's commitment schemes with the vector-matrix-vector multiplication structure in evaluation queries, to improve other costs. Specifically, the pre-processing time can be reduced from linear to square root in the degree of the committed polynomial. And unlike in Section 14.3, this improvement does not come at the cost of increasing the size of the commitment. This technique has the added benefit that polynomial evaluation queries can be answered with $O(n^{1/2})$ rather than $O(n)$ group operations by the prover (on top of the $O(n)$ $\mathbb{F}_p$ operations required to simply evaluate the polynomial at the requested point).

Commitment Phase of the Improved Protocol. Let $u \in \mathbb{F}_p^{m \times m}$ be the matrix such that for any $z \in \mathbb{F}_p$, $q(z) = b^T \cdot u \cdot a$ for some vectors $b, a \in \mathbb{F}_p^m$. The prover "in its own head" computes a Pedersen-vector commitment c_i in $\mathbb{G}$ to each column i of u, using random generator vector $\mathbf{h} = (h_1, \ldots, h_m) \in \mathbb{G}^m$ as the commitment key. Rather than sending $(c_1, \ldots, c_m) \in \mathbb{G}^m$ explicitly to the verifier, the prover instead just sends an inner-pairing-product commitment c^* to $(c_1, \ldots, c_m)$ using $\mathbf{g} = (g_1, \ldots, g_m)$ as the commitment key. In other words, the commitment is

$$c^* := \sum_{j=1}^{m} e \left(\sum_{i=1}^{m} u_{i,j} \cdot h_i, g_j \right) = \sum_{j=1}^{m} \sum_{i=1}^{m} e \left(u_{i,j} \cdot h_i, g_j \right).$$

This is just a single element of $\mathbb{G}_t$.

Evaluation Phase of the Improved Protocol. If the verifier requests the evaluation $q(z)$, let $w, x \in \mathbb{F}_p^m$ be vectors such that $q(z) = w^T \cdot u \cdot x$, and let v denote the claimed value of $q(z)$.

Both vectors w and x themselves have the same tensor structure exploited to maintain polylogarithmic verifier time in Section 15.4.4. Recall that that protocol allowed a prover to establish knowledge of an opening $\mathbf{t} \in \mathbb{G}^m$ of a given inner-pairing-product commitment such that $\langle \mathbf{t}, y \rangle = v$, where $y \in \mathbb{F}^m$ is any public vector that can be written as a $(\log m)$-dimensional tensor product of length-2 vectors.

Denote $u \cdot x \in \mathbb{F}_p^m$ by $\mathbf{d}$. The prover first sends the verifier a Pedersen-vector commitment $c' \in \mathbb{G}$, whose prescribed value is $\langle \mathbf{d}, \mathbf{h} \rangle$. It suffices for the prover to establish three things.

- The prover knows an opening $\mathbf{t} = (t_1, \ldots, t_m) \in \mathbb{G}^m$ of the inner-pairing-product commitment c^*.

- $\langle \mathbf{t}, x \rangle = c'$. Combined with the first bullet above, this means that, if u is the matrix with column commitments given by the entries of $\mathbf{t}$, then c' is a Pedersen-vector commitment to $u \cdot x$ using key $\mathbf{h}$, i.e., $c' = \sum_{i=1}^{m} (u \cdot x)_i \cdot h_i$.

- The prover knows an opening $\mathbf{d} = (d_1, \ldots, d_m) \in \mathbb{F}_p^m$ of c' such that $\langle w, \mathbf{d} \rangle = v$. Combined with the bullet above, this means that $w^T \cdot u \cdot x = v$ as claimed by $\mathcal{P}$.

The first two items together can be established directly by the protocol of Section 15.4.4.

Since w also has tensor structure, it is tempting to also apply the protocol of Section 15.4.4 to establish that the third bullet point holds. This does not work directly because c' is not an AFGHO-commitment to $\mathbf{d}$ but rather a Pedersen-vector commitment to $\mathbf{d}$. To address this, the verifier simply transforms c' into an AFGHO-commitment as follows: for a public, randomly chosen $g \in \mathbb{G}$, the verifier lets $c'' = e(c', g)$. Then $c'' \in \mathbb{G}_t$ is an AFGHO-commitment to $\mathbf{d}$ with commitment keys $\mathbf{h} \in \mathbb{G}^n$ and $g \in \mathbb{G}$. Indeed, by bilinearity of e:

$$c'' = e(\sum_{i=1}^{m} d_i h_i, g) = \sum_{i=1}^{n} e(d_i \cdot h_i, g) = \sum_{i=1}^{n} e(h_i, d_i \cdot g).$$

Hence, the prover can invoke the protocol of Section 15.4.4 to prove it knows an opening $\mathbf{d}$ of c'' such that $\langle w, \mathbf{d} \rangle = v$.

15.4.6 Achieving $O(\log n)$ Communication and Verification Time

Recall that in Round 1 of the protocol of Section 15.4.3, the verifier is able to use the pre-processing outputs $\Delta_L^{(1)}$ and $\Delta_R^{(1)}$ to compute a commitment $c_{\mathbf{g}^{(1)}}$ to the newly-updated vector $\mathbf{g}^{(1)} = \alpha_1^{-1} \mathbf{g}_L^{(0)} + \alpha_1 \mathbf{g}_R^{(0)}$ under key $\Gamma^{(1)}$. However, the verifier is *not* able to derive a commitment to $\mathbf{u}^{(1)} = \alpha_1 u_L^{(0)} + \alpha_1^{-1} u_R^{(0)}$ under key $\Gamma^{(1)}$. Rectifying this turns out to lead to improved verification costs, of $O(\log n)$ instead of $O(\log^2 n)$.

The protocol below conceptually proceeds in $\log n$ *rounds* in close analogy with Bulletproofs and the protocol of Section 15.4.3, with each round halving the lengths of the vectors under consideration. But each round in the protocol below actually consists of 4 messages. So the number of actual rounds of communication in the final protocol is $2 \log n$ rather than $\log n$.

The Setup. Suppose at the start of Round i, the prover has claimed to know two vectors $u^{(i-1)}, \mathbf{g}^{(i-1)} \in \mathbb{G}^{n \cdot 2^{-(i-1)}}$ satisfying the following three equations:

$$\langle u^{(i-1)}, \mathbf{g}^{(i-1)} \rangle = c_1, \tag{15.17}$$

$$\langle u^{(i-1)}, \Gamma^{(i-1)} \rangle = c_2 \tag{15.18}$$

$$\langle \mathbf{g}^{(i-1)}, \Gamma^{(i-1)} \rangle = c_3. \tag{15.19}$$

In Round 1, the following choices ensure that the three equations above capture $\mathcal{P}$'s claim that the protocol as a whole is meant to verify, namely that $\mathcal{P}$ knows $u^{(0)}$ satisfying

$$\langle u^{(0)}, \mathbf{g}^{(0)} \rangle = c_{u^{(0)}}. \tag{15.20}$$

Set $\Gamma^{(0)} = \mathbf{g}^{(0)}$, and set $c_1 = c_2 = c_{u^{(0)}}$. Finally, set $c_3 = \langle \mathbf{g}^{(0)}, \mathbf{g}^{(0)} \rangle$, which is a quantity that can be included in the output of pre-processing, as it is independent of $u^{(0)}$.[14] Under the above settings of $\Gamma^{(0)}$, c_1, c_2, and c_3, the validity of Equations (15.17)-(15.19) for $i = 1$ is equivalent to the validity of Equation (15.20).

Description of Round i. The purpose of Round i is to reduce the three equations above to three equations of the same form, but over vectors $u^{(i)}$ and $g^{(i)}$ that are shorter than $u^{(i-1)}, \mathbf{g}^{(i-1)}$ by a factor of 2. This is done as follows (below, we intermingle the description of each step of the protocol with intuitive justification for the step. A standalone protocol description is in Protocol 14).

- The prover begins by sending four quantities $D_{1L}, D_{1R}, D_{2L}, D_{2L} \in \mathbb{G}_t$ claimed to be AFGHO-commitments to the left and right halves of $u^{(i-1)}$ and $\mathbf{g}^{(i-1)}$ under key $\Gamma^{(i)}$. Conceptually, the point of sending these four commitments is to enable the verifier to homomorphically compute commitments under $\Gamma^{(i)}$ to $u^{(i)}$ and $\mathbf{g}^{(i)}$ (defined later in the protocol).

- The verifier chooses a random $\beta \in \mathbb{F}_p$ and sends it to $\mathcal{P}$. Conceptually, β is used to "take a random linear combination" of the three equations, yielding a single "equivalent" equation. Specifically, observe that if Equations (15.17)–(15.19) hold, then so does the following equation:

$$\langle u^{(i-1)} + \beta\Gamma^{(i-1)}, \mathbf{g}^{(i-1)} + \beta^{-1}\Gamma^{(i-1)} \rangle$$
$$= c_1 + \beta^{-1}c_2 + \beta c_3 + \langle \Gamma^{(i-1)}, \Gamma^{(i-1)} \rangle. \tag{15.21}$$

---

[14]More generally, Round i of the protocol will require that the pre-processing also output the quantity $\langle \Gamma^{(i-1)}, \Gamma^{(i-1)} \rangle$.

Meanwhile, it turns out that if the prover can establish that it knows $u^{(i-1)}$ and $\mathbf{g}^{(i-1)}$ such that Equation (15.21) holds even for just three values of β, then in fact $u^{(i-1)}$ and $\mathbf{g}^{(i-1)}$ satisfy Equations (15.17)–(15.19). This is because, if any one of Equations (15.17)–(15.19) fail to hold, then Equation (15.21) can only hold for at most 2 values of $\beta \in \mathbb{F}_p$, as the left hand and right hand sides of Equation (15.21) are distinct Laurent polynomials in β, and hence can agree on at most 2 points.

So, conceptually speaking, the remainder of Round i will be devoted to proving that Equation (15.21) holds for the verifier's random choice of β. As we detail below, the remainder of the round accomplishes this essentially by applying the standard Bulletproofs iteration to Equation (15.21), i.e., of randomly choosing an $\alpha \in \mathbb{F}_p$ and using it to "randomly combine" the left and right halves of $u^{(i-1)}$ and $\mathbf{g}^{(i-1)}$ respectively to obtain new vectors $u^{(i)}$ and $\mathbf{g}^{(i)}$ of half the length.

To this end, let

$$w_1 = u^{(i-1)} + \beta \Gamma^{(i-1)} \tag{15.22}$$

and

$$w_2 = \mathbf{g}^{(i-1)} + \beta^{-1} \Gamma^{(i-1)}, \tag{15.23}$$

and let w_{1L} and w_{1R} denote the left and right halves of w_1 and similarly for w_{2L} and w_{2R}.

- The prover sends cross-terms v_L and v_R claimed to equal $\langle w_{1L}, w_{2R} \rangle$ and $\langle w_{1R}, w_{2L} \rangle$.

- The verifier chooses a random $\alpha \in \mathbb{F}_p$ and sends it to the prover.

- The prover defines:

$$u^{(i)} = \alpha \cdot w_{1L} + \alpha^{-1} w_{1R} \tag{15.24}$$

$$\mathbf{g}^{(i)} = \alpha^{-1} \cdot w_{2L} + \alpha w_{2R}. \tag{15.25}$$

- The verifier does not know $u^{(i)}$ or $\mathbf{g}^{(i)}$ but can homomorphically compute the following three quantities:

    – $\langle u^{(i)}, \mathbf{g}^{(i)} \rangle$. Indeed, if Equations (15.17)–(15.19) hold and v_L, v_W are prescribed, then a straightforward consequence of Equation (15.21) is that

$$\langle u^{(i)}, \mathbf{g}^{(i)} \rangle = c_1 + \beta^{-1} c_2 + \beta c_3 + \langle \Gamma^{(i-1)}, \Gamma^{(i-1)} \rangle + \alpha v_L + \alpha^{-1} v_R.$$

$$(15.26)$$

    Note that the verifier has access to all terms on the right hand side of Equation (15.26) (as mentioned in Footnote 14, $\langle \Gamma^{(i-1)}, \Gamma^{(i-1)} \rangle$ can be computed in pre-processing.)

    – $\langle u^{(i)}, \Gamma^{(i)} \rangle$. Indeed, if D_{1L} and D_{1R} are as prescribed, then Equations (15.22) and (15.24) imply that:

$$\langle u^{(i)}, \Gamma^{(i)} \rangle = \alpha D_{1L} + \alpha^{-1} D_{1R} + \alpha \beta \Delta_L^{(i)} + \alpha^{-1} \beta \Delta_R^{(i)}. \quad (15.27)$$

    Recall that, here, $\Delta_L^{(i)} = \langle \Gamma_L^{(i-1)}, \Gamma^{(i)} \rangle$ and $\Delta_R^{(i)} = \langle \Gamma_R^{(i-1)}, \Gamma^{(i)} \rangle$ are commitments to the left and right halves of $\Gamma^{(i-1)}$ computed during pre-processing.

    – $\langle \mathbf{g}^{(i)}, \Gamma^{(i)} \rangle$. If D_{2L} and D_{2R} are as prescribed, then Equations (15.23) and (15.25) imply that

$$\langle \mathbf{g}^{(i)}, \Gamma^{(i)} \rangle = \alpha^{-1} D_{2L} + \alpha D_{2R} + \alpha^{-1} \beta^{-1} \Delta_L^{(i)} + \alpha \beta^{-1} \Delta_R^{(i)}.$$

$$(15.28)$$

- Let c_1', c_2', and c_3' denote the above three quantities that the verifier homomorphically computes. Round $i + 1$ is then devoted to showing that indeed the prover knows $u^{(i)}, \mathbf{g}^{(i)}$ such that the following three equations indeed hold:

$$\langle u^{(i)}, \mathbf{g}^{(i)} \rangle = c_1'$$

$$\langle u^{(i)}, \Gamma^{(i)} \rangle = c_2',$$

$$\langle \mathbf{g}^{(i)}, \Gamma^{(i)} \rangle = c_3'.$$

The above protocol is summarized in Protocol 14.

Sketch of the Extraction Analysis. The knowledge extractor proceeds similarly to the one for the protocol of Section 15.4.3. First, it constructs a 3-transcript tree for the protocol, of depth $2 \log n$ (the 2 comes in because each of the $\log n$ "conceptual rounds" in the protocol description actually consists of 2 communication rounds). For the remainder of this sketch, we use the phrase "round" to refer to a conceptual round.

As usual, the extractor proceeds from the leaves toward the root. At each node of distance $2i$ from the root (capturing the start of round $i + 1$ of the protocol), it constructs vectors $u^{(i)}$ and $\mathbf{g}^{(i)}$ that "explain" the prover's messages in all transcripts of the sub-tree rooted at that node.

Suppose by way of induction that the extractor has already succeeded in reconstructing such vectors for all vertices in the tree corresponding to rounds $i + 1$ and later. Consider a tree vertex corresponding to round $i + 1$ of the protocol, and let α, β denote the random group elements selected by the verifier in round i. Because AFGHO commitments are computationally binding and the extractor is efficient, one can argue that for the vector $u^{(i+1)}$ reconstructed by the extractor for that vertex, there is an (efficiently computable) vector $z = (z_L, z_R)$ such that

$$u^{(i+1)} = \alpha z_L + \alpha^{-1} z_R + \alpha\beta\Gamma_L^{(i-1)} + \alpha^{-1}\beta\Gamma_R^{(i-1)}.$$

This is because Equation (15.27) ensures that the commitment to $u^{(i+1)}$ is a commitment to a vector of this form. Similarly, one can argue that there is an (efficiently computable) vector $t = (t_L, t_R)$ such that the reconstructed vector $\mathbf{g}^{(i+1)}$ is of the form

$$\alpha^{-1} t_L + \alpha t_R + \alpha^{-1}\beta^{-1}\Gamma_L^{(i-1)} + \alpha\beta\Gamma_R^{(i-1)}.$$

Now consider any node of the transcript tree capturing the second message of round i of the protocol. Because the second message of Round i applies the Bulletproofs update procedure to commitments to w_1 and w_2 under commitment key $\Gamma^{(i)}$, the Bulletproofs extractor is able to reconstruct vectors w_1 and w_2 such that Equations (15.24) and (15.25) hold, i.e., w_1 and w_2 "explain" the reconstructed vectors $u^{(i+1)}$ and $\mathbf{g}^{(i+1)}$ for all child vertices of the node. Moreover, the previous paragraph implies that there are efficiently computable vectors $u^{(i-1)}$ and $\mathbf{g}^{(i-1)}$

such that Equations (15.22) and (15.23) hold, i.e., $w_1 = u^{(i-1)} + \beta \Gamma^{(i-1)}$ and $w_2 = \mathbf{g}^{(i-1)} + \beta^{-1} \Gamma^{(i-1)}$.

All that is left is to argue that $u^{(i-1)}$ and $\mathbf{g}^{(i-1)}$ satisfy Equations (15.17)–(15.19). That $u^{(i-1)}$ and $\mathbf{g}^{(i-1)}$ satisfy Equation (15.21) for the three values of β appearing in the 3-transcript tree follows from the following three facts. First, the verifier's commitment computation in Equation (15.26) applies the Bulletproofs update procedure to confirm that the prover knows vectors $w_1 = u^{(i-1)} + \beta \Gamma^{(i-1)}$ and $w_2 = \mathbf{g}^{(i-1)} + \beta^{-1} \Gamma^{(i-1)}$ such that Equation (15.21) holds. Second, as argued above, w_1 and w_2 "explain" the reconstructed vectors $u^{(i+1)}$ and $\mathbf{g}^{(i+1)}$ and hence they are exactly the vectors that the Bulletproofs knowledge extractor would compute if the Bulletproofs update procedure were applied to Equation (15.21). This means that the vectors computed by the extractor satisfy Equation (15.21). Finally, as explained in the protocol description itself, if $u^{(i-1)}$ and $\mathbf{g}^{(i-1)}$ satisfy Equation (15.21) for three or more values of β, then they also satisfy Equations (15.17)–(15.19).

Protocol 14 A transparent argument of knowledge of vectors $u, \mathbf{g} \in \mathbb{G}^n$ such that $\langle u, \mathbf{g} \rangle = c_1$, $\langle u, \Gamma \rangle = c_2$, and $\langle \mathbf{g}, \Gamma \rangle = c_3$, where $\Gamma \in \mathbb{G}^n$ is a public vector summarized via a linear-time pre-processing phase (Section 15.4.3). Here, $\mathbb{G}$ is an additive group and $\langle u, \mathbf{g} \rangle = \sum_{i=1}^{n} e(u_i, g_i)$ denotes the inner-pairing-product between u and $\mathbf{g}$. The protocol consists of $2 \log_2 n$ communication rounds, with 6 $\mathbb{G}_t$ elements communicated from prover to verifier per round. Total verifier time is dominated by $O(\log n)$ scalar multiplications in $\mathbb{G}_t$. For simplicity, we present the protocol for a symmetric pairing, though inner-pairing-product commitments are only binding for asymmetric pairings (in particular, under the SXDH assumption, which only holds for asymmetric pairings).

1: Let $\mathbb{G}$ be an additive cyclic group of prime order p with with bilinear map $e \colon \mathbb{G} \times \mathbb{G} \to \mathbb{G}_t$.

2: Input is $c_1 = \langle u, \mathbf{g} \rangle$, $c_2 = \langle u, \Gamma \rangle$, and $c_3 = \langle \mathbf{g}, \Gamma \rangle$, where $u, \mathbf{g}, \Gamma \in \mathbb{G}^n$. Verifier only knows c_1, c_2, c_3 and the following quantities computed during pre-processing: $\langle \Gamma, \Gamma \rangle$, as well as AFGHO commitments $\Delta_L = \langle \Gamma_L, \Gamma' \rangle$ and $\Delta_R = \langle \Gamma_R, \Gamma' \rangle$ to the left and right halves of Γ under public commitment key $\Gamma' \in \mathbb{G}^{n/2}$.

3: If $n = 1$, Prover sends u, $\mathbf{g}$, and Γ, to the verifier and the verifier checks that $c_1 = \langle u, \mathbf{g} \rangle$, $c_2 = \langle u, \Gamma \rangle$, $c_3 = \langle \mathbf{g}, \Gamma \rangle$, $\Delta_L = \langle \Gamma_L, \Gamma' \rangle$ and $\Delta_R = \langle \Gamma_R, \Gamma' \rangle$.

4: Otherwise, $\mathcal{P}$ sends $D_{1L}, D_{1R}, D_{2L}, D_{2L} \in \mathbb{G}_t$ claimed to be AFGHO-commitments to the left and right halves of u and $\mathbf{g}$ under key Γ'.

5: $\mathcal{V}$ chooses a random $\beta \in \mathbb{F}_p$ and sends it to $\mathcal{P}$.

6: $\mathcal{P}$ sets $w_1 = u + \beta\Gamma$ and $w_2 = \mathbf{g} + \beta^{-1}\Gamma$. Let w_{1L} and w_{1R} denote the left and right halves of w_1 and similarly for w_{2L} and w_{2R}.

7: $\mathcal{P}$ sends $v_L, v_R \in \mathbb{G}_t$ claimed to equal $\langle w_{1L}, w_{2R} \rangle$ and $\langle w_{1R}, w_{2L} \rangle$.

8: $\mathcal{V}$ chooses a random $\alpha \in \mathbb{F}_p$ and sends it to $\mathcal{P}$

9: $\mathcal{P}$ sets $u' = \alpha \cdot w_{1L} + \alpha^{-1} \cdot w_{1R}$ and $\mathbf{g}' = \alpha^{-1} \cdot w_{2L} + \alpha \cdot w_{2R}$.

10: $\mathcal{V}$ sets:

$$c_1' = c_1 + \beta^{-1}c_2 + \beta c_3 + \langle \Gamma, \Gamma \rangle + \alpha v_L + \alpha^{-1}v_R.$$
$$c_2' = \alpha D_{1L} + \alpha^{-1}D_{1R} + \alpha\beta\Delta_L + \alpha^{-1}\beta\Delta_R.$$
$$c_3' = \alpha^{-1}D_{2L} + \alpha D_{2R} + \alpha^{-1}\beta^{-1}\Delta_L + \alpha\beta^{-1}\Delta_R.$$

11: $\mathcal{V}$ and $\mathcal{P}$ apply the protocol recursively to prove that $\mathcal{P}$ knows vectors $u', \mathbf{g}' \in \mathbb{G}^{n/2}$ such that $\langle u', \mathbf{g}' \rangle = c_1$, $\langle u', \Gamma' \rangle = c_2$, and $\langle \mathbf{g}', \Gamma' \rangle = c_3$.

16

Wrap-Up of Polynomial Commitments

16.1 Batch Evaluation of Homomorphically Committed Polynomials

In some applications of polynomial commitment schemes to SNARKs, the verifier will wish to open many committed polynomials at the same point—see for example Section 10.3.2. We now explain that, if the polynomial commitment scheme is homomorphic (as all polynomial commitment schemes in this section are), all openings can be verified with essentially the same prover and verifier costs as a single opening.

Suppose for concreteness that the prover claims that $p(r) = y_1$ and $q(r) = y_2$ where p and q are committed polynomials over field $\mathbb{F}$, with commitments c_1 and c_2 respectively. Rather than verifying both claims independently, the verifier can instead verify a random linear combination of the claims, i.e., check that

$$a \cdot p(r) + q(r) = a \cdot y_1 + \cdot y_2 \tag{16.1}$$

for randomly chosen $a \in \mathbb{F}$. Clearly Equation (16.1) is true if both original claims are true. Meanwhile, because the left hand side and right hand side of Equation (16.1) are both linear functions of a, so if either one of the original claims is false, Equation (16.1) will be false except with probability at most $1/|\mathbb{F}|$ over the random choice of a.

So up to soundness error $1/|\mathbb{F}|$, verifying both claims is equivalent to verifying Equation (16.1), which is an evaluation claim about a single polynomial $ap + q$, of the same degree as p and q are individually. Via homomorphism, the verifier can compute a commitment c_3 to the polynomial $a \cdot p + q$ unaided. Hence, the prover and verifier can apply the polynomial commitment's evaluation procedure directly to this polynomial to check Equation (16.1).

This means the evaluation procedure has to be applied only *once* to check both original claims. The only extra work the prover does to reduce the two original claims to the one derived claim is to compute the polynomial $a \cdot p + q$, and the only extra work the verifier does is to compute the derived commitment c_3 from c_1 and c_2, and $a \cdot y_1 + y_2$ from y_1 and y_2. Both of these extra computations are typically low-order costs, i.e., far cheaper than computing and verifying an evaluation proof respectively.

More general batching techniques are also known, which can handle evaluating multiple different homomorphically-committed polynomials at distinct points [64].

16.2   Commitment Scheme for Sparse Polynomials

Let us call a degree-D univariate polynomial *dense* if the number of nonzero coefficients is $\Omega(D)$, i.e., at least a constant fraction of the coefficients are nonzero. Similarly, call an ℓ-variate multilinear polynomial dense if the number of coefficients over the Lagrange basis is $\Omega(2^\ell)$. If a polynomial is not dense, we call it *sparse*.

An example of sparse polynomials that we have seen in this survey are $\widetilde{\text{add}}_i$ and $\widetilde{\text{mult}}_i$, the multilinear extensions of the functions add_i and mult_i that arose in our coverage of the GKR protocol (Section 4.6) and the related functions $\widetilde{\text{add}}$ and $\widetilde{\text{mult}}$ appearing in the MIP of Section 8.2. Indeed, $\widetilde{\text{add}}$ and $\widetilde{\text{mult}}$ are defined over $\ell = 3 \log |\mathcal{C}|$ variables, and the number of Lagrange basis polynomials over this many variables is $2^\ell = |\mathcal{C}|^3$. However, the number of nonzero coefficients of $\widetilde{\text{add}}$ and $\widetilde{\text{mult}}$ in the Lagrange basis is just $|\mathcal{C}|$.

As discussed in Section 4.6.6, when $\widetilde{\mathrm{add}}$ and $\widetilde{\mathrm{mult}}$ cannot be evaluated in time sublinear in $|\mathcal{C}|$, one technique to save the verifier time is for a trusted party to commit to these polynomials in a pre-processing phase with a polynomial commitment scheme (this can be done transparently, so that any party willing to put in the effort can confirm that the commitment was computer correctly). Then whenever the GKR protocol or MIP of Sections 4.6 and 8.2 (or SNARKs derived thereof) is applied to $\mathcal{C}$ on a new input, the verifier need not evaluate $\widetilde{\mathrm{add}}$ and $\widetilde{\mathrm{mult}}$ on its own to perform the necessary checks of the prover's messages. Rather, the verifier can ask the prover to reveal the evaluations, using the evaluation phase of the polynomial commitment scheme. This reduces the verifier's runtime after the pre-processing phase from $\Theta(|\mathcal{C}|)$ to whatever is the verification time of the evaluation phase of the polynomial commitment scheme. Note that in this application of the polynomial commitment scheme, there is no need for the protocol to be zero-knowledge or extractable; it only needs to be binding to save the verifier work in the resulting zero-knowledge arguments for circuit satisfiability.

We have now seen several polynomial commitment schemes in which the committer's runtime is dominated by doing a number of group exponentiations that is linear in the number of coefficients for *dense* univariate and multilinear polynomials (e.g., Section 14.3). However, these schemes do not offer any additional runtime savings for the committer if the polynomials are sparse. For example, applying these schemes directly to $\widetilde{\mathrm{add}}$ and $\widetilde{\mathrm{mult}}$ requires $\Omega(|\mathcal{C}|^3)$ time, which is totally impractical.[1]

In this section, we sketch a commitment scheme proposed by Setty [226] for any polynomial q such that the runtime of the committer is proportional to the *nonzero coefficients* M of q. The commitment scheme uses any polynomial commitment scheme for *dense, multilinear polynomials* as a subroutine. This result is analogous to the holography achieved in Section 10.3.2, which gave a way to commit to any sparse *bivariate* polynomial given a commitment scheme for dense *univariate*

---

[1] Directly applying the KZG-based scheme for multilinear polynomials of Section 15.3 would allow the commitment to be computed in $O(|\mathcal{C}|)$ time, but the SRS would have length $|\mathcal{C}|^3$, and the evaluation phase may take time $\Omega(|\mathcal{C}|^3)$ for the committer.

polynomials. The schemes of this section and Section 10.3.2 share conceptual similarities, but also key differences.

For presentation purposes, we first describe a protocol that achieves the above goals up to a logarithmic factor. That is, the committer will have to apply a dense multilinear polynomial commitment scheme to a multilinear polynomial defined over $\ell' = \log_2 M + \log_2 \ell$ variables. Assuming M is $2^{\Omega(\ell)}$ (as is the case for $\widetilde{\mathrm{add}}$ and $\widetilde{\mathrm{mult}}$), $O(M\ell) \leq O(M \log M)$, so the dense polynomial to be committed is an $O(\log M)$ factor larger than can be hoped for.

At the end of this section we sketch a technique to remove even this extra $\ell = \Theta(\log M)$ factor from the committer's runtime by exploiting additional structure in $\widetilde{\mathrm{add}}$ and $\widetilde{\mathrm{mult}}$. For brevity, our sketch is very high-level, and deviates in certain details from Setty's scheme–the interested reader is directed to [137, Section 6] for a self-contained exposition of Setty's full scheme.

Simple Scheme with Logarithmic Factor Overhead.   The idea is to identify a layered arithmetic circuit $\mathcal{C}'$ of fan-in two that takes as input a description of a sparse ℓ-variate multilinear polynomial q (we specify the input description shortly) and a second input $z \in \mathbb{F}^\ell$, and such that $\mathcal{C}'$ outputs $q(z)$. We will ensure that the input to $\mathcal{C}'$ consists of $O(M\ell)$ field elements, and $\mathcal{C}'$ has size $O(M\ell)$ and depth $O(\log M)$. Also, $\mathcal{C}'$ will have wiring predicates $\widetilde{\mathrm{add}}_i$ and $\widetilde{\mathrm{mult}}_i$ that can be evaluated any point in $O(\log(M\ell))$ time.

If s denotes the input to $\mathcal{C}'$ specifying q, the commitment to q in our sparse polynomial commitment scheme will simply be a commitment to the multilinear extension $\tilde{s}$ of s using any commitment scheme for dense multilinear polynomials. The reveal phase of our sparse polynomial commitment scheme works as follows. When the verifier requests the committer reveal $q(z)$ for a desired $z \in \mathbb{F}^\ell$, the committer sends the claimed value v of $q(z)$, and then the committer and verifier apply the GKR protocol to the claim that $\mathcal{C}'(s, z) = v$.[2] At the end of the GKR protocol, the verifier needs to evaluate the multilinear extension

---

[2]They could also apply the MIP of Section 8.2 to verify this claim, replacing the second prover with a polynomial commitment scheme for dense multilinear polynomials.

of the input (s, z) at a random point. Since the verifier knows z but not s, using an observation analogous to Equation (7.1), the multilinear extension of (s, z) can be efficiently evaluated at any desired point so long as the verifier learns an evaluation of $\tilde{s}$ at a related point. The verifier can obtain this evaluation from the prover using the reveal phase of the dense polynomial commitment scheme.

Since $\mathcal{C}'$ has size $O(M\ell)$, the GKR protocol prover applied to $\mathcal{C}'$ can be implemented in $O(M\ell)$ total time, and committing to $\tilde{s}$ using an appropriate dense polynomial commitment scheme requires a multi-exponentiation of size $O(M\ell)$. Since $\widetilde{\text{add}}_i$ and $\widetilde{\text{mult}}_i$ for $\mathcal{C}'$ can be evaluated in $O(\log(M\ell))$ time, the verifier's runtime in the protocol is dominated by the cost of the evaluation phase of the dense polynomial commitment scheme.

Here is how the input to $\mathcal{C}'$ will specify the polynomial q. Let $T_1, \ldots, T_M \in \{0, 1\}^\ell$ denote the Lagrange basis polynomials $\chi_{T_1}, \ldots, \chi_{T_M}$ that have nonzero coefficients $c_1, \ldots, c_M$ in q. That is, let

$$q(X) = \sum_{i=1}^{M} c_i \cdot \prod_{j=1}^{\ell} (T_{i,j} X_j + (1 - T_{i,j})(1 - X_j)). \tag{16.2}$$

The description s of q will consists of two lists $L[1], \ldots, L[M]$ and $B[1], \ldots, B[M]$, where $L[i] = c_i \in \mathbb{F}_p$ and $B[i] = T_i \in \{0, 1\}^\ell$. The circuit $\mathcal{C}'$ will simply evaluate Equation (16.2) at input z. It is not hard to verify that Equation (16.2) can be evaluated by an arithmetic circuit with $O(M\ell)$ gates, such that the multilinear extensions of the wiring predicates add_i and mult_i for each layer of $\mathcal{C}'$ can be evaluated in $O(\log(M\ell))$ time.

Saving a logarithmic factor (sketch). The idea to shave a factor of ℓ from the size of $\mathcal{C}'$ and the length of its input when committing to $q = \widetilde{\text{add}}$ or $q = \widetilde{\text{mult}}$ is as follows. First, modify the description of q, so as to reduce the description length from $O(M \cdot \ell)$ field elements down to $O(M)$ field elements. Then identify a Random Access Machine $\mathcal{M}$ that takes as input this modified description of q and an input $z \in \mathbb{F}^\ell$ and outputs $q(z)$. We make sure that $\mathcal{M}$ runs in time $O(M)$, and that $\mathcal{M}$ can be transformed into a circuit of size that is just a constant factor larger than its runtime.

Here is how to modify the description of $q = \widetilde{\text{add}}$. Rather than having the identities of the nonzero Lagrange coefficients of $\widetilde{\text{add}}$ be specified via a list of bit-strings $T_1, \ldots, T_M \in \{0,1\}^{3\log|\mathcal{C}|}$, we instead specify their identities with triples of *integers* $(u_1, u_2, u_3) \in \{1, \ldots, |\mathcal{C}|\}^3$, and interpret a triple as indicating that the u_1'st gate of $\mathcal{C}$ is an addition gate with in-neighbors assigned integer labels u_2 and u_3.

The Random Access Machine $\mathcal{M}$ works as follows. It is given as input the modified description of $q = \widetilde{\text{add}}$ and a point $z = (r_1, r_2, r_3) \in \left(\mathbb{F}_p^{\log|\mathcal{C}|}\right)^3$, runs in $O(M)$ time and outputs $q(z)$. Recall from Section 8.2 that $\text{add}(a, b, c) : \{0,1\}^{3\log S} \to \{0,1\}$ interprets its input as three gate labels a, b, c and outputs 1 if and only if b and c are the in-neighbors of gate a, and a is an addition gate. This means that

$$\widetilde{\text{add}}(X, Y, Z) = \sum_{a \in \{0,1\}^{\log|\mathcal{C}|} \,:\, a \text{ an add gate}} \chi_a(X) \cdot \chi_{\text{in}_1(a)}(Y) \cdot \chi_{\text{in}_2(a)}(Z),$$

(16.3)

where $\text{in}_1(a)$ and $\text{in}_2(a)$ respectively denote the labels in $\{0,1\}^{\log|\mathcal{C}|}$ of the first and second in-neighbors of gate a in $\mathcal{C}$. Recall in addition from Lemma 3.8 that evaluating all $(\log|\mathcal{C}|)$-variate Lagrange basis polynomials at a specified input $r \in \mathbb{F}^{\log|\mathcal{C}|}$ can be done in $O(|\mathcal{C}|)$ time. So to evaluate $\widetilde{\text{add}}$ at an input $(r_1, r_2, r_3) \in \left(\mathbb{F}^{\log|\mathcal{C}|}\right)^3$ in $O(|\mathcal{C}|)$ time, it suffices for $\mathcal{M}$ to operate in two phases. In the first phase, $\mathcal{M}$ evaluates all $(\log|\mathcal{C}|)$-variate Lagrange basis polynomials at the three inputs $r_1, r_2, r_3 \in \mathbb{F}^{\log|\mathcal{C}|}$ in $O(|\mathcal{C}|)$ time (this can be done without even examining the list of triples (u_1, u_2, u_3)), and stores the $3 \cdot |\mathcal{C}|$ results in memory. In the second phase, $\mathcal{M}$ evaluates $\widetilde{\text{add}}$ at (r_1, r_2, r_3) via Equation (16.3) in $O(|\mathcal{C}|)$ additional time, given random access to the memory contents. Note that the the memory accesses made by $\mathcal{M}$ depend only on the committed polynomial q and are independent of the evaluation point z.

Using the computer-programs-to-circuit-satisfiability transformation of Section 6, specifically using the fingerprinting-based memory-checking procedure described in Section 6.6.2, $\mathcal{M}$ can be transformed into a circuit-satisfiability instance for a circuit $\mathcal{C}'$. As described in Sections 6.6.2 and 6.6.3, the transformation procedure from $\mathcal{M}$ to the circuit-satisfiability instance is itself interactive, but the transformation can be rendered non-interactive in the random oracle model using the Fiat-Shamir transformation.

16.3 Polynomial Commitment Schemes: Pros and Cons

We have seen three approaches to the construction of practical polynomial commitment schemes. The first is based on IOPs, specifically FRI (Section 10.4.2), and Ligero-and Brakedown-commitments (Section 10.5). The second (Section 14) builds in sophisticated ways on homomorphic commitment schemes such as Pedersen commitments [206], and Schnorr-style [223] techniques for proving inner product relations between a committed vector and a public vector; this approach based binding on the assumed hardness of the discrete logarithm problem. The third (Section 15) is derived from work of KZG [164] and is based on bilinear maps and requires a trusted setup. Roughly, the practical pros and cons of the three approaches to polynomial commitment schemes are the following.

Pros and Cons of the IOP-Based Polynomial Commitments. The IOP approach is the only one of the three approaches that is plausibly quantum-secure (it can lead to security in the quantum random oracle model [99]). The other two approaches assume hardness of the discrete logarithm problem, which is a problem that quantum computers can solve in polynomial time. Another advantage of the IOP approach is that it uses very small public parameters (these simply specify one or more cryptographic hash functions) that moreover can be generated at random, i.e., they simply specify a randomly chosen hash function from a collision-resistant hash family. That is, unlike the third approach, the first (and also the second) approach is transparent, meaning it does not require a structured reference string (SRS) generated by a trusted party who will have the power to forge proofs of evaluations if they fail to discard toxic waste.

The downsides of the IOP-based schemes include the following. FRI's evaluation proofs, while polylogarithmic in size and the smallest amongst known IOP-based schemes, are concretely rather large, especially relative to commitment schemes from other approaches with logarithmic or constant size proofs, e.g., Bulletproofs (Section 14.4), Dory (Section 15.4), and KZG commitments (Section 15).

FRI also has relatively high concrete costs for the prover. To be more precise, FRI exhibits a strong tension between prover costs and verification costs, with the tradeoff between the two determined by the *rate* of the Reed-Solomon code used in the protocol (see Section 10.4.4 for details). Under current security analyses, if FRI is configured to have a slower prover than other polynomial commitment schemes (e.g., using Reed-Solomon code rate 1/16), the size of evaluation proofs at 100 bits of security is substantially over 100 KBs. See, for example, [145] for details. When configured to have a faster prover, the proof sizes are considerably larger. For example, when using rate rate 1/2 rather than rate 1/16, the proofs are roughly 4× larger though the prover is roughly 8× faster.

Ligero- and Brakedown-commitments are faster for the prover than FRI, but have significantly bigger proofs. Some approaches toward mitigating their proof sizes via SNARK composition [95], [253] are discussed in Section 19.

Another major disadvantage of the IOP approach is that the other two approaches yield homomorphic commitments (i.e., given two commitments c_p, c_q to two polynomials p and q, a commitment c to the sum of $p + q$ can be derived). This homomorphism property leads to excellent batch-opening properties (Section 16.1) and is essential in some applications of polynomial commitment schemes (see for example Section 18.5 later in this survey). FRI and Ligero also require the prover to perform FFTs, which can place some restrictions on the field used and for large instances can be a bottleneck in prover time and space.

Pros and Cons of Discrete-Logarithm Based Polynomial Commitments. The second approach is also transparent because the public parameters are simply random group elements— though depending on the commitment scheme, there can be a lot of them, and generating many random elements of elliptic-curve groups can be expensive in practice. This approach does not require FFTs, and the committer performs $O(n)$ many group exponentiations in any group for which the discrete logarithm problem is hard (with a Pippenger-style multi-exponentiation speedup possible, with the exception of Bulletproof's evaluation proofs). Hence, this approach currently has very good concrete efficiency for the committer, roughly comparable to Ligero- and Brakedown-commitments for large enough polynomials. Until the advent of Dory (Section 15.4), this approach did require larger verifier runtime than the other two approaches. For example, in Hyrax's commitment scheme (Section 14.3), the verifier computes a multi-exponentiation of size $O(\sqrt{n})$, while in Bulletproofs (Section 14.4) the multi-exponentiation done by the verifier has *linear size*, $\Theta(n)$. Dory reduces the verifier time to $O(\log n)$ group exponentiations, at the cost of constant-factor increase in the time to compute commitments, mostly due to Dory's need to operate in a pairing-friendly group, which can lead concretely slower group operations. The costs of the transparent polynomial commitment schemes covered in this survey are summarized in Table 16.1.

Pros and Cons of KZG-Based Polynomial Commitments. The primary benefit of the third approach is its superior verification costs when applied to univariate polynomials. Specifically, both the commitment and proofs of evaluation consist of a constant number of group elements, and can be verified with a constant number of group operations and two bilinear map evaluations. For multilinear polynomials (Section 15.3) these costs are logarithmic in the number of coefficients instead of constant.

A significant downside of the third approach is that it requires an SRS, with toxic waste that must be discarded to avoid forgeability of evaluation proofs. There has been significant work to mitigate the trust assumptions required, and it is now known how to make the SRS "updatable". This means that the SRS can be updated at any point by any party, such that if even a single party is honest—meaning a single party discards their toxic waste—then no one can forge proofs of evaluation [187]. The rough idea for why this is possible is that the SRS consists of powers of a random nonzero field element $\tau \in \{1, \ldots, p-1\}$ in the exponent of a group generator g, so any party can "rerandomize the choice of τ" by picking a random $s \in \{1, \ldots, p-1\}$ and updating the ith element of the SRS from g^{τ^i} to $(g^{\tau^i})^{s^i} = g^{(\tau s)^i}$. That is, by

Table 16.1: Costs of transparent polynomial commitment schemes covered in this survey. For simplicity, this table restricts its focus to univariate polynomials of degree N with coefficients over the standard monomial basis. λ denotes the security parameter. Commit time and $\mathcal{P}$ time columns respectively list a dominant operation to produce the commitment and an evaluation proof. $\mathcal{V}$ time lists a dominant operation to verify any evaluation proof. FRI and Ligero-commit are plausibly post-quantum, but not homomorphic; the others are homomorphic, but not post-quantum. Dory requires operations over a pairing-friendly group and a pre-processing phase costing $O(\sqrt{N})$ group exponentiations. The public parameters for FRI and Ligero simply specify a cryptographic hash function. For Bulletproofs, they are $O(N)$ random group elements, while for all other rows they are $O(\sqrt{N})$ random group elements. The term exp is short for group exponentiation, and the term field ops is short for field operations.

Scheme	Commit Size	Evaluation Proof Size	$\mathcal{V}$ Time	Commit Time	$\mathcal{P}$ Time
FRI (Sections 10.4.4 and 10.4.2)	one hash value	$O(\log^2(N) \cdot \lambda)$ hash values	$O(\log^2(N) \cdot \lambda)$ hash evaluations	$O(N \log N)$ field ops	$O(N \log N)$ field ops
Ligero-commit (Section 10.5)	one hash value	$O(\sqrt{N} \cdot \lambda)$ field elements	$O(\sqrt{N} \cdot \lambda)$ field ops	$O(N \log N)$ field ops	$O(N)$ field ops
Hyrax-commit (Section 14.3)	$O(\sqrt{N})$ group elements	$O(\sqrt{N})$ group elements	multi-exp of size $\sqrt{N}$	$\sqrt{N}$ multi-exps of size $\sqrt{N}$	$O(N)$ field ops
Bulletproofs (Section 14.4)	one group element	$O(\log N)$ group elements	multi-exp of size $O(N)$	multi-exp of size $O(N)$	$O(N)$ group exps
Hyrax-commit+ Bulletproofs (Section 14.4.2)	$O(\sqrt{N})$ group elements	$O(\log N)$ groups elements	multi-exp of size $\sqrt{N}$	$\sqrt{N}$ multi-exps of size $\sqrt{N}$	$O(N)$ field ops
Dory (Section 15.4)	one group element	$O(\log N)$ group elements	multi-exp of size $O(\log N)$	$\sqrt{N}$ multi-exps of size $\sqrt{N}$	$O(N)$ field ops

raising the ith entry of the SRS to the power s^i, τ is effectively updated to $\tau \cdot s \mod p$, which is a random element of $\{1, \ldots, p-1\}$.

KZG commitments can also be more computation-intensive for the committer than alternatives. For example, it requires a similar number of public-key cryptographic operations (i.e., group exponentiations) as the second approach, but as with Dory these operations must be in pairing-friendly groups, for which group operations may be concretely more expensive.

16.4 Additional Approaches

Recent polynomial commitment schemes that we do not discuss in this survey include [13], [57], [83], which are based on a cryptographic notion called groups of unknown order. Specifically, so-called DARKs [83] claimed a polynomial commitment scheme with similar asymptotic verifier complexity to Dory (logarithmic size evaluation proofs and verifier time), but contained a flaw in the security analysis. This was rectified in [57] and a later version of [83], and [13] improved the size of the evaluation proof from a logarithmic number of group elements to constant (verification time remains logarithmic, and prover costs increase substantially). Current constructions of groups of unknown order require a trusted setup or appear to be impractical. One construction is based on so-called class groups, which are currently impractical in this context [108] (see [179, Table 2] for microbenchmarks), and the other is based on so-called RSA groups modulo $\{-1, 1\}$, which require a trusted setup.

Another example is recent work [22], [71] that operates in a manner similar to Bulletproofs (Section 14.4), but modifies it in order to base security on lattice assumptions that are believed to be post-quantum secure. This approach currently appears to yield significantly larger proofs than the discrete-logarithm based protocols that it is inspired by.

17

Linear PCPs and Succinct Arguments

17.1 Overview: Interactive Arguments From "Long", Structured PCPs

"Short" PCPs for circuit satisfiability were covered in Section 9—by short, we mean the PCP proof has length quasilinear in the circuit size. Recall (Section 9.2) that Kilian [168] showed that short PCPs can be transformed into succinct arguments by first having the prover cryptographically commit to the PCP string π via Merkle-hashing. Then the argument-system verifier can simulate the PCP verifier, who queries a small number of symbols of π. The argument system prover can reveal these symbols of the committed PCP proof π, along with succinct authentication information to establish that the revealed symbols are indeed consistent with the committed string.

Unfortunately, short PCPs are quite complicated and remain impractical.[1] This section covers succinct arguments obtained via a similar methodology, but without resorting to complicated and impractical short PCPs.

---

[1] Though interactive analogs of PCPs called IOPs can achieve reasonable concrete performance (Section 10).

439

Arguments Without Short PCPs.   Why is the prover inefficient if one instantiates Kilian's argument system [168] with a PCP of superpolynomial length $L = n^{\omega(1)}$? The problem is that $\mathcal{P}$ has to materialize the full proof π in order to compute its Merkle-hash and thereby commit to π. Materializing a proof of superpolynomial length clearly takes superpolynomial time.

But Ishai *et al.* [156] (IKO) showed that if π is highly structured in a manner made precise below, then there is a way for $\mathcal{P}$ to cryptographically commit to π *without* materializing all of it. This enables IKO to use structured PCPs of exponential length to obtain succinct interactive arguments. Such "long" PCPs turn out to be much simpler than short PCPs. The commitment protocol of [156] is based on any semantically secure, additively-homomorphic cryptosystem, such as ElGamal encryption [110]. Here, an additively-homomorphic encryption scheme is analogous to the notion of an additively-homomorphic commitment scheme (Section 12.3) which we exploited at length in Sections 13 and 14. It is an encryption scheme for which one can compute addition over encrypted data without decrypting the data.

Linear PCPs. The type of structure in the PCP proof that IKO [156] exploit is linearity. Specifically, in a *linear PCP*, the proof is interpreted as a function mapping $\mathbb{F}^v \to \mathbb{F}$ for some integer $v > 0$. A linear PCP is one in which the "honest" proof is (the evaluation table of) a linear function π. That is, π should satisfy that for any two queries $q_1, q_2 \in \mathbb{F}^v$ and constants $d_1, d_2 \in \mathbb{F}$, $\pi(d_1 q_1 + d_2 q_2) = d_1 \pi(q_1) + d_2 \pi(q_2)$. This is the same as requiring that π be a v-variate polynomial of total degree 1, with constant term equal to 0. Note that in a linear PCP, soundness should hold even against "cheating" proofs that are non-linear. So the only difference between a linear PCP and a PCP is that in a linear PCP, the honest proof is guaranteed to have special structure.

Putting it All Together. Summarizing the above, the arguments of IKO [156] conceptually proceed in the same two steps as Kilian's argument based on short PCPs. In the first step, the prover commits to the proof π, but unlike in Kilian's approach, here the prover can leverage the linearity of π to commit to it without ever materializing π in full. In the second step, the argument system verifier simulates the linear PCP verifier, asking the prover to reveal certain evaluations of π, which the prover does using the reveal phase of the commitment protocol.

Hence, in order to give an efficient argument system based on linear PCPs, IKO [156] had to do two things. First, give a linear PCP for arithmetic circuit satisfiability. Second, give a commit/reveal protocol for linear functions.

In the results of IKO's seminal paper, there are downsides to both of the steps above. First, when applied to circuits of size S, IKO's linear PCP has length $|\mathbb{F}|^{O(S^2)}$, i.e., exponential in the *square* of the circuit size. To achieve practicality, this needs to be reduced to exponential in S itself rather than its square. Second, IKO's commit/reveal protocol for linear functions is *interactive*. This means that the arguments obtained thereof are also interactive. Moreover, the arguments cannot be rendered non-interactive via the Fiat-Shamir transformation because they are not public-coin. Interactivity, and associated lack of public verifiability, renders the arguments unusable in many practical scenarios.

Subsequent work addressed both of the downsides above. First, Gennaro *et al.* (GGPR) [125] give a linear PCP[2] of length $|\mathbb{F}|^{O(S)}$. Second, alternate transformations were given to turn linear PCPs into succinct *non-interactive* arguments [56], [125]. These transformations use pairing-based cryptography in a manner reminiscent of KZG commitments (Section 15.2). Applying these transformations to GGPR's linear PCP yields SNARKs, variants of which are widely used in practice today.[3]

Characteristics of the Resulting Arguments. A downside of long PCPs is that if the proof π has length L, then even writing down one of the verifier's queries to π requires $\log L$ field elements. If L is exponential in the circuit size $S = |\mathcal{C}|$, then even $\log(L)$ is *linear* in the circuit size. This means that even *specifying* the linear PCP verifier's queries takes time $\Omega(S)$. Compare this to the MIPs, PCPs, and IOPs from Sections 8–10, where the verifier's total runtime was $O(n + \text{polylog}(S))$, where

---

[2]The observation that GGPR's protocol is actually a linear PCP as defined by IKO was made in later work [56], [227].

[3]A variant of the SNARK due to Groth [142] is especially popular. See Section 17.5.6.

n is the size of the public input to $\mathcal{C}$. In the zk-SNARKs we obtain in this section, these long messages from the PCP verifier to specify its queries to π will translate into a long structured reference string, of length $\Omega(S)$, the generation of which produces "toxic waste" that could be used to forge "proofs" of false statements if it is not discarded.

This is analogous to how many SNARKs for circuit-satisfiability that use KZG-polynomial commitments (Section 15.2) require an SRS of size $\Omega(S)$. An important difference is that the SRS in KZG-based SNARKs depends only on the size S of the circuit under consideration, while the SRS arising in the SNARKs of this section is *circuit-specific*. If one tweaks the circuit under consideration even slightly, a new trusted setup must be run.

However, the communication in the reverse direction of the linear PCP, from prover to verifier, is very small (a constant number of field elements) and the verifier's online verification phase is especially fast as a consequence. This will ultimately lead to SNARKs with state-of-the-art proof length and verification costs.

Outline for the Section. Section 17.2 covers IKO's commit/reveal protocol for linear functions. Section 17.3 describes IKO's linear PCP of length $|\mathbb{F}|^{O(S^2)}$. Section 17.4 covers GGPR's linear PCP of length $|\mathbb{F}|^{O(S)}$. Section 17.5 covers transformations from linear PCPs to SNARKs via pairing-based cryptography.

17.2　Committing to a Linear PCP without Materializing It

Let π be a linear function $\mathbb{F}^v \to \mathbb{F}$. This section sketches the technique of IKO [156] for allowing the prover to first commit to π in a "commit phase" and then answer a series of k queries $q^{(1)}, \ldots, q^{(k)} \in \mathbb{F}^v$ in a "reveal phase". Roughly speaking, the security guarantee is that at the end of the commit phase, there is *some* function π' (which may not be linear) such that, if the verifier's checks in the protocol all pass and $\mathcal{P}$ cannot break the cryptosystem used in the protocol, then the prover's answers in the reveal phase are all consistent with π'.[4]

---

[4]This section actually sketches a refinement of IKO's commitment/reveal protocol, due to Setty *et al.* [228]. The original protocol of IKO guaranteed that for each

In more detail, the protocol uses a semantically secure homomorphic cryptosystem. Roughly speaking, semantic security guarantees that, given a ciphertext $c = \text{Enc}(m)$ of a plaintext m, any probabilistic polynomial time algorithm cannot "learn anything" about m. Semantic security is an analog of the hiding property of commitment schemes such as Pedersen commitments (Section 12.3). A cryptosystem is (additively) homomorphic if, for any pair of plain texts (m_1, m_2) and fixed constants $d_1, d_2 \in \mathbb{F}$, it is possible to efficiently compute the encryption of $d_1 m_1 + d_2 m_2$ from the encryptions of m_1 and m_2 individually. Here, in the context of linear PCPs, m_1 and m_2 will be elements of the field $\mathbb{F}$, so the expression $d_1 m_1 + d_2 m_2$ refers to addition and scalar multiplication over $\mathbb{F}$.

Many additively homomorphic encryption schemes are known, such as the popular ElGamal encryption scheme, whose security is based on the Decisional Diffie-Hellman assumption introduced in Section 15.1.

Commit Phase. In the commit phase, the verifier chooses a vector $r = (r_1, \ldots, r_v) \in \mathbb{F}^v$ at random, encrypts each entry of r and sends all v encryptions to the prover. Since π is linear, there is some vector $d = (d_1, \ldots, d_v) \in \mathbb{F}^v$ such that $\pi(q) = \sum_{i=1}^v d_i \cdot q_i = \langle d, q \rangle$ for all queries $q = (q_1, \ldots, q_v)$. Hence, using the homomorphism property of the encryption scheme, the prover can efficiently compute the encryption of $\pi(r)$ from the encryptions of the individual entries of r. Specifically, $\text{Enc}(\pi(r)) = \text{Enc}(\sum_{i=1}^v d_i r_i)$, and by the homomorphism property of Enc, this last expression can be efficiently computed from $\text{Enc}(r_1), \ldots, \text{Enc}(r_v)$. The prover sends this encryption to the verifier, who decrypts it to obtain (what is claimed to be) $s = \pi(r)$.

Remark 17.1. At the end of the commit phase, using the homomorphism property of Enc and the linearity of π, the honest prover has managed to send to the verifier an encryption of $\pi(r)$, even though the prover has no idea what r is (this is what semantic security of Enc

---

query i, there is a separate function π_i to which $\mathcal{P}$ was committed. Setty *et al.* [228] tweaked the protocol of IKO in a way that both reduced costs and guaranteed that $\mathcal{P}$ was committed to answering all k queries using a single function π' (which is possibly non-linear).

guarantees). Moreover, the prover has accomplished this in $O(v)$ time. This is far less than the $\Omega(|\mathbb{F}|^v)$ time required to evaluate π at all points, which would be required if the prover were to build a Merkle tree with the evaluations of π as the leaves.

One may wonder whether the use of an additively homomorphic *encryption* scheme Enc can be replaced with an additively homomorphic *commitment* scheme such as Pedersen commitments. Indeed, given a Pedersen commitment to each entry of r, the prover could compute a Pedersen commitment c^* to $\pi(r)$ using additive homomorphism, despite not knowing r, just as the prover in this section is able to compute $\mathrm{Enc}(\pi(r))$ given $\mathrm{Enc}(r_1), \ldots, \mathrm{Enc}(r_v)$. The problem with this approach is that the verifier, who does not know π, would not be able to open c^* to $\pi(r)$. In contrast, by using an encryption scheme, the verifier can decrypt $\mathrm{Enc}(\pi(r))$ to $\pi(r)$ despite not knowing π.

Reveal Phase. In the reveal phase, the verifier picks k field elements $\alpha_1, \ldots, \alpha_k \in \mathbb{F}$ at random, and keeps them secret. The verifier then sends the prover the queries $q^{(1)}, \ldots, q^{(k)}$ in the clear, as well as $q^* = r + \sum_{i=1}^{k} \alpha_i \cdot q^{(i)}$. The prover returns claimed answers $a^{(1)}, \ldots, a^{(k)}, a^* \in \mathbb{F}$, which are supposed to equal $\pi(q^{(1)}), \ldots, \pi(q^{(k)}), \pi(q^*)$. The verifier checks that $a^* = s + \sum_{i=1}^{k} \alpha_i \cdot a^{(i)}$, accepting the answers as valid if so, and rejecting otherwise.

Clearly the verifier's check will pass if the prover is honest. The proof of binding roughly argues that the only way for $\mathcal{P}$ to pass the verifier's checks, if $\mathcal{P}$ does not answer all queries using a single function, is to know the α_i's, in the sense that one can efficiently compute the α_i's given access to such a prover. But if the prover knows the α_i's, then the prover must be able to solve for r, since $\mathcal{V}$ reveals $q^* = r + \sum_{i=1}^{k} \alpha_i \cdot q^{(i)}$ to the prover. But this would contradict the semantic security of the underlying cryptosystem, which guarantees that the prover learned nothing about r from the encryptions of r's entries.

17.2.1   Detailed Presentation of Binding Property When $k = 1$

We present the main idea of the proof of binding, in the case that only one query is made in the reveal phase, i.e., $k = 1$. What does it mean for the prover *not* to be bound to a fixed function after the commitment phase of the protocol? It means that there are at least two runs of the reveal protocol, where in the first run, the verifier sends queries q_1 and $q^* = r + \alpha \cdot q_1$, and the prover responds with answers a_1 and a^*, while in the second run the verifier sends queries q_1 and $\hat{q} = r + \alpha' \cdot q_1$, and the prover responds with answers $a'_1 \neq a_1$ and $\hat{a}$. That is, in two different runs of the reveal protocol, the prover responded to the same query q_1 with two different answers, and managed to pass the verifier's checks.

As indicated above, we will argue that in this case, the prover must know α and α'. But, as we now explain, this breaks the semantic security of the encryption scheme.

Why the prover knowing α and α' means semantic security is broken. Roughly speaking, this is because if the prover really learned nothing about r from $\text{Enc}(r_1), \ldots, \text{Enc}(r_v)$, as promised by semantic security of Enc, then it should be impossible for the prover to determine α with probability noticeably better than random guessing, even given $q_1, q^* = r + \alpha \cdot q_1$, and $\hat{q} = r + \alpha' \cdot q_1$. This is because, without knowing r, all that the equations

$$q^* = r + \alpha q_1 \tag{17.1}$$

and

$$\hat{q} = r + \alpha' \cdot q_1 \tag{17.2}$$

tell the prover about α and α' is that they are two field elements satisfying $q^* - \hat{q} = (\alpha - \alpha')q_1$. This is because, for every pair $\alpha, \alpha' \in \mathbb{F}$ satisfying Equations (17.1) and (17.2) for r, and any $c \in \mathbb{F}$, the pair $\alpha + c, \alpha' + c$ also satisfy both equations when r is replaced by $r - cq_1$. So without knowing anything about r, Equations (17.1) and (17.2) reveal no information whatsoever about α itself. Equivalently stated, if the prover knows α, then the prover must have learned something about r, in violation of semantic security of Enc.

Showing that the prover must know α and α'. Recall that s is the decryption of the value sent by the prover in the commit phase, which is claimed to be $\text{Enc}(\pi(r))$. Since the prover cannot decrypt, the prover does not know s. Even so, if the verifier's checks in the two runs of the reveal phase pass, then the prover does know that:

$$a^* = s + \alpha a_1, \tag{17.3}$$

and

$$\hat{a} = s + \alpha' a_1. \tag{17.4}$$

Subtracting these two equations means that the prover knows that

$$(a^* - \hat{a}) = \alpha a_1 - \alpha' a_1', \tag{17.5}$$

Similarly, even though the prover doesn't know r, the prover does know that Equations (17.1) and (17.2) hold. Subtracting those two equations implies that $q^* - \hat{q} = (\alpha - \alpha')q_1$.

We may assume that none of the queries are the all-zeros vector, since any linear function π evaluates to 0 on the all-zeros vector. Hence, if we let j denote any nonzero coordinate of q_1, then:

$$q_j^* - \hat{q}_j = (\alpha - \alpha')q_{1,j}. \tag{17.6}$$

Since $a_1 \neq a_1'$, Equations (17.5) and (17.6) express α and α' via two linearly independent equations in two unknowns, and these have a unique solution. Hence, the prover can solve these two equations for α and α' as claimed.

17.3　A First Linear PCP for Arithmetic Circuit Satisfiability

Let $\{\mathcal{C}, x, y\}$ be an instance of arithmetic circuit satisfiability (see Section 6.5.1). For this section, we refer to a setting $W \in \mathbb{F}^S$ of values to each gate in $\mathcal{C}$ as a transcript for $\mathcal{C}$.

The linear PCP of this section is from IKO [156], and is based on the observation that W is a correct transcript if and only if W satisfies the following $\ell = S + |y| - |w|$ constraints (there is one constraint for every other non-output gate of $\mathcal{C}$, there are two constraints for each output gate of $\mathcal{C}$, and there are no constraints for any witness elements).

- For each input gate a, there is a constraint enforcing that $W_a - x_a = 0$. This effectively insists that the transcript W actually corresponds to the execution of $\mathcal{C}$ on input x, and not some other input.

- For each output gate a there is a constraint enforcing that $W_a - y_a = 0$. This effectively insists that the transcript W actually correspond to an execution of C that produces outputs y, and not some other set of outputs.

- If gate a is an addition gate with in-neighbors $\text{in}_1(a)$ and $\text{in}_2(a)$, there is a constraint enforcing that $W_a - \left(W_{\text{in}_1(a)} + W_{\text{in}_2(a)} \right) = 0$.

- If gate a is a multiplication, there is a constraint enforcing that $W_a - W_{\text{in}_1(a)} \cdot W_{\text{in}_2(a)} = 0$.

Together, the last two types of constraints insist that the transcript actually respects the operations performed by the gates of C. That is, any addition (respectively, multiplication) gate actually computes the addition (respectively, product) of its two inputs. Note that the constraint for gate a of C is always of the form $Q_a(W) = 0$ for some polynomial Q_a of degree at most 2 in the entries of W.

For a transcript W for $\{C, x, y\}$, let $W \otimes W$ denote the length-(S^2) vector whose (i, j)th entry is $W_i \cdot W_j$. Let $(W, W \otimes W)$ denote the vector of length $S + S^2$ obtained by concatenating W with $W \otimes W$. Let

$$f_{(W, W \otimes W)}(\cdot) := \langle \cdot, (W, W \otimes W) \rangle.$$

That is, $f_{(W, W \otimes W)}$ is the linear function that takes as input a vector in $\mathbb{F}^{S+S^2}$ and outputs its inner product with $(W, W \otimes W)$. Consider a linear PCP proof π containing all evaluations of $f_{(W, W \otimes W)}$. π is typically called the *Hadamard encoding* of $(W, W \otimes W)$. Notice that π has length $|\mathbb{F}|^{S+S^2}$, which is enormous. However, $\mathcal{P}$ will never need to explicitly materialize all of π.

$\mathcal{V}$ needs to check three things. First, that π is a linear function. Second, assuming that π is a linear function, $\mathcal{V}$ needs to check that π is of the form $f_{(W, W \otimes W)}$ for some transcript W. Third, $\mathcal{V}$ must check that W satisfies all ℓ constraints described above.

First Check: Linearity Testing.   Linearity testing is a considerably simpler task than the more general low-degree testing problems considered in the MIP of Section 8.2 (linearity testing is equivalent to testing that an m-variate function equals polynomial of total degree 1 (with no constant term), while the low-degree testing problem considered in Section 8.2 tested whether an m-variate function is multilinear, which means its total degree can be as large as m).

Specifically, to perform linearity testing, the verifier picks two random points $q^{(1)}, q^{(2)} \in \mathbb{F}^{S+S^2}$ and checks that $\pi(q^{(1)} + q^{(2)}) = \pi(q^{(1)}) + \pi(q^{(2)})$, which requires three queries to π. If π is linear then the test always passes. Moreover, it is known that if the test passes with probability $1 - \delta$, then there is some linear function f_d such that π is δ-close to f_d [60], at least over fields of characteristic 2.[5]

Second Check. Assuming π is linear, π can be written as f_d for some vector $d \in \mathbb{F}^{S+S^2}$. To check that d is of the form $(W, W \otimes W)$ for some transcript W, $\mathcal{V}$ does the following.

- $\mathcal{V}$ picks $q^{(3)}, q^{(4)} \in \mathbb{F}^S$ at random.

- Let $(q^{(3)}, \mathbf{0})$ denote the vector in $\mathbb{F}^{S+S^2}$ whose first S entries equal $q^{(3)}$ and whose last S^2 entries are 0. Similarly, let $(\mathbf{0}, q^{(3)} \otimes q^{(4)})$ denote the vector whose first S entries equal 0, and whose last S^2 entries equal $q^{(3)} \otimes q^{(4)}$. $\mathcal{V}$ checks that $\pi(q^{(3)}, \mathbf{0}) \cdot \pi(q^{(4)}, \mathbf{0}) = \pi(\mathbf{0}, q^{(3)} \otimes q^{(4)})$. This requires three queries to π.

The check will pass if π is of the claimed form, since in this case

$$\pi(q^{(3)}, \mathbf{0}) \cdot \pi(q^{(4)}, \mathbf{0}) =$$

$$\left(\sum_{i=1}^{S} W_i q_i^{(3)} \right) \cdot \left(\sum_{j=1}^{S} W_j q_j^{(4)} \right) = \sum_{1 \leq i,j \leq S} W_i W_j q_i^{(3)} q_j^{(4)} = \langle q^{(3)} \otimes q^{(4)}, W \otimes W \rangle$$

$$= \pi(\mathbf{0}, q^{(3)} \otimes q^{(4)}).$$

If π is not of the claimed form, the test will fail with high probability over the choice of $q^{(3)}$ and $q^{(4)}$. This holds because $\pi(q^{(3)}, \mathbf{0}) \cdot \pi(q^{(4)}, \mathbf{0}) = f_d(q^{(3)}, \mathbf{0}) \cdot f_d(q^{(4)}, \mathbf{0})$ is a quadratic polynomial in the entries of $q^{(3)}$ and

---

[5]See [9, Theorem 19.9] for a short proof of this statement based on Discrete Fourier analysis. Over fields of characteristic other than 2, the known soundness guarantees of the linearity test are weaker. See [227, Proof of Lemma A.2] and [27, Theorem 1.1].

$q^{(4)}$, as is $f_d\left(\mathbf{0}, q^{(3)} \otimes q^{(4)}\right)$, and the Schwartz-Zippel lemma (Lemma 3.3) guarantees that any two distinct low-degree polynomials can agree on only a small fraction of points.

Third Check. Once $\mathcal{V}$ is convinced that $\pi = f_d$ for some d of the form $(W, W \otimes W)$, $\mathcal{V}$ is ready to check that W satisfies all ℓ constraints described above. This is the core of the linear PCP.

In order to check that $Q_i(W) = 0$ for all constraints i, it suffices for $\mathcal{V}$ to pick random values $\alpha_1, \ldots, \alpha_\ell \in \mathbb{F}$, and check that $\sum_{i=1}^{\ell} \alpha_i Q_i(W) = 0$. Indeed, this equality is always satisfied if $Q_i(W) = 0$ for all i; otherwise, $\sum_{i=1}^{\ell} \alpha_i Q_i(W)$ is a nonzero multilinear polynomial in the variables $(\alpha_1, \ldots, \alpha_\ell)$, and the Schwartz-Zippel lemma guarantees that this polynomial is nonzero at almost all points $(\alpha_1, \ldots, \alpha_\ell) \in \mathbb{F}^\ell$.

Notice that $\sum_{i=1}^{\ell} \alpha_i Q_i(W)$ is itself a degree-2 polynomial in the entries of W, which is to say that it is a linear combination of the entries of $(W, W \otimes W)$. Hence it can be evaluated with one additional query to π.

Soundness Analysis. A formal proof of the soundness of the linear PCP just described is a bit more involved than indicated above, but not terribly so. Roughly it proceeds as follows. If the prover passes the linearity test with probability $1 - \delta$, then π is δ-close to a linear function f_d. Hence, as long as the 4 queries in the second and third checks are distributed uniformly in $\mathbb{F}^{S+S^2}$, then with probability at least $1 - 4 \cdot \delta$, the verifier will never encounter a point where π and f_d differ, and we can treat π as f_d for the remainder of the analysis. However, the queries in the second and third checks are not uniformly distributed in $\mathbb{F}^{S+S^2}$ as described. Nonetheless, they can be made uniformly distributed by replacing each query q with two random queries q' and q'' subject to the constraint that $q' + q'' = q$. This way, the marginal distributions of q' and q' are uniform over $\mathbb{F}^{S+S^2}$. And by linearity of f_d, it holds that $f_d(q)$ can be deduced to equal $f_d(q') + f_d(q'')$. With this change, the soundness analysis of the second and third steps are as indicated above.

Costs of the Argument System. One obtains an argument system by combining the above linear PCP with IKO's commitment/reveal protocol for linear functions (Section 17.3). The costs of this argument system are summarized in Table 17.1. Total communication from $\mathcal{V}$ to $\mathcal{P}$ is $\Theta(S^2)$, and hence $\mathcal{V}$ and $\mathcal{P}$'s runtime is also $\Theta(S^2)$. On the positive side, the communication in the reverse direction is just a constant number of field elements per input. Also, if $\mathcal{V}$ is simultaneously verifying $\mathcal{C}$'s execution over a large *batch* of inputs, then the $\Theta(S^2)$ communication and time costs can be amortized over the entire batch.

Such $\Theta(S^2)$ costs are very high, precluding practicality. Conceptually, the reason for the $\Theta(S^2)$ costs above is that the prover is forced to materialize the vector $W \otimes W$, whose (i, j)'th entry is $W_i \cdot W_j$. This is effectively forcing the prover to compute the product of every two gates i and j in the circuit, irrespective of the circuit's wiring pattern. That is, the prover must compute the product of every pair of gates in the circuit, irrespective of whether those two gates are actually multiplied together by another gate in the circuit. Then the third check in the linear PCP above effectively ignores almost all of those S^2 products, checking the validity only of the at most S products that actually correspond to multiplication gates in the circuit.

Section 17.4 below explains how to "cut out" the unnecessary products above, reducing the $\Theta(S^2)$ costs to $\Theta(S)$.

Table 17.1: Costs of the argument system from Section 17.3 for arithmetic circuit satisfiability when run on a circuit $\mathcal{C}$ of size S. Note that the verifier's cost and the communication cost can be amortized when simultaneously outsourcing $\mathcal{C}$'s execution on a large *batch* of inputs. The stated bound on $\mathcal{P}$'s time assumes $\mathcal{P}$ knows a witness w for $\mathcal{C}$.

$\mathcal{V} \to \mathcal{P}$ Communication	$\mathcal{P} \to \mathcal{V}$ Communication	$\mathcal{V}$ Time	$\mathcal{P}$ Time
$O(S^2)$ field elements	$O(1)$ field elements	$O(S^2)$	$O(S^2)$

17.4   GGPR: A Linear PCP of Size $O(|\mathbb{F}|^S)$ for Circuit-SAT and R1CS

In a breakthrough result, Gennaro *et al.* [125] gave a linear PCP of length $O(|\mathbb{F}|^S)$ for arithmetic circuit satisfiability, where S denotes the size of the circuit.[6] In fact, their linear PCP also solves the more general problem of R1CS satisfiability (see Section 8.4 for a detailed introduction to R1CS and how to transform arithmetic circuit satisfiability instances into R1CS-satisfiability instances).[7,8] In this section, we choose to present the linear PCPs of [125] in the context of R1CS rather than arithmetic circuits because we feel this leads to a clearer description of the protocol, and is more general. The linear PCPs of [125] have been highly influential, and form the foundation of many of the implementations of argument systems.

Recap of R1CS.   For the reader's convenience, we briefly recall the definition of R1CS. An R1CS instance over field $\mathbb{F}$ is of the form

$$A z \circ B z = C z, \tag{17.7}$$

where A, B, and C are public matrices in $\mathbb{F}^{\ell \times S}$. Here, $\circ$ denotes entrywise-wise product. An R1CS instance is satisfiable if there is some vector $z \in \mathbb{F}^S$ satisfying Equation (17.7). Note that z can be thought of as the R1CS-analog of the circuit transcript W appearing in Section 17.3.

Equivalently, if $a_i, b_i, c_i \in \mathbb{F}^S$ respectively denote the ith rows of A, B, and C, then an R1CS instance consists of ℓ *constraints*, with the ith constraint of the form

$$\langle a_i, z \rangle \cdot \langle b_i, z \rangle - \langle c_i, z \rangle = 0. \tag{17.8}$$

The linear PCPs of [125] crucially exploit that the left hand side of Equation (17.8) can be evaluated in constant time given three linear

---

[6]The argument system of Gennaro *et al.* can be understood in multiple ways, and [125] did not present it within the framework of linear PCPs. Subsequent work [56], [227] identified the protocol of Gennaro *et al.* as an example of a linear PCP.

[7]Gennaro *et al.* referred to R1CS satisfiability problems as *Quadratic Arithmetic Programs* (QAPs).

[8]IKO's linear PCP covered in Section 17.3 also applied to R1CS satisfiability, though we only presented it in the context of circuit satisfiability.

functions evaluated at z, namely $\langle a_i, z \rangle$, $\langle b_i, z \rangle$, and $\langle c_i, z \rangle$. This is a stronger notion of structure than was exploited Section 17.3. Section 17.3 only exploited that each circuit gate corresponds to a constraint involving a polynomial (in the entries of the circuit transcript W) of total degree at most 2. This meant that the constraint is a linear function of the entries of the vector $W \otimes W$, but this vector has length S^2, leading to quadratic costs in the linear PCP of that section.

The linear PCP. Our ultimate goal is to associate any vector $z \in \mathbb{F}^S$ with a univariate polynomial $g_z(t)$ that vanishes on H if and only if z satisfies the R1CS instance (Equation (17.7)). To define g_z, we must first define several constituent polynomials that together capture the R1CS matrices.

Polynomials capturing matrix columns. Let $H := \{\sigma_1, \ldots, \sigma_\ell\}$ be a set of ℓ arbitrary distinct elements in $\mathbb{F}$, one for each constraint in the R1CS instance. For each $j \in \{1, \ldots, S\}$, we define three univariate polynomials $\mathcal{A}_j$, $\mathcal{B}_j$, and $\mathcal{C}_j$, meant to "capture" the j'th column of A, B, and C respectively. Specifically, for each $j \in \{1, \ldots, S\}$, define three degree-$(\ell - 1)$ polynomials via interpolation as follows.

$$\mathcal{A}_j(\sigma_i) = A_{i,j} \text{ for all } i \in \{1, \ldots, \ell\}.$$
$$\mathcal{B}_j(\sigma_i) = B_{i,j} \text{ for all } i \in \{1, \ldots, \ell\}.$$
$$\mathcal{C}_j(\sigma_i) = C_{i,j} \text{ for all } i \in \{1, \ldots, \ell\}.$$

Turning z into a polynomial that vanishes on H if and only if z is a satisfying assignment. Let $g_z(t)$ denote the following univariate polynomial:

$$\left(\sum_{\text{columns } j \in \{1,\ldots,S\}} z_j \cdot \mathcal{A}_j(t) \right) \cdot \left(\sum_{\text{columns } j \in \{1,\ldots,S\}} z_j \cdot \mathcal{B}_j(t) \right)$$
$$- \left(\sum_{\text{columns } j \in \{1,\ldots,S\}} z_j \cdot \mathcal{C}_j(t) \right). \tag{17.9}$$

By design, g_z vanishes on H if and only all R1CS constraints are satisfied, i.e., if and only if z is a satisfying assignment for the R1CS instance. Indeed,

$$g_z(\sigma_i) = \left(\sum_{\text{columns } j} z_j \cdot A_{i,j} \right) \cdot \left(\sum_{\text{columns } j} z_j \cdot B_{i,j} \right)$$
$$- \left(\sum_{\text{columns } j} z_j \cdot C_{i,j} \right) = \langle a_i, z \rangle \cdot \langle b_i, z \rangle - \langle c_i, z \rangle,$$

where a_i, b_i, and c_i the ith rows of A, B, and C respectively (see Equation (17.8)). Hence $g_z(\sigma_i) = 0$ if and only if the ith constraint in the R1CS instance is satisfied by z.

Checking Whether g_z Vanishes on H. To check whether g_z vanishes on H, we rely on Lemma 9.3, which also played a key role in our constructions of efficient PCPs and IOPs (Sections 9 and 10) and is restated here for the reader's convenience.

Lemma 17.1. (Ben-Sasson and Sudan [50]) Let $\mathbb{F}$ be a field and $H \subseteq \mathbb{F}$. For $d \geq |H|$, a degree-d univariate polynomial g over $\mathbb{F}$ vanishes on H if and only if the polynomial $\mathbb{Z}_H(t) := \prod_{\alpha \in H}(t - \alpha)$ divides g, i.e., if and only if there exists a polynomial h^* with $\deg(h^*) \leq d - |H|$ such that $g = \mathbb{Z}_H \cdot h^*$.

By inspection, the degree of the polynomial g_z is at most $d = 2(\ell-1)$, where ℓ is the number of constraints. By Lemma 9.3, to convince $\mathcal{V}$ that g_z vanishes on H, the proof merely needs to convince $\mathcal{V}$ that $g_z = \mathbb{Z}_H \cdot h^*$ for some polynomial h^* of degree $d - |H| = \ell - 1$. To be convinced of this, $\mathcal{V}$ can pick a random point $r \in \mathbb{F}$ and check that

$$g_z(r) = \mathbb{Z}_H(r) \cdot h^*(r). \tag{17.10}$$

Indeed, because any two distinct degree $(\ell - 1)$ polynomials can agree on at most $\ell - 1$ points, if $g_z \neq \mathbb{Z}_H \cdot h^*$, then this equality will fail with probability at least $1 - (\ell - 1)/|\mathbb{F}|$.

To this end, a correct proof represents two linear functions. The first is $f_{\text{coeff}(h^*)}$, where $\text{coeff}(h^*)$ denotes the vector of coefficients of h^*

(recall that f_v for any vector $v \in \mathbb{F}^\ell$ denotes the ℓ-variate linear function $f_v(x) := \langle v, x \rangle$). The second is f_z. Note that

$$f_{\text{coeff}(h^*)}(1, r, r^2, \ldots, r^{\ell-1}) = h^*(r), \tag{17.11}$$

so $\mathcal{V}$ can evaluate $h^*(r)$ with a single query to the proof. Similarly, $\mathcal{V}$ can evaluate g_z at r by evaluating f_z at the three vectors $(\mathcal{A}_1(r), \ldots, \mathcal{A}_S(r))$, $(\mathcal{B}_1(r), \ldots, \mathcal{B}_S(r))$, and $(\mathcal{C}_1(r), \ldots, \mathcal{C}_S(r))$.

Remark 17.2. In applications, there will in fact be a public input $x \in \mathbb{F}^n$ to the R1CS instance, and it will be required that the satisfying vector z have $z_i = x_i$ for $i = 1, \ldots, n$ (and these requirements are not otherwise included in the R1CS constraints). One can easily modify the linear PCP to enforce this by letting $z' = (z_{n+1}, \ldots, z_S)$ and replacing the linear function f_z in the proof with $f_{z'}$. Whenever the linear PCP verifier wants to query f_z at some vector $q = (q'', q') \in \mathbb{F}^n \times \mathbb{F}^{S-n}$, note that $f_z(q) = \left(\sum_{j=1}^{n} q''_j \cdot x_j \right) + f_{z'}(q')$. Hence, the the verifier can query the proof $f_{z'}$ at q' to obtain $v = f_{z'}(q')$ and set $f_z(q) = \left(\sum_{j=1}^{n} q''_j \cdot x_j \right) + v$.

Just as in the linear PCP of Section 17.3, the verifier also has to perform linearity testing on $f_{\text{coeff}(h^*)}$ and f_z. The verifier must also replace the four queries described above with two queries each to ensure that all queries are uniformly distributed. These complications arise because we required that a linear PCP be sound against proofs that are *non-linear* functions of queries. We remark that for purposes of the non-interactive argument system of the next section (Section 17.5), the linear PCP verifier need not perform linearity testing nor ensure that any of its queries are uniformly distributed. This is because the cryptographic techniques in that section bind the argument system prover to *linear functions*, so the underlying information-theoretic protocol does not need to bother testing whether the function is in fact linear. In contrast, the cryptographic techniques of Section 17.2 only bind the prover to some function which was not necessarily linear, hence the need for the underlying linear PCP to be sound against proofs that are non-linear functions.

Argument System Costs. One can obtain an argument system by combining the linear PCP above with the commitment protocol for linear functions of Section 17.2. This argument system is not currently used in practice; one reason for this is that it is interactive. Still, it is instructive to examine the costs of the resulting argument system. They next section (Section 17.5) will provide a different transformation of the linear PCP above into a succinct argument that addresses the downsides of Section 17.2 while essentially preserving the costs.

The costs of the argument system are summarized in Table 17.2. The honest prover $\mathcal{P}$ needs to perform the following steps, assuming $\mathcal{P}$ knows a satisfying assignment z for the R1CS instance. First, compute the polynomial $g_z(t)$. Second, divide g_z by $\mathbb{Z}_H$ to find the quotient polynomial h^*. Third, run the linear commitment/reveal protocol described in Section 17.2, to commit to $f_{\mathrm{coeff}(h^*)}$ and f_z and answer the verifier's queries.

For simplicity, let us assume that the number of R1CS constraints (matrix rows) ℓ is less than or equal to the number of columns S, and that $O(S)$ many entries of the matrices A, B, and C are non-zero— this is the case for R1CS instances resulting from circuit-satisfiability instances of size S, see Section 8.4. The third step can clearly be done in time $O(S)$.[9] The first step, of computing g_z, can be done in time $O(S \log^2 S)$ using standard multipoint interpolation algorithms based on the Fast Fourier Transform (FFT).[10] The second step can be done in time $O(S \log S)$ using FFT-based polynomial division algorithms.

Total communication from $\mathcal{V}$ to $\mathcal{P}$ is $\Theta(S)$ as well, but the communication in the reverse direction is just a constant number of field elements per input. Because the communication from $\mathcal{V}$ to $\mathcal{P}$ is so

---

[9]More precisely, this step requires taking a linear combination of $O(S)$ ciphertexts of a homomorphic encryption scheme.

[10]In somewhat more detail, the polynomial g_z can be expressed as $\mathcal{A} \cdot \mathcal{B} - \mathcal{C}$ where $\mathcal{A}$, $\mathcal{B}$, and $\mathcal{C}$ are degree-$(\ell - 1)$ polynomials whose coefficients over the Lagrange basis corresponding to the set H can be computed in time proportional to the number of nonzero entries of each matrix. Given these coefficients, fast multi-point interpolation algorithms can evaluate g_z at any desired set $H' \subseteq \mathbb{F}$ of size ℓ in $\mathbb{F}$ in time $O(S \log^2 S)$. Since g_z has degree $2(\ell - 1)$, if H' is disjoint from H, then the 2ℓ evaluations of g_z at points in $H \cup H'$ uniquely specify g_z. In fact, for all $\sigma \in H'$, $h^*(\sigma)$ can be computed directly from $g_z(\sigma)$, via: $h^*(\sigma) = g_z(\sigma) \cdot \mathbb{Z}_H(\sigma)^{-1}$. Since h^* has degree at most $\ell - 1$, these evaluations uniquely specify h^*. The coefficients of h^* in the standard monomial basis can be computed in $O(S \log S)$ time using FFT-based algorithms.

Table 17.2: Costs of the argument system from Section 17.4 when run on a circuit satisfiability instance $\{\mathcal{C}, x, w\}$ of size S, or R1CS instance with $O(S)$ nonzero entries in each of the matrices A, B, C. The $\tilde{O}$ notation hides polylogarithmic factors in S. Note that the verifier's cost and the communication cost can be amortized when outsourcing the circuit $\mathcal{C}$'s execution on a *batch* of inputs. The stated bound on $\mathcal{P}$'s time assumes $\mathcal{P}$ knows a witness w for $\mathcal{C}$ or a solution vector z for the R1CS instance.

$\mathcal{V} \to \mathcal{P}$ Communication	$\mathcal{P} \to \mathcal{V}$ Communication	$\mathcal{V}$ Time	$\mathcal{P}$ Time
$O(S)$ field elements	$O(1)$ field elements	$\tilde{O}(S)$	$\tilde{O}(S)$

large, i.e., $\Theta(S)$, $\mathcal{V}$'s runtime is also $\Theta(S)$. So this argument system in uninteresting if applied to a *single input* to $\mathcal{C}$: the verifier would be just as fast in the trivial protocol in which the prover sends a witness w to the verifier, and the verifier checks on her own that $\mathcal{C}(x, w) = y$. However, if $\mathcal{V}$ is simultaneously verifying $\mathcal{C}$'s execution over a large batch of inputs, then the $\Theta(S)$ cost for $\mathcal{V}$ can be amortized over the entire batch.

Note that the verifier's check does require $\mathcal{V}$ to evaluate $\mathbb{Z}_H(r)$, where $\mathbb{Z}_H(X) = \prod_{\sigma \in H}(X - \sigma)$ is the vanishing polynomial of H. Since the verifier requires $O(S)$ time just to specify the linear PCP queries, $\mathcal{V}$'s asymptotic time bound in the linear PCP is not affected by computing $\mathbb{Z}_H(r)$ directly via S subtractions and multiplications. Nonetheless, H could be chosen carefully to ensure that $\mathbb{Z}_H(x)$ is sparse, thereby enabling $\mathbb{Z}_H(r)$ to be evaluated in $o(S)$ time. For example, if H is chosen to be a multiplicative subgroup of $\mathbb{F}$ of order ℓ (the setting considered in Section 10.3, see Equation (10.1)), then $\mathbb{Z}_H(X) = X^\ell - 1$. Clearly, then $\mathbb{Z}_H(r)$ can be evaluated with $O(\log n)$ field multiplications.

In the non-interactive argument presented in the next section, $\mathbb{Z}_H(r)$ can simply be provided to the verifier as part of the trusted setup procedure, which takes time $O(S)$ regardless of whether or not H is chosen to ensure $\mathbb{Z}_H$ is a sparse polynomial.

17.5 Non-Interactivity and Public Verifiability

17.5.1 Informal Overview

We have already seen (Section 17.2) how to convert the linear PCP of the previous section to a succinct interactive argument using any additively-homomorphic encryption scheme. We cannot apply the Fiat-Shamir transformation to render this argument system non-interactive because it is not public coin—the argument system makes use of an additively homomorphic encryption scheme for which the verifier chooses the private key, and if the prover learns the private key it can break soundness of the argument system.

Instead, linear PCPs can be converted to non-interactive arguments using pairing-based techniques extremely similar to the KZG polynomial commitment scheme of Section 15.2. The idea is as follows (we simplify slightly in this informal overview, deferring a complete description of the protocol until Section 17.5.3).[11] Rather than having the verifier send the linear PCP queries to the prover "in the clear" as in the interactive argument of Section 17.2, the entries of the linear PCP queries $q^{(1)}, \ldots, q^{(k)}$, will be *encoded* in the exponent of a group generator $\mathbf{g}$ for pairing-friendly group $\mathbb{G}$, and the encodings provided to the prover via inclusion in a structured reference string. The argument system then exploits the additive homomorphism of the encoding, i.e., that the encoding $\mathbf{g}^{x+y}$ of $x + y \in \mathbb{F}_p$ equals the product of the encodings $\mathbf{g}^x, \mathbf{g}^y$ of x and y individually, so long as $|\mathbb{G}| = p$.[12] If $\pi(x) = \sum_j c_j x_j$ denotes a linear PCP proof, the additive homomorphism allows the prover to evaluate the encodings of $\pi(q^{(1)}), \ldots, \pi(q^{(k)})$ and send them to the verifier. Finally, the argument system verifier accepts if and only if the linear PCP verifier would accept the responses $\pi(q^{(1)}), \ldots, \pi(q^{(k)})$. Since the argument system prover did not send $\pi(q^{(1)}), \ldots, \pi(q^{(k)})$ in

---

[11]In this section, we use the serif font $\mathbf{g}$ rather than g to denote a generator of a pairing-friendly group $\mathbb{G}$, to distinguish the group generator from the polynomial $g_{x,y,w}$ defined in the previous section.

[12]The encoding $\mathbf{g}^x$ of x is an (unblinded) Pedersen commitment to x (Section 12.3). But in the SNARK of this section, neither the prover nor the verifier can open these "commitments", i.e., the exponents of the group elements in the structured reference string are "computationally hidden" from both prover and verifier. This is why we refer to an SRS entry g^x as an encoding of x rather than a commitment to x.

the clear, but rather *encodings* $g^{\pi(q^{(1)})}, \ldots, g^{\pi(q^{(k)})}$, it is not immediately obvious how the argument system verifier can make this determination. This is where pairings come in.

Observe that the verifier's check in the linear PCP is a total-degree-2 function of the responses to the PCP queries. Indeed, recall that the linear PCP verifier checks that $g_z(r) = \mathbb{Z}_H(r) \cdot h^*(r)$. Letting

$$q^{(1)} = (A_1(r), \ldots, A_S(r)),$$

$$q^{(2)} = (B_1(r), \ldots, B_S(r)),$$

and

$$q^{(3)} = (C_1(r), \ldots, C_S(r)),$$

then

$$g_z(r) = f_z(q^{(1)}) \cdot f_z(q^{(2)}) - f_z(q^{(3)}),$$

which is clearly a function of total degree two in the linear PCP prover responses $f_z(q^{(1)})$, $f_z(q^{(2)})$, and $f_z(q^{(3)})$, with a single multiplication operation. Similarly, letting $q^{(4)} = (1, r, \ldots, r^S)$, the right hand side of the verifier's check is a linear (i.e., total degree 1) function of the linear PCP prover response $f_{\text{coeff}(h^*)}(q^{(4)})$.

Recall from Section 15.1 that the entire point of pairings is that they allow for a single "multiplication check" to be performed on encoded values, without the need to decode the values. This enables the argument system verifier to perform the linear PCP verifier's check "in the exponent". That is, if the argument system prover responds to the ith query with g^{v_i}, the verifier can use the bilinear map associated with $\mathbb{G}$ to check whether the PCP verifier would have accepted if the PCP prover had answered query $q^{(i)}$ with value v_i.

17.5.2   A Complication: Linear Interactive Proofs vs. Linear PCPs

The argument system sketched above runs into the following complication. While (under appropriate Knowledge of Exponent assumptions) the pairing-based cryptography forces the argument system prover to answer each encoded linear PCP query in a manner consistent with a linear function, it does not ensure that all queries are answered with *the same* linear function.[13] That is, for the argument system to be sound, we really need the underlying linear PCP to be sound against provers that use a different linear function to answer each query.[14] Such a linear PCP is called a (2-message) *linear interactive proof* (LIP) [56].

Bitansky *et al.* [56] give a simple and efficient method for translating any linear PCP into a LIP. Specifically, if soundness of the linear PCP requires that queries $q^{(1)}, \ldots, q^{(k')}$ be answered with the same linear function, the LIP verifier simply adds an extra query $q^{(k+1)} = \sum_{i=1}^{k'} \beta_i q^{(i)}$ to the linear PCP, where $\beta_1, \ldots, \beta_{k'}$ are randomly chosen field elements known only to the verifier. That is, $q^{(k+1)}$ is a random linear combination of the relevant linear PCP queries. The LIP verifier checks that the answer a_{k+1} to the $(k+1)$'st query equals $\sum_{i=1}^{k'} \beta_i a_i$, and if so, feeds answers $a_1, \ldots, a_k$ to the linear PCP verifier. It can be shown that if the linear PCP is complete and knowledge-sound, then the resulting LIP is as well. We omit the proof of this fact, but the idea is to argue that if the LIP prover does not answer all $k' + 1$ queries $q^{(1)}, \ldots, q^{(k')}, q^{(k+1)}$ using the same linear function for each query, then there is some nonzero linear function π such that the prover will pass the LIP verifier's final check only if $\pi(\beta_1, \ldots, \beta_{k'}) = 0$. Since $\beta_1, \ldots, \beta_{k'}$ are chosen uniformly at random from $\mathbb{F}$, the Schwartz-Zippel lemma (Lemma 3.3) implies that this occurs with probability at most $1/|\mathbb{F}|$.

17.5.3   Complete Description of the SNARK

Here is the entire non-interactive argument system. Recall that $q^{(1)}, \ldots, q^{(4)}$ were defined in Section 17.5.1. Accounting for the transformation from a linear PCP to an LIP of Section 17.5.2, we define a 5th query vector $q^{(5)} := \sum_{i=1}^{3} \beta_i q^{(i)}$, where $\beta_1, \ldots, \beta_3$ are randomly chosen elements of $\mathbb{F}_p$. We do not include the 4th query in this random linear combination because soundness of the linear PCP from Section 17.4 only requires that the first 3 queries be answered with the same linear

---

[13]In fact, the cryptography does not prevent the prover from answering the ith (encoded) query $q^{(i)}$ with (an encoding of) a linear combination of entries of *all of the queries* $q^{(1)}, \ldots, q^{(3)}$.

[14]More precisely, owing to Footnote 13, the linear PCP needs to be secure against provers that answer each of the four queries with different linear function of all four queries.

function f_z, and completeness in fact requires that the 4th query be answered with a different linear function, namely $f_{\text{coeff}(h^*)}$.

For every entry $q_j^{(i)}$ of each of the five LIP queries $q^{(1)}, \ldots, q^{(5)}$, the SRS contains the pair $(g^{q_j^{(i)}}, g^{\alpha q_j^{(i)}})$ where α is chosen at random from $\{1, \ldots, p-1\}$. The verification key (i.e., the information provided to the verifier by the trusted setup procedure) contains the quantities g, g^α, $g^{\mathbb{Z}_H(r)}$, g^{β_1}, g^{β_2}, g^{β_3}. Note that all quantities in the SRS can be computed during the setup phase because they depend only on the R1CS matrices, not on the witness vector z.

Using the SRS and additive homomorphism, the prover computes and sends to the verifier five pairs of group elements $(g_1, g_1') \ldots$, $(g_4, g_4'), (g_5, g_5')$ claimed to equal

$$(g^{f_z(q^{(1)})}, g^{\alpha \cdot f_z(q^{(1)})}),$$

$$(g^{f_z(q^{(2)})}, g^{\alpha \cdot f_z(q^{(2)})}),$$

$$(g^{f_z(q^{(3)})}, g^{\alpha \cdot f_z(q^{(3)})}),$$

$$(g^{f_{\text{coeff}(h^*)}(q^{(4)})}, g^{\alpha \cdot f_{\text{coeff}(h^*)}(q^{(4)})}),$$

and

$$(g^{f_z(q^{(5)})}, g^{\alpha \cdot f_z(q^{(5)})}).$$

The verifier performs the following checks. First, it checks that

$$e(g_1, g_2) = e(g_3, g) \cdot e\left(g^{\mathbb{Z}_H(r)}, g_4\right). \tag{17.12}$$

Second, it checks that

$$\prod_{i=1}^{3} e(g^{\beta_i}, g_i) = e(g_5, g). \tag{17.13}$$

Third, for each of the five pairs (g_i, g_i') for $i = 1, \ldots, 5$, the verifier checks that

$$e(g_i, g^\alpha) = e(g, g_i'). \tag{17.14}$$

17.5.4 Establishing Completeness and Knowledge-Soundness

Completeness of the SNARK holds by design. Indeed, by bilinearity of e, the first check of the verifier (Equation (17.12)) is specifically designed to pass if $g_{x,y,W}(r) = Z_H(r) \cdot h^*(r)$ and the prover returns the prescribed proof elements. The second check (Equation (17.13)) will pass if and only if $g_5 = \prod_{i=1}^{3} g_i^{\beta_i}$, which will be the case if the prover behaves as prescribed. Similarly, the final set of checks (Equation (17.14)) will pass if indeed $g_i' = g_i^{\alpha}$ for all i.

The proof of knowledge-soundness relies on the following two cryptographic assumptions. These are mild variants of the two assumptions (PKoE and SDH) that we relied upon for the pairing-based polynomial commitment of Section 15.2.

Knowledge of Exponent Assumption (KEA). This is a Variant of the PKoE assumption. Recall that the SRS for the SNARK of this section consists of $t = O(S)$ many pairs of the form (g_i, g_i^{α}) for $i = 1, \ldots, t$. The Knowledge of Exponent assumption essentially guarantees that for any polynomial-time algorithm that is given such an SRS as input and is capable of outputting pairs (f, f') such that $f' = f^{\alpha}$, there is an efficient extractor algorithm that outputs coefficients $c_1, \ldots, c_t$ explaining (f, f'), in the sense that $f = \prod_{i=1}^{t} g_i^{c_i}$. See Section 15.2 for discussion of the intuition behind such an assumption and why it is reasonable.

Poly-Power Discrete Logarithm is Hard. This assumption posits that, if r is chosen at random from $\mathbb{F}_p$, then any polynomial time algorithm, when given as input the encodings of $t \leq \text{poly}(S)$ many powers of r (i.e., $g, g^r, g^{r^2}, \ldots, g^{r^t}$), is incapable of outputting r except with negligible probability.

Informally, the final set of five checks the SNARK verifier performs (Equation (17.14)) guarantees by KEA that the SNARK prover answers all of the LIP queries using linear functions, and in fact the prover "knows" these linear functions. To clarify, since in the SNARK the LIP queries are encoded in the exponent of g, the SNARK prover is applying the linear function to the exponents, by taking products of constant powers of the encoded query entries in the SRS.

The remaining two checks that the SNARK verifier performs ensures that these linear functions would convince the verifier to accept in the LIP obtained by applying the transformation of Section 17.5.2 to the linear PCP of Section 17.4. Knowledge-soundness of the SNARK then follows from that of the LIP.

In more detail, the analysis establishing that the SNARK is knowledge sound shows how to transform any argument system prover that convinces the argument system verifier to accept with non-negligible probability into either a witness vector z for the R1CS instance, or a polynomial time algorithm $\mathcal{A}$ that breaks the poly-power discrete logarithm assumption. Because the SNARK prover passes the final set of 5 checks performed by the verifier (Equation (17.14)) with non-negligible probability, the KEA implies that there is an efficient extractor $\mathcal{E}$ outputting linear functions $\pi_1, \ldots, \pi_5 \colon \mathbb{F}^t \to \mathbb{F}$ that "explain" the query responses as linear combinations (in the exponent) of SRS elements. That is, for $i = 1, \ldots, 5$, if the SRS σ consists of pairs of group elements (f_j, f_j^α) for $j = 1, \ldots, |\sigma|$, let $c_{i,1}, \ldots, c_{i,|\sigma|}$ denote the coefficients of π_i. Then for $i \in \{1, 2, 3, 4, 5\}$,

$$g_i = \prod_{j=1}^{|\sigma|} f_j^{c_{i,j}}.$$

For notational convenience, let us write π_1 as f_z, and π_4 as $f_{\mathrm{coeff}(h^*)}$. Let g_z and h^* be the polynomials implied by z and h^* via Equations (17.9) and (17.11). The argument system's verifier's first and second checks ensure that these linear functions convince the LIP verifier to accept with non-negligible probability. In particular, the LIP soundness analysis then implies that $\pi_1 = \pi_2 = \pi_3 = f_z$ and hence that $g_z(r) = \mathbb{Z}_H(r) \cdot h^*(r)$.

If $g_z = \mathbb{Z}_H \cdot h^*$, then z satisfies the R1CS instance, so to prove knowledge-soundness it suffices to suppose that $g_z \neq \mathbb{Z}_H \cdot h^*$ and show that this would contradict the poly-power discrete logarithm assumption.

If $g_z \neq \mathbb{Z}_H \cdot h^*$, then since both the left hand side and right hand side are polynomials of degree most 2ℓ, there are at most 2ℓ points r' for which $g_z(r') = \mathbb{Z}_H(r') \cdot h^*(r')$, and all such points r' can be enumerated in $\mathrm{poly}(S)$ time using a polynomial factorization algorithm. Consider the algorithm $\mathcal{A}$ that selects one of these points r' at random. Clearly $\mathcal{A}$ runs in polynomial time, and with non-negligible probability (at least $1/(2\ell)$), it outputs r. We claim that this violates the poly-power discrete logarithm assumption. Indeed, since $\mathcal{A}_1, \ldots, \mathcal{A}_S, \mathcal{B}_1, \ldots, \mathcal{B}_S, \mathcal{C}_1, \ldots, \mathcal{C}_S$, are all polynomials of degree at most ℓ that are all computable in $\mathrm{poly}(S)$ time, the SRS for the SNARK of this section consists entirely of encodings of known linear combinations of powers-of-r (i.e., of products of known powers of g, g^r, $g^{r^2}, \ldots, g^{r^{\ell-1}}$), plus additional group elements equal to these values raised to either α, β_1, β_2, β_3, $\alpha \cdot \beta_1$, $\alpha \cdot \beta_2$, or $\alpha \cdot \beta_3$, where $\alpha, \beta_1, \beta_2, \beta_3$ are uniform random elements of $\{1, \ldots, p - 1\}$. Hence, a string distributed identically to the entire SRS of the SNARK (which $\mathcal{A}$ is given access to) can be computed in polynomial time given the input encodings referred to in the poly-power discrete logarithm assumption. Since $\mathcal{A}$ outputs r with non-negligible probability, $\mathcal{A}$ violates the assumption.

17.5.5 Handling Public Input

For clarity, the presentation of the SNARK above elided the following detail. As per Remark 17.2, in many applications, there will in fact be a public input $x \in \mathbb{F}^n$ to the R1CS instance, and it will be required that the satisfying vector z have $z_i = x_i$ for $i = 1, \ldots, n$, with these requirements not otherwise included in the R1CS constraints. Remark 17.2 explained how to modify the linear PCP to enforce this. Essentially, the prover is forced to "ignore" the first n entries of z. Since the verifier knows x, the verifier on its own can "determine the contributions" of those entries of z to the verification checks.

This translates into the following modifications to the SNARK. First, let $z' = (z_{n+1}, \ldots, z_S)$ and replace the linear function f_z in the prescribed SNARK proof with $f_{z'}$. In more detail, letting $q^{(i)'} \in \mathbb{F}^{S-n}$ denote the last $S - n$ entries of $q^{(i)}$, the SNARK proof elements (g_1, g_1'), (g_2, g_2'), (g_3, g_3'), and (g_5, g_5') are now respectively claimed to equal:

$$\left(g^{f_{z'}(q^{(1)'})}, g^{\alpha \cdot f_{z'}(q^{(1)'})}\right),$$

$$\left(g^{f_{z'}(q^{(2)'})}, g^{\alpha \cdot f_{z'}(q^{(2)'})}\right),$$

$$\left(g^{f_{z'}(q^{(3)'})}, g^{\alpha \cdot f_{z'}(q^{(3)'})}\right),$$

and

$$\left(g^{f_{z'}(q^{(5)'})}, g^{\alpha \cdot f_{z'}(q^{(5)'})}\right).$$

Second, the SRS entries $g^{q_1^{(i)}}, \ldots, g^{q_n^{(i)}}$ for $i \in \{1, 2, 3, 5\}$ get added to the verification key. Note that the prover does not need to know these entries so they can be omitted from the proving key. *Neither* the prover nor verifier need to know the α'th powers of these entries, and in fact, those α'th powers *must* be omitted from the proving and verification keys for the SNARK to be sound.[15]

For $i \in \{1, 2, 3\}$, let $g^{(x,i)} = g^{\sum_{j=1}^n x_j \cdot q_j^{(i)}}$, which can be computed by the verifier using the now-expanded verification key. Finally, the verifier's first check (Equation (17.12)) changes to

$$e\left(g_1 \cdot g^{(x,1)}, g_2 \cdot g^{(x,2)}\right) = e\left(g_3 \cdot g^{(x,3)}, g\right) \cdot e\left(g^{Z_H(r)}, g_4\right). \quad (17.15)$$

Remark 17.3. It is often asserted that the verifier's work in the SNARK above is dominated by the handful of evaluations of the bilinear map e performed across all of its checks. There are 17 such bilinear map evaluations in the SNARK presented above; as discussed in Section 17.5.6, Groth [142] gave a variant SNARK that reduces this number to 3. In fact, these bilinear map evaluations will only dominate the verifier's costs if the size n of the public input is reasonably small. Otherwise, the verifier's processing of the public input, specifically the computation of $g^{(x,i)}$ above, will dominate, as this requires a multi-exponentiation of size n. Fortunately, in many applications, the public input is merely a *commitment* to a much larger witness, and hence is small.

17.5.6   Achieving Zero-Knowledge

The SNARK above is not zero-knowledge. One reason for this is that the proof contains encodings of f_z evaluated at various points, where z

---

[15] A variant SNARK given in [46] accidentally included these group elements in the SRS. Gabizon [121] gave an attack on the resulting SNARK, showing that these group elements' inclusion enables any prover to take a valid proof of knowledge of a witness w such that $C(x, w) = y$, and for any $x' \neq x$ turn it into a "proof" for the potentially invalid statement that $C(x', w) = y$. This flawed SNARK was deployed for several years in the cryptocurrency ZCash before the vulnerability was discovered. if exploited, it could have permitted unlimited counterfeiting of currency.

is a satisfying assignment for the R1CS instance. This leaks information to the verifier that the verifier cannot compute on its own, since the verifier does not know z.

To render the SNARK zero-knowledge, we modify the underlying LIP to be honest-verifier zero-knowledge. This ensures that the resulting SNARK is zero-knowledge even against dishonest verifiers, by the following reasoning. Because the SNARK verifier does not send any message to the prover, honest-verifier and malicious-verifier zero-knowledge are equivalent for the SNARK. The SNARK verifier only sees the verification key, which is generated in polynomial time and is independent of the witness vector z, and encodings of the LIP prover's responses to the LIP verifier's queries. Once the proving and verification keys are generated, these encodings are deterministic, efficiently computable functions of the responses. Hence, since the LIP is honest-verifier perfect zero-knowledge, so is the resulting SNARK. That is, the simulator for the SNARK verifier's view simply runs the simulator for the LIP verifier's view, and outputs encodings of the LIP prover's messages instead of the messages themselves.

Rendering the LIP Honest-Verifier Zero-Knowledge. Recall that in the nonzero-knowledge LIP, the prover established that $g_z = \mathbb{Z}_H \cdot h^*$ for an R1CS solution vector z, where

$$g_z(t) = \left(\sum_{\text{columns } j \in \{1,\dots,S\}} z_j \cdot \mathcal{A}_j(t) \right) \cdot \left(\sum_{\text{columns } j \in \{1,\dots,S\}} z_j \cdot \mathcal{B}_j(t) \right)$$
$$- \left(\sum_{\text{columns } j \in \{1,\dots,S\}} z_j \cdot \mathcal{C}_j(t) \right).$$

This required the LIP verifier to pick a random $r \in \mathbb{F}$ and obtain from the prover the following four evaluations:

$$h^*(r),$$
$$\sum_{\text{columns } j} z_j \cdot \mathcal{A}_j(r),$$
$$\sum_{\text{columns } j} z_j \cdot \mathcal{B}_j(r),$$

and
$$\sum_{\text{columns } j} z_j \cdot \mathcal{C}_j(r).$$

These four values leak information to the LIP verifier, who cannot efficiently compute W or h^*.

To render the LIP zero-knowledge, the prover picks three random values $r_A, r_B, r_C \in \mathbb{F}$, and considers a "perturbed" version g_z' of g_z, in which each constituent function comprising g_z has added to it a random multiple of the vanishing polynomial $\mathbb{Z}_H$ of H. Specifically, letting

$$\mathcal{A}(t) := \sum_{\text{columns } j} z_j \cdot \mathcal{A}_j(t),$$

$$\mathcal{B}(t) := \sum_{\text{columns } j} z_j \cdot \mathcal{B}_j(t),$$

$$\mathcal{C}(t) := \sum_{\text{columns } j} z_j \cdot \mathcal{C}_j(t),$$

define:

$$g_z'(t) := (\mathcal{A}(t) + r_A \mathbb{Z}_H(t)) \cdot (\mathcal{B}(t) + r_B \mathbb{Z}_H(t)) - (\mathcal{C}(t) + r_C \mathbb{Z}_H(t)). \tag{17.16}$$

Note that $g_z'(t) = g_z(t) + r_B \mathbb{Z}_H(t)\mathcal{A}(t) + r_A \mathbb{Z}_H(t)\mathcal{B}(t) + r_A r_B (\mathbb{Z}_H(t))^2 - r_C \mathbb{Z}_H(t)$. Just as g_z vanished on H if and only if z is a satisfies the R1CS instance, the same can be said for g_z', because the "added factors" in g_z' are multiples of the polynomial $\mathbb{Z}_H$, which vanishes on H.

To prove that g_z' vanishes on H, it is sufficient for the prover to establish that there exists a polynomial h' such that $g_z' = h' \cdot \mathbb{Z}_H$. Note that this is satisfied by

$$h' = h^* + r_B \cdot \mathcal{A}(t) + r_A \cdot \mathcal{B}(t) + r_A r_B \mathbb{Z}_H - r_C.$$

The LIP verifier can (with soundness error at most $2\ell/(|\mathbb{F}| - \ell)$) check that this equality of formal polynomials holds by confirming that the right hand and left hand sides agree at a random point $r \in \mathbb{F} \setminus H$.

The zero-knowledge LIP proof consists of two linear functions. The first is claimed to equal $f_{\text{coeff}(h')}$, defined as usual so that $f_{\text{coeff}(h')}(1, r, r^2, \ldots, r^{\deg(h')}) = h'(r)$. The second is prescribed to equal $f_{z'}$ where W' is the vector $z \circ r_A \circ r_B \circ r_C \in \mathbb{F}^{S+3}$, where $\circ$ denotes concatenation. That is, z' is the satisfying R1CS vector z, with the random values r_A, r_B, r_C that are chosen by the prover appended.

The honest LIP verifier will query $f_{z'}$ at three locations:

$$q^{(1)} = (\mathcal{A}_1(r), \ldots, \mathcal{A}_S(r), \mathbb{Z}_H(r), 0, 0),$$
$$q^{(2)} = (\mathcal{B}_1(r), \ldots, \mathcal{B}_S(r), 0, \mathbb{Z}_H(r), 0),$$

and

$$q^{(3)} = (\mathcal{C}_1(r), \ldots, \mathcal{C}_S(r), 0, 0, \mathbb{Z}_H(r))$$

to obtain the three values:

$$v_1 := r_A \cdot \mathbb{Z}_H(r) + \sum_{\text{columns } j} z_j \cdot \mathcal{A}_j(r),$$

$$v_2 := r_B \cdot \mathbb{Z}_H(r) + \sum_{\text{columns } j} z_j \cdot \mathcal{B}_j(r),$$

and

$$v_3 := r_C \cdot \mathbb{Z}_H(r) + \sum_{\text{columns } j} z_j \cdot \mathcal{C}_j(r).$$

The honest LIP verifier will then pick a point $r \in \mathbb{F} \setminus H$ at random and query $f_{\text{coeff}(h')}$ at a single point $q^{(4)} := (1, r, r^2, \ldots, r^{\ell-1})$ to obtain a value v_4 claimed to equal $h'(r)$. Then the verifier will check that

$$v_1 \cdot v_2 - v_3 = v_4 \cdot \mathbb{Z}_H(r).$$

Finally, following Section 17.5.2, in order to confirm that the LIP prover answered the queries $q^{(1)}$, $q^{(2)}$, and $q^{(3)}$ with the same linear function, the verifier will also choose $\beta_1, \beta_2, \beta_3$ at random from $\mathbb{F}$ and query $f_{z'}$ at location $q^{(5)} = \sum_{i=1}^{3} \beta_i q^{(i)}$ to obtain response v_5, and check that $\sum_{i=1}^{3} \beta_i v_i = v_5$. By the discussion in Section 17.5.2, if the LIP prover passes this check, then with high probability a single linear function $f_{z'}$ was used to answer $q^{(1)}$, $q^{(2)}$, and $q^{(3)}$.

Analysis of the LIP. Completeness of this LIP holds by design. Soundness holds because for any linear functions $f_{\text{coeff}(h')}$ and $f_{z'}$ that cause the LIP verifier to accept, $\text{coeff}(h')$ must specify the coefficients of a polynomial h' and z' must specify a witness $z \in \mathbb{F}^S$ followed by three values r_A, r_B, r_C such that

$$h'(r) \cdot \mathbb{Z}_H(r) = g_z'(r),$$

where $g_z'(t)$ is as defined in Equation (17.16). This implies that z is a valid circuit transcript.

The LIP is honest-verifier zero-knowledge by the following reasoning. Since $r \notin H$, we may conclude that $\mathbb{Z}_H(r) = \prod_{a \in H}(r-a) \neq 0$. Combined with the fact that r_A, r_B, and r_C are independent, uniform random field elements, it follows that $\mathbb{Z}_H(r) \cdot r_A$, $\mathbb{Z}_H(r) \cdot r_B$, and $\mathbb{Z}_H(r) \cdot r_C$ are uniform random field elements as well. Hence, $f_{z'}(q^{(1)})$, $f_{z'}(q^{(2)})$, and $f_{z'}(q^{(3)})$ are themselves uniform random field elements, as each is some fixed quantity plus a uniform random field element (e.g., $f_{z'}(q^{(1)}) = f_z(\mathcal{A}_1(r), \ldots, \mathcal{A}_S(r)) + \mathbb{Z}_H(r) \cdot r_A$).

Meanwhile, for any choice of $r \in \mathbb{F}$, $v_4 = h'(r)$ is always equal to

$$(v_1 \cdot v_2 - v_3) \, \mathbb{Z}_H(r)^{-1}. \tag{17.17}$$

Hence, the simulator can choose r at random from $\mathbb{F}$, and simply set v_1, v_2, v_3 (i.e., the simulated responses to queries $q^{(1)}$, $q^{(2)}$, $q^{(3)}$) to be uniform random field elements, and then set v_4 as per Equation (17.17). Finally, the simulator chooses $\beta_1, \beta_2, \beta_3$ at random from $\mathbb{F}$, and computes the simulated response v_5 to $q^{(5)}$ as $\sum_{i=1}^{3} \beta_i v_i$. This is a perfect simulation of the LIP verifier's view.

Historical Notes. The zk-SNARK described above is nearly identical to the one for QAPs given in [125]. Minor differences arise in our treatment, stemming from our use of the linear-PCP-to-LIP from subsequent work [56] in the construction and analysis of the SNARK presented here. [203] provided concrete improvements to the zk-SNARK from [125], and implemented the resulting variant. Other optimized variants were presented in [42], [46], [121].

Groth's SNARK. Groth [142] gave an influential variant of the zk-SNARK of this section, in which the proof consists of only 3 group elements, and proved his SNARK to be knowledge sound in the generic group model. Roughly speaking, this reduction in proof size can be traced to two differences from the SNARK covered in this section. First, he gave an LIP in which the verifier only makes 3 queries, rather than 5 as in the LIP we cover. This alone reduces the number of group elements from 10 to 6. Second, establishing security in the generic group model rather than relying on Knowledge of Exponent assumptions allows for a halving of the number of group elements, as it is possible to ensure that each group element g_i in the proof need not be paired with g_i^α. Fuchsbauer *et al.* [117] extended the security proof of Groth's SNARK to the Algebraic Group Model.

18

SNARK Composition and Recursion

18.1 Composing Two Different SNARKs

Consider two SNARK systems, $\mathcal{I}$ and $\mathcal{O}$, say for arithmetic circuit-satisfiability, with different cost profiles. The prover in $\mathcal{I}$ is very fast (say, linear in the size of the statement being proven), but the proofs and verification time are fairly large (though still sublinear in the size of the statement being proven, e.g., square root of the circuit size). In contrast, the prover in $\mathcal{O}$ is slower—say, superlinear in the size of the circuit by logarithmic factors, and with a large leading constant factor—but the proofs and verification time are very short and fast (say, of length logarithmic or even constant in the circuit size). Is it possible to combine them to get the best of both worlds? That is, we seek a SNARK $\mathcal{F}$ with the fast prover speed of $\mathcal{I}$ and the short proof length and fast verification of $\mathcal{O}$.

The answer is yes, at least in principle, via a technique called proof composition. This works as follows. Suppose the $\mathcal{F}$-prover $\mathcal{P}_{\mathcal{F}}$ claims to know a witness w such that $\mathcal{C}(w) = 1$, where $\mathcal{C}$ is a specified circuit. $\mathcal{P}_{\mathcal{F}}$ can use $\mathcal{I}$ to generate a SNARK proof π of the claim at hand. But since π is pretty big and verifying it is somewhat slow, $\mathcal{P}_{\mathcal{F}}$ doesn't want to explicitly send π to the $\mathcal{F}$ verifier. Rather, $\mathcal{P}_{\mathcal{F}}$ can use the $\mathcal{O}$-SNARK system to *prove* to the $\mathcal{F}$-verifier that it knows π. It is this $\mathcal{O}$-proof π' that $\mathcal{P}_{\mathcal{F}}$ actually sends to the verifier. Put another way, $\mathcal{P}_{\mathcal{F}}$ uses the fast-verification SNARK $\mathcal{O}$ to establish knowledge of an $\mathcal{I}$-proof π that would have convinced the $\mathcal{I}$ verifier that $\mathcal{P}_{\mathcal{F}}$ knows a w such that $C(w) = 1$.

The above procedure requires taking the verification procedure of $\mathcal{I}$ and feeding it through the proof machinery of $\mathcal{O}$. That is, the $\mathcal{I}$-verifier must be represented as an arithmetic circuit C' and the $\mathcal{O}$ prover then applied to C' to establish knowledge of a π such that $C'(\pi) = 1$.[1]

Let $\mathcal{F} = \mathcal{O} \circ \mathcal{I}$ denote the above composed proof system. Here, $\mathcal{O}$ stands for the "outer" SNARK and $\mathcal{I}$ stands for the "inner" SNARK. The motivation for this terminology is that one thinks of the $\mathcal{O}$-proof π' that is actually sent to the verifier in $\mathcal{F}$ as having an $\mathcal{I}$-proof π "living inside of it": the $\mathcal{O}$-proof π' attests that whoever generated the proof knows some $\mathcal{I}$-proof π for the claim at hand.

Costs of the composed proof system. The final proof length and verification time of $\mathcal{F}$ is the size of the proof generated by $\mathcal{O}$ applied to the $\mathcal{I}$ verifier circuit C'. Since the $\mathcal{O}$-proof and verification procedure are respectively short and fast, the $\mathcal{F}$-proof and verification procedure are short and fast as well.

The $\mathcal{F}$ prover first has to generate the $\mathcal{I}$-proof π for C (which is by assumption fast), and then has to generate the $\mathcal{O}$-proof for C'. While the $\mathcal{O}$ prover is slow, the key point is that C' should be *much smaller* than C, since the verification procedure of $\mathcal{I}$ is sublinear (e.g., square root) in the size of C. Hence, the time required by the $\mathcal{F}$ prover to generate the $\mathcal{I}$-proof that $C'(\pi) = 1$ should be dwarfed by the time required to compute π in the first place. Hence, the $\mathcal{F}$ prover time is extremely close to that of the $\mathcal{I}$ prover, which by assumption is fast. The best of both worlds has been achieved.

---

[1]There is nothing special about circuit-satisfiability in this example. What matters is that the verification procedure of $\mathcal{I}$ be represented in whatever format $\mathcal{O}$ requires to allow $\mathcal{P}$ to establish that it knows an $\mathcal{I}$-proof π that would have caused the $\mathcal{I}$ verifier to accept. See Section 6 and Section 8.4 for additional discussion of intermediate representations other than circuits, including R1CS.

There are other potential benefits of proof composition beyond reducing verification costs. For example, if the inner SNARK $\mathcal{I}$ is not zero-knowledge, but the outer SNARK $\mathcal{O}$ is zero-knowledge, the composed SNARK $\mathcal{F}$ will be zero-knowledge. Hence, composition can be used to transform a highly efficient but non-zero-knowledge SNARK $\mathcal{I}$ into a new SNARK $\mathcal{O} \circ \mathcal{I}$ that is zero-knowledge.

18.2 Deeper Compositions of SNARKs

As in the previous section, imagine a SNARK $\mathcal{I}$ for circuit satisfiability instances of size S in which the verification procedure, when itself represented as an arithmetic circuit, has size $O(S^{1/2})$, and proofs have size $O(S^{1/2})$ as well. That is, verification is sublinear relative to the cost of evaluating the circuit gate-by-gate on a witness w, but is still more expensive than we might like. In principle, self-composition can be used to obtain a SNARK with lower verification cost.

Composing $\mathcal{I}$ with *itself* yields a new SNARK $\mathcal{F} = \mathcal{I} \circ \mathcal{I}$ with proof size and verification time $O\left((S^{1/2})^{1/2}\right) = O\left(S^{1/4}\right)$. One more invocation of composition, say with $\mathcal{F}$ as the outer SNARK and with $\mathcal{I}$ as the inner SNARK, yields yet another SNARK, now with verification time $O\left((S^{1/4})^{1/2}\right) = O(S^{1/8})$. In this way, the more invocations of composition, the smaller the proofs and faster the verification time of the resulting SNARK. One can fruitfully continue this process until the verification circuit of the composed SNARK is smaller than the so-called *recursion threshold* of the base SNARK $\mathcal{I}$. This refers to the smallest circuit size S^* such that the verification procedure of $\mathcal{I}$ cannot be represented by a circuit-satisfiability instance of size smaller than S^*. On circuits smaller than the recursion threshold, composing the SNARK with itself does not reduce verification costs, and in fact may increase them.

Of course, the deeper the recursion, the more work the prover has to do. For example, if $\mathcal{I}$ is composed with itself three times, then the prover has to "in its own head" first produce a proof π that would convince the $\mathcal{I}$ verifier of the claim at hand, then produce a proof π' that it knows π, then produce a proof π'' that it knows π'.[2] This is naturally more work than just producing the proof π for the non-composed proof system.

Establishing knowledge-soundness of composed SNARKs. When considering the composition $\mathcal{F}$ of two SNARKs $\mathcal{I}$ and $\mathcal{O}$ (Section 18.1), we presented $\mathcal{F}$ in a manner that hopefully made intuitively clear that it is knowledge-sound: the $\mathcal{F}$-prover $\mathcal{P}_{\mathcal{F}}$ establishes using the outer SNARK $\mathcal{O}$ that it knows a proof π that would have caused the $\mathcal{I}$-verifier to accept the claim at hand, namely that $\mathcal{P}_{\mathcal{F}}$ knows a w such that $\mathcal{C}(w) = 1$. In turn, since $\mathcal{I}$ is knowledge-sound, any efficient party $\mathcal{P}_{\mathcal{F}}$ who knows such a proof π must also know such a witness w.[3]

Still, it is instructive to carefully write out a description of the procedure $\mathcal{E}_{\mathcal{F}}$ that extracts the witness w from $\mathcal{P}_{\mathcal{F}}$. This will help us understand knowledge-extraction for the "deeper" compositions considered in this section. As we will see, the natural knowledge extractor for a composed SNARK will have runtime that grows exponentially with the depth of the composition. This means that super-constant depth compositions will yield a superpolynomial-time knowledge-extractor. Hence, the knowledge-soundness of such deep compositions is not on firm theoretical footing.[4]

Knowledge extractor for $\mathcal{F} = \mathcal{O} \circ \mathcal{I}$. Given an efficient prover $\mathcal{P}_{\mathcal{F}}$ that can generate accepting proofs for $\mathcal{F}$, $\mathcal{E}_{\mathcal{F}}$ must identify a witness w such that $\mathcal{C}(w) = 1$. $\mathcal{E}_{\mathcal{F}}$ works as follows. Since a convincing proof for $\mathcal{F}$ establishes via the outer SNARK system $\mathcal{O}$ that $\mathcal{P}_{\mathcal{F}}$ knows a proof

---

[2]By in its own head, we mean the prover performs a computation without sending the result to the verifier.

[3]Note that if $\mathcal{O}$ satisfies only standard soundness rather than knowledge-soundness, the composed proof system $\mathcal{O} \circ \mathcal{I}$ may not even satisfy standard soundness. This is because $\mathcal{O}$ will only establish the *existence* of a proof π that would have caused the $\mathcal{I}$-verifier to accept. And there will typically *exist* convincing proofs of false statements under the SNARK $\mathcal{I}$: computational soundness of $\mathcal{I}$ only guarantees that such proofs are difficult for a cheating prover to find.

[4]While we cannot prove knowledge-soundness of superconstant-depth SNARK recursions, that does not necessarily mean we think deep recursions are *not* knowledge-sound, just that we don't know how to provably reduce their knowledge-soundness to that of the underlying base SNARK. Indeed deep recursions of SNARKs are beginning to see practical deployment in distributed environments (e.g., [65]. See also Sections 18.4 and 18.5).

π causing the $\mathcal{I}$-verifier to accept, $\mathcal{E}_\mathcal{F}$ can first apply the following sub-routine: "run the knowledge-extractor $\mathcal{E}_\mathcal{O}$ for $\mathcal{O}$ to extract from $\mathcal{P}_\mathcal{F}$ such a proof π". This sub-routine itself represents an efficient convincing prover algorithm $\mathcal{P}_\mathcal{I}$ for the inner SNARK $\mathcal{I}$. Hence, $\mathcal{E}_\mathcal{F}$ can apply the knowledge-extractor $\mathcal{E}_\mathcal{I}$ to extract from $\mathcal{P}_\mathcal{I}$ a witness w such that $\mathcal{C}(w) = 1$.

How efficient is $\mathcal{E}_\mathcal{F}$? $\mathcal{E}_\mathcal{F}$ has to apply the inner-SNARK knowledge-extractor $\mathcal{E}_\mathcal{I}$ to a prover $\mathcal{P}_\mathcal{I}$ that itself runs the outer-SNARK knowledge-extractor $\mathcal{E}_\mathcal{O}$ on $\mathcal{P}_\mathcal{F}$. Hence, $\mathcal{E}_\mathcal{F}$ may be significantly slower than $\mathcal{E}_\mathcal{I}$ or $\mathcal{E}_\mathcal{O}$ individually (though $\mathcal{E}_\mathcal{F}$ still runs in polynomial time as long as $\mathcal{E}_\mathcal{I}$ and $\mathcal{E}_\mathcal{O}$ both do). For example, if A denotes the number of times $\mathcal{E}_\mathcal{I}$ calls[5] $\mathcal{P}_\mathcal{I}$ to extract w from it, and B denotes the number of times $\mathcal{E}_\mathcal{O}$ calls $\mathcal{P}_\mathcal{F}$ to extract π from it, then the entire extraction procedure $\mathcal{E}_\mathcal{F}$ may call $\mathcal{P}_\mathcal{F}$ up to $A \cdot B$ times.[6]

Knowledge extractor for deeper compositions. Now consider a SNARK $\mathcal{O}$ composed with itself, say, four times, and denote the composition by $\mathcal{O}^4 := \mathcal{O} \circ \mathcal{O} \circ \mathcal{O} \circ \mathcal{O}$. We can view $\mathcal{O}^4$ as $\mathcal{O}^2 \circ \mathcal{O}^2$, where $\mathcal{O}^2 := \mathcal{O} \circ \mathcal{O}$. The previous paragraph shows that if A denotes the number of times that the knowledge extractor $\mathcal{E}_\mathcal{O}$ for $\mathcal{O}$ must run a convincing prover $\mathcal{P}_\mathcal{O}$ to extract a witness, then the number of times that the natural knowledge extractor for $\mathcal{O}^2$ must run a convincing prover $\mathcal{P}_{\mathcal{O}^2}$ to extract a witness is A^2. Then applying the same analysis to $\mathcal{O}^2 \circ \mathcal{O}^2$ means that the number of times the natural knowledge extractor for $\mathcal{O}^4$ must run a convincing prover is A^4.

In general, composing $\mathcal{O}$ with itself t times will yield a knowledge extractor that runs a prover generating convincing proofs at most A^t times. If A is polynomial in the size of the statement that the SNARK is applied to, then A^t will be superpolynomial unless t is constant.

---

[5]When we say that a knowledge extractor "calls" a prover more than once, we refer to the fact that the extractor might repeatedly "rewind and restart" the prover from which it is extracting a witness. We saw examples of this in the context of forking-lemma-based extractors for Σ-protocols (see Remark 12.1 in Section 12.2.1 and Section 14.4.1), and for SNARKs obtained thereof via the Fiat-Shamir transformation (Section 12.2.3).

[6]A and B may depend on the size of the statement being proven, but we suppress this dependence from our notation for simplicity.

Practical considerations of composition.   For many popular SNARKs $\mathcal{O}$, there can be considerable concrete overhead in attempting to represent the $\mathcal{O}$-verifier as an equivalent instance of arithmetic circuit-satisfiability or R1CS, or whatever intermediate representation is "consumed" by the outer SNARK. Here, we highlight one particularly common and important issue, and describe how it is has been addressed to date.

As we have seen in Sections 14 and 17, many popular SNARKs require the verifier to perform operations in cryptographic groups in which the discrete logarithm problem is intractable (and for many SNARKs, the groups must furthermore be pairing-friendly, see Section 15.1). Modern instantiations of such cryptographic groups use elliptic curves (Section 12.1.2.2). Recall that elements of an elliptic curve group correspond to pairs of points $(x, y) \in \mathbb{F} \times \mathbb{F}$ that satisfy an equation of the form $y^2 = x^3 + ax + b$ for field elements a and b. $\mathbb{F}$ is referred to as the *base field* of the curve. When designing a discrete-logarithm-based SNARK for arithmetic circuit-satisfiability or R1CS-satisfiability over a field $\mathbb{F}_p$ of prime order p, one requires that the *order* of the elliptic curve group $\mathbb{G}$ be p (in this case, $\mathbb{F}_p$ is called the *scalar field* of $\mathbb{G}$). The crucial point here is that the base field $\mathbb{F}$ and the scalar field $\mathbb{F}_p$ of $\mathbb{G}$ are *not* the same field (see Section 12.1.2.2). This means that, in a discrete-log-based SNARK $\mathcal{O}$ for an arithmetic circuit $\mathcal{C}$ defined over field $\mathbb{F}_p$, the verifier has to perform field operations over a base field $\mathbb{F}$ that *differs* from $\mathbb{F}_p$.

Recall that in order to compose a SNARK $\mathcal{O}$ for circuit-satisfiability with itself, one must represent the verification procedure of $\mathcal{O}$ as an arithmetic circuit $\mathcal{C}'$ to which $\mathcal{O}$ can be applied. If $\mathcal{O}$ uses a cryptographic group $\mathbb{G}$ as per the above paragraph, then it is natural to define $\mathcal{C}'$ over the base field $\mathbb{F}$ of $\mathbb{G}$ rather than the scalar field $\mathbb{F}_p$ of $\mathbb{G}$, so that $\mathcal{C}'$ can "natively" perform the operations over $\mathbb{F}$ required to perform group operations in $\mathbb{G}$ (while it is possible to "implement" $\mathbb{F}$ operations via a circuit defined over a different field $\mathbb{F}_p$ using techniques discussed in Section 6, it is currently quite expensive, despite efforts from many researchers to make it less so). But in order to apply $\mathcal{O}$ to $\mathcal{C}'$, one needs to know *another* cryptographic group $\mathbb{G}'$ whose scalar field (rather than base field) is $\mathbb{F}$.

Accordingly, to support arbitrary-depth compositions of $\mathcal{O}$ with itself (or with other SNARKs), it is useful to identify a *cycle* of elliptic curves. The simplest form of such a cycle has length two. This is a pair of elliptic curve groups $\mathbb{G}$ and $\mathbb{G}'$ such that the base field $\mathbb{F}_p$ of $\mathbb{G}$ is the scalar field $\mathbb{F}$ of $\mathcal{G}'$ and vice versa. Using such a cycle of elliptic curves ensures that the verifier of $\mathcal{O}$ applied to a circuit over field $\mathbb{F}$ can be efficiently implemented via a circuit over field $\mathbb{F}_p$, and vice versa.

To walk through the specific example of depth-two recursive composition: let $\mathcal{O}$ be a SNARK for arithmetic circuit-satisfiability. It will be helpful to use a subscript $\mathcal{O}_{\mathbb{F}}$ to clarify what field the circuit-satisfiability instance is defined over. Then $\mathcal{O}^3 := \mathcal{O}_{\mathbb{F}_p} \circ \mathcal{O}_{\mathbb{F}} \circ \mathcal{O}_{\mathbb{F}_p}$ will work as follows to establish knowledge of a w such that $\mathcal{C}(w) = 1$, where $\mathcal{C}$ is defined over $\mathbb{F}_p$. First, the $\mathcal{O}^3$ prover $\mathcal{P}$ in its own head will generate a proof π that convinces the $\mathcal{O}_{\mathbb{F}_p}$-verifier of the claim. The $\mathcal{O}_{\mathbb{F}_p}$ verifier for this claim can be efficiently represented by a circuit $\mathcal{C}'$ over $\mathbb{F}$. So (in its own head once again) the $\mathcal{O}^3$ prover will generate an $\mathcal{O}_{\mathbb{F}}$-proof π' that it knows such an $\mathcal{O}_{\mathbb{F}_p}$-proof π. The $\mathcal{O}_{\mathbb{F}}$-verifier for this claim can in turn be efficiently implemented by a circuit $\mathcal{C}''$ over $\mathbb{F}_p$, so the $\mathcal{O}^3$ prover finally computes a proof π'' that it knows such an $\mathcal{O}_{\mathbb{F}}$-proof π'. And $\mathcal{P}$ sends this proof explicitly to the $\mathcal{O}^3$ verifier.

More generally, given a cycle of elliptic curves, arbitrary-depth composition of $\mathcal{O}_{\mathbb{F}}$ and $\mathcal{O}_{\mathbb{F}_p}$ can be supported. Every time the prover needs to produce a proof π' that it knows a proof π that the $\mathcal{O}_{\mathbb{F}_p}$-verifier would accept, it represents the $\mathcal{O}_{\mathbb{F}_p}$-verifier as a circuit over $\mathbb{F}$ and applies the $\mathcal{O}_{\mathbb{F}}$ SNARK to this circuit, and similarly with the roles of $\mathbb{F}_p$ and $\mathbb{F}$ reversed.

Currently, a popular cycle of (non-pairing-friendly) curves are Pasta curves,[7] which are reasonably close in efficiency to some of the best curves that don't support cycles (e.g., Curve25519, see Section 12.1.2.2). Cycles of pairing-friendly curves are also known, e.g., via so-called MNT curves [96], but, at the time of writing, for a given security level these remain significantly less efficient than popular pairing-friendly curves for SNARK design that don't support cycles (e.g., BLS12-381, see Section 15.1). This owes to a need of the cycle-supporting curves

---

[7]https://electriccoin.co/blog/the-pasta-curves-for-halo-2-and-beyond/.

to work over significantly larger finite fields, which leads to slower group operations. While *cycles* of pairing-friendly curves are currently very expensive, efficient depth-one composition of two pairing-based SNARKs does not require a cycle of curves; rather, it only requires two pairing-friendly curves such that the base field of one is the scalar field of the other. This is currently offered by an efficient curve known as BLS12-377 and a sister curve called BW6-761 [74], [154].

Another common practical consideration arising in recursive SNARK composition is that the verifier in many transparent SNARKs performs Merkle hash path verifications, which means cryptographic hash operations must be expressed as a circuit- or R1CS-satisfiability instance. As mentioned in Section 6, there has been considerable effort devoted to developing "SNARK-friendly" hash functions, meaning plausibly collision-resistant hash functions that can be efficiently expressed in such a form.

18.3   Other Applications of SNARK Composition

We have seen that composition of SNARKs can be used to improve efficiency: a SNARK with fast prover and somewhat slow verification can be composed with itself or with another SNARK to improve the verification costs. There are other reasons to compose SNARKs.

Incremental computation.   One, which we detail later in this section (Sections 18.4 and 18.5), uses recursion more directly to construct efficient SNARKs tailored for iterative computation, i.e., to prove that for some designated input x and specified function F that $F(F(F(F(F(F(x)))))) = y$. More generally, let $F^{(i)}(x)$ denote the i-fold iterative application of F to x, e.g., $F^{(3)}(x) = F(F(F(x)))$. A quintessential application of such proof systems is to let F be a *delay function*, meaning a simple function that requires some non-trivial sequential computation to compute. Then a SNARK for many iterative applications of F yields a *verifiable delay function*: a function that requires substantial sequential time to compute, the result of which can be verified very quickly.

Incrementally Verifiable Computation (IVC). Certain applications (to be discussed momentarily) actually call for a primitive called *incrementally verifiable computation* [239]. This means that after each application j of F to x, a prover can output y_j and a SNARK proof π_j that $F^{(j)}(x) = y_j$, and moreover, given y_j and π_j, *any* other party can apply F to y_j to obtain an output y_{j+1} and efficiently compute a new SNARK proof π_{j+1} that $F^{(j+1)}(x) = y_{j+1}$.

Applications to distributed computing environments. In fact, our SNARKs for iterative computation will be able more generally to handle non-deterministic computations F. That is, F can take two inputs, a public input x and a witness w, and produce some output $y = F(x, w)$. The SNARKs we present hereon in this section will be able to[8] establish knowledge of witnesses $w_1, \ldots, w_i$ such that

$$F(F(\ldots F(F(F(x, w_1), w_2), w_3), \ldots, w_{i-1}), w_i) = y_i.$$

Here is one example of a possible application to public blockchains. Think of F as taking as input the current state of an "accumulation" (e.g., Merkle-hash, see Section 7.3.2.2) of all account balances for a public blockchain, and think of each witness w_i as specifying a new valid transaction t_i along with associated proof-of-work, and such that F outputs an updated accumulation (i.e., F outputs the accumulation of the new account balances following the processing of transaction t_i). Then a SNARK for the above yields a proof that y_i is a valid accumulation of account balances after i transactions. This can enable computationally weak nodes in a blockchain network to very efficiently learn from any untrusted party an accumulation of the global state of the network (i.e., the current account balances), with a proof that the accumulation actually captures a sequence consisting of a certain number of valid transactions and associated proofs-of-work. This may be important for protocols that designate the current state of the network to be that of the "longest chain", i.e., the longest known sequence of valid transactions. Hence, nodes can trustlessly learn the accumulation

---

[8]For simplicity, we do not present the SNARKs in this level of generality but they will support it without modification.

of the network state, with no need to download the entire transaction history of the network or even the current account balances.

Proof aggregation. Another application of SNARK composition is proof aggregation, which can be explained via the following example application. Suppose that a prover $\mathcal{P}$ claims for some public input x and function F that $F(x) = y$, but computing F is highly computation-intensive. Imagine that the computation is broken up into ℓ more manageable pieces, say, $F_1(x), \ldots, F_\ell(x)$, that can be performed independently of each other. $\mathcal{P}$ farms each piece out to a different machine (possibly untrusted even by the prover, who is in turn untrusted by the verifier), to produce outputs $y_1, \ldots, y_\ell$, which are then combined via some aggregation function G to produce the final output y.

In order to prove that $F(x) = y$, each machine can produce a proof π_i that $y_i = F_i(x)$, and send both π_i and the result y_i back to $\mathcal{P}$. Then it suffices for $\mathcal{P}$ to (a) prove knowledge of the convincing proofs $\pi_1, \ldots, \pi_\ell$ for the ℓ claims $y_i = F_i(x)$, and (b) prove that $G(y_1, \ldots, y_\ell) = y$. One can accomplish this by applying a SNARK to the computation that first *verifies* the proofs $\pi_1, \ldots, \pi_\ell$ and then computes $G(y_1, \ldots, y_\ell)$.

18.4   SNARKs for Iterative Computation via Recursion

Recall that $F^{(i)}(x)$ denote the i-fold iterative application of F to x. Suppose we want to design a SNARK for the claim that $F^{(i)}(x) = y$.

One could of course apply any of the (non-composed) SNARKs from earlier sections of this survey to $F^{(i)}$, but these come with various downsides and tradeoffs, delineated in detail in the next section, Section 19. For starters, they do not support IVC (Section 18.3). Turning to efficiency, if one desires the shortest possible proofs and fastest verification, the SNARKs with these properties require a trusted setup (see Section 17). They also tend to be quite space-intensive for the prover due in part to their use of FFTs, so applying them to very large computations may not be feasible, and their use of pairing-friendly groups can lead to slow prover time. While many of the transparent SNARKs of earlier sections avoid FFTs and pairings, they have much larger proofs and verification costs than the trusted-setup SNARKs with fastest verification.

The recursive-composition-of-SNARKs approach. Can we address the above issues by taking a base SNARK $\mathcal{O}$ and applying recursive composition? Let us imagine for a moment that we have already designed a SNARK $\mathcal{O}_{i-1}$ for the claim that $F^{(i-1)}(x) = y_{i-1}$. Then here is a SNARK $\mathcal{O}_i$ for the claim that $F^{(i)}(x) = y_i$: the prover $\mathcal{P}$ uses the base SNARK $\mathcal{O}$ to prove that

(a) it knows an $\mathcal{O}_{i-1}$-proof π_{i-1} that $F^{(i-1)}(x) = y_{i-1}$, and

(b) that $F(y_{i-1}) = y_i$.[9]

This recursive-composition-of-SNARKs approach to incremental computation has been pursued (e.g., [45]) using the trusted-setup SNARK with fastest known verification, which is now due to Groth [142] (Section 17.5.6).[10] A major benefit of the recursive approach is that it yields

---

[9]An important practical issue here is that, in order to identify a single arithmetic circuit confirming both (a) and (b), it is essential that the $\mathcal{O}_{i-1}$-verifier's computation and F itself both be efficiently expressible as a circuit over the same field. This can be challenging for SNARKs that perform elliptic curve operations, because as discussed in Section 18.2, such SNARK verifiers are only efficiently representable as circuits over the *base* field $\mathbb{F}$ of the curve, which differs from the (scalar) field $\mathbb{F}_p$ that F is presumably efficiently representable over. One way to sidestep this issue is to identify a cycle of curves with scalar and base fields $\mathbb{F}_p$ and $\mathbb{F}$ such that F is efficiently computable by circuits over *both* $\mathbb{F}_p$ and $\mathbb{F}$. This way, at each step i, the $\mathcal{O}_{i-1}$ verifier will be efficiently expressible as a circuit over one of the two fields (which one depends on whether i is odd or even), and F will also be efficiently expressible as a circuit over the same field. If F is only efficiently computable by a circuit over $\mathbb{F}_p$, then one will run into the issue that the $\mathcal{O}_{i-1}$-verifier is efficiently representable as a circuit only over $\mathbb{F}$, and F itself is not. To address this, one can define $\mathcal{O}_i$ via *two* steps of SNARK composition, rather than one. In the first step, the prover represents the $\mathcal{O}_{i-1}$-verifier as a circuit over $\mathbb{F}$, and in its own head computes an $\mathcal{O}_{\mathbb{F}}$-proof π that it knows an $\mathcal{O}_{i-1}$-proof π_{i-1} that $F^{(i-1)} = y_{i-1}$. Then, since (unlike the $\mathcal{O}_{i-1}$-verifier) the $\mathcal{O}_{\mathbb{F}}$-verifier *is* efficiently representable as a circuit over $\mathbb{F}_p$, there is a small circuit over $\mathbb{F}_p$ to establish that both (a) the prover knows such a proof π and and (b) that $F(y_{i-1}) = y_i$. Hence, $\mathcal{O}_{\mathbb{F}_p}$ can be applied to this circuit to yield a proof that $F^{(i)}(x) = y_i$.

[10]More recent work has studied recursive-composed SNARKs with a universal rather than circuit-specific trusted setup, but this leads to even higher overheads for the prover [96].

IVC (Section 18.3): for each iteration $j - 1$, the prover could output y_{j-1} and the proof π_{j-1} that $y_{j-1} = F^{(j-1)}(x)$, and any other party could "pick up the computation from there", computing $F(y_{j-1})$ and using π_{j-1} to compute a proof π_j that $y_j = F^{(j)}(x)$.

Relative to the direct application of the non-composed base SNARK, the above recursive solution also reduces the prover's space cost, because the prover only ever applies the base SNARK to a *single* application of F, one after the other (i.e, it does not apply the base SNARK "all at once" to an entire circuit computing $F^{(i)}$). That is, at any time j during its computation of the proof π_i, the prover only needs to remember the preceding proof π_{j-1} and the preceding output y_{j-1} of $F^{(j-1)}$.

On the other hand, a significant downside of the recursive approach when applied to a SNARK that uses pairings such as Groth's [142] is that the prover is quite slow, in large part owing to the need to use cycles of pairing-friendly elliptic curves to support arbitrary-depth recursion (Section 18.2). On top of this, there is additional overhead for the prover that can be traced to a notion we term the *overhead of recursion*.

The overhead of recursion.   Effectively, the final SNARK proof π_i for $F^{(i)}$ establishes that for all $j \leq i$, the prover $\mathcal{P}$ not only faithfully applied F to y_{j-1} to obtain y_j (as per (b) above), but *also* that $\mathcal{P}$, in its own head, faithfully verified the proof π_{j-1} as per (a) above.[11] Put another way, the above recursive approach replaces the computation of $F(y_{j-1})$ with a *larger* computation $F'(y_{j-1}, \pi_{j-1})$ that outputs $F(y_{j-1})$ and verifies π_{j-1}, and it applies the base SNARK to F' for all $j \leq i$. (This perspective will come up again in Section 18.5).

We refer to the added cost to the prover of establishing that it verified π_{j-1} for each iterative application j of F as the "overhead of recursion". This is because non-recursive solutions—i.e., a direct application of a SNARK to a circuit computing $F^{(i)}$—require the prover to establish only that it faithfully applied F all i times, not that it verified any proofs of its own faithfulness along the way. Hence, the

---

[11]To clarify, π_i establishes all of this without even "telling the verifier" what y_{j-1} or π_{j-1} even were.

"overhead of recursion" is purely extra work for the prover, which does not arise in non-recursive solutions.

This overhead is naturally measured by the number of gates in a circuit, or other intermediate representation as appropriate, implementing the base SNARK's verifier.[12] This will be the dominant contributor to the prover's costs if this circuit is larger than the circuit required to implement F itself. Specifically, this happens if the circuit representing F is smaller than the *recursion threshold* of the base SNARK $\mathcal{O}$ (see Section 18.2).

Trusted-setup SNARKs with state-of-the-art verification costs [142] have a reasonably low recursion threshold. Still, we will see later (Section 18.5) that this overhead can be reduced further via other approaches that moreover can avoid a trusted setup and pairing-friendly groups (the use of pairings both increases the recursion threshold and, as mentioned above, leads to concretely high prover costs).[13]

Recursively composing transparent SNARKs. To recap, there are a number of downsides to above approach of recursively composing a SNARK with state-of-the-art verification costs: the base SNARK's need for a trusted setup, the very high prover overheads due to the use of cycles of pairing-friendly curves, and the concretely sub-optimal "overhead of recursion".

The most straightforward approach to address the first two issues is to replace the trusted-setup SNARKs with transparent SNARKs that moreover do not require pairing-friendly groups. These SNARKs all utilize transparent polynomial commitment schemes—e.g., based on FRI (Section 10.4), Ligero's polynomial commitment scheme (Section 10.5),

---

[12]The issue described at the end of Footnote 9 can further increase the overhead of recursion, by forcing *two* statements about SNARK verification circuits to be proved for every application of F, rather than one.

[13]Verification of Groth's SNARK [142] involves 3 pairing computations, which are concretely fairly expensive, especially once represented as a circuit or R1CS. Hence, there is room to reduce this overhead further. We will see an approach later in this section (Section 18.5) that reduces the "three pairing computations" down to roughly two group exponentiations in a *non*-pairing-friendly group, which concretely can be represented by a significantly smaller circuit or R1CS than three pairing computations.

Hyrax's polynomial commitment scheme (Section 14.3), or Bulletproofs (Section 14.4). The problem with a naive implementation of this approach is that the verification of evaluation proofs of such polynomial commitment schemes is quite expensive and hence the overhead of recursion is very large. For example, if the popular Bulletproofs polynomial commitment is used, then while proofs are short (logarithmic in size), the verification cost is linear. Even FRI-based polynomial commitments (Section 10.4.4), while achieving polylogarithmic verification time, has proofs that are concretely quite large for appropriate security levels, and verification involve many Merkle hash path authentication operations, which can be somewhat expensive to represent as a circuit or R1CS (see the end of Section 18.2).

To address the overhead of recursion in this case, a line of works starting with Halo [64], [75], [81], [82], [175] has roughly shown how to avoid feeding verification of evaluation proofs of polynomial commitment schemes through the proof machinery. The verifier in these transparent SNARKs can be split into two parts: (a1) verifying all parts of the proof other than evaluations of committed polynomials and (a2) verifying evaluations of committed polynomials. Essentially, the SNARK is modified to simply *omit* the verification check (a2). This means that, each time the prover, in its own head, generates a "proof"[14] π_j that $F^{(j)}(x) = y_j$ (having already computed a "proof" π_{j-1} that $F^{(j-1)}(x) = y_{j-1}$), π_j does *not* directly attest to the validity of any claimed evaluations of committed polynomials involved in the "proof". So these evaluation claims must be checked separately. What these works roughly do is show how to use homomorphism properties of known polynomial commitment schemes to cheaply "batch-check" *all* evaluations of *all* committed polynomials across all "proofs" $\pi_1, \ldots, \pi_i$ that the prover generated in its own head. That is, all such evaluation claims regarding committed polynomials across $\pi_1, \ldots, \pi_i$ are "accumulated" into a single claim, which can then be checked at the same cost as a *single* claim. In Section 16.1, we covered details of this technique in

---

[14]Here, we are putting the word "proof" in quotes, because π_j omits essential verification information, namely verification of evaluations of committed polynomials. Hence, π_j is not actually a complete SNARK proof for the claim at hand, that $F^{(j)}(x) = y_j$.

the case of homomorphic polynomial commitments all being evaluated at the same point.

The most recent works in this line have taken the above approach to its logical extreme and derived SNARKs for iterative computation $F^{(i)}$ purely from homomorphic vector commitment schemes (i.e., without first developing a "base SNARK" that is recursively applied i times). See Footnote 24 in Section 18.5.4 for additional discussion of this perspective. The following section describes one such result, yielding a proof system called Nova [175].

18.5 SNARKs for Iterative Computation via Homomorphic Commitments

Our goal in this section is to design a SNARK for iterative computation directly from homomorphic vector commitment schemes. The resulting SNARK is transparent, avoids the need for pairing friendly curves, and has state-of-the-art overhead of recursion. These last two properties together ensure a significantly faster prover relative to the recursive composition of pairing-based SNARKs (Section 18.4).

18.5.1 Informal Overview of the SNARK

The SNARK will roughly work as follows. Using the front-end techniques of Section 6, one first transforms F into an equivalent R1CS instance, i.e., three public matrices $A, B, C \in \mathbb{F}^{n \times n}$ such that $F(x) = y$ if and only if there exists a vector z of the form (x, y, w) for some witness w such that $(A \cdot z) \circ (B \cdot z) = C \cdot z$. Here $\circ$ denotes the element-wise product of two vectors.[15]

---

[15]Previous sections in this section referred to SNARKs for arithmetic circuit satisfiability for simplicity and concreteness, but as pointed out in Footnote 1, they apply without modification to SNARKs for R1CS. In this section, we use the formalism of R1CS rather than circuits because Nova is most naturally described in the R1CS setting. Of course, R1CS is a generalization of a circuit (see Section 8.4), so any SNARK for R1CS representations also yields a SNARK for circuit representations.

Let $y_0 = x$. Then proving that $F^{(i)}(x) = y_i$ is equivalent to showing the existence of vectors $w_1, \ldots, w_i$ such that for

$$z_j := (y_{j-1}, y_j, w_j), \tag{18.1}$$
$$(A \cdot z_j) \circ (B \cdot z_j) = C \cdot z_j : j = 1, \ldots, i. \tag{18.2}$$

The rough idea of the SNARK is that $\mathcal{P}$ will commit to all of the vectors $z_1, \ldots, z_i$ using a homomorphic vector-commitment scheme, and prove that each one has the form Equation (18.1) and satisfies Equation (18.2). It will do this by repeatedly applying a primitive called a "folding scheme"—roughly, a way of taking two R1CS instances of the form Equation (18.2) and transforming them into a single R1CS instance such that the derived instance is satisfied if and only if both original instances are satisfied.[16] The folding scheme can be repeatedly applied to reduce all i instances of Equation (18.2) into a single instance. For simplicity, we will focus on the "sequential" folding pattern whereby instance one of Equation (18.2) is folded with instance two, and then the resulting derived instance is folded with instance three, and then the resulting derived instance is folded with instance four, and so on until all i instances have been folded into a single one.[17] The folding scheme is interactive, but the interaction can be removed with the Fiat-Shamir transformation.

The validity of this final R1CS instance can be proven with any SNARK for R1CS instances of the form $(A \cdot z) \circ (B \cdot z) = C \cdot z$ in which the prover commits to the witness vector z via the same homomorphic vector commitment scheme used by the prover to commit to $z_1, \ldots, z_i$. This includes, for example, SNARKs that make use of the Bulletproofs

---

[16]This folding scheme is reminiscent several earlier protocols in this text. Most directly, in each round of Bulletproofs (Section 14.4), a claim about an inner product of committed vectors of length n is reduced to a derived claim about an inner product of vectors of length $n/2$. Also, in each round of the sum-check protocol (Section 4.2), a claim about a sum over 2^ℓ terms is reduced to a claim about a sum over $2^{\ell-1}$ terms. In fact, there have been works that view these protocols through a unified lens [70], [174].

[17]In general, any folding pattern can be used. That is, we can treat the i instances as the leaves of any binary tree, with any internal node of the tree representing the "folding" of its two children into a single instance. The root of the tree represents the final R1CS instance that results from all of the folding operations.

polynomial commitment scheme (Section 14.4) as the commitment in Bulletproofs is just a generalized Pedersen commitment to the coefficient vector of the polynomial. If Bulletproofs is used, the length of the SNARK proof for the final R1CS instance that results from folding can be made $O(\log n)$, though the verification time will be $O(n)$.[18]

The above brief description glosses over a number of details. First, the folding scheme will take two R1CS instances and not yield another R1CS instance, but rather a generalization that we call *committed-R1CS-with-a-slack-vector*. Second, because each folding operation will require a message from the prover to the verifier (and a random challenge sent from verifier to prover), the proof length of the resulting protocol will be linear in i, when we would really like a proof length that is *independent* of i. We will ultimately achieve the desired proof length via a variant of recursive proof composition (Section 18.5.4). We additionally have not explained how to check that each committed vector z_j has the form of Equation (18.1).

18.5.2 A Folding Scheme for Committed-R1CS-with-a-Slack-Vector

The problem of committed-R1CS-with-a-slack-vector. In an instance of this problem, there are three public $n \times n$ matrices A, B, and C with entries from a field $\mathbb{F}$, as well as a public scalar $u \in \mathbb{F}$ and a public vector $s \in \mathbb{F}^m$. In addition to those public objects, there are two committed vectors $w \in \mathbb{F}^{n-m}$ and E in $\mathbb{F}^n$. Let $z = (s, w) \in \mathbb{F}^n$. One should think of the prover as having already committed to w and E using a homomorphic vector-commitment scheme (e.g., Pedersen vector commitments from Section 14.2). The prover claims that

$$(A \cdot z) \circ (B \cdot z) = u \cdot (C \cdot z) + E.$$

Folding two instances. Consider having two instances of committed-R1CS-with-a-slack-vector, in which the public matrices in the two

---

[18]For iterative computation, one typically thinks of the number of iterations i as very large, and function F applied at each iteration as small, perhaps even computed by a constant-size circuit. In this case, $O(n)$ can be thought of as a constant and $O(\log n)$ as an *even smaller* constant.

instances are identical. That is, the prover has claimed that:

$$(A \cdot z_1) \circ (B \cdot z_1) = u_1 \cdot C \cdot z_1 + E_1, \tag{18.3}$$

$$(A \cdot z_2) \circ (B \cdot z_2) = u_2 \cdot C \cdot z_2 + E_2. \tag{18.4}$$

Here, $A, B, C \in \mathbb{F}^{n \times n}$ are public matrices, $u_1, u_2 \in \mathbb{F}$ are public scalars, $s_1, s_2 \in \mathbb{F}^m$ are public vectors, $w_1, w_2 \in \mathbb{F}^{n-m}$ and $E_1, E_2 \in \mathbb{F}^n$ are committed vectors, and $z_1 = (s_1, w_1)$ and $z_2 = (s_2, w_2)$. $\mathcal{V}$ would like to check both of these claims. The naive way to do this would be to have the prover open the commitments to w_1, w_2, E_1, and E_2, so $\mathcal{V}$ can check both claims directly, but this naive approach is too expensive for our purposes. Instead, imagine the verifier $\mathcal{V}$ would like to "take a random linear combination" of the two claims, to derive a single claim of the same form, such that the derived claim is true (up to some negligible soundness error) if and only if both of the original claims are true.

Here is a way the verifier could try to accomplish this.

A first attempt that doesn't work. The verifier could choose a random field element $r \in \mathbb{F}$, and let

$$s \leftarrow s_1 + r \cdot s_2 \tag{18.5}$$

$$w \leftarrow w_1 + r \cdot w_2 \tag{18.6}$$

$$u \leftarrow u_1 + r \cdot u_2 \tag{18.7}$$

$$E \leftarrow E_1 + r^2 E_2. \tag{18.8}$$

Observe that $\mathcal{V}$ can directly compute s and u because $s_1, s_2 \in \mathbb{F}^m$ and $u_1, u_2 \in \mathbb{F}$ are public. Also, by homomorphism of the commitment scheme used by $\mathcal{P}$ to commit to w_1, w_2, E_1, and E_2, the verifier can on its own compute commitments to w and E. The verifier might *hope* that under these definitions, Equation (18.3) and (18.4) imply the following (and vice versa):

$$(A \cdot z) \circ (B \cdot z) = u \cdot (C \cdot z) + E. \tag{18.9}$$

If this were the case, then the verifier, on its own, could derive a single new instance of committed-R1CS-with-a-slack-vector that is *equivalent* to the validity of the two original instances (Equations (18.3) and (18.4)).

Unfortunately, even if Equation (18.3) and (18.4) both hold, Equation (18.9) does *not* hold. But as we will see, we can slightly modify the definition of E so that Equation (18.9) does hold.

What does work. Let us redefine E to include an extra "cross-term", namely, throw away Equation (18.8) and replace it with:

$$E \leftarrow E_1 + r^2 E_2 + r \cdot T \tag{18.10}$$

where

$$T \leftarrow (A \cdot z_2) \circ (B \cdot z_1) + (A \cdot z_1) \circ (B \cdot z_2) - u_1 \cdot C \cdot z_2 - u_2 \cdot C \cdot z_1. \tag{18.11}$$

Then it can be checked via elementary algebra that Equation (18.9) holds for every choice of $r \in \mathbb{F}$.

Calculation showing that Equation (18.9) holds for every $r \in \mathbb{F}$.
The left hand side of Equation (18.9) is:

$$(A \cdot z) \circ (B \cdot z) = (A \cdot z_1 + r \cdot A \cdot z_2) \circ (B \cdot z_1 + r \cdot B \cdot z_2)$$
$$= (A \cdot z_1) \circ (B \cdot z_1) + r^2 \cdot (A \cdot z_2) \circ (B \cdot z_2) + r$$
$$\cdot ((A \cdot z_1) \circ (B \cdot z_2) + (A \cdot z_2) \circ (B \cdot z_1))$$
$$\tag{18.12}$$

while the right hand side equals:

$$u \cdot (C \cdot z) = (u_1 + r u_2) \cdot C \cdot (z_1 + r z_2)$$
$$= u_1 \cdot C \cdot z_1 + E_1 + r^2 (u_2 \cdot C \cdot z_2 + E_2)$$
$$+ r (u_2 \cdot C \cdot z_1 + u_1 \cdot C \cdot z_2) \tag{18.13}$$

By Equations (18.3) and (18.4), we can rewrite Expression (18.12) as:

$$u_1 \cdot C \cdot z_1 + E_1 + r^2 \cdot (u_2 \cdot C \cdot z_2 + E_2)$$
$$+ r \cdot ((A \cdot z_1) \circ (B \cdot z_2) + (A \cdot z_2) \circ (B \cdot z_1)). \tag{18.14}$$

The difference between Expression (18.14) and the right hand side of Equation (18.13) is exactly r times the value assigned to T by Equation (18.11).

Accordingly, consider the following simple interactive protocol that seeks to "reduce" checking that Equation (18.3) and (18.4) both hold to the task of checking that Equation (18.9) holds: First, $\mathcal{P}$ commits to a vector v claimed to equal the cross-term T (Equation (18.11)) using the same homomorphic vector-commitment scheme used to commit to w_1, w_2, E_1, and E_2. Next, $\mathcal{V}$ chooses r at random from $\mathbb{F}$ and sends it to $\mathcal{P}$. Observe that, given the commitments to E_1, E_2, and v, $\mathcal{V}$ can use the homomorphism to compute a commitment to the vector $E_1 + r^2 E_2 + r \cdot v$, which, if v is as claimed, equals the right hand side of Equation (18.10).

We have already explained that if the committed vector v equals T (Equation (18.11)) as prescribed, then Equation (18.10) holds with probability 1 over the random choice of r. Meanwhile, it is not hard to see that if the prover commits to a vector v that *differs* from T, then with probability $1 - 2/|\mathbb{F}|$ over the random choice of r, Equation (18.9) will fail to hold. This is because, if $v_j \neq T_j$ for some $j \in \{1, \ldots, n\}$, then the jth entries of the vectors on the left hand side and right hand side of Equation (18.9) will be two distinct degree-2 univariate polynomials in r, and hence will disagree at a randomly chosen input with probability $1 - 2/|\mathbb{F}|$. Here, it is essential that the prover is forced to commit to the cross-term vector T before learning the verifier's choice of $r \in \mathbb{F}$. Similarly, if either Equation (18.3) or (18.4) does not hold, then there is no vector T that the prover can commit to that would render every entry of the right hand and left hand sides of Equation (18.9) to be the same polynomials in r.

Formally, to be useful in designing a SNARK for iterative computation, we need to show that the above folding scheme is a proof of knowledge, meaning given any efficient prover that can convince the verifier of the validity of the folded instance with non-negligible probability, we can extract openings of the vectors w_1, E_1, w_2, E_2 that respectively satisfy the instances that were folded together (Equations (18.3) and (18.4)). We omit the details, as the paragraph above conveys the key intuition as to why a prover that does not behave as prescribed will, with overwhelming probability over the choice of r, be left to establish a false claim after the folding, namely that it can open the commitments to w and E to vectors satisfying Equation (18.9).[19]

While this folding scheme is interactive, it is public coin, and hence can be rendered non-interactive via the Fiat-Shamir transformation (i.e, replace the verifier's challenge with a hash of the public inputs and the prover's message in the folding scheme).

18.5.3 A Large Non-Interactive Argument

A non-interactive argument of knowledge for an iterative computation $F^{(i)}(x)$ with proof length linear in i can be obtained by repeatedly applying the above folding scheme in the manner sketched in Section 18.5.1. This proof length is far too large to be interesting in applications, but it will be a useful object to have considered when we turn to designing the final SNARK (Section 18.5.4).

We will describe the proof as being produced and processed in "rounds", even though it is non-interactive. Since there is no message sent from $\mathcal{V}$ to $\mathcal{P}$, the entire proof is obtained by simply concatenating all prover messages across all "rounds".

At the start of each "round" $j > 1$ of the protocol, there is already a "running folded instance" I of committed-R1CS-with-slack-vector that captures the result of having folded across the first j rounds the R1CS instances capturing the first $j - 1$ applications of F (as per Equation (18.2)), and the purpose of round $j > 1$ is to fold into this running instance the R1CS capturing the jth application of F (again, as per Equation (18.2)). This means that at the start of round $j > 1$, the verifier will be tracking a commitment c_w to the "witness vector" w for I, and a commitment c_E for the "slack vector" E for I. The verifier at all times keeps track of the following variables:

- *round-count* (meant to track the number j of applications of F that have been processed so far).

- *prev-output* (meant to track $y_{j-1} = F^{(j-1)}(x)$)

---

[19]Readers are referred to the knowledge-soundness analysis of the Bulletproofs polynomial commitment (Section 14.4) for an example of a knowledge-soundness analysis for a folding scheme.

- *cur-output* (meant to track $y_j = F^{(j)}(x)$)

- $u \in \mathbb{F}$ (meant to track the scalar u of the running folded instance I)

- $s \in \mathbb{F}^m$ (meant to track the public input s to the running folded instance I)

- c_w (meant to track the commitment to the witness vector w of the running folded instance I)

- c_E (meant to track the commitment to the slack vector E of the running folded instance I).

Let us introduce some notation to capture this state of affairs at the start of round j. We denote the prover's claim in running folded instance I at the very start of round j by

$$(A \cdot z) \cdot (B \cdot z) = u \cdot (C \cdot z) + E, \qquad (18.15)$$

with the verifier's variables c_w, c_E being a commitments to w and E respectively, and recall that $z = (s, w)$. As per Equation (18.2), there is an R1CS instance that is satisfiable if and only if $F(y_{j-1}) = y_j$. This R1CS instance has the form

$$(A \cdot z_j) \cdot (B \cdot z_j) = C \cdot z_j, \qquad (18.16)$$

where $z_j = (s_j, w_j) \in \mathbb{F}^m \times \mathbb{F}^{n-m}$, and $s_j = (y_{j-1}, y_j)$. Let us refer to this R1CS instance as I_j.

The prover's work in round j. At the start of round j, the prover sends the claimed value of y_j. This reveals to the verifier the public vector $s_j = (y_{j-1}, y_j)$, as $\mathcal{V}$ learned the claimed value of y_{j-1} in the previous round. The prover also sends a commitment c_{w_j} to vector w_j. Together, these quantities specify the committed-R1CS instance I_j given in Equation (18.16). The purpose of round $j > 1$ is then to fold I_j into the running folded instance I. Accordingly, the prover sends a commitment c_T to the claimed cross-term T (Equation (18.11)). In round $j = 1$, there is no folding operation to perform, as the verifier will simply set the running folded instance to I_1; see next paragraph for details.

How the verifier $\mathcal{V}$ processes round j. Upon reading the prover's message in round $j = 1$, $\mathcal{V}$ sets its variables in accordance with the running folded instance becoming I_1. Specifically, $\mathcal{V}$ sets *round-count* to 1, *prev-output* to x, *cur-output* to the claimed value of y_1, u to 1, s to (*prev-output*, *cur-output*), c_w to c_{w_1}, and c_E to a commitment to the all-0s vector.

Upon receiving the prover's message in round $j > 1$, the verifier increments *round-count* from $j - 1$ to j, sets *prev-output* to *cur-output*, and updates *cur-output* to (the claimed value of) y_j. In a truly interactive protocol, the verifier would randomly choose the field element $r \in \mathbb{F}$ used for that round's folding operation and send it to the prover, but in the non-interactive setting, both prover and verifier can determine r via the Fiat-Shamir transformation as per Section 18.5.2. After r is chosen, using homomorphism of the vector commitment scheme, $\mathcal{V}$ updates c_w to a commitment to $w + rw_j$ (as per Equation (18.6)).[20] $\mathcal{V}$ also updates c_E to a commitment to $E + rT$ (as per Equation (18.10)).[21] $\mathcal{V}$ updates $u \leftarrow u + r$ (as per Equation (18.7))[22] and updates $s \leftarrow s + r \cdot s_j$, where $s_j = (\textit{prev-output}, \textit{cur-output})$ (as per Equation (18.5)).

In this manner, after processing all i "rounds" of the proof, the verifier has computed a single folded committed-R1CS-with-slack-vector instance as per Equation (18.15), whose validity, up to a negligible soundness error, is equivalent to the validity of all i applications of F. In this final "round", the prover can establish the validity of the instance using any SNARK for committed-R1CS-with-slack-vector. Such a SNARK can in turn be easily obtained from any SNARK for R1CS satisfiability that commits to witness vectors via the same homomorphic vector commitment scheme used throughout the folding protocol. This includes the SNARK for R1CS from Section 8.4 when combined with, say, the Bulletproofs polynomial commitment scheme (Section 14.4).

---

[20] i.e., $c_w \leftarrow c_w \cdot (c_{w_j})^r$ where $\cdot$ denotes the group operation of the multiplicative group over which the Pedersen vector commitments used by the protocol are defined (see Section 14.2).

[21] Note that Equation (18.10) simplifies due to the fact that there is no slack vector in the R1CS instance of Equation (18.16)—equivalently, the slack vector is zero.

[22] Note that Equation (18.7) simplifies due to the fact that in the right hand side of Equation (18.16), $C \cdot z_j$ is multiplied by the trivial scalar 1.

18.5.4   The Final SNARK: Nova

Unfortunately, the argument of the previous section yields a proof π that grows linearly with i, the number of applications of F. Roughly speaking, we now address this by forcing the SNARK prover to, in its own head, perform the verifier's processing of π across i "rounds" of the protocol, and thereby avoid having the prover explicitly send π to the verifier.

Conceptual overview: folding as deferral of proof checking.   The protocol of the previous section can be thought of as an argument system for incremental computation that works by reducing the checking of *all* applications of F (or more precisely, of R1CS instances equivalent to F) to checking a single derived folding of the applications of F. That is, the validity of the single folded instance is equivalent to the validity of every one of the applications of F that the prover claims to have faithfully executed.

With this in mind, the (validity of) the running folded committed-R1CS-with-slack-vector instance I at the start of each "round" $j > 1$ itself acts a "proof" π_j that $F^{(j-1)}(x) = y_{j-1}$. The folding procedure that occurs in "round" $j > 1$ should then be thought of as a way to *defer* checking the validity of π_j to a later point. Moreover, the folding has the effect of "accumulating" all i such checks into a single statement that can be checked at the same cost as performing any one of the validations individually. Specifically, the checks are deferred until all i foldings have occurred, at which point the prover finally establishes that the final running folded instance is valid.

The above method of "deferring/accumulating" the checking of each "proof" π_j is in contrast to the recursive-composition-of-SNARKs approach covered in Section 18.4, in which the prover explicitly proves that it verified a SNARK proof π_j in its own head for all $j = 1, \ldots, i-1$.[23] Intuitively, it is cheaper to defer/accumulate the checks than it is to

---

[23]More precisely, the prover establishes that it knows a π_j that would have convinced the SNARK verifier to accept. But this effectively means that the prover has itself applied the SNARK verifier's accept/reject computation to π_j, since the prover knows that the outcome of this computation is "accept".

actually explicitly perform each check, thereby reducing the overhead of recursion relative to the recursive-composition-of-SNARKs approach of Section 18.4 (we discuss exactly what is the overhead of recursion of Nova later).[24]

The augmented function F'. Now we come to obtaining a SNARK from the folding scheme via recursive proof composition. Let us "augment" the computation of F to a larger computation F' that not only 1) applies F but also 2) does the verifier's work in one step of the folding scheme. This is analogous to how, in Section 18.4, the honest prover in round j of proof generation applied a base SNARK $\mathcal{O}$ to a circuit $\mathcal{C}'$ that not only applied F to y_{j-1}, but also applied a verification circuit to the proof π_{j-1} computed in the previous round $j - 1$.

In more detail, F' will take as public input values for the variables maintained by the verifier in round j of the folding scheme (see the bulleted list in Section 18.5.3), and will also take as non-deterministic input the prover's message in the folding scheme (except for the claimed value of y_j). F' will output the new values of the verifier's variables in the folding scheme upon processing the prover's message—see the paragraph entitled "How the verifier processes round j" of Section 18.5.3. The one exception is that whereas the verifier in the folding scheme updates the value of the variable *cur-output* to a *claimed* value for y_j provided by the prover, F' will instead output the *actual* value of y_j. That is, F' will apply F to the relevant input and include the result in its output.

The SNARK. The final SNARK applies the folding-based proof of the previous section with F' in place of F.[25] But rather than outputting

---

[24]The deferral/accumulation of these checks is also analogous to earlier results such as Halo [75], that deferred/accumulated only *part* of the verification of the SNARK proof π_j, namely the verification of evaluations of committed polynomials, via a folding-like procedure.

[25]This description elides the following subtlety, which requires a tweak to the definition of F' to address. The folding-scheme is applied to force the prover to faithfully compute $(F')^{(i)}$, which means that for $j \leq i$, the output of the $(j - 1)$'st application of F' has to be fed as public input to the j'th application of F'. One "piece" of the output of F' is the folding-verifier's variable s representing a "running

the entire proof, which consists of i "rounds", the final SNARK proof provides only the information sent by the prover in the final "round". This information comprises the following:

- A specification of the running folded instance I at the start of round i (Equation (18.15)), and a description of the final R1CS instance I_j to be folded in (Equation (18.16) with $j = i$). This latter description includes the claimed output of $(F')^{(i)}(x)$. This includes both the variable *round-count* (Section 18.5.3) and the claimed output y_i of $F^{(i)}(x)$. The SNARK verifier must confirm that *round-count*$= i$ and reject if not, as this ensures that the proof actually refers to $F^{(i)}$ and not $F^{(j)}$ for some $j \neq i$. If all of the SNARK verifier's remaining checks (described below) pass, then the verifier is convinced that indeed $y_i = F^{(i)}(x)$.

- The information provided by the prover in the "final round" of the protocol of the previous section to perform the final folding operation, specifically a commitment c_T to the cross-term used in this folding operation.

- A SNARK proof that the final folded instance is satisfiable.

In summary, the honest prover performs each "round" of the previous section's protocol in its own head, only outputting a transcript of the

---

folding" of all public inputs to previous applications of F'. This means that the vector s that is (just one piece of the) input to the jth application of F' has to be at least as big as the entire public input to the previous application of F'. But since there are other outputs of the $(j-1)$'st application of F' as well (see the bulleted list of verifier values in Section 18.5.3), this forces the length of the public input to the jth application of F' to be *strictly bigger* than that of the previous application. Thus, the public input length for F' grows with each application of F'. To address this issue, one can modify F' to not include in its output $s \in \mathbb{F}^m$, but only a cryptographic hash $H(s)$, thereby ensuring that the output length of F' is independent of the length of s. F' will then take s as an additional non-deterministic input rather than as public input and as part of its computation it will confirm that s is indeed the pre-image of the associated public input value $H(s)$. In summary, without this modification, the public input size to F' grows iteration-by-iteration, because the vector s (the folding of prior public inputs) grows with each iteration. The modification replaces s in the input and output of F' with a hash $H(s)$, which addresses the issue because the size of the hash $H(s)$ does not depend on the length of the vector s.

final "round" of the protocol. This is analogous to how the prover in the recursive-SNARK solution of Section 18.4 for $F^{(i)}$ generated in its own head a sequence of SNARK proofs $\pi_1, \ldots, \pi_i$, with each π_j attesting to a correct execution of F to input y_{j-1} (as well as knowledge of π_{j-1}). But ultimately, only the final proof π_i needs to be sent to the verifier to guarantee the correctness of the claimed output of $F^{(i)}$.

Essentially, each time that the Nova prover $\mathcal{P}$ performs a folding operation in its own head, thereby folding I_j into the running folded instance I, the very next application of F' performs the verifier's work in the folding operation, in addition to applying F for a $(j+1)$'st time. This is the sense in which the final Nova SNARK forces the prover of the previous section's protocol to perform in its own head the verifier's work of that protocol.

The overhead of recursion. In this SNARK, the overhead of recursion refers to the amount of extra work that F' does beyond simply applying F (or more precisely, the number of constraints in the R1CS instance over field $\mathbb{F}_p$ representing F' relative to the R1CS instance over $\mathbb{F}_p$ representing F). This extra work done in F' simply implements the verifier's variable updates in the folding scheme; see the final paragraph of Section 18.5.3. This consists of a handful of field multiplications and additions over $\mathbb{F}_p$, one invocation of a cryptographic hash function per the Fiat-Shamir transformation, and the homomorphic updating of the two commitments c_w and c_E to obtain commitments to $w + rw_j$ (as per Equation (18.6)), and $E + rT$.

If a SNARK-friendly hash function is used for Fiat-Shamir, then it is the two homomorphic commitment updates that dominate the overhead of recursion. If the commitments are Pedersen vector commitments over a multiplicative group $\mathbb{G}$, then each of these updates requires one group exponentiation and one group multiplication; it is the two group exponentiations that dominate the cost, as a group exponentiation takes approximately $\log|\mathbb{G}| \approx 2\lambda$ group multiplications. This overhead of recursion is concretely cheaper than that of recursive-SNARK solutions considered earlier in this section (see Footnote 13 in Section 18.4).[26]

---

[26] This description elides an important implementation issue that is essentially identical to the one described in Footnote 9 in the context of IVC from recursive

Overall prover runtime. Assuming the number of iterations i is not very small, the prover's runtime is dominated by the cost of computing a Pedersen vector commitment at every iteration $j \leq i$ to the witness vector w_j and the cross-term T. Both of these vectors have length at most n', where n' is the number of rows of the R1CS instance capturing F'. Hence, this is two multi-exponentiations of size n' per iteration. As per the above overhead-of-recursion analysis, n' is quite close to n, the number of rows of the R1CS capturing F alone. One does need to use a cycle of elliptic curves, but the curves need not be pairing friendly, ensuring fast group operations (see Section 18.2).

SNARKs. Specifically, Pedersen vector commitments that are homomorphic over field $\mathbb{F}_p$ are elements of an elliptic curve group $\mathbb{G}$ in which the *scalar field* is $\mathbb{F}_p$ and the *base field* is another field, $\mathbb{F}$. And group operations over $\mathbb{G}$ can be efficiently implemented by a circuit or R1CS defined over the base field, but unfortunately not the scalar field. Similar to Footnote 9, one way to sidestep this issue is to identify a cycle of curves $\mathbb{G}$ and $\mathbb{G}'$ with scalar and base fields $\mathbb{F}_p$ and $\mathbb{F}$ such that F is efficiently computable by circuits or R1CS over *both* $\mathbb{F}_p$ and $\mathbb{F}$. One then maintains two different sequences of R1CS instances, with one sequence defined over field $\mathbb{F}_p$ and the other defined over field $\mathbb{F}$. Since F is efficiently computable in R1CS over both fields, one can efficiently define two different augmented functions, say, F', and F'', computing F and performing folding operations when commitments are sent over $\mathbb{G}'$ and $\mathbb{G}$ respectively. One then alternates performing folding operations on each sequence. Specifically, a folding of two committed-R1CS-with-slack-vector instances defined over $\mathbb{F}_p$ (and associated application of F') can be efficiently computed by F'' and hence by the R1CS sequence defined over field $\mathbb{F}$, and similarly a folding operation of two instances defined over $\mathbb{F}$ can be efficiently computed by F' and hence by the R1CS sequence defined over $\mathbb{F}_p$. The final SNARK proof consists of the final folding operation for *both* sequences, and SNARK proofs for both sequences that the final folded instance is satisfied. Also similar to Footnote 9, if F is only efficiently implementable over $\mathbb{F}_p$ one will still have two functions F' and F'', but only F' will both apply F and implement folding; F'' will only implement folding. This will double the number of folding operations required to obtain a SNARK for $F^{(i)}$. Effectively only applications of F' perform the "useful work" of applying F; applications of F'' are only used to "switch" which of the two fields folding operations can be efficiently computed over.

19

Bird's Eye View of Practical Arguments

We have covered four approaches to the construction of practical SNARKs. In each of the four, an underlying information-theoretically secure protocol is combined with cryptography to yield an argument. The first approach is based on the interactive proof for arithmetic circuit evaluation of Section 4.6 (the GKR protocol), the second is based on the MIPs for circuit or R1CS satisfiability of Sections 8.2 and 8.4, the third is based on the constant-round polynomial IOP for circuit or R1CS satisfiability of Section 10.3, and the fourth is based on the linear PCP of Section 17.4. We presented a unified view of the first three approaches, and the pros and cons of each, in Section 10.6, via the lens of polynomial IOPs.

We have also covered a fifth approach to argument design, based on commit-and-prove techniques (Section 13.1), which can be viewed as combining a trivial static (i.e., **NP**) proof system with cryptographic commitments. Commit-and-prove based arguments have been studied in several works, e.g., [23], [107], [248]. These arguments are not succinct, and recent works on this approach yield interactive protocols; for both of these reasons, these arguments are not SNARKs.

For each of the first three approaches (IP-based, MIP-based, and constant-round-polynomial-IOP-based), one can combine the information-theoretically secure protocol with any extractable polynomial commitment scheme of the protocol designer's choosing to obtain a succinct argument (there is essentially just one technique to to turn linear PCPs into publicly-verifiable SNARKs, based on pairings and very similar to KZG polynomial commitments, see Section 17.5). For the IP-based and MIP-based argument systems, the polynomial commitment scheme must allow committing to *multilinear* polynomials. For the IOP-based argument system, the polynomial commitment scheme must allow committing to *univariate* polynomials. Of course, the resulting argument system will inherit the cryptographic and setup assumptions as well as any efficiency bottlenecks of the chosen polynomial commitment scheme.

We have in turn covered three broad approaches to polynomial commitment schemes in this survey, though some of these approaches have multiple instantiations with various cost tradeoffs. The first is via IOPs combined with Merkle hashing, where we saw FRI in Section 10.4.2 and Ligero- and Brakedown-commitments in Section 10.5. The second is based on transparent Σ-protocols that assume hardness of the discrete logarithm problem, where we saw Hyrax-commit (Section 14.3), Bulletproofs (Section 14.4), and Dory (Section 15.4).[1] The third is based on the approach of KZG [164] and uses pairings and a trusted setup (Section 15.2). Below, we call these respective approaches to polynomial commitments "IOP-based", "discrete-log-based", and "KZG-based". We discussed the pros and cons of the various polynomial commitment schemes in Section 16.3.

19.1 A Taxonomy of SNARKs

The research literature on practical succinct arguments is a veritable zoo of built systems and theoretical protocols. In this section, we attempt

---

[1]We also saw that it is possible to combine various commitment schemes to obtain different cost tradeoffs, e.g., Section 15.4. We omit such combinations from this section to avoid a combinatorial explosion of commitment schemes to discuss.

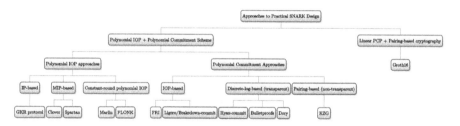

Figure 19.1: Our taxonomy of SNARK design. Leaves depict selected example protocols covered or discussed in this survey. Every combination of polynomial IOP and polynomial commitment scheme yields a SNARK, though constant-round polynomial IOPs need a commitment scheme for univariate polynomials, while IPs and MIPs need one for multilinear polynomials. SNARKs using transparent polynomial commitments are transparent. SNARKs using IOP-based polynomial commitments are plausibly post-quantum.

to tame this zoo with a coherent taxonomy of the primary approaches that have been pursued.

Outside of the linear-PCP-based SNARKs, most known SNARKs are obtained by combining some IP, MIP, or constant-round polynomial IOP with a polynomial commitment scheme. As we have covered at least six polynomial commitment schemes in this survey, this yields at least 18 possible SNARKs (even ignoring the fact that there are multiple MIPs and constant-round polynomial IOPs to choose from). Most of these combinations have been explored; below, we list which implemented systems use which combination.[2] Our taxonomy is depicted in Figure 19.1.

(a) IPs combined with FRI-based (multilinear) polynomial commitments (Section 10.4.5) were explored in [256], producing a system called Virgo.

(b) IPs combined with discrete-log-based (multilinear) polynomial commitments (Bulletproofs, and Hyrax-commit) were explored in [244], producing a system called Hyrax.

---

[2]This list is surely not exhaustive.

(c) IPs combined with KZG-based (multilinear) polynomial commitments were explored in [251], [257], [258], producing systems called zk-vSQL and Libra.

(d) MIPs combined with many different multilinear polynomial commitments were explored in [137], [226], [230], producing systems including Spartan, Xiphos, Kopis, Brakedown, and Shockwave. Spartan, Kopis, and Xiphos use various discrete-logarithm-based multilinear commitments, while Brakedown naturally uses the Brakedown-commitment and Shockwave the Ligero-commitment.

(e) Constant-round polynomial IOPs combined with FRI-based (univariate) polynomial commitments were explored in a series of works, most recently [43], [100], [165], producing systems called Aurora, Fractal, and Redshift. Other related works in this series include [33]–[36], [41], [221].

(f) Constant-round polynomial IOPs combined with KZG-based (univariate) polynomial commitments were explored in popular systems called Marlin [98] and PlonK [123]. Marlin uses the polynomial IOP for R1CS from Section 10.3, while PlonK gives a different polynomial IOP, for circuit-satisfiability. A predecessor to these works is Sonic [187].

"Halo 2"[3] combines the PlonK constant-round polynomial IOP with the Bulletproofs polynomial commitment scheme. "PlonKy2"[4] uses a FRI-based polynomial commitment scheme rather than Bulletproofs.

(g) Ligero [7] combines a constant-round polynomial IOP with the polynomial commitment of the same name, and Ligero++ [53] replaces the polynomial commitment with a "combination" of Ligero's commitment and FRI.

(h) A very large number of systems have been derived from the linear PCP of Genarro, Gentry, Parno, and Raykova [125] (Section 17.5).

---

[3]https://zcash.github.io/halo2/.
[4]https://github.com/mir-protocol/PlonKy2/blob/main/PlonKy2.pdf.

These include [42], [203]. The most popular variant of the SNARK derived from GGPR's linear PCP is due to Groth [142], who obtained a proof length of just 3 elements of a pairing-friendly group, and proved the SNARK secure in the Generic Group Model that was briefly discussed in Section 15.2 ([117] extended the security proof to the Algebraic Group Model). This variant is colloquially referred to as Groth16.

More SNARKs via composition. On top of the taxonomy of SNARKs delineated above, one can take any two SNARKs designed via one of the 18 above approaches, and compose them one or more times. As discussed in Section 18.1, by taking a "fast-prover, larger-proof" SNARK and composing it with a "slower prover-smaller proof" SNARK, one can in principle obtain a "best-of-both-worlds" SNARK with a fast prover and small proofs. Such compositions are growing increasingly popular and already yield state-of-the-art performance.

To name some recent examples, PlonKy2 self-composes the SNARK obtained by combining the PlonK polynomial IOP with the FRI polynomial commitment scheme. In the first SNARK application, FRI can be configured to have a fast prover but to generate a large proof π. Since π is large, it is not actually sent to the verifier. Rather, subsequent applications of the same SNARK are used to establish knowledge of π. Since these later applications of the SNARK are applied to a relatively small computation (the procedure for *verifying* π), FRI can be configured in these later applications to have a slower prover and smaller proofs.

Relatedly, Polygon Hermez is composing such a FRI-based SNARK with Groth16, in order to inherit Groth16's attractive verification costs, while keeping both the prover time and size of the trusted setup smaller than in a direct application of Groth16 to the original statement being proved [25] (the use of Groth16 does relinquish the plausible post-quantum security and transparency of the FRI-based SNARK).

As other examples, Orion [253] composes Brakedown with Virgo to reduce proof size. deVirgo [252] in turn composes Virgo with Groth16. Filecoin uses a technique called SnarkPack [124] to aggregate many Groth16 proofs into one; such aggregation of SNARK proofs can be viewed as a form of SNARK composition (see Section 18.3). zkSync has similarly used recursive aggregation of PlonK proofs since 2020.

Other approaches. There are a handful of approaches to the design of arguments that do not necessarily fall into the categories above. One example is called MPC-in-the-head, which takes any secure multiparty computation (MPC) protocol[5] and transforms it into a (zero-knowledge) IOP [7], [127], [157].[6] The IOP can in turn be transformed into a non-interactive argument via Merkle-hashing and the Fiat-Shamir transformation, as we have described in this survey.

Arguments derived via MPC-in-the-head typically have a cost profile loosely analogous to commit-and-prove arguments: much larger proof sizes and higher verifier costs than the approaches above, but they can have good concrete costs on small instance sizes, and good prover runtimes. This has led, for example, to an interesting family of candidate post-quantum secure digital signatures, called Picnic [93], [106], [162], [163], [166].[7]

We do not cover MPC-in-the-head because, in our view, it is not truly distinct from the approaches covered in this survey. In particular, all known *succinct* arguments (i.e., with sublinear proof size) that were originally discovered or presented via the MPC-in-the-head framework in fact comprise a polynomial IOP combined with one of the IOP-based polynomial commitment schemes that we have covered [7].

---

[5] An MPC protocol allows $t \geq 2$ parties to compute some function f of their inputs, say, $f(x_1, \ldots, x_t)$ where x_i is the i'th party's input. Very roughly speaking, the guarantee of an MPC protocol is that each party i learns no other information about the other parties' inputs, other than $f(x_1, \ldots, x_t)$.

[6] Very roughly speaking, the IOP is obtained as follows. If the IOP prover claims to know a witness w such that $\mathcal{C}(w) = 1$, it simulates, in its own head, the secret-sharing of w amongst several parties. It then simulates an MPC protocol for evaluating $\mathcal{C}$ on w, using verifier-supplied randomness within the MPC protocol. The IOP proof string is then a (claimed) transcript of the MPC protocol. The IOP verifier inspects the proof string to try to ascertain whether it is indeed a valid transcript for the MPC protocol. The security properties of the MPC protocol are used to ensure that the resulting IOP is complete, sound, and zero-knowledge.

[7] Other related techniques also derive zero-knowledge proofs from MPC protocols [114], [149], [159], with broadly similar cost profiles to MPC-in-the-head (long proofs and verification time, but good prover runtime and small hidden constants).

Another example approach not covered in this survey is that linear PCPs can be combined with *non*-pairing-based cryptosystems to yield designated-verifier (i.e., non-publicly-verifiable) SNARKs, including some based on the assumed hardness of lattice problems that are plausibly post-quantum secure [56]. To date, this approach has not led to practical protocols.

19.2 Pros and Cons of the Approaches

Every combination of {IP, MIP, constant-round polynomial IOP} and polynomial commitment scheme naturally inherits the pros and cons of the two components of the combination. Sections 10.6 and 16.3 respectively discussed the pros and cons of the individual components. In this section, we aim to do the same for the various combinations, as well as for SNARKs derived from linear PCPs.

Approaches minimizing proof size. There are two approaches that achieve proofs consisting of a constant number of group elements, captured in items (f) and (h) of the previous section—namely, constant-round polynomial IOPs combined with KZG-based polynomial commitments, and linear PCPs (transformed into SNARKs using pairing-based cryptography). The linear PCP approach is the ultimate winner in proof size, as its proofs consist of as few as 3 group elements [142]. For comparison, Marlin [98] (which uses the former approach), produces proofs that are roughly 4 times larger than that of Groth's SNARK [142].

The downsides of the two approaches are also related. First, both require a trusted setup (as they make use of a structured reference string), which produces toxic waste (also called a trapdoor) that must be discarded to prevent forgeability of proofs. In the case of IOPs combined with KZG-based polynomial commitments, the downsides of the SRS are not as severe as for linear PCPs, for two reasons. First, the SRS for the former approach is *universal*: a single SRS can be used for *any* R1CS-satisfiability or circuit-satisfiability instance up to some specified size bound. This is because the SRS simply consists of encodings of powers of a random field element τ, and hence is independent of the circuit or R1CS instance. In contrast, the SRS in the linear PCP approach is *computation-specific*: in addition to including encodings of powers-of-τ, the SRS in the linear PCP approach also has to include encodings of evaluations of univariate polynomials capturing the wiring pattern of the circuit or the matrix entries specifying the R1CS instance.[8] Second, the SRS for the former approach is *updatable* (see Section 16.3 for discussion of this notion), while the SRS for the linear PCP approach is not, again owing to the fact that the SRS contains elements other than encodings of powers-of-τ.

The second downside of both of these two approaches is that they are computationally expensive for the prover, for two reasons. First, in both approaches, the prover needs to perform FFTs or polynomial division over vectors or polynomials of size proportional to the circuit size S, or number K of nonzero entries of constraints in the R1CS instance. This is time-intensive as well as highly space intensive and difficult to parallelize and distribute [250]. Second, in both approaches the prover also needs to perform several multi-exponentiations of size $\Theta(S)$ or $\Theta(K)$ in a pairing-friendly group. See Section 16.3 for discussion of the concrete costs of these operations.

SNARKs such as Marlin and PlonK that are derived from constant-round polynomial IOPs have a significantly slower prover than Groth's SNARK for a given circuit or R1CS size.[9] This increased prover cost

---

[8]One can render universal a SNARK with a computation-specific SRS by applying the SNARK to a so-called universal circuit, which takes as input both a description of another circuit $\mathcal{C}$ and an input-witness pair (x, w) for $\mathcal{C}$ and evaluates $\mathcal{C}$ on (x, w). This introduces significant overhead, despite several mitigation efforts [46], [172]; see [243] for some concrete measurements of overhead.

[9]In Groth's SNARK, the prover performs three multi-exponentiations in $\mathbb{G}_1$ and one in $\mathbb{G}_2$, all of size linear in the number of gates of the circuit or number of constraints in the R1CS. With popular pairing-friendly groups such as BLS12-381, this cost is comparable to that of applying KZG polynomial commitments to roughly six polynomials of this size. Marlin and PlonK require the prover to commit to more and/or larger polynomials than this. This is especially so as these systems are typically applied in the holographic setting (Sections 10.3.2 and 16.2), whereby polynomials capturing the "wiring" of the circuit or R1CS are committed in pre-processing, to enable sublinear verification time. These pre-processing polynomials are larger than the others by a constant factor, and there are several of them, and the prover must reveal evaluations of these committed polynomials as part of the SNARK proof. In contrast, Groth's SNARK, with its circuit-specific pre-processing,

can be mitigated in certain applications by the fact that polynomial-IOP derived SNARKs, compared to linear-PCP derived SNARKs such as Groth's, have more flexibility in the intermediate representation used—see Section 19.3.3 for details.

In the remainder of this section, we describe broad tradeoffs of the remaining approaches.

Transparency. In contrast to the two approaches that minimize proof size, all of the remaining approaches are *transparent* unless they choose to use KZG-based polynomial commitments. That is, they use a uniform reference string (URS) rather than a structured reference string, and hence no toxic waste is produced. Transparency of the SNARK is totally determined by the polynomial commitment scheme used—if the commitment scheme uses a URS, then the entire SNARK uses a URS.

Post-quantum security. The approaches that are plausibly post-quantum secure are comprised of those that utilize an IOP-based polynomial commitment (FRI, Ligero, Brakedown).[10] That is, quantum security is determined entirely by the polynomial commitment scheme–IOPs are plausibly post-quantum, but the other two classes of polynomial commitments are not, due to their reliance on the hardness of discrete log.

Dominant contributor to cost: polynomial commitments. When MIPs and constant-round polynomial IOPs are combined with any polynomial commitment, it is the polynomial commitment that typically dominates the most relevant costs: prover time, proof length, and verifier time (the lone exception is that, if an MIP is combined with KZG commitments, it is the MIP and not the polynomial commitment that dominates verification costs).

This may or may not be the case for IPs for circuit-satisfiability as well—IPs have larger proofs "outside of the polynomial commitment"

"bakes" circuit wiring information into the SRS generation procedure, and thereby does not have to "pay" in prover efficiency to achieve holography.

[10]The MPC-in-the-head approach, by virtue of yielding IOPs, also gives plausibly post-quantum secure protocols [7], [127].

than MIPs and constant-round IOPs, and that may or may not dominate verification costs, depending on the polynomial commitment scheme used, how small the witness is relative to the rest of the circuit, and how deep the circuit is.

Detailed asymptotic costs of the transparent polynomial commitments covered in this survey were provided in Table 16.1. Here is a brief summary of how concrete costs compare. Broadly speaking, in terms of prover costs, FRI[11] and Bulletproofs[12] are the most expensive polynomial commitment schemes, followed by those using pairings (Dory and KZG commitments). Hyrax, Ligero and Brakedown's commitments all have similar prover costs, though Brakedown is slightly faster and applies over fields that the others do not (see Section 19.3.1 for details). In terms of the sum of commitment size and evaluation proof length (which is what ultimately determines SNARK proof length), Brakedown is the largest, followed by Ligero, followed by Hyrax—all three yield roughly square-root size proofs, but with different constant factors. After that is FRI (polylogarithmic proof size). Next is Dory and Bulletproofs (logarithmic size proofs, with Bulletproofs shorter than Dory by a significant constant factor). KZG-commitments for univariate polynomials are the smallest (constant size).

Recent work called Orion [253] reduces the size of Brakedown's evaluation proofs via depth-one SNARK composition, but in so doing it relinquishes the field-agnostic nature of Brakedown and the proofs remain large (megabytes). Hyperplonk [95] proposes to reduce the proof size much further, to under 10 KBs, by combining Brakedown or

---

[11] As discussed in detail in Section 16.3, FRI exhibits a strong tension between prover costs and verification costs, with the tradeoff between the two determined by the *rate* of the Reed-Solomon code used in the protocol (see Section 10.4.4 for details). It can be configured to have a relatively fast prover, but then proofs are large (multiple hundreds of KBs), or a slower prover with smaller proofs (though still close to 100 KBs when run at 100 bits of security under current analyses [145]).

[12] A principle reason for high prover costs in Bulletproofs prover is that evaluation proofs are concretely expensive to compute: they require a linear number of exponentiations, as opposed to the single multi-exponentiation of linear size that suffices to compute the commitment itself. This high prover cost can be mitigated in contexts where many polynomials are committed and then evaluated, owing to efficient batch-verification of homomorphic polynomial commitments (Section 16.1).

Orion with KZG commitments, though this relinquishes transparency in addition to field-agnosticism.

Constant-round IOPs vs. MIPs and IPs. Broadly speaking, SNARKs from constant-round IOPs tend to be much slower and more space intensive for the prover than SNARKs from MIPs and IPs. This is because constant-round IOPs require the prover to commit to many polynomials (often 10 or more), while in SNARKs from MIPs or IPs, the prover only needs to commit to a single polynomial (which is no bigger than each of the polynomials arising in known constant-round IOPs).[13] This leads to prover time and space costs that are often one or more orders of magnitude larger than for MIP- and IP-derived SNARKs. The large number of committed polynomials in SNARKs from constant-round IOPs does not effect verification costs as much, owing to techniques for efficiently "batch-verifying" the claimed evaluations of multiple committed polynomials at the same input.

On pre-processing and work-saving for the verifier. The approaches requiring an SRS (i.e., linear PCPs, or any approach using KZG-based polynomial commitments) inherently require a pre-processing phase to generate the SRS, and this takes time proportional to the size of the circuit or R1CS instance and must be performed by a trusted party.[14] But the other approaches (combining any IP, MIP, or IOP with IOP-based or discrete-log-based polynomial commitments) can achieve a work-saving verifier *without pre-processing*, if applied to computations with a "regular" structure. By work-saving verifier, we mean that $\mathcal{V}$ runs faster than the time required simply to check a witness—in particular, $\mathcal{V}$'s runtime is sublinear in the size of the circuit or R1CS instance

---

[13]These statistics about the number of polynomials committed ignore the cost of holography/computation commitments, which requires even more (and even larger) committed polynomials (see Sections 10.3.2 and 16.2 and Footnote 9.). Even in the holographic setting, the qualitative comparison is similar.

[14]A partial exception is that combining IPs for circuit-satisfiability with KZG-based polynomial commitments has a setup phase of cost proportional to the size of the witness w rather than the entire circuit $\mathcal{C}$. Also, [84] gives a variant of KZG-based polynomial commitments with square-root-sized SRS, but logarithmic- rather than constant-sized evaluation proofs.

under consideration. For example, the MIP of Section 8.2 achieves a work-saving verifier without pre-processing so long as the multilinear extensions $\widetilde{\text{add}}$ and $\widetilde{\text{mult}}$ of the circuit's wiring predicate can be efficiently evaluated at any input, and any RAM of runtime T can be transformed into such a circuit of size $\tilde{O}(T)$ (Section 6).

That said, not all implementations of these approaches seek to avoid pre-processing for the verifier. One reason for this is that guaranteeing that the intermediate representation (whether a circuit, R1CS instance, or other representation) has a sufficiently regular structure to avoid pre-processing can introduce large concrete overheads to the representation size. Another is that "paying for" an expensive pre-processing phase can enable improved verification costs in the online phase of the protocol. For example, a primary ethos of SNARKs derived from linear PCPs, as well as constant-round polynomial IOPs combined with KZG commitments, is that, while it is expensive to generate the (long) SRS and distribute it to all parties wishing to act as the prover, checking proofs is extremely fast (only a constant number of group operations and bilinear map (pairing) evaluations). We elaborate further on these points at the end of this section.

To give a few examples from the research literature, STARKs [35], [128], [235] implement an IOP specifically designed to avoid pre-processing and achieve a polylogarithmic time verifier for *any* computation, with considerable effort devoted to mitigating the resulting overheads in the size of the intermediate representation. Although STARKs achieve considerable improvements over earlier instantiations of this approach [33], the resulting intermediate representations remain very large in general. Meanwhile, many IP and MIP implementations avoid or minimize pre-processing in data parallel settings [237], [242], [244] (see Section 4.6.7). These systems are able to exploit data parallel structure to ensure that the verifier can efficiently compute the information it needs about the computation in order to check the proof. Specifically, the time required for the verifier is independent of the number of parallel instances executed. They achieve this without incurring large concrete overheads in the size of the intermediate representation (see Section 6.6.4 for a sketch of how such overheads can arise when supporting work-saving verifiers for arbitrary computations).

Still other systems, such as Marlin [98], RedShift [165], PlonK [123], and Spartan [226] implement IOPs and MIPs targeted for the pre-processing setting, where a party can commit to polynomials encoding the wiring of the circuit or R1CS instance during pre-processing,[15] and thereafter, every time the circuit or R1CS is evaluated on a new input, the verifier can run in time sublinear in the circuit size. This is sometimes referred to as *holography* or *computation commitments*.

Finally, many systems do not seek a work-saving verifier even after potential pre-processing—these include [7], [43], [66], [80], [120].

Prover time in holographic vs. non-holographic SNARKs. In systems that implement holography, producing evaluation proofs for the "wiring" polynomials committed in pre-processing is typically the dominant cost in terms of prover time, for reasons discussed in Footnote 9. Hence, care should be taken when comparing prover time of holographic SNARKs to non-holographic ones (i.e., SNARKs that either don't seek to save work for the verifier, or that do seek to save work but only for circuits with "regular" wiring patterns). Non-holographic systems may achieve faster prover time as measured on a per-gate basis, but they may have to use much bigger circuits to achieve a work-saving verifier in general, or else limit themselves to applications that naturally perform the same "small' computation many times, to ensure "regular" wiring without significant blowups in circuit size.

19.3 Other Issues Affecting Concrete Efficiency

There are many subtle or complicated issues that can affect the concrete efficiency of a SNARK. This section provides an overview of some of them.

19.3.1 Field Choice

A subtle aspect of the various approaches to SNARK design that can have a significant effect on practical performance is the many ways in

---

[15]The pre-processing may or may not be transparent, depending on the polynomial commitment scheme used.

which the designer's choice of field to work over can be limited. One reason this matters is that many cryptographic applications naturally work over fields that do not satisfy the properties required by many SNARKs. Examples include proofs regarding encryption or signature schemes, many of which work over elliptic curve groups that are defined over fields that are not FFT-friendly; this is problematic for the many SNARKs in which the prover needs to perform FFTs.

Another reason flexibility in field choice matters is that for certain fields, addition and multiplication are particularly efficient on modern computers. For example, when working over Mersenne-prime fields ($\mathbb{F}_p$ where p is a prime of the form $2^k - 1$ for some positive integer k), reducing an integer modulo p can be implemented with simple bit-shifts and addition operations, and field multiplication can be implemented with a constant number of native (integer) multiplications and additions, followed by modular reduction. Mersenne primes include $2^{61} - 1$, $2^{127} - 1$, and $2^{521} - 1$. Similarly fast arithmetic can be implemented more generally using any pseudo-Mersenne prime, which are of the form $2^k - c$ for small odd constant c (e.g., $2^{224} - 2^{96} + 1$). In contrast, modular reduction in an arbitrary prime-order field potentially requires division by p, and this is typically slower than reduction modulo pseudo-Mersenne primes by a factor of at least 2.[16] As another example of fields with fast arithmetic, some modern CPUs have built-in instructions for arithmetic operations in fields of sizes including 2^{64} and 2^{192}.

Limitations on the choice of field size for SNARKs come in multiple ways. Here are the main examples.

Guaranteeing soundness. All of the IPs, IOPs, MIPs, and linear PCPs that we have covered have soundness error that is at least $1/|\mathbb{F}|$ (and often larger by significant factors). Of course, so long as the soundness error is at most, say, $1/2$, the soundness error can always be driven to $2^{-\lambda}$ by repeating the protocol λ times, but this is expensive (often, only certain "soundness bottleneck" components need to be repeated, and this can mitigate the blowup in some costs, see for example Section 10.4.4).

---

[16]More information on efficient techniques for modular reduction in arbitrary prime-order fields can be found, for example, at https://en.wikipedia.org/wiki/Montgomery_modular_multiplication.

Regardless, $|\mathbb{F}|$ must be chosen sufficiently large to ensure the desired level of soundness.

Limitations coming from discrete-logarithm- or KZG-based polynomial commitments. SNARKs making use of discrete-logarithm-based or KZG-based polynomial commitments (Section 14), or linear PCPs (which are compiled into SNARKs via pairings) must use a field of size equal to the order of the cryptographic group that the polynomial commitment is defined over.[17] In contrast, SNARKs using polynomial commitment schemes derived from IOPs do not suffer such limitations, as the only cryptographic primitive they make use of is a collision-resistant hash function (to build a Merkle-tree over the evaluations of the polynomial to be committed), and such hash functions can be applied to arbitrary data.

Limitations coming from FFTs. SNARKs derived from IOPs (Section 10) and linear PCPs (Section 17) require the prover to perform FFTs over large vectors, and different finite fields support FFT algorithms of different complexities. In particular, standard FFT algorithms running in time $\tilde{O}(n)$ on vectors of length n work only for prime fields $\mathbb{F}_p$ if $p-1$ has many small prime factors.

Many, but not all, desirable fields do support fast FFT algorithms.[18] As an example, all fields of characteristic 2 do have efficient FFT algorithms, though until relatively recently, the fastest known algorithm ran in time $O(n \log n \log \log n)$. The extra $\log \log n$ factor was removed only in 2014 by Lin *et al.* [182]. Very recent work [37], [38] does show how to obtain $O(n \log n)$-time FFT-like algorithms and associated argument systems over arbitrary fields (after a more expensive field-dependent

---

[17]For any large enough prime p, it is typically possible to identify an elliptic curve group $\mathbb{G}$ with scalar field $\mathbb{F}_p$, such that discrete logarithms are presumed difficult to compute in $\mathbb{G}$. See for example [236]. However, the curve may not support pairings, and it is generally undesirable to have to design a new elliptic curve group every time a SNARK protocol designer wishes to change the field order p.

[18]By desirable, we either mean that the field supports fast arithmetic and meets the other desiderata described in this section, or that a particular cryptographic application calls for use of the field, say, because a SNARK is being used to prove a statement about an existing cryptosystem that performs arithmetic over the field.

pre-processing phase), but at the time of writing, its concrete efficiency remains unclear.

A related issue is that known constant-round polynomial IOPs [98], [123] require the field to have multiplicative or additive subgroups of specified sizes. For example, the polynomial IOP in Section 10.3 requires $\mathbb{F}$ to have a subgroup H of size roughly the number variables of the R1CS system, and a second subgroup $L_0 \supset H$ of size a constant factor larger than H. This is one reason SNARK designers may choose to work over a field of size 2^k, as this field has additive subgroups of size $2^{k'}$ for every $k' \le k$ (see Remark 10.1 in Section 10.3.1).

Limitations coming from program-to-circuit transformations. IOP-derived SNARKs that seek to emulate arbitrary computer programs (Random Access Machines (RAMs)) while being work-saving for the verifier and avoiding pre-processing typically use transformations from RAMs to circuits or other intermediate representations that only work over fields of characteristic 2. We saw an example of this in Section 9.4.1, and modern instantiations such as STARKs [33], [35] also have this property.

Other considerations in field choice. There are other considerations when choosing a field to work over, beyond the limitations described above. For example, as discussed in Section 6.5.4.1, a prime field of size p naturally simulates integer addition and multiplication so long as one is guaranteed that the values arising in the computation always lie in the range $[-p/2, p/2]$ (if the values grow outside of this range, then the field, by reducing all values modulo p, will no longer simulate integer arithmetic). Such an efficient simulation is not possible in fields of characteristic 2. Conversely, addition in fields of characteristic 2 is equivalent to bitwise-XOR. Hence, aspects of the computation being fed through the proof machinery will affect which choice of field is most desirable: arithmetic-heavy computations may be more efficiently simulated when working over prime fields, and computations heavy on bitwise operations may be better suited to fields of characteristic 2.

Example field choices. To give some examples from the literature: Aurora [43], which is based on IOPs, chooses to work over the field of size 2^{192}. This is large enough to provide good soundness error while supporting FFT algorithms requiring $O(n \log n)$ group operations, and some modern processors have built-in support for arithmetic over this field. Virgo [256] chooses to work over the field of size p^2 where $p = 2^{61} - 1$ is a Mersenne prime, to take advantage of the fast field operations offered by such primes. [35] chooses to work of the field of size 2^{64}. This field is not large enough to ensure cryptographically-appropriate soundness error on its own, so aspects of the protocol are repeated several times to drive the soundness error lower. PlonKy2 works over (an extension of) the field of size $2^{64} - 2^{32} + 1$. This field has is increasingly popular due features such as its fast arithmetic, its ability to support FFTs of length up to 2^{32} or larger, and the fact that it is large enough to represent the product of two 32-bit unsigned integer data types (which is at most $(2^{32} - 1)^2 = 2^{64} - 2^{33} + 1$).

The three systems above use FRI-based polynomial commitments, meaning they do not have to work over a field of size equal to the order of some cryptographically-secure group (though they do need the field to support FFTs and have subgroups of specified sizes for other reasons as well). SNARKs based on pairings or discrete-logarithm-based polynomial commitments are not able to work over these fields.

Hyrax [244] and Spartan [226], both of which combine IPs or MIPs with discrete-logarithm-based polynomial commitments, work over the field whose size is equal to the order of (a subgroup of) the elliptic curve group Curve25519 [52] (see Section 12.1.2.2), with this group chosen for its fast group arithmetic and popularity.

Systems that use pairings (e.g., all linear-PCP-derived SNARKs, as well as any SNARK using KZG-based polynomial commitments or Dory) work over a field of size equal to the order of (a subgroup of) chosen pairing-friendly elliptic curves. There have been significant efforts to design such pairing-friendly curves with fast group arithmetic while ensuring, e.g., that the order of the chosen subgroup is a prime p such that the field $\mathbb{F}_p$ supports fast FFTs. The most popular such curve today is perhaps BLS12-381—see the references in Footnote 3 in Section 15.1.

The choice of field can make a significant concrete difference in the efficiency of field arithmetic. For example, experiments in [226], [256] suggests that the field used in Virgo (of size $(2^{61} - 1)^2 \approx 2^{122}$) has arithmetic that is at least 4× faster than the field used in Hyrax and Spartan (of size close to 2^{252}). Much of this 4× difference can be attributed to the fact that Virgo's field is roughly square root of the size of Hyrax and Spartan's, and hence field multiplications operate over smaller data types. However, some of the difference can be attributed to extra structure in the Mersenne prime $2^{61} - 1$ that is not present in the prime order field used by Hyrax and Spartan.

Currently, Brakedown [137], which combines an MIP with the Brakedown-commitment, is the only implemented SNARK that neither requires the field to support FFTs nor to match the order of a cryptographic group. The same would hold if combining an IP with the Brakedown commitment, but not a constant-round polynomial IOP.[19]

19.3.2   Relative Efficiency of Different Operations

Of course, the speed of field arithmetic is just one factor in determining overall runtime of a SNARK. In some SNARKs, the bottleneck for the prover is performing FFTs over the field, in others the bottleneck is group operations, and in still others the bottleneck may be processes that have nothing to do with the field choice (e.g., building a Merkle tree). To give one example, in SNARKs for R1CS-satisfiability derived from constant-round polynomial IOPs, the prover typically has to perform an FFT over a vector of length $\Theta(K)$, where K is the number of nonzero matrix entries of the R1CS system, and also must build one or more Merkle trees over vectors of length $\Theta(K)$. For reasonably large values of K, the $O(K \log K)$ runtime of the FFT will be larger than the time required to perform the $\Theta(K)$ evaluations of a cryptographic hash function that are needed to build the Merkle tree(s). But for very small values of K, the $\log K$ factor in the FFT runtime may be concretely smaller

---

[19]This is because Brakedown-commitment applies to univariate polynomials represented over the standard monomial basis, but the univariate polynomials arising in constant-round polynomial IOPs are specified via their evaluations over a subgroup H of $\mathbb{F}$. Efficiently converting from these evaluations to the standard monomial basis requires an FFT.

than the time required to evaluate a cryptographic hash evaluation, particularly if the field supports fast arithmetic, ensuring the hidden constant in the FFT runtime is small. So which part of the protocol is the bottleneck (FFT vs. Merkle-tree building) likely depends on how large a computation is being processed.

As another example, if an MIP is combined with many of the discrete-logarithm-based or KZG-based polynomial commitment schemes, the prover does not have to do any FFTs, and the bottleneck is typically in performing one multi-exponentation of size proportional to K. Via Pippenger's algorithm, the multiexponentiation can be done using $O(K \log(|\mathbb{G}|)/\log(K))$ group multiplications. In many other SNARKs the prover would have to at least perform an FFT over a vector of length at least K, and this will cost $O(K \log K)$ field operations.

For small R1CS instances, the FFT is likely to be faster than the multi-exponentiation, for three reasons. First, each operation in a cryptographic group $\mathbb{G}$ is often an order of magnitude more expensive than a field multiplication. Second, when K is small, $\log(|\mathbb{G}|)/\log(K) \gg \log K$, so even ignoring differences in the relative cost of a group vs. field operation, $O(K \log(|\mathbb{G}|)/\log K)$ is larger than $O(K \log K)$. Third, if the SNARK uses IOP-based polynomial commitments, it has the flexibility to work over a field whose size is not the order of an elliptic-curve group, and these fields can potentially support faster arithmetic. However, once K is large enough that $\log |\mathbb{G}| \ll \log^2 K$, the $O(K \log K)$ field operations required by the FFT will take more time than the $O(K \log(|\mathbb{G}|)/\log(K))$ group multiplications required to perform the multiexponentiation.

19.3.3 Intermediate Representations (IRs) Other than Arithmetic Circuits and R1CS

This survey described a variety of SNARKs for arithmetic circuit-satisfiability and R1CS. The SNARKs for arithmetic circuits supported addition and multiplication gates of fan-in two. R1CS systems are conceptually similar to arithmetic circuits augmented to allow "linear combination" gates of arbitrary fan-in (see Section 8.4.1). In both cases, all gates compute degree-two operations, meaning the output of each gate or constraint is a polynomial in the gate's inputs of total degree at most 2.

However, SNARKs based on polynomial IOPs can typically be modified to support more general intermediate representations. For example, they can typically be modified to handle circuits with gates computing operations of total degree up to some bound d, with an increase in prover time that grows linearly with d.[20]

The proof size will typically also grow with the degree bound d, but in many cases this growth will be a low-order effect. For example, in MIP-based SNARKs using certain polynomial commitment schemes, the proof length, when applied to a circuit of size S in which gates compute operations of degree at most d, will be $O(S^{1/2} + d \log S)$. The $d \log S$ term, which grows linearly with d, will be dominated by the $S^{1/2}$ term unless the circuit size S is tiny.

The use of such expanded gate sets can be fruitful. To give a simple example, suppose that allowing gates computing degree-3 operations rather than degree-2 operations reduces the size S of the resulting circuit by a factor of 2, while the prover's runtime as a function of S increases by a factor of only 4/3 due to the degree of gate operations increasing from 2 to 3. Then using the expanded gate set yields a faster prover: the total prover time decreases by a factor of $2 \cdot (3/4) > 1$.[21]

---

[20]Such modifications require understanding how the SNARK works and modifying it in a non-black-box manner. To give a very rough indication of how this might work: the MIP of Section 8.2 uses a $(3 \log S)$-variate polynomial $g(a, b, c) = \widetilde{\text{mult}}(a, b, c) \left(\widetilde{W}(a) - \widetilde{W}(b) \cdot \widetilde{W}(c) \right)$ to "check" that the value that $\widetilde{W}$ "assigns" to a multiplication gate a is the product of the values assigned to the two in-neighbors of a. To support multiplication gates of fan-in three rather than two, with the MIP one would replace g with the following modified polynomial defined over $4 \log S$ variables, with total degree four instead of three: $g(a, b, c, e) = \widetilde{\text{mult}}(a, b, c, e) \left(\widetilde{W}(a) - \widetilde{W}(b) \cdot \widetilde{W}(c) \cdot W(e) \right)$.

[21]Intermediate representations that are *more restrictive* than arithmetic circuits or R1CS can also be useful for some applications. This will be the case if one manages to design a SNARK with improved prover time or proof size for these limited IRs, and the improvements outweigh the negative effects of any resulting increase in representation size. For one example, see the notion of "R1CS-Lite" in [86]. Highly efficient SNARKs for incremental computation (Sections 18.4 and 18.5) can also be thought of as utilizing restricted IRs to obtain efficiency benefits, as can the various super-efficient IPs given for specific problems in Section 4.

The polynomial-IOP-derived SNARKs covered in this survey can all be modified in the manner sketched above to support operations of total degree higher than 2. This does *not* appear to be the case for linear-PCP derived SNARKs such as Groth's [142]: their use of pairing-based cryptography appears to rely heavily on the linear PCP verifier computing a degree-2 function of the proof string, which in turn relies on the circuit or R1CS instance computing only degree-2 operations. It is also not clear that recursive-composition-based SNARKs for iterative computation, e.g., Nova (Section 18.5) can be modified support operations with degree $d > 2$, at least not without a blowup in prover time or proof size that outweighs the benefits.

There has been particular recent interest in modifications of the PlonK SNARK to support expanded and modified IRs. For example, the cryptocurrency Zcash incorporates so-called "PlonKish arithmetization" into its Orchard protocol.[22] This refers to a modification of PlonK[23] to support an IR reminiscent of circuits with gates of degree up to 9.[24] There is also considerable interest in backends for a related IR called AIR [128], [235].

As SNARK protocol designers move beyond arithmetic circuits and R1CS to variant IRs, the line between "front-ends" (Section 6) and "back-ends" (i.e., SNARK proof machinery) becomes blurred. Protocol designers may tailor the chosen IR to the desired back-end, and in turn have to modify the chosen back-end to support the resulting IR.

There may be tradeoffs to such efforts. On the one hand, the use of more expressive or idiosyncratic IRs may yield important efficiency gains. On the other, it may increase the burden on protocol designers or render it more difficult to develop or reuse infrastructure. For example, protocol designers may find themselves painstakingly designing "circuits" in the modified IRs by hand to adequately take advantage of the expanded set of primitive operations supported. And if one decides to swap out

---

[22]https://zips.z.cash/zip-0224.

[23]More precisely, to a modification of the SNARK obtained by combining the constant-round polynomial IOP underlying PlonK with the Bulletproofs polynomial commitment scheme.

[24]See, for example, https://zcash.github.io/halo2/concepts/arithmetization.html and, in particular, sections on "gadgets" within the same document, such as https://zcash.github.io/halo2/design/gadgets/sha256/table16.html.

one back-end for another with a different cost profile, one may have to change the IR, and hence repeat the entire protocol design process, or at least alter the front-end.

Acknowledgements

This monograph began as a set of lecture notes accompanying the Fourteenth Bellairs' Crypto-Workshop in 2015. I am indebted to Claude Crépeau and Gilles Brassard for their warm hospitality in organizing the workshop, and to all of the workshop participants for their generosity, patience, and enthusiasm. The notes were further expanded during the Fall 2017 and 2020 offerings of COSC 544 at Georgetown University, and benefited from comments provided by students in the course. Two reading groups organized around the ZK Hack Discord in 2021 and 2022 provided spectacular feedback and support that transformed this monograph into its present form.

The knowledge and feedback of a number of people heavily influenced the development of this monograph, including Sebastian Angel, Bryan Gillespie, Thor Kamphefner, Michael Mitzenmacher, Srinath Setty, Luís Fernando Schultz Xavier da Silveira, abhi shelat, Michael Walfish, and Riad Wahby. I owe a special thanks to Riad for his patient explanations of many cryptographic tools covered in this survey, and his willingness to journey to the end of any rabbit hole he encounters. There are many fewer errors in this monograph because of Riad's help; any that remain are entirely my own.

A major benefit of taking 7 years to complete this monograph is the many exciting developments that can now be included. This survey would have looked very different had it been completed in 2015, or even in 2020 (over 1/3 of the content covered did not exist 7 years ago). During this period, the various approaches to the design of zero-knowledge arguments, and the relationships between them, have come into finer focus. Yet owing to the sheer volume of research papers, it is increasingly challenging for those first entering the area to extract a clear picture from the literature itself.

Will the next 5–10 years bring a similar flood of developments? Will this be enough to render general-purpose arguments efficient enough for routine deployment in diverse cryptographic systems? It is my hope that this survey will make this exciting and beautiful area slightly more accessible, and thereby play some role in ensuring that the answer to both questions is "yes."

References

[1] B. Abdolmaleki, K. Baghery, H. Lipmaa, and M. Zajac, "A subversion-resistant SNARK," in *Advances in Cryptology – ASIACRYPT 2017 – 23rd International Conference on the Theory and Applications of Cryptology and Information Security, Hong Kong, China, December 3–7, 2017, Proceedings, Part III*, T. Takagi and T. Peyrin, Eds., ser. Lecture Notes in Computer Science, vol. 10626, pp. 3–33, Springer, 2017.

[2] M. Abe, G. Fuchsbauer, J. Groth, K. Haralambiev, and M. Ohkubo, "Structure-preserving signatures and commitments to group elements," in *Annual Cryptology Conference*, Springer, pp. 209–236, 2010.

[3] W. Aiello and J. Hastad, "Statistical zero-knowledge languages can be recognized in two rounds," *Journal of Computer and System Sciences*, vol. 42, no. 3, pp. 327–345, 1991.

[4] M. Albrecht, L. Grassi, C. Rechberger, A. Roy, and T. Tiessen, "MiMC: Efficient encryption and cryptographic hashing with minimal multiplicative complexity," in *International Conference on the Theory and Application of Cryptology and Information Security*, Springer, pp. 191–219, 2016.

[5]   J. Alman and V. V. Williams, "A refined laser method and faster matrix multiplication," in *Proceedings of the 2021 ACM-SIAM Symposium on Discrete Algorithms (SODA)*, SIAM, pp. 522–539, 2021.

[6]   A. Aly, T. Ashur, E. Ben-Sasson, S. Dhooghe, and A. Szepieniec, "Efficient symmetric primitives for advanced cryptographic protocols (A Marvellous contribution)," *IACR Cryptol. ePrint Arch.*, vol. 2019, p. 426, 2019.

[7]   S. Ames, C. Hazay, Y. Ishai, and M. Venkitasubramaniam, "Ligero: Lightweight sublinear arguments without a trusted setup," in *Proceedings of the 2017 ACM SIGSAC Conference on Computer and Communications Security*, pp. 2087–2104, 2017.

[8]   B. Applebaum, I. Damgård, Y. Ishai, M. Nielsen, and L. Zichron, "Secure arithmetic computation with constant computational overhead," in *Annual International Cryptology Conference*, Springer, pp. 223–254, 2017.

[9]   S. Arora and B. Barak, *Computational Complexity: A Modern Approach*, 1st edn. New York, NY, USA: Cambridge University Press, 2009.

[10] S. Arora, C. Lund, R. Motwani, M. Sudan, and M. Szegedy, "Proof verification and the hardness of approximation problems," *Journal of the ACM (JACM)*, vol. 45, no. 3, pp. 501–555, 1998.

[11] S. Arora and S. Safra, "Probabilistic checking of proofs: A new characterization of NP," *J. ACM*, vol. 45, no. 1, pp. 70–122, 1998.

[12] S. Arora and M. Sudan, "Improved low-degree testing and its applications," *Combinatorica*, vol. 23, no. 3, pp. 365–426, 2003.

[13] A. Arun, C. Ganesh, S. Lokam, T. Mopuri, and S. Sridhar, Dew: Transparent constant-sized zksnarks, Cryptology ePrint Archive, Report 2022/419, 2022. URL: https://ia.cr/2022/419.

[14] T. Attema, S. Fehr, and M. Klooß, fiat-shamir transformation of multi-round interactive proofs, Cryptology ePrint Archive, Report 2021/1377, 2021. URL: https://ia.cr/2021/1377.

[15] L. Babai, "Trading group theory for randomness," in *STOC*, R. Sedgewick, Ed., pp. 421–429, ACM, 1985.

[16] L. Babai, "Graph isomorphism in quasipolynomial time," in *Proceedings of the Forty-Eighth Annual Acm Symposium on Theory of Computing*, pp. 684–697, 2016.

[17] L. Babai, L. Fortnow, and C. Lund, "Non-deterministic exponential time has two-prover interactive protocols," *Computational Complexity*, vol. 1, pp. 3–40, 1991.

[18] E. Bangerter, J. Camenisch, and S. Krenn, "Efficiency limitations for Σ-protocols for group homomorphisms," in *Theory of Cryptography Conference*, Springer, pp. 553–571, 2010.

[19] B. Barak and O. Goldreich, "Universal arguments and their applications.," in *IEEE Conference on Computational Complexity*, pp. 194–203, IEEE Computer Society, 2002.

[20] N. Barić and B. Pfitzmann, "Collision-free accumulators and fail-stop signature schemes without trees," in *International Conference on the Theory and Applications of Cryptographic Techniques*, Springer, pp. 480–494, 1997.

[21] J. Bartusek, L. Bronfman, J. Holmgren, F. Ma, and R. D. Rothblum, "On the (in) security of Kilian-based SNARGs," in *Theory of Cryptography Conference*, Springer, pp. 522–551, 2019.

[22] C. Baum, J. Bootle, A. Cerulli, R. del Pino, J. Groth, and V. Lyubashevsky, "Sub-linear lattice-based zero-knowledge arguments for arithmetic circuits," in *Advances in Cryptology – CRYPTO 2018 – 38th Annual International Cryptology Conference, Santa Barbara, CA, USA, August 19–23, 2018, Proceedings, Part II*, H. Shacham and A. Boldyreva, Eds., Lecture Notes in Computer Science, vol. 10992, pp. 669–699, Springer, 2018.

[23] C. Baum, A. J. Malozemoff, M. B. Rosen, and P. Scholl, "Mac'n' Cheese: Zero-knowledge proofs for boolean and arithmetic circuits with nested disjunctions," in *Annual International Cryptology Conference*, Springer, pp. 92–122, 2021.

[24] S. Bayer and J. Groth, "Efficient zero-knowledge argument for correctness of a shuffle," in *Annual International Conference on the Theory and Applications of Cryptographic Techniques*, Springer, pp. 263–280, 2012.

[25] J. Baylina, "Verifying STARKs with SNARKs," zk7 Zero Knowledge Summit 7 on April 21, 2022. URL: https://youtu.be/j7An-33Zs0.

[26] M. Bellare, A. Boldyreva, and A. Palacio, "An uninstantiable random-oracle-model scheme for a hybrid-encryption problem," in *International Conference on the Theory and Applications of Cryptographic Techniques*, Springer, pp. 171–188, 2004.

[27] M. Bellare, D. Coppersmith, J. Håstad, M. A. Kiwi, and M. Sudan, "Linearity testing in characteristic two," *IEEE Transactions on Information Theory*, vol. 42, no. 6, pp. 1781–1795, 1996.

[28] M. Bellare, G. Fuchsbauer, and A. Scafuro, "NIZKs with an untrusted CRS: security in the face of parameter subversion," in *Advances in Cryptology – ASIACRYPT 2016 – 22nd International Conference on the Theory and Application of Cryptology and Information Security, Hanoi, Vietnam, December 4–8, 2016, Proceedings, Part II*, J. H. Cheon and T. Takagi, Eds., ser. Lecture Notes in Computer Science, vol. 10032, pp. 777–804, 2016.

[29] M. Bellare and P. Rogaway, "Random oracles are practical: A paradigm for designing efficient protocols," in *Proceedings of the 1st ACM conference on Computer and communications security*, pp. 62–73, 1993.

[30] A. Belling and O. Bgassat, *Using GKR inside a SNARK to reduce the cost of hash verification down to 3 constraints*, 2020. URL: https://ethresear.ch/t/using-gkr-inside-a-snark-to-reduce-the-cost-of-hash-verification-down-to-3-constraints/7550.

[31] V. E. Beneš, "Mathematical theory of connecting networks and telephone traffic," *Academic Press*, 1965.

[32] M. Ben-Or, S. Goldwasser, J. Kilian, and A. Wigderson, "Multiprover interactive proofs: How to remove intractability assumptions," in *Proceedings of the 20th Annual ACM Symposium on Theory of Computing, May 2–4, 1988*, Chicago, Illinois, USA, ACM, pp. 113–131, 1988.

[33] E. Ben-Sasson, I. Bentov, A. Chiesa, A. Gabizon, D. Genkin, M. Hamilis, E. Pergament, M. Riabzev, M. Silberstein, E. Tromer, *et al.*, "Computational integrity with a public random string from quasi-linear PCPs," in *Annual International Conference on the Theory and Applications of Cryptographic Techniques*, Springer, pp. 551–579, 2017.

[34] E. Ben-Sasson, I. Bentov, Y. Horesh, and M. Riabzev, "Fast reed-solomon interactive oracle proofs of proximity," in *45th International Colloquium on Automata, Languages, and Programming (ICALP 2018)*, Schloss Dagstuhl-Leibniz-Zentrum fuer Informatik, 2018.

[35] E. Ben-Sasson, I. Bentov, Y. Horesh, and M. Riabzev, "Scalable zero knowledge with no trusted setup," in *Advances in Cryptology – CRYPTO 2019 – 39th Annual International Cryptology Conference, Santa Barbara, CA, USA, August 18-22, 2019, Proceedings, Part III*, A. Boldyreva and D. Micciancio, Eds., ser. Lecture Notes in Computer Science, vol. 11694, pp. 701–732, Springer, 2019.

[36] E. Ben-Sasson, D. Carmon, Y. Ishai, S. Kopparty, and S. Saraf, "Proximity gaps for Reed–Solomon codes," in *2020 IEEE 61st Annual Symposium on Foundations of Computer Science (FOCS)*, IEEE, pp. 900–909, 2020.

[37] E. Ben-Sasson, D. Carmon, S. Kopparty, and D. Levit, "Elliptic curve fast fourier transform (ECFFT) part I: Fast polynomial algorithms over all finite fields," *CoRR*, vol. abs/2107.08473, 2021.

[38] E. Ben-Sasson, D. Carmon, S. Kopparty, and D. Levit, "Scalable and transparent proofs over all large fields, via elliptic curves," *Electron. Colloquium Comput. Complex.*, vol. TR22-110, 2022.

[39] E. Ben-Sasson, A. Chiesa, M. A. Forbes, A. Gabizon, M. Riabzev, and N. Spooner, "Zero knowledge protocols from succinct constraint detection," in *Theory of Cryptography Conference*, Springer, pp. 172–206, 2017.

[40] E. Ben-Sasson, A. Chiesa, D. Genkin, and E. Tromer, "Fast reductions from rams to delegatable succinct constraint satisfaction problems: Extended abstract," in *ITCS*, R. D. Kleinberg, Ed., pp. 401–414, ACM, 2013.

[41] E. Ben-Sasson, A. Chiesa, D. Genkin, and E. Tromer, "On the concrete efficiency of probabilistically-checkable proofs," in *STOC*, pp. 585–594, 2013.

[42] E. Ben-Sasson, A. Chiesa, D. Genkin, E. Tromer, and M. Virza, "SNARKs for C: Verifying program executions succinctly and in zero knowledge," in *Advances in Cryptology – CRYPTO 2013 – 33rd Annual Cryptology Conference, Santa Barbara, CA, USA, August 18–22, 2013. Proceedings, Part II*, R. Canetti and J. A. Garay, Eds., ser. Lecture Notes in Computer Science, vol. 8043, pp. 90–108, Springer, 2013.

[43] E. Ben-Sasson, A. Chiesa, M. Riabzev, N. Spooner, M. Virza, and N. P. Ward, "Aurora: Transparent succinct arguments for R1CS," in *Annual International Conference on the Theory and Applications of Cryptographic Techniques*, Springer, pp. 103–128, 2019.

[44] E. Ben-Sasson, A. Chiesa, and N. Spooner, "Interactive oracle proofs," in *Theory of Cryptography – 14th International Conference, TCC 2016-B, Beijing, China, October 31 – November 3, 2016, Proceedings, Part II*, M. Hirt and A. D. Smith, Eds., ser. Lecture Notes in Computer Science, vol. 9986, pp. 31–60, 2016.

[45] E. Ben-Sasson, A. Chiesa, E. Tromer, and M. Virza, "Scalable zero knowledge via cycles of elliptic curves," in *Advances in Cryptology – CRYPTO 2014 – 34th Annual Cryptology Conference, Santa Barbara, CA, USA, August 17–21, 2014, Proceedings, Part II*, J. A. Garay and R. Gennaro, Eds., ser. Lecture Notes in Computer Science, vol. 8617, pp. 276–294, Springer, 2014.

[46] E. Ben-Sasson, A. Chiesa, E. Tromer, and M. Virza, "Succinct non-interactive zero knowledge for a von Neumann architecture," in *Proceedings of the 23rd USENIX Security Symposium, San Diego, CA, USA, August 20–22, 2014*, pp. 781–796, 2014.

[47] E. Ben-Sasson, L. Goldberg, and D. Levit, *Stark friendly hash – survey and recommendation*, Cryptology ePrint Archive, Report 2020/948, 2020. URL: https://eprint.iacr.org/2020/948.

[48] E. Ben-Sasson, O. Goldreich, P. Harsha, M. Sudan, and S. P. Vadhan, "Short PCPs verifiable in polylogarithmic time," in *20th Annual IEEE Conference on Computational Complexity (CCC 2005), 11–15 June 2005, San Jose, CA, USA*, pp. 120–134, 2005.

[49] E. Ben-Sasson, S. Kopparty, and S. Saraf, "Worst-case to average case reductions for the distance to a code," in *33rd Computational Complexity Conference, CCC 2018, June 22-24, 2018, San Diego, CA, USA*, R. A. Servedio, Ed., ser. LIPIcs, vol. 102, 24:1–24:23, Schloss Dagstuhl – Leibniz-Zentrum für Informatik, 2018.

[50] E. Ben-Sasson and M. Sudan, "Short PCPs with polylog query complexity," *SIAM J. Comput.*, vol. 38, no. 2, pp. 551–607, 2008.

[51] D. Bernhard, O. Pereira, and B. Warinschi, "How not to prove yourself: Pitfalls of the Fiat-Shamir heuristic and applications to Helios," in *International Conference on the Theory and Application of Cryptology and Information Security*, Springer, pp. 626–643, 2012.

[52] D. J. Bernstein, "Curve25519: New Diffie-Hellman speed records," in *International Workshop on Public Key Cryptography*, Springer, pp. 207–228, 2006.

[53] R. Bhadauria, Z. Fang, C. Hazay, M. Venkitasubramaniam, T. Xie, and Y. Zhang, "Ligero++: A new optimized sublinear IOP," in *CCS '20: 2020 ACM SIGSAC Conference on Computer and Communications Security, Virtual Event, USA, November 9-13, 2020*, J. Ligatti, X. Ou, J. Katz, and G. Vigna, Eds., pp. 2025–2038, ACM, 2020.

[54] E. Birrell and S. Vadhan, "Composition of zero-knowledge proofs with efficient provers," in *Theory of Cryptography Conference*, Springer, pp. 572–587, 2010.

[55] N. Bitansky and A. Chiesa, "Succinct arguments from multi-prover interactive proofs and their efficiency benefits," in *CRYPTO*, R. Safavi-Naini and R. Canetti, Eds., ser. Lecture Notes in Computer Science, vol. 7417, pp. 255–272, Springer, 2012.

[56] N. Bitansky, A. Chiesa, Y. Ishai, R. Ostrovsky, and O. Paneth, "Succinct non-interactive arguments via linear interactive proofs," in *TCC*, pp. 315–333, 2013.

[57] A. R. Block, J. Holmgren, A. Rosen, R. D. Rothblum, and P. Soni, "Time-and space-efficient arguments from groups of unknown order," in *Annual International Cryptology Conference*, Springer, pp. 123–152, 2021.

[58] M. Blum, "How to prove a theorem so no one else can claim it," in *Proceedings of the International Congress of Mathematicians*, Citeseer, vol. 1, p. 2, 1986.

[59] M. Blum, W. Evans, P. Gemmell, S. Kannan, and M. Naor, "Checking the correctness of memories," *Algorithmica*, pp. 90–99, 1995.

[60] M. Blum, M. Luby, and R. Rubinfeld, "Self-testing/correcting with applications to numerical problems," *J. Comput. Syst. Sci.*, vol. 47, no. 3, pp. 549–595, 1993.

[61] A. J. Blumberg, J. Thaler, V. Vu, and M. Walfish, "Verifiable computation using multiple provers," *IACR Cryptology ePrint Archive*, vol. 2014, p. 846, 2014.

[62] D. Boneh and X. Boyen, "Short signatures without random oracles," in *International Conference on the Theory and Applications of Cryptographic Techniques*, Springer, pp. 56–73, 2004.

[63] D. Boneh, B. Bünz, and B. Fisch, "Batching techniques for accumulators with applications to IOPs and stateless blockchains," in *Annual International Cryptology Conference*, Springer, pp. 561–586, 2019.

[64] D. Boneh, J. Drake, B. Fisch, and A. Gabizon, "Halo infinite: Proof-carrying data from additive polynomial commitments," in *Annual International Cryptology Conference*, Springer, pp. 649–680, 2021.

[65] J. Bonneau, I. Meckler, V. Rao, and E. Shapiro, "Coda: Decentralized cryptocurrency at scale.," *IACR Cryptol. ePrint Arch.*, vol. 2020, p. 352, 2020.

[66] J. Bootle, A. Cerulli, P. Chaidos, J. Groth, and C. Petit, "Efficient zero-knowledge arguments for arithmetic circuits in the discrete log setting," in *Annual International Conference on the Theory and Applications of Cryptographic Techniques*, Springer, pp. 327–357, 2016.

[67] J. Bootle, A. Cerulli, E. Ghadafi, J. Groth, M. Hajiabadi, and S. K. Jakobsen, "Linear-time zero-knowledge proofs for arithmetic circuit satisfiability," in *Advances in Cryptology – ASIACRYPT 2017 – 23rd International Conference on the Theory and Applications of Cryptology and Information Security, Hong Kong, China, December 3–7, 2017, Proceedings, Part III*, T. Takagi and T. Peyrin, Eds., ser. Lecture Notes in Computer Science, vol. 10626, pp. 336–365, Springer, 2017.

[68] J. Bootle, A. Cerulli, J. Groth, S. Jakobsen, and M. Maller, "Arya: Nearly linear-time zero-knowledge proofs for correct program execution," in *International Conference on the Theory and Application of Cryptology and Information Security*, Springer, pp. 595–626, 2018.

[69] J. Bootle, A. Chiesa, and J. Groth, "Linear-time arguments with sublinear verification from tensor codes," in *Theory of Cryptography – 18th International Conference, TCC 2020, Durham, NC, USA, November 16–19, 2020, Proceedings, Part II*, R. Pass and K. Pietrzak, Eds., ser. Lecture Notes in Computer Science, vol. 12551, pp. 19–46, Springer, 2020.

[70] J. Bootle, A. Chiesa, and K. Sotiraki, "Sumcheck arguments and their applications," in *Annual International Cryptology Conference*, Springer, pp. 742–773, 2021.

[71] J. Bootle, V. Lyubashevsky, N. K. Nguyen, and G. Seiler, *A non-PCP approach to succinct quantum-safe zero-knowledge*, Cryptology ePrint Archive, Report 2020/737, To appear in CRYPTO, 2020. URL: https://eprint.iacr.org/2020/737.

[72] R. B. Boppana, J. Hastad, and S. Zachos, "Does co-NP have short interactive proofs?" *Inf. Process. Lett.*, vol. 25, no. 2, pp. 127–132, 1987.

[73] P. Bottinelli, An illustrated guide to elliptic curve cryptography validation, 2021.

[74] S. Bowe, A. Chiesa, M. Green, I. Miers, P. Mishra, and H. Wu, "Zexe: Enabling decentralized private computation," in *2020 IEEE Symposium on Security and Privacy (SP)*, IEEE, pp. 947–964, 2020.

[75] S. Bowe, J. Grigg, and D. Hopwood, "Recursive proof composition without a trusted setup," *Cryptol. ePrint Arch., Tech. Rep*, vol. 1021, p. 2019, 2019.

[76] Z. Brakerski, V. Koppula, and T. Mour, "NIZK from LPN and trapdoor hash via correlation intractability for approximable relations," in *Annual International Cryptology Conference*, Springer, pp. 738–767, 2020.

[77] G. Brassard, D. Chaum, and C. Crépeau, "Minimum disclosure proofs of knowledge," *Journal of Computer and System Sciences*, vol. 37, no. 2, pp. 156–189, 1988.

[78] G. Brassard, P. Høyer, and A. Tapp, "Quantum cryptanalysis of hash and claw-free functions," in *Latin American Symposium on Theoretical Informatics*, Springer, pp. 163–169, 1998.

[79] B. Braun, A. J. Feldman, Z. Ren, S. Setty, A. J. Blumberg, and M. Walfish, "Verifying computations with state," in *Proceedings of the Twenty-Fourth ACM Symposium on Operating Systems Principles*, ACM, pp. 341–357, 2013.

[80] B. Bünz, J. Bootle, D. Boneh, A. Poelstra, P. Wuille, and G. Maxwell, "Bulletproofs: Short proofs for confidential transactions and more," in *2018 IEEE Symposium on Security and Privacy (SP)*, IEEE, pp. 315–334, 2018.

[81] B. Bünz, A. Chiesa, W. Lin, P. Mishra, and N. Spooner, "Proof-carrying data without succinct arguments," in *Annual International Cryptology Conference*, Springer, pp. 681–710, 2021.

[82] B. Bünz, A. Chiesa, P. Mishra, and N. Spooner, "Proof-carrying data from accumulation schemes.," *IACR Cryptol. ePrint Arch.*, vol. 2020, p. 499, 2020.

[83] B. Bünz, B. Fisch, and A. Szepieniec, "Transparent snarks from DARK compilers," in *Advances in Cryptology – EUROCRYPT 2020 – 39th Annual International Conference on the Theory and Applications of Cryptographic Techniques, Zagreb, Croatia, May 10–14, 2020, Proceedings, Part I*, A. Canteaut and Y. Ishai, Eds., ser. Lecture Notes in Computer Science, vol. 12105, pp. 677–706, Springer, 2020.

[84] B. Bünz, M. Maller, P. Mishra, N. Tyagi, and P. Vesely, "Proofs for inner pairing products and applications," in *International Conference on the Theory and Application of Cryptology and Information Security*, Springer, pp. 65–97, 2021.

[85] D. Butler, A. Lochbihler, D. Aspinall, and A. Gascón, "Formalising Σ-Protocols and Commitment Schemes Using CryptHOL," *Journal of Automated Reasoning*, vol. 65, no. 4, pp. 521–567, 2021.

[86] M. Campanelli, A. Faonio, D. Fiore, A. Querol, and H. Rodríguez, "Lunar: A toolbox for more efficient universal and updatable zksnarks and commit-and-prove extensions," in *International Conference on the Theory and Application of Cryptology and Information Security*, Springer, pp. 3–33, 2021.

[87] M. Campanelli, D. Fiore, and A. Querol, "Legosnark: Modular design and composition of succinct zero-knowledge proofs," in *Proceedings of the 2019 ACM SIGSAC Conference on Computer and Communications Security*, pp. 2075–2092, 2019.

[88] R. Canetti, Y. Chen, J. Holmgren, A. Lombardi, G. N. Rothblum, R. D. Rothblum, and D. Wichs, "Fiat-Shamir: From practice to theory," in *Proceedings of the 51st Annual ACM SIGACT Symposium on Theory of Computing*, pp. 1082–1090, 2019.

[89] R. Canetti, Y. Chen, and L. Reyzin, "On the correlation intractability of obfuscated pseudorandom functions," in *Theory of cryptography conference*, Springer, pp. 389–415, 2016.

[90] R. Canetti, Y. Chen, L. Reyzin, and R. D. Rothblum, "Fiat-shamir and correlation intractability from strong kdm-secure encryption," in *Advances in Cryptology – EUROCRYPT 2018 – 37th Annual International Conference on the Theory and Applications of Cryptographic Techniques, Tel Aviv, Israel, April 29–May 3, 2018 Proceedings, Part I*, J. B. Nielsen and V. Rijmen, Eds., ser. Lecture Notes in Computer Science, vol. 10820, pp. 91–122, Springer, 2018.

[91] R. Canetti, O. Goldreich, and S. Halevi, "The random oracle methodology, revisited," *Journal of the ACM (JACM)*, vol. 51, no. 4, pp. 557–594, 2004.

[92] A. Chakrabarti, G. Cormode, A. McGregor, and J. Thaler, "Annotations in data streams," *ACM Transactions on Algorithms*, vol. 11, no. 1, p. 7, 2014, Preliminary version by the first three authors in *ICALP*, 2009.

[93] M. Chase, D. Derler, S. Goldfeder, C. Orlandi, S. Ramacher, C. Rechberger, D. Slamanig, and G. Zaverucha, "Post-quantum zero-knowledge and signatures from symmetric-key primitives," in *Proceedings of the 2017 Acm Sigsac Conference on Computer and Communications Security*, pp. 1825–1842, 2017.

[94] D. L. Chaum, "Untraceable electronic mail, return addresses, and digital pseudonyms," *Communications of the ACM*, vol. 24, no. 2, pp. 84–90, 1981.

[95] B. Chen, B. Bünz, D. Boneh, and Z. Zhang, "HyperPlonk: Plonk with linear-time prover and high-degree custom gates," *Cryptology ePrint Archive*, 2022.

[96] W. Chen, A. Chiesa, E. Dauterman, and N. P. Ward, "Reducing participation costs via incremental verification for ledger systems.," *IACR Cryptol. ePrint Arch.*, vol. 2020, p. 1522, 2020.

[97] A. Chiesa, M. A. Forbes, T. Gur, and N. Spooner, "Spatial isolation implies zero knowledge even in a quantum world," in *59th IEEE Annual Symposium on Foundations of Computer Science, FOCS 2018, Paris, France, October 7–9, 2018*, M. Thorup, Ed., pp. 755–765, IEEE Computer Society, 2018.

[98]   A. Chiesa, Y. Hu, M. Maller, P. Mishra, N. Vesely, and N. Ward, "Marlin: Preprocessing zkSNARKs with universal and updatable SRS," in *Annual International Conference on the Theory and Applications of Cryptographic Techniques*, Springer, pp. 738–768, 2020.

[99]   A. Chiesa, P. Manohar, and N. Spooner, "Succinct arguments in the quantum random oracle model," in *Theory of Cryptography Conference*, Springer, pp. 1–29, 2019.

[100]   A. Chiesa, D. Ojha, and N. Spooner, "Fractal: Post-quantum and transparent recursive proofs from holography," in *Annual International Conference on the Theory and Applications of Cryptographic Techniques*, Springer, pp. 769–793, 2020.

[101]   D. Clarke, S. Devadas, M. Van Dijk, B. Gassend, and G. E. Suh, "Incremental multiset hash functions and their application to memory integrity checking," in *International Conference on the Theory and Application of Cryptology and Information Security*, Springer, pp. 188–207, 2003.

[102]   G. Cormode, M. Mitzenmacher, and J. Thaler, "Practical verified computation with streaming interactive proofs," in *ITCS*, S. Goldwasser, Ed., pp. 90–112, ACM, 2012.

[103]   G. Cormode, J. Thaler, and K. Yi, "Verifying computations with streaming interactive proofs," *Proc. VLDB Endow.*, vol. 5, no. 1, pp. 25–36, 2011.

[104]   R. Cramer and I. Damgård, "Zero-knowledge proofs for finite field arithmetic, or: Can zero-knowledge be for free?" In *Annual International Cryptology Conference*, Springer, pp. 424–441, 1998.

[105]   I. B. Damgård, "On the existence of bit commitment schemes and zero-knowledge proofs," in *Conference on the Theory and Application of Cryptology*, Springer, pp. 17–27, 1989.

[106]   I. Dinur, D. Kales, A. Promitzer, S. Ramacher, and C. Rechberger, "Linear equivalence of block ciphers with partial nonlinear layers: Application to lowmc," in *Annual International Conference on the Theory and Applications of Cryptographic Techniques*, Springer, pp. 343–372, 2019.

[107] S. Dittmer, Y. Ishai, and R. Ostrovsky, Line-point zero knowledge and its applications, Cryptology ePrint Archive, Report 2020/1446, 2020. URL: https://eprint.iacr.org/2020/1446.

[108] S. Dobson, S. D. Galbraith, and B. Smith, *Trustless unknown-order groups*, Cryptology ePrint Archive, Report 2020/196, 2020, URL: https://ia.cr/2020/196.

[109] M. Driscoll, *The animated elliptic curve*, Github source code, 2022, URL: https://github.com/syncsynchalt/animated-curves.

[110] T. ElGamal, "A public key cryptosystem and a signature scheme based on discrete logarithms," *IEEE Transactions on Information Theory*, vol. 31, no. 4, pp. 469–472, 1985.

[111] A. Fiat and A. Shamir, "How to prove yourself: Practical solutions to identification and signature problems," in *Conference on the Theory and Application of Cryptographic Techniques*, Springer, pp. 186–194, 1986.

[112] L. Fortnow, "The complexity of perfect zero-knowledge," in *Proceedings of the Nineteenth Annual ACM Symposium on Theory of Computing*, pp. 204–209, 1987.

[113] L. Fortnow, J. Rompel, and M. Sipser, "On the power of multi-power interactive protocols," in *Structure in Complexity Theory Conference, 1988. Proceedings., Third Annual*, IEEE, pp. 156–161, 1988.

[114] T. K. Frederiksen, J. B. Nielsen, and C. Orlandi, "Privacy-free garbled circuits with applications to efficient zero-knowledge," in *Advances in Cryptology – EUROCRYPT 2015 – 34th Annual International Conference on the Theory and Applications of Cryptographic Techniques, Sofia, Bulgaria, April 26-30, 2015, Proceedings, Part II*, E. Oswald and M. Fischlin, Eds., ser. Lecture Notes in Computer Science, vol. 9057, pp. 191–219, Springer, 2015.

[115] R. Freivalds, "Probabilistic machines can use less running time," in *IFIP congress*, vol. 839, p. 842, 1977.

[116] G. Fuchsbauer, "Subversion-zero-knowledge SNARKs," in *Public-Key Cryptography – PKC 2018 – 21st IACR International Conference on Practice and Theory of Public-Key Cryptography, Rio de Janeiro, Brazil, March 25–29, 2018, Proceedings, Part I*, M. Abdalla and R. Dahab, Eds., ser. Lecture Notes in Computer Science, vol. 10769, pp. 315–347, Springer, 2018.

[117] G. Fuchsbauer, E. Kiltz, and J. Loss, "The algebraic group model and its applications," in *Annual International Cryptology Conference*, Springer, pp. 33–62, 2018.

[118] E. Fujisaki and T. Okamoto, "Statistical zero knowledge protocols to prove modular polynomial relations," in *Annual International Cryptology Conference*, Springer, pp. 16–30, 1997.

[119] M. Furer, O. Goldreich, Y. Mansour, M. Sipser, and S. Zachos, "On completeness and soundness in interactive proof systems," *Randomness and Computation (Volume 5 of Advances in Computing Research)*, pp. 429–442, 1989.

[120] A. Gabizon, Auroralight: Improved prover efficiency and srs size in a soniclike system, IACR Cryptology ePrint Archive, 2019: 601, 2019.

[121] A. Gabizon, "On the security of the BCTV Pinocchio zk-SNARK variant.," *IACR Cryptol. ePrint Arch.*, vol. 2019, p. 119, 2019.

[122] A. Gabizon and Z. J. Williamson, *Plookup: A simplified polynomial protocol for lookup tables*, Cryptology ePrint Archive, Report 2020/315, 2020. URL: https://ia.cr/2020/315.

[123] A. Gabizon, Z. J. Williamson, and O. Ciobotaru, "PlonK: Permutations over Lagrange-bases for Oecumenical Noninteractive arguments of Knowledge.," *IACR Cryptol. ePrint Arch.*, vol. 2019, p. 953, 2019.

[124] N. Gailly, M. Maller, and A. Nitulescu, "SnarkPack: Practical snark aggregation," *Cryptology ePrint Archive*, 2021.

[125] R. Gennaro, C. Gentry, B. Parno, and M. Raykova, "Quadratic span programs and succinct NIZKs without PCPs," in *EUROCRYPT*, pp. 626–645, 2013.

[126] C. Gentry and D. Wichs, "Separating succinct non-interactive arguments from all falsifiable assumptions," in *Proceedings of the 43rd ACM Symposium on Theory of Computing, STOC 2011, San Jose, CA, USA, 6–8 June 2011*, L. Fortnow and S. P. Vadhan, Eds., pp. 99–108, ACM, 2011.

[127] I. Giacomelli, J. Madsen, and C. Orlandi, "ZKBoo: Faster zero-knowledge for boolean circuits," in *25th USENIX Security Symposium*, pp. 1069–1083, 2016.

[128] L. Goldberg, S. Papini, and M. Riabzev, *Cairo? A Turing-complete STARK-friendly CPU architecture*, Cryptology ePrint Archive, Paper 2021/1063, URL: https://eprint.iacr.org/2021/1063, 2021.

[129] O. Goldreich, *On post-modern cryptography*, Cryptology ePrint Archive, Report 2006/461, URL: https://eprint.iacr.org/2006/461, 2006.

[130] O. Goldreich, *Foundations of cryptography: Volume 1, Basic tools.* Cambridge university press, 2007.

[131] O. Goldreich, S. Micali, and A. Wigderson, "Proofs that yield nothing but their validity or all languages in np have zero-knowledge proof systems," *Journal of the ACM (JACM)*, vol. 38, no. 3, pp. 690–728, 1991.

[132] O. Goldreich, S. P. Vadhan, and A. Wigderson, "On interactive proofs with a laconic prover," *Computational Complexity*, vol. 11, no. 1–2, pp. 1–53, 2002.

[133] S. Goldwasser, S. Micali, and C. Rackoff, "The knowledge complexity of interactive proof systems," *SIAM J. Comput.*, vol. 18, pp. 186–208, 1989, Preliminary version in STOC 1985. Earlier versions date to 1982.

[134] S. Goldwasser and Y. T. Kalai, "On the (in) security of the Fiat-Shamir paradigm," in *44th Annual IEEE Symposium on Foundations of Computer Science, 2003. Proceedings.*, IEEE, pp. 102–113, 2003.

[135] S. Goldwasser, Y. T. Kalai, and G. N. Rothblum, "Delegating computation: Interactive proofs for muggles," in *Proceedings of the 40th Annual ACM Symposium on Theory of Computing*, ser. STOC '08, pp. 113–122, New York, NY, USA: ACM, 2008.

[136] S. Goldwasser and M. Sipser, "Private coins versus public coins in interactive proof systems," in *STOC*, J. Hartmanis, Ed., pp. 59–68, ACM, 1986.

[137] A. Golovnev, J. Lee, S. T. V. Setty, J. Thaler, and R. S. Wahby, "Brakedown: Linear-time and post-quantum snarks for R1CS," *IACR Cryptol. ePrint Arch.*, p. 1043, 2021.

[138] L. Grassi, D. Kales, D. Khovratovich, A. Roy, C. Rechberger, and M. Schofnegger, "Starkad and poseidon: New hash functions for zero knowledge proof systems.," *IACR Cryptol. ePrint Arch.*, vol. 2019, p. 458, 2019.

[139] M. D. Green, J. Katz, A. J. Malozemoff, and H.-S. Zhou, "A unified approach to idealized model separations via indistinguishability obfuscation," in *International Conference on Security and Cryptography for Networks*, Springer, pp. 587–603, 2016.

[140] J. Groth, "A verifiable secret shuffle of homomorphic encryptions," *Journal of Cryptology*, vol. 23, no. 4, pp. 546–579, 2010.

[141] J. Groth, "Short pairing-based non-interactive zero-knowledge arguments," in *ASIACRYPT*, M. Abe, Ed., ser. Lecture Notes in Computer Science, vol. 6477, pp. 321–340, Springer, 2010.

[142] J. Groth, "On the size of pairing-based non-interactive arguments," in *Annual International Conference on the Theory and Applications of Cryptographic Techniques*, Springer, pp. 305–326, 2016.

[143] J. Groth, *Homomorphic trapdoor commitments to group elements*, Cryptology ePrint Archive, Report 2009/007, 2009, URL: https://ia.cr/2009/007.

[144] J. Groth and Y. Ishai, "Sub-linear zero-knowledge argument for correctness of a shuffle," in *Annual International Conference on the Theory and Applications of Cryptographic Techniques*, Springer, pp. 379–396, 2008.

[145] U. Haböck, A summary on the FRI low degree test. Cryptology ePrint Archive, Paper 2022/1216, URL: https://eprint.iacr.org/2022/1216, 2022.

[146] T. Haines, S. J. Lewis, O. Pereira, and V. Teague, "How not to prove your election outcome," in *2020 IEEE Symposium on Security and Privacy*, pp. 644–660, 2020. DOI: 10.1109/SP40000. 2020.00048.

[147] M. Hamburg, "Decaf: Eliminating cofactors through point compression," in *Annual Cryptology Conference*, Springer, pp. 705–723, 2015.

[148] H. Hasse, "Zur Theorie der abstrakten elliptischen Funktionenkörper, I–III.," *Journal für die reine und angewandte Mathematik*, vol. 175, 1936.

[149] D. Heath and V. Kolesnikov, "Stacked garbling for disjunctive zero-knowledge proofs," in *Advances in Cryptology – EURO-CRYPT 2020 – 39th Annual International Conference on the Theory and Applications of Cryptographic Techniques, Zagreb, Croatia, May 10-14, 2020, Proceedings, Part III*, A. Canteaut and Y. Ishai, Eds., ser. Lecture Notes in Computer Science, vol. 12107, pp. 569–598, Springer, 2020.

[150] J. Holmgren and A. Lombardi, "Cryptographic hashing from strong one-way functions (or: One-way product functions and their applications)," in *59th IEEE Annual Symposium on Foundations of Computer Science, FOCS 2018, Paris, France, October 7-9, 2018*, M. Thorup, Ed., pp. 850–858, IEEE Computer Society, 2018.

[151] J. Holmgren, A. Lombardi, and R. D. Rothblum, "Fiat-shamir via list-recoverable codes (or: Parallel repetition of GMW is not zero-knowledge)," in *STOC '21: 53rd Annual ACM SIGACT Symposium on Theory of Computing, Virtual Event, Italy, June 21-25, 2021*, S. Khuller and V. V. Williams, Eds., pp. 750–760, ACM, 2021.

[152] J. Holmgren and R. Rothblum, "Delegating computations with (almost) minimal time and space overhead," in *2018 IEEE 59th Annual Symposium on Foundations of Computer Science (FOCS)*, IEEE, pp. 124–135, 2018.

[153] D. Hopwood, S. Bowe, T. Hornby, and N. Wilcox, "Zcash protocol specification," *GitHub: San Francisco, CA, USA*, 2016.

[154] Y. E. Housni and A. Guillevic, "Optimized and secure pairing-friendly elliptic curves suitable for one layer proof composition," in *International Conference on Cryptology and Network Security*, Springer, pp. 259–279, 2020.

[155] R. Impagliazzo and A. Wigderson, "P= bpp if e requires exponential circuits: Derandomizing the xor lemma," in *Proceedings of the Twenty-Ninth Annual ACM Symposium on Theory of Computing*, pp. 220–229, 1997.

[156] Y. Ishai, E. Kushilevitz, and R. Ostrovsky, "Efficient arguments without short PCPs," in *22nd Annual IEEE Conference on Computational Complexity (CCC 2007), 13–16 June 2007, San Diego, California, USA*, pp. 278–291, IEEE Computer Society, 2007.

[157] Y. Ishai, E. Kushilevitz, R. Ostrovsky, and A. Sahai, "Zero-knowledge proofs from secure multiparty computation," *SIAM Journal on Computing*, vol. 39, no. 3, pp. 1121–1152, 2009.

[158] R. Jawale, Y. T. Kalai, D. Khurana, and R. Zhang, "SNARGs for bounded depth computations and PPAD hardness from sub-exponential LWE," in *Proceedings of the 53rd Annual ACM SIGACT Symposium on Theory of Computing*, pp. 708–721, 2021.

[159] M. Jawurek, F. Kerschbaum, and C. Orlandi, "Zero-knowledge using garbled circuits: How to prove non-algebraic statements efficiently," in *2013 ACM SIGSAC Conference on Computer and Communications Security, CCS'13, Berlin, Germany, November 4-8, 2013*, A.-R. Sadeghi, V. D. Gligor, and M. Yung, Eds., pp. 955–966, ACM, 2013.

[160] Y. Kalai, "A new perspective on delegating computation," Talk at Workshop on Probabilistically Checkable and Interactive Proofs @ STOC 2017 Theory Fest, 2017.

[161] Y. T. Kalai, G. N. Rothblum, and R. D. Rothblum, "From obfuscation to the security of Fiat-Shamir for proofs," in *Advances in Cryptology – CRYPTO 2017 – 37th Annual International Cryptology Conference, Santa Barbara, CA, USA, August 20–24, 2017, Proceedings, Part II*, J. Katz and H. Shacham, Eds., ser. Lecture Notes in Computer Science, vol. 10402, pp. 224–251, Springer, 2017.

[162] D. Kales, S. Ramacher, C. Rechberger, R. Walch, and M. Werner, "Efficient FPGA implementations of LowMC and picnic," in *Cryptographers' Track at the RSA Conference*, Springer, pp. 417–441, 2020.

[163] D. Kales and G. Zaverucha, "Improving the performance of the picnic signature scheme," *IACR Transactions on Cryptographic Hardware and Embedded Systems*, pp. 154–188, 2020.

[164] A. Kate, G. M. Zaverucha, and I. Goldberg, "Constant-size commitments to polynomials and their applications," in *Advances in Cryptology – ASIACRYPT 2010 – 16th International Conference on the Theory and Application of Cryptology and Information Security, Singapore, December 5–9, 2010. Proceedings*, M. Abe, Ed., ser. Lecture Notes in Computer Science, vol. 6477, pp. 177–194, Springer, 2010.

[165] A. Kattis, K. Panarin, and A. Vlasov, "Redshift: Transparent snarks from list polynomial commitment iops," *IACR Cryptol. ePrint Arch.*, vol. 2019, p. 1400, 2019.

[166] J. Katz, V. Kolesnikov, and X. Wang, "Improved non-interactive zero knowledge with applications to post-quantum signatures," in *Proceedings of the 2018 ACM SIGSAC Conference on Computer and Communications Security*, pp. 525–537, 2018.

[167] J. Katz, C. Zhang, and H.-S. Zhou, *An analysis of the algebraic group model*, Cryptology ePrint Archive, Report 2022/210, URL: https://ia.cr/2022/210, 2022.

[168] J. Kilian, "A note on efficient zero-knowledge proofs and arguments (extended abstract)," in *Proceedings of the Twenty-Fourth Annual ACM Symposium on Theory of Computing*, ser. STOC '92, pp. 723–732, New York, NY, USA: ACM, 1992.

[169] A. R. Klivans and D. Van Melkebeek, "Graph nonisomorphism has subexponential size proofs unless the polynomial-time hierarchy collapses," *SIAM Journal on Computing*, vol. 31, no. 5, pp. 1501–1526, 2002.

[170] N. Koblitz and A. J. Menezes, "The random oracle model: A twenty-year retrospective," *Designs, Codes and Cryptography*, vol. 77, no. 2–3, pp. 587–610, 2015.

[171] A. E. Kosba, Z. Zhao, A. Miller, Y. Qian, T.-H. H. Chan, C. Papamanthou, R. Pass, A. Shelat, and E. Shi, "How to use SNARKs in universally composable protocols.," *IACR Cryptol. ePrint Arch.*, vol. 2015, p. 1093, 2015.

[172] A. Kosba, D. Papadopoulos, C. Papamanthou, and D. Song, "MIRAGE: Succinct arguments for randomized algorithms with applications to universal zk-SNARKs," in *USENIX Security Symposium*, 2020.

[173] A. Kosba, Z. Zhao, A. Miller, Y. Qian, H. Chan, C. Papamanthou, R. Pass, A. Shelat, and E. Shi, *C∅C∅: A framework for building composable zero-knowledge proofs*, Cryptology ePrint Archive, Report 2015/1093, 2015.

[174] A. Kothapalli and B. Parno, "Algebraic reductions of knowledge," *Cryptology ePrint Archive*, 2022.

[175] A. Kothapalli, S. Setty, and I. Tzialla, "Nova: Recursive zero-knowledge arguments from folding schemes," in *Annual International Cryptology Conference*, Springer, pp. 359–388, 2022.

[176] D. Kozen, *Theory of Computation*, ser. Texts in Computer Science. Springer, 2006.

[177] E. Kushilevitz and N. Nisan, *Communication Complexity*. New York, NY, USA: Cambridge University Press, 1997.

[178] F. Le Gall, "Powers of tensors and fast matrix multiplication," in *Proceedings of the 39th International Symposium on Symbolic and Algebraic Computation*, ACM, pp. 296–303, 2014.

[179] J. Lee, "Dory: Efficient, transparent arguments for generalised inner products and polynomial commitments," in *Theory of Cryptography Conference*, Springer, pp. 1–34, 2021.

[180] F. T. Leighton, *Introduction to Parallel Algorithms and Architectures: Array, Trees, Hypercubes*. Morgan Kaufmann Publishers Inc., 1992.

[181] G. Leurent and T. Peyrin, "SHA-1 is a shambles: First chosen-prefix collision on SHA-1 and application to the PGP web of trust," in *29th USENIX Security Symposium (USENIX Security 20)*, pp. 1839–1856, 2020.

[182] S.-J. Lin, T. Y. Al-Naffouri, Y. S. Han, and W.-H. Chung, "Novel polynomial basis with fast fourier transform and its application to reed-solomon erasure codes," *IEEE Trans. Inf. Theory*, vol. 62, no. 11, pp. 6284–6299, 2016, Preliminary version in FOCS 2014.

[183] R. J. Lipton, *Fingerprinting sets*. Princeton University, Department of Computer Science, 1989.

[184] R. J. Lipton, "Efficient checking of computations," in *STACS*, pp. 207–215, 1990.

[185] A. Lombardi and V. Vaikuntanathan, "Correlation-intractable hash functions via shift-hiding," in *13th Innovations in Theoretical Computer Science Conference, ITCS 2022, January 31 – February 3, 2022, Berkeley, CA, USA*, M. Braverman, Ed., ser. LIPIcs, vol. 215, 102:1–102:16, Schloss Dagstuhl – Leibniz-Zentrum für Informatik, 2022.

[186] C. Lund, L. Fortnow, H. Karloff, and N. Nisan, "Algebraic methods for interactive proof systems," *J. ACM*, vol. 39, pp. 859–868, 1992.

[187] M. Maller, S. Bowe, M. Kohlweiss, and S. Meiklejohn, "Sonic: Zero-knowledge SNARKs from linear-size universal and updatable structured reference strings," in *Proceedings of the 2019 ACM SIGSAC Conference on Computer and Communications Security*, pp. 2111–2128, 2019.

[188] U. Maurer, "Abstract models of computation in cryptography," in *IMA International Conference on Cryptography and Coding*, Springer, pp. 1–12, 2005.

[189] U. Maurer, "Unifying zero-knowledge proofs of knowledge," in *International Conference on Cryptology in Africa*, Springer, pp. 272–286, 2009.

[190] O. Meir, "IP = PSPACE using error-correcting codes," *SIAM J. Comput.*, vol. 42, no. 1, pp. 380–403, 2013.

[191] R. Merkle, "Secrecy, authentication, and public key systems," Ph.D. dissertation, Electrical Engineering, Stanford, 1979.

[192] S. Micali, "Computationally sound proofs," *SIAM J. Comput.*, vol. 30, no. 4, pp. 1253–1298, 2000.

[193] P. B. Miltersen and N. V. Vinodchandran, "Derandomizing Arthur–Merlin games using hitting sets," *Computational Complexity*, vol. 14, no. 3, pp. 256–279, 2005.

[194] D. Moshkovitz, "An alternative proof of the Schwartz-Zippel lemma.," in *Electronic Colloquium on Computational Complexity (ECCC)*, vol. 17, p. 96, 2010.

[195] D. Moshkovitz and R. Raz, "Sub-constant error low degree test of almost-linear size," *SIAM J. Comput.*, vol. 38, no. 1, pp. 140–180, 2008.

[196] M. Naehrig, P. S. L. M. Barreto, and P. Schwabe, "On compressible pairings and their computation," in *Progress in Cryptology – AFRICACRYPT 2008*, ser. Lecture Notes in Computer Science, vol. 5023, pp. 371–388, Springer, 2008.

[197] M. Naor, "On cryptographic assumptions and challenges," in *Annual International Cryptology Conference*, Springer, pp. 96–109, 2003.

[198] C. A. Neff, "A verifiable secret shuffle and its application to e-voting," in *Proceedings of the 8th ACM conference on Computer and Communications Security*, pp. 116–125, 2001.

[199] J. B. Nielsen, "Separating random oracle proofs from complexity theoretic proofs: The non-committing encryption case," in *Annual International Cryptology Conference*, Springer, pp. 111–126, 2002.

[200] A. Ozdemir, R. Wahby, B. Whitehat, and D. Boneh, "Scaling verifiable computation using efficient set accumulators," in *29th USENIX Security Symposium*, pp. 2075–2092, 2020.

[201] P. Paillier and D. Vergnaud, "Discrete-log-based signatures may not be equivalent to discrete log," in *International Conference on the Theory and Application of Cryptology and Information Security*, Springer, pp. 1–20, 2005.

[202]   C. Papamanthou, E. Shi, and R. Tamassia, "Signatures of correct computation," in *Theory of Cryptography Conference*, Springer, pp. 222–242, 2013.

[203]   B. Parno, J. Howell, C. Gentry, and M. Raykova, "Pinocchio: Nearly practical verifiable computation," in *Proceedings of the 2013 IEEE Symposium on Security and Privacy*, ser. SP '13, pp. 238–252, Washington, DC, USA: IEEE Computer Society, 2013.

[204]   R. Pass, "On deniability in the common reference string and random oracle model," in *Annual International Cryptology Conference*, Springer, pp. 316–337, 2003.

[205]   A. Pavan, A. L. Selman, S. Sengupta, and N. V. Vinodchandran, "Polylogarithmic-round interactive proofs for coNP collapse the exponential hierarchy," *Theor. Comput. Sci.*, vol. 385, no. 1-3, pp. 167–178, 2007.

[206]   T. P. Pedersen, "Non-interactive and information-theoretic secure verifiable secret sharing," in *Annual International Cryptology Conference*, Springer, pp. 129–140, 1991.

[207]   C. Peikert and S. Shiehian, "Noninteractive zero knowledge for NP from (plain) learning with errors," in *Advances in Cryptology – CRYPTO 2019 – 39th Annual International Cryptology Conference, Santa Barbara, CA, USA, August 18–22, 2019, Proceedings, Part I*, A. Boldyreva and D. Micciancio, Eds., ser. Lecture Notes in Computer Science, vol. 11692, pp. 89–114, Springer, 2019.

[208]   D. Petersen, (URL: https://math.stackexchange.com/users/677/dan-petersen). How to prove that a polynomial of degree n has at most n roots? Mathematics Stack Exchange. URL: https://math.stackexchange.com/q/25831 (version: 2011-03-08).

[209]   N. Pippenger, "On the evaluation of powers and monomials," *SIAM Journal on Computing*, vol. 9, no. 2, pp. 230–250, 1980.

[210]   S. C. Pohlig and M. E. Hellman, "An improved algorithm for computing logarithms over GF(p) and its cryptographic significance," *IEEE Trans. Inf. Theory*, vol. 24, no. 1, pp. 106–110, 1978.

[211] D. Pointcheval and J. Stern, "Security arguments for digital signatures and blind signatures," *Journal of Cryptology*, vol. 13, no. 3, pp. 361–396, 2000.

[212] A. Polishchuk and D. A. Spielman, "Nearly-linear size holographic proofs," in *Proceedings of the Twenty-Sixth Annual ACM Symposium on Theory of Computing, 23–25 May 1994, Montréal, Québec, Canada*, pp. 194–203, 1994.

[213] J. M. Pollard, "Monte Carlo methods for index computation mod *p*," *Mathematics of Computation*, vol. 32, pp. 918–924, 1978.

[214] O. Reingold, G. N. Rothblum, and R. D. Rothblum, "Constant-round interactive proofs for delegating computation," in *Proceedings of the Forty-eighth Annual ACM Symposium on Theory of Computing*, ser. STOC '16, pp. 49–62, New York, NY, USA: ACM, 2016.

[215] N. Ron-Zewi and R. Rothblum, "Local proofs approaching the witness length," *Electron. Colloquium Comput. Complex.*, vol. 26, p. 127, 2019, Accepted to Foundations of Computer Science (FOCS), 2020.

[216] G. Rothblum, "Delegating computation reliably : Paradigms and constructions," Ph.D. dissertation, Massachusetts Institute of Technology, 2009.

[217] G. N. Rothblum, S. P. Vadhan, and A. Wigderson, "Interactive proofs of proximity: Delegating computation in sublinear time," in *Symposium on Theory of Computing Conference, STOC'13, Palo Alto, CA, USA, June 1-4, 2013*, pp. 793–802, 2013.

[218] R. Rothblum, "The Fiat-Shamir transformation," Talk at The 9th BIU Winter School on Cryptography – Zero Knowledge. 2019. URL: https://www.youtube.com/watch?v=9cagVtYstyY.

[219] R. Rubinfeld and M. Sudan, "Robust characterizations of polynomials with applications to program testing," *SIAM Journal on Computing*, vol. 25, no. 2, pp. 252–271, 1996.

[220] A. D. Sarma, R. J. Lipton, and D. Nanongkai, "Best-order streaming model," in *Proc. Annual Conference on Theory and Applications of Models of Computation*, 2009.

[221]   E. B. Sasson, L. Goldberg, S. Kopparty, and S. Saraf, "DEEP-FRI: sampling outside the box improves soundness," in *11th Innovations in Theoretical Computer Science Conference, ITCS 2020, January 12–14, 2020, Seattle, Washington, USA*, T. Vidick, Ed., ser. LIPIcs, vol. 151, pp. 5: 1–5: 32, 2020.

[222]   W. J. Savitch, "Relationships between nondeterministic and deterministic tape complexities," *Journal of Computer and System Sciences*, vol. 4, no. 2, pp. 177–192, 1970.

[223]   C.-P. Schnorr, "Efficient identification and signatures for smart cards," in *Conference on the Theory and Application of Cryptology*, Springer, pp. 239–252, 1989.

[224]   J. T. Schwartz, "Fast probabilistic algorithms for verification of polynomial identities," *J. ACM*, vol. 27, no. 4, pp. 701–717, 1980.

[225]   R. Seidel, "On the all-pairs-shortest-path problem in unweighted undirected graphs," *J. Comput. Syst. Sci.*, vol. 51, no. 3, pp. 400–403, 1995.

[226]   S. Setty, "Spartan: Efficient and general-purpose zkSNARKs without trusted setup," in *Annual International Cryptology Conference*, Springer, pp. 704–737, 2020.

[227]   S. T. V. Setty, B. Braun, V. Vu, A. J. Blumberg, B. Parno, and M. Walfish, "Resolving the conflict between generality and plausibility in verified computation," in *EuroSys*, Z. Hanzálek, H. Härtig, M. Castro, and M. F. Kaashoek, Eds., pp. 71–84, ACM, 2013.

[228]   S. T. V. Setty, R. McPherson, A. J. Blumberg, and M. Walfish, "Making argument systems for outsourced computation practical (sometimes)," in *19th Annual Network and Distributed System Security Symposium, NDSS 2012, San Diego, California, USA, February 5–8, 2012*, 2012.

[229]   S. Setty, S. Angel, T. Gupta, and J. Lee, "Proving the correct execution of concurrent services in zero-knowledge," in *13th USENIX Symposium on Operating Systems Design and Implementation (OSDI)*, pp. 339–356, 2018.

[230] S. Setty and J. Lee, *Quarks: Quadruple-efficient transparent zksnarks*, Cryptology ePrint Archive, Report 2020/1275, 2020. URL: https://eprint.iacr.org/2020/1275.

[231] A. Shamir, "IP = PSPACE," *J. ACM*, vol. 39, pp. 869–877, 1992, Preliminary version in STOC 1990.

[232] A. Shen, "IP = PSPACE: Simplified Proof," *J. ACM*, vol. 39, pp. 878–880, 1992.

[233] P. W. Shor, "Algorithms for quantum computation: Discrete logarithms and factoring," in *Proceedings 35th Annual Symposium on Foundations of Computer Science*, IEEE, pp. 124–134, 1994.

[234] V. Shoup, "Lower bounds for discrete logarithms and related problems," in *International Conference on the Theory and Applications of Cryptographic Techniques*, Springer, pp. 256–266, 1997.

[235] StarkWare, *EthSTARK documentation*, Cryptology ePrint Archive, Paper 2021/582, 2021. URL: https://eprint.iacr.org/2021/582,

[236] H. Sun, H. Sun, K. Singh, A. S. Peddireddy, H. Patil, J. Liu, and W. Chen, *The inspection model for zero-knowledge proofs and efficient zerocash with secp256k1 keys*, Cryptology ePrint Archive, Paper 2022/1079, 2022. URL: https://eprint.iacr.org/2022/1079,

[237] J. Thaler, "Time-optimal interactive proofs for circuit evaluation," in *Proceedings of the 33rd Annual Conference on Advances in Cryptology*, ser. CRYPTO'13, Berlin, Heidelberg: Springer-Verlag, 2013.

[238] J. Thaler, *A note on the GKR protocol*, 2015. URL: http://people.cs.georgetown.edu/jthaler/GKRNote.pdf.

[239] P. Valiant, "Incrementally verifiable computation or proofs of knowledge imply time/space efficiency," in *Theory of Cryptography Conference*, Springer, pp. 1–18, 2008.

[240] A. Vlasov and K. Panarin, "Transparent polynomial commitment scheme with polylogarithmic communication complexity.," *IACR Cryptol. ePrint Arch.*, vol. 2019, p. 1020, 2019.

[241] V. Vu, S. T. V. Setty, A. J. Blumberg, and M. Walfish, "A hybrid architecture for interactive verifiable computation," in *2013 IEEE Symposium on Security and Privacy, SP 2013, Berkeley, CA, USA, May 19–22, 2013*, pp. 223–237, 2013.

[242] R. S. Wahby, Y. Ji, A. J. Blumberg, A. Shelat, J. Thaler, M. Walfish, and T. Wies, "Full accounting for verifiable outsourcing," in *Proceedings of the 2017 ACM SIGSAC Conference on Computer and Communications Security*, ACM, pp. 2071–2086, 2017.

[243] R. S. Wahby, S. Setty, Z. Ren, A. J. Blumberg, and M. Walfish, "Efficient ram and control flow in verifiable outsourced computation," in *NDSS*, 2015.

[244] R. S. Wahby, I. Tzialla, A. Shelat, J. Thaler, and M. Walfish, "Doubly-efficient zkSNARKs without trusted setup," in *2018 IEEE Symposium on Security and Privacy, SP 2018, Proceedings, 21–23 May 2018, San Francisco, California, USA*, pp. 926–943, IEEE Computer Society, 2018.

[245] A. Waksman, "A permutation network," *Journal of the ACM*, vol. 15, no. 1, pp. 159–163, 1968.

[246] H. Wee, "On round-efficient argument systems.," in *ICALP*, pp. 140–152, 2005.

[247] H. Wee, "Zero knowledge in the random oracle model, revisited," in *International Conference on the Theory and Application of Cryptology and Information Security*, Springer, pp. 417–434, 2009.

[248] C. Weng, K. Yang, J. Katz, and X. Wang, "Wolverine: Fast, scalable, and communication-efficient zero-knowledge proofs for Boolean and arithmetic circuits," in *2021 IEEE Symposium on Security and Privacy (SP)*, IEEE, pp. 1074–1091, 2021.

[249] D. Wikström, *Special soundness in the random oracle model*, Cryptology ePrint Archive, Report 2021/1265, URL: https://ia.cr/2021/1265, 2021.

[250] H. Wu, W. Zheng, A. Chiesa, R. A. Popa, and I. Stoica, "DIZK: A distributed zero knowledge proof system," in *27th USENIX Security Symposium* (USENIX Security), pp. 675–692, 2018.

[251] T. Xie, J. Zhang, Y. Zhang, C. Papamanthou, and D. Song, "Libra: Succinct zero-knowledge proofs with optimal prover computation," in *Annual International Cryptology Conference*, Springer, pp. 733–764, 2019.

[252] T. Xie, J. Zhang, Z. Cheng, F. Zhang, Y. Zhang, Y. Jia, D. Boneh, and D. Song, "Zkbridge: Trustless cross-chain bridges made practical," *arXiv preprint arXiv:2210.00264*, 2022.

[253] T. Xie, Y. Zhang, and D. Song, "Orion: Zero knowledge proof with linear prover time," in *Annual International Cryptology Conference*, Springer, pp. 299–328, 2022.

[254] R. Yuster, "Computing the diameter polynomially faster than APSP," *arXiv preprint arXiv:1011.6181*, 2010.

[255] J. Zhang, T. Liu, W. Wang, Y. Zhang, D. Song, X. Xie, and Y. Zhang, "Doubly efficient interactive proofs for general arithmetic circuits with linear prover time," in *CCS '21: 2021 ACM SIGSAC Conference on Computer and Communications Security, Virtual Event, Republic of Korea, November 15–19, 2021*, Y. Kim, J. Kim, G. Vigna, and E. Shi, Eds., pp. 159–177, ACM, 2021.

[256] J. Zhang, T. Xie, Y. Zhang, and D. Song, "Transparent polynomial delegation and its applications to zero knowledge proof," in *2020 IEEE Symposium on Security and Privacy*, IEEE, pp. 859–876, 2020.

[257] Y. Zhang, D. Genkin, J. Katz, D. Papadopoulos, and C. Papamanthou, "A zero-knowledge version of vSQL," *IACR Cryptol. ePrint Arch.*, vol. 2017, p. 1146, 2017.

[258] Y. Zhang, D. Genkin, J. Katz, D. Papadopoulos, and C. Papamanthou, "VSQL: Verifying arbitrary SQL queries over dynamic outsourced databases," in *2017 IEEE Symposium on Security and Privacy, SP 2017, San Jose, CA, USA, May 22–26, 2017*, pp. 863–880, 2017.

[259] Y. Zhang, D. Genkin, J. Katz, D. Papadopoulos, and C. Papamanthou, "VRAM: Faster verifiable RAM with program-independent preprocessing," in *2018 IEEE Symposium on Security and Privacy, SP 2018, Proceedings, 21–23 May 2018, San Francisco, California, USA*, pp. 908–925, IEEE Computer Society, 2018.

[260] R. Zippel, "Probabilistic algorithms for sparse polynomials," in *EUROSAM*, E. W. Ng, Ed., ser. Lecture Notes in Computer Science, vol. 72, pp. 216–226, Springer, 1979.

[261]   ZKProof Community Reference, Version 0.3, 2022. URL: https://
         docs.zkproof.org/pages/reference/versions/ZkpComRef-0-3.
         pdf.

CPSIA information can be obtained
at www.ICGtesting.com
Printed in the USA
LVHW052225140723
752120LV00005B/66